Modeling Experimental and Observational Data

Modeling Experimental and Observational Data

Clifford E. Lunneborg

University of Washington
The Open University, Milton Keynes, UK

Duxbury Press
An Imprint of Wadsworth Publishing Company
Belmont, California

Duxbury Press
An Imprint of Wadsworth Publishing Company
A division of Wadsworth, Inc.

Editor: *Curt Hinrichs*
Assistant Editor: *Jennifer Burger*
Editorial Assistant: *Michelle O'Donnell*
Production: *The Wheetley Company, Inc.*
Cover and Text Designer: *Cloyce Wall*
Print Buyer: *Barbara Britton*
Compositor: *Interactive Composition Corporation*
Printer: *Arcata Graphics/Fairfield*

 This book is printed on acid-free recycled paper.

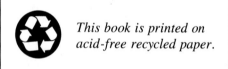

International Thompson Publishing
The trademark ITP is used under license

Printed in the United States of America
1 2 3 4 5 6 7 8 9 10—98 97 96 95 94

Library of Congress Cataloging-in-Publication Data

Lunneborg, Clifford E.
    Modeling experimental and observational data / Clifford E.
Lunneborg.
       p.   cm.
    Includes bibliographical references and index.
    ISBN 0-534-21426-6 (acid-free paper)
    1. Linear models (Statistics) 2. Biometry. 3. Social sciences—
Statistical methods. I. Title.
QA279.L86 1994
001.4′34—dc20
                                      93-11598

Brief Contents

1   Models for Experimental and Observational Data   **1**

2   The Measured Response Variable   **27**

3   Simple Linear Regression: An Introduction   **49**

4   Simple Linear Regression: Estimation   **71**

5   Simple Linear Regression: Inference About Models   **99**

6   Categorical Explanatory Variables: One-Way ANOVA   **119**

7   Several Explanatory Variables: Multiple Regression   **153**

8   Comparing Fuller with Less Full Models   **195**

9   Assessing a Model's Adequacy: Individual Observations   **211**

10   Assessing a Model's Adequacy: Checking Assumptions   **240**

11   Categorical Explanatory Variables: ANOVA Models   **269**

12   Auxiliary Variable Models: Enhancing Model Sensitivity   **311**

13   Auxiliary Variable Models: Moderating Explanatory Variable Influence   **331**

14   Introduction To Modeling Repeated Observations   **349**

15   The Categorical Response Variable: Characteristics   **399**

16   Logistic Regression: Modeling the Proportion of Successes   **409**

17   Grouped Logistic Regression Models   **439**

18   Logistic Regression for Multiple Response Categories   **465**

19   Poisson Regression for Counts in Time or Space   **497**

Appendix 1   **A1**

Appendix 2   **A11**

Contents

CHAPTER 1 Models for Experimental and Observational Data

1.1   The Uses of Models   **1**

1.2   The Elements of Models   **5**

1.3   The Development of Models   **12**

1.4   Collecting Data for Models   **18**

1.5   Model Assessment and Variable Type   **23**

1.6   Summary   **26**

CHAPTER 2 The Measured Response Variable

2.1   Observational Samples, Populations, and Models   **27**

2.2   Explaining Response Variability in the Observational Population   **28**

2.3   What Characterizes a Response Variable as Measured?   **32**

2.4   Characteristics of Measured Response Samples   **35**

2.5   A Population of Responses   **41**

2.6   Sample and Population, Statistics and Parameters   **42**

2.7   Explaining Response Variability: A Review   **43**

2.8   Experimental Studies and Conditional Response Populations   **45**

2.9   Summary   **47**

CHAPTER 3 Simple Linear Regression: An Introduction

3.1   Regression   **49**

3.2   Linear Regression   **52**

3.3   Linear Model Inference: Assumptions   **57**

3.4   The Heights of Adolescent Males: An Example   **60**

3.5   Covariability and Correlation   **61**

3.6   Summary   **69**

CHAPTER 4   Simple Linear Regression: Estimation

4.1   The Linear Model: A Review   **71**

4.2   Estimates of Linear Model Parameters   **74**

4.3   Sampling Distribution of Estimates   **88**

4.4   Summary   **97**

CHAPTER 5   Simple Linear Regression: Inference About Models

5.1   Sampling Distribution of Estimates and
        Inferences About Parameters   **99**

5.2   Confidence Intervals and Magnitude Inference   **104**

5.3   Comparing Linear Models: Relation Inference   **110**

5.4   Output from a Regression Command   **114**

5.5   Summary   **115**

        Exercises   **115**

CHAPTER 6   Categorical Explanatory Variables: One-Way ANOVA

6.1   Categorical Explanatory Variables   **119**

6.2   Categories and Conditional Response Populations   **121**

6.3   Models for the Categorical Explanatory Variable   **124**

6.4   Response Population Estimates and Sampling   **126**

6.5   Full and Null Models for the Two-level Category   **130**

6.6   Full and Null Models: The Multilevel Explanatory Variable   **138**

6.7   The Explanatory Variable with Ordered Categories   **148**

6.8   Summary   **149**

        Exercises   **150**

CHAPTER 7   Several Explanatory Variables: Multiple Regression
7.1   Growth Study: A Second Explanatory Variable   **153**
7.2   A Linear Model for Two Explanatory Variables   **154**
7.3   Parameter Estimates for the Two-variable Model   **160**
7.4   Sampling Distributions: Multiple Linear Model   **169**
7.5   Model Comparisons: Multiple Explanatory Variables   **172**
7.6   Linear Models with k Explanatory Variables   **181**
7.7   Summary   **188**
       Exercises   **188**

CHAPTER 8   Comparing Fuller with Less Full Models
8.1   The Fuller/Less Full Relation   **195**
8.2   Models That Add or Delete x-variables   **196**
8.3   Models That Combine x-variables   **198**
8.4   Models That Constrain Parameters   **199**
8.5   Linear Constraints and Weighted Sums of Variables   **200**
8.6   Motivation for a Less Full Model   **204**
8.7   Summary   **205**
       Exercises   **205**

CHAPTER 9   Assessing a Model's Adequacy: Individual Observations
9.1   Fitted Values and Residuals   **211**
9.2   Leverage of Design Points   **212**
9.3   Residuals and Residual Plots   **220**
9.4   Outliers   **223**
9.5   Influential Observations   **228**
9.6   Resolving Troublesome Data Points   **231**
9.7   Summary   **236**
       Exercises   **236**

CHAPTER 10   Assessing a Model's Adequacy: Checking Assumptions

10.1   Residuals and Modeling Assumptions   **240**

10.2   Assessing the Linearity of Regression   **243**

10.3   Assessing Homogeneity of Response Variance   **252**

10.4   Assessing Normal Characteristics of Response   **261**

10.5   Residuals and Modeling Strategies   **266**

10.6   Summary   **266**

         Exercises   **266**

CHAPTER 11   Categorical Explanatory Variables: ANOVA Models

11.1   Two Categorical Influences: Additive Model   **269**

11.2   Two Categorical Variables: Interactive Model   **279**

11.3   Factorial Designs   **293**

11.4   Nested Designs   **303**

11.5   Fixed and Random Factors   **306**

11.6   Summary   **308**

         Exercises   **308**

CHAPTER 12   Auxiliary Variable Models: Enhancing Model Sensitivity

12.1   Increasing Model Sensitivity: Some General Ideas   **311**

12.2   Increasing Model Sensitivity: An Example   **313**

12.3   Technique 1: Blocking   **314**

12.4   Technique 2: Concomitant Variable Analysis   **319**

12.5   Technique 3: Analysis of Covariance   **321**

12.6   Summary   **327**

         Exercises   **327**

CHAPTER 13   Auxiliary Variable Models: Moderating Explanatory Variable Influence

13.1   Auxiliary Variables in Interaction   **331**

13.2   Group Regression: External Categorical Moderation   **333**

13.3   Segmented Regression: Internal Categorical Moderation   **338**

13.4   Moderated Regression: External Measured Moderation   **341**

13.5   Polynomial Regression: Internal Measured Moderation   **345**

13.6   Summary   **345**

Exercises   **346**

CHAPTER **14**   Introduction To Modeling Repeated Observations

14.1   Repeated Measures   **349**

14.2   A Single Response Variable from Repeated Measures   **353**

14.3   Blocking on Individual Subjects   **356**

14.4   A Single Within-subjects Categorical Variable or Factor   **358**

14.5   Two or More Within-subjects Categorical Explanatory Variables   **359**

14.6   Mixed Models: Within- and Between-subjects Variables in the Same Design   **365**

14.7   Coding Efficiencies for Repeated-measures Model Comparisons   **375**

14.8   Covariates in Repeated-measures Designs   **382**

14.9   Crossover Designs   **387**

14.10   Advanced Repeated-measures Analysis: Beyond Blocking on Subjects   **394**

14.11   Summary   **395**

Exercises   **396**

CHAPTER **15**   The Categorical Response Variable: Characteristics

15.1   Categorical Responses: Population Characteristics   **399**

15.2   Certainty and the Categorical Response   **402**

15.3   Modeling and the Categorical Response   **406**

15.4   A Uniform Approach to Categorical Modeling   **407**

15.5   Summary   **407**

CHAPTER 16   Logistic Regression: Modeling the Proportion of Successes

16.1   Simple Linear Regression: A Review   **409**

16.2   The Dichotomous Response: Censored Measurement   **410**

16.3   Logistic Regression: An Introduction   **413**

16.4   Logistic Regression Models   **415**

16.5   Fitting the Logistic Regression Model   **418**

16.6   An Example: Law School Grades and Bar Examination Performance   **420**

16.7   Assessing the Fit of a Logistic Regression Model   **422**

16.8   Comparing Logistic Regression Models   **426**

16.9   Odds of Success: A Multiplicative Model   **432**

16.10   Summary   **436**

      Exercises   **436**

CHAPTER 17   Grouped Logistic Regression Models

17.1   Design Points with Multiple Observations   **439**

17.2   Logistic Regression and Categorical Explanatory Variables   **449**

17.3   Example: Death Penalty and Murder Convictions   **452**

17.4   Multiplicative Models and Grouped Logistic Regression   **455**

17.5   Summary   **460**

      Exercises   **460**

CHAPTER 18   Logistic Regression for Multiple Response Categories

18.1   The Ordered Categorical Response: Degrees of Success   **465**

18.2   Logistic Regression Models for the Ordered Response   **466**

18.3   The Proportional Odds Model   **467**

18.4   Proportional Odds with Multiple x-variables   **477**

18.5   An Alternative Cumulative Odds Model   **481**

18.6   Nominal Response Categories: Polychotomous Logistic Regression   **490**

18.7   Summary   **495**

      Exercises   **495**

CHAPTER 19 Poisson Regression for Counts in Time or Space

19.1   Counting Independently Occurring Events   **497**

19.2   Poisson Regression   **498**

19.3   Model Fitting and Comparisons   **500**

19.4   Poisson Regression Model Interpretation   **501**

19.5   An Example of Poisson Regression Model Comparison   **501**

19.6   Summary   **504**

Exercises   **504**

APPENDIX 1 Tables of Statistical Distributions   **A1**

APPENDIX 2 Advanced Topics   **A11**

References   **A33**

Sources of Data Used in End-of-Chapter Exercises   **A35**

Index   **A37**

Preface

Introduction

Modeling Experimental and Observational Data introduces statistical modeling as a quite general and highly insightful approach to data analysis. Research in the empirical sciences—physical as well as biological and behavioral—almost exclusively focuses on explanatory relations: What factors explain or influence some phenomenon of interest? How great is their influence? Statistical models provide answers to just such questions. They allow researchers not only to test hypotheses but, thanks to the availability of quick, inexpensive computing, to learn far more about and from their data than has been possible heretofore. In particular, modeling emphasizes assessing the strength of influences and comparing alternative models, alternative explanatory structures.

Audience

This text was written for undergraduates and graduates throughout the biological and behavioral sciences. It assumes only a limited familiarity with basic ideas of statistics, the most important of which are thoroughly reviewed, and is thus appropriate for use in a wide variety of second level statistics and data analysis courses. The mathematical content is kept low to broaden its instructional applicability and to insure that it can be used effectively as well in self-instruction by researchers wanting to "modernize" their approach to data analysis.

Approach

Modeling as a data analysis approach has fully blossomed only in the past decade. It can be thought to be the result of interactions between recent developments in statistical theory, in the collection of empirical data, and in the asking of questions about those data, all of these developments facilitated, if not fueled, by the rapid extension of inexpensive computing resources. We collect more data, of a more complex kind, and consequently have more questions to ask of those data. At the same time we have the capacity to perform more computations, more rapidly, over those data.

Modeling provides coherence to this rapidly expanding universe of data, questions, and computations. It provides the necessary structure to each and to their connections. An important aspect to this is the near universality of modeling concepts. Their implementation, in statistical theory and in computational programs, is now well enough developed that modeling as a data analysis approach can and should be made widely available.

Features

In preparing this introduction to modeling for market, several characteristics emerged as important, defining characteristics of the final text:

- A carefully paced introduction to statistical models and to statistical inference. The first five chapters should provide the student or independent reader with a leisurely review of those ideas needed to build a modeling orientation to data analysis.

- Low mathematical detail. Formulae and the development of formulae should be kept to a minimum. The emphasis is on data, not on mathematics. With computations largely in the hands of the "computer," there is little practicable reason to emphasize computational details.

- Emphasis on the generality of the (linear) modeling approach. Owing largely to their separate origins, linear regression and logistic regression and its extensions have been taught as two quite different techniques. This text focuses on the continuity of modeling as an approach, whatever the characteristics of the response variable. Similarly, models for data collected in a classic analysis of variance context are developed in parallel to those for multiple regression. The intent is that the student appreciate the continuity of modeling.

- Model comparison as the focus of data analysis. Researchers approach their data with not one but several explanatory models in mind. Further models may surface as the data are examined. The major task in data analysis, then, is sorting out competing models, deciding which to abandon, which to modify, which to describe as "better." Chapters 8 through 14, as well as sections of earlier and later chapters, concentrate on the formulation and comparison of models.

- Models should describe explanatory strength. The text takes the position that hypothesis testing (or, model choice) is only part of the data analyst's task. Once one or more "better" models have been identified, it is important that the analyst describe the strength of influence of each of the factors present in those models. These descriptions, to be appropriate, need to take model elements and sampling scheme into account. Emphasis is given in the text to the interpretation of regression parameters, to the reformulation of interaction or polynomial models, and to the use of a parallel, multiplicative model in logistic regression.

■ Interpreting computational results. The text does not depend upon a particular statistics program. Linear and logistic regression commands are widely available in personal computer statistical packages and the text emphasizes the interpretation of "results" common to these packages rather than to a specific one.

Course Use

The entire text can be covered in a course extending over two academic quarters or a single semester. However, shorter or more specialized courses may use the text in several ways. Depending on the emphasis of the course, some materials may be skipped. The classical linear models course might omit the later chapters dealing with the categorical response variable, Chapters 15–19. Chapters on "designed studies," notably Chapters 11, 12, and 14, might be omitted where students are unlikely to encounter data from such studies. Conversely, an introductory experimental design course may want to omit material on regression diagnostics (Chapters 9 and 10) and on moderated regression (Chapter 13) as well as parts of the Chapters 15–18. (However, Chapter 19, on Poisson regression, could be a valuable addition to such a course.) Finally, Chapters 18 and 19 may be omitted where computational support for the multi-category or counted response is not available.

Acknowledgments

The text is based on courses taught at the University of Washington over a number of years. The students in those courses are primarily responsible for the present content and emphasis. Development of the text has benefitted considerably from the wise advice and lively commentary on modeling issues provided by my colleagues at the University of Washington, notably June Morita and David Madigan, and at the Open University, notably Fergus Daly, David Hand, and Dan Lynn. I am grateful to the patient reviewers of earlier drafts of the text: John W. Cotton, University of California, Santa Barbara; Robert P. Abelson, Yale University; Thomas E. Nygren, Ohio State University; Jeffrey S. Berman, Memphis State University; Ulf Bockenholt, University of Illinois; and Jan De Leeuw, University of California, Los Angeles, for materially improving the understandability of my message as well as for saving me from error on more than one occasion. Publishers Michael Payne, initially, and Alex Kugushev, more recently, have sustained my belief in the project and a talented crew for Wadsworth including Curt Hinrichs, Jennie Burger, Cloyce Wall, Michelle O'Donnell, Sandra Craig, and Bonnie Crutcher has seen it through to its handsome conclusion. Finally, without the unflagging encouragement and help of Patricia Lunneborg none of it could ever have happened.

1

Models for Experimental and Observational Data

The purpose of this chapter is to introduce some basic ideas associated with models for data and modeling as an orientation to data analysis. Models for data summarize a set of observations in the behavioral or biological sciences so that we may communicate with our colleagues and the public. The *data model* we will be interested in is both an *explanatory and a statistical model*. It is *explanatory* in that it is formulated to describe the influence of one or more (explanatory) variables on another (response) variable. By *statistical* we mean that we will use variability in the data to assess how well our model *fits* those data.

Modeling refers to processes by which models are originated, evaluated, and modified. The refinement of a model requires, at each stage, an integration of substantive considerations with the relations found in the data.

We focus on modeling as a very productive approach to data analysis. Because it is both structured and flexible, it invites researchers to learn more from data than a strictly *confirmatory* or hypothesis-testing orientation permits. At the same time, substantively grounded modeling avoids excessive reliance on data, which sometimes is true of *exploratory data analysis*. Modeling should assure that both theoretical issues and data characteristics are properly addressed in the analysis.

1.1
The Uses of Models

The observations made by scientists contain vital information about what goes on in the social and natural world. Extracting this information can be difficult, particularly if the observations are numerous or complex. The task is simpler, of course, if the scientist has some idea about what is to be looked for in the data. Then, she or he knows where to start looking, and how to begin *organizing* the data.

- Women sales clerks might be expected to score higher, in general, than men clerks on the Customer Courtesy Scale.
- Students' GPAs might be hypothesized to rise as hours of study increase.
- Chick weight might be thought to go down as the number of chicks in the hatch goes up.

Ideas phrased in this manner, as hypotheses to be confirmed or just hunches to be explored, suggest how the data may be usefully structured or sorted out—by gender, by hours of study, by hatch size. Whether a proposed structuring proves useful or not, it serves as a framework for looking at the observations and for coming to grips with what they have to tell us.

Ideas we articulate about the structure of data are called *models*. Modeling is also the process by which we compare these ideas to data, often with the goal of satisfying ourselves and our colleagues that we have found a good model. A good model is one that provides a good fit to our data. Modeling is what this book is about, so a complete definition lies in the chapters ahead.

1.1.1   Models Communicate Data

Models and modeling may sound very sophisticated. Not every model, though, is a Theory of Evolution or Relativity. Indeed, many models will strike us as not very profound at all. Sometimes, the model behind the summarization of a set of data isn't given explicitly. We may be able to infer a particular model from the summarization. And we may be wrong.

> After scoring the Spatial Visualization tests completed by all eleventh graders in a suburban high school, the psychologist in charge of testing summarizes the results by calculating an average score (55 score points) and a standard deviation (9 score points).

A set of data may be summarized in more than one way. Why would the psychologist have chosen to summarize the results in this way, rather than, for example, reporting the lowest and highest scores or the proportion of students earning scores above 50? The average, you may recall from an introductory statistics course, is the result of adding up all of the scores and dividing by their number. It often is indicative of the general size of scores in a set. The standard deviation, another common staple of introductory statistics, is the square root of the average squared deviation of the scores from their average. It is used as a measure of how much variability exists in a set of numbers. If all are close to the average, the standard deviation will be small. If some observations are markedly smaller or larger than the average, the standard deviation will be large.

Taking the two summary calculations together, the scores of the students are described as if they made up *one set* with two important characteristics. The scores are distributed about a *central point* (the average) with a certain amount of *variability* (the standard deviation). Is this the model of the data the psychologist had in mind? We can't know that she wanted to portray the scores as all belonging to one collection, but this agrees with the summarization. Had the gender of the students been of interest to the psychologist—had she a different model for the data—she might have calculated separate means and standard deviations for the men and women, thus describing two sets of scores.

The average score and the standard deviation *summarized* the observations. The psychologist now can report the results of testing all eleventh graders with these two summary statistics.

Summarization of a set of data can occur, of course, only after we have decided *how to summarize* those data. That decision depends on our having a model, whether we make that model explicit or not. *Without a model, we do not know how to summarize!*

Our summarization of data depends on our model for the data. We would not summarize the data as making up a single set unless we had such a model for the data. In addition to depending on the model, our data summary should reflect accurately that model.

Summarization is essential to *communication*. We cannot expect colleagues to take the time to look through all of our data, observation by observation, case by case. Others depend on our summaries. Yet, summarized data may not be sufficient to communicate results. Our readers will ask themselves why the observations were summarized as they were. We chose a particular summary because we were guided by a certain model for the data. We can either tell readers what the model was or we can ask that they play Sherlock Holmes, as we did with the Spatial Visualization scores summary, and decide for themselves. The latter has two drawbacks. Drawing the inference takes the reader's time and, more serious, he or she may infer the *wrong model* and misinterpret our results. We don't want to keep readers guessing. Scientific communication can only be facilitated if we describe our models as well as summarize our observations.

Our idea of the psychologist's model for the Spatial Visualization scores is that they all belonged to one set. The simple descriptive model (Average and Standard Deviation) allows her to communicate, perhaps to the school board, the general size and variability of Spatial Visualization scores among her eleventh grade students. But what *purpose* would this model serve?

1.1.2   Models Are to Explain Data

Scientists, of course, are not passive summarizers of the data that chance to fall their way. Often, we collect data because we are interested to "show that" or "see if" a particular way of summarizing those data makes sense, or is better than some other summarization. That is, we are interested in whether one model rather than another provides a better *explanation* of the data.

Our school psychologist, in reporting to the school board the average Spatial Visualization score among eleventh graders, may wish to draw attention to how different this average is from that in an adjoining school district in an attempt to influence the curriculum in her district. She may wish to *explain* the lower overall performance in her school as owing to a lack of emphasis in coursework on the development of spatial visualization skills. That explanation, though, would not be grounded in her summary. The model that led to that summary was not an *explanatory* one.

It is useful to think of two prototypic kinds of explanatory models. We'll call the two *confirmation models* and *hypothesis models*. The names describe models at the two ends of a continuum and many models fall between the two. Indeed, the most useful data analyses often are those that yield models that are a blend of the two types.

Models to Confirm Earlier Hypotheses

A model will be referred to as a confirmation model if it originates *outside* the set of observations being summarized and is specified in advance of any data analysis. Such models may be suggested by some *substantive theory*:

> The time taken to respond to a word flashed on the screen should be inversely related to the frequency with which that word occurs in ordinary conversation.

Or they may be suggested by what has been found in *earlier studies*:

> One should observe the same dependence of educational attainment on educational aspiration among Japanese students as has been found for North Americans.

Such models are confirmation models in the sense that, having been stated in advance, the model fitting can make use of information in the new observations to confirm (or disconfirm) these "hypotheses."

Models to Develop New Hypotheses

A model not stated in advance, but stimulated wholly by the data modeling itself, is a hypothesis model.

> In the process of sorting through data on the failure of small businesses, a researcher noticed that businesses founded in the winter months appeared more likely to make it through a first year than did those that opened their doors in the summer. He used that model to summarize the data and it seemed to "fit."

Because the model came from those same data, however, the fit does not provide any confirmation of the researcher's hypothesis. Rather, at the end of data analysis, the model remains a hypothesis. Confirmation of the hypothesis awaits the application of the model to a *new* set of observations.

1.1.3 Models Integrate Data and Theory

We do not pursue the different purposes of models—*communication, hypothesis confirmation*, and *hypothesis development*—isolated from one another. At the same time that we are summarizing a new set of data according to some old but useful model, we are checking to see if a hypothesis carried over from the last data set makes sense here *and* we are looking for clues in the new data that might help us further refine our explanation of the response behavior.

How then *should* we summarize our observations? That is the basic question that modeling answers. Because modeling requires that we go back and forth between what we already know and what our new data have to say, it is unrivaled as an approach to the explanation of scientific observations.

1.2
The Elements of Models

How does a model lead to a summarization of a set of observations? How can we translate an idea we have about what is going on in a set of observations into a model? What characteristics should a model have if it is to serve its explanatory purposes?

An explanatory model describes *how one variable influences or explains another*.

"Variable" is used here in a very general sense. It means any characteristic that can take on two or more observationally distinct levels or values. The following are all variables:

- The gender of lawyers
- The number of dollars appropriated by a state to support higher education
- The type of wine preferred by diners

A model also should describe *where* or *when* the explanation operates. *Observational units* to which the model applies may be individuals, aggregations of individuals, institutions, species, geographic areas, or time periods—to mention only some of the possibilities.

Oxygen uptake by the blood is not related to blood type in the human infant

states a model. Blood type and rate of oxygen uptake are variables. The first does not explain the second at all. Human infants (for example, between 3 and 9 months of age) are the appropriate observational units. The model speculates that if we *summarize by blood type* the rates of oxygen uptake among a sample of human infants, we should see no difference in those rates among the several blood types.

1.2.1 The Response Variable: To Be Explained

The focus of models is on what is to be explained.

- Why are there greater numbers of Merganser nests along some shoreline tracts than others?
- Why do some car buyers purchase Nissans and others Chevrolets?
- Why do high school seniors earn different Scholastic Aptitude Test Verbal scores?

Nesting sites, makes of cars, and SAT Verbal scores are all *response variables*.

To be of interest, responses must show some variability. If the density of Merganser nests was the *same* across all tracts or if *all* high school seniors earned exactly the same SAT Verbal scores, these responses would offer nothing to be explained. You may know the response variable under another name. Some texts refer to dependent, criterion, or target variables. "Response," we think, provides the clearest indication of this variable's role in a model.

The central importance of the response variable in a model is reinforced by our speaking of *modeling the response variable*. This is a shorthand way of saying that we want to explain the variability in the response.

1.2.2   The Explanatory Variable: Source of Explanation

Response variable suggests that the variable *responds* to something. Our candidates for this something are termed *explanatory variables*. Quite simply, an explanatory variable explains *some part* of the variability we observe in a response variable.

Too much should not be read into our use of the term *explanatory*.

Older children run faster than younger children

states an explanatory model. It states a belief that *some of the variability* in the running speeds of children can be explained by their ages. Our model, however, is silent about any underlying "mechanism."

- Do older children run faster because of better muscular coordination?
- Or is it their greater strength?
- Or their longer limb length?
- Or an increased motivation to do well at the task?

Calling a variable explanatory, then, is not intended to have any deep, metaphysical implications. It merely points out the *direction of explanation*. Here, we are interested in how age explains running speed, not in how running speed explains age.

Just as there must be variability in the response, so there must be variability in the postulated explanatory source. If we looked at running speeds among children *of the same age*, we would learn nothing of the explanatory power of age.

1.2.3   The Explanatory Relation

All explanatory models specify the *direction* of the explanation.

- Blood type variability explains (an appreciable amount of the) variability in oxygen uptake.
- Extent of cortical lesion explains (some of the) variability in amount of time a rat spends grooming.
- Age of interviewees explains (in part) how favorably they view the building of a new freeway.

Occasionally, we may be unsure of the direction of explanation.

Does human intelligence explain socioeconomic status or does socioeconomic status explain intelligence?

Explanatory Variables ──────────► Response Variables

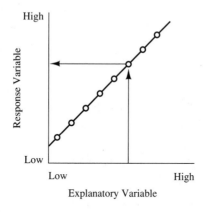

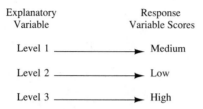

Explanatory Variable	Response Variable Scores
Level 1 ──────────►	Medium
Level 2 ──────────►	Low
Level 3 ──────────►	High

FIGURE 1.1
Relations between
Response Variables
and Explanatory
Variables

To shed light on questions similar to this one, we have to *decide* among models, some offering explanation in one direction and others offering explanation in the opposite direction.

The explanatory direction of a model is indicated by the directed arrow in the top panel of Figure 1.1. *Variability in the explanatory variable* explains variability in the response variable.

Increasing/Decreasing Relation

One of the commonest forms postulated for explanation is that the magnitude of the response variable will *increase* or *decrease* as the magnitude of the explanatory variable increases.

> Among children aged 7 to 17 years, running speed (in meters per minute over a 100-meter course) increases with age (in months).

Such a model specifies not only the direction of explanation but the *direction of change* in the response, up or down.

Rate of Change Relation

The *rate of change* in the response as well as the direction of change may be specifed. For example, the rate of change in the response may be postulated to be constant across the range of the explanatory variable. In that case, there is a straight line or *linear* explanatory relation.

The middle panel of Figure 1.1 describes a linear, increasing explanatory relation. As the value of the explanatory variable increases, the result is a *steady increase* in the value of the response variable.

Response Difference Relation

Another common form of explanatory relation is to postulate simply that differences in the explanatory variable are associated with *differences* in the response variable.

> U.S., Canadian, and Mexican legislators will be, in that order, progressively less favorable of U.S. immigration policy.

The response variable is a measure of favorability to U.S. immigration policy. Our explanatory model speculates on how the magnitude of this measure will change as we move among three groups of potential respondents. In this case, it *orders* the three with respect to the response.

The third panel of Figure 1.1 describes an explanatory relation similar to this— one between a *categorical* explanatory variable, such as nationality, and a *measured* response variable.

On occasion, a model can postulate *only* differences. For example, if three experimental drugs are administered, each to a different sample of respondents, we may be able to speculate in advance only that the magnitude of the response (for example, the proportion of the sample showing marked symptom relief) will be *different* among the three treatments.

1.2.4   Explanatory Relations and Variable Types

The kind of explanatory relation our model can posit is affected by the types of our explanatory and response variables. Not all variables can enter into the full range of relations. Distinctions among variable types can be made quite complex. However, modeling goals will be met by a principal division of variables into *measured, counted*, and *categorical*, and a secondary division of categorical variables into *dichotomous, ordered*, and *nonordered*.

Measured Variables

An observed variable is regarded as *measured* if it has the following four properties:

- Observations of the variable take a large number of values.
- The values of the variable are all numeric.
- When arranged from smallest to largest, these numeric values reflect progressively greater amounts of the variable.
- The numeric values of the variable are linked by a consistent unit of measurement.

In principle, our measured variable could take a very large number of values, but our measuring instruments typically limit our observed measurements; our observations are only to the closest centimeter, gram, or second. For now, we can be a bit arbitrary about what is a "large number" of values. If the other conditions are met, a variable with 20 or more distinct values typically will have the necessary fineness to be treated as measured. The measured variable, then, takes numeric values that can be arranged from smallest to largest, corresponding to lesser to greater amounts of the variable. What does it mean, though, for the variable to have a consistent *unit of measurement*?

A variable possesses a (consistent) unit of measurement if a *difference* of one unit in the scale of measurement (1 hour, 1 pound, 1 degree *C*, etc.) has the same meaning wherever that difference occurs. Having a unit of measurement allows us to interpret *differences in value* of observations of the measured variable. The larger the difference between two values of the variable, the larger the difference in the two amounts of the variable.

The weight of an experimental animal (measured to the closest gram, or gm) is a measured variable. The animal weighing 186 gm weighs more than the one weighing 175 gm. Furthermore, the difference in weights between these two animals (11 gm) is less than the difference in weights between an animal weighing 170 gm and one weighing 190 gm. The gram provides a unit of measurement for weight; it has a *consistent interpretation* across the range of numeric values that weight may take.

Counted Variables

A numeric variable that tells, for each observational unit, the number of times some event has occurred in or happened to that unit is a *counted variable*. They are, perhaps, easiest described by example.

- The number of arrests among juvenile males subsequent to first juvenile court appearance
- The number of children among the female Harvard MBAs of 1975
- The number of traffic citations among municipal bus drivers in Chicago in 1991

The counted variable takes only nonnegative integer values—0, 1, 2, ... etc. A number between 1 and 2 would not be possible no matter how good our "measuring instrument."

Categorical Variables

If our variable takes nonnumeric values or only a (very) limited number of numeric values, we refer to it as a *categorical variable*. The values of the categorical variable may or may not conform to a unit of measurement. Indeed, the values of the categorical variable need not be numeric. We require only that the categorical variable establish differences among observations by assigning them to different categories, not by measuring those differences. Within that broad characterization, it is useful to distinguish among three types of categorical variables: *ordered*, *nonordered*, and *dichotomous*.

Ordered Categories

The ordered categorical variable, as the name implies, has categories that are arranged in a strict order, reflecting the amount of the variable.

> Students in an architecture studio course have their term projects graded on a 5 point scale ranging from 1 for an Unsatisfactory performance through 5 for an Outstanding one.

The values of the term project grade are arranged in a definite order to reflect the relative merits of the students' projects. Despite this clear ordering, we may be reluctant to conclude that the difference of one "unit" between grades of 2 (Fair) and 1 has the same meaning as the difference in one unit between grades of 5 and 4 (Very Good). We may be unwilling to assume a *unit of measurement* in the grading.

Where the few values assumed by the variable may be ordered unambiguously, even in the absence of a unit of measurement, we speak of those values as describing *ordered categories*. Student projects assigned a grade of 2 fall into a quality of performance category located between the two categories 1 and 3 (Good). Numeric values or "labels" for the categories are not necessary; the descriptions Unsatisfactory, Fair, Good, Very Good, and Outstanding would serve equally well—as long as we make it clear that we intend the labels to be used to establish an ordering of the categories.

Nonordered Categories

Our modeling variables need not take values that are orderable.

> Students at MidAmerica College are categorized by ethnic origin as either American Indian, Asian-American, Black, Hispanic, or White.

The categories of ethnic origin possess no inherent "amount of" ordering and we refer to them as *nonordered* or *nominal categories*. They simply have different names.

Dichotomous Variables

If a variable can take only two values, assigning observations to one of two categories, we refer to it as *dichotomous*.

- The gender of a fourth-grade student is either male or female.
- Those taking the Bar Examination either pass or fail that examination.
- Some architecture students are left-handed; all others are right-handed.

The dichotomous variable enjoys a special status among categorical variables. As it has only two categories, there can be only one ordering of the categories (and its reversal). Also, as there are only two "points" at which the variable is observed, there is a single "unit" separating those two points. We exploit these properties of the dichotomous variable both in developing and interpreting explanatory models.

Importance of Variable Type

Variable types have been described as measured, counted, ordered, nonordered, or dichotomous. How do these distinctions affect the way in which explanatory relations are described?

The *increasing/decreasing* relation requires that the values of both explanatory and response variables be ordered from smallest to largest. Thus, the explanatory and response variables each must be either measured, counted, ordered, or dichotomous variables.

The *rate of response change* relation requires a unit of measurement for both the explanatory and response variables. As a result, each is either measured, dichotomous, or (possibly) an ordered categorical variable with a unit of measurement.

For *simple response difference* relations, explanatory and response variables may be any of the types.

1.2.5 Where Explanation Holds

Models must specify where the explanatory relation is thought to hold. Species, size, age, or other restrictions on the respondents may be important parts of a model. Does the explanation hold for all humans, only for females, or only for females over 13 years of age?

The *level of aggregation* of data is usually important; models for the behavior of individuals are likely to be different from those for groups. Time and place also may be relevant. Our model may explain the career choices made by college graduates in the 1960s but fail to explain the behavior of students in the 1990s.

To summarize this section, every model—once we have it—consists of the following four elements:

- *Identification of one or more explanatory variables (x_1, x_2) and a response variable (y).* The value of y is thought to be explained by the value of x_1, of x_2, or of both. We must specify the variables and the direction of explanatory relation.

- *Specification of how the variables are to be assessed.* What instruments or manipulations will be employed? Which variables will be measured and which categorical? How does this limit what we can specify about the explanatory relation?

- *Description of the explanatory relation.* Does the value of y increase/decrease with an increase in the value of x_1? If so, is the rate of change in y constant over the range of x_1? Or, can we only postulate that differences in the value of x_1 will be associated with differences in the value of y?

- *Nomination of appropriate respondents.* From what populations of potential subjects or observational units should we sample? Where, when, and to whom does our model apply?

1.3
The Development of Models

Where do our models come from? How do we create them? In answering these questions, we will distinguish between an *initial model*, the one we need to develop to get us started investigating a particular problem, and later models, those we develop as we continue our research.

1.3.1   The Initial Model: Starting with a Substantive Idea

Our initial model is invariably one based on a *substantive* question. We depend on past knowledge, theoretical and empirical, to raise some problem of sufficient interest that we want to look for an explanation. How do we start with such a question and refine it into a model with the elements described in the preceding section?

Our substantive interest may be as vague an idea as "something like Construct A ought to have an effect on something like Construct B." Clearly, much needs to be done before this idea becomes a model. Here are the steps we would take, the first being to specify what we mean by Constructs A and B.

Selecting Constructs

The behavioral sciences (as well as the biological) are marked by an abundance of constructs, many with closely connected "cousins." In everyday conversation, we may get away with using "angry," "aggressive," and "hostile" as if they were interchangeable. As scientific constructs, however, Anger, Aggression, and Hostility have distinctive definitions. We need to be certain to which constructs we want our model to refer: Do we want to study how Anger affects Hostility, or how Hostility influences Aggression?

In which constructs are we interested? If we choose our manipulations and assessments without careful consideration of the underlying constructs, we run the risk of investigating an unintended model.

Let's assume that we are interested in the influence of Anger (our explanatory variable) on Hostility (our response variable).

Selecting Assessments

Once we know the constructs we want our model to refer to, we can choose our variables. Unless the level of the construct is assigned (or *manipulated*), it must be *assessed*. Our assessment should possess *construct validity*. In our example, having decided it is the construct Hostility that we want represented by the response or *y* variable in our model, we need to insure that that variable really does assess Hostility and not, for example, Anger.

This stage requires attention to recent research literature. What evidence is there for the use of alternate approaches to assessment? In deciding which is the best approach, we must take into account the setting in which the assessments are to be made. Assessing Hostility is a different matter among 5 year olds than among middle-level managers in a commercial organization.

We may have decided, on this basis, that counting the number of times the third-grade boy hits the punching bag (after receiving news, perhaps false, about how well he did on his spelling test) provides an assessment of his Hostility level.

The urge to build our own assessment instruments should be resisted. Establishing the construct validity of an assessment *and* evaluating the role of a construct in a substantive model requires extensive work. It is important to realize that it is impossible to use the same set of observations both to establish that a variable is assessing what it was intended to *and* that the construct assessed is playing the role in the model that was hypothesized for it.

A second but no less important reason for using an established assessment whenever possible is that we can compare our results with those of other investigators employing the same instrument.

Checking Manipulations

We need to have just as much concern about the construct validity of manipulated variables as we do for those that are assessed. Does the manipulation "work"? A *manipulation check* is often desirable. It is mandatory for any previously untried manipulation.

First, though, what is a manipulated variable?

We referred above to counting the number of times a third-grade boy strikes a punching bag after being told his, perhaps spurious, spelling test results. This is a shorthand way of describing the model we are designing around the hypothesis that increasing Anger leads to higher levels of Hostility. We have reason to believe that striking the bag assesses Hostility—the greater the level of Hostility, the more strikes delivered. Counting the number of strikes provides an *assessment* of the level of Hostility.

Our model also assumes that the information given about spelling test performance *manipulates* Anger level. In designing our study, we *choose* to tell some boys that they did well and others that they did poorly *irrespective of how they actually did* in the expectation that those told they had done poorly will be angrier (and, thus, more hostile) than those told they had done well. If this expectation is warranted, we can speak of having *manipulated* Anger levels rather than of having assessed them.

Before we can interpret more punching bag striking among the "poor" spellers than among the "good" spellers as evidence of an Anger/Hostility link, we need some assurance, independent of punching bag striking, that the spelling test messages do indeed manipulate Anger. A manipulation check is needed to support our conclusion that the messages "worked," that Anger was induced or increased by the "poor performance" message, but not by the "good performance" one.

Choosing Respondents

Substantive considerations related to the choice of constructs, assessments, and manipulations should suggest the observational units or respondents appropriate to our model. Over which human or animal populations, for which institutions, in what locations, or at what times will variability in x, the explanatory variable, explain variability in y, the response variable? These are questions that must be considered in model development.

We choose to study the effect of manipulating spelling test performance on punching bag behavior among third-grade boys. While there may be some human populations—certain clinically depressed groups, for instance—for which we would not expect Anger to influence Hostility, it is probably a general relation. However, our choice of explanatory (spelling test performance manipulation) and response variables (punching bag striking) places constraints on the respondents appropriate to our model. The manipulation or assessment, or both, may be inappropriate guides to the constructs and their relation among airline pilots, United States Senators, or—perhaps—third grade girls.

The choice of respondents depends not only on the model's constructs but also on the chosen assessments or manipulations. Theory, assessment, and choice of respondents must each be rationalized against the others.

Deciding the Explanatory Relation

Our model needs to specify not only the explanatory and response constructs but the *form* of the explanatory relation linking their assessments or manipulations. For our example, we can specify the *direction* of response change; as Anger increases, so too, we postulate, will Hostility. We are able to specify not just that the two levels of the manipulated Anger (two levels of the variable x) ought to yield different levels of Hostility (the y variable), but that the higher Anger level will produce higher Hostility scores (greater numbers of hits on the punching bag).

Because our choice of explanatory variable manipulation allows us only two levels of Anger, we *cannot* specify any rate of response change as part of the model. Why is this true?

Most biological and behavioral responses are complexly determined. Any one model and its corresponding experiment or observational study can look at only a part of a complex theoretical structure. Often that means the postulated explanation may be relatively weak; variables other than the specific explanatory variables employed in the study also influence the response. We should, however, have some reasonable expectation of the *strength* of the explanatory relation when we design the study. The number of respondents to be sampled, for example, should reflect this anticipated strength.

Considering Alternative Explanations

We should always have in mind more than one model.

If there is a competing *theoretical model*—a different arrangement of constructs on the explanatory and response sides—we should anticipate this as much as possible by including additional assessments or manipulations.

If there is a potentially competing *interpretation*—because of our choice of manipulations, assessments, or respondents—we should anticipate that too. Auxiliary variables or samples may be appropriate.

If we have another *hunch*, not firmly grounded in any theory but one we can gain insight from without compromising our more firmly based goals, we should certainly attempt to investigate it as well. It may not be true that we only pass this way once, but it certainly costs to come back a second time!

1.3.2   Later Models: Using Observations to Improve Models

After we've taken the initial plunge, developing a substantive-based model and collecting data for that model, where do we go? In all likelihood, we will want to use those data to develop a *new model*, different from and, we hope, better than our initial one. After the first, every explanatory model has roots both in theory and in data we've collected. In this section, we preview how we look at our data to take us on to the next model—how to develop data-and-theory-based models.

We've said that the purpose of a model is to *explain* the variability in some response variable. All models are not equally good at this. Some models explain more of the variability than others. A model that explains more of the response variability is said to provide a *better fit* to the response observations. We use the data we've collected to determine the fit of one or more models. Those fits, in turn, give us a basis for deciding upon a new model; based on our substantive knowledge and the data we've just collected, do we now have a better way to explain our response variable?

Should we change our initial model? If so, how? Which of the four model elements of Section 1.2.5 should we address?

- Could we make a better selection of explanatory constructs?
- Are some assessments of our constructs better than others?
- Should we change the form of the explanatory relation?
- Do we have the right specification of respondents or should some be excluded or others added?

These are all questions we *might* pursue using the data of our initial model to suggest answers. Which questions we feel are appropriate will be influenced by how firmly we are committed to our original model and how open we are to letting the data suggest new models. In this section, which owes much to Leamer's (1978) excellent but more advanced discussion of model modification, we describe a range of model decision strategies, what can be done once we have evaluated our initial model against the data.

Rejection

At one end of this range of modeling decisions is the strategy of considering the fit to the data of only one model, the original one. If the fit is good enough, if enough of the response variability is explained by our model, it is retained. On the other hand, if the fit is not good enough, the model is rejected.

This modeling approach bears a close resemblance to the *classical hypothesis testing* tradition of statistical analysis. An all-or-none decision is made with respect to our theory-based model. We return to theory to develop a new model, again along the lines of Section 1.3.1.

Selection

We may have begun our data collection considering two or more *alternative models*—ways of explaining the response variable. Each model is fit to the data and the modeling task is to decide which one among the adequately fitting models provides the best fit. This best-fitting model is retained and the others are rejected.

We may then choose to evaluate our best-fitting model against data from a new population of respondents:

> Will the educational level of first-time employees explain variability in trade-union membership in Great Britain as well as it does in the United States?

Or, we may want to try out an alternate assessment of a key construct:

> Can we use self-reported annual income to explain job tenure or must we use employer-reported salary data?

Minor Modification

Model modification pays attention to our data in suggesting a new model, but *modifications* make less extreme changes in models than do *revisions*, taken up next.

Depending again on how firmly wedded we are to the details of an initial model, we may regard a modified model either as a brand new model or as one essentially equivalent to the old one, differing from it in no substantively important way. Not all scientists agree on how "serious" the following four modifications are. They are presented, though, in increasing order of potential seriousness.

- *Elimination of Outliers.* Our initial model may provide a good fit to most of our observations, but a few data points may stick out like the proverbial sore thumb. These observations—labeled *outliers*—would appear not to belong with the others and can occur for a variety of reasons.

  There may be errors in recording data or stray observations from wrong populations (e.g., male rather than female). By chance alone, a very small or very large response may be observed. We may choose to modify our model by fitting it not to all of our observations but to a reduced set of respondents by eliminating these outliers from consideration. Issues in the detection and resolution of outliers are addressed in Chapter 9.

- *Transformation of Explanatory Relation.* We may find, for example, that the fit of our model is improved if we replace the values of an explanatory variable (or the response variable) with their square roots. If we had postulated only an *increasing/decreasing* relation, such a transformation would do no "damage" to our original model. On the other hand, if we had reason to believe there was a *linear* relation between explanatory and response variables, this transformation would give us a "new" model. Transformation of model variables is discussed in Chapter 10.

- *Model Contraction.* We may find from our data that one or more of the explanatory variables originally specified in our model is not necessary. That is, these variables may be dropped from the model without leading to a poorer fit of the model to the data. The data may suggest a "new" model that is simpler than the older one. The search for parsimonious explanations, for simple but useful models is a hallmark of science. As a result, model contraction is very often guided at least as much by substantive considerations as by the data. The search for simpler but adequately fitting and substantively meaningful models is at the heart of modeling. As such, it will receive considerable attention. Chapters 8 through 14 effectively describe strategies for identifying such models.

- *Model Expansion.* Alternatively, we may find—again from our data or from subject matter considerations—that we can improve the fit of our model by including explanatory variables other than those in the original model. To discover this, of course, we must have included these additional variables in our data collection! Model expansion creates a "new" model that is more complex than the older one. Owing to the importance of parsimonious explanation, we shall emphasize model contraction over model expansion, moving from the more complex to the less complex rather than the reverse, whenever possible.

Seriousness of Model Modification

For the rejection and selection strategies, the evaluated models were all *confirmation models*. That is, all were specified in advance and we could use our data set to make "final" decisions among them.

What is the status of a *modified model*? Under what circumstances will a "new" model be a confirmation model, one that can be evaluated against the data already collected? And, when should we have to collect additional data to evaluate the modified model? These are not simple data analysis or statistical issues. Substantive judgment certainly has to be exercised and not everyone will agree with the judgment.

One recommendation is safe, however. It is imperative that we *always report* each model that we consider and the reasoning that we used to take us from one model to another. Only with this information can our colleagues make reasonable judgments about the status of our models and conclusions.

Major Revision

Model *revision* depends much more heavily than does *modification* on the data. Just as model rejection could be likened to hypothesis testing or classical confirmatory data analysis, revision has some of the same flavor as exploratory data analysis—asking the data to structure themselves, with minimal theoretical guidance.

An extreme example of model revision is the technique of subset regression analysis. Given a set of, say, 10 possible explanatory variables, subset regression is a technique by which we can find the subset of, say, 4 variables that provides the "best" fit to our data set. The choice of these 4 is dictated *solely* by relations among the observations. No substantive theory enters into that particular decision.

Model revision need not be divorced completely from substantive considerations. The thorough data analyst may spot relations in the data that—after the fact—make perfectly good theoretical sense. A *revised model*, though, is surely a *hypothesis model*, needing further data for confirmation.

Making Progress

At some point in time in the progress of any research project, we may have several tentative models for a particular behavioral or biological response. While there may be no one "right" model, there may be several "useful" ones.

Some of our models will be better developed than others, more "in the mainstream." One may be no better than a wild hunch. Another may be backed by a long series of research projects. We need, though, to carry them all forward, each in its own stage of development. That means that in any particular data analysis, modeling will lead us to reject some models, modify or revise others, and outright "invent" yet additional ones.

1.3.3   Strength of Explanatory Relation

An extremely important aspect of the modeling approach to data analysis is that there is a *strength* to each explanatory relation. We want not just to find one or more good models via comparison, modification, or revision, but to assess and report explanatory strength as well. Perhaps more than anything else, it is this emphasis on "how big is the influence" that sets modeling apart from more classical, hypothesis-testing approaches to data analysis.

1.4
Collecting Data for Models

There are two traditions in science for collecting data: the experiment and the observational study. In practice, most scientists do not think about which might be "better" for a particular study. Rather, we all get used to using one or the other. However, there is an important distinction between the two methods in what we mean by *explanation* and, consequently, in how we interpret our models.

1.4.1   Experiments

The hallmark of the experiment from a modeling perspective is that at least one of the explanatory variables is *manipulated* by the experimenter. That is, it is the experimenter who determines which experimental units are to be observed at which value of an explanatory variable. Often, the explanatory variable is one identifying the treatment to which a respondent is assigned and we speak of an experimental unit as having been *assigned to a treatment level*. (In more complex experiments, as we will see in Chapter 14, assignment may be to a particular *sequence* of treatment levels rather than to a particular level.)

Here are three examples of an experiment, not all, as we'll see shortly, of the same quality:

- Ten rats are assigned at random to each of four restricted diets. Following 10 days of dieting, their maze-running speeds are measured.

- At the beginning of the school year, 20 fifth-grade classrooms are selected at random from among those in a particular school district. The selected classrooms are then assigned to one of two arithmetic instruction conditions, depending on whether the classroom is in the north or south half of the district. At the end of the school year, the arithmetic achievements of students in those classrooms are measured.

- A random sample of 50 mothers of low-birth-weight babies born in Central Hospital between January and July of 1991 is identified. The mothers are provided a special infant formula and the weights of their low-birth-weight children at two years of age are compared with those of a random sample of 50 normal-birth-weight children born in Central during the same period.

In each instance, a respondent—rat, classroom, or baby—is assigned by an experimenter to a particular *treatment level*.

The assignment of respondents to an explanatory variable value can take one of two forms, *random* or *constrained*. Choice of assignment strategy has implications for model interpretation.

Random Assignment

In the first example above, individual rats were assigned at random among the four diets. One purpose of random assignment is to protect against the *confounding* of some other characteristic of respondents with treatment assignment. Thus, littermates (having the same parents) were not assigned, except by chance, the same treatment. Nor were earlier-born litters systematically assigned to one diet and later-born ones to a second.

Absence of confounding makes it more certain that any observed response differences are due to the manipulated explanatory variable rather than to something merely correlated with it.

We are now in a position to say something more about the explanatory relation. Under those circumstances in which we can be certain that observed response differences are due to explanatory variable differences, the explanatory relation can be typified as *causal*. Our use of *causal* is restricted to meaning that the explanatory relation has been assessed in a particular way. This view of causality in science is inspired by the excellent discussion of the question in Cook and Campbell (1979). We follow their prescription that only the randomized experiment offers evidence of a causal relation. Both a manipulated explanatory variable and a random assignment of respondents to levels of that variable are necessary to assert that differences in the explanatory variable *caused* the observed differences in the response variable.

Our position notwithstanding, the question of establishing causality in science is far from settled. The interested reader may want to consult such recent discussions as those of Cox (1992) or of Rubin (1991), who offer quite different views on when causality might be inferred from an experimental result.

For our modeling purposes, random assignment will be treated as providing *explanatory control*, giving considerable assurance that we can interpret the manipulation as responsible for any observed shift in the response. If we were to invoke the manipulation in the future, we would expect to see the response shift again. We have reason to believe *we can make it happen*.

Random assignment cannot *insure* a lack of confounding, but it can reduce the likelihood of confounding to that of a chance event. There is some small probability that the 10 fattest rats would be assigned, at random, to the same diet. It is prudent, in developing or assessing models, to be alert to competing explanations even when assignment is random.

Constrained Assignment

The other two experiments listed above did not involve random assignment of respondents. Let us see how this influences our interpretation of those studies.

In the arithmetic instruction example, classrooms were assigned to treatments not at random but in *blocks*—all the classrooms sampled from the southern part of the district received one treatment, those sampled from the northern part received another. The nonrandom assignment may have been for administrative convenience—it is easier to have all schools in a geographical region using the same instruction—or it may have been linked to some other consideration.

In any event, the nonrandom assignment makes the interpretation of results difficult. A difference in year-end achievement between the two blocks of classrooms could be due to *any variable* on which the blocks differ systematically. One variable differentiating the blocks is arithmetic instruction; but the blocks might differ as well in characteristics of students, teachers, or community. Because one or more of these may be *confounded* with treatment, explanatory control has been lost.

The same is true for the low-birth-weight study. There, constrained assignment may have been used to assure that a "better" treatment was provided those who "really needed it"—only the low-birth-weight babies were provided the special formula. Treatment—regular or special diet—is confounded with another characteristic of the infants—normal or low birth weight. Any effect of the special formula cannot be separated from the effect of differences in birth weight—and of anything correlated with that weight difference, such as mother's age or health.

From the perspective of explanatory control, random assignment of respondents is always preferred. There are situations in which, for political, ethical, or other insurmountable reasons, randomization is not feasible. Cook and Campbell (1979) provide an extensive discussion of a variety of experimental designs involving constrained assignment. They term these designs *quasi-experimental* to stress the absence of random assignment and, hence, of explanatory control.

1.4.2   Observational Studies

If the levels of all explanatory variables are assessed or *observed* rather than assigned or manipulated, the study is *observational* rather than experimental. The following are examples of observational studies.

- One hundred households are selected at random from among those sending children to the public schools in a large North American city. Heads of these households are then interviewed and it is observed that those with more formal education express a more positive attitude towards the school district's multicultural curriculum planning.

- A survey is made of deaths recorded during the first 6 months of 1992. The survey reveals that white males dying in Alaska were considerably younger than those dying in Florida.

- In a study of Graduate Record Examination (GRE) scores, it is reported that women graduating from MidWestern State University earned higher verbal subtest scores than did men graduating from NorthEastern State University.

No treatment was manipulated in any of these examples. No experimenter assigned respondents to levels of education, state of residence, alma mater, or gender! Hence, it would be inappropriate to conclude that invoking any implied manipulation necessarily would have the effect suggested by the study.

If the less educated interviewees in the first study were somehow "made" to get more education, there is no assurance their attitudes towards multiculturalism in the schools would change. Attitude may be a function not of education itself, but of some unobserved (in this study) factor that encourages people to continue or to leave school. That is, what we observed may be an example of the influence of a "third variable," something not assessed but correlated with both the explanatory and the response variable.

Similarly, we should pause before concluding that we could prolong the lives of Alaskan males by moving them to Florida. The migration of large numbers of young men to Alaska and of older men to Florida—hence their overrepresentation in those populations—is enough in itself to explain the discrepancy in ages at death. Nothing need be assumed about the effect of state of residence on the individual's life expectancy once he arrives there.

The GRE example provides an extra dose of confounding. Gender and institution are both confounded here with (a) whatever leads students to choose one school over another and (b) whatever differential treatment the institutions may provide one gender.

These examples were chosen to illustrate a point about the limitations that observational studies impose on inferences about manipulation and causality. The shortcomings of these examples, though, should not be construed as damning observational research. Useful models can be constructed for observational data, ones that do not infer that "if we were to manipulate the explanatory variable we would observe change in the response."

Similarly, observational studies may be carefully enough designed that we can "rule out" the more important competing or alternative explanations by including additional assessments or collecting data in other populations.

The hallmark of the observational study is that respondents are *selected* rather than assigned. In the absence of any experimental manipulation, any relation between the explanatory and response variables has to be a function of that selection of respondents. We must take pains to insure that the selection neither "forces" the relation nor precludes it. How should respondents be selected? Just as random assignment plays a key role in interpreting experimental outcomes, *random selection* is important in observational studies.

Random Selection

We usually wish to generalize our findings, to have some confidence that our model fits not just the data we collect, but other data we might encounter in the future. For this, we need to be able to model the "behavior" of the explanatory and response variables in our observations as a "sample" of their behavior in the larger, to-be-generalized-to world of potential observations.

The surest way to pursue this goal is to select the respondents at random from that larger world or "population." Random selection, as we see beginning with Chapter 3, is a vital element in the assumptions we need to make if we are to evaluate and compare models.

Samples of Convenience

When we can't sample from the population we prefer, we have to ask if the population which is available is suitable for evaluating our model. How do the two populations differ? Will the explanatory response relation differ? Will we introduce contaminating or confounding factors?

For example, we might have a model we think describes the influence of parental social attitudes on the social attitudes of their 17-year-old children. We can collect data only by sampling (at random, of course) from among those enrolled in metropolitan high schools and living with their parents. How might these limitations affect our results and their interpretation?

Anticipating potential problems allows us to redesign our study. We may choose to select our sample in a different fashion, or—barring that—we may choose to include additional variables, permitting us to evaluate alternative models for our response observations.

It is important to question whether *samples of convenience*, those most readily available or most readily collected, are suitable. When in doubt, we must at least describe characteristics of the data set that we think may limit the generalizability of our findings. Again, Cook and Campbell (1979) provide a useful catalog of factors that are potentially threatening to the validity of interpretation of the observational study. Lack of randomness in sample selection is both a serious bar to generalization and, alas, a common fault in observational study design. The mathematical or statistical side to modeling—assessing model fit and comparing the fit of one model to that of another—assumes we have sampled at random. Any conclusions we reach on the basis of these fits in the absence of random sampling are likely to possess little *dependability*; the results for a new sample could be strikingly different.

Predictive Explanatory Relations

Explanatory models for randomized experiments, wherein respondents or other units of observation are randomly allocated among the levels of one or more manipulated explanatory variables (the *alternate treatment levels*), were earlier described as *causal*. The random assignment of units of observation among treatments makes it likely that any systematic response differences among treatments are due to differences in treatment (or explanatory variable level); we have reason to believe that an explanatory variable difference causes a response variable difference.

In well-designed observational studies, with respondents randomly sampled from well-defined populations, we also employ a characterization of the explanatory relation. We call it *predictive*. This term emphasizes that, given an explanatory relation, we can make useful response predictions for new observations. Thus, based on the results of our first observational study example, we might be able to predict a certain more positive attitude towards multiculturalism in the schools for a "new" householder who was a college graduate than for one who was a high school dropout. These new observations may even be characterized by explanatory variable scores slightly different from those encountered in the original observational study. We can't say that an increasing amount of education *causes* more favorable attitudes, but we can utilize the explanatory relations to *predict* response variable behavior from explanatory variable performance. Prediction, when sufficiently accurate, is in itself an important scientific goal.

1.5
Model Assessment and Variable Type

We now have a vocabulary to describe or characterize models. Now we can begin developing and evaluating them. Although we will emphasize and exploit a common approach to modeling, the nuts and bolts of assessing models, fitting them to our data, and comparing those fits will vary a bit depending on the types of our explanatory and response variables. We take this into account in the organization of this book, as summarized in Table 1.1.

1.5.1 Organization by Response Variable Type

The mechanics of how an explanatory model is fit to a set of data are determined primarily by the type of the response variable. This, then, is our major organizational principle. The topics in the first block of chapters, those dealing with the modeling of a *measured response*, make up the study of *multiple regression* , and, in the case of designed experiments, what is known as the *fixed-effects model* of the *analysis of variance* (ANOVA). Chapters 15 through 18 develop *logistic regression* as an approach to the modeling of the *categorical response*. The *dichotomous response* is the topic of Chapters 16 and 17, while the multicategory *ordered* and *nonordered response* variables are examined in Chapter 18. Finally, Chapter 19 extends these regression ideas to the modeling of the *counted response*, making use of the technique of *Poisson regression*.

A minor organizing principle to the book is the type and number of explanatory variables present in our models. Within each of the response types, we move from single explanatory variable models to more complex ones.

Historically, multiple regression, ANOVA, count data, and categorical data analysis have been treated separately. There have been two reasons for this. First, the technical or statistical underpinning becomes more complex as one moves from the single measured response to the counted or categorical response. This has encouraged postponing the study of models for the nonmeasured response until the student was more "sophisticated" statistically and mathematically.

Second, parallel to this increasing statistical complexity, the computational aspects of modeling across the different response types appears rather differentially complicated. Until computer support of the kind we are now accustomed to became widely available, the researcher had to be familiar with several different statistical theories to do the computations. Now, freed of these interrelated burdens, we can benefit from the generality of the modeling approach across the variety of potential observational or experimental responses.

T A B L E 1.1
Organization of Modeling Topics

Models with a Measured Response Variable:

Chapter 2	The Measured Response Variable
Chapter 3	Simple Linear Regression: An Introduction
Chapter 4	Simple Linear Regression: Estimation
Chapter 5	Simple Linear Regression: Inference About Models
Chapter 6	Categorical Explanatory Variables: One Way ANOVA
Chapter 7	Several Explanatory Variables: Multiple Regression
Chapter 8	Comparing Fuller with Less Full Models
Chapter 9	Assessing a Model's Adequacy: Individual Observations
Chapter 10	Assessing a Model's Adequacy: Checking Assumptions
Chapter 11	Categorical Explanatory Variables: ANOVA Models
Chapter 12	Auxiliary Variable Models: Enhancing Model Sensitivity
Chapter 13	Auxiliary Variable Models: Moderating Explanatory Variable Influence
Chapter 14	Introduction to Modeling Repeated Observations

Models with a Categorical Response Variable:

Chapter 15	The Categorical Response Variable: Characteristics
Chapter 16	Logistic Regression: Modeling the Proportion of Successes
Chapter 17	Group Logistic Regression Models
Chapter 18	Logistic Regression for Multiple-response Categories

Models with a Counted Response Variable:

Chapter 19	Poisson Regression for Counts in Time or Space

Several chapters listed under *Models with a Measured-response Variable* in Table 1.1 have greater generality that this organization would suggest. Chapters 3 through 5 review statistical ideas of populations, samples, and the sampling distribution of estimates of population characteristics, ideas that are equally useful when the response population is categorical or counted as when it consists of measured observations. The conventions for including the levels of one or more categorical explanatory variable in a linear model, developed in Chapters 6 and 11, are applicable with all response types, as are the concept of comparing the fits of a Fuller and Less Full model (Chapter 8), the use of auxiliary variables in models (Chapters 12 and 13), and modeling repeated observations of the same response variable (Chapter 14).

1.5.2   Scope of Coverage

Something should be said to the reader who already has some training in applied statistics about what this book does not cover. The major goals here are to introduce a coherent set of modeling ideas and to illustrate their application to a broad range of observational and experimental data sets, characterized by different data types. In emphasizing coherency of approach, we necessarily neglect in varying degrees alternate, more specialized data-analysis techniques and topics. Here are some examples of this. Early in Chapter 6, we will see how to use our linear-models approach to assess the magnitude of the difference between the means in two response populations. This gives the same result as readers may have already learned to associate with the "independent groups *t-test*." Because we want to place the stress on the inferred *magnitude* of the mean difference rather than on the *decision* as to whether that mean difference is "significantly larger than zero," we do our work in the *regression* rather than the *t-testing* context.

Similarly, throughout our linear models development of topics that are elsewhere developed in the analysis of variance (ANOVA) context (in Chapters 6, 11, 12, and 14), we will be concerned with the size of between treatments response differences rather than with the significance of effects. As a result, we will report and discuss linear model parameter estimates and their confidence intervals more often than classical ANOVA tables breaking down the sum of squared response observations. Along this same line, rather than focus on the significance of an *interaction* between effects, we will look, in similar circumstances, at the size of explanatory influences in models we describe as *modular*.

Importantly, in modeling both observational and experimental data, we will treat all of our explanatory variables as taking *fixed* rather than *random* values. What this means, essentially, is that, for purposes of drawing inferences, we consider what would happen if we were to repeat our study over and over, sampling from the response variable anew each time while keeping the explanatory variable scores— and, hence, the response populations from which we sample—as they were in the original study, *fixed at those initial values*. We do this for two reasons.

In the case of an observational study, we are interested in the dependability of our estimate of the magnitude of an explanatory variable's influence on the response *given the design of that particular study*, which we tend to think of as the only one available to us. Were we interested, say, in estimating the degree of correlation between two variables rather than a directional influence of one on the other, we would want to treat the observations of *both* variables as randomly determined by our sampling. The analysis of a particular data set by *regression* methods may be neither more nor less legitimate than the analysis of those same data in terms of a *bivariate* (or *multivariate*) *correlation model*. The two simply answer different questions. In this book, we are interested in the questions posed by the regression model.

In the case of an experimental study, we regard the levels of all explanatory variables as fixed because we are interested in estimating the magnitude of response differences between treatments or groups rather than in accounting for response variance. Again, the choice between a *fixed-effects* analysis of variance and a *variance components model* depends on the questions we want to ask of the experimental results.

1.6
Summary

Models are essential to science. They go straight to the heart of the scientific enterprise by expressing the scientist's belief, supported by observation, that one variable helps to *explain* a second. Models both communicate the specific goals and results of a study and advance our systematic understanding. This chapter proposes modeling as a *general* approach to the posing of scientific questions and the analysis of data collected to shed light on those questions. The vocabulary of modeling is introduced and the dependence of models, both on substantive knowledge and on data, is established.

2

The Measured Response Variable

The data analyses most commonly reported in the behavioral and biological sciences are applications of *linear regression* and the *analysis of variance*. The two approaches, closely related as we will see in Chapters 6 and 11, are appropriate to the study of many explanatory models where the response variable is *measured*. To prepare the way for the introduction of these standard modeling applications, this chapter is devoted to describing more fully the measured response variable.

We learn in this chapter what it means for a response to be considered as measured, how to describe a *sample* and a *population* of measured responses, and the role of an explanatory variable with respect to a population or populations of responses.

Most of the sample description ideas will be familiar to readers. On the other hand, some of the population description notions—particularly those relating to *conditional* populations—are likely to be new. They are important concepts, however, for modeling and the reader should become very comfortable with them. To make these new ideas as accessible to readers as possible we begin with a leisurely discussion of their modeling implications, first for observational studies and then for experiments.

2.1
Observational Samples, Populations, and Models

Before we say much about the characteristics of the measured response, we need to expand a bit on two points in Chapter 1. The first relates to the role of samples and populations in models. The second relates to "explaining" variability in a response.

We say that we are interested in modeling as a way of explaining what is going on in our data. Taken quite literally, that would seem to mean that we are interested only in the particular observations we have collected in an experiment or field study. Is that true?

Later in this chapter, we will introduce a set of response variable scores, the heights at 18 years of age of 28 boys born in Berkeley, California. Are we interested in the heights of these particular 28 boys? No. There is nothing so distinctive about them that they should be singled out for special study. There is variability in the heights of these boys, but why would we be interested in explaining that variability?

Our interest more likely is in the *general question* of why some adolescent boys are taller than others. We are interested in explaining the variability in height among 18-year-old boys *in general*.

Put in statistical terms, for observational studies like the adolescent height one we are interested in explaining the response variability, not in any specific sample, but *in some population*, namely the population from which that sample was selected. *Models are for populations, not for samples.*

We use sample data in developing and assessing models not because of any special interest in the sample, but because we believe that samples provide valuable information about populations. To justify this belief, certain precautions must be taken in collecting our samples and certain assumptions must be met by the sampled observations. These assumptions are taken up in Chapter 3.

2.2
Explaining Response Variability in the Observational Population

We say we want our models for observational data to *explain* response variability in some population. In Chapter 1 we learned a bit about the different *meanings* that could attach to explanation. In particular, we singled out two paradigms for which specific, and quite different, interpretations could be given explanation. Throughout this book, these two paradigms will be of central interest and it is worth emphasizing their characteristics.

In the *randomized experiment*, subjects, usually representative members of some larger population, are randomly allocated among alternate treatments (i.e., among the levels of an explanatory variable). If we subsequently observe systematic differences in the response variable for those allocated to different treatments, this random allocation provides support for the notion that treatment differences *caused* the response differences. That is, we have reason to believe that if we were to allocate new subjects from that same population randomly among these treatments we could create similar response variable differences. Later in this chapter we'll take up the relationship between this *causal* notion of explanation and the characteristics of response populations.

In the *observational study*, we cannot assign or manipulate the values of the explanatory variable. Rather, the explanatory values we observe are a consequence of the participants selected. If participants are *randomly sampled* from one or more well-defined populations, we describe the explanatory relation as *predictive*. By that we mean that we expect to be able to use the relation to make useful predictions of the response variable for new samples drawn from those populations.

Let's look now at this notion of *predictive* explanation from a response population perspective. What will it mean for an explanatory variable to provide a predictive explanation for a population of measured responses? First, to repeat something from Chapter 1, our models will never *fully* explain the response population. The phenomena we study in the biological and behavioral sciences are subject to so many influences that we can never expect to capture them all in our research. Rather, the explanatory variables in any single model will explain only some part of the response variability reflected in the population.

But what does it mean for an explanatory variable to explain, even in part, the population response variability? To answer this question, we'll return to the adolescent height example, illustrate it with a picture, and introduce some new ideas that we'll return to in the final parts of the chapter.

The new ideas go by the names *population mean, certainty, unconditional response population*, and *conditional response population*. Let's see how we use those ideas.

Suppose someone tells you that a boy has been selected at random from among all 18-year-old boys. You are asked to predict his height. What should you predict? You know only that the selected boy's height belongs to the population of all 18-year-old boys' heights. These heights, measured, say, in centimeters, meet our Chapter 1 ideas of observations on a measured variable. They will take on many different values; there is considerable variability in the heights of boys of a given age. And, we have in the centimeter a consistent unit of measurement.

A reasonable prediction for the height of our randomly selected boy is that it will be a *typical* height in that population. You wouldn't expect the shortest or the tallest boy to have been picked out. For a measured variable like height, "typical" usually translates into *average*. Thus, you could predict the boy to be of average height. Or in statistical terms, you'd *estimate* the height of the randomly chosen boy to be the *mean* of the heights in the population from which he was selected or, equivalently, the *population mean* of those heights.

Right, you've made an estimate. But what's your *certainty* about the correctness of your estimate? You know that you might be wrong. Not all 18-year-old boys have the same height. There is variability in their heights and you can't be certain that the chosen boy will have a height exactly at the population mean. Your certainty about the correctness of your prediction of that population mean, however, will be greater the smaller the *variability* in the population. For a measured response, it is convenient to use as our index of variability the *standard deviation* (SD) of the response observations making up a population. If all the heights are very close to the population mean, the SD (the square root of the average of the squared distances of the response observations about their mean) will be small and you can be fairly certain of your estimate. On the other hand, if the population of heights has a large SD (or variance, the square of the SD), you can be quite wrong about the boy's real height when you predict it to be the population mean. You'd have little certainty in the correctness of your estimate. (We'll have more to say about the standard deviation and its definition and computation in Section 2.4. For now, it can be thought of as a numeric index of response variability. The larger the SD, the greater the variability.)

Now, let's bring an explanatory variable into play. Suppose someone again tells you that an 18-year-old boy has been selected at random and you are to predict his height. This time, though, you are also told that this particular boy is known to have stood 85 cm tall when he was 2 years old. What do you predict his height to be? A reasonable estimate, by the same logic as before, again would be a population mean. Now, though, it would be the mean of the population of heights, not of all 18-year-old boys, but of *just those* who were 85 cm tall as 2 year olds. We refer to this new population as a *conditional response population*; it is a response population *conditional* upon an explanatory variable taking a certain value.

How certain should you be about your prediction this second time? There is still variability in the heights of these 18-year-olds; not all boys who stood 85 cm tall at age 2 grew up to be the same height at age 18. When you give as your prediction the mean of that population you still may be wrong. Again, the SD of the conditional response population tells you how certain you can be about the correctness of your prediction.

In this second example, the random selection of an 18-year-old boy happened to turn up someone who was 85 cm tall at 2 years of age. You then used that information in making your estimate; you estimated as his height the mean of the population of age-18 heights of those who were 85 cm tall at age 2. If the random selection of an 18-year-old had turned up a boy who was 90 cm tall at 2 years of age, you would have used that information in making your prediction. You would have used as your estimate the mean of a second conditional population, the population of age-18 heights for boys who were 90 cm tall at age 2. Similarly, if the randomly chosen 18-year-old had been 80 cm tall at age 2, your estimate of his present height would use that fact. Your prediction would be the mean of the population of heights of 18-year-old boys who were 80 cm tall at 2 years, the mean of a third conditional population.

We could continue in this way, describing a different conditional population of age-18 heights for each possible value of the explanatory variable, age-2 height. Each of these conditional (measured) response populations has a mean and an SD.

Given information about these conditional response populations, you would then be able to *tailor* your estimate of an 18-year-old boy's height, making it dependent on the particular value of the explanatory variable by using the mean for the appropriate conditional population. You would also be able to assess the certainty of your prediction: The smaller the SD in the conditional population, the greater your certainty.

Now, let's change the prediction task slightly. Instead of predicting the height of just one 18-year-old boy, you are to estimate the heights of each of a large number of 18-year-old boys. In fact, you can think of estimating the height of every 18-year-old boy in the population. For any one boy, though, you know his age-2 height. In making each of your predictions, you take into account the value of this explanatory variable. Taking an explanatory variable into account means that you are using an *explanatory model*.

How good is this model? It is good to the extent that when you use it you *increase the certainty* of your predictions, assessed across all these predictions. The certainty of any one of your predictions depends on the SD of the corresponding conditional response population. If that conditional SD—one taking a particular height at age 2 into account—is *smaller* than the SD of the *unconditional population*—that for all 18-year-olds, whatever their infant height—then you have increased your certainty about the correctness of that particular estimate.

If the SD in *each* of the *conditional response populations* (one for each distinct explanatory variable value) is smaller than the SD of the *unconditional population*, then you clearly have increased certainty in each of your predictions. You will have explained at least some of the variability in the response and your model has some explanatory power.

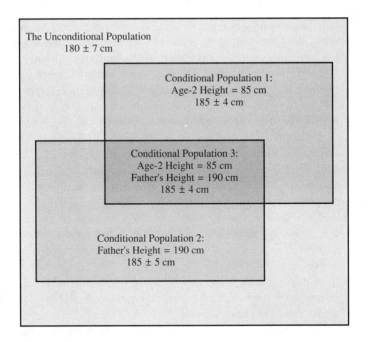

FIGURE 2.1
Unconditional and Conditional Response Populations: Heights of 18-Year-Old Boys

We've just said what it means for an explanatory variable in an observational study to explain some of a response's population variability. It means that when we include that variable in our model, we increase our certainty overall. Knowing height at age 2—using that as an explanatory variable—may increase our certainty about the heights of 18-year-old boys.

These ideas about *unconditional* and *conditional response populations, population means,* and *certainties* are illustrated in Figure 2.1. The figure as a whole represents the unconditional population of age 18 heights and we have given it a mean of 180 cm and an SD of 7 cm (180 ± 7 cm). The figure depicts, within this unconditional population, several conditional populations. Each of these conditional populations is a population of 18-year-old boys' heights in which the boys all share the same value on one or more explanatory variables.

One conditional population is that for 18-year-olds whose height at age 2 was 85 cm. It has an expected value of 185 cm and an SD of 4 cm. This conditional SD is smaller than the unconditional one, so we would increase the certainty of our prediction of a boy's age if we were to take his infant height into account. A second conditional response population is illustrated for the heights of 18-year-old boys whose fathers were 190 cm tall. Father's height is an alternate explanatory variable. This conditional population has an expected value of 185 cm and an SD of 5 cm. The conditional SD is again less than the unconditional one and taking into account father's height when estimating a boy's height will make us more certain of our estimate.

Finally, a third conditional population is sketched in Figure 2.1. It is the population of heights of boys who were 85 cm tall at age 2 *and* whose fathers were 190 cm tall. This conditional population takes *both* explanatory variables into account. The conditional expected value is 185 cm and the conditional SD is 4 cm.

Assuming similar hypothetical results for the conditional populations associated with other values of the two explanatory variables, taken singly and together, we interpret Figure 2.1 as telling us that using information about *either* age 2 height or father's height or *both* will increase our certainty about age-18 heights. Of the two, knowledge of infant height appears to increase our certainty more—the conditional SD taking that variable into account is smaller. The example also suggests that, while taking either explanatory variable into account increases certainty, there may be no advantage to taking both into account; the conditional SD for the model with *both* explanatory variables is no smaller than that for the model that includes only height at age 2.

The "best" model for age-18 height, then, may be the one with age 2 height as the single explanatory variable. We will judge models for observational studies by how much they increase our certainty about the response (reduce the unconditional response variability).

We will return to the consideration of conditional response populations, their means and certainties, particularly as we encounter these in experimental studies, in the final section of this chapter.

For now, though, let us learn a bit more about the measured response variable.

2.3
What Characterizes a Response Variable as Measured?

In Chapter 1 we sketched briefly the characteristics of a *measured variable*. We'll review those ideas now in the context of the variable being a *response*.

2.3.1   Smaller and Larger Responses

The measured variable takes numeric values that can be arranged in order from smallest to largest. The first implication of a measured-response variable is that the response must also possess *orderable magnitudes*.

> Susan, Joe, and Karen participate in a foot race together, completing the 200-meter distance in 32, 34, and 38 seconds, respectively. We say that Karen took longer to complete the run than did Joe, who in turn took longer than Susan. The response associated with Joe is between those for Susan and Karen.

Ordering the values of the response variable (the *y* values when we come to represent the explanatory model as a regression model) orders the responses in a sensible way.

2.3.2 Unit of Response Measurement

The hallmark of the measured variable is a *unit of measurement.* If the response variable is to be treated as measured, we also think of the response as varying in "units" of a constant meaning.

The presence of a unit of measurement permits us to compare *differences* among responses as well as the responses themselves. We can say that the difference in running times between Susan and Joe (2 seconds) is less than the difference in running times between Joe and Karen (4 seconds). We accept the "second" as a *constant unit of measurement* of running time. We believe the second has the same meaning when, for example, it is the difference in running times of 32 and 33 seconds as when it is the difference in running times of 37 and 38 seconds.

2.3.3 Many Values of the Response Variable

In Chapter 1, we additionally described our measured variable as *capable* of assuming many different values. For a response variable to be treated as measured, it is practically important to make a stronger statement. The measured response *actually* must assume in our study a reasonably large number of values. In our running time example, we would want to observe more values than the three, 32, 34, and 38 seconds. Two reasons for this will be developed. First, we will learn that reasonably large samples (hence, potentially many different response values) are needed if we are to learn from the sample about explanatory relations in a population. Second, and more technical, observing many different response values is important to us if we are to check the statistical assumptions we depend on for fitting and comparing models for a measured response.

2.3.4 Distinguishing Measured and Ordered Responses

Let's change the scenario on Susan, Joe, and Karen.

> Susan, Joe, and Karen participate in a learning experiment. They are given an opportunity to learn 20 pairs of words. At the end of the learning period, they are tested to see how many of the pairs they are able to recall correctly. Susan, Joe, and Karen correctly recalled 10, 14, and 16 of the word pairs, respectively.

Again, Joe's value on the response variable is *between* those of Susan and Karen; he recalled more word pairs than Susan, but fewer than Karen. We would probably accept that the ordering of the response variable values also reflects the ordering of the responses; Joe "learned" more than Susan but less than Karen.

But what about the sizes of the *differences* in the response values? The difference between the numbers of word pairs correctly recalled by Susan and Joe is 4 word pairs. The difference for Joe and Karen is 2 word pairs. Does the first difference reflect a greater difference in "amount learned" than the second difference? Is it, in fact, twice as great? Are we willing to accept the "word pair recalled" as a *unit of measurement*?

We'll distinguish two possible modeling goals. If we wish to explain "number of word pairs correctly recalled," then the response variable of that same name may qualify as a measured response variable. "One word pair" would be an acceptable unit of measurement. We'd like assurance, though, that our variable *actually* takes "many" values. Twenty-one values (0 through 20) are *possible* . If some number of participants in the learning experiment earns each of these 21 scores, it would be appropriate to regard the response variable as measured. However, in practice, all of the learning scores may be in a narrower range, perhaps the 10–16 range identifd by Susan, Joe, and Karen. If so, we'd then have too few values to seriously treat the response variable as *measured*. Rather, with these few response options, it would be better to treat the scores as describing ordered response categories. But just a moment, our response variable is a *count*, isn't it, a count of word pairs correctly recalled? Wouldn't it be most appropriate to treat it as a *counted response*? We'll take that question up in the next section.

On the other hand, if we wish to explain not just "number of word pairs correctly recalled," but a more abstract "amount learned," we must also decide whether "number of word pairs" faithfully reflects the amount learned, or if it serves only to *order* respondents on that response. The decision requires that we be well-informed about the construct validity of our response variable. As a result, it is a substantive rather than a modeling decision. (In Chapter 18, we will give special attention to models for which the response is ordered, not continuous.)

In Chapter 1, we discussed the need for the *construct validation* of our assessments. We should choose variables that reflect as accurately as possible the constructs we wish to model. In this and the chapters that follow, we will assume the researcher has done that and is using the best available assessment as the response variable.

2.3.5   Distinguishing Counted from Measured or Ordered Response Variables

In Chapter 1, we distinguished *counted* from *measured*, or *ordered* variables. We said the score for an experimental or observational unit on a counted variable was the number of times some event occurred to (or happened in) that unit. Now, in the context of response variables, we need to extend that definition just a bit. Anticipating the techniques to be explored in Chapter 19, the *counted response variable* is strictly one that registers the number of events occurring in a specified *time period*: for example, the number of telephone inquiries in a 24-hour period, the number of arrests in a five-year period, and the number of relapses in the year following treatment for alcohol addiction. In principle, any number of events may occur in the time period and, hence, there is no upper bound to the value the counted response variable may take. As a result, models with such a response are best fit in a special way.

We need, then, to distinguish the "time-count" variable from near-related "counts." For example, the number of word pairs correctly recalled *out of a possible*

20 would not be a counted response variable. It results from observing, not over a time period but over a *fixed number* of opportunities. Response variables such as those just discussed are best treated as *measured* (where appropriate) or as *ordered.*

2.4
Characteristics of Measured Response Samples

Now we concentrate on a set or *sample* of measured response variable observations. What are the characteristics of such a sample? There are three that are important to us (and will be familar from any introductory study of statistics): the typical *size* of the response in the sample, the *variability* of the response sizes, and the "shape" of the sample of responses.

2.4.1   An Example: Heights of Adolescent Males

Table 2.1 lists a sample of observations on a measured response. These are the heights, at age 18, of 28 boys in the Berkeley Growth Study (Tuddenham & Snyder 1954), which followed the development of children born in the late 1920s. The centimeter is the unit of measurement of height. The values on this variable, which we refer to by the shorthand name *ht18*, indeed show variability in the sample. The heights of the 28 boys range from a shortest of 166.8 cm to a tallest of 195.1 cm.

These age-18 heights are *responses* for which we develop models in the following chapters to explain variability among the heights of adolescent boys.

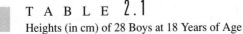

T A B L E 2.1
Heights (in cm) of 28 Boys at 18 Years of Age

179.0	183.5
195.1	178.1
183.7	177.0
178.7	172.9
171.5	188.4
181.8	169.4
172.5	180.2
174.6	189.0
190.4	182.4
173.8	185.8
172.6	180.7
185.2	178.7
178.5	169.6
177.6	166.8

2.4.2   Typical Size of the Response Variable: Sample Mean and Median

We usually begin the description of a sample of numeric values by saying something about *general magnitude*, the size of a typical member of the sample. How large is the response, typically?

The Sample Mean

The classical description of typical size for a collection of scores on a numeric variable with a unit of measurement is that provided by the arithmetic average or mean. The mean is simply the result of adding together all of the responses and dividing by the number of them. Here, this computation gives the result

$$\left[\frac{179 \text{ cm} + 195.1 \text{ cm} + \cdots + 166.8 \text{ cm}}{28} \right] = 179.2 \text{ cm.}$$

And we report this as $M(ht18) = 179.2$ cm. The "M" stands for the mean of a collection of values and we include the name of the variable in parentheses following to remind us of what it is the mean. The mean of the age-18 heights in our sample is 179.2 cm. Note that the unit of measurement is a necessary part of the mean.

We express the idea of finding the mean of a sample, using summation notation

$$M(y) = \left[\frac{\sum_{i=1}^{N} y_i}{N} \right] \tag{2.1}$$

The sample consists of N observations on the y variable. Equation [2.1] sums these, $\sum_{i=1}^{N} y_i$, and then divides this sum by N, the number of observations summed.

The mean of a sample of values is *always reported in the same unit of measurement* as the values themselves. Here, the heights were in centimeters and the mean height is also in centimeters.

We introduced the sample mean as describing the size of the *typical observation* in a sample. Let's give this idea of typicality a little more substance, expanding on the "prediction" task we introduced at the beginning of the chapter.

Suppose that one boy has been chosen from our sample of 28 and you are asked to predict his height. What value will you pick as his height?

You know that not all of the boys' heights are the same; the selected boy's height may be as small as 166.8 cm and as large as 195.1 cm. You don't know which boy was chosen; he may be the shortest or he may be the tallest or he may be somewhere in between. All you know is that he is one of the 28. What do you predict his height to be?

Knowing nothing else about him, most of us would guess that the selected boy is typical of the sample from which he was selected and that he is of average height. We'd predict that he is 179.2 cm tall, the sample mean height. Predicting the value of an unknown observation to be equal to the mean of the sample from which the observation came is a standard statistical notion. We use the idea over and over in developing and evaluating explanatory models for a measured response.

The Sample Median

Occasionally, often to contrast with the mean, we compute a second index of the typical size, the *sample median*. The median is the "middlemost value" in a sample, the result of arranging the values from smallest to largest and then counting in from either end until we reach a point where there are just as many values smaller as there are larger.

If the sample consists of an odd number of values, the median is the value of the middlemost member of the sample. If the sample contains an even number of values, the median is the average of the two middlemost observations. Here, the two middlemost values (the 14th and 15th, counting from the smallest or largest) are identical and the median is computed as

$$\mathrm{Mdn}(ht18) = \left[\frac{178.7 \text{ cm} + 178.7 \text{ cm}}{2} \right] = 178.7 \text{ cm}.$$

We abbreviate the sample median as Mdn. For our sample of 28 heights, the two indices of typical size, the mean and median, are close to each other. We'll have more to say about this later.

2.4.3 Variability of the Response: Sample Variance and SD

Not all of the boys' heights were equal to the typical height. The heights showed variability about the mean. We use two statistics to describe the amount of this variability, the *variance* and, closely related to it, the *standard deviation*.

The variance of a set of measures is defined as the mean of the squared distances (or deviations) of the observations from their mean. This definition can be expressed, as was that for the mean, using summation notation:

$$\mathrm{Var}(y) = \frac{\sum_{i=1}^{N}[y_i - M(y)]^2}{N}. \tag{2.2}$$

From each observation on the measured response variable, the sample mean for that sample of scores is subtracted. Each of the resulting *deviations* is then squared. The sample variance, abbreviated to Var, is the mean of these squared deviations. You will note that we divide by N and not by $(N-1)$; our variance is the variance of the sample and not an estimate of a population variance.

For our sample of 28 heights, we find the variance as

$$\frac{(179 - 179.2)^2 + (195.1 - 179.2)^2 + \cdots + (166.6 - 179.2)^2}{28} = 45.96 \text{ cm}^2$$
$$= \mathrm{Var}(ht18).$$

Notice that the variance has as its unit of measurement the *square* of the units of measurement of the response. The variance of our heights is in *squared centimeters*.

If the response measurements are all closely packed about the sample mean, the deviances, their squares and, consequently, the variance will be small. If some observations are considerably smaller or larger than the mean, the variance will be larger. If there is no variability in the responses—if all of the sample measurements are equal to the sample mean—the variance will be 0. Otherwise, the variance, based as it is on squared deviations, will be positive—greater than 0.

It is usually handier to describe the variability of the responses with an index that is in the same unit of measurement as the response values. The *standard deviation* provides such a description. The *standard deviation* of a sample is simply the (positive) square root of the variance:

$$\mathrm{SD}(y) = \sqrt{\mathrm{Var}(y)}. \tag{2.3}$$

The standard deviation (SD) is the square root of the mean of the squared deviations of a sample of measures about their mean.

For our boys' heights the SD is

$$\mathrm{SD}(\mathit{ht18}) = \sqrt{\mathrm{Var}(\mathit{ht18})} = \sqrt{45.96 \ \mathrm{cm}^2} = 6.779 \ \mathrm{cm}.$$

The typical height (mean) in our sample is 179.2 cm. There is variability about this typical value, however, and we report this with the sample SD of 6.779 cm. We intend Var(y) and SD(y) to be *descriptive* of the variability in a sample of observations and not *estimates* of the variability in some larger population. We will learn about estimators in later chapters.

In discussing the sample mean, we reintroduced our "prediction" game: One boy was chosen from among the 28 and you were to predict his height. Thinking him to be typical of the sample, you predicted his height to be the sample mean height, 179.2 cm.

Not all of the boys in the sample stand 179.2 cm tall; so, depending on which boy was selected, our predicting the sample mean can lead to an error. An important interpretation of the SD is that it tells us by how much we are likely to be wrong when we predict an observation to be equal to the mean. The larger the SD, the more we are likely to be "off" when we use the mean as the estimate of the height of the selected boy. In terms of the concepts introduced in Section 2.2, the larger the SD, the less certainty you have in the accuracy of that estimate.

2.4.4   Shape of the Response Sample

The third characteristic of a collection of numeric observations with a unit of measurement is its *shape*. Means are fairly easily understood, but the interpretation of the SD needs to take into account the *shape* of the response sample. By shape, we mean the shape of the *frequency histogram* for the sample. The histogram represents the sample as a series of side-by-side rectangles, each corresponding to a selected interval or range of measured variable scores. The width of each rectangle is proportional to the size of the interval and the area of each rectangle is proportional to the number of observations (frequency) falling within that interval. (If the intervals are all of the same width, then the heights of the rectangles, as well as their areas, will be proportional to these frequencies.) Figure 2.2 shows three histograms, each constructed over the score ranges 1–5, 6–10, 11–15, 16–20, and 21–25. They reveal contrasting response "shapes."

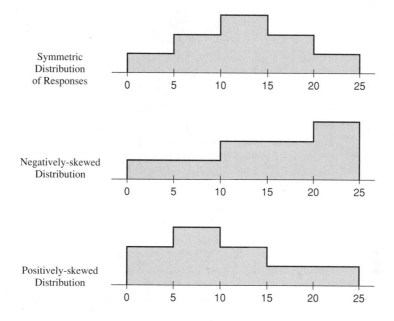

Symmetric
Distribution
of Responses

Negatively-skewed
Distribution

FIGURE 2.2
Frequency
Histograms with
Contrasting Shapes

Positively-skewed
Distribution

The distribution of responses in the top panel of Figure 2.2 is *symmetric* about the mean. The shape of the histogram above the mean is the mirror image of its shape below the mean. The mean stands in the middle of the distribution.

With symmetric samples like the one described by this first histogram, where the histogram falls off progressively above and below the mean, about two-thirds of the observations lie within one SD either way of the mean and the remaining one-third is divided equally between the two remaining "tails." This "two-thirds" interpretation for the symmetric, declining tails histogram we will see in subsequent chapters is based on an ideal of a "normal" distribution of scores in which 68% of the observations are within one SD of the mean.

Collections of numeric observations with asymmetric histograms are referred to as *skewed* and Figure 2.2 shows two. We call a distribution of numbers *positively skewed* if the long tail is towards the positive, larger-valued end and *negatively skewed* if the opposite is true. The SD for skewed distributions does not have the same neat interpretation as it does for "normal" distributions.

While the three illustrative histograms of Figure 2.2 certainly do not exhaust the potential shapes, most collections of measured observations have frequency histograms of one of these three general *types*. That is, most such collections will be *unimodal*; their histograms have a single "peak". This peak may be in the middle (a symmetric distribution of scores) or displaced to one side (positively or negatively skewed).

To avoid overinterpreting the mean and SD, it is a good idea (indeed, an invaluable idea) to *look* at the shape of the sample of responses. Every statistical package provides several tools for doing this. The histogram is one such tool. Another, sometimes called a *description,* reports some key values. A description of our boys' heights from a typical statistics package follows.

```
Col Name Size  Mean StDev   Min     LQ Median   UQ    Max

  1 ht18 28 179.196 6.904 166.8 173.35 178.7 183.6 195.1
```

Among the 28 values in the sample (*ht18*) the smallest (Min) was 166.8 and the largest (Max) was 195.1. The median was 178.7. The Lower Quartile (LQ), sometimes called the first quartile, of 173.35 separates the lowest one-quarter or 25% of the observations from the remaining 75%, while the Upper Quartile (UQ), also known as the third quartile, of 183.6 separates the lower three-quarters or 75% from the remaining 25%. (The median is also the second quartile, separating the lowest two-quarters from the remaining 50%. The quartiles divide the set of scores into quarters.) The *middle 50%* of the responses, then, were between 173.35 (LQ) and 183.6 (UQ). The distance separating the two is called the *interquartile range*: 50% of the responses are in the range 173.35 cm to 183.6 cm.

For a symmetric sample, the median (50%) will be midway between the *quartiles* (25% and 75% values). Symmetric or not, the interquartile range has a constant interpretation, as does the median. In the display above, the reader will note that the standard deviation (StDev) is reported as 6.904 cm rather than the 6.779 cm we computed earlier. Many computer programs for statistics, including the one that produced this display, routinely calculate not the SD for a set of measures but an estimated population standard deviation. That is, in the variance computation, the sum of squared deviations is divided by $(N-1)$ rather than by N. We can get the sample SD for our set of 28 heights from the estimate in the computer report by multiplying it by the square root of the ratio $(N-1)$ to N:

$$\sqrt{\frac{27}{28}}(6.904) = 6.78.$$

Graphic representations of the sample, too, help us understand its shape—and, perhaps, to recognize certain errors or irregularities. The *stem-and-leaf plot* (sometimes called a frequency plot) is available in many statistical packages and gives us something very much like a "vertical" histogram, one turned on its side. Each score is divided into larger (stem) and smaller (leaf) parts. In this example, the stem for each of our heights consists of the first two digits in the heights, rounded to the nearest cm. The leaf part is the final digit.

The "row" of the stem-and-leaf plot reading,

```
17|023334
```

"plots" the six responses: 170 cm, 172 cm, 173 cm, 173 cm, 173 cm, and 174 cm.

Our stem-and-leaf plot suggests a certain positive skew. There is some bunching up of values at the low end and something of a (positive) tail at the high end.

```
16|79
17|023334
17|57889999
18|012244
18|5689
19|0
19|5
```

Because each line of this stem-and-leaf plot represents a constant interval of scores (or stem width) of 5 cm, the length of the leaf part (to the right of the vertical divider) corresponds to the proportion of observations falling in that interval. It is a sideways histogram.

A second graphic shows the tail more clearly. The *box-and-whisker plot* (or boxplot) provides a picture of some of the key values reported by a *descriptive statistics* command, extending it pictorially.

The asterisk in the middle of the box corresponds to the median and the left and right margins of the box mark the lower and upper quartiles, respectively—25% on the left and 75% on the right. The width of the box, the interquartile range, includes the middle 50% of the sample. In the version of the boxplot displayed above, only the values of the largest and smallest observations are reported. Other statistical packages give the values of the median and of the quartiles as well.

Whiskers extend on either side of the box a distance that ought to include about 95% of the observations in a normal distribution. If the sample is symmetric, the asterisk should appear in the middle of the box and the two whiskers should be of the same length. Measures that are farther than a whisker's length away from the box describe a "long" tail and may be "outliers," observations that should not be included, for some reason, in the sample.

We will learn more about using these sample summaries in modeling. Here, they serve to suggest that the tallest of our boys, at 195.1 cm, may be markedly taller than the other sample members. Were he not in the sample, the distribution of height responses would appear considerably more symmetric.

2.5
A Population of Responses

Our 28 boys were only a sample of all those born in Berkeley during the period of the Growth Study. As we noted at the beginning of this chapter, it is the age-18 height variability in this larger population we would like to explain, not just the sample variability. How do we describe populations of response variable observations?

You probably have an intuitive idea of what a population is and how it differs from a sample. Despite the differences, some of the same descriptions pertain to each. We can see this most easily if we think of a population of responses as a very large collection of responses. What we can do with a smaller collection of measures, the sample, we can at least *think* of doing with the population. It may not be feasible actually to carry out the operations, but we want simply to consider what the results would be *if we could*. Remember, the calculations fancied or real are to be carried out on observations from a measured variable—one with a unit of measurement.

2.5.1   Population Mean of the Response Variable

We begin, as we did in describing the sample, by considering what we have if we add up all the response values making up the population and then divide by the number of responses that contributed to that sum. What we'd have is a mean response—the mean of the entire response population.

Just like the sample mean, this *population mean* describes the size of the typical response—in this case, in the population. To distinguish it from a sample mean, $M(y)$, we'll use the notation $\mu(y)$ to indicate the population mean of the variable y. Thus, $M(ht18)$ is the mean height in a *particular sample* of age-18 males, while $\mu(ht18)$ is the mean height in a population of 18-year-old males.

2.5.2   Population Response Variance

There is variablility among the large number of observations making up a population, just as there is among the smaller number in a sample. Indeed, we couldn't observe variability in the sample *unless* there was variability in the population from which the sample came.

The variability of responses in the population is described by the population response *variance*. In principle, the population variance is "computed" in the same way as the sample variance; it is the mean, over the entire population, of the squared deviations of the response scores from the population mean.

We'll use the notation $\sigma^2(y)$ to indicate the *population* response variance and $Var(y)$, introduced earlier, for the *sample* response variance. Similarly, $SD(ht18)$ denotes the standard deviation of the age-18 heights in a sample and $\sigma(ht18)$ denotes the standard deviation of heights in a population of 18-year-olds. The positive square root of $\sigma^2(y)$ is $\sigma(y)$.

We have seen that the population standard deviation, $\sigma(y)$, assesses our certainty about the accuracy of the population mean as a guess or estimate of the value of an observation chosen from that population. The smaller $\sigma(y)$ is, the greater our certainty in the accuracy of the estimate provided by $\mu(y)$, the population mean.

2.6
Sample and Population, Statistics and Parameters

The mean, median, variance, and standard deviation we computed for the *sample* of boys' heights in Section 2.4 are *sample statistics*. The mean, variance, and standard deviation of a *population* are *parameters* of that population. Statistics describe a sample and are readily calculable from the sample. Parameters describe a population—conditional or unconditional—and are calculable only in principle. We very rarely have all of the population laid out in front of us so that we actually may find its mean or variance.

We made the point in Section 2.1 that *models are for populations, not samples*. We can now add to that. It is the characteristics of populations of response observations—their means and their standard deviations—that we want to understand. Do the conditional (population) means differ one from another? Is the conditional standard deviation smaller than the unconditional one? *Models are for population parameters*.

2.7
Explaining Response Variability: A Review

In Section 2.2, you were introduced to the ideas of certainty and of conditional response populations for the measured response in observational studies. Because those ideas are so important to modeling, we'll review them and introduce a notation that will make it easier for us to describe these ideas and their application.

2.7.1 Unconditional Response Certainty

Scientific questions arise because we cannot be certain about the value of a response variable. We note variability in some response and set out to explain or account for it. That variability is to be explained, to the extent that it can be, by one or more explanatory variables.

In observational studies, the variability to be explained is that contained within some *unconditional response population*, that is, in a population made up of "all (potential) respondents" without regard to the value of any explanatory variable. This unconditional population is the *most general* population our models are to consider. For the measured response variable, the standard deviation in the unconditional population assesses the variability potentially to be explained. The larger this standard deviation, the less our certainty about the value of the response. That is, if we think about an observation chosen at random from the population, we will be less certain about the value of that observation the larger the population standard deviation.

In modeling, it is often convenient to refer to two characteristics of the unconditional response population. It has a mean and a variance (and a standard deviation—its square root). Our notation for the unconditional (population) mean of the response variable, generally symbolized as y, is $\mu(y)$, and for the unconditional response variance, $\sigma^2(y)$. The unconditional standard deviation is written $\sigma(y)$.

Thus, $\mu(ht18)$ is the mean of the heights in a population of 18-year-old boys, irrespective of any explanatory variable score, and $\sigma(ht18)$ is the standard deviation of that population of age-18 heights.

2.1.2   Conditional Response Certainty

When we introduce an explanatory variable in an attempt to explain the variability of an observational response, we can think of "dividing up" the unconditional response population into a number of *conditional response populations*, one for each value of the explanatory variable. The conditional population $(ht18 \mid ht2 = 85 \text{ cm})$ consists of the age-18 heights of all boys who stood 85 cm tall at 2 years of age.

The mean of the conditional population, $\mu(ht18 \mid ht2 = 85 \text{ cm})$, is the average age-18 height for a boy who was 85 cm tall at age 2. The standard deviation of the conditional population, $\sigma(ht18 \mid ht2 = 85 \text{ cm})$, describes the variability in the conditional response population and our certainty in the conditional mean as a description of the age-18 height of a boy picked from that conditional population. If the conditional standard deviation is small compared with the unconditional standard deviation, we have increased certainty in the mean as an estimate of the response. Taking the value of the explanatory variable into account increases our certainty about the value of the response whenever the conditional standard deviation is smaller than the unconditional one.

In our notation, we make clear the dependence of a conditional population on the value of an explanatory variable. For example,

$$\mu(ht18 \mid ht2 = 85 \text{ cm})$$

is the mean of the population of heights of 18-year-olds *who were 85 cm tall at age 2*. It is the age-18 height we estimate for boys who were of that infant height. We read this conditional expression as "the mean value of *ht18 given that ht2* is equal to 85 cm."

Similarly,

$$\sigma(ht18 \mid ht2 = 85 \text{ cm})$$

designates a *conditional response standard deviation*. It is the standard deviation of age-18 heights among all boys who were 85 cm tall at 2 years.

The conditional response standard deviations describe our certainty about the value of the measured response *when we take into account* the value of an explanatory variable.

Explanatory models for measured responses are always based in conditional response populations. The two go hand in glove and we can look at the goal of finding a best model as equivalent to deciding *which conditional populations* we should use to describe our response variable observations.

The unconditional response standard deviation indicates our certainty about the measured response when we use no explanatory variable information in arriving at our guess or estimate of the response value for an observation. The conditional response standard deviations, analogously, describe our certainty about the response when our estimate, the appropriate conditional mean, takes into account the value of some explanatory variable.

An explanatory model is one for which the conditional standard deviations are smaller than the unconditional one; it is one that explains, at least partially, the response by increasing our certainty about its value.

Some models—some selections of explanatory variables—will clearly be better than others. Intuitively, we have reason for believing that the conditional standard deviations,

$$\sigma\,(ht18 \mid ht2),$$

one for each of the conditional populations based on a particular age-2 height, will all be smaller than the unconditional standard deviation, $\sigma\,(ht18)$.

On the other hand, the conditional standard deviations,

$$\sigma\,(ht18 \mid \textit{left handed}) \text{ and } \sigma\,(ht18 \mid \textit{right handed}),$$

for the heights of left-handed and right-handed 18-year-old boys, respectively, are probably not any smaller than the unconditional standard deviation of age-18 heights. We are no more certain about the height of an 18-year-old after learning his preferred hand than we were before.

While "handedness" probably does nothing to explain adolescent height, the example does serve to show us that all our notions of conditional populations, expectations, and certainties are as useful for models with *categorical explanatory variables* as for models with measured explanatory variables.

In the above, we stressed whether, in general terms, $\sigma\,(y\,|\,x)$—the conditional response SDs—are smaller than $\sigma\,(y)$—the unconditional response SD. If they are, the explanatory variable x helps to explain the measured response variable y. For what follows, we need to appreciate a consequence of this: The conditional SDs will all be smaller than the unconditional SD *only if* the conditional response means, the $\mu\,(y\,|\,x)$s, differ among themselves. The converse makes this clearer: If all the conditional means are identical, if we are led to make the same prediction of the response variable value for all values of the explanatory variable, then we have not increased our certainty about the response when we take that explanatory variable into account. Increased certainty is accompanied by variability in the $\mu\,(y\,|\,x)$s. Indeed, of central interest in explanatory modeling is by how much the $\mu\,(y\,|\,x)$s differ.

2.8
Experimental Studies and Conditional Response Populations

We have developed the ideas of conditional and unconditional response populations, with their means and variances, in the context of observational studies. Our observational sample is taken from some larger population, an unconditional distribution with respect to measurements of the response. And, we can think of *subdividing* that population according to the values of one or more explanatory variables to create conditional (response) populations. If our explanatory variable(s) influences the response, the resulting conditional response populations will have different means and SDs that are smaller than in the unconditional population.

We'd like to use this notion of conditional response distributions to undergird our explanatory modeling for experimental studies as well as for observational ones. Because there are sufficient differences, though, between the two kinds of study, we need to proceed carefully with the translation to the experimental setting. A simple example will highlight the issues.

A sample of N = 30 first grade students, with parental consent, is randomly divided into three treatment groups of 10, receiving either 1,000 mg, 500 mg, or 0 mg (a placebo instead) of ascorbic acid (vitamin C) with each school lunch. Of interest is the number of school days missed owing to illness.

Our explanatory variable is size of daily dose of *ascorbic acid* (0 mg, 500 mg, or 1,000 mg) and the response variable is school days missed owing to *illness*. Our sample of observational units is of first grade students.

In the prototypical observational study, we define the conditional response populations as fractions of the unconditional response population. In our experimental study, it will be fairly easy to see how to define conditional response populations, but they will be of a somewhat different kind. We define three conditional response populations symbolized as

$$(illness \,|\, ascorbic\ acid = 0\ \text{mg}),$$
$$(illness \,|\, ascorbic\ acid = 500\ \text{mg}),\ \text{and}$$
$$(illness \,|\, ascorbic\ acid = 1,000\ \text{mg}).$$

The first is the population of *illness* scores (days out ill) that would result *if* all first graders were given a placebo (0 mg *ascorbic acid*) with their school lunches. The second is the population of *illness* scores *if* all first graders were given 500 mg *ascorbic acid* daily. And the third is the population of *illness* scores *if* all first graders were given 1,000 mg *ascorbic acid* daily. These are *conditional populations* in the sense that each is conditional on the value of the explanatory variable. Since the response variable is measured, each of these conditional populations will have a mean,

$$\mu(illness \,|\, ascorbic\ acid = 0\ \text{mg}),$$
$$\mu(illness \,|\, ascorbic\ acid = 500\ \text{mg}),\ \text{and}$$
$$\mu(illness \,|\, ascorbic\ acid = 1,000\ \text{mg}),$$

and a standard deviation,

$$\sigma(illness \,|\, ascorbic\ acid = 0\ \text{mg}),$$
$$\sigma(illness \,|\, ascorbic\ acid = 500\ \text{mg}),\ \text{and}$$
$$\sigma(illness \,|\, ascorbic\ acid = 1,000\ \text{mg}).$$

These are the conditional response means and standard deviations.

If *ascorbic acid* dose influences or partially explains days of *illness*, we would find that the conditional means differ. Indeed, if our experiment is driven by the hypothesis that regular administration of vitamin C will reduce illness in young school children, then we would hope to find either that

$$\mu(illness \,|\, ascorbic\ acid = 1,000\ \text{mg}) < \mu(illness \,|\, ascorbic\ acid = 0\ \text{mg})$$

or that

$$\mu(\textit{illness} \mid \textit{ascorbic acid} = 500 \text{ mg}) < \mu(\textit{illness} \mid \textit{ascorbic acid} = 0 \text{ mg})$$

or both, and, perhaps, that

$$\mu(\textit{illness} \mid \textit{ascorbic acid} = 1,000 \text{ mg}) < \mu(\textit{illness} \mid \textit{ascorbic acid} = 500 \text{ mg}).$$

What can we say about these conditional SDs? There is no natural unconditional SD against which they may be compared because there is, in the typical experimental study, no natural unconditional response population. There is no mixture of the several treatments which constitutes a population.

We've identifed two ways, then, in which our idea of conditional response populations differs between observational and experimental studies. For observational studies, the conditional populations are subdivisions of a larger unconditional population. For experimental studies, there is no unconditional population and the conditional populations, rather than being subdivisions of a larger population, are themselves "complete" populations, each conditional on the value of the experimental variable—conditional on the treatment administered. In either case, we will say that the explanatory variable is influential (or predictive) if the conditional response populations have different means.

2.9
Summary

The measured response is very common in behavioral and biological studies. When we model a response, our goal is to explain that response by increasing our certainty about the value it takes. This chapter introduces terminology and notation useful to describing how we use information about an explanatory variable to increase our certainty about a measured response. Central is the idea of *conditional response populations*—one for each value of an explanatory variable. These are subdivisions of a larger *unconditional response population*, one that ignores the value of any explanatory variable, in the case of sampled or *observational studies*. In the case of manipulated or *experimental studies*, the conditional response populations are hypothetical, each describing responses *if* a particular treatment were given all members of a population. In either paradigm, variability in the means of these conditional response populations provides evidence of an explanatory effect. A good explanatory model reveals differences in levels of response, that is, it reveals differences among conditional response means.

3

Simple Linear Regression: An Introduction

This chapter introduces the basic idea of *regression*, that of a systematic relation between the conditional population means for a response variable, on the one hand, and the values of an explanatory variable, on the other. It is an extremely powerful idea and provides the framework for the most often used modeling and data-analysis techniques.

In many real world instances, that systematic relation can be expressed usefully as a *linear regression*. Because this affords a particularly easy-to-use approach to model development and comparison, we begin in this chapter our focus on *linear models*. This starts with an orientation to simple linear models and their *parameters*.

Because models are for populations rather than samples, we conclude the chapter by laying the groundwork for the task of *estimating* linear model parameters and their accuracies from sample data. This includes a review of the sample descriptive techniques of scatterplots, covariance, and product moment correlation.

3.1
Regression

In Sections 2.2, 2.7, and 2.8, we introduced the idea of response variable (y) populations that were *conditional* upon the value of an explanatory variable (x). We think of a separate conditional response population for each value of the explanatory variable. If that explanatory variable in fact influences the response, we should be able to detect that in aspects of these conditional populations.

- First, the averages or means of these conditional populations would differ. To continue with our boys' heights example, we would predict or estimate a different age-18 height for a boy who stood 80 cm tall at 2 years than for one who was 90 cm tall.

- Second, for observational studies, the conditional populations are subdivisions of a larger, unconditional population. There, the standard deviations (or variances) in the conditional response populations ought to be smaller than that in the un-conditional population, where no attention is paid to the value of the explanatory variable.

We would interpret these signs as evidence that, by taking the value of x into account, we have *increased our certainty* about the value of the y. Equivalently, using the explanatory variable in our model for the response we would explain some of the variability in the response.

Now, when we consider an explanatory model—when we think that the mean of our response may be different for different values of some explanatory variable—we almost certainly think that those means differ not in some haphazard fashion, but in a way that reflects *form* or *lawfulness* to the explanatory relation. For example, if we were to speculate on the values of these three conditional response means,

$$\mu(ht18 \,|\, ht2 = 80 \text{ cm}), \quad \mu(ht18 \,|\, ht2 = 85 \text{ cm}), \text{ and } \mu(ht18 \,|\, ht2 = 90 \text{ cm}),$$

we would probably think that the leftmost value would be smaller than the middle one, which, in turn, should be smaller than that on the far right. The three ought to reflect the idea that the smaller a boy is as a 2-year-old, the smaller we predict him to be at 18.

Regression is the name given to the idea that the conditional mean of the response variable may be *functionally related* to the value of the explanatory variable. We write this basic idea in the form of a general equation:

$$\mu(y \,|\, x = x_i) = g(x_i). \tag{3.1}$$

What Equation [3.1] says is that the conditional mean of the response (y) is some function of the value of the explanatory variable, $g(x)$. If we knew the particulars of $g(x)$, we could substitute different quantities for x_i, different explanatory variable values into the right-hand side of the equation and receive conditional means or predicted values for the response variable on the left-hand side.

The existence of an underlying function relating the x_is to the $\mu(y \,|\, x = x_i)$s suggests that if we were to plot values of $\mu(y \,|\, x = x_i)$ against values of x_i, the result would be a "smooth" curve, one describing the "lawful" dependence of the (conditional) response mean on the value of the explanatory variable. That curve is the *curve of regression*. For example, if we could plot the response means

$$\mu(ht18 \,|\, ht2 = 80 \text{ cm}),$$
$$\mu(ht18 \,|\, ht2 = 81 \text{ cm}),$$
$$\vdots$$
$$\mu(ht18 \,|\, ht2 = 90 \text{ cm})$$

against the corresponding *ht2* values (80 cm, 81 cm, 82 cm, ..., 90 cm) the result ought to be not a jumble of points, but a "pattern" that shows how adolescent height, on the average, is dependent on infant height.

Our general notion of the dependence of adolescent height on infant height simply may be that taller infants tend to grow up to be taller adults. Figure 3.1 illustrates three of the many curves of regression that would be appropriate to this model.

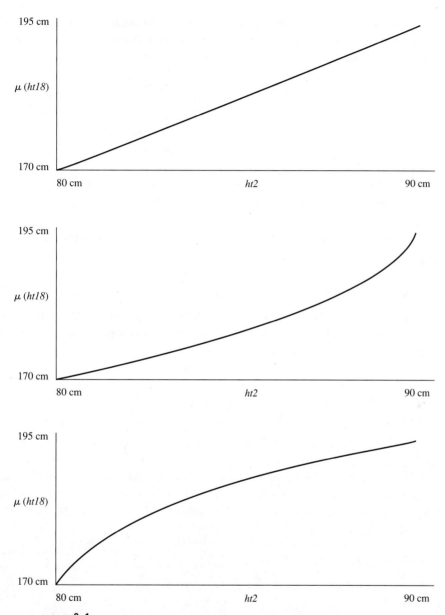

FIGURE 3.1   Curves of Regression: An Increasing Explanatory Relation

In each of the three curves, an increase in age-2 height (along the X axis) is accompanied by an increase in the mean or *predicted* age-18 height (along the Y axis). The three curves of regression are different, however, in what they say about the *rate* at which the mean of the response increases. In the top figure, the rate of change is *constant*; every 1 cm increase in age-2 height is accompanied by the same increase in the mean age-18 height. By contrast, in the second figure we see an *accelerating* influence of infant height; a difference of 1 cm in height has less importance for shorter than for taller infants. This situation is reversed in the third curve; the impact of an additional cm of infant height decreases as infant height increases.

Which curve, if any, is the correct one? Each of the curves in Figure 3.1 is associated with a different explanatory function, a different "$g(x_i)$" in Equation [3.1]. Might the correct function be

$g(x_i) = a + bx_i^2$, an accelerating, increasing function of the positively valued x;

or is it

$g(x_i) = c + dx_i$, a steadily increasing function of x; or could it be

$g(x_i) = e + f\sqrt{x_i}$, a decelerating, increasing function of x?

What is the correct form for the function on the right-hand side of Equation [3.1]? Deciding which of the alternative forms is the explanatory relation is one of the important modeling tasks.

3.2
Linear Regression

If the curve of regression is a straight line, we have linear regression. The linear form is particularly attractive to modelers because it lends itself so easily to model development, interpretation, and comparison. We will emphasize the use of linear regression in modeling. Not every explanatory relation is linear, but we develop techniques in later chapters for converting many nonlinear models into linear ones so that we may study them with the same set of techniques.

For *linear regression*, the general functional relation between the (conditional) response mean and the explanatory variable of Equation [3.1] is expressed in this special form:

$$\mu(y \mid x = x_i) = \beta_0 + \beta_1 x_i. \tag{3.2}$$

The previously quite general function, $g(x_i)$, has been replaced by a very specific function. The $\beta_0 + \beta_1 x_i$ on the right-hand side of Equation [3.2] is the equation for a straight line. If we plot values of $\beta_0 + \beta_1 x_i$ against values of x_i, keeping β_0 and β_1 constant, all of the plotted points will lie on a straight line. The two *constants* describe the *intercept* (β_0) and *slope* (β_1) of that line. Shortly, we'll explain the role of these two constants in explanatory models.

Equation [3.2] describes a *structural model*, one that specifies the *form of the explanatory relation*; it structures the relation between the x and the expected value of the y.

Putting this all together, we'll refer to Equation [3.2] as a *linear structural equation*. We'll also refer to β_0 and β_1 as *parameters* of the linear structural equation.

What do we mean when we say that β_0 and β_1 are parameters? In Section 2.6, we said that the mean of a population was a parameter of that population. If Equation [3.2] accurately describes the explanatory relation, then the means of *all* of the conditional response populations *depend on* the values of β_0 and β_1. As a result, these two values can themselves be thought of as parameters of the conditional response populations.

What interpretation can we give the two linear structural equation parameters, β_0 and β_1? Look at the illustrations in Figure 3.2. Each shows $\mu(y \mid x)$ plotted as a linear function of x, but the two parameters have different values for the three plots.

We'll start with a definition of the slope parameter, β_1. The slope of the regression line tells us the amount by which $\mu(y \mid x)$ changes when x increases by one unit. A positive β_1 means that $\mu(y \mid x)$ increases with an increase in x. A negative slope coefficient indicates that $\mu(y \mid x)$ *decreases* as x increases. And, a β_1 of 0 tells us that $\mu(y \mid x)$ does not change in response to an increase in x. When the slope parameter is 0, the (conditional) mean of the response is the *same* for all values of the explanatory variable.

Each of the three panels of Figure 3.2 shows the effect on $\mu(y \mid x)$ of changing the value of x by one unit. In the top panel, we have set $\beta_0 = 10$ and $\beta_1 = 5$. The slope parameter is positive and the line slopes upward as we move from left to right, as the value of x increases. Substituting the two selected values of x, 0 and 1, into the linear model yields expected values of 10 and 15, respectively. The increase of one unit in the explanatory variable—from 0 to 1—has been accompanied by an increase of five units—from 10 to 15—in the mean of the response. This increase is equal to the value of the slope parameter, β_1.

In the middle panel, we have set $\beta_0 = 15$ and $\beta_1 = -2$. The slope parameter is negative now and the line slopes downward as the value of x increases. Substituting the two selected values of x, 5 and 6, into the linear model yields $\mu(y \mid x)$s of 5 and 3, respectively. The increase of one unit in the explanatory variable—from 5 to 6—has been accompanied by a *decrease* of two units—from 5 to 3—in the mean of the response. The increase is equal to β_1, which is negative in sign.

Finally, in the bottom panel, we have set $\beta_0 = 100$ and $\beta_1 = 0$. The slope parameter of 0 produces a flat regression line. Increasing the value of x has no effect on $\mu(y \mid x)$. Substituting the two selected values of the explanatory variable, 50 and 51, into the linear model yields response variable means of 100 in both instances. An increase of one unit in the explanatory variable—from 50 to 51—has been accompanied by an increase of zero units—from 100 to 100—in the mean of the response. This increase is equal again to the value of the slope parameter, β_1.

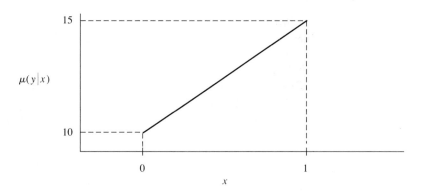

$$\mu(y \mid x = x_i) = \beta_0 + \beta_1 x_i$$
$$\mu(y \mid x = x_i) = 10 + 5x_i$$
$$\mu(y \mid x = 0) = 10 + (5)(0) = 10, \mu(y \mid x = 1) = 10 + (5)(1) = 15$$

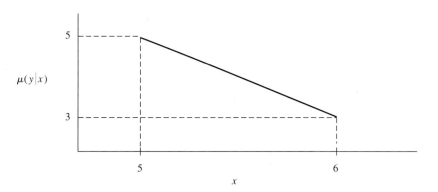

$$\mu(y \mid x = x_i) = \beta_0 + \beta_1 x_i$$
$$\mu(y \mid x = x_i) = 15 + (-2)x_i$$
$$\mu(y \mid x = 5) = 15 + (-2)(5) = 5, \mu(y \mid x = 6) = 15 + (-2)(6) = 3$$

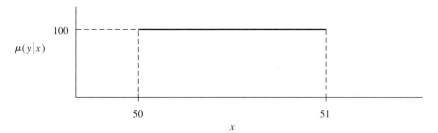

FIGURE 3.2

Three Illustrative
Linear Models

$$\mu(y \mid x = x_i) = \beta_0 + \beta_1 x_i$$
$$\mu(y \mid x = x_i) = 100 + 0x_i$$
$$\mu(y \mid x = 50) = 100 + (0)(50) = 100, \mu(y \mid x = 51) = 100 + (0)(51) = 100$$

What interpretation do we give the *intercept* parameter, β_0? It is the (conditional) mean of the response when the value of the explanatory variable is 0. We can see this if we substitute 0 for x in Equation [3.2]:

$$\mu(y \mid x = x_i) = \beta_0 + \beta_1 x_i,$$
$$\mu(y \mid x = 0) = \beta_0 + \beta_1 0,$$
$$\mu(y \mid x = 0) = \beta_0.$$

This interpretation is reinforced by the illustration in the top panel of Figure 3.2. There, an x of 0 leads to a $\mu(y \mid x)$ of 10, the value of the intercept parameter, $\beta_0 = 10$. Were we to substitute a 0 for x in the linear models illustrated in the middle and bottom panels, the conditional means for y would be 15 and 100, respectively.

Let's assume that Equation [3.2], the linear model, correctly describes the explanatory relation between boys' infant and adolescent heights:

$$\mu(ht18 \mid ht2 = x_i) = \beta_0 + \beta_1 x_i.$$

And, we'll further assume that the values of the two parameters are

$$\beta_0 = 30 \text{ and } \beta_1 = 2.$$

Then, the predicted age-18 height of an 80-cm-tall 2-year-old boy, the mean age-18 height of those who were 80 cm tall at age 2 would be

$$\mu(ht18 \mid ht2 = 80 \text{ cm}) = 30 + (2)80 = 190,$$

while the mean age-18 height, conditional upon an age-2 height of 81 cm, would be

$$\mu(ht18 \mid ht2 = 81 \text{ cm}) = 30 + (2)81 = 192.$$

The difference in (conditional) mean *ht18* scores here, 2, is that associated with a one-unit increase in *ht2* and, hence, is equal to the assumed value of the slope parameter.

With both age-2 and age-18 heights measured in centimeters, β_1 tells us the amount in centimeters by which we should estimate the age-18 heights of two boys to differ if those two boys differed in height at age 2 by 1 cm. Given our choice of slope parameter, $\beta_1 = 2$, the 1 cm difference in age-2 heights of the boys would be accompanied by a 2-cm difference in the expected values of their age-18 heights.

Just as there are scales of measurement or metrics for x and y, there are metrics for the two regression parameters. The slope parameter is a rate-of-change measure and its metric reflects this. It is measured in "y units per x unit." For the height data, both x and y are measured in centimeters so the metric for β_1 is "cm per cm," the number of centimeters difference in $\mu(ht18 \mid ht2)$ per 1-cm difference in *ht2*.

For our example, we have

$$\beta_1 = 2 \frac{\text{cm}}{\text{cm}}.$$

Because the intercept is a (conditional) mean for the response variable, the metric for the intercept is the same as that for the response variable. For the height example, β_0 has the same metric as that for *ht18*, centimeters, and we have $\beta_0 = 30$ cm.

Let's rewrite our two conditional mean equations, putting in the metrics for the variables and the parameters:

$$\mu(ht18 \mid ht2 = 80 \text{ cm}) = 30 \text{ cm} + (2\frac{\text{cm}}{\text{cm}})\, 80 \text{ cm} = 190 \text{ cm},$$

and

$$\mu(ht18 \mid ht2 = 81 \text{ cm}) = 30 \text{ cm} + (2\frac{\text{cm}}{\text{cm}})\, 81 \text{ cm} = 192 \text{ cm}.$$

It is good practice to include the metric whenever we specify the value of a variable or a parameter. This reminds us that far from being abstract numbers, these values have interpretations specific to our model and the metrics in which our explanatory and response variables have been assessed.

The intercept is necessary to describe a straight line and, so, it is a necessary part of any linear model. Together with the slope, it allows us to describe a complete set of conditional expected values. The slope parameter *always* is of interest to us. In our height example, we want to know what a difference in height at age 2 *implies* for heights at adolescence. The slope tells us that. By contrast, the intercept often is uninteresting and, indeed, can be misinterpreted. Our height example provides a good illustration of this.

The intercept for our linear model of heights, quite literally, is the age-18 height expected among boys who, at age 2, stood *0 cm tall*! We recognize that it is nonsense, of course, to say that we expect the 2 year old with no height at all to grow into a 30-cm-tall 18 year old. We have enough real world knowledge, to know that there is no boy whose 2-year-old height is 0 cm and, therefore, that it is absurd to speculate on what his height might be at 18.

How can we translate such real world knowledge into model knowledge, so that we aren't led, unawares, by a model into errors such as this one? An important start is to recognize that our model is much more limited than Equation [3.2] might suggest. That equation, taken by itself, looks as if we could put into it *any value* of x and get back a conditional response mean, a $\mu(y \mid x = x_i)$. But our model is not one that applies for every number that might be substituted for x_i in Equation [3.2].

We should *always* have in mind *particular values* of x that are possible or for which $\mu(y \mid x)$ is of interest. These may be selected, isolated values (e.g., the number of children in the family is 0, 1, 2, or 3—but not 1.5, 2.25, etc.), or they may be a range of values (e.g., infant heights between 60 cm and 90 cm). The important thing is that we *specify* what those values are. Having done so, we are then careful not to *overinterpolate* the model—interpret it as applying to values of x lying between possible values—or to *overextrapolate* it—interpret it as applying to values outside the specified x range. Trying to interpret the intercept in the height study is an example of an *extrapolation error*; a value of 0 for our x is outside the range of infant heights to which our model is meant to apply.

In experimental studies, the range of interest for x usually is specified in advance and the observations collected to cover that range. In some observational studies, the x range may not be specifiable until after data are collected. When this is true, it often will make sense to restrict the extrapolation range to the range actually observed.

If we are careful in our interpolations and extrapolations, we can go a long way towards not misinterpreting our model.

Why should regression be used as the name for this powerful idea of a systematic explanatory relation? It seems an odd choice and is, in fact, the result of a phenomenon noted in one of the earliest "regression" analyses.

Sir Francis Galton, a distinguished English gentleman-scientist of the late nineteenth century, was interested in, among many other things, the dependency of mens' heights on the heights of their fathers. He was not, of course, the first to notice that tallness tended to be passed on from one generation to the next. Galton did assemble, however, an impressive collection of adult height data for fathers and sons.

Galton divided up sons' heights according to their fathers' heights, forming, in effect, a number of conditional populations of sons' heights. When he examined these, he was intrigued by what he found. The sons of the taller fathers were, rather than being as tall as their fathers, on the whole, somewhat shorter. Similarly, the sons of the shorter fathers tended to be taller than their fathers.

From these results, Galton concluded that the sons' heights tended to *regress* or to move back towards the (unconditional) mean height for all fathers. The extremes in one generation, it would appear, became less extreme in the generation following.

The name *regression* was carried over as a name for the general technique of describing the partial dependency of a response variable on an explanatory one, whether or not the two are measures of the "same thing." In the next chapter, when we describe sample estimates of the regression parameters, we will see why it is that Galton observed a generational "regression towards the mean" in his data.

3.3
Linear Model Inference: Assumptions

In this and the preceding chapter, we have stressed the view that the goal of models for the measured response is to learn about the parameters of conditional response populations. In particular, we are interested in the *pattern* of conditional response means, the $\mu(y\,|\,x)$s, and the *magnitudes* of the conditional standard deviations, the $\sigma(y\,|\,x)$s. The first tells us the form of the explanatory relation, and the second something of its strength. We've seen in Chapter 2 that, for observational studies, the smaller the conditional standard deviations relative to $\sigma(y)$—the standard deviation of the unconditional-response population—the stronger the relation. Though, as we've also seen in the last chapter, we do not have unconditional response populations for experimental studies, we also will develop ways of using conditional response SDs (or variances) to assess explanatory strength for experimental studies.

Now, we can't observe the contents of any conditional response population. As a result, we can't apply our computational definitions of these parameters to know the values of these means and standard deviations. What we can do is observe *samples* from these response populations. Can we use a sample to learn about population model parameters?

In this section, we describe three sampling *assumptions*. If these assumptions are justified, then there are techniques we can use first to *estimate* parameters of the conditional populations from sample observations, and second to draw defensible *inferences* about those parameters.

An *estimate* of a population parameter is a sample-based "guess" at the value of the parameter.

An *inference* is a decision we make about a population parameter based on a sample.

The three assumptions we need for our linear model follow. If these assumptions are unwarranted, it may not be possible for us to bridge the gap between sample and population.

3.3.1   Independence of Sample Observations

The first assumption is that the *N* response variable observations making up the sample are *independent* of one another. We can best insure that this assumption has been met if we sample our observational units at random from some larger collection of potential units of observation. For experimental studies, we should, as well, randomly allocate the sampled units among the levels of treatment.

Why is this assumption critical? It was noted in Chapter 1 that, unless we could regard our sample of responses as *randomly representative* of some population, we would be unable to generalize any of our findings from the sample to the population. And, it is the population explanatory relation that we wish to understand, not any sample phenomena.

Independence is the *one* assumption among the three that the researcher can guarantee has been satisfied. Random sampling or random sampling and allocation are sufficient to insure independence.

3.3.2   Homogeneity of Conditional Response Variances

The second assumption is that *each* of the conditional response populations has the *same variance*. At each level of *x*, the variance of *y* is the same. The (conditional) mean of the response may change as the value of the explanatory variable changes— Equation [3.2] expresses how we think it does—but the (conditional) variance of the response is assumed to remain constant. Statisticians say the variances are *homogeneous*.

Why is such an assumption necessary?

Our sample consists of *N* response observations. In some samples, *each observation* will have come from a *different* conditional population. It would be impossible to estimate a different variance for each of the populations with but one observation apiece.

One way of resolving this dilemma is to be able to *assume* that the variances are the same in all of the conditional populations. This provides the needed simplification. Only one conditional variance must be estimated from the sample and this can be done.

Unlike independence, constant response variance cannot be assured. We cannot know at the outset of a study that the $\sigma^2(y \mid x = x_i)$s, the conditional *y* variances, will be homogeneous. We must examine each sample, once collected, for evidence of the *reasonableness* of this assumption. When we detect a violation of homogeneity, we will need to correct it. Failure to do so can only reduce the confidence we have in our modeling inferences. In Chapter 10, we learn how to examine data for homogeneity and what we can do when the assumption seems unwarranted.

3.3.3 Normal Characteristics of Conditional Response Populations

We not only want to estimate the parameters of our conditional response populations, we need to know how accurate those estimates are. Unless we know how accurate our estimmnates are we cannot choose between explanatory models. The best assessments of estimate accuracy are available to us if the frequency histograms for each of our conditional response populations share certain characteristics with what statisticians know as the *probability density function of the Normal random variable*. This probability density function is more popularly known simply as the "Normal curve."

The characteristics of the Normal curve that we want to see in our conditional response histograms are these three:

Unimodality: The Normal curve has a single peak or mode. The same should be true of our response variable histograms.

Symmetry: That single peak is in the middle of the Normal curve and the height of the curve descends at the same rate either side of the middle. We want our response variable histograms to be similarly non-skewed, without a long "tail" extending either to the left or right.

Normal Kurtosis: Finally, we require that our frequency histograms have tails that are neither "thicker" nor "thinner" than the tails of the Normal curve. Statisticians refer to the relative thickness of a symmetric histogram as *kurtosis*; a histogram with thinner-than-Normal tails is said to be *leptokurtic*, one with thicker-than-Normal tails is *platykurtic*.

If our conditional response population histograms have these three Normal probability density function characteristics, the mathematical abstraction that is the Normal random variable can be safely used to assess the accuracy of our parameter estimates. *Notice that we do not say that the response variable must be Normal.* The Normal random variable is a very useful mathematical abstraction, but our observed, measured response variable can never have all of the characteristics imparted to the Normal variable by its mathematical theory.

Fortunately, many response variable conditional population histograms really are rather close to Normal in the ways mentioned above. That is, scores close to the mean are fairly frequent while those farther away—smaller or larger—are progressively less common. A symmetric, bell-shaped histogram is quite common for the conditional *y* population. A reason for this is that responses that are contributed to by many causes (have many influences) tend to have Normal-like histograms. Even when the conditional response population histograms depart a bit from our Normal standards—so long as our homogeneity of variance assumption is appropriate—the accuracies established via the normality assumption are known to remain valid.

Like homogeneity of variance, normality of conditional response populations cannot be assured. Samples of response observations must be inspected to detect violations of modality, skewness and kurtosis severe enough to invalidate our inferences. Detection and correction techniques for all sampling assumptions are discussed in Chapter 10.

3.4
The Heights of Adolescent Males: An Example

We looked earlier at the age-18 heights in a sample of 28 boys who participated in the Berkeley Growth Study (Tuddenham & Snyder, 1954) which followed the development of children born in Berkeley, California in the late 1920s. We now add to those data the heights of these *same* boys at 2 years of age.

We'll continue the use of the abbreviations *ht2* for height at age 2 and *ht18* for height at age 18. Table 3.1 repeats the *ht18* data summarized earlier, together with the new, infant heights.

Let's begin by describing the infant heights as we did the adolescent data. The 28 Berkeley boys were not all the same height at 2 years of age, anymore than they were at 18. Their infant heights ranged from the shortest at 81.30 cm to the tallest at 92.20 cm with a mean of 88.16 cm:

$$\frac{90.20 + 91.40 + \cdots + 86.20}{28} = 88.16 \text{ cm} = M(ht2).$$

A *typical* 2-year-old height in this sample is 88 cm.

The age-2 heights are not all of this typical value, however, and our usual measure of how they spread out from the mean, because height is a measured variable,

T A B L E 3.1
Heights (in cms) of 28 Boys at Two Ages

2 Years	18 Years	2 Years	18 Years
90.20	179.0	91.40	183.5
91.40	195.1	90.00	178.1
86.40	183.7	86.40	177.0
87.60	178.7	90.00	172.9
86.70	171.5	91.40	188.4
88.10	181.8	81.30	169.4
82.20	172.5	90.60	180.2
83.80	174.6	92.20	189.0
91.00	190.4	87.10	182.4
87.40	173.8	91.40	185.8
84.20	172.6	89.70	180.7
88.40	185.2	92.20	178.7
87.70	178.5	83.80	169.6
89.60	177.6	86.20	166.8

is the standard deviation or SD, the square root of the variance or the square root of the mean of the squared deviations of the variable's scores from their mean.

For the age-2 heights we compute the SD first by finding the mean of the squared deviations from the mean,

$$\frac{(90.20 - 88.16)^2 + (91.40 - 88.16)^2 + \cdots + (86.20 - 88.16)^2}{28} = 9.099 \text{ cm}^2$$
$$= \text{Var}(ht2),$$

and then by taking the positive square root:

$$\sqrt{9.099 \text{ cm}^2} = 3.016 \text{ cm} = \text{SD}(ht2).$$

The mean and standard deviation in this sample for *ht18* were found earlier to be $\text{M}(ht18) = 179.2$ cm and $\text{SD}(ht18) = 6.779$ cm. Not only were these boys taller at age 18, but their heights became more variable. This contrast in variability is made graphically clear if we look at box-and-whisker plots for the two variables:

```
81.30                   |-------|92.20
     o X-------|    *    |- X
              |-------|

166.8               |------------------|
     X---------|         *          |- X      195.1
              |------------------|               o
```

3.5
Covariability and Correlation

When we have measures of two variables on the same set of observational units, we can describe not only the variability in each of the measures but how the two vary in unison. We use the closely related ideas of *covariance* and the *product-moment correlation* to describe this joint variability of a pair of variables, each with a unit of measurement.

It should be noted at the outset that this joint variability does *not* take into account any direction to the relation as does regression. Covariability and correlation merely reflect how much and in which direction two variables vary together, in unison.

We are interested in covariance and correlation because they provide *summary descriptive statistics* that will prove useful in developing and understanding linear models. Of the two, correlation will be the more important to us.

To start, we'll look at some pictures of joint variability.

3.5.1   Scatterplots

We produce a very interesting picture of how the two sets of heights jointly vary by using the 28 pairs of scores in Table 3.1 to position each boy as a point in a two-dimensional plot. We use the *ht2* value to position the point along the *X*-axis (from left to right as the value of *ht2* increases) and the *ht18* value to position it along the *Y*-axis (from the bottom upward as the value of *ht18* increases). When we have finished, the 28 points will be scattered over the plot. In fact, we refer to the result, in Figure 3.3, as a *scatterplot*.

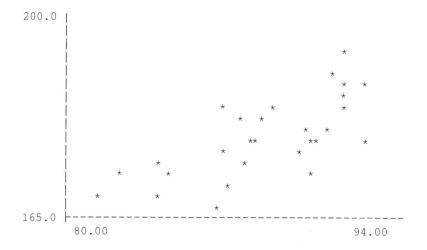

FIGURE 3.3
Scatterplot: Age-18
Heights v. Age-2
Heights

Where one variable, *x*, is explanatory and the other, *y*, is a response, it is conventional to let *x* vary along the horizontal or *X*–axis and *y* vary along the vertical or *Y*–axis. Our scatterplot anticipates Chapter 4 where we will develop a model with *ht2* as the explanatory and *ht18* as the response variable. As we continue to describe scatterplots, we will assume the *X*–axis variable is explanatory and the *Y*–axis variable is a response.

The scatterplot can tell us a good bit about the relation between a pair of variables. Figure 3.4 displays six different patterns. Panels a and d depict examples of a *positive* relation between the two variables—as the value of *x* increases, the value of *y* tends to increase as well (moving from left to right, the cloud of points tends to rise from the baseline).

Panels b and e, by contrast, illustrate *negative* relations—as *x* increases, *y* tends to take smaller values. In panel c, there is no discernible relation between the two variables—the value of *y* seems uninfluenced by the level of *x*. Finally, panel f shows a *nonlinear* relation—as *x* increases, *y* first increases and then decreases. This is a different picture from the one painted in panels a, b, d, or e. In those, the change in *y* is fairly steady over the range of *x*—the relations appear to be *linear* ones.

The scatterplot also gives information about the *strength* of the relation as well as its direction. Consider how the scatterplots a and d in Figure 3.3 differ in their

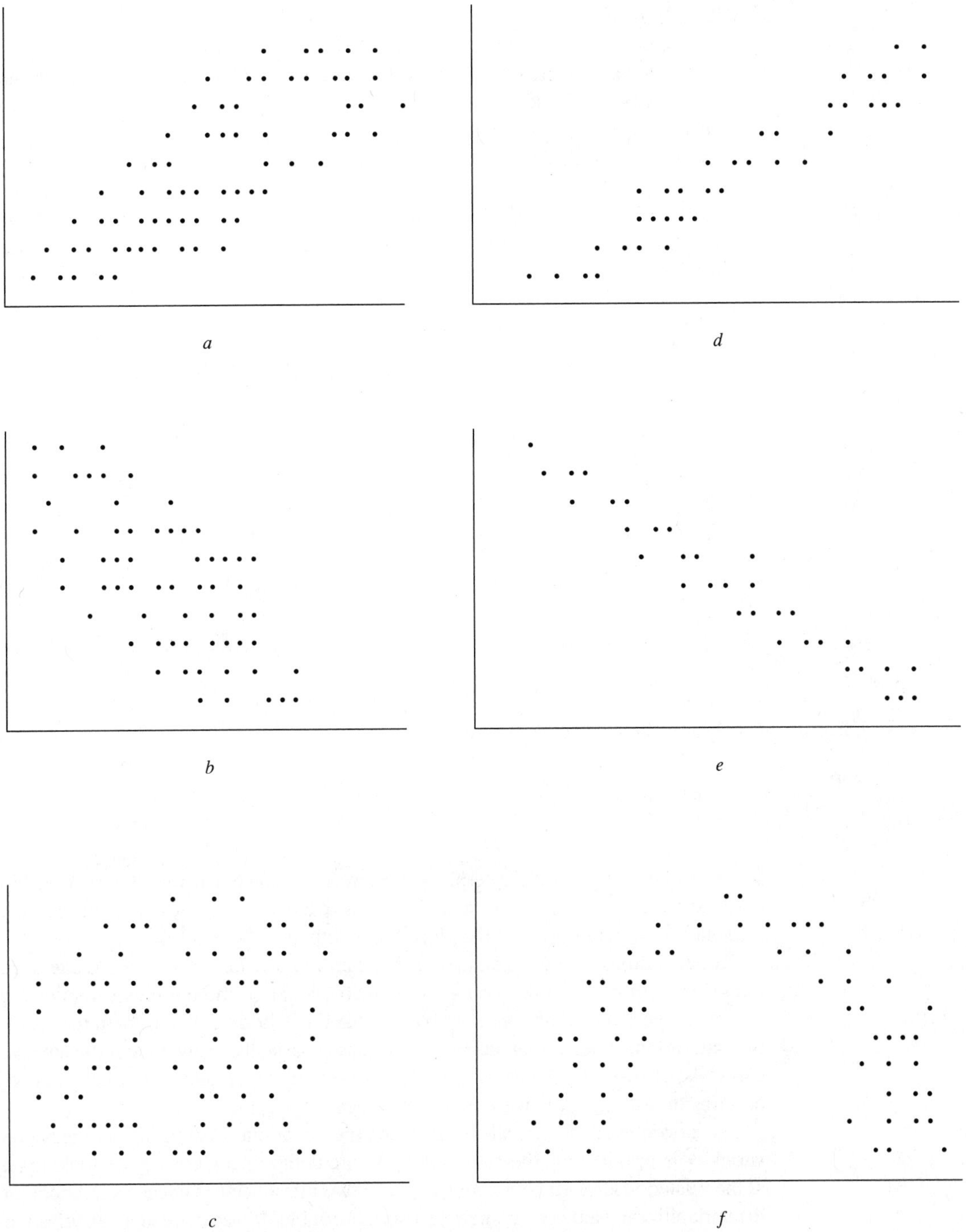

a

b

c

d

e

f

FIGURE **3.4** Scatterplot Patterns

vertical scatter for any x value. We can think of this vertical scatter as a pictorial representation of the conditional response variance. In both scatterplots a and d, the response is steadily increasing, a linear function of x. In scatterplot d, however, our *certainty* about the value the response will take, when we know the value of the explanatory variable, is much greater than it is in scatterplot a .

This point is further illustrated by Figure 3.5. Scatterplots a and d are those from Figure 3.4. A narrow slice of each scatterplot, corresponding to a small range of x values, has been marked off with an additional pair of vertical lines. The *conditional variability* of y—that for a prescribed narrow range of x—is quite a bit larger in the a scatterplot than in d.

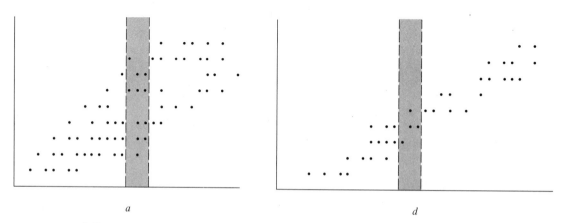

a   d

FIGURE 3.5   Conditional Variability of the Y Variable

3.5.2   Covariance

In describing the several scatterplots in Figure 3.4, we noted that the relationship between the two variables was sometimes positive and sometimes negative and that it seemed stronger in some of the plots than in others.

We can almost always pick up the *direction of covariation* from the scatterplot. Saying something about the *strength* of that covariation is more difficult. Intuitively, we see greater covariation in scatterplots d than in a and in e than in b. In those sets of observations, the varying values of the x and y variables show greater unison. We can make at least rough comparisons among sets of observations, but how can we describe the strength of covariation in any one set?

A conventional numerical summary of the covariation between two measured variables is provided by the *covariance*. Before defining covariance, we look again at the related idea of *variance*. In Chapter 2, we introduced variance as an index of the variability in values of a single measured variable. It was defined as the mean of the squared deviations of those values about their mean:

$$\text{Var}(x) = \frac{\sum_{i=1}^{N} [x_i - M(x)]^2}{N}. \tag{3.3}$$

Returning to our observations of the heights of 28 Berkeley boys at ages 2 and 18, we have

$$\text{Var}(ht2) = 9.099 \text{ cm}^2 \text{ and } \text{Var}(ht18) = 45.96 \text{ cm}^2$$

as measures of the variability of each of the two sets of heights taken separately.

The *joint variability* of the two sets may be assessed by their covariance. The covariance is defined analogously to the variance. Instead of computing the mean of the squared distances from the mean, we find the *mean of the products of pairs of distances from their respective means*:

$$\text{Cov}(x, y) = \frac{\sum_{i=1}^{N} [x_i - M(x)][y_i - M(y)]}{N}. \tag{3.4}$$

The contributing product will be positive if the observations on the x and y variables are either both above or both below their respective means and negative if one is above and the other below. The covariance, as the mean of these products, will itself be positive, 0, or negative depending on the balance over the sample between instances of positive and of negative association.

For the height data, the covariance is computed as

$$(\frac{1}{28})[(90.2 - 88.16)(179.0 - 179.2) + (91.4 - 88.16)(195.1 - 179.2)$$
$$+ \cdots + (86.2 - 88.16)(166.8 - 179.2)] = 14.42 \text{ cm}^2.$$

The covariance for the two sets of heights is positive, consistent with the shape of the Figure 3.3 scatterplot. It is expressed in cm^2 as it is an average of products of terms, each in cm units. If the x and y variables had different metrics—if, for example, the response variable were weight in pounds and the explanatory variable height in inches—the covariance would be expressed in (pounds × inches).

Covariances are not easily interpretable. In general, the covariance can be no bigger—in absolute value—than the larger of the two variances, and, typically, it will be considerably smaller than this upper limit.

The covariance is sensitive not only to the strength of the relation between x and y variables but to the units in which the two are measured. *If* heights at both age 2 and age 18 had been measured in inches rather than centimeters, the SDs and covariance would have been

$$\text{SD}(ht2) = 1.19 \text{ in}, \quad \text{SD}(ht18) = 2.67 \text{ in}, \text{ and } \text{Cov}(ht2, ht18) = 2.24 \text{ in}^2.$$

The numeric values of the variances and covariances are different for the inches and centimeters measurements. We believe, of course, that the relation between the boys' heights at the two ages hasn't changed; only the metric has.

3.5.3   Correlation

How can we express the strength of the covariation between two variables undisturbed by differences in metrics, means, or variances? We turn to the correlation coefficient for that. In fact, the *product moment correlation* provides an answer to the question

> What would be the value of the covariance if the two measures did not differ in metric (the two were measured in the same units), or in general magnitude (the two had equal means), or in variability (the two had equal variances)?

More specifically, we develop the correlation coefficient by finding what the covariance would be if each set of scores were *transformed* to a set of *standard scores*, each set with a mean of 0 and an SD of 1. The standard score transformation looks like this:

$$z(x)_i = \frac{x_i - M(x)}{SD(x)}. \tag{3.5}$$

A standard score, $z(x)_i$, expresses how far—and in which direction—an original score, x_i, is displaced from its mean in standard deviation units. If x_i exceeds $M(x)$, $z(x)_i$ is positive, and if x_i is below the mean, $z(x)_i$ is negative.

Thus, the first boy in the sample had heights expressed in standard score form as

$$z(ht2)_1 = \frac{90.2 \text{ cm} - 88.16 \text{ cm}}{3.016 \text{ cm}} = \frac{2.04 \text{ cm}}{3.016 \text{ cm}} = 0.68$$

and

$$z(ht18)_1 = \frac{179.0 - 179.2}{6.779} = \frac{-0.2}{6.779} = -0.03.$$

His age-2 height was 0.68 SDs *above* the age-2 mean and his age-18 height was 0.03 SDs *below* the age-18 mean. Note that the deviation from the mean, in cm, is divided by the standard deviation, also in cm, with the result that the standard score has no metric—other than SD units—associated with it.

The computation of the covariance based on standard scores for the two variables is simplified. Because the mean of a set of standard scores is always 0 and the SD always 1, the covariance between two sets of standard scores is just the mean of the products of those standard scores:

$$Cov[z(x), z(y)] = \frac{\sum_{i=1}^{N}[z(x)_i z(y)_i]}{N}.$$

But, the covariance between two variables, each transformed to standard scores, is also the *product moment correlation* between the two variables!

$$r(x, y) = Cov[z(x), z(y)] = \frac{\sum_{i=1}^{N}[z(x)_i z(y)_i]}{N}. \tag{3.6}$$

As a covariance, $r(x, y)$ may be negative or positive. Similarly, the absolute value of $r(x, y)$ cannot be greater than the larger of the two variances, $Var[z(x)]$ and $Var[z(y)]$. Since the variance of a set of standard scores is 1.0, the product moment correlation can take values only in the interval from -1.0 to 1.0.

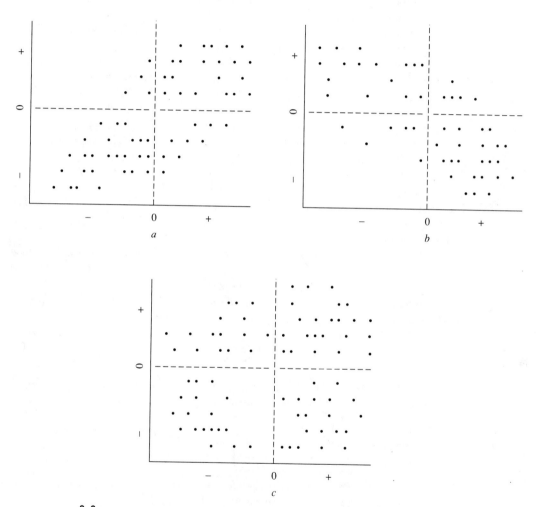

FIGURE 3.6   Correlations and Standard Score Products

The scatterplots in Figure 3.6 help us see how Equation [3.6] works. These are scatterplots of standard scores. The lines bisecting the plots horizontally divide the Y–axis variable values at the mean, and the lines bisecting the plots vertically divide the X–axis variable values at the mean. As a result, points in the upper-right quadrant correspond to observations that are above the mean on both variables. Similarly, points in the lower-left quadrant represent observations that are below the mean on both variables. Points falling in the other two quadrants describe observations that are above the mean on one variable and below it on the other: In the upper-left quadrant Y–axis variable scores are above the mean and X–axis variable scores are below. This is reversed in the lower-right quadrant.

In computing a correlation with Equation 3.6, we first find a product of standard scores for each of these points. This product is *positive* for points in the upper-right (both standard scores are positive) and lower-left (both standard scores are negative) quadrants, and it is *negative* for points in the upper-left and lower-right quadrants (where one standard score is positive and the other negative).

Continuing the computation of the correlation, these products of standard scores are then summed. For the situation depicted in panel a of Figure 3.6, most of the standard score products will be positive—the bulk of the points falls in the upper-right and lower-left quadrants—and so the sum of the products clearly will be positive. Dividing by the number of points, the resulting correlation will also be positive.

The standard score products for panel b will, by contrast, nearly all be negative as the points tend to fall in the two "off" quadrants. The sum of products and the mean of the products—the correlation—will also be negative. In the last panel, the points are distributed over all four quadrants. There will be, roughly, as many negative as positive products, and, when they are summed, the result will be a very small number. Dividing by the number of observations will give a correlation for scatterplot c close to 0.

Despite its ease of interpretation, the correlation coefficient is not usually defined as the mean of a set of standard score products. In the following equation, we show that this definition is equivalent to the more standard one.

If we replace each of the two standard scores in Equation [3.6] with its Equation [3.5] definition, we can write the product moment correlation as

$$r(x, y) = \text{Cov}[z(x), z(y)] = \left(\frac{1}{N}\right) \sum_{i=1}^{N} \left(\frac{[x_i - M(x)]}{\text{SD}(x)}\right) \left(\frac{[y_i - M(y)]}{\text{SD}(y)}\right).$$

Neither standard deviation changes as we sum over the pairs of mean deviations and, as a result, the SDs can be brought outside the summation to give us

$$r(x, y) = \left(\frac{1}{\text{SD}(x)\text{SD}(y)}\right) \frac{\sum_{i=1}^{N}[x_i - M(x)][y_i - M(y)]}{N}.$$

Now, we have the reciprocal of the product of the standard deviations multiplied by the covariance between x and y, as given in Equation [3.4].

This results in a much more common way of defining the correlation:

$$r(x, y) = \left(\frac{\text{Cov}(x, y)}{\text{SD}(x)\text{SD}(y)}\right). \tag{3.7}$$

Introductory statistics students typically learn that the product moment correlation is the ratio of the covariance between two variables to the product of their standard deviations.

Equation [3.6], however, provides a far better way of *thinking about* the extent of covariation between two variables. Our product moment correlation coefficient is simply the average product of deviations from the mean expressed in standard deviation units. Equation [3.6] is not a good computational formula—we need not compute standard scores just to find the correlation—but it possesses conceptual clarity.

If we substitute into Equation [3.7] the covariances and standard deviations we reported earlier for the different metric scalings of heights, we can compute the correlation between the two sets of heights as

$$r[ht2(\text{cm}), ht18(\text{cm})] = \frac{14.42 \text{ cm}^2}{(3.02 \text{ cm})(6.78 \text{ cm})} = 0.705$$

or as

$$r[ht2(\text{in}), ht18(\text{in})] = \frac{2.24 \text{ in}^2}{(1.19 \text{ in})(2.67 \text{ in})} = 0.705.$$

Notice how the metrics—centimeters or inches—cancel out in the formation of the correlation coefficient. The two correlations are identical. The two sets of heights—age 2 and age 18—have a product moment correlation of .70.

The positive correlation is consistent with the scatterplot for these data given in Figure 3.2. As height at age 2 increases (as we move from left to right), height at age 18 also increases,—the scatter rises. But, what can we make of the magnitude of the correlation? How strong a relation does the correlation of .70 indicate?

The question is an important one and it has an answer, important in linear modeling. We will see it in the next chapter when we report the results of estimating our linear structural model parameters.

3.6
Summary

This chapter introduced the framework for *linear models*, ones in which the expected value of the response is a linear function of the value of the explanatory variable. The linear model has associated with it *slope* and *intercept* parameters. The slope parameter is the more interesting from a modeling perspective. It describes the magnitude of the explanation, the amount of change in $\mu(y \mid x = x_i)$ associated with a one-unit change in x. The linear model is a population model and, consequently, its characteristics can only be *estimated* from sample observations. To provide estimates whose accuracies can be known, three *assumptions* are introduced as companions to the linear model. We shall need to assume (a) that the N response observations making up a sample are *independent* one of another, (b) that each conditional response population has the *same variance* , and (c) that each conditional response population has a histogram with characteristics common to the Normal random variable. In preparation for estimating the linear model parameters, this chapter reviewed the descriptive statistics *covariance* and *correlation* and the graphic technique of *scatterplots*.

4

Simple Linear Regression: Estimation

Chapter 3 introduced *regression* and the *linear model*. The linear model proposes that the mean of the response variable (*y*) is a linear function of the value of the explanatory variable (*x*). This is a very simple and convenient way to express the explanatory relation. Despite its simplicity, the linear model is exceptionally adaptable. It will meet our modeling needs in a very wide variety of experiments and observational studies, essentially whenever the response is measured.

    Because of its importance, we review the linear model here. We then go on to show how to *estimate* the parameters of the linear model and develop the idea of a *sampling distribution* for an estimate to allow us to appreciate the accuracy of these estimates.

4.1
The Linear Model: A Review

Let's begin with a review of the very important linear model ideas that were introduced in the last chapter. We'll use Figure 4.1 to help us see those ideas even more clearly.

    Our model begins with the selection of a response variable, *y*, and a population of potential respondents. For an *observational* or sampling study, we think of the totality of the scores on *y* for these respondents as making up a single, unconditional response population. The histogram for this population is sketched along the *Y*-axis on the left-hand border of Figure 4.1. This unconditional response population has a variance of $\sigma^2(y)$, the unconditional response variance. It describes our certainty about the response variable. The smaller $\sigma^2(y)$ is, the greater our certainty about the value of *y* for a randomly chosen member of the unconditional population.

    Now, our purpose in modeling is that we think we may be able to *increase our certainty* about the value of *y* if we take into account the value of an associated explanatory variable, *x*. In particular, again for the observational study, we think that if we were to divide our unconditional response population into several populations, one for each relevant value of *x*, the resulting *conditional response populations* would have two properties:

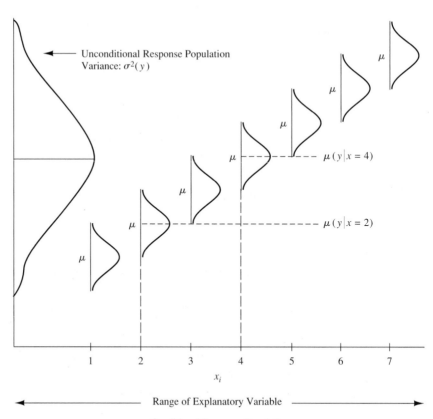

FIGURE 4.1

The Linear Model,
Conditional and
Unconditional
Observational
Response
Populations

Range of Explanatory Variable

Conditional Response Populations
• Linear Model:
  $\mu(y \mid x = x_i) = \beta_0 + \beta_1 x_i$
• Assumptions:
  • Normal Shapes
  • Same Variances: $\sigma^2(y \mid x)$

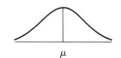

- The conditional response means, the $\mu(y \mid x = x_i)$s, will differ among them-selves.

- The conditional response variances, the $\sigma^2(y \mid x = x_i)$s, will be smaller than the the unconditional response variance.

The first property conveys our idea of how y is influenced by x: The mean of the response is different for different values of the explanatory variable. The second property is a consequence of the first. By taking the value of x into account, we should increase our certainty about y, hence, the smaller variance in the conditional population. We should be more certain about the value of an observation randomly sampled from one of the conditional populations than we are about one sampled from the unconditional population.

The smaller histograms, ranging from the lower left to upper right in Figure 4.1, represent a set of seven conditional response populations. Their expected values—the centers of the baselines of the histograms—take different values along the Y-axis and the conditional populations show less variability than does the unconditional response population.

For *experimental* or random assignment studies, the picture is different than that shown in Figure 4.1. We can again start with the selection of a response variable, *y*, and a population of potential respondents. The conditional response populations are hypothetical ones rather than subdivisions of a real population. Each would be the result of measuring the response over the whole population of respondents assigned to a particular level of treatment (level of the explanatory variable, *x*). Thus, the seven conditional response populations of Figure 4.1 would be populations of responses from the same respondents but under seven different treatments. As in observational studies, our explanatory model is motivated by the suspicion that the conditional response populations may have different means. We do not have, as we do for observational studies, an unconditional response population, so no comparison can be made between conditional and unconditional response variances.

The *linear model* provides a structure to this idea of different means for the conditional response populations. The means are postulated to vary *systematically* with the value of the explanatory variable. In particular, $\mu(y \mid x = x_i)$ is a *linear function* of the value of *x*:

$$\mu(y \mid x = x_i) = \beta_0 + \beta_1 x_i. \tag{3.2}$$

Thus, in Figure 4.1, the expected values of the seven conditional response histograms (noted by the μs) have been made to line up. Each is a point on the straight line whose equation is given by Equation [3.2]. This line is known as the *regression line*.

Finally, in Chapter 3, we described two *assumptions* about the conditional response populations. These assumptions are in anticipation of our need to make decisions about a population model on the basis of a sample of observations. The two assumptions are the following.

■ The several conditional response populations all have the same variance:

$$\sigma^2(y \mid x = 1) = \sigma^2(y \mid x = 2) = \ldots = \sigma^2(y \mid x = 7) = \sigma^2(y \mid x).$$

■ The several conditional response population histograms are unimodal, symmetric, and have the same degree of kurtosis as the Normal random variable.

In Figure 4.1, the seven conditional histograms have been drawn to differ only in their expected values—where their centers are along the *Y*-axis. Their spreads and shapes are the same.

The linear model and accompanying assumptions allow us to capture the important elements of Figure 4.1, and of linear regression models, in four statements:

■ The conditional response populations—a separate population for each level of *x*—have means that are a *linear function* of *x*:
  $\mu(y \mid x = x_i) = \beta_0 + \beta_1 x_i.$

■ The conditional response populations have a common variance, $\sigma^2(y \mid x)$.

■ The conditional response population histograms have Normal characteristics.

- In observational, but not in experimental studies, there is an unconditional population of response scores—the result of pooling over explanatory variable levels—that has a variance, $\sigma^2(y)$, termed the *unconditional response variance*, that is typically larger than the conditional response variance.

Four unknown population parameters are referred to in these statements: β_0, β_1, $\sigma^2(y\,|\,x)$, and, for observational studies, $\sigma^2(y)$.

Together, β_0 and β_1 tell us the mean of *each* of the conditional populations. In particular, β_1 is the *slope* of the line connecting the conditional means. If β_1 is 0, all of the means are identical. Otherwise, the slope tells us the amount by which the response mean changes with a change of one unit in the explanatory variable. Figure 4.1 illustrates this for x values of 2 and 4. The difference between $\mu(y\,|\,x=2)$ and $\mu(y\,|\,x=4)$ will be $2\,\beta_1$ inasmuch as the two x values are separated by two points.

A most critical question about a linear model is whether the slope parameter is 0 or not. If it is 0, knowledge of the x level does not increase our certainty about y. In an observational study, the conditional response variance, $\sigma^2(y\,|\,x)$, would be no smaller than the unconditional response variance, $\sigma^2(y)$.

How can we ascertain the sizes of these parameters, β_0, β_1, $\sigma^2(y\,|\,x)$, and, for observational studies, $\sigma^2(y)$?

4.2
Estimates of Linear Model Parameters

A *parameter*, we have noted, describes a *population characteristic*. Thus, the numeric value of $\sigma^2(y)$ describes the variance of an unconditional response population. The values of the parameters $\sigma^2(y\,|\,x)$, β_0 and β_1, will describe the variance and means of all of the response populations conditional on values of our explanatory variable, x, assuming our linear model is appropriate.

A number computed from a *sample* of observations, on the other hand, is termed a *statistic*. We have mentioned in the past two chapters such statistics as the sample mean, median, variance, covariance, and correlation. We compute these and other statistics for a *purpose*. In fact, we do so typically for one of three purposes:

- Statistics describe samples. The sample variance, Var(*ht2*), describes variability in the sample of age-2 heights and is a *descriptive statistic*.

- Statistics estimate population parameters. We may choose, for example, to interpret the sample mean, M(*ht18*), as an *estimate* of the mean of the population, μ(*ht18*).

- Statistics can be used to draw inferences about populations. In Chapter 5, we will use Student's t statistic, calculated from a sample, to "test the hypothesis" that $\beta_1 = 0$. The t is an *inferential statistic*.

Statistics are interpreted as descriptive, inferential, or estimates. We now introduce estimates of the four linear model parameters. In Chapter 5, we develop some inferential statistics important to the linear model. Both estimates and inferential statistics make use of the descriptive statistics we reviewed in earlier chapters.

How should we use the sample observations to estimate our linear model parameters? The answers—certainly for the slope and intercept parameters—are not obvious. The estimates we describe here are based on some of our Chapter-3 assumptions and on statistical estimation techniques that make them "good" estimates. In the section following this, we will say a little about what is meant by a good estimate and how these estimates were obtained. For now, however, let's look at the estimates.

4.2.1   Estimates of Slope and Intercept Parameters

The estimates of the two linear equation parameters are expressed conveniently in terms of sample descriptive statistics reviewed in Chapters 2 and 3. This makes it easy to describe them. The estimate of the *regression slope* is

$$\widehat{\beta}_1 = r(x, y)\frac{SD(y)}{SD(x)}. \tag{4.1}$$

The slope estimate is the product of the sample correlation between explanatory and response variables and the *ratio* of the sample SDs, response to explanatory. We've put a "hat" ($\widehat{}$) on β_1 to remind us that what we have is an *estimate* of the parameter, not the real thing!

The slope estimate is then used in the definition of the *intercept estimate*:

$$\widehat{\beta}_0 = M(y) - \widehat{\beta}_1 M(x). \tag{4.2}$$

The intercept estimate is the result of subtracting the product of the slope estimate and the sample mean for the explanatory variable from the sample mean for the response variable.

When we substitute these two parameter estimates into the linear model (Equation [3.2]) we have an equation for *estimating the conditional mean of the response*:

$$\widehat{\mu}(y \mid x = x_i) = \widehat{\beta}_0 + \widehat{\beta}_1 x_i. \tag{4.3}$$

Let's apply these three estimation equations to our boys' heights example. We have, from Chapter 3, the following descriptive statistics:

$$M(x) = M(ht2) = 88.16 \text{ cm}, \ SD(x) = SD(ht2) = 3.016 \text{ cm},$$

$$M(y) = M(ht18) = 179.2 \text{ cm}, \ SD(y) = SD(ht18) = 6.779 \text{ cm},$$

$$N = 28, \text{ and } r(x, y) = r(ht2, ht18) = 0.705.$$

The estimated slope of regression, from Equation [4.1], for these sample data is

$$\widehat{\beta}_1 = r(x, y)\frac{SD(y)}{SD(x)} = r(ht2, ht18)\frac{SD(ht18)}{SD(ht2)} = (0.705)\left(\frac{6.779 \text{ cm}}{3.016 \text{ cm}}\right)$$
$$= 1.585 \text{ cm/cm}.$$

Our estimate of the difference in average age-18 heights of 2 boys whose age-2 heights were separated by 1 cm is a little bit less than 1.6 cm. The metric for the slope estimate is a rate one, units of *y per unit* of *x*. For our example, both *x* and *y* are measured in cm.

The estimated value of the regression intercept is calculated from Equation [4.2] as

$$\widehat{\beta}_0 = \mathrm{M}(y) - \widehat{\beta}_1 \mathrm{M}(x) = \mathrm{M}(ht18) - \widehat{\beta}_1 \mathrm{M}(ht2) = 179.2 \text{ cm} - (1.585 \text{ cm/cm})(88.16 \text{ cm})$$
$$= 39.47 \text{ cm}.$$

The metric of the intercept is *always the same* as that for *y*. Height at age 18 is measured in cm—so, too, is the intercept of the regression line.

From these numeric results, we use Equation [4.3] to estimate (conditional) mean response values of *ht18*, each as a function of the value of *ht2*:

$$\widehat{\mu}(y \mid x = x_i) = \widehat{\mu}(ht18 \mid ht2 = x_i) = \widehat{\beta}_0 + \widehat{\beta}_1 x_i = 39.47 \text{ cm} + (1.585 \text{ cm/cm})(x_i \text{ cm}).$$

We'll use this equation to predict the adolescent height first for an 85-cm-tall two year old,

$$\widehat{\mu}(ht18 \mid ht2 = 85 \text{ cm}) = 39.47 \text{ cm} + (1.585 \text{ cm/cm})(85 \text{ cm}) = 174.20 \text{ cm},$$

and then for a 90-cm-tall infant,

$$\widehat{\mu}(ht18 \mid ht2 = 90 \text{ cm}) = 39.47 \text{ cm} + (1.585 \text{ cm/cm})(90 \text{ cm}) = 182.12 \text{ cm}.$$

The 5-cm difference in infant heights leads to a predicted 7.92-cm difference in adolescent heights: $(5 \text{ cm})(1.585 \text{ cm/cm}) = 7.925 \text{ cm}$.

4.2.2   Estimated Regression Line

Equation [4.3] is the equation for a straight line, the *estimated regression line*. Were we to plot several values of $\widehat{\mu}(y \mid x = x_i)$ against the corresponding values of x_i, all the points would fall on this straight line. Look at this line to better understand the parameter estimates.

Figure 4.2 is the scatterplot of the boys' heights data with this estimated regression line overlaid on it. The estimated regression line slopes clearly upward in this figure.

Let's relate this picture to some features of the estimated regression slope, as defined in Equation [4.1] ,

$$\widehat{\beta}_1 = \mathrm{r}(x, y) \frac{SD(y)}{SD(x)}. \tag{4.1}$$

Three things are noteworthy in this equation:

- Because both SDs are positive, $\widehat{\beta}_1$ will have the *same sign* as the correlation, $\mathrm{r}(x, y)$. A positive regression slope for the height data is consistent with the positive correlation, $\mathrm{r}(ht2, ht18) = 0.705$.

- The slope estimate will be 0—the estimated slope flat—only if the correlation is 0.

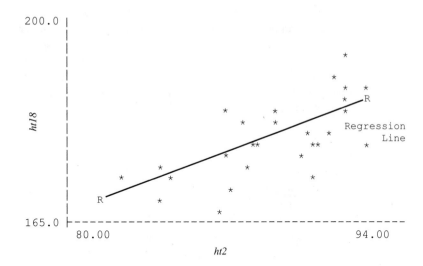

FIGURE 4.2
Estimated Regres-
sion Line for Boys'
Heights

- The *steepness* of the slope depends both on the size of the correlation and on the relative sizes of the x and y sample SDs.

- For given x and y sample SDs, the maximum steepness of the estimated regression line occurs when the correlation is 1.0 (or -1.0) and will be equal to $SD(y)/SD(x)$.

For the boys' heights example, we had $SD(ht2) = 3.016$ cm and $SD(ht18) = 6.779$ cm. The ratio of the two,

$$\frac{SD(ht18)}{SD(ht2)} = \frac{6.779 \text{ cm}}{3.016 \text{ cm}} = 2.25 \text{ cm/cm},$$

gives the maximum slope for the estimated regression line. The predicted difference in the average heights at age 18 associated with a 1-cm difference in height at age 2 could not be greater than 2.25 cm, whatever the correlation between x and y.

The equation for the estimated regression line tells another interesting property of that line, one we can verify from a scatterplot. If we replace $\widehat{\beta}_0$ on the right-hand side of Equation [4.3],

$$\widehat{\mu}(y \mid x = x_i) = \widehat{\beta}_0 + \widehat{\beta}_1 x_i, \qquad \textbf{(4.3)}$$

with the right-hand side of Equation [4.2],

$$\widehat{\beta}_0 = M(y) - \widehat{\beta}_1 M(x), \qquad \textbf{(4.2)}$$

we have another way of describing the estimated regression line:

$$\widehat{\mu}(y \mid x = x_i) = M(y) - \widehat{\beta}_1 M(x) + \widehat{\beta}_1 x_i = M(y) + \widehat{\beta}_1 [x_i - M(x)]. \qquad \textbf{(4.4)}$$

Equation [4.4] provides, in many ways, a more useful way of looking at the estimated regression line than does Equation [4.3].

For example, when the value of x is its sample mean, when $x_i = M(x)$, Equation [4.4] makes it clear that the estimated conditional response mean is simply the sample response mean, $M(y)$.

In terms of our estimated regression line, this means that the line must pass through the point whose value along the X-axis is $M(x)$ and whose value along the Y-axis is $M(y)$. This point, which always will serve to anchor an estimated regression line, is called the *point of means*.

The regression line in Figure 4.2 passes through the point $ht2 = M(ht2) = 88.16$ cm, $ht18 = M(ht18) = 179.2$ cm. That is the point of means for the heights sample data.

It is an important property of the estimated regression line that it always passes through the point common to the x and y sample means. The estimated regression line is completely known when we know this point of means and the slope of the line, as computed from Equation [4.1].

Knowing that the regression line passes through the point of means is of greater interest to us than knowing the estimated value of the intercept. The reliance of the regression line on the point of means and the slope is illustrated in Figure 4.3.

Both panels show the estimated regression line passing through two points. One of these points is the point of means. The second point is positioned (a) one unit, in the metric of x, to the right of $M(x)$ and (b) $\widehat{\beta}_1$ units, in the metric of y, above $M(y)$. The slope of the connecting line, then, is $\widehat{\beta}_1$.

The point was made previously that the slope of the regression line had to fall between 0 and the ratio of $SD(y)$ to $SD(x)$. We provide a graphic illustration of this in Figure 4.4.

The scatterplot and (estimated) regression line of Figure 4.2, for the boys' height sample, are reproduced in Figure 4.4. To that have been added two additional lines, both passing through the point of means. The first new line, that with 0 slope, is called the *mean line*. Its height is constant, equal here to $M(y) = M(ht18) = 179.2$ cm. The second new line has a slope equal to the ratio $[SD(y)/SD(x)] = SD(ht18)/SD(ht2) = 2.25$ cm.

We refer to this second line as the *SD line*. The slope of the SD line is what we earlier noted to be the maximum possible slope for the regression line, given the SDs of the explanatory and response variables. The mean line, by contrast, gives the minimum possible slope for the regression line, the slope when $r(x, y) = 0.0$.

The estimated regression line will always fall *between* the mean and SD lines. If the (x, y) correlation is 0, the regression line will fall on top of the mean line. If the (x, y) correlation is perfect (1.0 or -1.0), the regression line will fall on top of the SD line. (If the correlation is negative, we revise our definition of the SD line to $-[SD(y)/SD(x)]$ so that it, like the regression line, will have a negative slope.)

In practice, the slope of the regression line is always flatter than that of the SD line. The rather sizable correlation in the boys' heights sample, $r(ht2, ht18) = 0.705$ is reflected in the position of the regression line closer to the SD than to the mean line.

The regression line rises above the mean line towards the SD line, approaching the SD line as the correlation in the sample between x and y approaches 1.0.

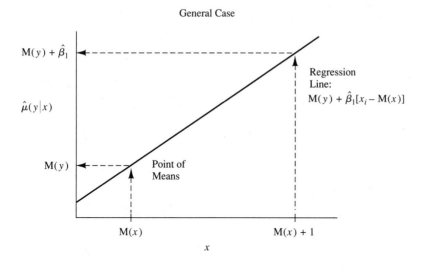

General Case

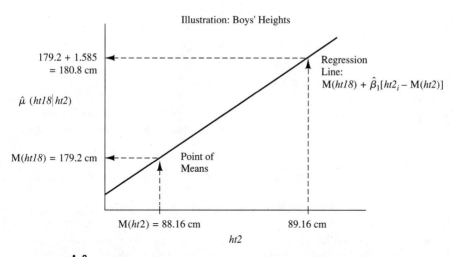

Illustration: Boys' Heights

FIGURE 4.3   Slope of Regression Line and the Point of Means

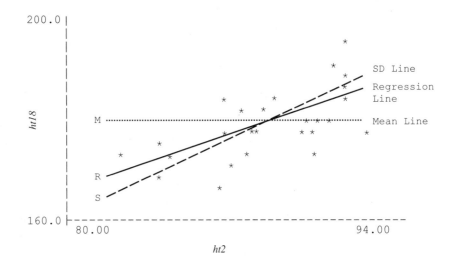

FIGURE 4.4

Regression, Mean,
and SD Lines for
the Height Sample

4.2.3   Explaining Response Variance in Observational Samples Using the Linear Model

The farther the regression line is away from the mean line and the closer it is to the SD line, the greater the amount of *y* variability—in the sample—that has been explained by *x* through our linear model. To appreciate this, we will look back at the "predict the age-18 height of the randomly chosen boy" examples of Chapter 2.

This time, though, we will think about the prediction strategies solely in terms of this particular sample.

If we predict the value of *ht18* *unconditionally*, (not taking *ht2*, the explanatory variable, into account) then we predict it to be the sample *ht18* mean, M(*y*), whichever boy is chosen.

The accuracy of that prediction strategy is reflected, graphically, in Figure 4.5. This describes the *ht2*, *ht18* scatterplot with the mean line overlaid. Whichever boy is chosen, our prediction is the height given by mean line. The *vertical distance* separating this line and the actual age-18 height of the randomly chosen boy is the amount by which our prediction would be in error. The error can be quite small—if a boy with height close to 179.2 cm is chosen—or quite large—if one of the shortest or tallest is picked out. Two of these potential errors are indicated in Figure 4.5.

If, now, we predict *conditionally*, we let our prediction vary according to the selected boy's infant height—his *x* value. We now use as our prediction what we believe to be the conditional response mean—the mean *ht18* for boys with a particular *ht2* score. Our prediction is the (estimated) conditional mean provided by Equation [4.4]:

$$\widehat{\mu}(y \mid x = x_i) = M(y) + \widehat{\beta}_1[x_i - M(x)].\tag{4.4}$$

The unconditional prediction, remember, was just M(*y*). The conditional prediction modifies this on the basis of x_i, the value of the explanatory variable. Our conditional prediction will be one of the values that fall along the regression line.

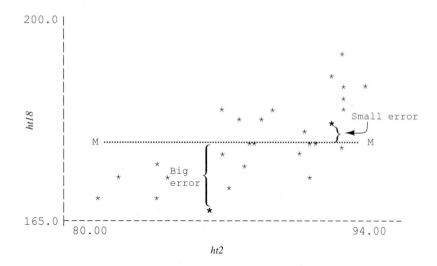

FIGURE 4.5

Errors in Uncondi-
tional Prediction

Our linear model (conditional) prediction is a point on the regression line, so, again in Figure 4.6, it is the vertical distance separating that point on the line from the boy's actual adolescent height that tells us how much our prediction was in error. The error can be smaller or larger, as illustrated in Figure 4.6.

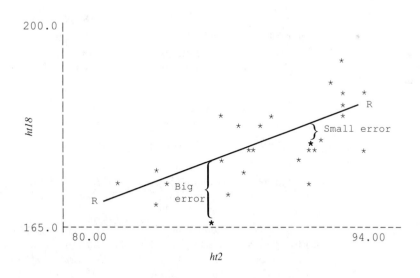

FIGURE 4.6

Errors in Condi-
tional Prediction

Big and small errors are possible whether we guess the value of *ht18* for the randomly chosen boy conditionally or unconditionally. A visual comparison of Figures 4.5 and 4.6 suggests, however, that the vertical distances to the scatterplot points tend to be greater when taken from the mean line than when taken from the regression line. Across the boys who might be randomly chosen, the possible errors seem smaller, overall, for our conditional predictions than for the unconditional ones.

In fact, it is very useful to have numerical indices of the overall size of errors associated with the two prediction strategies. The index used most often is the *mean squared error* (MSE), the mean of the squares of the errors that result if we apply one of the prediction strategies to each of the sample observations.

For the unconditional predictions, the mean squared error is

$$\text{MSE(Unconditional)} = \frac{\sum_{i=1}^{N}[y_i - M(y)]^2}{N}, \tag{4.5}$$

where y_i is the y score for the ith case in the sample and $M(y)$ is the sample response mean, the value we would predict for each of the N cases making up the sample. We square the difference between the two and find the mean of these squared errors.

In terms of Figure 4.5, the MSE(Unconditional) is the mean of the squared vertical distances of the 28 points from the mean line.

The right-hand side of Equation [4.5] is also the equation for the sample y variance, the mean of the squared deviations from the mean. So, the MSE for the unconditional guesses is the sample variance:

$$\text{MSE(Unconditional)} = \text{Var}(y). \tag{4.6}$$

For our conditional predictions, the mean squared error is

$$\text{MSE(Conditional)} = \frac{\sum_{i=1}^{N}[y_i - \widehat{\mu}(y\,|\,x = x_i)]^2}{N}.$$

Each of the N predictions, $\widehat{\mu}(y\,|\,x = x_i)$, now takes the value of x into account. Since these (estimated) conditional response means are based on the linear model, they are given by Equation [4.3] and the resulting MSE is

$$\text{MSE(Linear Model)} = \frac{\sum_{i=1}^{N}[y_i - (\widehat{\beta}_0 + \widehat{\beta}_1 x_i)]^2}{N}. \tag{4.7}$$

With reference to Figure 4.6, the MSE(Linear Model) is the mean of the squared vertical distances of the 28 points from the regression line.

"Eyeballing" Figures 4.5 and 4.6 leads us to believe the MSE ought to be smaller for the linear model predictions than for the unconditional ones. Will the computed MSE values confirm this?

From our earlier computation of Var($ht18$), we already know the MSE(Unconditional) for the boys' heights data. We could first use Equation [4.3] to calculate a prediction for each of the 28 boys and then Equation [4.7] to find the mean of the squares of the errors in those guesses.

We are spared the effort of computing MSE(Linear Model) in this way because there is a very simple relation between the two MSEs:

$$\text{MSE(Linear Model)} = [1 - r(x, y)^2]\text{MSE(Unconditional)}$$
$$= [1 - r(x, y)^2]\text{Var}(y). \tag{4.8}$$

The difference between the two MSEs depends on the size of the sample correlation between explanatory and response variables. If the correlation is 0, the two MSEs are the same. The linear model predictions are the same as the unconditional ones when x and y are uncorrelated.

If the sample (x, y) correlation is perfect (1.0 or -1.0), the MSE for the linear model predictions drops to 0! We predict each of the N sample y values with complete accuracy when the correlation is perfect. For absolute values of the sample correlation between 0.0 and 1.0, the MSE(Linear Model) will be *smaller* than the MSE(Unconditional).

For the boys' heights sample pictured in Figures 4.5 and 4.6, the two MSEs are

$$\text{MSE(Unconditional)} = \text{Var}(ht18) = 45.96 \text{ cm}^2$$

and

$$\text{MSE(Linear Model)} = [1 - 0.705^2]45.962 \text{ cm}^2 = 23.18 \text{ cm}^2.$$

A smaller MSE error for the conditional predictions, in the language of Chapter 2, provides evidence for the increased certainty we have in those predictions.

Now, we must sound a warning about the interpretation we have just placed on the relationship between the two MSEs. These MSEs are *sample descriptive statistics*. They describe aspects of the scatterplot for this particular sample.

We are much more interested in variability, conditional and unconditional, in the *populations* from which we have sampled than in the sample itself. What do the sample MSEs—descriptive statistics—tell us about the population variances?

4.2.4 Estimates of Response Variances

The *estimate* of the unconditional response variance, the variance in y scores before the subdivision of an observational population on the basis of x values, is given by the formula

$$\widehat{\sigma}^2(y) = \frac{\sum_{i=1}^{N} [y_i - \text{M}(y)]^2}{N - 1}. \tag{4.9}$$

Except for dividing the sum of squared distances from the mean line of Figure 4.5 by $(N - 1)$ rather than N, this is the unconditional MSE or sample y variance, Var(y), described in Equations [4.5] and [4.6]. A brief explanation of the difference can be given. The variance of a population of scores is defined in terms of squared deviances from the population mean, $\mu(y)$. Because we don't know that population parameter, we have had to replace it in Equation [4.9] with an *estimate* of the population mean, namely the sample mean, $\widehat{\mu}(y) = \text{M}(y)$. We have used up some of the information in the sample to estimate the one parameter, $\mu(y)$. In statistical parlance, we have lost a *degree of freedom*. To properly average the N squared discrepancies, we must now divide by one less than the number of observations in the sample. Throughout this book, we will see how good statistical inference requires that we take account of our dependence on information extracted from samples.

The estimate of the common *conditional response variance*, the variance in y at *each* level of x, is given by this formula:

$$\widehat{\sigma}^2(y \mid x) = \frac{\sum_{i=1}^{N}[y_i - (\widehat{\beta}_0 + \widehat{\beta}_1 x_i)]^2}{N - 2}.$$ (4.10)

Except for dividing the sum of squared distances from the estimated regression line of Figure 4.6 by $(N - 2)$ rather than N, Equation [4.10] is the linear model conditional MSE described earlier by Equations [4.7] and [4.8]. The use of $(N - 2)$ in the denominator is again linked to a loss of degrees of freedom. In estimating the conditional response variance, we would like to average the squared deviances about the *true* conditional means, about $\mu(y \mid x = x_i)$ for each value of x_i. But we do not know those conditional means. Our linear model, though, assumes them to be a linear function of the value of the explanatory variable

$$\mu(y \mid x = x_i) = \beta_0 + \beta_1 x_1$$ (3.2)

and we would be able to calculate them *if* we knew the values of the parameters β_0 and β_1. Alas, we don't know those parameters either, but in this chapter we have learned how to estimate them. In turn, we can use the estimated linear model parameters to provide estimates of the conditional response means:

$$\widehat{\mu}(y \mid x = x_i) = \widehat{\beta}_0 + \widehat{\beta}_1 x_i.$$ (4.3)

It is our need to estimate the two parameters, β_0 and β_1, that costs us two degrees of freedom, one for each, and calls for us to average the squared deviances about the estimated means by $(N - 2)$ rather than N in getting our conditional response variance estimate.

For the boys' heights sample, the estimated unconditional and conditional *ht18* population variances are

$$\widehat{\sigma}^2(ht18) = 47.66 \text{ cm}^2$$

and

$$\widehat{\sigma}^2(ht18 \mid ht2) = 24.88 \text{ cm}^2.$$

If we compare these with the sample unconditional and conditional MSEs,

$$\text{MSE(Unconditional)} = 45.96 \text{ cm}^2$$

and

$$\text{MSE(Linear Model)} = 23.18 \text{ cm}^2,$$

we see that the MSEs are a bit smaller. Sample MSEs *underestimate* the population variances. Equations [4.9] and [4.10] define the best sample statistics to use as estimates of our population response variances.

The important thing to note about the heights results is that the difference in the two sample MSEs tells the same story as the difference in the two estimated variances. Our linear model predictions are superior to our unconditional ones. If the MSE difference, though, had been quite small it might have disappeared or even been reversed on the calculation of the more useful variance estimates.

There should be no doubt, given these results, that we have, by taking *ht2* into account, increased our certainty about *ht18*.

4.2.5 Linear Model Estimates: A Summary

A series of figures will help summarize what we've learned about the estimation of linear model parameters in observational studies. Figure 4.7 is a repetition of Figure 4.1, describing linear model conditional and unconditional response populations.

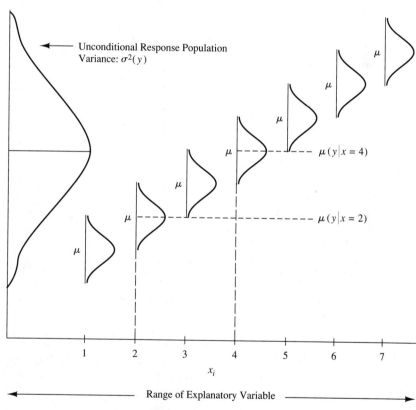

FIGURE 4.7

The Linear Model, Conditional and Unconditional Observational Response Populations

Figures 4.8 and 4.9 are based on having sampled, randomly, three times each from the seven conditional populations illustrated in Figure 4.7. The scatterplot for the resulting 21 observations appears in Figures 4.8 and 4.9.

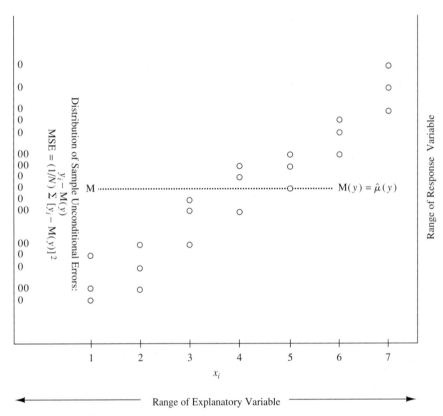

FIGURE 4.8   Sample Scatterplot, Unconditional Predictions and Mean Squared Error (MSE) of Prediction

In Figure 4.8, we focus on the unconditional prediction of the response based on sample data. In the absence of any other information, we have to make the same prediction of a response variable score for each observation. That common prediction is simply the mean response score in the sample. The horizontal dashed line is the mean line for the sample. The unconditional errors—the errors associated with the unconditional prediction—are given by the vertical distances separating each of the scatterplot points from this mean line.

The sample histogram for these errors is given along the left margin of Figure 4.8. We summarize the magnitudes of these errors of prediction by computing the mean of their squares—the MSE(Unconditional), as indicated in the Figure.

In Figure 4.9, the estimated regression line is shown passing through the scatterplot of 21 sample points. The vertical distances of the points from this line are the

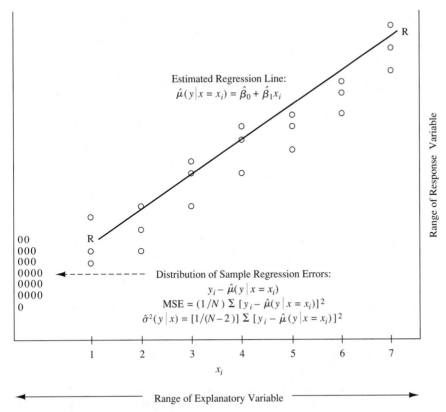

Within the figure (text labels):

Estimated Regression Line:
$\hat{\mu}(y \mid x = x_i) = \hat{\beta}_0 + \hat{\beta}_1 x_i$

Distribution of Sample Regression Errors:

$y_i - \hat{\mu}(y \mid x = x_i)$

$MSE = (1/N) \Sigma [y_i - \hat{\mu}(y \mid x = x_i)]^2$

$\hat{\sigma}^2(y \mid x) = [1/(N-2)] \Sigma [y_i - \hat{\mu}(y \mid x = x_i)]^2$

Range of Response Variable

Range of Explanatory Variable

x_i

F I G U R E 4.9   Sample Scatterplot, Conditional Errors, Mean Squared Error (MSE) and Conditional Variance Estimate

linear model or regression errors. The sample histogram for these errors appears in the lower-left corner of Figure 4.9.

The histogram for the regression errors is notably more compact than that for the unconditional errors. This regression error histogram provides the sample analog to the one common to the several conditional response populations, sketched along the diagonal of Figure 4.7. The conditional or linear model MSE and the estimate of the conditional response variance are computed from this collection of errors.

In Figure 4.9, as in Figure 4.6, the estimated regression line goes through the middle of the scatterplot points. In fact, the estimates of the slope and intercept,

$$\widehat{\beta}_1 = r(x, y)\frac{SD(y)}{SD(x)} \tag{4.1}$$

and

$$\widehat{\beta}_0 = M(y) - \widehat{\beta}_1 M(x), \tag{4.2}$$

are defined so that the MSE about the resulting estimated regression line is *smaller* than it would be about any other straight line that might be drawn through the scatterplot. The two are *least squares* estimates of their respective parameters; any other estimates would give a line with a larger MSE in the sample.

4.2.6 Random Sampling and Linear Model Estimation

In Chapter 3, we noted that for the kinds of explanatory models in which we are interested, model estimation and inference require that the response observations in our sample be obtained independently of one another. The hypothetical sample illustrated in Figures 4.8 and 4.9, taken together with our continuing boys' heights example, illustrate the two principal ways in which this requirement is met.

The boys' heights sample was the result of sampling, at random, 28 times from an *unconditional* response population—that of heights of 18-year-old boys. Each of the resulting age-18 heights was, however, also a random observation from some conditional age-18 height population. We couldn't know in advance just which conditional populations would be represented in the resulting sample, but our random sampling assures that whatever conditional populations were represented, they were sampled randomly.

In the example underlying Figures 4.8 and 4.9, several conditional populations were settled on in advance—$x_i = 1, 2, 3, 4, 5, 6$, and 7—and each of these conditional populations was randomly sampled exactly three times.

In either case, two or more conditional response populations were each randomly sampled. That provides the necessary independence of response observations.

The two approaches to sampling are related to the *experimental-observational study* distinction discussed in Chapter 1. The experiment is marked by the careful preselection of the values of x or explanatory variable scores, while in the observational study, the values of x are more often randomly determined.

You may note that while Figure 4.8 makes mention of *unconditional predictions*, predictions of the response that do not take explanatory variable scores into account, it does not refer to an *unconditional response population*. In experimental studies where we choose the conditional response populations to sample from, there is no unconditional population. While we compute and utilize unconditional prediction errors, their squares, and averages of their squares for experimental as well as observational data sets, there is no unconditional response variance to be estimated from experimental data sets.

4.3
Sampling Distribution of Estimates

We have seen how to compute estimates of the linear model βs and σ^2s from a sample. In particular, for our sample of 28 boys' heights, we obtained estimates of

$$\textit{regression slope } \widehat{\beta}_1 = 1.585 \text{ cm/cm,}$$
$$\textit{unconditional response variance } \widehat{\sigma}^2(ht18) = 47.66 \text{ cm}^2,$$

and

conditional response variance $\widehat{\sigma}^2(ht18 \mid ht2) = 24.88$ cm^2.

We *estimate* that a 1-cm difference in infant height will lead to a difference in expected adolescent heights of about 1.6 cm. That estimate, though, is based on just one sample of 28 boys. If we were to collect information from a second sample, what would a second estimate of the slope parameter be like? How close to 1.585 cm/cm would the new estimate be? Might a second $\widehat{\beta}_1$ be as large as 2.50 cm/cm, as small as 1.0 cm/cm, or even 0.0 cm/cm?

Similarly, our sample gave us an estimate of the conditional response variance— $\widehat{\sigma}^2(ht18 \mid ht2) = 24.88$ cm^2—which was much smaller than the estimated unconditional variance—$\widehat{\sigma}^2(ht18) = 47.66$ cm^2, the sign of a useful explanatory model. Would we find a similar difference in the two in a new sample? Might the difference be much smaller, or even vanish?

The confidence we place in our estimates—and, hence, the model they estimate—clearly is affected by the extent of this potential sample-to-sample variability. If a new estimate of β_1 were 1.60 cm/cm or 1.57 cm/cm, we would put more faith in our 1.585 cm/cm than if the new estimate were to come in at 1.0 cm/cm or 2.5 cm/cm.

What would happen in a new sample? Almost without exception, we cannot answer the question by doing the study over again. To repeat the actual study simply would cost too much. There is, however, another route to the answer.

4.3.1   A Sampling Distribution

Let's look again at how the boys' heights sample was obtained and how we look at the observations making up that sample from the point of view of an explanatory model. A random sample of 28 boys was drawn from the population of Berkeley Study 18 year olds. For each boy sampled, we learn two things: his present height (score on the variable *ht18*) and his height at 2 years of age (score on *ht2*).

We have in mind an explanatory model. Height at age 2, we believe, partially explains height at age 18. Let's look at the first boy drawn. His heights were $ht2_1 = 90.2$ cm and $ht18_1 = 179.0$ cm. From our modeling perspective, we have an observation from the conditional response population ($ht18 \mid ht2 = 90.2$ cm) that takes a value of 179.0 cm.

Similarly, the second boy drawn, with heights of $ht2_2 = 91.4$ cm and $ht18_2 = 195.1$ cm, represents an observation of 195.1 cm from the conditional response population ($ht18 \mid ht2 = 91.4$ cm). The heights of each of the 28 boys sampled tell us two things:

- The conditional response population from which the *y* observation—age-18 height—was drawn.
- The value of the *y* observation.

Because the entire sample was drawn at random, we can assume that each *y* observation was randomly drawn from its conditional population and independently of any of the other 27 draws.

This interpretation of the boys' heights sample is illustrated in Figure 4.10. After the 28 boys have been drawn, we see that they represent a random sample from each of 28 specific, and different conditional populations—no two of the boys, it turns out, had the same *ht2* scores. These 28 conditional populations are symbolized by the buckets along the left-hand side of Figure 4.10. The first bucket, for example, corresponds to a conditional population of age-18 heights—that for boys who were 90.2 cm tall at 2 years of age.

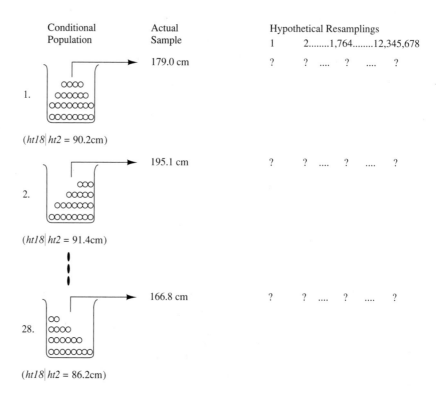

Population Parameters	Sample Estimates						
	Actual Sample	Hypothetical Resamplings					
$\beta_0 = ?$	$\hat{\beta}_0 = 39.47$ cm	?	?	....	?	....	?
$\beta_1 = ?$	$\hat{\beta}_1 = 1.585$ cm/cm	?	?	....	?	....	?
$\sigma^2(ht18 \mid ht2) = ?$	$\hat{\sigma}^2(ht18 \mid ht2) = 24.88$ cm^2 ?		?	....	?	....	?
$\sigma^2(ht18) = ?$	$\hat{\sigma}^2(ht18) = 47.66$ cm^2	Not available for Resamples					

FIGURE 4.10

Illustrating the Development of Sampling Distributions

Again, from our modeling perspective, the actual sample of age-18 heights was the result of sampling at random once each from the 28 conditional buckets of Figure 4.10. The results are shown in the second column of the Figure. We obtained age-18 heights of 179.0 cm and 195.1 cm from the first two populations, and a *y* score of 166.8 cm from the 28th population sampled.

Based on this sample, we estimated the four parameters with the results given at the bottom of the second column in Figure 4.10.

Now, let's *imagine* resampling, again once each from these same 28 conditional populations. We'd end up with another set of age-18 heights. The results are given in column "1" under the heading "Hypothetical Resampling" in Figure 4.10 by "?s" since we're only imagining doing the sampling. While we are at it, though, we can also imagine computing estimates of β_0, β_1, and $\sigma^2(ht18 \mid ht2)$ from this second sample. These results, also "?s," are at the base of this column in Figure 4.10.

You will note that we would not compute estimates of any unconditional population variance, $\sigma^2(y)$, in these resamples. Why is this? For a sample to provide a good basis for estimating a population variance, it should be a random sample from that population. According to the typical observational study design, our sample of actual respondents should be drawn at random from some population of potential respondents, the unconditional response population. From *that* sample, we can estimate the unconditional response variance. Our hypothetical resamplings, however, are not random samples from a response population. These hypothetical resamplings, to be useful to us in drawing accurate inferences from our actual sample results, *must follow* the same sampling plan as the original sample. By this, we mean that the re-samplings must contain *exactly the same set* of explanatory variable scores as were in the actual sample. For our resamples, we must sample the same number of times from the same conditional response populations as we did for the actual sample. Put another way, we resample *y* observations but we keep our *x* values *fixed* at those observed in the actual sample. This is as much true for the modeling of observational studies, where the original sampling plan or selection of *x* values was random, as for experimental studies where we explicitly chose the values of *x*.

Well, if we can imagine the results of one resampling, according to a fixed sampling plan from our conditional populations, we can imagine the results of a second and a third just as easily. Each resampling gives us a randomly drawn age-18 height from each of the 28 conditional populations and an estimate of each of the three parameters computed, by the formulae of this chapter, from each set of 28 observations.

Let's give our imagination full rein and think of resampling a very large number of times. As Figure 4.10 suggests, we might obtain a 1,764th resample or—as this is all hypothetical—even a 12,345,678th one! From each resample of observations from the 28 conditional response populations, we'd have a computed estimate of, say, β_1, the slope parameter.

Now, let's think of going across the line at the bottom of Figure 4.10 on which we have recorded the 12,345,678—or some equally impossibly large number—estimates of β_1, collecting them together into what is called the *sampling distribution* of that estimate, $\widehat{\beta}_1$. Let's repeat this for each of the other two terms at the bottom of Figure 4.10, each time collecting the millions of estimates into another sampling distribution.

As a result of the assumptions about the characteristics of the conditional populations from which we have sampled (and resampled) as outlined in the last chapter, the resulting three sampling distributions will have histograms—plots of the frequencies of occurrence of different values—that look something like the three displayed in the top half of Figure 4.11.

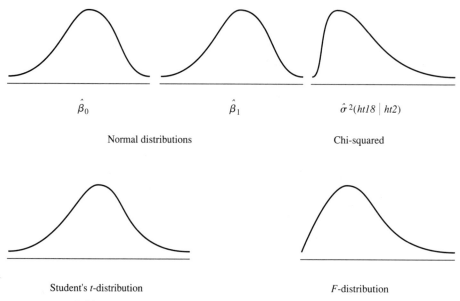

$\hat{\beta}_0$ $\hat{\beta}_1$ $\hat{\sigma}^2(ht18 \mid ht2)$

Normal distributions   Chi-squared

Student's *t*-distribution   *F*-distribution

FIGURE 4.11   Some Sampling Distributions

The shapes of the sampling distributions for the estimates of the βs are different than those for the estimate of $\sigma^2(y \mid x)$. We'll learn about the importance of these shapes as we go along. First, the hypothetical sampling distribution "histogram" for each of the two β estimates is again the normal curve. The sampling distribution of the conditional response variance estimates is shaped like the probability density function for the *Chi-squared random variable*. The Normal random variable curves, we earlier noted, are symmetric. In contrast, the Chi-squared probability density functions are skewed. They have longer tails stretching out to the right. We'll return to the Chi-squared sampling distribution in the next chapter.

Theoretical sampling distributions for statistics take many different shapes. At the bottom of Figure 4.11 are histograms descriptive of two others. We'll encounter the Student *t* distribution in the next chapter when we look more closely at the sampling distribution of the slope estimator and the *F* becomes important from Chapter 7 as we begin to study models with more than one explanatory variable. The *t*-distributions are symmetric, the *F*-distributions skewed.

Figure 4.12 provides a closer look at the sampling distribution of $\widehat{\beta}_1$. An extract from the bottom of Figure 4.10 has been included at the top of the new figure to remind us of the source of the hypothetical data. Sketched in Figure 4.12 is the limiting *probability density function* for the sampling distribution of the slope estimate, $\hat{\beta}_1$. It summarizes some of the features of the "millions" of estimates we have imagined could be created by resampling again and again, always according to the same "sampling plan," the one laid down by our actual sample. That sampling plan tells us which conditional response populations to sample from.

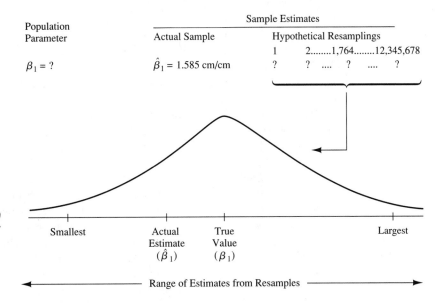

| Population Parameter | Actual Sample | Hypothetical Resamplings |

Sample Estimates

| Population Parameter | Actual Sample | Hypothetical Resamplings |

$$\beta_1 = ? \qquad \hat{\beta}_1 = 1.585 \text{ cm/cm}$$

1   2........1,764........12,345,678
?   ? .... ? .... ?

FIGURE 4.12
Probability Density Curve for the Sampling Distribution of $\widehat{\beta}_1$

Smallest   Actual Estimate $(\hat{\beta}_1)$ True Value (β_1) Largest

Range of Estimates from Resamples

The height of the curve varies. If values of the estimate occur a large number of times in a particular narrow range, the curve's height above that range will be high. If another narrow range of values is represented in the sampling distribution only infrequently, the curve is low over that range. Somewhere in the total range represented by the sampling distribution is the "true value" of the slope parameter, β_1. If our method of estimation is a good one, it should produce estimates "close to" this true value more often than estimates that are far away. Somewhere also in the range of this hypothetical sampling distribution is the value of the "actual estimate," the one we calculated from our single, actual sample. We've indicated in Figure 4.12 where the true value and actual estimate might fall in the range of the sampling distribution.

The sampling distribution of the slope estimate is, in fact, a hypothetical population of slope estimates. The actual, single slope estimate we computed from the actual, single sample we have is but one observation from that population. Our sample was a particular one of the very large number of samples (even larger, perhaps, than 12,345,678) possible as a result of our random sampling. That particular sample gave us our particular estimate. *We could have gotten any one of the estimates* that make up the sampling distribution. We could have gotten any one of the values in the range of the histogram of Figure 4.12.

We can't ever really know just where our actual estimate falls in this range relative to the true value of the parameter we are estimating. For the purpose of making a drawing, we've shown in Figure 4.12 our estimate of the slope to be less than the true slope, but this need not be so. The estimate could just as well be larger than the parameter.

Like other populations, however, the sampling distribution of an estimate has a mean and a standard deviation.

If we knew the standard deviation of the sampling distribution we would know how much we should expect the estimate to fluctuate if we were to resample from the same conditional response populations and estimate our parameter again.

If we knew, as well, the mean for the sampling distribution and the probability density function for the curve describing that continuous distribution, we would know how close we should expect our single estimate to be to the true value of the parameter we are estimating.

We come now to the importance of our Chapter 3 assumptions—independent response observations drawn from conditional response populations all with Normal random variable characteristics and all with the same variance. These assumptions permit us to stipulate, to an acceptable degree of accuracy, the means, standard deviations, and probability densities of the sampling distributions of our $\widehat{\beta}$s and $\widehat{\sigma}^2$s. The linkage between these assumptions and the sampling distribution characteristics we are about to describe is well established by statisticians, but to trace that linkage here would take considerable time away from developing our main interest in modeling. So, to keep us moving along without undue delay, we accept that those assumptions make possible the results presented in the balance of this chapter.

Let's see what we can say about the sampling distributions of our linear model estimates, starting with the sampling distributions for the slope and intercept estimates.

4.3.2   Sampling Distributions: Slope and Intercept Estimates

Figure 4.13 gives the theoretical probability densities, the sampling distributions of $\widehat{\beta}_0$, the intercept estimate, and $\widehat{\beta}_1$, the slope estimate. We'll use the figure as an aid in describing the characteristics of these two sampling distributions.

First, the means or *expected values* of the sampling distributions for $\widehat{\beta}_0$ and for $\widehat{\beta}_1$ are each equal to the true values of the parameters being estimated:

$$\mu(\widehat{\beta}_0) = \beta_0 \tag{4.11}$$

and

$$\mu(\widehat{\beta}_1) = \beta_1. \tag{4.12}$$

The sampling distributions of the two estimates are *centered* around the true values of the two parameters as indicated in Figure 4.13. Any given estimate of β_0 or β_1 may be too large or too small. But $\widehat{\beta}_1$ will not be consistently either too small or too large. The same is true for $\widehat{\beta}_0$.

If the expected value of the sampling distribution of an estimate is equal to the value of the parameter being estimated, the estimate is *unbiased*. This is a good property for an estimate to have. Both $\widehat{\beta}_0$ and $\widehat{\beta}_1$ are unbiased estimates.

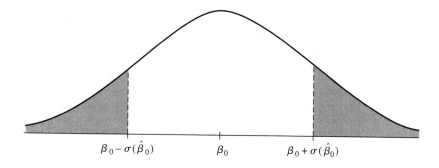

$$\beta_0 - \sigma(\hat{\beta}_0) \qquad \beta_0 \qquad \beta_0 + \sigma(\hat{\beta}_0)$$

FIGURE 4.13
Sampling Distribution Probability Densities: $\widehat{\beta}_0$ and $\widehat{\beta}_1$

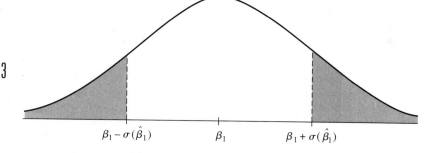

$$\beta_1 - \sigma(\hat{\beta}_1) \qquad \beta_1 \qquad \beta_1 + \sigma(\hat{\beta}_1)$$

Our sampling distributions of $\widehat{\beta}_0$ and $\widehat{\beta}_1$ also have standard deviations. The smaller the standard deviation of the sampling distribution, the closer the population of estimates is clustered about the true value of the parameter and the more likely it is that our particular estimate is close to the truth.

We will express the two standard deviations in terms of statistics with which we are familiar. Even so, the resulting formulae appear complicated, particularly that for the standard deviation of the intercept estimate. We present the two standard deviations in the following two equations to see what makes them larger and smaller.

$$\sigma(\widehat{\beta}_0) = \sqrt{\frac{\sigma^2(y \mid x)[\mathrm{Var}(x) + \mathrm{M}(x)^2]}{N\,\mathrm{Var}(x)}} \qquad \textbf{(4.13)}$$

$$\sigma(\widehat{\beta}_1) = \sqrt{\frac{\sigma^2(y \mid x)}{N\,Var(x)}} \qquad \textbf{(4.14)}$$

The sizes of these standard deviations are influenced by four factors: the conditional response variance, $\sigma^2(y \mid x)$; the sample size, N; the variance of the explanatory variable, $\mathrm{Var}(x)$; and, in the case of $\sigma(\widehat{\beta}_0)$, the square of the mean of the explanatory variable in the sample plan, $\mathrm{M}(x)^2$.

- Both sampling distribution standard deviations are directly proportional to the conditional response variance, $\sigma^2(y \mid x)$.

- Both sampling distribution standard deviations are inversely proportional to N, the sample size.

- The standard deviation of the sampling variability of the estimate of the regression slope, $\widehat{\beta}_1$, is inversely proportional as well to the variance of the explanatory variable, Var(x).

- For a given Var(x), the standard deviation of the sampling distribution of the intercept estimate, $\widehat{\beta}_0$, is minimized if M(x) is 0.

A small standard deviation for the sampling distribution means the estimate will fluctuate little as a result of sampling. A small standard deviation, therefore, is a good thing. What do these four dependencies tell us about achieving a small standard deviation? Which of the factors are under our control and how should we use that control?

The sizes of the conditional response variance and its estimate depend solely on our choice of model and sampling plan. Once we've decided on the population of potential respondents—the response and explanatory variables—$\sigma^2(y \mid x)$ is established. As a goal of modeling, of course, we seek to identify xs that help explain y and will make the conditional response variances small.

The dependency of the sampling distribution standard deviations on the sample size may be the most interesting of the four results. We typically have some control over the size of the sample for a study and this result tells us that the larger we make the sample, the more accurate we can expect our estimates of slope and intercept to be.

In the design of some studies, notably experimental or manipulative ones, we also may set the sampling plan, i.e., choose the values for the explanatory variable. Where we do this, the above tells us that the greater the variance in x scores, the more accurate we can expect our slope estimate to be.

Similarly, the last point tells us that if we can choose our x scores so that they have a mean near 0, we will have a more accurate estimate of the intercept. Where interpretation of the intercept is important, this is a point to remember and we encounter designs in later chapters that exploit this principle.

Finally, what can we say about the theoretical probability densities of the sampling distributions of our slope and intercept estimates? Importantly, each follows a well know statistical form, that of a Normal random variable.

As shown in Figure 4.13, these Normal densities are symmetric about their expected values. Their curves are higher in the middle and fall off towards the lower and upper ends of the range of values for the estimates. Because the height of the density curve describes the relative popularity of different values in the population, Figure 4.13 suggests that estimates close to the true values of either β_0 or β_1 should be fairly common.

In Chapter 5, we use the three characteristics of these sampling distributions of the $\widehat{\beta}$s—their expected values, standard deviations, and Normality—in drawing model inferences from our sample estimates.

4.3.3   Sampling Distribution: Conditional Response Variance Estimates

A glance at the bottom of Figure 4.10 reminds us that each hypothetical resampling from the conditional response populations will be accompanied by a new estimate of the common conditional response variance as well as new estimates of the regression slope and intercept.

We can think, then, of the "millions" of resamples producing an additional sampling distribution, for the $\widehat{\sigma}^2(y \mid x)$s.

We make less direct use in modeling of the sampling distribution of the conditional variance estimates than we do of those for the slope and intercept estimates. However, certain properties of the sampling distributions are worth noting.

First, the expected value of the sampling distribution is equal to the true value of the conditional response variance:

$$\mu[\widehat{\sigma}^2(y \mid x)] = \sigma^2(y \mid x). \tag{4.15}$$

The sampling distribution is centered at the true value of the parameter estimated. Our estimates will not consistently over or under estimate the conditional population variances. Like the estimates of slope and intercept, the variance estimate is *unbiased*.

Second, the standard deviation of the sampling distribution of conditional variance estimates is influenced, as were the standard deviations of the sampling distribution of the slope and intercept estimates, by the size of the sample. The larger the sample size, the smaller the standard deviation will be.

Finally, the sampling probabilities, under our linear model assumptions, are well matched by a well known statistical form. The probability density of our hypothetical sampling distribution of conditional response variance estimates is proportional to that of a particular Chi-squared random variable, that with $(N - 2)$ degrees of freedom.

The linear model estimates of slope, intercept, and conditional response variances introduced in this chapter are the best estimates of those parameters. Given the linear modeling assumptions we've made, the sampling distributions of our estimates share two important characteristics:

- Each of the three sampling distributions has as its expected value, the value of the parameter being estimated.

- Our estimates are not the only unbiased estimates of these parameters, but they are the unbiased estimates whose sampling distributions have the smallest standard deviations.

4.4
Summary

The linear model introduced in Chapter 3 is a powerful device for understanding explanatory relations between variables. It describes *populations* of response variable observations. All we ever have, however, are *samples* from those populations.

In this chapter, we described *estimates* of the linear model *parameters*. Those estimates are sample based and, hence, are likely to be different in any hypothetic resampling. The notion of a *sampling distribution* for each estimate was introduced. The expected value, variability, and shape of the sampling distribution allows us to assess the accuracy of our estimates and, in Chapter 5, provides the foundation for the all-important task of making *inferences* about our models: Is our model a good one? Is one model better than another?

5

Simple Linear Regression: Inference About Models

The linear model introduced in Chapter 3 describes what we think is true for a collection of conditional response populations. These may be the result of "dividing up" an unconditional response population into separate populations, one for each value of an explanatory variable in the case of observational studies. Or, they may anticipate what would happen if all the members of a population of potential respondents could be assigned to each of several levels of treatment, a conditional response population for each treatment.

Do we have a good model? Do the expected values of the conditional response populations actually change as the value of the explanatory variable changes? Is the common conditional response variance small? Have we increased our certainty about a randomly selected response observation by taking into account the value of an explanatory variable?

In this chapter, we see how to answer these questions—that is, *to make inferences* about our conditional response populations from a sample of observations. The search for these answers starts with our Chapter 4 sampling distributions.

5.1
Sampling Distribution of Estimates and Inferences About Parameters

In Chapter 4, we learned that the sampling distributions of our estimates of the linear model slope and intercept parameters

- *were centered at the true values of those parameters,*
- *had Normal probability densities, and*
- *had standard deviations that depended upon several factors:*
  (a) *the conditional response population variance, $\sigma^2(y\,|\,x)$,*
  (b) *the sample size, N,*
  (c) *the variance of explanatory variable scores, $Var(x)$ and*
  (d) *the mean of x, $M(x)$.*

Not all of the factors entering into the sampling distribution standard deviations are available to us. We can obtain N, $\text{Var}(x)$ and $M(x)$ from the sample. We can't, however, compute a value for the *conditional response variance*. It is *unknown* to us. Equation [4.10], though, gives us a way of *estimating* it.

5.1.1   Standard Errors of Slope and Intercept Estimates

If we replace the unknown value of $\sigma^2(y\,|\,x)$ in Equations [4.13] and [4.14] with our estimate of it, we have, in turn, estimates of these two sampling distribution standard deviations. We refer to the estimated standard deviation of the sampling distribution of an estimate as the *standard error* (SE) of that estimate.

From Equations [4.13] and [4.14], the standard errors of the intercept and slope estimates are given by

$$SE(\widehat{\beta_0}) = \sqrt{\frac{\widehat{\sigma}^2(y\,|\,x)[\text{Var}(x) + M(x)^2]}{N\,\text{Var}(x)}} \tag{5.1}$$

and

$$SE(\widehat{\beta_1}) = \sqrt{\frac{\widehat{\sigma}^2(y\,|\,x)}{N\,\text{Var}(x)}}. \tag{5.2}$$

There are no unknowns here. We can calculate these SEs from our sample data.

5.1.2   Student's *t*-distributions

When we must estimate the standard deviation of a sampling distribution that would otherwise have a *Normal density*, we change that density. Assuming a proper estimate of σ, the sampling distribution instead will have the probability density of one of the family of *Student t-random variables* These *t*-random variables, like the Normal, are symmetric and peaked in the middle but, as if to compensate for the estimated standard deviations, they have greater spread or *longer tails*. Just how much greater the spread is depends upon the sample size; the larger the sample size, the more closely the *t*-density curve resembles that of a Normal random variable.

Reflecting this dependence upon sample size, the family of *t*-random variables is indexed by a parameter called the *degrees of freedom* (d.f.). We have some familiarity with this idea of degrees of freedom. Let's review it. We begin with a sample of N independent response variable observations. As we estimate parameters, based on these y observations, we use up sample information and reduce our degrees of freedom. In our simple linear regression context, we "lose" two degrees of freedom as a result of having to estimate β_0 and β_1, estimates that we rely on for our subsequent estimates of the sampling variability of these estimates. As a result, we must replace the Normal density with that for the *t*-variate with $(N - 2)$ degrees of freedom to reflect adequately the sampling variability of the slope or intercept estimates.

Figure 5.1 illustrates the sampling distribution for $\widehat{\beta}_1$ when the estimate is computed from a sample of $N = 28$ independent y observations. The numeric values used in the figure can be obtained either from computer inquiry where your statistics

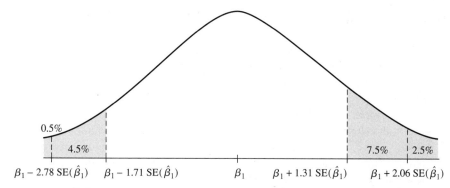

FIGURE 5.1   Sampling Distribution for $\widehat{\beta}_1$, $N = 28$

package can provide information about t and other standard statistical probability functions, or from the appropriate line in the Table of Central Proportions of t-Distributions in the Appendix, that for d.f. $= (N - 2) = (28 - 2) = 26$:

Central Proportions of *t*-Distribution

$(1 - \alpha)$

d.f.	.80	.90	.95	.99
26	1.31	1.71	2.06	2.78

We interpret these tabled values as follows. The central or middlemost 90% of the entries in a sampling distribution with the shape of a t-distribution with 26 d.f. will lie in an interval from 1.71 SEs (estimated standard deviations) *below* the expected value to 1.71 SEs *above* the expected value. Because the t-distribution is symmetric, this also tells us, for example

- that 45% of the sampling distribution lies between the expected value and 1.71 SEs above the expected value and

- that 5% of the sampling distribution is below 1.71 SEs below the expected value.

The symbol α is used to indicate the *proportion* of the sampling distribution lying *outside* the symmetric, central interval. Thus,

- $(1 - \alpha)$ is the central proportion,
- $(1 - \alpha)100\%$ is the central percentage,
- $(\alpha/2)$ is the proportion above or greater than the central interval, and
- $(\alpha/2)100\%$ is the percentage below the central interval.

The sampling distribution for $\widehat{\beta}_1$ has the true value of the slope parameter, β_1, as its expected value. As a result, 50% of the estimates will be *greater* than β_1 and 50% *lower*.

5.1.3   Interpreting the Standard Error (SE) of Slope Estimates

In Figure 5.1, we have used the symmetry of the *t*-variate with the tabled values to show that only 5% of the estimates of the slope parameter will be smaller than $[\beta_1 - 1.71 \ SE(\widehat{\beta}_1)]$ and only 2.5% of the estimates will be larger than $[\beta_1 + 2.06 \ SE(\widehat{\beta}_1)]$.

The *t*-variate density curve, we noted, has tails that are a little "fatter" than those of the Normal; a greater proportion of the *t*-variate observations are out in the two tails. An example will illustrate the difference. We need to go out either way from the expected value of the Normal random variable 1.96 standard deviations to enclose the middle 95% of the population. However, to enclose the middle 95% of a *t*-variate with 26 d.f., the tabled figures listed previously tell us that we have to go out further, 2.06 standard deviations each way. The larger the sample size—and, hence, the d.f.—the closer the *t*-variate density curve comes to that of the Normal.

Here is one more example, based on our *t*-variate with 26 d.f. The middle 80% of the slope estimates will be within 1.31 standard errors of the expected or true value of the slope parameter. Given the symmetry of the *t*-variate, this means that 10% of the slope estimates will be larger than $\beta_1 + 1.31 \ SE(\widehat{\beta}_1)$ and 10% will be smaller than $\beta_1 - 1.31 \ SE(\widehat{\beta}_1)$.

Let's put this last statement in the context of our boys' height data by computing the SE of the slope estimate (the estimated standard deviation of the slope estimate's sampling distribution). Substituting into Equation [5.2] gives

$$SE(\widehat{\beta}_1) = \sqrt{\frac{\widehat{\sigma}^2(y \mid x)}{N \ Var(x)}} = \sqrt{\frac{\widehat{\sigma}^2(ht18 \mid ht2)}{N \ Var(ht2)}} = \sqrt{\frac{24.88 \ cm^2}{(28)(9.099 \ cm^2)}} = 0.313 \ cm/cm.$$

Whatever the *true* value of β_1, there is a 10% chance that our estimate will be larger than that true value by at least 1.31 SEs. For our example, this means a 10% chance that our estimate of $\widehat{\beta}_1 = 1.585$ cm/cm will be at least $(1.31)(.313$ cm/cm$)$ = .410 cm/cm larger than β_1. Similarly, there is a 10% chance that our particular estimate of β_1 will be at least .410 cm/cm smaller than β_1. That is, there is a 10% chance that our particular estimate is one of those in the upper tail of the *t*-density curve of Figure 5.1, out beyond $\beta_1 + 1.31 \ SE(\widehat{\beta}_1)$. By the same token, there is one chance in ten that it is one of those in the lower tail of Figure 5.1, down below $\beta_1 - 1.31 \ SE(\widehat{\beta}_1)$.

Taking another look at the tabled *t*-values and at Figure 5.1, there is only one chance in a hundred that our sample estimate of β_1 will be "off" the true value (either way, plus or minus) by as much as 2.78 $SE(\widehat{\beta}_1)$.

It is important to keep in mind, throughout this and subsequent chapters, what chances, proportions, and percentages mean when we are talking about a sampling distribution. The reference is to occasions on which we compute the estimate and its SE from a sample. That is, for the last illustration, we expect that for every

100 times that we compute $\widehat{\beta}_1$ and $SE(\widehat{\beta}_1)$ from a sample of $N = 28$ independent observations, on only *one* occasion will the distance separating the estimate, $\widehat{\beta}_1$, from the parameter's true value, β_1, exceed 2.78 $SE(\widehat{\beta}_1)$. Alas, we can't predict which one of the 100 will be that singular occasion!

5.1.4 The SE of the Slope Estimate and Sample Size

Our computation of $SE(\widehat{\beta}_1)$, the standard error of the slope estimate, for the height data provides an opportunity to illustrate one of the points made in the last chapter about the determinants of the standard deviation of the slope estimate's sampling distribution: A larger sample means a smaller SE.

Let's pretend for the moment that our sample included not 28 boys, but four times that number, $4 \times 28 = 112$, and that it yielded the same values for $Var(ht2)$ and for $\widehat{\sigma}^2(y \mid x)$ that we found in the actual sample. If we were then to compute $SE(\widehat{\beta}_1)$ from Equation [5.2],

$$SE(\widehat{\beta}_1) = \sqrt{\frac{\widehat{\sigma}^2(y \mid x)}{N \, Var(x)}} = \sqrt{\frac{\widehat{\sigma}^2(ht18 \mid ht2)}{N \, Var(ht2)}} = \sqrt{\frac{24.88 \text{ cm}^2}{(112)(9.099 \text{ cm}^2)}} = 0.157 \text{ cm/cm},$$

we would find our hypothetical standard error to be *exactly one-half* the actual value obtained.

This relation between sample size and the magnitude of the standard error of an estimate is called the *square root* law. If we make the sample four times as large, the standard error of the estimate is one-half what it otherwise would have been. If we make the sample 9 times as large, $SE(\widehat{\beta}_1)$ will be one-third what it would have been. And, if we make the sample 100 times as large, $SE(\widehat{\beta}_1)$ will be only one-tenth what it would have been. Certainty increases as the square root of the increase in sample size.

5.1.5 Population Parameter Inferences for a Linear Model

Our certainty about the slope estimate is greater with a larger sample size. Whatever the sample size, this certainty and the value of the estimate determine the *inferences* that can be made about population parameters.

In modeling, an inference is a decision about populations based upon a sample of observations. We deal here with two kinds of modeling inferences. The first is a *magnitude inference*. For example, what is the "true" size of the slope parameter, given our estimate of it and our beliefs about the sampling distribution of the estimate? Magnitude inferences about parameters are made in the form of *confidence intervals* for those parameters, and this is the topic of Section 5.2.

The second kind of inference about parameters is *relation inference*. It focuses not on the actual sizes of parameters but on relations between parameters or to some other "standard." For example, can we infer from an observational sample that $\sigma^2(y \mid x)$ is smaller than $\sigma^2(y)$? Or, in either the observational or experimental setting, can we conclude that β_1 is greater than 0?

Relation inference, the statistically experienced reader may anticipate, is related to the older tradition of testing hypotheses about population parameters—for example, that the conditional and unconditional response variances are the same size or that the slope parameter is equal to 0. Magnitude and relation inference are linked and we will take up relation inference in Section 5.3.

5.2
Confidence Intervals and Magnitude Inference

Our $\widehat{\beta}_1$ of 1.585 cm/cm for the height data is the best estimate of the slope parameter that we can obtain from our sample. But, what we've just learned from the sampling distribution is that even the best may not be very good. Our estimate *could be* off the mark by some amount.

5.2.1   Reporting Confidence in an Estimate

When we report our estimate, we must also report its accuracy. How do we do that? The statistician's way is to report a *confidence interval* (CI) for the estimate.

What is a CI? Where does it come from? Let's use a specific example. From this example, we'll see first how to interpret the CI and, from that, how to form it. Our specific example will be the 90% CI for the slope parameter based on our estimate, $\widehat{\beta}_1 = 1.585$ cm/cm.

This 90% CI ranges, in fact, from 1.050 cm/cm to 2.120 cm/cm. Soon, we will see from where those numbers came.

We think β_1 is "about" 1.585 cm/cm, but it might be as small as 1.050 cm/cm or as large as 2.120 cm/cm. In fact, it could be smaller or larger than the limits of the 90% CI. We can never be *absolutely certain* about the value of the parameter. But, we can be *90% confident* that β_1 is between 1.050 cm/cm and 2.120 cm/cm.

What does it mean to have 90% confidence that the true value of the parameter is in the 90% CI? And, how do we calculate the width of a 90% CI? The answers to the two questions are linked and we can get at them by looking again at some of the ideas we used in exploring sampling distributions, particularly that for the regression slope estimate.

5.2.2   Intervals and the Sampling Distribution

In Chapter 4, we imagined resampling from each of 28 conditional age-18 height distributions (those pictured in Figure 4.10) to provide a second "sample" from which could be computed a second estimate of β_1. We then imagined resampling in this same way many, many times, creating a very large number of slope estimates.

Now, let's imagine doing all of this again! But, this time we will also imagine forming an interval each time rather than computing a specific numeric or point estimate of the slope. How wide do we make the interval? For the moment, we'll leave that question unanswered. We'll assume only that we have a rule that tells us how to calculate the width. The important thing is that the rule is a constant one. For each imagined sample, we apply this rule to construct a slope interval.

Figure 5.2 provides a picture of what the first few intervals we compute in this way might look like. The top line in the figure corresponds to the interval for our real sample. Each of the other lines shows an interval computed, always by the same rule, from an imagined resampling of the 28 conditional response populations.

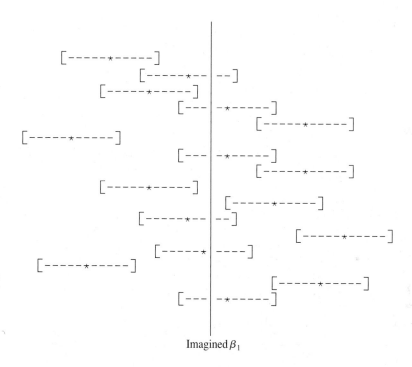

FIGURE 5.2

Slope Intervals
Constructed From
Imagined
Resamples

Imagined β_1

Since this is an imaginary exercise, let's also imagine where in the range of our estimates the true value of the slope parameter, β_1, lies. We've indicated this at the bottom of the figure. The important thing about Figure 5.2 is that it shows that *some* of the intervals *include* the true value of the parameter, while *others do not*. In this hypothetical example, only six of the first sixteen intervals (2, 4, 7, 11, 13 and 16) overlap β_1.

We also can see from Figure 5.2 that if the interval construction rule were changed to give consistently *narrower* intervals, *fewer* than six of the sixteen would include the parameter value. Conversely, if the rule gave intervals that were consistently *wider* than those pictured, a *greater proportion* of the intervals would overlap β_1.

5.2.3   Definition of a Confidence Interval

The idea behind a 90% CI is that it is constructed by a rule such that *if* an interval were constructed about every estimate in the sampling distribution following that same rule, *exactly 90%* of those intervals would overlap the true value of the parameter.

It is in this sense that we are 90% confident that the parameter value lies within our 90% CI; 90% of intervals we construct in this way do include the true parameter value.

How do we find a rule that will have this result? We look again at the sampling distribution of our slope estimate to answer that.

5.2.4   Confidence Intervals for the Slope Parameter

Figure 5.3 is another picture of the $\widehat{\beta}_1$ sampling distribution, based on samples of $N = 28$ independent observations. It is drawn to emphasize that 90% of the samples would provide estimates of β_1 that are within ± 1.71 SE$(\widehat{\beta}_1)$ of the true value of that parameter.

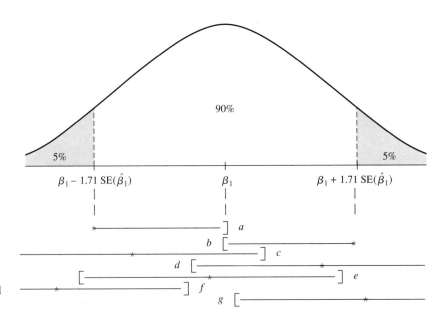

FIGURE 5.3

Illustrating a 90%
Confidence Interval
for β_1, $N = 28$

We can use this information to see how to compute a 90% CI.

We want to compute the width of our 90% CI so that, if we were to form intervals in that same way about each of the millions of estimates that make up the sampling distribution, exactly 90% of those intervals would overlap the true value of the parameter. We would then be 90% confident that a randomly chosen one, the one we computed from our actual random sample, would include β_1 in its range.

Because the true value of the slope parameter is right in the middle of the sampling distribution pictured in Figure 5.3, the intervals that are most likely to include β_1 are those intervals that are themselves towards the middle of the sampling distribution. In fact, we can formalize this idea. In establishing a 90% CI, we will want to use a rule that insures that *all* intervals constructed by this rule for those resamples that give the middlemost 90% of the estimates will overlap the true slope value and that none of the intervals constructed for samples yielding slope estimates outside the middlemost 90% will do so.

To find this rule, we ask what we must do when we are *right at the edge* of this central cluster of 90% of the estimates. How wide do we have to make the interval so that we *just reach* the parameter value from there? Remember, we want to reach down to or up to β_1 when we are right at the edge of the middle 90% of slope estimates but not when we are any further out on either tail.

If we had an estimate at the *very bottom* of the middle 90% of the distribution, we would want the interval about that estimate to extend *to the right* just far enough to reach the true parameter value, β_1. This situation is illustrated by the line labeled *a* at the bottom of Figure 5.3. If we add the length of this line to the estimate, we just reach β_1. The length of the line is $1.71\,\mathrm{SE}(\widehat{\beta}_1)$.

Adding this amount to the value of the estimate gives us the *upper limit* of our 90% CI:

$$\widehat{\beta}_1 + 1.71\mathrm{SE}(\widehat{\beta}_1).$$

Similarly, if we had an estimate at the *very top* of the middle 90% of the sampling distribution, we would want the interval about that estimate to extend *to the left* just far enough to reach the true parameter value. This is the situation illustrated by the line labeled *b* at the figure's bottom. If we subtract the length of this line from the estimate, we just reach β_1 from above. The length of the line is, again, $1.71\,\mathrm{SE}(\widehat{\beta}_1)$.

Subtracting this amount from the value of the estimate gives us the *lower limit* of our 90% CI:

$$\widehat{\beta}_1 - 1.71\mathrm{SE}(\widehat{\beta}_1).$$

Our 90% CI for β_1 based on a sample of 28 observations, then, extends from $[\widehat{\beta}_1 - 1.71\,\mathrm{SE}(\widehat{\beta}_1)]$ to $[\widehat{\beta}_1 + 1.71\,\mathrm{SE}(\widehat{\beta}_1)]$.

Figure 5.3 helps us see that the resulting CI has the right width. As long as the estimate is one of the middle 90%, the interval will be wide enough to reach to the parameter value. This is illustrated by the lines labeled *c*, *d*, and *e* at the bottom of the figure. On the other hand, if the estimate is one of the smallest 5% or one of the largest 5% of the estimates, the interval will not be wide enough to include the true value of the parameter. The final two lines, *f* and *g*, in Figure 5.3 picture these results.

Our *actual sample* may provide an estimate that is one of the middlemost 90% in the sampling distribution so that our 90% CI does include the true value of the parameter. Or, it may provide an estimate that is in one of the tails of the sampling distribution so that our 90% CI does not include β_1. We can never be certain which sample we have and we can never be certain that our 90% CI includes the true parameter value. But, we do have 90% confidence (not 100% confidence) that β_1 lies in the 90% CI.

The 90% CI for the regression slope based on the boys' heights sample works out to be

$$[\widehat{\beta}_1 - 1.71\,\mathrm{SE}(\widehat{\beta}_1)] \text{ to } [\widehat{\beta}_1 + 1.71\,\mathrm{SE}(\widehat{\beta}_1)]$$
$$[1.585 - (1.71)(0.313)] \text{ to } [1.585 + (1.71)(0.313)]$$
$$[1.585 - 0.535] \text{ to } [1.585 + 0.535]$$
$$[1.050\,\mathrm{cm/cm} \text{ to } 2.120\,\mathrm{cm/cm}].$$

We are 90% confident that the true value of the slope parameter is between 1 cm/cm and 2 cm/cm. That is, we are 90% confident that a difference of 1 cm in age-2 height means a difference in the expected value of adolescent height of between 1 and 2 cm.

5.2.5 Choice of Degree of Confidence for CI

The CI computation traced above was for a particular degree of confidence, $(1 - \alpha)100\% = 90\%$, and for a particular sample size, $N = 28$. The procedure we outlined, however, generalizes to other sample sizes and other degrees of confidence. The equation below provides a succinct summary of how to compute the lower and upper limits for the $(1 - \alpha)100\%$ CI for the slope parameter:

$$\mathrm{CI}[\beta_1, \ (1 - \alpha)100\%] = [\widehat{\beta}_1 \pm t_{(N-2),(1-\alpha)}\,\mathrm{SE}(\widehat{\beta}_1)]. \tag{5.3}$$

The degree of confidence, $(1 - \alpha)100\%$, for the CI usually is chosen to be 90%, 95%, or 99%. We want to be reasonably confident that our CI does include the true parameter value.

Equation [5.3] directs us to compute the lower limit for the $(1 - \alpha)100\%$ CI by subtracting from the slope estimate, $\widehat{\beta}_1$, the product of two quantities:

- $t_{(N-2),(1-\alpha)}$, *the value (from the table) of the t-variate with (N − 2) degrees of freedom such that the central (1 - α)100% of t-variate scores are between* $-t_{(N-2),(1-\alpha)}$ *and* $t_{(N-2),(1-\alpha)}$, *and*
- $\mathrm{SE}(\widehat{\beta}_1)$, *the standard error of the slope estimate.*

By Equation [5.3], the upper limit for the $(1 - \alpha)100\%$ CI is computed by adding this same product to the slope estimate.

We illustrate the application of Equation [5.3] by computing a 95% CI for the slope parameter in our boys' height model. The slope estimate and its standard error have been found to be

$$\widehat{\beta}_1 = 1.585 \text{ cm/cm}$$

and

$$\mathrm{SE}(\widehat{\beta}_1) = 0.313 \text{ cm/cm}.$$

The slope estimate was based on $N = 28$ observations. So, the $t_{(N-2),(1-\alpha)}$ for the CI limits is, as follows, from the t-distribution with $(N-2) = 26$ d.f.:

Central Proportions of *t*-Distribution

d.f.	.80	.90	.95	.99
26	1.31	1.71	2.06	2.78

For a 95% CI, the *t*-distribution value needed is the one that encloses the central 95% of that distribution:

$$t_{(N-2),(1-\alpha)} = t_{26,0.95} = 2.06.$$

The central 95% of the *t*-distribution with 26 d.f. is within 2.06 SEs of its expected value.

From Equation [5.3], the lower limit for the 95% CI is

$$1.585 \text{ cm/cm} - (2.06)(0.313 \text{ cm/cm}) =$$
$$1.585 \text{ cm/cm} - 0.645 \text{ cm/cm} = 0.940 \text{ cm/cm},$$

and the upper limit is

$$1.585 \text{ cm/cm} + 0.645 \text{ cm/cm} = 2.230 \text{ cm/cm}.$$

The 95% CI, then, is

$$CI[\beta_1, \ 95\%] = [0.940 \text{ cm/cm}, \ 2.230 \text{ cm/cm}].$$

When we compare this 95% CI for the slope parameter with the 90% CI for the same parameter computed earlier,

$$CI[\beta_1, \ 90\%] = [1.050 \text{ cm/cm}, \ 2.120 \text{ cm/cm}],$$

we see that the 95% CI is wider. For any sample, we must make the CI wider if we are to increase our confidence that the interval includes the parameter.

5.2.6 Sample Size and CI Width

Equation [5.3] points up the role played by the standard error of the slope estimate in determining the width of the CI. For any particular degree of confidence, $(1 - \alpha)$ 100%, a smaller $SE(\widehat{\beta}_1)$ means a narrower CI.

Earlier in this chapter, we saw how increasing the sample size would decrease the standard error of the slope estimate and we gave the name *square root law* to the relation between the two. For example, if we make the sample 4 times as large, we can expect the standard error to be reduced to one-half its original size.

Put these two facts together and the square root law works equally well to forecast the effect of changing the sample size on the width of the CI. If we make the sample 9 times as large, the 95% CI should be only one-third its original width. Our degree of confidence would remain the same but in a much *narrower range* of possible values for the parameter. Our *certainty* about the true value of the parameter would increase.

Purely hypothetically, but in keeping with the square root law, a sample of height data for $9 \times 28 = 252$ boys yielding the same SE would provide a 95% CI for the slope of

$$\text{CI}[\beta_1, 95\%] = [1.370 \, \text{cm/cm}, \ 1.800 \, \text{cm/cm}]$$

rather than the actual ($N = 28$) one,

$$\text{CI}[\beta_1, 95\%] = [0.940 \, \text{cm/cm}, \ 2.230 \, \text{cm/cm}].$$

We would have a much clearer idea about the true value of β_1 with the larger sample.

5.2.7   CIs for Intercepts and Response Population Variances

Although we have been talking about CIs for the regression slope, everything we've done for the slope could be done as well for the intercept, whose estimate also has a sampling distribution with probability density based on a Student's *t*-distribution with $(N - 2)$ d.f. We are interested less often in CIs for the intercept, but they may be obtained from an equation similar to that for the slope:

$$\text{CI}[\beta_0, (1 - \alpha)100\%] = [\widehat{\beta}_0 \pm t_{(N-2),(1-\alpha)}\text{SE}(\widehat{\beta}_0)] \qquad \textbf{(5.4)}$$

The standard error of the intercept estimate is defined by Equation [5.1].

Confidence intervals for conditional variances can be developed as well, based on the relation of their hypothetical sampling distributions to those of random variables known by statisticians as Chi-squared. We will not have any cause in the chapters following, however, to refer to such confidence intervals.

5.2.8   Magnitude Inference

We use confidence intervals to infer the magnitude of a population parameter. We conclude, on the basis of our sample of observations, that the true value of the parameter is one of those included in the CI. This conclusion, that the true value of the parameter is inside the CI, implies a second conclusion, that the true value does *not lie outside the CI*. This second conclusion emphasizes what we believe, on the basis of our sample, cannot be true of the parameter and exemplifies relation inference, important to the topic of Section 5.3.

5.3
Comparing Linear Models: Relation Inference

The most important conclusion we reach about any explanatory model is whether it is useful or not. In this section, we see how that conclusion depends on comparing that model with another simpler model and how that, in turn, requires a *relation inference* for one of our model population parameters.

5.3.1 The Simple Linear Regression Model

This chapter and the two preceding it have developed *simple linear regression*. Regression is the name we give to explanatory models that postulate conditional means for the measured response variable that vary, systematically, as a function of the values of one or more measured explanatory variables. Linear regression is the name we give to models that stipulate that this function is linear. And, simple linear regression is the name we give to models for which the conditional y mean is a linear function of a *single x*:

$$\mu(y \mid x = x_i) = \beta_0 + \beta_1 x_i. \tag{3.2}$$

We have seen how to *interpret* the parameters of this linear model, how to *estimate* their values from a sample of observations, and, in Section 5.2, how to *infer* their true values. We have learned a good bit about the simple linear regression model. What we haven't learned yet, though, is how to tell whether it is a useful model or not.

5.3.2 Comparison of Models

Chapter 1 established that our goal in modeling is to select, among alternative models, the *better* ones. Much remains to be said in this and later chapters about how to state alternative models for any given study and how to choose among them. We are reminded, however, that the question of whether a particular simple linear regression model is a good one or not really is a question of whether it is *better* than some other model. Evaluating a model always involves *comparing* it with an alternative.

Let's consider a specific simple linear regression model—the one that links the expected heights of adolescent boys to their infant heights:

$$\mu(ht18 \mid ht2 = x_i) = \beta_0 + \beta_1 x_i.$$

With what model or models should this be compared to conclude whether it is a good model? We say that a *simple* linear regression model is "good", if, on comparison, we conclude that is better than the *null model*. Perhaps the only comparison of interest for our simple linear model is that with the null model.

5.3.3   The Null Model

The null model takes its name from the idea that the explanatory variables have *no influence* on the response variable. As an alternative regression model, it hypothesizes that all of the conditional response means are identical:

$$\mu(y \mid x = x_i) = \beta_0. \tag{5.5}$$

The single parameter in the null model equation, β_0, is the common value of the conditional means. The right-hand side of Equation [5.5] does not change with changes in the value of x.

The null model for the boys' height study,

$$\mu(ht18 \mid ht2 = x_i) = \beta_0,$$

states a belief that the predicted value of a boy's height at age 18 should be the same, *whatever* his age-2 height.

5.3.4   Comparing the Simple Linear and Null Models

The null model is expressed in the form of Equation [5.5] to facilitate its comparison with other regression models. The comparison of a regression model with the null model requires two steps:

- Identifying the conditions under which the regression model is identical to the null model.

- Concluding, on the basis of a sample of observations, whether these null model conditions could be true.

If the null model conditions *could be true*, then we conclude that the regression model is no better than the null model. Only by concluding that the null model could not be true can we go on to conclude that the regression model is better than the null model and, hence, that it is a good model.

5.3.5   The Null Model and the Slope Parameter

What are the conditions under which the simple linear regression model,

$$\mu(y \mid x = x_i) = \beta_0 + \beta_1 x_i, \tag{3.2}$$

is the same as the null model,

$$\mu(y \mid x = x_i) = \beta_0? \tag{5.5}$$

If the value of the slope parameter, β_1, in the linear model were 0, then the right-hand side of Equation [3.2] would give the same value, β_0, for all values of x. If $\beta_1 = 0$, the linear model is identical to the null model.

A simple linear regression model will be a good model if it is concluded that the slope parameter for that model *could not be 0*.

5.3.6 The Slope Parameter CI: Inferring that $\beta_1 \neq 0$

Section 5.2 ended by noting that the CI for a parameter represents a *conclusion reached* (with a specified degree of confidence) that the true value of that parameter is one of the values within that interval. We conclude, for example, that the value of the slope parameter is within the interval, CI[β_1, 95%].

We conclude that $\beta_1 \neq 0$, that the true value of the slope parameter could not be 0, if 0 is outside the CI. Put another way, β_1 *could be 0* if 0 is within the CI for the slope.

We conclude that our simple linear regression model is a good model if the CI for the slope parameter in that model does not include 0. On the other hand, we conclude that our simple linear model is no better than the null model if the CI for the slope parameter includes 0.

The linear model should not be labeled good unless we are "sure" that the null model could not be true. Consequently, we typically use 95% or 99% CIs in reaching our conclusion. We want to be 95% or 99% confident that the null model is not true before concluding that the linear model with an active explanatory variable is the better one.

5.3.7 The Boys' Height Model

Can we conclude that the infant height of boys influences their adolescent height?

We earlier worked out the 95% CI for the slope parameter to be

$$\text{CI}[\beta_1, \; 95\%] = [0.940\,\text{cm/cm}, \; 2.230\,\text{cm/cm}].$$

Zero is outside the range of this interval. To be more certain, however, let's use Equation [5.3] to compute the wider 99% CI:

$$\text{CI}[\beta_1, \; (1-\alpha)100\%] = [\widehat{\beta_1} \pm t_{(N-2),(1-\alpha)} \; \text{SE}(\widehat{\beta_1})]. \tag{5.3}$$

We begin with our estimate of the slope parameter,

$$\widehat{\beta_1} = 1.585\,\text{cm/cm},$$

and its standard error,

$$\text{SE}(\widehat{\beta_1}) = 0.313\,\text{cm/cm}.$$

These were obtained from a sample of $N = 28$ observations, so the $t_{(N-2),(1-\alpha)}$ refers to the t-distribution with $(N-2) = 26$ d.f.:

Central Proportions of t-Distribution

d.f.	.80	.90	.95	.99
26	1.31	1.71	2.06	2.78

For a 99% CI, this fragment of the table gives

$$t_{(N-2),(1-\alpha)} = t_{26,0.99} = 2.78.$$

From these results, we compute the product on the right-hand side of Equation [5.3]:

$$t_{(N-2),(1-\alpha)} \, SE(\widehat{\beta_1}) = (2.78)(0.313 \, cm/cm) = 0.870 \, cm/cm.$$

The resulting quantity, 0.870 cm/cm, is subtracted from and added to the slope estimate to give lower and upper limits to the new CI:

$$CI[\beta_1, \, 99\%] = [(1.585 - 0.870), \, (1.585 + 0.870)] = [0.715 \, cm/cm, \, 2.455 \, cm/cm].$$

The 99% CI for the slope parameter does not include 0 either. We can be at least 99% confident that $\beta_1 \neq 0$ and, hence, the linear regression model is a good model, better than the null model.

We can conclude that an increase in infant height is accompanied by an increase in the expected adolescent height. Because of the small sample size, we cannot be too precise about how great the expected increase will be. We are 99% confident, though, that a difference of 1 cm in infant height will be associated with an expected difference in adolescent heights somewhere between 0.7 cm and 2.5 cm.

5.4
Output from a Regression Command

This and earlier chapters have presented the linear model computations in terms of basic sample statistics. As we move beyond simple linear regression, however, we will find it progressively more awkward to continue doing that. We will have to entrust our computations to one or another *regression commands* built into a statistics package. In preparation for this, let's see how the linear (and null) models for the boys' heights data set are reported by a typical regression program.

```
                        Response: ht18
Column Name          Coeff      StErr   Pvalue              SS

   0 Constant       39.470     27.568   0.164       899082.250
   1 ht2             1.585      0.313   0.000          639.983

   df:26         RSq:0.497   s:4.988             RSS:646.995
```

Above are the results for the simple linear regression model, *ht18*, the response, and *ht2*, the explanatory variable.

The results can be compared with the "hand" calculations reported here and in earlier chapters, making some allowances for the effects of rounding errors in the earlier, piecemeal computations!

The regression output gives us all we need to compute confidence intervals and to conclude whether our linear model is a good one or not.

The Coeff listed opposite Constant is the intercept estimate, $\widehat{\beta_0}$, and that opposite *ht2* is the slope estimate. Their standard errors (StErr) are listed in the adjacent column. The df are the degrees of freedom for our linear model—$N - 2 = 26$, in this instance. The estimated conditional response standard deviation, $\widehat{\sigma}(y \mid x)$, is reported here as s:4.988.

These results all square with our earlier computations. This regression output provides some additional information about the model, some of which we will use in later chapters. RSq:0.497 reports the *square* of the correlation between *ht2* and *ht18*. RSS:646.995 is the sum of the squares of the differences between the *y* values and the model's estimate of their respective conditional means:

$$\text{RSS} = \sum_{i=1}^{N} [y_i - \widehat{\mu}(y \mid x = x_i)]^2 = \sum_{i=1}^{N} [y_i - (\widehat{\beta}_0 + \widehat{\beta}_1 x_i)]^2.$$

The RSS is a summary computation that contributes to the estimate of the conditional response variance,

$$\widehat{\sigma}^2(y \mid x) = \frac{\text{RSS}}{\text{df}} = \frac{646.995}{26} = 24.884.$$

The square root of this ratio is the estimated conditional response standard deviation,

$$\widehat{\sigma}(y \mid x) = \sqrt{\frac{\text{RSS}}{\text{df}}} = \sqrt{\frac{646.995}{26}} = 4.988.$$

And, as we have seen in this chapter, $\widehat{\sigma}(y \mid x)$ is used, in turn, in the computation of the SEs for the slope and intercept estimates.

5.5
Summary

In this chapter, we use the idea of a *sampling distribution* for the estimate of each of our linear model parameters—slope, intercept, and conditional response variance—to draw conclusions about the true sizes of those parameters or to say whether our explanatory variable *explains* variability in the response variable—whether we have a good model. These are described here as *inference tasks*, the first being a magnitude inference task and the second a relation inference task. Both tasks are dependent on computing a *confidence interval* for one of the population parameters. In the case of a linear regression model with just one measured *x* variable, inference focuses on just one parameter—the slope of the regression line.

Exercises

1 Below are data related to the use of airborne observers to estimate the size of snow geese flocks. A pair of observers were flown over 45 flocks. A photo was also taken of each flock. Photo counts are given in column 1 and the estimates of observers 1 and 2, respectively, in columns 2 and 3. We take the photo count as the response variable. Why?

Construct and evaluate a separate linear model for each observer. Is either of the observers accurate? Use scatterplots to see if you can detect whether either explanatory relation is linear.

Col 1	Col 2	Col 3
56	50	40
38	25	30
25	30	40
48	35	45
38	25	30
22	20	20
22	12	20
42	34	35
34	20	30
14	10	12
30	25	30
9	10	10
18	15	18
25	20	30
62	40	50
26	30	20
88	75	120
56	35	60
11	9	10
66	55	80
42	30	35
30	25	30
90	40	120
119	75	200
165	100	200
152	150	150
205	120	200
409	250	300
342	500	500
200	200	300
73	50	40
123.	75	80
150	150	120
70	50	60
90	60	100
110	75	120
95	150	150
57	40	40
43	25	35
55	100	110
325	200	400
114	60	120
83	40	40
91	35	60
56	20	40

2 In this second data set, we have the head lengths and breadths, columns 1 and 2, of the first-born sons from 25 families. In columns 3 and 4 are the head lengths and breadths of second-born sons from those same families. Use first-born head lengths to predict second-born head lengths. How accurate is the prediction? Do the same for head breadths.

Col 1	Col 2	Col 3	Col 4
191	155	179	145
195	149	201	152
181	148	185	149
183	153	188	149
176	144	171	142
208	157	192	152
189	150	190	149
197	159	189	152
188	152	197	159
192	150	187	151
179	158	186	148
183	147	174	147
174	150	185	152
190	159	195	157
188	151	187	158
163	137	161	130
195	155	183	158
181	145	182	146
175	140	165	137
192	154	185	152
174	143	178	147
197	167	200	158
190	163	187	150
186	153	173	148
176	139	176	143

6

Categorical Explanatory Variables: One-Way ANOVA

Some important explanatory sources for our models are not measured or counted or even ordered variables. Eye color, political orientation, or country of origin, for example, may influence a measured response variable of interest to us. How can we model these influences? If we can use the same approach we have learned to use with an explanatory variable possessing a unit of measurement, it will make modeling easier. For one thing, having a common approach to measured and nonmeasured influences allows us to include both in the same model, something we frequently want to do. So, in this chapter we discuss how the linear modeling approach introduced in Chapters 3 through 5 can be used with *categorical explanatory variables*. In doing this, we lay the groundwork as well for Chapter 7 in which we learn about models with more than one explanatory variable.

6.1
Categorical Explanatory Variables

In the last three chapters, we've been concerned with models in which the explanatory variable (our x variable) possessed a *unit of measurement*. We used the unit of measurement as a basis for interpreting the regression slope, the change in the mean of the response for a *unit increase* in x. Without the definition of a unit for the explanatory variable, the slope parameter—and inferences about it—lack meaning.

Height at age 2, in our boys' heights example, possessed a unit of measurement. The 85-cm-tall boy is taller than the 80-cm-tall boy. Further, the difference in their heights, 5 cm, is greater than the difference in the heights of a 90-cm-tall boy and an 87-cm-tall one. We rely on our idea of the centimeter being a fixed, constant unit of height in making this last judgment. The centimeter, in other words, provides a unit of measurement for our boys' heights.

If a variable does not possess a unit of measurement, we refer to it as a *categorical variable*. The values assumed by such a variable categorize observations rather than measure them. Note that, on the explanatory side, *count* variables are similar to measured variables in that they possess a unit of measurement. It is only on the response side where we need to distinguish between count and measured variables.

6.1.1   Categories Ordered, But No Unit of Measurement

Not all explanatory variables can pass the "tests" of order of scores and order of differences required of measured or count variables. For some explanatory variables, the score order may be obvious but the order of differences not at all clear. Let's look at an example:

- A group of randomly chosen psychiatric in-patients are assigned to an experimental therapy. Before the therapy begins, each of the patients is rated by a psychiatrist as "Unlikely to benefit from treatment," "Moderately likely to benefit from treatment," or "Very likely to benefit from treatment."

The scores or levels of this Likelihood of Benefiting from Treatment variable are ordered, "moderately likely" lying between "unlikely" and "very likely." But we haven't a clue about the interpretation of *differences between levels*. Is the difference between "unlikely" and "moderately likely" greater than, less than, or the same as the difference between "moderately" and "highly" likely? We don't know. The variable does not have a unit of measurement.

Likelihood of Benefiting from Treatment is an *ordered categorical variable*. It is used to assign patients to categories—levels of the variable—that are ordered.

6.1.2   Unordered or Nominal Categories

For other categorical variables, even the order of scores may not be specifiable:

- Survey respondents are asked to identify their Religious Affiliation by selecting one of the following: Jewish, Catholic, Protestant, Muslim, Other, or None.

There is no obvious way to order these different "scores" with respect to one another. For example, we cannot say where Other belongs relative to Jewish and Protestant. The six possible responses correspond to *distinct categories* of Religious Affiliation, but thay are categories that cannot be ordered. Such categories are called *nonordered* or *nominal* categories, and Religious Affiliation is a *nominal categorical variable* As a variable, it can take any one of six different "names."

6.1.3   Category Levels

Where the alternative scores for an explanatory variable comprise a set of categories rather than a set of unit-based measures, we will refer to those distinct scores as the *levels* of the explanatory variable. These levels may be ordered or they simply may be distinct (nominal).

6.2
Categories and Conditional Response Populations

In Chapter 2, we introduced a set of ideas relating to conditional populations for the measured response variable (y). There is a separate population of y scores associated with each distinct score of interest on an explanatory variable (x). These are conditional response populations. Certain characteristics of these populations, notably their means, may be conditional upon the value of x.

Just as there is a separate population of y scores for each score on a measured or count variable x, there is a separate conditional response population *for each level* of the categorical explanatory variable.

We begin with an exemplar study that is in the observational tradition. Later in the chapter, we look at an experimental study in which the explanatory variable is categorical. Let's say we are interested in the attitudes of parents of New York City (NYC) high-school students towards pregnancy counseling in the schools. We think attitude may be influenced by parents' religious affiliation.

Attitude towards counseling is our y and is assessed on a scale with a unit of measurement, yielding scores from 0 (very unfavorable) to 20 (very favorable). The categorical variable described above, Religious Affiliation, is our explanatory variable. The explanatory model linking the two postulates six conditional response populations, each a population of parents' attitudes towards pregnancy counseling scores. One conditional response population consists of the measured attitudes of all parents who describe their religious affiliation as Jewish. A second conditional population consists of the attitudes of all parents describing themselves as Catholics. Similarly, there are separate populations of attitudes towards counseling scores for the complete collections of Protestant, Muslim, Other, and None NYC high-school parents. There also is an unconditional response population containing the measured attitudes of all NYC high-school parents, without regard to their expressed religious affiliations. In this hypothetical, observational study, this unconditional population is the sum of the several conditional ones.

6.2.1 Response Population Characteristics

Each of our conditional response populations possesses characteristics of interest to us in modeling. For the measured response, these are the *mean,* the *variance,* and the *histograms* that characterize the distribution of responses.

Means of Response Populations

The mean of a population is the mean of the collection of values that makes up that population. Thus, the mean of the unconditional response population described above is the mean attitude towards pregnancy counseling among all NYC high-school parents. We express the unconditional response mean as $\mu(y)$ or, for a specific response variable, as

$$\mu(Att\ Pregnancy\ Couns).$$

The *mean* of a conditional response population, $\mu(y\,|\,x = x_i)$, is a mean again. Thus,

$$\mu(\textit{Att Pregnancy Couns}\,|\,\textit{Jewish})$$

is the mean of the attitude scores among all NYC Jewish parents, and

$$\mu(\textit{Att Pregnancy Couns}\,|\,\textit{Catholic})$$

is the mean of the attitude towards pregnancy counseling scores of all NYC Catholic parents.

Variances of Response Populations

Each response population has a variance, the mean of the squared deviations from the mean of the scores making up that population. For our illustrative model, the variance of the unconditional response population variance would be written as

$$\sigma^2(\textit{Att Pregnancy Couns}),$$

while the variances in the several conditional response populations would be

$$\sigma^2(\textit{Att Pregnancy Couns}\,|\,\textit{Jewish}), \sigma^2(\textit{Att Pregnancy Couns}\,|\,\textit{Catholic}), \textit{etc.}$$

Proportions of Response Scores

Figure 6.1 shows a set of idealized histograms for the conditional response populations in our attitudes towards pregnancy counseling model. The conditional response populations are ordered, top to bottom, in the same arbitrary way they were listed previously. Each histogram is higher in y regions where there are larger proportions of observations and lower where the proportions are smaller.

As a convenience to description, the conditional population histograms in Figure 6.1 have all been constructed to reflect the same conditional response variance. The conditional histograms also have been drawn to be unimodal, symmetric, and of the same kurtosis. Only the means, the locations of the peaks or modes, are shown to differ among these histograms. In these hypothetical figures, the mean for the No Religious Affiliation population of attitudes is higher than that for the Jewish population of parents. The Jewish conditional population, in turn, has a higher mean than does the Catholic parents' one.

As described at the bottom of Figure 6.1, the spread—or variance—of expressed attitudes is considerably greater in the unconditional response population, the population that contains the attitudes of all NYC high-school parents of all religious affiliations, than in any one of the conditional populations.

Because these histograms plot proportions of attitude scores, rather than their absolute frequencies, we have drawn all of the histograms the same size. The conditional populations would not, of course, all contain the same number of scores—there are more Jewish than Muslim parents of NYC high-school students. Similarly, the unconditional population would be much larger than the conditional ones inasmuch as it contains all of the conditional populations. What is important is not

Conditional Response Population

Jewish Parents

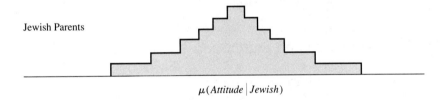

$\mu(Attitude \mid Jewish)$

Catholic Parents

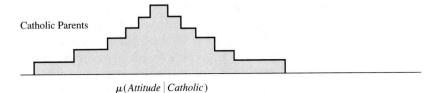

$\mu(Attitude \mid Catholic)$

No-religious-affiliation Parents

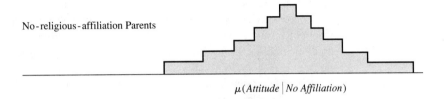

$\mu(Attitude \mid No\ Affiliation)$

Unconditional Response Population

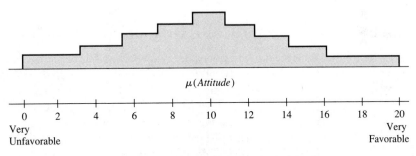

$\mu(Attitude)$

FIGURE 6.1
Conditional and
Unconditional Re-
sponse Population
Histograms

0   2   4   6   8   10   12   14   16   18   20
Very   Very
Unfavorable   Favorable

Attitude Towards Pregnancy Counseling in Schools

the absolute sizes of these populations but how the scores are distributed relatively within each of them.

6.2.2   Modeling and Increased Response Certainty

In Chapter 2, we saw that, in observational studies with a measured response, the variance of a response population (or its square root, the standard deviation) indicates our *certainty* about the value of an observation randomly chosen from that y population. The smaller the variance, the greater our certainty that the observation will be close to the mean of that response population.

If an explanatory variable is a good one, it leads to increased certainty about the response variable. To increase certainty, the conditional response populations must have smaller variances than the unconditional response population variance. When the conditional response populations have smaller variances, the conditional response populations will have different means. The hallmark of a good explanatory variable is that the means are different among the conditional response populations.

This way of thinking about the usefulness of explanatory models for a measured response is just as relevant when the explanatory variable is categorical. We will continue to ask about differences among the means of conditional response populations.

We look now at how we can develop and evaluate explanatory models for the categorical explanatory variable.

6.3
Models for the Categorical Explanatory Variable

Where both the explanatory and response variables have units of measurement we are able to specify the *form of the explanatory relation*. We did this in Chapters 3 through 5 in developing the *linear model*. The situation is quite different for the categorical explanatory variable; as it has no unit of measurement, our models cannot prescribe a form for the relationship of conditional response means to category "levels." In fact, when the category levels are not ordered, our models cannot postulate even an increasing or decreasing relationship between the two.

What categorical explanatory variable models can do is to hypothesize *differences among the conditional response means*. We'll describe categorical explanatory models as *full*, *null*, or *constrained* depending upon the mean differences they hypothesize.

6.3.1   Full Explanatory Models

A *full model* is one that hypothesizes that the mean of the response for any category level will be different from those for all other category levels. No two are the same.

Also, the full model prescribes *no pattern,* no prespecified ordering to these conditional means. They are hypothesized, simply, to be different. The full model, then, for our Religious Affiliation example is that the six conditional means,

$$\mu(\textit{Att Pregnancy Couns} \,|\, \textit{Jewish}),$$
$$\mu(\textit{Att Pregnancy Couns} \,|\, \textit{Catholic}),$$
$$\mu(\textit{Att Pregnancy Couns} \,|\, \textit{Protestant}),$$
$$\mu(\textit{Att Pregnancy Couns} \,|\, \textit{Muslim}),$$
$$\mu(\textit{Att Pregnancy Couns} \,|\, \textit{Other}),$$

and

$$\mu(\textit{Att Pregnancy Couns} \,|\, \textit{None}),$$

all take *different* values.

6.3.2 Null Explanatory Models

A *null model*, as we saw in Chapter 5, is one that hypothesizes that the response mean is the same at *all explanatory variable levels*. All of the conditional response means are equal to one another. In observational studies, they are equal to the mean of the unconditional response population.

For the Religious Affiliation example, the null model is that all six of the conditional means are identical to one another (and to the unconditional response mean).

The null model specifies that the categorical explanatory variable has *no influence* on the response variable mean.

6.3.3 Constrained Explanatory Models

The full model allows the conditional means to all be different. The null model demands that they all be the same. Between these two extremes are models that stipulate *some pattern* to the means; for example, that certain means will be identical but different from other means. We refer to such models as *constrained*. The means are not as free to vary as in the full model, nor are they as completely restricted as they are in the null model.

As an example of a constrained model for the religious affiliation study, we might hypothesize only that the mean attitude towards pregnancy counseling will be the same in the populations of Protestant and Other parents,

$$\mu(\textit{Att Pregnancy Couns} \,|\, \textit{Protestant}) = \mu(\textit{Att Pregnancy Couns} \,|\, \textit{Other}),$$

and have no hypotheses about the other four conditional response populations.

You may have formulated one or more constrained models of your own for this study. Whether or not you have, you probably have concluded that constrained models are the really interesting ones. The full model hypothesizes only that the six means differ among themselves in some unspecified way, and the null model that they differ not at all. Neither promises to teach us much about how differences in religious affiliation influence parental attitude towards pregnancy counseling. We need models more specific than either the null or the full if we are to understand this topic.

The null and full models serve primarily to *anchor* the two extremes: All category levels have the same influence and all levels have different influences. What we are curious about is which specific levels differ in their influence from which other levels.

6.4
Response Population Estimates and Sampling

Comparing one model with another to find a best one amounts to *drawing conclusions* about the parameters of our conditional response populations. Are the two conditional means $\mu(Att\ Pregnancy\ Couns\,|\,Protestant)$ and $\mu(Att\ Pregnancy\ Couns\,|\,Other)$ equal or are they different?

The conditional means and variances, like the populations they come from, are unknown and unknowable to us. We cannot completely inventory the response populations in order to compute their parameters. Instead, our conclusions about those parameters must be in the form of *inferences* we can draw about them on the basis of *estimates* of those parameters obtained from a *sample* of response observations.

6.4.1 Assumptions Needed for Estimation and Inference

Just as for the measured explanatory model developed in Chapters 3 through 5, the certainty of our sample-based inferences about models with explanatory categories depends upon a set of assumptions made about the conditional response populations and about the samples drawn from those populations.

In fact, inasmuch as the reasons for the assumptions are the same as they are for the linear model with measured x, the assumptions we are asked to make are also the same.

We make two assumptions about the conditional response populations:

- At each level of the categorical explanatory variable the population of response variable observations has the same variance, $\sigma^2(y\,|\,x)$.

- At each level of the categorical explanatory variable, the population response histogram possesses the Normal random variable characteristics of unimodality, symmetry, and kurtosis.

A third assumption, again in common with our measured x linear model, is that the response observations are sampled *independently* of one another. For observational studies, independence is insured by random sampling of participants, either from the unconditional response population or from each conditional response population. For experimental studies, independence can be achieved by the random assignment among levels of treatment (category levels) of participants who were randomly selected from a relevant population of potential respondents.

Because we cannot propose for our categorical explanatory variable a simple linear model that "links" together the several conditional response population means, we have to impose one additional condition on the sample. The sample *must contain more than one response observation at each explanatory level*. In fact, our sample should include several response observations at each level. In Section 6.4.3, we see how the size of the sample at an explanatory level influences the certainty we have in our estimate of the response mean for that level.

6.4.2   Estimates of Response Population Parameters

We'll let N be the number of observations in our sample and k the number of explanatory variable levels. If we have *designed* our study, as we do for many experiments, we may have the same number of observations at each explanatory level, making N a multiple of k. Were we to sample 50 times from each of the six conditional response distributions associated with the six levels of religious affiliation, the total sample size would be $50 \times 6 = 300$. More generally, the sample size, N, will be equal to the sum of the number of observations at each of the k explanatory levels:

$$N = N(a) + N(b) + \cdots + N(j) + \cdots + N(k),$$

where $N(j)$ is the number of sample observations at the jth explanatory level. We use letters rather than numbers to identify the levels, thus stressing that there may be no order to the category levels.

The parameter estimates described here are based on the *same estimation principles* used earlier to estimate the simple linear model parameters.

Means of Response Populations

Assuming random selection of respondents from the unconditional response population, the mean of that population, $\mu(y)$, is estimated by the *overall sample mean* of the response,

$$\widehat{\mu}(y) = M(y), \tag{6.1}$$

the mean of the N response observations. In experimental studies or in observational studies, where respondents are drawn from prespecified conditional populations rather than from a single unconditional one, we will not estimate unconditional population parameters.

The estimate of $\mu(y\,|\,j)$, the mean of the conditional response population for the jth explanatory level, is simply the mean of the $N(j)$ sample y observations drawn from that conditional population:

$$\widehat{\mu}(y\,|\,j) = M(y\,|\,j). \tag{6.2}$$

For categorical explanatory models, means are estimated by sample means. This only appears to contrast with the simple linear model for a measured explanatory variable where the conditional means are estimated through an estimated slope and intercept.

Variances of Response Populations

The estimate of the unconditional response variance, where it is appropriate to estimate it, is given by the sum of squared deviations of the N response observations about the estimated unconditional response mean divided by $(N - 1)$,

$$\widehat{\sigma}^2(y) = \frac{\displaystyle\sum_{i=1}^{N}[y_i - M(y)]^2}{N - 1}. \tag{4.9}$$

As the equation number indicates, this definition is identical to that given in Chapter 4 for the unconditional response variance. As noted at that time, the loss of one degree of freedom in the denominator is the result of having first to estimate the unconditional response mean, having to use $M(y)$ rather than $\mu(y)$.

The common conditional response variance, the response variance in any one of the conditional populations, is estimated by the sum of squared deviations of the response observations from their estimated conditional means divided by $(N - k)$:

$$\widehat{\sigma}^2(y\,|\,j) = \frac{\displaystyle\sum_{j=a}^{k}\sum_{i=1}^{N(j)}[y_i - M(y\,|\,j)]^2}{N - k}. \tag{6.3}$$

We've now had to estimate k population means, each by a sample mean, with a consequent loss of k degrees of freedom in the divisor.

6.4.3 Sampling Distribution: Estimates of Conditional Means

Just as we did in Chapter 4, we can imagine resampling another

$$N = N(a) + N(b) + \cdots + N(j) + \cdots + N(k)$$

times according to the same sampling plan from the *same conditional response populations* using the *same subsample sizes* as in the actual study and then computing another set of estimates of the k conditional means. We can imagine repeating this hypothetical resampling a very large number of times until we have "millions" of estimates of each of the k conditional means, each estimate from a different hypothetical resampling of the conditional response populations.

Finally, we can imagine assembling the millions of hypothetical estimates of any one of the conditional means into a *sampling distribution* of estimates. Figure 6.2 illustrates some of the characteristics of this hypothetical sampling distribution of estimates of a conditional mean.

The sampling distribution of estimates of the conditional mean sketched in Figure 6.2, is centered at the true value of that conditional mean:

$$\mu[\widehat{\mu}(y\,|\,j)] = \mu(y\,|\,j). \tag{6.4}$$

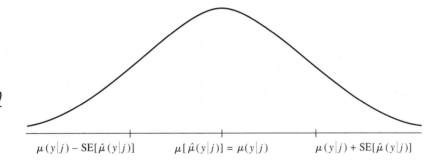

FIGURE 6.2
Sampling Distri-
bution Histogram:
$\widehat{\mu}(y\,|\,j)$

The standard error of the estimated conditional mean (the estimated standard deviation of its sampling distribution) is given by

$$\mathrm{SE}[\widehat{\mu}(y\,|\,j)] = \sqrt{\frac{\widehat{\sigma}^2(y\,|\,j)}{N(j)}}. \tag{6.5}$$

On the right-hand side of Equation [6.5], the estimated conditional response variance is divided by the number of observations at the jth explanatory level and the square root of the result is taken.

By assumption, the conditional response variance is estimated to be the same at all explanatory levels. The number of observations though may vary. Because of the division by $N(j)$, a large sample at any explanatory level yields a small standard error for the estimate of the response mean at that level. If the sample sizes are the same at all categorical levels, all conditional means are estimated with the same certainty. Otherwise, the means at levels with larger sample sizes are estimated with greater certainty than those at levels with smaller sample sizes.

The sampling distribution for each of the estimated conditional means, again by assumption, is approximated by the probability density function of the Student's t-variate with $(N-k)$ degrees of freedom. This is conveyed in the unimodal, symmetric form of Figure 6.2.

We use all of these characteristics of the sampling distribution of the estimates of a conditional mean to establish a confidence interval (CI) for the actual conditional mean. In fact, we compute these CIs exactly as we did the CIs for the slope parameter in Chapter 5. We illustrate this in Section 6.5.

6.4.4 Sampling Distribution of Estimated Conditional Response Variance

We can imagine, just as well, building up a sampling distribution of estimates of the conditional response variance by letting each additional hypothetical resampling from the conditional response populations contribute another estimate until we have a very large number of such imagined estimates.

The resulting sampling distribution is centered about the true value of the conditional response variance, in the sense that our estimate is an unbiased one:

$\mu[\widehat{\sigma}^2(y\,|\,j) = \sigma^2(y\,|\,j)$. The hypothetical sampling distribution, however, is not symmetric but is well approximated by the shape of that of the *Chi-squared random variable* with $(N - k)$ degrees of freedom.

Now, let's look at the application of these ideas. We'll do this first with an example in which the number of levels of the categorical explanatory variable is just two. This will make it easy for us to link up with what we already have done for measured simple linear models. Once we've done that, we'll consider a model in which the category levels are more numerous than two.

6.5
Full and Null Models for the Two-level Category

Two levels of the explanatory variable mean just two conditional response populations, one for each level. Assuming that those conditional populations have the same variance and have Normal characteristics of unimodality, symmetry, and kurtosis, they can differ only in their means. Our *full* model for these conditional response populations is that these two means differ. Our *null* model is that they are identical.

6.5.1   Gender and the SATV: A Two-level Example

The Scholastic Aptitude Test (SAT) with its verbal and quantitative parts, is taken by large numbers of U.S. high-school students seeking admissions to college or university study. Scores on the test are often used by institutions in selecting candidates for admission. High schools may also use the scores to monitor their educational accomplishments:

- The superintendent of schools in a large city asked her research officer to find out whether the mean score on the Verbal Part of the SAT for women graduating from high schools in that city and taking the SAT in 1988 was higher than the mean score for the men.

Let's look at the superintendent's question from a modeling perspective.

Scores on the SAT verbal part (SATV) for all the city's high-school graduates tested in 1988 make up an unconditional response population. Two conditional populations result when this population of SATV scores is divided into two categories, one for women graduates and one for men. Gender of test taker is the explanatory variable for these conditional response populations.

The superintendent's question is whether the two conditional populations have the same mean or if the mean for the women exceeds that for the men.

However large the city, the two conditional response populations each contain a finite number of scores and, in principle, the superintendent's question could be answered by computing the two conditional population means. We'll assume, though, that to inventory the conditional populations completely would be too expensive and that the research officer elects to *infer* an answer to the question based on a sample of observations.

The research officer adopts the following strategy for our hypothetical study: To sample, randomly, 50 times from among those students taking the SAT in 1988; to record the resulting SATV scores; and to note, for each score, whether it was earned by a woman or a man. This study design results in $N(W)$ independent observations from the $(SATV \mid Women)$ conditional response population and $N(M)$ independent observations from the $(SATV \mid Men)$ conditional response population, with $N(W) + N(M) = 50$.

Table 6.1 displays the results. The sample of 50 SATV scores included those for $N(W) = 22$ women and $N(M) = 28$ men.

T A B L E **6.1**

SAT Verbal Scores for a Sample of 50 Women and Men High-School Graduates

Women	Men
336	380
450	392
480	400
480	400
480	420
500	450
500	450
500	460
510	480
520	480
520	490
532	520
540	530
580	530
580	540
580	550
590	558
600	590
670	590
690	600
710	600
740	610
	630
	643
	650
	650
	720
	780

6.5.2   Confidence Intervals for Conditional Means

Because the sampling distributions for the estimates of the response mean at each category level are well approximated by the probability densities of Students' t-variates, we can use the confidence interval (CI) ideas developed in Chapter 5 to construct CIs for the conditional response means.

We can adapt Equation [5.3] to tell us how to compute the lower and upper limits for these means:

$$\text{CI}[\mu(y\,|\,j), (1-\alpha)100\%] = \widehat{\mu}(y\,|\,j) \pm t_{(N-k)(1-\alpha)}\text{SE}[\widehat{\mu}(y\,|\,j)]. \qquad \textbf{(6.6)}$$

We add to or subtract from our estimate of the conditional mean the product of the standard error of the mean and a value, $t_{(N-k)(1-\alpha)}$, from the t-variate table: The central $(1-\alpha)100\%$ of the t-distribution with $(N-k)$ degrees of freedom is within $\pm t_{(N-k)(1-\alpha)}$ of the expected value of that t-distribution.

We'll illustrate the application of Equation [6.6] for the sample data introduced in the last section, computing 95% CIs for the two conditional means, $\mu(SATV\,|\,Women)$ and $\mu(SATV\,|\,Men)$.

First, we'll compute the estimated conditional means, the $\widehat{\mu}(y\,|\,j)$s.

From the 50 SATV scores of Table 6.1 and on the basis of Equation [6.2], we compute estimates of the two response means:

$$\widehat{\mu}(SATV\,|\,Women) = \frac{336 + 450 + \ldots + 710 + 740}{22} = 549.45$$

and

$$\widehat{\mu}(SATV\,|\,Men) = \frac{380 + 392 + \ldots + 720 + 780}{28} = 539.04.$$

We note that the estimated mean of the women's SATV scores is, in fact, greater than that of the men's.

Next, our CI equation requires the standard errors of these two estimated means. Before these can be obtained from Equation [6.5],

$$\text{SE}[\widehat{\mu}(y\,|\,j)] = \sqrt{\frac{\widehat{\sigma}^2(y\,|\,j)}{N(j)}}, \qquad \textbf{(6.5)}$$

we must estimate the conditional response variance. From Equation [6.3], we compute this to be

$$\widehat{\sigma}^2(SATV\,|\,Gender) = \frac{(336 - 549.45)^2 + \ldots + (780 - 539.04)^2}{50 - 2} = 9765.10.$$

We substitute this result in Equation [6.5] and compute standard errors for the two estimated means:

$$\text{SE}[\widehat{\mu}(SATV\,|\,Women)] = \sqrt{\frac{9765.10}{22}} = 21.07$$

and

$$\text{SE}[\widehat{\mu}(SATV\,|\,Men)] = \sqrt{\frac{9765.10}{28}} = 18.67.$$

The standard error for the Men's mean is somewhat smaller than that for the Women's, a direct consequence of the greater number of men in the sample.

We have estimates of the conditional means and their standard errors as needed for Equation [6.6]. All we need now is the $t_{(N-k)(1-\alpha)}$ value to complete the computation of the CIs.

For our sample of $N = 50$ high-school graduates, this value will come from the *t*-distribution with $(N - k) = (50 - 2) = 48$ d.f. The relevant line from the *t*-distribution table in the Appendix is

Central Proportions of *t*-Distribution

d.f.	.80	.90	.95	.99
48	1.30	1.68	2.01	2.68

From these table entries, we see that for our 95% CIs the appropriate multiplier of the standard error in Equation [6.6] is 2.01.

Finally, we have everything we need to compute CIs. The 95% CI for the Women's SATV mean is

$$[549.45 \pm (2.01)(21.07)] = [549.45 \pm 42.35] = [507.10, 591.80].$$

The 95% CI for $\mu(SATV \mid Men)$ is

$$[539.04 \pm (2.01)(18.67)] = [539.04 \pm 37.53] = [501.51, 576.57].$$

We are 95% confident, based on our sample of $N(W) = 22$ observations, that the mean of the women's population of SATV scores is somewhere between 507 and 592. Similarly, we are 95% confident, based on $N(M) = 28$ observations from the men's population of SATV scores, that the mean of that population is somewhere between 501 and 577.

While our estimate of the mean of the Women's SATV population (549.45) is greater than our estimate of that for the men (539.04), the two 95% CIs we've just computed overlap one another to a considerable extent. They have many values in common. Could it be that, despite the difference in estimates, the two conditional populations have the same means?

That question, calling for a comparison of full and null models, is not readily answered by our study of the sampling distributions of the two estimated means. We turn now to an alternative way of looking at the two conditional populations investigated here, one that makes the full and null model comparisons.

6.5.3   Linear Model for Two-Category Levels

The purposes of modeling with the two-level categorical explanatory variable include estimating the two conditional response means as we did in the last section. They also include estimating the *difference between the two conditional means,*

- By how much does $\mu(SATV \mid Women)$ exceed $\mu(SATV \mid Men)$?

and, most importantly, concluding whether the two means differ at all.

The latter two purposes focus on the *difference in the two means.* How big is it? Could the difference be zero? It is easier to pursue these purposes if our full model takes this mean difference explicitly into account. There is more than one full model that will do that. Among such full models are those that also tie directly into the linear model we developed in Chapters 3 through 5. Using one of these full models will give us an edge—we can take advantage of what we already know about the βs and σ^2s of the linear model.

Linear Model with One Dummy Variable

The heart of our earlier linear model is the equation that links the conditional response means to the *numeric values* of some x,

$$\mu(y \mid x = x_i) = \beta_0 + \beta_1 x_i. \tag{3.2}$$

How can we use this linear model with its measured x for the present problem where our explanatory variable has just the two nominal levels, Women and Men? All that is required is that the x in Equation [3.2] take two distinct numeric values, one for an observation at the first explanatory level and a different one for an observation at the second explanatory level.

Dummy Variable

One simple way of providing "scores" for the two levels is to have x take values of 0 for one explanatory level and 1 for the other.

Let's see how this works.

To be specific, let's define a variable, *Gender*, that takes the value 0 for each of the observations for Men and 1 for each of the observations for women. A 0/1 variable used in this way, to differentially code two categorical levels, is called a *dummy variable*. The name derives from the notion that the measured variable "stands in" for one of the categories.

When we use this dummy variable as the x in Equation [3.2], we see the following results:

$$\mu(SATV \mid Women) = \mu(SATV \mid x = 1) = \beta_0 + \beta_1(1) = \beta_0 + \beta_1$$

and

$$\mu(SATV \mid Men) = \mu(SATV \mid x = 0) = \beta_0 + \beta_1(0) = \beta_0.$$

Dummy Variable Slope and Intercept

These results are very promising. If we employ the dummy variable in our linear model, both the slope and intercept parameters have very *direct interpretations* in terms of the two conditional response populations.

First, the linear model equation with $x = 0$ can be rearranged to give the following:

$$\beta_0 = \mu(y \mid x = 0) = \mu(SATV \mid Men).$$

The linear model with a single dummy variable x has an *intercept* that is equal to the conditional response mean for the level coded 0. The level coded 0 by the dummy variable is called the *comparison level*.

Next, the two dummy variable linear model equations can be solved for the slope parameter by subtracting the equation where $x = 0$ from that where $x = 1$:

$$\beta_1 = (\beta_0 + \beta_1) - \beta_0 = \mu(y\,|\,x = 1) - \mu(y\,|\,x = 0)$$
$$= \mu(SATV\,|\,Women) - \mu(SATV\,|\,Men).$$

The regression slope for the dummy variable linear model is equal to the difference between the response mean for the explanatory level coded 1 and that for the level coded 0.

The two parameters in the dummy variable model, β_0 and β_1, insure that it is a *full model* for the two-category level study. The two conditional means are hypothesized by the linear dummy variable model to differ freely by an unknown amount, given by the model parameter, β_1.

It is exactly this difference in conditional means, corresponding to the linear model population parameter β_1, that is of *greatest interest* in the analysis of models with a two-level categorical explanatory variable.

The interpretation of the slope parameter for the dummy variable linear model may not be our common sense idea of a slope. Figure 6.3, however, makes clearer how the dummy variable slope fits the more general linear model definition.

If we plot our straight line in a system of *X-Y* coordinates, as in Figure 6.3, the slope of the line is the amount the line rises in the *Y*-dimension, top to bottom, as we move one unit in the *X*-dimension, left to right. So, as the dummy variable "increases" from 0 to 1—moving one unit to the right along the *X*-axis—the response mean "increases" from $\mu(y\,|\,x = 0) = \beta_0$ to $\mu(y\,|\,x = 1) = \beta_0 + \beta_1$, an increase of β_1. *The slope of the line is* β_1.

FIGURE 6.3

Conditional Response Means for the Two-level Explanatory Variable: Dummy Variable Coding

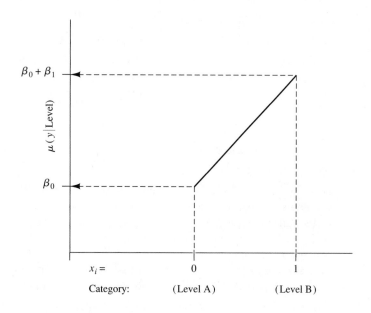

Estimation in the Single Dummy Variable Model

The use of the 0/1 dummy variable to represent the two-level category makes it easy for us to use the regression techniques of Chapters 4 and 5 to make inferences about the size of the difference in conditional response population means. All we have to do is compute a 95% or 99% CI for the slope parameter.

Let's use a statistical package's regression command to do this. We describe the SATV scores as the response observations and our 0/1 dummy variable (called *Women* here as it takes values of 1 for Women and 0 for Men) as the x variable. The regression results look like this:

```
                     Response: SATV
Column Name         Coeff      StErr Pvalue              SS

    0 Constant     539.036     18.675  0.000          1.47761e7
    2 Women         10.419     28.154  0.713           1337.361


  df:48            RSq:0.003 s:98.818        RSS:468724.406
```

The estimated intercept (the Constant Coeff in this output) is the sample SATV mean for the Men in the sample, and the estimated slope, $\widehat{\beta}_1$ (the Coeff for the dummy variable, *Women*), is the *difference* between the Women's and Men's sample SATV means:

$$549.455 - 539.036 = 10.419.$$

The SE for $\widehat{\beta}_0$ of 18.675 is the same as computed earlier for the SE of the Men's mean. The $\widehat{\sigma}(SATV \mid Gender)$, reported by the program as s: 98.818, is the square root of the estimated conditional response variance calculated earlier:

$$\sqrt{9765.10} = 98.818.$$

And the estimated conditional response variance itself can be obtained from the program output (RSS and df) as

$$\frac{RSS}{df} = \frac{468724.406}{48} = 9765.09.$$

CI for the Difference in Means

Dummy variable regression is just a special case of simple linear regression, one in which the x variable is a 0/1 variable. Whatever we can do in the general case we can do in the special case. In particular, we can compute and interpret a CI for the regression slope just as we did in Sections 5.2 and 5.3. For dummy variable models, however, this leads to inferences about the *difference* in response means for the two explanatory levels.

Let's compute a 95% CI for the slope in our dummy variable model for the Gender and SATV study. It will be a 95% CI for the *difference in means*,

$[\mu(SATV\,|\,Women) - \mu(SATV\,|\,Men)]$. We refer to Equation [5.3] for the computation:

$$CI[\beta_1, (1-\alpha)100\%] = [\widehat{\beta}_1 \pm t_{(N-2),(1-\alpha)}SE(\widehat{\beta}_1)].$$

The present sample size, $N = 50$, refers us to the t-distribution with $(N - 2) = 48$ d.f.:

Central Proportions of t-Distribution

d.f.	.80	.90	.95	.99
48	1.30	1.68	2.01	2.68

The lower and upper limits of the interval are given, utilizing the regression output, as

$$10.42 - (2.01)(28.15) = 10.42 - 56.58 = -46.16$$

and

$$10.42 + (2.01)(28.15) = 10.42 + 56.58 = 67.00$$

and the 95% CI is

$$CI[\mu(SATV\,|\,Women) - \mu(SATV\,|\,Men)], 95\% = [-46.16, 67.00].$$

We see immediately that the CI includes zero. We cannot be confident that the difference between means is positive *or* negative, that $\mu(SATV\,|\,Women)$ is larger or smaller than $\mu(SATV\,|\,Men)$.

The estimated difference in means, 10.42, was too small relative to its standard error, 28.15, for us to conclude that $\mu(SATV\,|\,Women)$ actually is greater than $\mu(SATV\,|\,Men)$.

The Dummy Variable Model v. the Null Model

As we saw in Section 5.3, asking whether the 95% CI (or the 99 % CI) for the slope parameter includes zero compares the simple linear model—our dummy variable model—with the *null model*. In this instance, we conclude that our Gender model for SATV scores,

$$\mu(SATV\,|\,Women) = \beta_0 + \beta_1,$$
$$\mu(SATV\,|\,Men) = \beta_0,$$

which hypothesizes that the two conditional populations have different means (different by an unknown amount, β_1), is no better than the null model,

$$\mu(SATV\,|\,Women) = \beta_0,$$
$$\mu(SATV\,|\,Men) = \beta_0,$$

which hypothesizes the two means to be the same.

Though we did it in the context of linear regression models, we have effectively carried out a statistical "test" that will be familiar to many readers, a t-test of the (null) hypothesis that the population SATV means are the same for Men and

Women. Although our computations look different from those for the independent groups *t*-test, the conclusions from dummy variable regression and the *t*-test would be identical for any data set.

6.6
Full and Null Models: The Multilevel Explanatory Variable

We saw in Section 6.5 how we could use our simple linear regression concepts to develop and evaluate a model in which the explanatory variable was not measured and assumed two levels. In this section, we generalize these results to models in which the categorical explanatory variable has more than two levels. As a result of this generalization, we will pass, quietly, from simple linear regression to *multiple linear regression*.

6.6.1 Spatial Problem Solving Instruction

An educational psychologist is interested in the effectiveness of each of two short instructional interventions in improving the performance of students in solving problems related to the spatial arrangement of objects. One intervention involves watching a videotape of other students successfully solving such spatial problems. The other involves attending a lecture on the principles of problem solving.

- The psychologist conducts an experiment. Thirty students are randomly selected from among those in the ninth grade at the Jackson School. These students are randomly assigned, ten a piece, to one of three "treatments":

  Treatment Level A: Videotape

  Treatment Level B: Lecture

  Treatment Level C: Control

  Students assigned to the Control level receive no problem solving intervention. Rather, during the time the other students are watching the videotape or attending the lecture, they develop outlines for a story titled "Getting to Know Grandmother."

- One week after these interventions, all 30 students are asked to solve 25 spatial arrangement problems.

Table 6.2 shows the number of problems correctly solved by each student.

The psychologist is interested in concluding whether the Video or Lecture interventions result in improved spatial problem solving. The Control "intervention" is included to provide data on problem solving accuracy in the absence of any special instruction.

T A B L E 6.2

Effect of Spatial Problem Solving Instruction

Instruction	Number of Problems Correctly Solved									
Videotape	11	12	19	13	17	15	17	14	13	16
Lecture	11	14	10	9	12	13	10	8	14	11
Control	7	18	16	11	9	10	13	14	12	12

6.6.2 CIs for k Conditional Means

From our modeling point of view, the 30 response observations listed in Table 6.2 consist of 10 observations from each of three distinct conditional response populations:

(Problem Solving Scores | Videotape Instruction),

(Problem Solving Scores | Lecture Instruction), and

(Problem Solving Scores | Control Instruction).

Because levels of our explanatory variable are being manipulated or assigned in this example rather than passively observed as was the case with Gender, these are somewhat hypothetical populations. Each is the population of Problem Solving Scores that *would result* if all ninth grade students in the Jackson School, the population from which participating students were sampled, were given that particular instruction.

In randomly sampling from the population of ninth grade students, randomly allocating the selected students among the three levels of instruction, and measuring Problem Solving for the instructed students, the psychologist effectively has sampled independently from these three conditional response populations.

To be able to reach conclusions about the means of these conditional populations, we assume, at least tentatively, that they all have the same variance and share the Normal random variable characteristics of unimodality, symmetry, and kurtosis. These are the assumptions made generally for categorical explanatory models as described in Section 6.4.1.

Under these assumptions, we can use the results of Section 6.5.2 to compute CIs that will show our conclusions about the magnitudes of these three conditional response population means. The computational formula is the one given earlier in this chapter:

$$\text{CI}[\mu(y \mid j), (1 - \alpha)100\%] = \widehat{\mu}(y \mid j) \pm t_{(N-k)(1-\alpha)} \text{SE}[\widehat{\mu}(y \mid j)]. \qquad \textbf{(6.6)}$$

Let's compute 90% CIs for the three means. To do this, we'll need

- estimates of the response means,
- standard errors for these estimates, and
- the "t-multiplier" from one of the t-distributions.

The response means are estimated, as they were earlier, by the sample response means at the different levels:

$\widehat{\mu}(Problem\ Solving\,|\,Video) = M(Problem\ Solving\,|\,Video) = 14.70,$

$\widehat{\mu}(Problem\ Solving\,|\,Lecture) = M(Problem\ Solving\,|\,Lecture) = 11.20,$ and

$\widehat{\mu}(Problem\ Solving\,|\,Control) = M(Problem\ Solving\,|\,Control) = 12.20.$

These results provide some evidence that the Video instruction may improve Problem Solving, though the students receiving Lecture instruction did less well, on the average, than those who received no instruction at all, those in the Control group.

The estimate of the common conditional response variance, $\widehat{\sigma}^2(Problem\ Solving\,|\,Instruction\ Level)$, is computed from the squares of the deviations of the sample Problem Solving scores from these estimated means using Equation [6.3],

$$\widehat{\sigma}^2(y\,|\,j) = \frac{\displaystyle\sum_{j=a}^{k}\sum_{i=1}^{N(j)}[y_i - M(y\,|\,j)]^2}{N - k}. \tag{6.3}$$

For the observations of Table 6.2, the conditional response variance is estimated at

$$\widehat{\sigma}^2(Problem\ Solving\,|\,Instruction\ Level) = 7.085.$$

We use this estimated population variance in Equation [6.5],

$$SE[\widehat{\mu}(y\,|\,j)] = \sqrt{\frac{\widehat{\sigma}^2(y\,|\,j)}{N(j)}}, \tag{6.5}$$

to find the standard errors of the three response means. Because in this study the number of observations was the same at each instructional level,

$$N(Video) = N(Lecture) = N(Control) = 10,$$

the three means have identical standard errors,

$$SE[\widehat{\mu}(Problem\ Solving\,|\,Video)] =$$
$$SE[\widehat{\mu}(Problem\ Solving\,|\,Lecture)] = \sqrt{\frac{7.085}{10}} = 0.84.$$
$$SE[\widehat{\mu}(Problem\ Solving\,|\,Control)] =$$

Lastly, the "*t*-multiplier" required to compute from Equation [6.6] the 90% CIs for the three expected values is the 90% central inclusion one from the *t*-distribution with $(N - k) = (30 - 3) = 27$ d.f.

Central Proportions of *t*-Distribution

d.f.	.80	.90	.95	.99
27	1.31	1.70	2.05	2.77

This gives: $t_{(N-k),(1-\alpha)} = t_{27,0.90} = 1.70.$

The *t*-multipliers as well as the standard errors will be the same for the three CIs. Thus, the three CIs from Equation [6.6],

$$\text{CI}[\mu(y \,|\, j), (1 - \alpha)100\%] = \widehat{\mu}(y \,|\, j) \pm t_{(N-k)(1-\alpha)}\text{SE}[\widehat{\mu}(y \,|\, j)], \qquad \textbf{(6.6)}$$

will result from adding and subtracting the quantity

$$t_{(N-k)(1-\alpha)}\text{SE}[\widehat{\mu}(y \,|\, j)] = (1.70)(0.84) = 1.43$$

to and from each of the estimated means. This gives

CI[μ(*Problem Solving* | *Video*), 90%] = 14.70 ± 1.43 = [13.27, 16.13],

CI[μ(*Problem Solving* | *Lecture*), 90%] = 11.20 ± 1.43 = [9.77, 12.63], and

CI[μ(*Problem Solving* | *Control*), 90%] = 12.20 ± 1.43 = [10.77, 13.63].

It is noted that there is very little overlap between the CIs for the Video and Control levels but considerable overlap between the CIs for the Lecture and Control levels.

6.6.3 A Dummy Variable Linear Model for the *k*-Level Category

The CIs just developed certainly contribute to our knowledge of the three separate, conditional response means. We are 90% confident, for example, that, if all ninth grade students were provided Video instruction on spatial problem solving, the average student would earn a Problem Solving score somewhere between 13 and 17.

The psychologist conducting the study, though, is interested in *comparing the interventions*. Does the Video instruction result in higher scores? If so, how much higher? These questions are most easily answered, as they were in the case of the two-level explanatory variable, if our full model makes explicit reference to differences in the conditional means.

The dummy variable version of simple linear regression provided a full model for the two-level variable because the two parameters of the linear model allowed the two conditional means, one for each explanatory level, to take quite different values:

$$\mu(y \,|\, Level \text{ ``A''}) = \mu(y \,|\, x = 0) = \beta_0$$

and

$$\mu(y \,|\, Level \text{ ``B''}) = \mu(y \,|\, x = 1) = \beta_0 + \beta_1.$$

The presence in the dummy variable model of the unknown population parameter, β_1, allows the difference in the two conditional means to be of any magnitude. The two means are not *constrained* to be alike in any way by the full model.

This idea generalizes. A full linear model for the three-level explanatory variable should include three parameters if the relations among the three conditional response means are to be unconstrained. Similarly, a full linear model for a four-level explanatory variable must have four parameters. But how do we express a linear model with more than two parameters? So far, all we've dealt with are the two-parameter *simple linear model,*

$$\mu(y \mid x = x_i) = \beta_0 + \beta_1 x_i,$$

and the one-parameter null linear model,

$$\mu(y \mid x = x_i) = \beta_0.$$

How do we get beyond two parameters? We'll do it first with dummy variables.

Dummy Variable Scoring of the Multilevel Category

We generalize first the idea of using more than one dummy variable to score the levels of a categorical variable. In the SATV-Gender study, we introduced a dummy variable scored 0 for one explanatory level—the comparison level—and 1 for the other level. That definition of dummy-variable scoring works well for the two-level variable. We need to change it a bit, though, when the categorical variable has more than two levels. This extended dummy variable convention has two parts:

- The dummy variable is scored 1 for all observations at a particular level of the categorical variable and 0 for observations at all other levels.
- Observations at the comparison level are coded 0 on each dummy variable.

The first part of the convention tells us how to create a 0/1 variable for *each* level of the categorical variable. The second part tells us to omit creating a dummy variable for one level, the *comparison level*.

We first choose one of the explanatory levels to be a comparison level. Then for each of the remaining levels, we create a 0/1 dummy variable—coding that level 1 and all other levels 0. Observations at the comparison level, with no dummy variable of its own, will be coded 0 on each of these dummy variables.

The Linear Model for Multiple Dummy Variables

The dummy variable scoring rules just outlined result in the definition of $(k - 1)$ dummy variables for the k-level explanatory variable. Where $k = 2$, as it did in the SATV-Gender example, there is but one dummy variable, and that single variable is readily accommodated in our simple linear regression model:

$$\mu(y \mid x = x_i) = \beta_0 + \beta_1 x_i.$$

The slope parameter for the dummy variable and the intercept parameter provide the two parameters needed to represent, freely, the two conditional response means.

When there are more than two explanatory levels, though, dummy variable scoring produces more than one dummy variable. We bring these dummy variables into a linear model simply by introducing a slope parameter or multiplier for *each* of the dummy variables.

We'll illustrate for our Problem Solving Instruction example. Our explanatory variable, type of instruction, takes three levels: Video, Lecture, and Control. We'll score the levels using dummy variables. Let's designate the Control instruction as the comparison level. We'll see shortly why that is a logical choice. As a result, we create two dummy variables, one for each of the other two explanatory levels. The first of these dummy variables, designated x_1, carries a code of 1 for the 10 observations at the Video instruction level and a code of 0 for the remaining 20 observations. The second dummy variable, x_2, carries a code of 1 for the 10 observations at the Lecture instruction level and 0s for the other 20. The 10 observations at the Control level are scored 0 on both x_1 and x_2. The definition of these two dummy variables is summarized in the following table:

	x_1	x_2
Video Instruction	1	0
Lecture Instruction	0	1
Control	0	0

Now we extend our linear model to include these two variables, each with its own multiplier or slope parameter:

$$\mu[y \mid xs] = \mu[y \mid x_1 = x_{i1}, x_2 = x_{i2}] = \beta_0 + \beta_1 x_{i1} + \beta_2 x_{i2}. \qquad \textbf{(6.7)}$$

This is the first linear model we've encountered with more than a single explanatory variable on the right-hand side. It is a *multiple linear model*. We'll learn in this chapter about multiple linear models where the *xs* are all dummy variables. In Chapter 7, we'll take up more general multiple linear models, where the multiple *xs* may be any numeric variables.

Multiple Dummy Variable Parameters

For our choice of dummy variables for the Problem Solving treatment levels, Equation [6.7] gives the following results:

$$\mu(Problem\ Solving \mid Video) = \mu[y \mid x_1 = 1, x_2 = 0] = \beta_0 + \beta_1,$$
$$\mu(Problem\ Solving \mid Lecture) = \mu[y \mid x_1 = 0, x_2 = 1] = \beta_0 + \beta_2,$$

and

$$\mu(Problem\ Solving \mid Control) = \mu[y \mid x_1 = 0, x_2 = 0] = \beta_0.$$

These results provide interpretations of the multiple dummy variable model parameters that are very *direct generalizations* of the interpretation of the parameters for the simple linear model with a single dummy variable.

- The intercept parameter, β_0, is the response mean at the comparison level.
- Each of the dummy variable slope parameters is the difference between the response mean at the level indexed by the dummy variable and at the comparison level.

We see now why choosing Control instruction to be the comparison level makes good sense. The two slope parameters are *directly interpretable* as the amount of improvement (relative to no instruction or to Control instruction) associated with the Video and Lecture instruction methods, respectively.

These interpretations of the intercept and slope parameters are not specific to this example. They hold true for any multiple linear model consisting of a set of dummy variables created by the rules specified above to "score" the levels of a categorical explanatory variable.

Estimation of Multiple Dummy Variable Parameters

Let's look at the results of using a statistical package regression command to estimate the linear model of Equation [6.7] for the Problem Solving example.

```
                        Response: ProbSolv
Column Name              Coeff   StErr  Pvalue        SS

    0 Constant           12.2    0.842   0.000     4838.7
    2 video               2.5    1.190   0.045       60.0
    3 lecture            -1.0    1.190   0.408        5.0

  df:27          RSq:0.254   s:2.662          RSS:191.3
```

Here the response observations are given by our Problem Solving scores (Response: ProbSolv) and we have as the two *xs* dummy variables coding the Video and Lecture treatment conditions, respectively. From the regression output above, we see that the intercept estimate, $\widehat{\beta}_0$, is the sample mean for the comparison level, M(*Problem Solving | Control*) = 12.2.

The dummy variable slopes are each estimated by the *increase* in sample response mean for the coded levels over the comparison level:

$$\widehat{\beta}_1 = M(Problem\ Solving\,|\,Video) - M(Problem\ Solving\,|\,Control)$$
$$= 14.70 - 12.20 = 2.50$$
$$\widehat{\beta}_2 = M(Problem\ Solving\,|\,Lecture) - M(Problem\ Solving\,|\,Control)$$
$$= 11.20 - 12.20 = -1.00.$$

The estimated "increase" for the Lecture over the Control treatment is negative. Problem Solving scores were poorer, on the average, for students in the Lecture condition.

Finally, the estimate of the standard deviation common to the three conditional response populations, s: 2.662 in the regression command output, is the square root of the conditional response variance estimate computed earlier: $\sqrt{7.085} = 2.662$.

CIs for Differences in Response Means

If our assumptions about the nature of the conditional response populations from which we have sampled are warranted, the slope and intercept estimates for the *multiple linear model*, like those for the simple linear model, have sampling distributions that

- have the true values of the population parameters as their expected values,
- have estimable SEs, and

- have theoretical histograms that are well approximated by the probability density for the t-random variable with $(N - k)$ degrees of freedom, where N is the number of observations in the sample and k is the number of parameters in the linear model.

The simple linear model has two parameters, β_0 and β_1, and estimates of these parameters have sampling distributions, as we have seen in earlier chapters, whose histograms we approximate with t-variate distribution with $(N - 2)$ d.f. The dummy variable full linear model for the categorical explanatory variable with k levels has k parameters—the intercept plus the slopes for the $(k - 1)$ dummy variables—and our estimates of those parameters each have sampling distributions whose histograms are well fit by the density functions for the t-variate with $(N - k)$ d.f.

In Chapter 5, we learned how to compute confidence intervals for parameters of linear models. Although we did this specifically for the slope parameter in the simple linear model, the logic and the computation are the same for any parameter with an estimate whose sampling distribution is a t-distribution centered at the true value of the parameter. As a result, we can write Equations [5.3] and [5.4] in this more general form:

$$\text{CI}[\beta_j, (1 - \alpha)100\%] = [\widehat{\beta_j} \pm t_{(N-k),(1-\alpha)}\text{SE}(\widehat{\beta_j})], \text{ for } j = 0, 1, \ldots, k - 1 \quad \textbf{(6.8)}$$

where $\widehat{\beta_j}$ is the estimate of β_j, one of the k parameters in a linear model. The multiplier $t_{(N-k),(1-\alpha)}$ is the absolute value of the pair of t-values that include the central $(1 - \alpha)100\%$ of the t-distribution with $(N - k)$ d.f., and $\text{SE}(\widehat{\beta_j})$ is the standard error of $\widehat{\beta_j}$, the estimated standard deviation of that estimate's sampling distribution.

Computation of the CI for a parameter depends upon knowledge of this standard error. In Chapter 7, we learn about the factors influencing the standard errors of slope estimates in multiple linear models. Here we will simply substitute our regression command's numeric solutions for these standard errors in Equation [6.8] to find CIs for the slope parameters in our dummy variable model for the effect of Instruction Level on Problem Solving.

The regression command output gave the SEs for the two slope estimates as

$$\text{SE}(\widehat{\beta_1}) = \text{SE}[\widehat{\mu}(Problem\ Solving\,|\,Video) - \widehat{\mu}(Problem\ Solving\,|\,Control)] = 1.190$$

and

$$\text{SE}(\widehat{\beta_2}) = \text{SE}[\widehat{\mu}(Problem\ Solving\,|\,Lecture) - \widehat{\mu}(Problem\ Solving\,|\,Control)]$$
$$= 1.190.$$

To compute 95% CIs for these differences in conditional means, we refer to the tabled values of the t-distribution with $(N - k) = (30 - 3) = 27$ d.f. :

Central Proportions of t-Distribution

d.f.	.80	.90	.95	.99
27	1.31	1.70	2.05	2.77

The appropriate t-multiplier is $t_{27,0.95} = 2.05$.

The 95% CI for the expected improvement in Problem Solving for the Video instruction is computed from Equation [6.8] as

$$\text{CI}\{[\mu(\textit{Problem Solving} \,|\, \textit{Video}) - \mu(\textit{Problem Solving} \,|\, \textit{Control})], 95\%\}$$
$$= 2.50 \pm (2.05)(1.19) = [0.06, 4.94].$$

We are 95% confident, on the basis of our sample of $N = 30$ observations, that the Video instruction results in better Problem Solving performance than no instruction at all. The amount of improvement, however, *may be quite small* as attested to by the size of the lower bound of this 95% CI.

By way of contrast, the 95% CI for the difference in means for the Lecture and Control levels of instruction,

$$\text{CI}\{[\mu(\textit{Problem Solving} \,|\, \textit{Lecture}) - \mu(\textit{Problem Solving} \,|\, \textit{Control})], 95\%\}$$
$$= -1.00 \pm 2.44 = [-3.44, 1.44],$$

tells us that we cannot conclude that Lecture instruction is either better or worse than no instruction in Problem Solving. The CI includes zero.

Full, Null, and Constrained Dummy Variable Models

Our full model for the multilevel categorical variable is that the response means may be different at each of the levels. The use of a set of dummy variables in a multiple linear model provides a way of presenting that full model in terms of a set of linear parameters, the number of linear parameters being equal to the number of levels of the categorical variable.

For our three levels of Problem Solving instruction, the relation between the three linear parameters of the full, dummy variable model and the three conditional response means is summarized by the following three equations:

$$\mu(\textit{Problem Solving} \,|\, \textit{Video}) = \mu[y \,|\, x_1 = 1, x_2 = 0] = \beta_0 + \beta_1,$$
$$\mu(\textit{Problem Solving} \,|\, \textit{Lecture}) = \mu[y \,|\, x_1 = 0, x_2 = 1] = \beta_0 + \beta_2,$$

and

$$\mu(\textit{Problem Solving} \,|\, \textit{Control}) = \mu[y \,|\, x_1 = 0, x_2 = 0] = \beta_0.$$

Substantively, the *null model* states the belief that the levels of the explanatory variable have no differential impact on the response mean, that the several conditional means *all take the same value*. In terms of the three equations just given, what condition or conditions would we need to place on the full-model parameters to arrive at the null model? The three equations would all be equal to β_0 on the right-hand side if $\beta_1 = 0$ *and* $\beta_2 = 0$. To conclude that the full model is no better than the null model, we would have to conclude that *both slope parameters* could be equal to zero.

In the case of the simple linear model, the full and null models were separated only by the presence of one additional parameter in the full model. Comparison of the two models was then made on the basis of the CI for that additional parameter. Where, as in the present example, the null and full models differ by more than a single parameter, we use in place of the CI a special inferential statistic called the F-ratio to make the comparison. In Chapter 7, we learn about the use of this statistic.

We can defer learning about the *F*-ratio because, in terms of model comparisons, the educational psychologist's interest in the Problem Solving Instruction study did not lie in comparing a full and null model. She was not asking, "Are both Video and Lecture instructions ineffective in improving Problem Solving Performance?" Rather, she was asking whether Video instruction improved Problem Solving performance *and* whether Lecture instruction improved Problem Solving performance. Those two questions imply model comparisons, but not full model v. null model.

We have already seen that the question of whether Video instruction improves Problem Solving performance (over that following no instruction) is assessed by constructing an appropriate CI for β_1, the slope parameter for the the dummy variable coding the Video observations. We conclude either that β_1 could be zero or that it could not. To conclude that the slope parameter could be zero is the same as concluding that the full model,

$$\mu(Problem\ Solving \mid Instruction\ Level) = \beta_0 + \beta_1 x_{i1} + \beta_2 x_{i2},$$

is no better than the model,

$$\mu(Problem\ Solving \mid Instruction\ Level) = \beta_0 + 0 x_{i1} + \beta_2 x_{i2} = \beta_0 + \beta_2 x_{i2},$$

in which β_1 is *constrained* to be 0.

Since we found that zero was outside the 95% CI for β_1, we can conclude that the slope parameter could not be zero and, hence, that the full model is better than this constrained model.

However, when we compared our full model against a second constrained model,

$$\mu(Problem\ Solving \mid Instruction\ Level) = \beta_0 + \beta_1 x_{i1} + 0 x_{i2} = \beta_0 + \beta_1 x_{i1},$$

now with β_2 *constrained* to be zero, we found that the full model was no better than the constrained one. Here, zero was within our 95% CI for β_2.

As a result of these two model comparisons, we can conclude that the best model is this second constrained one which provides a different estimate of the population mean for Video instruction,

$$\mu(Problem\ Solving \mid Video) = \beta_0 + \beta_1 1 = \beta_0 + \beta_1,$$

than it does for Lecture or Control instructions:

$$\mu(Problem\ Solving \mid Lecture) = \beta_0 + \beta_1 0 = \beta_0,$$
$$\mu(Problem\ Solving \mid Control) = \beta_0 + \beta_1 0 = \beta_0.$$

Video, but not Lecture, instruction makes a difference and the magnitude of the difference is given by the CI for the Video dummy variable slope parameter, β_1.

We have let the comparison models emerge here from the interpretations we place on the possible results for slope CIs. Beginning with the next chapter, we will phrase our alternate models explicitly before making the model comparisons.

In this section, we have seen our first examples of *constrained models*, models which are the result of imposing on the parameters of the full model some, but not all, of the constraints necessary to produce the null model. We'll see in the chapters ahead that constrained models generally hold more interest for us than do either full or null models. This is because they are more specific about what explains the response—they say something other than "everything works" or "nothing works."

6.6.4   Alternative Scoring of the Categorical Explanatory Variable

The use of dummy variables is but one way of scoring the levels of the categorical explanatory variable so as to produce a linear model. It is particularly appropriate where one of the levels provides a natural comparison. In Chapter 8, we will explore two alternate ways of scoring the levels that can lead to more easily interpreted model parameters in certain kinds of studies. At that point, we will emphasize the importance to our choice of scoring of the constrained models we have in mind for the data.

6.6.5   One-way Analysis of Variance

Earlier in this chapter, we noted that the use of a single dummy variable to code the two-level variable led to linear model comparisons that are the same as the two independent groups *t*-test. When we expand our full linear model, as we have here, to include dummy variables for an explanatory variable with more than two levels, the subsequent comparison of that full model with the null and constrained models bears a close resemblance to what is elsewhere called the *one-way analysis of variance* (ANOVA). The full model v. null model comparison, developed in the next chapter, corresponds to the "overall" test of treatment effects in the ANOVA, while comparisons of the full and constrained models correspond to specific between treatments comparisons in the ANOVA.

The ANOVA, like the *t*-test, stresses testing hypotheses about means in conditional response populations. In our linear model approach to these same data, we will emphasize the estimation of the magnitudes of the differences among those conditional response population means. In later chapters, we explore, from a linear modeling perspective, a variety of ANOVA topics.

6.7
The Explanatory Variable with Ordered Categories

Chapters 3 through 5 provided a set of working tools for models with a single measured explanatory variable. The same has been accomplished in this chapter for the explanatory categories that are essentially *nominal*. What about models with a categorical explanatory variable possessing *well-ordered* categories? How do we work with these models?

The *ordered categorical variable* poses a challenge for statisticians. It has proven difficult to develop easy, widely applicable techniques that take advantage of the ordered nature of categories without assuming, at the same time, some unit of measurement underlying the order. In practice, we must choose between considering the ordinal explanatory variable as like a nominal set of categories or like a measured variable.

We suggest treating the ordinal more as a nominal variable. This means that the full and null models will look the same for ordinal and for nominal explanatory variables. However, the constrained models for the ordinal variable—our rival explanatory models—are very likely to take the ordering of levels explicitly into account.

Let's look at an example:

- What is the influence of social class on health behaviors? A random sample of males, aged 50 and employed in London, are queried about their lifestyles. Among the questions asked is one that elicits the total number of years, to date, during which each man smoked. On the basis of their occupations, the men are assigned to different social classes: I, II, IIIa, IIIb, IV, and V. Classes I and II include professionals and managers, classes IIIa and IIIb skilled clerical and manual workers, and classes IV and V the semiskilled and unskilled.

The full model for this study would specify different means for the six conditional populations of years of smoking—one population for each social-class strata of employed 50-year-old London males. The null model, of course, would postulate equal means for the six populations.

What are some constrained models that take the ordering of the social classes into account? Here are two examples. We might hypothesize that the response mean might be the *same for certain adjacent categories*. For example, a constrained model might propose that the mean number of smoking years is the same for social classes I and II. Or, our model might suggest that the difference in response means is *less between adjacent social classes* IIIb and IV than it is between the adjacent IV and V.

Both of these constraints take advantage of the classes being ordered. In Chapter 8, we will see how models involving constraints such as these can be evaluated.

To treat our ordinal explanatory variable more as a measured variable, we can assign scores or weights to the ordered categories, scores that reflect the ordering. Thus, we could score the six social classes on a single measured x, using the numbers 1, 2, 3, 4, 5, and 6 in place of the class "names" I, II, IIIa, IIIb, IV, and V. Unfortunately, these scores not only capture the order of the classes but also say something—perhaps unintended—about the "distances" between the groups. In this instance, each pair of adjacent categories differs by a constant amount, one unit on the x scale. Other scoring choices—for example, 1, 3, 7, 10, 13, 18—would also be faithful to the class ordering but say something very different about distances between classes.

If we know only that the classes are ordered, we don't know how such a set of scores should be chosen. Because of this indeterminacy, we prefer to treat the ordinal explanatory variable as a special case of the nominal variable.

6.8
Summary

In this chapter, we encountered our first multiple explanatory variable models. These arose as a result of our need to code the levels of a categorical explanatory variable. We did this with a set of dummy variables, taking values of 0 and 1.

Exercises

1   Below are the times (in seconds) taken by 14 individuals to perform a simple task. Task performance was assessed under four different circumstances: A—normal, quiet conditions; B—intermittent pneumatic drill in background; C—people conversing in background; and D—pop music playing in the background.

Choose one of the conditions as a comparison "level" and develop a model with dummy variables for the remaining conditions. How many and which of the conditions influence the response, that is, time to complete the task, differently from your chosen comparison level?

A	B	C	D
65	65	67	68
55	71	70	63
58	64	75	66
52	66		

2   Below are data on the survival of batches of insects exposed to six different insecticides. Each batch consisted of 50 insects, and the numbers are of those still alive after a fixed exposure time. Each column corresponds to a different insecticide. Each row corresponds to an independent trial of the experiment and shows the numbers (each out of 50) surviving exposure to each of the insecticides.

Develop 95% confidence intervals for the survival numbers for each insecticide. Do you find evidence that one (or more) insecticide is superior to the others?

10	11	0	3	3	11
7	17	1	5	5	9
20	21	7	12	3	15
14	11	2	6	5	22
14	16	3	4	3	15
12	14	1	3	6	16
10	17	2	5	1	13
23	17	1	5	1	10
17	19	3	5	3	26
20	21	0	5	2	26
14	7	1	2	6	24
13	13	4	4	4	13

3   Below are data on a blood component assessed for samples of normal and diabetic mice. Column 1 gives the data for normal mice, column 2 for diabetic mice receiving a drug (Alloxan), and column 3 for diabetic mice receiving Alloxan plus insulin. From a model using the normal mice as a control group, assess the departures of the means of the response variable for the two Alloxan groups.

Normals	Alloxan	Alloxan+insulin
156	391	82
282	46	100
197	469	98
297	86	150
116	174	243
127	133	68
119	13	228
29	499	131
253	168	73
122	62	18
349	127	20
110	276	100
143	176	72
64	146	133
26	108	465
86	276	40
122	50	46
455	73	34
655	*	44
14	*	*

7

Several Explanatory Variables: Multiple Regression

In Chapter 6, we introduced, in the context of dummy variable scoring, a linear model with more than one explanatory variable (multiple x-variables). Our interpretation of model parameters was specific to the dichotomous, 0 or 1, scoring of those dummy variables. In this chapter, we develop, more generally, the ideas of *multiple linear regression*.

We begin by extending our earlier model of adolescent height as a function of infant height to a multiple-x model by introducing a second explanatory variable, infant weight. This provides a vehicle for extending as well the Chapters 3–5 ideas about linear models and their parameters. Parameter estimates, our confidence in those estimates, and our inferences about model parameters will take almost the same form for multi-x linear models as they did for simple linear regression. The keys to the linkage of the simple and multiple linear regression models are contained in the ideas of *partial variables*, *partial correlation*, and *multiple correlation*, introduced here.

7.1
Growth Study: A Second Explanatory Variable

In Chapters 3–5, we examined the importance of height of boys at age 2 in determining height at age 18. Our linear model,

$$\mu(ht18 \mid ht2) = \beta_0 + \beta_1 ht2$$

expressed the idea that the height *predicted* for 18 years of age was likely to be influenced by a boy's height at 2 years of age. Specifically, the model states that the mean response—average age-18 height—is a *linear function* of the score on an explanatory variable—age-2 height. Based on a sample of 28 boys, we concluded that boys who differed in height at age 2 by 1 cm could be expected at 18 years to differ in height by about 1.6 cm (i.e., we estimated the slope of the regression line to be $\widehat{\beta}_1 = 1.585$cm/cm).

Height at age 2 is likely to be only one influence on height in late adolescence. In modeling growth in stature, we may want to evaluate the importance of infant height alongside that of other explanatory variables. We may believe, for example, that an infant's weight—as well as height—provides information about how tall we expect him to be as an adolescent. That is, we want a model of adolescent height that reflects *both sources of influence*, infant height and infant weight.

In developing a model with two explanatory variables, we'll want to do so in a way that allows us to compare that model with the one that includes only one of those variables. That is, an important question to be answered in modeling with two (or more) sources of explanation is whether we have better models when we add sources. Do we increase our certainty about adolescent height when we take *both* infant height and weight into account beyond that achieved when we take only infant height into account? The approach to linear modeling described in the next section facilitates this model comparison.

7.2
A Linear Model for Two Explanatory Variables

To insure that we can compare our two-variable model with the single variable linear model, we develop our new model using the same ideas outlined in Chapters 2 and 3.

7.2.1   Conditional Response Populations

Our simple linear regression model had its origins in the idea of *conditional response populations*. That is, we started in Chapter 2 with the notion that the heights of 18-year-old boys could be divided into separate populations, conditional upon the boys' heights when 2 years old. For example, there were *separate populations* of *ht18* scores for boys who, at 2 years of age, stood 85.0-cm, 86.0-cm, and 87.0-cm tall. We denoted these three conditional response populations $(ht18 \mid ht2 = 85.0 \text{ cm})$, $(ht18 \mid ht2 = 86.0 \text{ cm})$, and $(ht18 \mid ht2 = 87.0 \text{ cm})$.

The Chapter 2 idea of conditional response populations was that there was a separate population of response observations, real or hypothetical, for each explanatory variable score of interest to us. The conditional response population notion generalizes, however. We can just as easily imagine populations of response scores *conditional on the values of two variables*. Now, there is one population of *ht18* scores for boys who at 2 years had heights of 85.0 cm and weights of 11.0 kg,

$$\mu(ht18 \mid ht2 = 85.0 \text{ cm}, wt2 = 11.0 \text{ kg});$$

there is another for those who were 85.0 cm tall and weighed 12.0 kg,

$$\mu(ht18 \mid ht2 = 85.0 \text{ cm}, wt2 = 12.0 \text{ kg});$$

and there is a third for those with heights and weights at 2 years old of 86.0 cm and 11.0 kg, respectively,

$$\mu(ht18 \mid ht2 = 86.0 \text{ cm}, wt2 = 11.0 \text{ kg}).$$

In general, there is a separate, conditional response population for *each pattern of explanatory variable scores* that appears in a study:

$$[y \mid x_1 = x_{i1}, x_2 = x_{i2}].$$

Figure 7.1 illustrates response populations conditional upon the values of two variables. Notice that a conditional response population need not be postulated for every combination of scores on the two variables, only for those that are of interest to a study. Thus, Figure 7.1 does not show (conditional) populations of age-18 heights for those who, at age 2, would have been either "exceptionally" tall for their weights (88 or 89 cm with a weight of 11 kg) or "exceptionally" heavy for their heights (14 kg with a height of 85 or 86 cm).

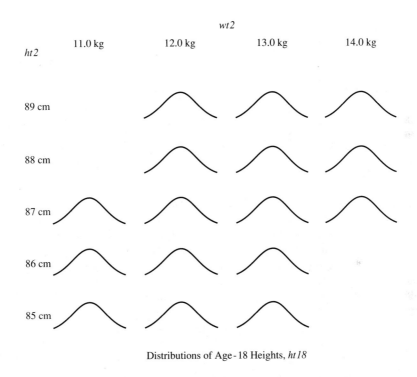

FIGURE 7.1
Conditional Response Populations and Design Points

Distributions of Age-18 Heights, *ht18*

If the study is *experimental*, the variable patterns will be those chosen by the researcher. If the study is *observational*, the score patterns may be the result of sampling. In either case, each distinct pattern of explanatory scores is referred to as a *design point* for the study.

Conditional Response Mean

The conditional response population at each design point has a mean,

$$\mu[y \,|\, x_1 = x_{i1}, x_2 = x_{i2}]$$

or

$$\mu[ht18 \,|\, ht2 = x_{i1}, wt2 = x_{i2}].$$

This last mean is the value of *ht18* we might predict if we were to anticipate the result of a draw at random from the population of heights of 18-year-old boys who, at 2 years, were x_{i1}-cm tall and weighed x_{i2} kg.

Conditional Response Variance

The variance in the conditional response population,

$$\sigma^2[y \mid x_1 = x_{i1}, x_2 = x_{i2}]$$

or

$$\sigma^2[ht18 \mid ht2 = x_{i1}, wt2 = x_{i2}],$$

reflects the certainty of this prediction. The smaller the conditional response variance, the more certain we are that the randomly chosen response will be close to our prediction, the mean in that population.

We earlier said that a model was a good model if it *increased our certainty* about the value of the response. The good model, one that helps to explain the response, yields conditional response means that differ from design point to design point, that are not all the same.

7.2.2 Multiple Regression Models

A natural form of explanatory model for the measured explanatory and response variables is one in which the means of the conditional response populations are postulated to be related *systematically* to the design point values. Such models are called *regression* models.

If there is but one numeric explanatory variable, $\mu(y \mid x = x_i) = g(x_i)$, we have a *simple regression* model. If there are two (or more) numeric xs, $\mu[y \mid x_1 = x_{i1}, x_2 = x_{i2}] = g(x_{i1}, x_{i2})$, it is a *multiple regression* model.

7.2.3 Multiple Linear Regression Models

Our substantive interest in the variables usually extends to the *form of the regression* relation. For simple regression models, as we noted in Chapter 4, it is very convenient to start with a regression that is *linear*, so that the relation between y and x can be expressed as

$$\mu(y \mid x = x_i) = \beta_0 + \beta_1 x_i. \tag{3.2}$$

A linear model is an equally convenient starting point when there are two explanatory sources. We write it as

$$\mu[y \mid x_1 = x_{i1}, x_2 = x_{i2}] = \beta_0 + \beta_1 x_{i1} + \beta_2 x_{i2}. \tag{6.7}$$

The equation is no longer that for a straight line but is described as *linear* because the equation's constants or parameters (the βs) are either additive constants (β_0)

or multipliers of explanatory variables (β_1 and β_2). The equation is linear in its parameters.

The linear model for a single x has been extended to one with two xs by adding the second x, with its own slope parameter, to the simple regression model. We see in the next section why we refer to β_1 and β_2 as slope parameters.

Equation [6.7] was introduced in Chapter 6 where x_1 and x_2 were both dummy variables, taking only values of 0 and 1. Now, in the multiple linear regression model, we are going to let the xs be any numeric variables possessing an interpretable unit of measurement. Extended in this way, Equation [6.7] permits us to construct and compare explanatory models for a very wide variety of empirical studies. We see only a bit of this range in this chapter but a great deal more in Chapters 8 and 11 through 14.

7.2.4 Interpreting the Multiple Linear Model Parameters

The three parameters of our linear model, Equation [6.7], have substantive interpretations quite similar to those of the intercept and slope for the simple linear model.

Additive Constant

We continue to refer to the additive constant, β_0, as an *intercept*. It is the response mean when *both* xs take the value of 0:

$$\mu[y \,|\, x_1 = 0, x_2 = 0] = \beta_0 + \beta_1 0 + \beta_2 0 = \beta_0. \qquad \text{(7.1)}$$

As with single x models, the intercept is interpretable only when 0 is in our range of interest, now for *each of the xs*. Thus, it had a very reasonable interpretation in Chapter 6 for the dummy variable linear model. By contrast, the intercept for Equation [7.1] for our Growth Study is not very illuminating:

$$\mu[ht18 \,|\, ht2 = 0, wt2 = 0] = \beta_0.$$

Multiplicative Constants

The multiplicative parameters in the multiple linear model are referred to as *slopes*, though their interpretation is a bit different from that given the single slope parameter in the simple model. The slope interpretation is better understood if we organize the terms on the right-hand side of Equation [6.7] and rewrite it first as

$$\mu[y \,|\, x_1 = x_{i1}, x_2 = x_{i2}] = [\beta_0 + \beta_2 x_{i2}] + \beta_1 x_{i1} \qquad \text{(7.2)}$$

and then as

$$\mu[y \,|\, x_1 = x_{i1}, x_2 = x_{i2}] = [\beta_0 + \beta_1 x_{i1}] + \beta_2 x_{i2}. \qquad \text{(7.3)}$$

Adding the square brackets prompts us to see each of the resulting Equations [7.2] and [7.3] as an equation for a series of straight lines.

This interpretation is made graphic in Figure 7.2. The top half of the figure shows, for the Growth Study, three lines based on Equation [7.2],

$$\mu[ht18 \mid ht2 = ht2_i, wt2 = wt2_i] = [\beta_0 + \beta_2 wt2_i] + \beta_1 ht2_i,$$

and the bottom half of the figure illustrates three lines obtained from Equation [7.3],

$$\mu[ht18 \mid ht2 = ht2_i, wt2 = wt2_i] = [\beta_0 + \beta_1 ht2_i] + \beta_2 wt2_i.$$

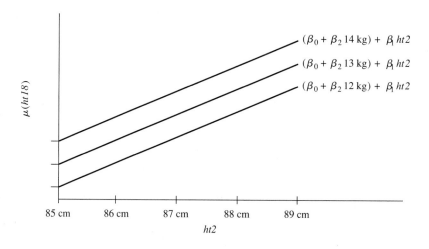

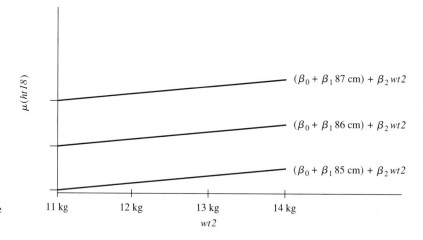

FIGURE 7.2
Illustrating the
Interpretation of the
Slope Parameters

The lines in the top of the figure describe the influence of *ht2* on $\mu(ht18)$ at three different levels of *wt2*. The *lines are parallel* to one another, having the same slope, and there is a separate line for each value of the second *x*, *wt2*. The slope common to the lines in the top half of Figure 7.2 is β_1, the multiplicative parameter for *ht2*. The intercepts for the lines differ, being a function of the three different values of *wt2*.

Thus, β_1 is the increase in $\mu(ht18)$ associated with a one-unit (one-cm) increase in *ht2 provided that* the value of *wt2 remains constant*. For example, β_1 is the amount by which we expect the age-18 heights of two 12-kg 2 year olds to differ if one stands 85-cm tall and the other 86-cm tall.

Similarly, the lower three lines in Figure 7.2 also have a *common slope*. Each describes the influence of *wt2* on $\mu(ht18)$ at a particular level of *ht2*. The slope to each line in this second set is β_2. We interpret this slope as the increase in $\mu(ht18)$ as *wt2* increases by one unit (one kg) and *ht2* remains fixed. Thus, a pair of 85-cm 2 year olds weighing 11 and 12 kg, respectively, can be expected to differ in their heights at age 18 by β_2.

The multiplicative constants have a *conditional* interpretation in multiple linear models. Each tells us the magnitude of the influence of one *x* on $\mu(y)$ when the other *x*s are *held constant*. As a result, before giving this interpretation to the multiplicative constant, we must ask whether it makes sense for the value of one *x* to remain constant while the value of a second is changing. Three examples will make the point.

If the *x* values can be chosen or manipulated independently by the experimenter, then the multiplicative constants can safely be given the "expected increase in response" interpretation. For example, an experimenter measures the number of seconds it takes 11 year olds to read a prose passage (*nsecs*) when both the number of words making up the prose passage (*nwords*) and the number of characters (*nchars*) appearing on each line of the printed passage are varied. The *y*-variate is *nsecs* and the two *x*-variates *nwords* and *nchars*.

It is easy enough for us to imagine a prose passage of 250 words printed either with 60 characters per line or with 80 characters per line. Similarly, we can imagine passages of 100 and 200 words, each printed with 75 characters per line. The value of either of the *x*s can be changed while that of the other remains fixed. As a result, the multiplicative constants in the linear model,

$$\mu(nsecs \mid nwords_i, nchars_i) = \beta_0 + \beta_1 nwords_i + \beta_2 nchars_i,$$

justify our "expected increase" interpretation:

- β_1: The expected increase in the number of seconds required to read a prose passage when that passage is increased in length by one word and when the length of the lines in which the passage is printed is kept constant.

- β_2: The expected increase in the number of seconds required to read a prose passage of fixed total length when the length of the lines in which the passage is printed is increased by one character.

However, we also can think of situations in which the value of one *x cannot change* while that of a second remains constant. For example, a researcher may be interested in representing the influence of number of older siblings (*nsibs*) on the number of hours female college students spend in athletic activities during a typical week (*hrsath*) with the following linear model:

$$\mu(hrsath \mid nsibs_i, nsibs_i^2) = \beta_0 + \beta_1 nsibs_i + \beta_2 nsibs_i^2.$$

Here, the two xs are the number of older sibs and the *square* of the number of older sibs. We cannot imagine how the value of one of these xs can change without the other being affected, so an "expected increase in y" interpretation of either β_1 or β_2 would not be sensible. In Chapters 10 and 13, we will see how the multiplicative parameters for models such as this can be given an alternative interpretation.

Many models fall between these two examples. The two xs may not be independent of one another nor may the value of one be completely determined by the value of the other. The Growth Study is a good example. We know that the heights and weights of 2 year olds are not unrelated. Taller infants tend to weigh more than shorter ones. At the same time, not all infants of 87-cm stature have identical weights. There is a certain amount of weight variability among infants of any given height.

The key to the interpretability of the multiplicative parameters for xs that are not independent of one another is whether there is sufficient variability in the one x at each level of the other to support the interpretation. Is there enough variability in weight among infants, all of whom are 87-cm tall, to make it sensible to talk about the influence on expected adolescent height of a 1-kg difference in weight?

This variability in one x at a level of a second x is not unlike the conditional variance we associate with y. We reserve the term *conditional*, though, to refer to y and in the following section we introduce the term *partial* to describe this x variability. In general, the stronger the correlation between the two xs, the smaller the partial variability and the less tenable the standard interpretation of the slope parameters.

7.3
Parameter Estimates for the Two-Variable Model

The linear model,

$$\mu[y \mid x_1 = x_{i1}, x_2 = x_{i2}] = \beta_0 + \beta_1 x_{i1} + \beta_2 x_{i2}, \qquad \text{(6.7)}$$

refers to conditional populations of responses or y scores. The βs are population parameters. So, too, is the conditional response variance, $\sigma^2[y \mid x_1 = x_{i1}, x_2 = x_{i2}]$. If we are to interpret our model and to compare it with other models, we must be able to *estimate* these unknown parameters from a sample of observations from the conditional response populations. Furthermore, these estimates must be well enough behaved that they allow us to make inferences about the parameters. The estimates we describe in this section are of this kind. They are also very similar to those developed earlier for the simple linear model.

7.3.1   Assumptions

To obtain inference-supporting estimates of the multiple linear model parameters, we make the same assumptions about the conditional response populations and our sampling that we made for the simple linear model:

- the N response observations making up the sample are obtained independently,
- each conditional response population has a histogram with Normal modality, skewness, and kurtosis characteristics, and
- each conditional response population has the same variance.

This common conditional response variance is expressed as $\sigma^2[y \mid x_1, x_2]$.

7.3.2   Partial Explanatory Variables

Before describing the estimators of our multiple linear model parameters and their characteristics, we will first consider the notion of a *partial explanatory variable*.

In the sample of N observations, our two xs have sample means and standard deviations of

$$M[x_1], \quad M[x_2], \quad SD[x_1], \quad \text{and} \quad SD[x_2]$$

and a sample correlation of

$$r[x_1, x_2].$$

If the correlation between the two xs is not 0, their values are not independent in the sample. There is some linear interdependence between the two. The closer the correlation is to 1.0 (or to -1.0 if the two xs are negatively related), the stronger is this interdependence.

The idea of a *partial explanatory variable* is that it is the result of "partialing" from one x its dependence upon a second x. The linear dependence of x_1 on x_2 can be partialed from x_1 by subtracting from each x_1 score a certain linear function of the corresponding x_2 score:

$$x_{(1.2)i} = x_{1i} - [a + bx_{2i}], \tag{7.4}$$

where the constants of that linear function are defined as

$$b = r[x_1, x_2] \left\{ \frac{SD[x_1]}{SD[x_2]} \right\} \tag{7.5}$$

and

$$a = M[x_1] - b \ M[x_2]. \tag{7.6}$$

Technically, it is the *linear dependence* of x_1 on x_2 that is partialed out. That is, in Equation [7.4], a linear function of x_2 is subtracted from x_1.

For our purposes, it will not be necessary to calculate actual scores for a partial variable. We need only an understanding of the properties of the partial explanatory variable.

The first property provides evidence that the linear dependence has been partialed out. The partial variable, $x_{(1.2)}$, will be uncorrelated with x_2,

$$r[x_{(1.2)}, x_2] = 0.0.$$

There is no linear dependence of $x_{(1.2)}$ upon x_2.

We can also partial *from* x_2 its linear dependence upon x_1. This second partial x is defined by

$$x_{(2.1)i} = x_{2i} - [c + d\,x_{1i}],$$

where the constants for the linear adjustment are

$$d = r[x_1, x_2]\left\{\frac{SD[x_2]}{SD[x_1]}\right\}$$

and

$$c = M[x_2] - d\,M[x_1].$$

Because $x_{(2.1)}$ has its linear dependence on x_1 partialed out, it will be uncorrelated with x_1:

$$r[x_{(2.1)}, x_1] = 0.0.$$

As a second property the partial xs have means of 0,

$$M[x_{(1.2)}] = M[x_{(2.1)}] = 0.0,$$

and standard deviations that reflect the effect of partialing out any linear dependency,

$$SD[x_{(1.2)}] = SD[x_1]\sqrt{1 - r[x_1, x_2]^2} \tag{7.7}$$

and

$$SD[x_{(2.1)}] = SD[x_2]\sqrt{1 - r[x_1, x_2]^2}. \tag{7.8}$$

On the right-hand side of Equation [7.7], the standard deviation of x_1 is multiplied by a term,

$$\sqrt{1 - r[x_1, x_2]^2},$$

which takes values between 0 and 1, depending on the value of the correlation between the two xs. The SD of the partial x is nearly as large as the SD of the original x if the correlation is quite close to 0. On the other hand, the SD of the partial x can be very close to 0 if the correlation between xs is very large.

Loosely speaking, the SDs of these partial xs describe the variability referred to in Section 7.2.4, the variability of one x at a particular level of the other. That is, we can think of

$$SD[wt2.ht2] = SD(wt2)\sqrt{1 - r(ht2, wt2)^2}$$

as the SD of weights among 2-year-old boys, all of the same height. If the correlation between heights and weights is at all large, this partial SD may be appreciably smaller than the overall SD for age-2 weights, $SD(wt2)$.

7.3.3   Estimates of Multiple Linear Model Parameters

We use the notion of partial explanatory variables to present the estimates of the parameters for the multiple linear model.

Estimates of Slope Parameters

Our best estimates of the two slope parameters can be expressed as

$$\widehat{\beta}_1 = r[y, x_{(1.2)}] \left\{ \frac{SD[y]}{SD[x_{(1.2)}]} \right\}$$

and

$$\widehat{\beta}_2 = r[y, x_{(2.1)}] \left\{ \frac{SD[y]}{SD[x_{(2.1)}]} \right\}. \tag{7.9}$$

These estimates have the *same form* as the single-slope estimate in the simple linear model,

$$\widehat{\beta}_1 = r[y, x] \left\{ \frac{SD[y]}{SD[x]} \right\}. \tag{4.1}$$

The correlation between x and y is multiplied by the ratio of the SDs of y and x. In Equation [7.9], however, each of the two xs is replaced by its *partial x*.

When the two xs are *uncorrelated* over the N sample points, the two-slope estimates simplify to

$$\widehat{\beta}_1 = r[y, x_1] \left\{ \frac{SD[y]}{SD[x_1]} \right\}$$

and

$$\widehat{\beta}_2 = r[y, x_2] \left\{ \frac{SD[y]}{SD[x_2]} \right\}.$$

These results exactly parallel the slope estimate for the single x.

Estimate of the Intercept Parameter

For the simple linear model, the intercept had as its estimate

$$\widehat{\beta}_0 = M(y) - \widehat{\beta}_1 M(x). \tag{4.2}$$

The intercept estimate for the multiple linear model is a straightforward generalization of this:

$$\widehat{\beta}_0 = M(y) - \widehat{\beta}_1 M(x_1) - \widehat{\beta}_2 M[x_2]. \tag{7.10}$$

Estimate of Conditional Response Means

The linear model equation,

$$\mu[y \mid x_1 = x_{i1}, x_2 = x_{i2}] = \beta_0 + \beta_1 x_{i1} + \beta_2 x_{i2}, \tag{6.7}$$

links the means of the conditional response populations with the values of the two xs. Substituting estimates of the βs for these unknown parameters in Equation [6.7] provides an equation for estimating these conditional means:

$$\widehat{\mu}[y \mid x_1 = x_{i1}, x_2 = x_{i2}] = \widehat{\beta}_0 + \widehat{\beta}_1 x_{i1} + \widehat{\beta}_2 x_{i2}. \tag{7.11}$$

If we substitute for $\widehat{\beta}_0$ from Equation [7.10], the estimated conditional means can also be expressed as

$$\widehat{\mu}[y \mid x_1 = x_{i1}, x_2 = x_{i2}] = M(y) + \widehat{\beta}_1[x_{i1} - M(x_1)] + \widehat{\beta}_2[x_{i2} - M(x_2)].$$

We can see that the estimate of the response mean on the left side of this equation, equals the sample y mean when both xs equal their sample mean values. This result represents a generalization of the Chapter 4 finding that the estimate of the simple regression line passes through the point of means, the intersection of the sample means of the explanatory and response variables.

Estimate of the Unconditional Response Variance

Our estimate of the unconditional response variance, for those observational studies in which such an estimate is warranted, is the same for the multiple linear model as it was for the models of Chapters 3–6. Indeed, since the unconditional response variance is the variance in the population of responses grouped together without regard to *any* x, however many we might be interested in, it will always be estimated by

$$\widehat{\sigma}^2(y) = \frac{\sum_{i=1}^{N}[y_i - M(y)]^2}{N - 1}. \qquad \textbf{(4.9)}$$

It is the "average" of the squared deviations of the sample response observations from the estimated mean of the unconditional response population, the population from which we assume the observations are drawn when the "null" model is the correct one.

Estimate of the Conditional Response Variance

Our model estimation assumes that there is a common variance for the several conditional response populations. Our estimate is again an "average" of the squared deviations of the response observations from the estimated means of the populations from which they were sampled. The estimated conditional means, though, are those obtained from Equation [7.11]. The result is

$$\widehat{\sigma}^2[y \mid x_1, x_2] = \frac{\sum_{i=1}^{N}[y_i - (\widehat{\beta}_0 + \widehat{\beta}_1 x_{i1} + \widehat{\beta}_2 x_{i2})]^2}{N - 3}. \qquad \textbf{(7.12)}$$

Equation [7.12] is of the same form as that for the estimated conditional variance in the simple linear model. It differs in that there are now three parameters, β_0, β_1, and β_2, that first must be estimated before the deviances about the estimated means can be computed. As a result, N must be reduced in the denominator by 3.

Model Residuals

Our multiple linear regression model,

$$\mu[y \,|\, x_1 = x_{i1}, x_2 = x_{i2}] = \beta_0 + \beta_1 x_{i1} + \beta_2 x_{i2}, \tag{6.7}$$

expresses the relationship between the mean of a conditional response population and the values of the *x*s. The individual *response observation*, y_i, can be thought of as the sum of the mean of the conditional population from which it was drawn *and* a deviation from that mean. This deviation from the mean,

$$\epsilon_i = y_i - \mu[y \,|\, x_1 = x_{i1}, x_2 = x_{i2}] = y_i - (\beta_0 + \beta_1 x_{i1} + \beta_2 x_{i2}), \tag{7.13}$$

is referred to as an "error." It is the error made in predicting that the value of the *i*th response observation will equal the mean of the population from which it is drawn. If the conditional response variance is small, the ϵs will be close to 0.

If we substitute estimates for the unknown means or βs on the right-hand side of Equation [7.13], we have an estimated error or *residual* on the left-hand side:

$$\widehat{\epsilon}_i = y_i - \widehat{\mu}[y \,|\, x_1 = x_{i1}, x_2 = x_{i2}] = y_i - (\widehat{\beta}_0 + \widehat{\beta}_1 x_{i1} + \widehat{\beta}_2 x_{i2}). \tag{7.14}$$

With the residual defined as the difference between a response observation and the estimate of its mean, it is convenient to define the estimated conditional response variance, from Equation [7.12], in terms of the sum of the squares of these residuals:

$$\widehat{\sigma}^2[y \,|\, x_1, x_2] = \frac{\sum\limits_{i=1}^{N} \widehat{\epsilon}_i^2}{N - 3}. \tag{7.15}$$

Estimates for the Growth Study

Let's look at what we've developed so far in this chapter in the context of our Growth Study. Table 7.1 reports weights (in kg) at 2 years of age, the explanatory variable *wt2*, as well as the two sets of heights for the sample of 28 boys studied in earlier chapters. Mean weight in the sample was M(*wt2*) = 13.5 kg and the standard deviation of the 28 observations was SD(*wt2*) = 1.57 kg.

The sample means, variances, standard deviations, and correlations for all three variables are given at the bottom of Table 7.1.

We'll use this sample first to estimate the parameters associated with the linear model,

$$\mu(ht18 \,|\, ht2_i, wt2_i) = \beta_0 + \beta_1 ht2_i + \beta_2 wt2_i,$$

and, later, to infer whether this is the best model for adolescent height.

We begin the review of the estimation computations by looking at the standard deviations of the two partial *x*s, *wt2·ht2* and *ht2·wt2*, and at the correlation between these partial variables and the *y*, *ht18*.

From Table 7.1, the SDs for the two *x*s are SD(*ht2*) = 3.016 cm and SD(*wt2*) = 1.567 kg, and the correlation between the two is r(*ht2, wt2*) = 0.5181. These data,

T A B L E 7.1
Growth Study Sample Data

	ht2	wt2	ht18
	90.20	13.60	179.0
	91.40	12.70	195.1
	86.40	12.60	183.7
	87.60	14.80	178.7
	86.70	12.70	171.5
	88.10	11.90	181.8
	82.20	11.50	172.5
	83.80	13.20	174.6
	91.00	16.90	190.4
	87.40	12.70	173.8
	84.20	11.40	172.6
	88.40	14.20	185.2
	87.70	17.20	178.4
	89.60	13.70	177.6
	91.40	14.20	183.5
	90.00	15.90	178.1
	86.40	14.30	177.0
	90.00	13.30	172.9
	91.40	13.80	188.4
	81.30	11.30	169.4
	90.60	14.30	180.2
	92.20	13.40	189.0
	87.10	12.20	182.4
	91.40	15.90	185.8
	89.70	11.50	180.7
	92.20	14.20	178.7
	83.80	12.60	169.6
	86.20	12.00	166.8
Mean	88.16	13.50	179.2
Variance	9.099	2.456	45.96
SD	3.016	1.567	6.779

Correlations Among Variables

	ht2	wt2	ht18
ht2	1.000	.5181	.7051
wt2		1.000	.3915

used in Equation [7.7], give us the SDs for the two partial xs:

$$SD[wt2.ht2] = SD(wt2)\sqrt{1 - r(ht2, wt2)^2}$$
$$= (1.567\,kg)\sqrt{1 - 0.51812^2}$$
$$= (1.567\,kg)(0.8553)$$
$$= 1.341\,kg$$

and

$$SD[ht2.wt2] = SD(ht2)\sqrt{1 - r(ht2, wt2)^2}$$
$$= (3.016\,cm)(0.8553)$$
$$= 2.580\,cm.$$

Each of the partial SDs is about 85% the size of the original SDs for the xs. The resulting values, 1.34 kg and 2.58 cm, appear to be large enough—absolutely as well as relative to the original SDs—to support the standard interpretation of the linear model slope parameter.

The correlations among the three Growth Study variables are given at the bottom of Table 7.1. These can be used, though the relation is not a simple one, to compute the correlations between each of the partial xs and y: $r(wt2.ht2, ht18) = 0.0306$ and $r(ht2.wt2, ht18) = 0.5873$.

While each of these correlations is smaller than the corresponding correlation with the unmodified x, $r(wt2, ht18) = 0.3915$ and $r(ht2, ht18) = 0.7051$, partialing the dependence on $ht2$ from $wt2$ has a particularly striking impact. The resulting partial x is *almost uncorrelated* with the response, $r(wt2.ht2, ht18) = 0.0306$.

We now have, though, what we need to use Equation [7.9] to compute estimated slope parameters:

$$\widehat{\beta}_1 = r(ht2.wt2, ht18)\frac{SD(ht18)}{SD(ht2.wt2)} = (0.5873)\frac{6.779\ cm}{2.580\ cm} = 1.543\ cm/cm$$

and

$$\widehat{\beta}_2 = r(wt2.ht2, ht18)\frac{SD(ht18)}{SD(wt2.ht2)} = (0.0306)\frac{6.779\ cm}{1.341\ kg} = 0.1548\ cm/kg.$$

We interpret the first of these estimates as follows: Two infants of the *same weight* but differing in height by 1 cm can be expected to differ in height at age 18 by 1.54 cm.

Similarly, for the second slope estimate, we can say: Two infants of the *same height* but differing in weight by 1 kg can be expected to differ in height at age 18 by 0.15 cm.

From these slope estimates and the sample means for the xs and y, we find, via Equation [7.10], the estimate of the regression intercept,

$$\widehat{\beta}_0 = M(ht18) - \widehat{\beta}_1 M(ht2) - \widehat{\beta}_2\,M(wt2)$$
$$= 179.2\,cm - (1.543\,cm/cm)(88.16\,cm) - (0.1548\,cm/kg)(13.5\,kg) = 41.07\,cm.$$

The three estimated βs are substituted into Equation [7.11] to give us the equation for estimating conditional response means:

$$\widehat{\mu}(ht18\,|\,ht2_i, wt2_i) = \widehat{\beta}_0 + \widehat{\beta}_1 ht2_i + \widehat{\beta}_2 wt2_i$$
$$= 41.07\,cm + (1.543\,cm/cm)\,ht2_i + (0.1548cm/kg)\,wt2_i.$$

Thus, the estimated mean of the conditional response population from which the first observation in Table 7.1 was drawn is found to be

$$\widehat{\mu}(ht18 \mid ht2 = 90.2\,\text{cm}, wt2 = 13.6\,\text{kg}) = 41.07 + (1.543)(90.2) + (0.1548)(13.6)$$
$$= 182.36\,\text{cm}.$$

In the fourth column of Table 7.2, under the heading $\widehat{\mu}$, the estimated means for the 28 sample *ht18* observations are listed. Each can be computed by substituting appropriate values of *ht2* and *wt2* in the last equation.

Table 7.2 also shows the set of *residuals* for this sample. Each entry in the column headed $\widehat{\epsilon}$ is a residual computed according to Equation [7.14] as the difference between the *y* observation and its estimated mean. Using the notation of Table 7.2, $\widehat{\epsilon}_i = ht18_i - \widehat{\mu}_i$.

T A B L E **7.2**

Estimated Conditional Means ($\widehat{\mu}$) and Residuals ($\widehat{\epsilon}$) for the Growth Study Sample

ht2	wt2	ht18	$\widehat{\mu}$	$\widehat{\epsilon}$
90.20	13.60	179.0	182.36	−3.36
91.40	12.70	195.1	184.08	11.02
86.40	12.60	183.7	176.35	7.35
87.60	14.80	178.7	178.54	.16
86.70	12.70	171.5	176.82	−5.32
88.10	11.90	181.8	178.86	2.94
82.20	11.50	172.5	169.69	2.81
83.80	13.20	174.6	172.43	2.17
91.00	16.90	190.4	184.11	6.29
87.40	12.70	173.8	177.90	−4.10
84.20	11.40	172.6	172.77	−.17
88.40	14.20	185.2	179.68	5.52
87.70	17.20	178.4	179.06	−.56
89.60	13.70	177.6	181.45	−3.85
91.40	14.20	183.5	184.31	−.81
90.00	15.90	178.1	182.41	−4.31
86.40	14.30	177.0	176.61	.39
90.00	13.30	172.9	182.01	−9.11
91.40	13.80	188.4	184.25	4.15
81.30	11.30	169.4	168.27	1.13
90.60	14.30	180.2	183.09	−2.89
92.20	13.40	189.0	185.42	3.58
87.10	12.20	182.4	177.36	5.04
91.40	15.90	185.8	184.57	1.23
89.70	11.50	180.7	181.27	−.57
92.20	14.20	178.7	185.54	−6.84
83.80	12.60	169.6	172.33	−2.73
86.20	12.00	166.8	175.94	−9.14

For example, we have in the fifth row of Table 7.2,

$$\widehat{\epsilon}_5 = ht18_5 - \widehat{\mu}_5 = 171.50 \text{ cm} - 176.82 \text{ cm} = -5.32 \text{ cm}.$$

For the Growth Study sample, we can use Equation [7.15] to estimate the conditional response variance, the variance in *ht18* for fixed values of *ht2* and *wt2*, by first computing the sum of squares of these residuals and then dividing this sum by $(N - 3) = (28 - 3) = 25$. The result is

$$\widehat{\sigma}^2(ht18 \mid ht2, wt2) = \frac{(-3.36)^2 + (11.02)^2 + \cdots + (-9.14)^2}{25} = \frac{645.8}{25}$$

$$= 25.83 \text{ cm}^2.$$

Finally, the estimated unconditional response variance is the sum of squared deviations of the *ht18* observations about their sample mean, M(*ht18*), divided by $(N - 1) = 27$:

$$\widehat{\sigma}^2(ht18) = \frac{(178.0 - 179.2)^2 + \cdots + (166.8 - 179.2)^2}{27} = \frac{1287}{27} = 47.67 \text{ cm}^2.$$

Certainty about *y* would appear to be considerably increased by taking the values of the two *x*s into account. The estimated conditional standard deviation,

$$\widehat{\sigma}(ht18 \mid ht2, wt2) = \sqrt{25.83 \text{ cm}^2} = 5.08 \text{ cm},$$

is smaller than the estimated unconditional standard deviation,

$$\widehat{\sigma}(ht18) = \sqrt{47.67 \text{ cm}^2} = 6.78 \text{ cm}.$$

Can we *infer* that the difference holds, as well, for the true values of the parameters? To answer this question, we must know about the *sampling variability* of our estimates.

7.4
Sampling Distributions: Multiple Linear Model

Under the assumptions described earlier, the estimates of the preceding section have sampling distributions very similar to those for the corresponding simple linear regression parameters. As a result, confidence intervals (CIs) can be computed, particularly for the slope parameters, β_1 and β_2, as an aid to model evaluation and comparison.

7.4.1 Sampling Distributions of Regression Slope and Intercept Estimates

The sampling distributions of the slope estimates have three properties:

- the mean of the sampling distribution is the value of the parameter being estimated—$\mu(\widehat{\beta}_1) = \beta_1$ and $\mu(\widehat{\beta}_2) = \beta_2$,

- the sampling distributions of slope estimates are well approximated by a Normal density function, and
- the sampling distributions of slope estimates have standard deviations

$$\sigma(\widehat{\beta}_1) = \sqrt{\frac{\sigma^2[y \,|\, x_1, x_2]}{\mathrm{Var}[x_{(1.2)}]N}} \quad \text{and} \quad \sigma(\widehat{\beta}_2) = \sqrt{\frac{\sigma^2[y \,|\, x_1, x_2]}{\mathrm{Var}[x_{(2.1)}]N}}.$$

The sampling distributions depend upon the unknown conditional response variance, $\sigma^2[y \,|\, x_1, x_2]$. When the estimated conditional response variance is used instead, the sampling distributions are approximated by the probability density of the t-variable with $(N - 3)$ d.f. with standard errors of

$$\mathrm{SE}(\widehat{\beta}_1) = \sqrt{\frac{\widehat{\sigma}^2[y \,|\, x_1, x_2]}{\mathrm{Var}[x_{(1.2)}]N}} \quad \text{and} \quad \mathrm{SE}(\widehat{\beta}_2) = \sqrt{\frac{\widehat{\sigma}^2[y \,|\, x_1, x_2]}{\mathrm{Var}[x_{(2.1)}]N}}. \tag{7.16}$$

The standard errors of the multiple linear model slope estimates have the same form as that for the slope estimate in the simple linear model,

$$\mathrm{SE}(\widehat{\beta}_1) = \sqrt{\frac{\widehat{\sigma}^2[y \,|\, x]}{\mathrm{Var}[x]N}}, \tag{5.2}$$

except that now the conditional response variance, in the numerator, has taken two xs into account, and the x variance in the denominator is for a partial x rather than an unmodified one.

We'll get a better idea of what influences the size of the slope-estimate standard errors if we substitute for the SDs of the partial xs from Equation[7.7]:

$$\mathrm{SE}(\widehat{\beta}_1) = \sqrt{\frac{\widehat{\sigma}^2[y \,|\, x_1, x_2]}{(1 - r[x_1, x_2]^2)\mathrm{Var}[x_1]N}}$$

and

$$\mathrm{SE}(\widehat{\beta}_2) = \sqrt{\frac{\widehat{\sigma}^2[y \,|\, x_1, x_2]}{(1 - r[x_1, x_2]^2)\mathrm{Var}[x_2]N}}.$$

There are three terms in the denominators of these standard errors. As is the case in simple linear regression,

- the larger the sample size (N), the smaller the standard errors of the slope estimates and
- the larger the SD (or variance) of an x-variable, the smaller the standard error of its slope estimate.

The third term in the denominator depends upon the correlation between the two xs.

If $r[x_1, x_2]$ is *large* (close to 1.0 or to -1.0), then $(1 - r[x_1, x_2]^2)$ is *small* (close to 0). As a result,

- the larger the correlation between the xs, the larger the standard errors of the slope estimates.

If the two xs are highly correlated, the slope coefficients will be estimated very imprecisely—there will be wide sample-to-sample variability in the estimates. This makes model interpretation and comparison difficult. Whenever possible, xs should be chosen or the sampling designed (design points selected) so that, in the sample, the xs are relatively uncorrelated.

7.4.2 Confidence Intervals for Regression Slope Parameters

Because the sampling distributions for the slope estimates are centered at the true values of the slopes, have the shape of t-distributions, and have calculable SEs, we can compute CIs for the two slope parameters just as we did for the single one in Chapter 5.

The only change to the computational rule provided by Equation [5.1] is that the needed t-value must be supplied from the tabled values for the t-distribution with $(N-3)$ d.f.:

$$\text{CI}[\beta_j, (1-\alpha)100\%] = [\widehat{\beta}_j \pm t_{(N-3),(1-\alpha)} \text{SE}(\widehat{\beta}_j)], \quad \text{for } j = 1, 2. \quad \textbf{(7.17)}$$

Let's bring the Growth Study example forward by computing standard errors for the slope estimates and CIs for the slopes themselves. For our linear model,

$$\mu(ht18 \mid ht2_i, wt2_i) = \beta_0 + \beta_1 ht2_i + \beta_2 wt2_i,$$

we already have estimates of

$$\widehat{\beta}_1 = 1.543 \text{ cm/cm}, \widehat{\beta}_2 = 0.155 \text{ cm/kg},$$

and

$$\widehat{\sigma}(ht18 \mid ht2, wt2) = 5.08 \text{ cm},$$

based on our sample of $N = 28$ observations in which the two xs had partial standard deviations of

$$\text{SD}(ht2.wt2) = 2.580 \text{ cm} \text{ and } \text{SD}(wt2.ht2) = 1.341 \text{ kg}.$$

These results give us what we need to compute from Equation [7.16] the standard errors for the slope estimates:

$$\text{SE}(\widehat{\beta}_1) = \widehat{\sigma}(ht18 \mid ht2, wt2)/[\text{SD}(ht2.wt2)\sqrt{N}]$$
$$= 5.08 \text{ cm}/[(2.580 \text{ cm})(\sqrt{28})]$$
$$= 0.37 \text{ cm/cm}$$

and

$$\text{SE}(\widehat{\beta}_2) = \widehat{\sigma}(ht18 \mid ht2, wt2)/[\text{SD}(wt2.ht2)\sqrt{N}]$$
$$= 5.08 \text{ cm}/[(1.341 \text{ kg})(\sqrt{28})]$$
$$= 0.72 \text{ cm/kg}$$

To compute 95% CIs for the two slope parameters, we note that, with $N = 28$, the t-value required in Equation [7.17] is, from the table in the Appendix, $t_{25,0.95} = 2.06$.

The 95% CIs are

$$\text{CI}[\beta_1, 95\%] = [1.543 \text{ cm/cm} \pm (2.06)(0.37 \text{ cm/cm})]$$
$$= [1.543 \text{ cm/cm} \pm 0.76 \text{ cm/cm}]$$
$$= [0.78 \text{ cm/cm}, 2.30 \text{ cm/cm}]$$

and

$$\text{CI}[\beta_2, 95\%] = [0.15 \text{ cm/kg} \pm (2.06)(0.72 \text{ cm/kg})]$$
$$= [0.15 \text{ cm/kg} \pm 1.48 \text{ cm/kg}]$$
$$= [-1.33 \text{ cm/kg}, 1.63 \text{ cm/kg}].$$

We can infer, with at least 95% confidence, that β_1 is positive, that taller infants (of the same weight) can be expected to be taller adolescents. On the other hand, the CI for β_2 overlaps 0 and we cannot infer that differences in infant weight, for those of the same height, should lead us to expect differences in adolescent height. We'll return to these results in Section 7.5 when we discuss model comparison.

7.4.3   Sampling Distributions for the Intercept and Response Variances

The sampling distributions for our estimates of β_0, and $\sigma^2[y \mid x_1, x_2]$ could also be used to compute CIs for those model parameters. We will not be interested directly in these parameters, so the sampling distributions of their estimates need only passing reference. The sampling distribution for the intercept estimate has the shape of a t-distribution with $(N - 3)$ degrees of freedom and is centered at the true value of the intercept. The sampling distribution of the estimate of the conditional response variances has the shape of a Chi-square distribution with $(N - 3)$ degrees of freedom.

7.5
Model Comparisons: Multiple Explanatory Variables

We want not only to estimate the parameters of the multiple linear model but also to reach some conclusions about that model. Given our sample of observations, *is it a good model*? That is, does taking the values of the *x*s into account increase our certainty about *y*? Or we may want to know whether accounting for several *x*s provides greater certainty than accounting for only one of them. Is our multiple linear model *better* than a simple linear one?

We need to be able to *compare* our multiple linear model with alternate ones.

7.5.1   Model Comparisons Based on the Confidence Interval for a Slope

To conclude, on the basis of the sample, that a simple linear model,

$$\mu(y \mid x = x_i) = \beta_0 + \beta_1 x_i$$

is better than the null model,

$$\mu(y \mid x = x_i) = \beta_0,$$

is the same—we learned in Chapter 5—as inferring that the slope parameter, β_1, is not 0. When $\beta_1 = 0$, the simple linear model is identical to the null model. We can conclude that β_1 is not 0 whenever we observe that the CI for β_1 does not include 0. Put another way, the CI describes a range we are confident includes the true value of the parameter given the sample observations, and, if 0 is not within that range, we infer the true value could not be 0.

Model Comparison and the CI for a Slope

We can use this same logic to compare our multiple linear model with alternate models. The logic tells us how—given a sample of observations—we can compare a linear model with two xs (x_1 and x_2),

$$\mu(y \mid x_1 = x_{i1}, x_2 = x_{i2}) = \beta_0 + \beta_1 x_{i1} + \beta_2 x_{i2}, \qquad \textbf{(Model 1)}$$

with either of the simple linear models employing just one of those xs,

$$\mu(y \mid x_1 = x_{i1}, x_2 = x_{i2}) = \beta_0 + \beta_1 x_{i1} \qquad \textbf{(Model 2)}$$

and

$$\mu(y \mid x_1 = x_{i1}, x_2 = x_{i2}) = \beta_0 + \beta_2 x_{i2}. \qquad \textbf{(Model 3)}$$

If β_2 is 0, Models 1 and 2 are identical. If β_1 is 0, Models 1 and 3 are the same.

We compare Models 1 and 2 by examining the CI for β_2 based on our Model 1 estimates. If that CI includes 0, we conclude that Model 2 is better than Model 1. However, if 0 is outside the CI for β_2, we conclude that Model 1 is the better of the two. In similar fashion, the Model 1 CI for β_1 gives us what we need to compare Models 1 and 3.

These model comparisons have substantive interpretations and, indeed, are substantively motivated. We compare Models 1 and 2 if we are interested in the question "Do we increase our certainty about y when we add x_2 to a linear model that already includes x_1?"

A Growth Study Example

Let's look at these model comparisons in the context of our Growth Study sample results. In Chapter 5, we concluded that knowledge of *ht2* increased our certainty about *ht18*, that

$$\mu(ht18_i \mid ht2_i) = \beta_0 + \beta_1 ht2_i$$

is a better model for *ht18* than

$$\mu(ht18_i \mid ht2_i) = \beta_0.$$

In this chapter, we introduced a second x, *wt2*, and a natural question is whether this second x further increases our certainty about adolescent height. Is

$$\mu(ht18_i \mid ht2_i, wt2_i) = \beta_0 + \beta_1 ht2_i + \beta_2 wt2_i$$

a better model than

$$\mu(ht18_i \mid ht2_i, wt2_i) = \beta_0 + \beta_1 ht2_i?$$

In Section 7.4.2, we computed a 95% CI for β_2,

$$CI[\beta_2, 95\%] = [0.15 \text{ cm/kg} \pm 1.48 \text{ cm/kg}]$$
$$= [-1.33 \text{ cm/kg}, 1.63 \text{ cm/kg}],$$

an interval that includes 0 in its range. We conclude that β_2 could be 0 and, hence, that the linear model with both *ht2* and *wt2* as explanatory variables is no better than the one assessing only *ht2*. Knowledge of an infant's weight as well as his height does not increase our certainty about his adolescent height over what is attained knowing only his infant height.

In the future we shall simplify our linear model equations by eliminating the names of explanatory variables from the left-hand side. We'll use the new notation for two reasons:

- Simplicity of notation. The right-hand side of the linear model equation will tell us which *x*s, if any, are involved in the equation.

- Centrality of the response. The new model notation, with its constant left-hand side, reminds us of the central importance to modeling of the response variable. As *y* remains constant, our task is to determine which, if any, *x*s to use in modeling *y*.

7.5.2   Other Model Comparisons: An Introduction

In the last section, we treated the Growth Study as if it were motivated by two specific questions:

- Does infant height help to explain adolescent height?
- If it does, does infant weight help further to explain adolescent height?

We answered the first question "Yes" when we concluded that

$$\mu(ht18_i) = \beta_0 + \beta_1 ht2_i$$

was a better model for the expected adolescent height of a 2 year old than

$$\mu(ht18_i) = \beta_0.$$

We answered the second question "No" when we concluded that

$$\mu(ht18_i) = \beta_0 + \beta_1 ht2_i + \beta_2 wt2_i$$

provided no better model of *ht18* than

$$\mu(ht18_i) = \beta_0 + \beta_1 ht2_i.$$

The Growth Study researcher, though, may not have had these two *particular* questions in mind. Let's assume instead that the explanatory roles of infant height and weight were thought of more generally—that the researcher posed this question:

Do infant height and weight, considered separately or together, influence adolescent height?

From a modeling perspective, this question is answered by deciding, on the basis of a sample of observations, that one of the following four is the best model of adolescent height:

$$\mu(ht18_i) = \beta_0 + \beta_1 ht2_i + \beta_2 wt2_i, \qquad \textbf{(Model 1)}$$

$$\mu(ht18_i) = \beta_0 + \beta_1 ht2_i, \qquad \textbf{(Model 2)}$$

$$\mu(ht18_i) = \beta_0 + \beta_2 wt2_i, \text{ or} \qquad \textbf{(Model 3)}$$

$$\mu(ht18_i) = \beta_0. \qquad \textbf{(Model 4)}$$

Model 1 postulates that both infant height and weight influence adolescent height, Model 2 that only infant height has an influence, Model 3 that influence is restricted to infant weight, and Model 4 that neither height nor weight in infancy helps to explain later height.

To choose among Models 1–4, the researcher must make comparisons among pairs of them. We have just seen how Model 1 might be compared with either Model 2 or Model 3, and we have reviewed from Chapter 5 how Models 2 or 3 might each be compared with Model 4. Each of these comparisons pits a pair of models that differ by the inclusion or exclusion of a *single slope parameter*. Evaluating the CI for that particular parameter provides all we need for making the comparison.

Not every pair of models in which we are interested differs in exactly this way. This is true, for example, of Growth Study Models 2 and 3. Model 2 includes *ht2* as an explanatory variable but Model 3 uses *wt2*. We cannot go from one of these models to the other simply by dropping a linear model term from one or by adding a linear-model term to the other. Also, we cannot get from Model 1 to Model 4 by eliminating a single slope parameter. We must postulate that *both* β_1 and β_2 are 0.

Neither of these model comparisons—between Models 2 and 3 or between Models 1 and 4—can be made by way of a CI. We make them differently and differently one from the other. We'll look first at the comparison of linear models such as Models 1 and 4, models that differ by the inclusion in one of two or more parameters not found in the other. For these model pairs, the parameters in one are a *subset* of the parameters in the other. Once we've done that, we'll describe a basis for comparing models, such as Models 2 and 3, that have *different* sets of parameters, neither one a subset of the other.

First, though, we'll use a set of terms introduced in Chapter 6 to typify the four Growth Study linear models. Model 1 is, for the question asked, the *full model*—all of the *x*s are in the model. Model 4 is the *null model*—it postulates a dependence of *y* on none of the study's *x*s. Models 2 and 3 are *intermediate* or *constrained models*—each assumes some constraints on the parameters of the full model but not all of those needed to convert the full model into the null model. The full model is converted to the null model by setting two constraints, $\beta_1 = 0$ and $\beta_2 = 0$. It is converted to either of the intermediate models by setting only one of the slope parameters to 0, a single constraint.

7.5.3   Comparing Fuller and Less Full Models

As we've just seen, a comparison of Models 1 and 4 for our Growth Study involves two constraints on the βs rather than one. Comparisons of this kind are common in multiple linear regression but cannot be handled through the computation of a slope CI. We need another model comparison strategy. We introduce this strategy for comparing fuller and less full models with some useful terminology.

Each of the explanatory models for a particular study can be thought to have a certain amount of fullness. A full model is fuller than an intermediate model because an intermediate model has fewer parameters. These fewer parameters are the result of placing constraints on full model parameters. Similarly, the null model is less full than an intermediate model because intermediate model parameters have been further constrained to produce the null model.

We use this idea of fullness to distinguish between the two models to be compared. We refer to one model as the *fuller model* and the second as the *less full model*. These are not only distinctive names for the two models. They imply a relation between the two. The less full model must be one that is the result of imposing some constraints on the parameters of the fuller model.

Not every pair of explanatory models has a fuller/less full relation. For example, among the four explanatory models for the Growth Study, the pair

$$\mu(ht18_i) = \beta_0 + \beta_1 ht2_i \quad \text{and} \qquad \textbf{(Model 2)}$$
$$\mu(ht18_i) = \beta_0 + \beta_2 wt2_i \qquad \textbf{(Model 3)}$$

does not have a fuller/less full relation. The parameters of one of the models *cannot be constrained* to provide the second model. In Section 7.5.4, we look at how to compare models such as these, models that are equally full.

Basis of a Model Comparison Strategy

One of the consequences of the fuller/less full relation is that the fuller model will have more parameters than the less full one. We'll represent the number of parameters in the less full model as p and the number of parameters in the fuller model as $(p + k)$. There are k more parameters in the fuller than in the less full model.

The idea behind our model comparison strategy can now be stated. For the fuller model to be judged better than the less full one, we have to conclude that the additional k parameters (and their xs) in the fuller model increase our certainty about y; in other words, we have to conclude that the (conditional) response variance for the fuller model, $\sigma^2(y \mid fuller\ model)$, really is smaller than the (conditional) response variance for the less full model, $\sigma^2(y \mid less\ full\ model)$.

A Model Comparison Strategy

We don't know the values of these response variances, but Equation [7.15] tells us that they may be estimated by

$$\widehat{\sigma}^2(y \mid fuller\ model) = \frac{\text{SSR}(fuller\ model)}{N - (p + k)} \qquad \textbf{(7.18)}$$

and

$$\widehat{\sigma}^2(y \mid less\ full\ model) = \frac{\text{SSR}(less\ full\ model)}{N-p} \qquad \textbf{(7.19)}$$

where the numerators are the sums of the squares of the residuals (SSR) associated with the estimates of the response means for each of the two linear models.

These estimates of the response variances, and the SSRs from which they are computed, are the sample evidence we have to go on in concluding whether $\sigma^2(y \mid less\ full\ model)$ really is larger than $\sigma^2(y \mid fuller\ model)$ and, hence, whether the fuller model is better than the less full one. How do we use these estimates to make the inference?

It would seem reasonable to conclude that the fuller model is the better of the two if $\widehat{\sigma}^2(y \mid less\ full\ model)$ is large *relative* to $\widehat{\sigma}^2(y \mid fuller\ model)$. We say "large relative to the fuller model estimate" because we might anticipate that when $\sigma^2(y \mid fuller\ model)$ is a large number (e.g., $\sigma^2 = 1,000,000$), its estimates will show greater variability than when it is a small number (e.g., $\sigma^2 = 0.001$). A natural model comparison statistic, then, would be

$$G = \frac{\widehat{\sigma}^2(y \mid less\ full\ model) - \widehat{\sigma}^2(y \mid fuller\ model)}{\widehat{\sigma}^2(y \mid fuller\ model)}. \qquad \textbf{(7.22)}$$

When G takes a "large" (positive) value, we would conclude that there is a difference in the true values of the two response variances and that the fuller model is better than the less full one.

In order to conclude that the value of a statistic, such as G, is a "large" one, we need to know what the sampling distribution of that statistic is. In the case of the statistic G, we are interested in its sampling distribution *when the less full model is the true model*, when there is no difference between $\sigma^2(y \mid fuller\ model)$ and $\sigma^2(y \mid less\ full\ model)$. Against this sampling distribution, we can judge whether a particular value of G is so large as to suggest that the two variances could not be the same.

In principle, the sampling distribution for G could be described, tabulated, and interpreted in this way. But it turns out that another closely related statistic can be used not only for our model comparisons but for a variety of related statistical tasks as well. This is the F-statistic, related to our G by

$$F = 1 + \left(\frac{N-p}{k}\right)G \qquad \textbf{(7.23)}$$

$$F = 1 + \left(\frac{N-p}{k}\right)\left\{\frac{\widehat{\sigma}^2(y \mid less\ full\ model) - \widehat{\sigma}^2(y \mid fuller\ model)}{\widehat{\sigma}^2(y \mid fuller\ model)}\right\}.$$

This F conveys the same sample information as G and behaves like G in that large values of F—relative to what we should expect when the less full model is the true one—provide evidence that the fuller model is better.

The F-Distributions

Figure 7.3 shows the sampling distribution for a particular F-statistic. It is not a symmetric distribution. The value of F would never be negative, and a long right-hand tail is needed to include the few very large positive values that would occur under the hypothetical re-sampling needed to create the sampling distribution.

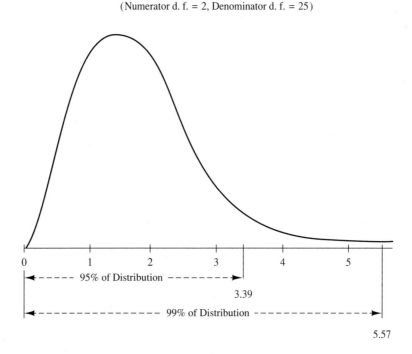

(Numerator d. f. = 2, Denominator d. f. = 25)

FIGURE 7.3
An F-probability
Density Curve

Under our linear model assumptions and under the assumption that the less full model is the correct one, the theoretical histogram for the sampling distribution of the F-statistic of Equation [7.23] is the same as the probability density function for one of the well-known F *random variables*. There is a large family of F-variables, just as there are several t-variables. And, similar to the t-variables, these F-variables are distinguished by their degrees of freedom. However, each F-distribution has two degree-of-freedom parameters, not just one. The two are referred to as the *numerator d.f.* and the *denominator d.f.* The model comparison statistic of Equation [7.23] has as its sampling distribution the F-distribution with numerator d.f. equal to k and denominator d.f. equal to $[N - (p + k)]$. The numerator d.f. is the difference between the number of parameters in the fuller and less full models, and the denominator d.f. is the sample size (N) less the number of parameters in the fuller model $(p + k)$.

If the variance estimates are replaced in Equation [7.23] by the right-hand sides of Equations [7.18] and [7.19], the result, after some algebraic manipulation, can be put in the form

$$F = \frac{\left(\frac{1}{k}\right)[SSR(\textit{less full model}) - SSR(\textit{fuller model})]}{\left(\frac{1}{N-p-k}\right)SSR(\textit{fuller model})}. \tag{7.24}$$

In this form, the F-statistic is a ratio and the numerator and denominator each have associated with them the numerator and denominator d.f.s mentioned above. Equation [7.24] is convenient if the SSRs are available.

Two tables of percentage points for the family of F-distributions are given in the Appendix. The columns of each table cover a range of numerator d.f.s and the rows a range of denominator d.f.s. Thus, an entry in the first table gives the 95% point for the F-distribution with numerator d.f. given at the head of the column and denominator d.f. given at the head of the row. The 99% points for these same F-distributions are given in the second table. Because of the asymmetry of the F-distributions, we refer to the percentage (or proportion) of observations above or below a particular value of F rather than to any "central proportions."

For example, if we are interested in the F-distribution with 2 (numerator) and 25 (denominator) degrees of freedom, we read from the two tables

	numerator d.f.: 2	
	95%	99%
denominator d.f.: 25	3.39	5.57

As illustrated in Figure 7.3, 95% of the sampling distribution for the F-statistic for $k = 2$ and $[N - (p + k)] = 25$ will fall below 3.39 and 99% will fall below 5.57.

Employing the Model Comparison Strategy

We single out these two percentage points because we will say that values of the F-statistic greater than the 95% point are "significantly" larger than we should expect when the less full model is correct and that F-statistic values greater than the 99% point are "very significantly" larger. We exploit this idea of *significantly* or *very significantly larger* in our model comparison. We conclude the fuller model is, in fact, better than the less full one only if the F-statistic takes a value so large as to significantly or very significantly exceed what we would expect if the less full model were appropriate.

Let's illustrate the use of the F-statistic with our Growth Study. For the linear model,

$$\mu(ht18) = \beta_0 + \beta_1 ht2_i + \beta_2 wt2_i,$$

we computed from the sample of $N = 28$ observations this estimate of the (conditional) response variance:

$$\widehat{\sigma}^2(ht18 \mid ht2, wt2) = 25.83 \text{ cm}^2.$$

For the linear model,

$$\mu(ht18) = \beta_0,$$

the estimated response variance is

$$\widehat{\sigma}^2(ht18) = 47.67 \text{ cm}^2.$$

First, we note that the two models can be compared because the less full model, $\mu(ht18) = \beta_0$, can be viewed as the result of imposing constraints on the parameters of the Fuller Model, $\mu(ht18) = \beta_0 + \beta_1 ht2 + \beta_2 wt2$. The constraints would be $\beta_1 = 0$ and $\beta_2 = 0$.

Our fuller model has $(p + k) = 3$ parameters, β_0, β_1, and β_2, while our less full model has only $p = 1$ parameter, β_0. The difference in number of parameters, is $k = 2$.

The F-statistic comparing the two models, based on Equation [7.23], takes the value

$$F = 1 + \left(\frac{N-p}{k}\right) \frac{\widehat{\sigma}^2(y \mid less\ full\ model) - \widehat{\sigma}^2(y \mid fuller\ model)}{\widehat{\sigma}^2(y \mid fuller\ model)}$$

$$F = 1 + \left(\frac{28-1}{2}\right) \left[\frac{47.67 - 25.83}{25.83}\right] = 12.41.$$

This is a very significantly large value for the F-distribution with $k = 2$ and $[N - (p + k)] = 25$ degrees of freedom, and we conclude that the fuller model is better than the less full alternative.

Equivalence of Approaches to Model Comparison

The development of the F-statistic was motivated by the need for a technique to compare models that differed with respect to more than one parameter—to complement the use of the CI in comparing models that differed on a single parameter. In application, evaluating the F-statistic looks quite different from evaluating the CI. However, the results are exactly the same.

Now that we have the F-statistic in place, it could be used to compare models that differ on only a single parameter. If we were to do so, we would reach the same conclusions: the 95% CI for the slope parameter computed for a model with p parameters from a sample of N observations will fail to include 0 under *exactly the same circumstances* that give an F-statistic that is significantly greater than the 95% percentage point. The technical reason for this is that the t-distribution with $(N - p)$ degrees of freedom—used to compute the slope CI—and the F-distribution with 1 and $(N - p)$ degrees of freedom—used to evaluate the F-statistic—have the same probability structure: The probability that a randomly chosen observation from the t-distribution with $(N - p)$ degrees of freedom will be within k SDs of the expected value of that distribution is exactly equal to the probability that a randomly chosen observation from the F-distribution with 1 and $(N - p)$ degrees of freedom will be less than k^2.

The technical details of the correspondence of the two approaches to model comparison are beyond our scope. The implications are not. We can continue to evaluate

CIs whenever we wish to compare two models differing on a single parameter, assured that the results are completely consistent with our use of the F-statistic where the models differ more drastically. We urge continued use of the CI approach because it provides additional information. In addition to facilitating model choice, the CI tells us about the magnitude of the slope. We learn how great the influence on y is, not just that there is or is not an influence.

7.5.4 Comparing Equally Full Models

Our general model comparison strategy is to prefer the less full model—to believe it is the correct one—unless the fuller model shows a real improvement in ability to explain y. It is not sufficient, as noted in Equations [7.22] and [7.23], for the estimated conditional response variance simply to be smaller for the fuller model than for the less full model. Our estimated certainty about y must have increased enough to warrant adopting a more complicated model, one with more parameters.

Now, let's return to the question of comparing

$$\mu(ht18) = \beta_0 + \beta_1 ht2 \quad \text{and} \qquad \textbf{(Model 2)}$$
$$\mu(ht18) = \beta_0 + \beta_2 wt2, \qquad \textbf{(Model 3)}$$

two models that do not have a fuller/less full relation. In this instance, the two models have the same number of parameters, two apiece, leading us to describe them as equally full.

Comparisons between equally full models are, from our point of view, both rare and of a different nature than fuller/less full ones. There is no question of *parsimony* involved in the comparison. We are not asked to choose between a simpler model (the less full model) and a smaller SSR (the fuller model). So, the choice between equally full models has to turn on some other criterion, perhaps cost of x-assessment or the theoretical clarity of one set of xs versus another set. It is not clear that the comparison should be made on a statistical basis. We shall restrict model comparisons to those between fuller and less full models. Chapter 8 develops these comparisons more fully.

7.6
Linear Models with k Explanatory Variables

In Sections 7.2 through 7.4, we extended the simple linear regression model to one with two xs. The presentation of a general model comparison statistic in Section 7.5 anticipates that we are often interested in explanatory models with more than two sources of influence, more than two xs. With this in mind, we review in this section the results of the earlier sections.

The linear regression model, its parameters, their estimates, and the model comparison inferences to be made are essentially the same whatever the number of xs. The ideas remain constant but the algebra and the arithmetic become more complex as the number of parameters increases. As a result, we will not give the same details for the general linear model with *k* *x* variables as we did for the one- and two-variable models. Rather, we will rely—as we must in practice—on the numeric solutions provided by the regression command in our statistical computing package.

7.6.1   A New and Hypothetical Growth Study

Let's assume that our Growth Study researcher, on the basis of what we learned earlier in this chapter, has concluded that infant weight has no influence on adolescent height but that infant height does. She decides to go a step further and investigate "how" infant height exerts this influence. Are some components to infant height more important than others?

Instead of measuring overall infant height (*ht2*), she measures, still at 2 years of age, three separate lengths: trunk length (*tl2*), upper-leg length (*ul2*), and lower-leg length (*ll2*).These three are the *x*s to be used in modeling adolescent height (*ht18*). Does *ht18* depend upon all three components of infant height? Or, to describe an alternative model, does *ul2* alone provide a better model?

This study will remain hypothetical. We'll offer no sample data but use this three-*x* study throughout this section simply to illustrate the more general *k* variable model.

7.6.2   Conditional Response Populations

At the heart of all explanatory models for the measured response, *y*, is the idea of a conditional response population. This is as true for models with three or more *x*s as it was for those with none, one, or two. For each pattern of scores across the *k* *x*-variables that is of interest to us—for each *design point* in our study—we postulate a separate population of *y* scores. These are our full model conditional response populations. We use the notation

$$[y \mid x_{i1}, x_{i2}, \ldots, x_{ik}]$$

to refer to the population of *y* scores conditional on the *k* *x*-variables taking a certain pattern of scores. This is the response population at that particular design point.

For the three-*x* Growth Study, we imagine that there is a population of age-18 heights for boys who at age 2 had trunk lengths of 36 cm, upper-leg lengths of 18 cm, and lower-leg lengths of 20 cm:

$$[ht18 \mid tl2 = 36 \text{ cm}, ul2 = 18 \text{ cm}, ll2 = 20 \text{ cm}].$$

There is another population of age-18 heights for those with trunk lengths of 36 cm and upper- and lower-leg lengths of 20 cm and 18 cm, respectively. Of course we recognize that the three measurements go together to some extent and that there are only certain patterns of scores on the three *x*s that are common among 2-year-old boys.

Mean of the Conditional Response Population

The hallmark of the linear regression model is that the mean response score at each design point is a linear function of the values of the xs that define the conditional populations. That is, as an extension of Equation [6.7], we can write the general linear model as

$$\mu[y \mid x_{i1}, x_{i2}, \ldots, x_{ik}] = \beta_0 + \sum_{j=1}^{k} \beta_j x_{ij}. \tag{7.25}$$

Thus, the full linear model for the "three-lengths" Growth Study looks like this:

$$\mu(ht18_i) = \beta_0 + \beta_1 tl2_i + \beta_2 ul2_i + \beta_3 ll2_i.$$

Conditional Response Variance and Population Histogram

In anticipation of the need to estimate and to make inferences about the parameters of the linear model on the basis of a sample of response observations, we make the usual two assumptions about the conditional y populations:

- At each design point, the conditional response variance is the same:

$$\sigma^2[y \mid x_1, x_2, \ldots, x_k].$$

- At each design point, the conditional response (population) histogram has Normal modality, skewness, and kurtosis characteristics.

7.6.3 Linear Model Parameters

The extended linear model of Equation [7.25] includes $(k+1)$ constants or parameters. These include the intercept, β_0, and a slope parameter for each x. The intercept can be interpreted as the y mean when each of the k x-variables takes the value 0,

$$\beta_0 = \mu[y \mid x_1 = 0, x_2 = 0, \ldots, x_k = 0],$$

provided that this pattern of all 0s for the xs is either one of the design points for the study or could have been a design point. For our hypothetical example, of course, the intercept, the expected age-18 height of a 2 year old with 0-length trunk and legs, would be uninterpretable.

Let's rearrange the right-hand side of Equation [7.25] to group with the intercept all of the terms except the one relating to the jth x:

$$\mu[y \mid x_{i1}, x_{i2}, \ldots, x_{ik}] = [\beta_0 + \sum_{m \neq j} \beta_m x_{im}] + \beta_j x_{ij}.$$

The notation $\sum_{m \neq j}$ indicates a sum over all values of m, from 1 through k, except $m = j$.

The resulting equation is similar to Equations [7.2] and [7.3] and suggests an extension of the interpretation of the slope parameter provided in Section 7.2. In particular, β_j can be interpreted as

- The increase in the mean of y associated with a one-unit increase in the value of the jth x-variable, provided that the values of all other xs remain unchanged.

Thus, for the linear model,

$$\mu(ht18_i) = \beta_0 + \beta_1 tl2_i + \beta_2 ul2_i + \beta_3 ll2_i,$$

we can interpret β_1 in this way: It is the difference in average $ht18$ between two boys whose trunk lengths differ by 1 cm but who have the same upper-leg lengths and the same lower-leg lengths.

As in the case of two-x models, the application of this interpretation to any particular model depends upon its reasonableness. Does it make sense that x_j can change by one unit while the values of all other xs remain unchanged?

7.6.4   Estimates of Linear Model Parameters

If we sample independently N observations from the conditional response populations described in the last two sections, the parameters of those populations have estimates that can be used in making model inferences. These estimates for the k x-variable model can be described, as were those for the two-x model, in terms of partial explanatory variables.

Higher Order Partial Variables

Equations [7.4] to [7.6] described the partialing from x_1 of its linear dependence upon x_2. The result was a partial variable, $x_{(1.2)}$, that was uncorrelated (in the sample) with x_2. We similarly partialed from x_2 its linear dependence upon x_1 in producing a second partial variable, $x_{(2.1)}$, one uncorrelated with x_1.

To describe certain properties of the estimates in the k-variable linear model, we'll want to extend this idea of partial variables. In the "three-lengths" model,

$$\mu(ht18) = \beta_0 + \beta_1 tl2 + \beta_2 ul2 + \beta_3 ll2,$$

any one of the three xs may be linearly dependent upon either or both of the remaining two. We can think of partialing from each x this linear dependence on the other two to give us the three partial variables

$$[tl2 \cdot ul2, ll2], [ul2 \cdot tl2, ll2], \text{ and } [ll2 \cdot tl2, ul2].$$

The "." in the notation separates the original x from the list of xs partialed from it.

Partialing out from one x the linear dependence on one or more other xs involves subtracting from that x a linear function of the others. Thus,

$$[tl2 \cdot ul2, ll2]_i = tl2_i - [a + b\,ul2_i + c\,ll2_i].$$

The constants of the linear function (a, b, and c) are such that the resulting partial variable will be uncorrelated with any one of the partialed-out variables:

$$r\{[tl2 \cdot ul2, ll2], ul2\} = r\{[tl2 \cdot ul2, ll2], ll2\} = 0,$$

$$r\{[ul2 \cdot tl2, ll2], tl2\} = r\{[ul2 \cdot tl2, ll2], ll2\} = 0, \text{ and}$$

$$r\{[ll2 \cdot tl2, ul2], tl2\} = r\{[ll2 \cdot tl2, ul2], ul2\} = 0.$$

When more than one x is partialed out, algebraic expressions corresponding to Equations [7.5] and [7.6] become very complicated. A numeric solution, though, is available. The linear function constants are those provided as the intercept and slopes by any regression command: "y" is the x from which dependencies are to be removed and the "x"s are those xs contributing the linear dependencies.

If one linear dependency is removed, the result is a first-order partial variable. Partialing out two xs describes a second-order partial variable.

The partial x-variables in which we are interested are those that result from partialing out the influence of all other xs. We'll use the notation,

$$[x_j \cdot x_{m \neq j}],$$

to indicate the partial variable that results from partialing from the jth explanatory variable, x_j, its linear dependency on each of the remaining $(k - 1)$ xs.

We emphasize that it is not necessary to compute the partial xs. It is useful to have in mind the idea of a partial x when discussing certain aspects of the multiple-x linear model.

Estimated Slope Parameters

Our estimate of the slope parameter for the jth x can be expressed as

$$\widehat{\beta_j} = r[y, x_j \cdot x_{m \neq j}] \frac{\text{SD}(y)}{\text{SD}(x_j \cdot x_{m \neq j})}. \tag{7.26}$$

It is the same form as given in Equation [7.9] for the two-variable model—the product of the correlation between the y and the partial variable and the ratio of their standard deviations in the sample. Depending upon the interrelations of the x-variables, the correlation with the partial-x may be quite different, even in sign, from $r[y, x_j]$. And, as we note in a later section, the SD for the partial-x may be quite a bit smaller than $\text{SD}[x_j]$.

Estimated Intercept and Response Variance

Our intercept estimate is the natural extension of Equation [7.10],

$$\widehat{\beta_0} = M(y) - \sum_{j=1}^{k} \widehat{\beta_j} M[x_j]. \tag{7.27}$$

If the estimates provided by Equations [7.26] and [7.27] are substituted for the parameters on the right-hand side of Equation [7.25], we have a way of estimating the means of different conditional response populations:

$$\widehat{\mu}(y \mid multi\text{-}x\ model) = \widehat{\beta_0} + \sum_{j=1}^{k} \widehat{\beta_j} x_{ij}.$$

The difference between y_i and its estimated mean is the residual (Equation [7.14]),

$$\widehat{\epsilon}_i = y_i - (\widehat{\beta}_0 + \sum_{j=1}^{k} \widehat{\beta}_j x_{ij}),$$

and we can use Equation [7.15] to describe the estimated common conditional response variance as the sum of squared residuals (SSR) divided by the difference between the number of sample observations (N) and the number of parameters in the model ($k + 1$):

$$\widehat{\sigma}^2[y \mid multi\text{-}x \ model] = \frac{1}{[N - (k+1)]} \sum_{i=1}^{N} \widehat{\epsilon}_i^2. \qquad \textbf{(7.28)}$$

7.6.5   Model Inference in Multi-x Models

We complete this section with some comments on the sampling distribution for the estimate of the regression slope for the *j*th *x* and on model comparisons. These comments are simply extensions of what was said in Sections 7.4 and 7.5 about the two-variable linear model.

Sampling Distribution of the Slope Estimate

Each of the *k* slope estimates has a sampling distribution that has three properties:

- The sampling distribution is centered at the true value of the slope parameter, $\mu(\widehat{\beta}_j) = \beta_j$.
- The sampling distributions have variances dependent upon the (unknown) conditional response variance and histograms with Normal random variable characteristics.
- After estimating the standard errors of the slope estimates,

$$SE(\widehat{\beta}_j) = \frac{\widehat{\sigma}[y \mid multi\text{-}x \ model]}{\sqrt{N} \ SD[x_j \cdot x_{m \neq j}]}, \qquad \textbf{(7.29)}$$

the slope estimates have *t*-variable sampling distributions with $(N - k - 1)$ d.f.

Equation [7.29] is in the same form as the SEs given earlier for two slopes in Equation [7.16]. The numerator of the SE is the estimated *y* standard deviation in each conditional population, the square root of Equation [7.28]. The denominator includes the square root of the sample size and the SD of the partial-*x*.

Multiple Correlation

We noted earlier that the SD for the partial-*x* may be considerably smaller than the SD for that *x*-variable itself. In fact, as an extension of Equation [7.7], this partial

SD can be expressed as

$$SD[x_j \cdot x_{m \neq j}] = SD[x_j] \sqrt{1 - R[x_j \; ; \; x_{m \neq j}]^2} \qquad \text{(7.30)}$$

where $R[x_j; x_{m \neq j}]$ denotes the *multiple correlation* between x_j and the remaining $(k - 1)$ other x variables.

The multiple correlation is a correlation between a single variable on the one hand and several variables on the other. In fact, it is the correlation between the single variable and a particular weighted sum of the several variables. Thus, $R[y; x, z]$, the multiple correlation between y, on the one hand, and x and z on the other, is the correlation between y and a particular weighted sum of x and z:

$$r[y, (a + b\,x + c\,z)],$$

where the weights a, b, and c are chosen so that

- the correlation of the weighted sum with y is positive and
- the correlation of the weighted sum with y is a maximum.

That is, no other weights would produce a higher correlation of the weighted sum of x and z with y.

The multiple correlation will be at least as large as the largest of the correlations between the single variable and one of the several variables.

We provide no algebraic representation for the multiple correlation. Many regression commands include in their output a multiple correlation (or a squared multiple correlation) between y and the set of xs.

CIs for the Slope Parameters

With several interrelated xs in a model, the multiple correlation between one x and the others can be quite large. As a consequence of this, the term

$$\sqrt{1 - R[x_j \; ; \; x_{m \neq j}]^2}$$

on the right of Equation [7.30] can be quite small. In turn, the SD for the partial-x also can be small. Finally, as the partial SD is in the denominator of the standard error for the slope estimate, we see that highly interrelated xs will have slope estimates with large standard errors.

The techniques of Section 7.4.2 can be used to compute CIs for any of the slope parameters in the k-variable model. We need only to draw our t-value from the tabled values for the t-distribution with $(N - k - 1)$ degrees of freedom. The slope CI can be used to compare two models that differ only with respect to the inclusion or exclusion of that slope parameter.

A large standard error for a slope estimate means a wide CI for that slope. This makes it likely that the CI will include 0 and, hence, that the model without the slope will be judged better than the one with it. Highly interrelated xs should be avoided whenever possible.

F-Statistic Model Comparisons

Section 7.5 provides the details for comparing models that differ on one or more parameters. The techniques outlined there are as relevant for models with more than two xs as for smaller models. An important aspect to multi-x designs, of course, is that the greater the number of xs in a study, the greater the number of potential intermediate models. Typically, only some of these models make good substantive sense. In the chapters that follow, we will see how to limit our model comparisons to those that are relevant to the questions we have about our data.

Matrix Formulation of Linear Models

We have presented only results in this chapter rather than offer any derivation of estimates and their sampling variabilities for the k-variable model and have relied on the idea of partial variables to convey a sense of continuity with the simple linear regression model. The reason for this brevity is that the algebra becomes rather unwieldy when the model contains more than a single explanatory variable. That is, the *scalar algebra* becomes unwieldy. If, however, we use the notation of vectors and matrices, the conventions of *linear algebra* (or matrix algebra) make it easy to express our linear modeling results, whatever the number of explanatory variables. This is done in the Advanced Topics Appendix for those readers familiar with linear algebra.

7.7
Summary

Very often our idea of what "explains" the variability in a response extends to the possible influence of more than one explanatory variable. In this chapter, we have extended the ideas of our simple linear model to include two or more xs. As tools in this extension, we described partial variables and partial and multiple correlations. Most importantly, a basis was established for comparing the explanatory powers of rival models.

Exercises

1   Below are selected data for the United States. To each of three random samples of 15 states, fit models that relate Expected Population Growth (the response) to the three explanatory variables: Percent Urban Population, Per Capita Income, and Percent Unemployment. What can you say about the influences of these three variables? How consistent are these results over your three samples?

State	% Urban 1985	Per Capita Income 1988	% Unemployment 1988	% Expected Growth 1990-2000
alabama	60	12604	7.2	5.5
alaska	64	19514	9.3	19.3
arizona	84	14887	6.3	23.1
arkansas	52	12172	7.7	4.2
california	91	18855	5.3	15.0
colorado	81	16417	6.4	11.0
connecticut	79	22761	3.0	5.1
delaware	71	17699	3.2	10.2
florida	84	16546	5.0	20.3
georgia	62	14980	5.8	19.4
hawaii	86	16898	3.2	17.9
idaho	54	12657	5.8	2.9
illinois	83	17611	6.8	-0.3
indiana	64	14721	5.3	-0.9
iowa	59	14764	4.5	-7.6
kansas	67	15905	4.8	1.5
kentucky	51	12795	7.9	-0.3
louisiana	69	12193	10.9	0.1
maine	48	14976	3.8	4.9
maryland	80	19314	4.5	11.5
massachusetts	84	20701	3.3	3.5
michigan	71	16387	7.6	-0.5
minnesota	67	16787	4.0	3.8
mississippi	47	10992	8.4	6.6
missouri	68	15492	5.7	3.7
montana	53	12670	6.8	-1.4
nebraska	63	15184	3.6	-2.0
nevada	85	17440	5.2	21.1
new hampshire	52	19016	2.4	16.7
new jersey	89	21882	3.8	8.2
new mexico	72	12481	7.8	20.6
new york	85	19299	4.2	1.2
north carolina	43	14128	3.6	11.9
north dakota	49	12720	4.8	-4.7
ohio	73	15485	6.0	-1.5
oklahoma	67	13269	6.7	2.8
oregon	68	14982	5.8	4.0
pennsylvania	69	16168	5.1	-2.7
rhode island	87	16793	3.1	4.7
south carolina	54	12764	4.5	10.1
south dakota	46	12475	3.9	0.8
tennessee	60	13659	5.8	5.9

State	% Urban 1985	Per Capita Income 1988	% Unemployment 1988	% Expected Growth 1990-2000
texas	80	14640	7.3	14.1
utah	84	12013	4.9	12.1
vermont	34	15382	2.8	5.2
virginia	66	17640	3.9	11.7
washington	74	16559	6.2	7.2
west virginia	36	11658	9.9	-7.2
wisconsin	64	15444	4.3	-0.5
wyoming	63	13718	6.3	-2.6

2   Below are data for selected U.S. four-year colleges and universities. What influences tuition cost?

a   What can you conclude from a model using only dummy variables for types of governance?

b   Begin with a model including the two explanatory variables, Number of Students Per Faculty Member and Percent of Applicants Admitted. Does either or do both influence tuition costs?

From left to right the columns represent:

```
1 = Serial number of college,
2 = Competitiveness (1=Most, 2=Highly, 3=Very,
      4=Competitive, 5=Less, 6=Noncompetitive)
3 = Number of full-time students
4 = Number of students per faculty member
5 = Tuition cost
6 = Percent of applicants admitted
7 = School governance: 1=private non-profit, 2=church-related,
      3=private for profit, 4=federal, 5=state, 6=city
```

1	1	850	9	12900	37	1
2	1	6505	10	13569	19	1
3	1	5183	2	14000	18	1
4	1	7236	8	12996	47	1
5	1	1333	11	14060	24	1
6	1	1570	9	14035	22	1
7	1	988	6	14310	49	1
8	1	4322	8	0	?	4
9	1	77	8	0	31	1
10	1	4650	?	13928	24	2
11	1	1159	13	13900	35	1
12	1	9181	5	13950	41	1
13	2	176	10	9500	79	2

14	2	1654	11	14050	44	1
15	2	21658	7	11016	60	5
16	2	2504	20	6331	73	5
17	2	1950	15	13985	55	2
18	2	872	11	0	15	4
19	2	2306	11	13840	42	1
20	2	2471	8	12100	86	1
21	2	2843	13	14232	57	1
22	2	4493	11	13550	71	1
23	2	2441	13	9074	50	2
25	3	3903	9	11775	79	1
26	3	9828	19	4076	38	5
27	3	1024	16	3100	80	2
28	3	1500	13	170	32	2
29	3	197	15	9705	62	1
30	3	403	6	11980	82	1
31	3	4141	6	5813	64	5
32	3	3241	11	8600	63	1
33	3	4728	15	4881	39	5
34	3	526	16	5550	69	2
35	3	5241	17	4392	52	5
36	3	17939	12	5706	66	5
37	4	1349	13	11450	86	2
38	4	1483	16	7980	95	2
39	4	980	12	4245	91	5
40	4	517	13	6182	88	2
41	4	2471	14	6975	51	1
42	4	1247	13	3420	91	2
43	4	19033	5	5340	61	5
44	4	530	12	6300	55	2
45	4	1172	19	6070	80	2
46	4	2135	20	4600	91	2
47	4	1865	17	8455	81	2
48	4	8262	20	5050	72	5
49	5	1603	17	7166	90	2
50	5	528	9	4152	100	2
51	5	2407	14	5150	100	2
52	5	893	24	4990	60	1
53	5	537	9	7800	68	2
54	5	389	10	10000	69	1
55	5	713	11	4140	96	5
56	5	962	20	5052	100	2
57	5	1026	20	3298	98	5
58	5	1081	14	3500	68	5
59	5	376	19	5500	100	1
60	5	481	20	4312	?	2
61	6	108	?	1740	100	2
61	6	418	14	3300	100	2
62	6	6078	18	1722	98	5
64	6	1321	?	3300	?	5
65	6	495	15	4300	96	2

66	6	8079	17	3300	98	5
67	6	665	16	3154	100	5
68	6	965	22	6195	95	5
69	6	95	19	5175	100	3
70	6	6129	15	4098	96	6
71	6	601	17	5187	?	5
72	6	1543	21	3780	99	2

3 Below are data for Chicago neighborhoods (1977–78) on the availability of home insurance. Use the data in Column 5 as the response variable. Propose and evaluate at least three different explanatory models. How would you get at the question of whether Percent Minority Residents influences insurance availability above and beyond the influence of risk factors (fire, theft, and housing age)? How might you tease apart the influences of Income and Minorities?

From left to right, the columns represent:

```
1 = percent minority race
2 = fires/1000 housing units
3 = thefts/1000 population
4 = percent of housing units built before 1940
5 = net new homeowner policies/100 housing units
6 = median family income ($1000s)
```

10.0	6.2	29	60.4	5.3	11.744
22.2	9.5	44	76.5	3.1	9.323
19.6	10.5	36	73.5	4.8	9.948
17.3	7.7	37	66.9	5.7	10.656
24.5	8.6	53	81.4	5.9	9.730
54.0	34.1	68	52.6	4.0	8.231
4.9	11.0	75	42.6	7.9	21.480
7.1	6.9	18	78.5	6.9	11.104
5.3	7.3	31	90.1	7.6	10.694
21.5	15.1	25	89.8	3.1	9.631
43.1	29.1	34	82.7	1.3	7.995
1.1	2.2	14	40.2	14.3	13.722
1.0	5.7	11	27.9	12.1	16.250
1.7	2.0	11	7.7	10.9	13.686
1.6	2.5	22	63.8	10.7	12.405
1.5	3.0	17	51.2	13.8	12.198
1.8	5.4	27	85.1	8.9	11.600
1.0	2.2	9	44.4	11.5	12.765
2.5	7.2	29	84.2	8.5	11.084

13.4	15.1	30	89.8	5.2	10.510
59.8	16.5	40	72.7	2.7	9.784
94.4	18.4	32	72.9	1.2	7.342
86.2	36.2	41	63.1	0.8	6.565
50.2	39.7	147	83.0	5.2	7.459
74.2	18.5	22	78.3	1.8	8.014
55.5	23.3	29	79.0	2.1	8.177
62.3	12.2	46	48.0	3.4	8.212
4.4	5.6	23	71.5	8.0	11.230
46.2	21.8	4	73.1	2.6	8.330
99.7	21.6	31	65.0	0.5	5.583
73.5	9.0	39	75.4	2.7	8.564
10.7	3.6	15	20.8	9.1	12.102
1.5	5.0	32	61.8	11.6	11.876
48.8	28.6	27	78.1	4.0	9.742
98.9	17.4	32	68.6	1.7	7.520
90.6	11.3	34	73.4	1.9	7.388
1.4	3.4	17	2.0	12.9	13.842
71.2	11.9	46	57.0	4.8	11.040
94.1	10.5	42	55.9	6.6	10.332
66.1	10.7	43	67.5	3.1	10.908
36.4	10.8	34	58.0	7.8	11.156
1.0	4.8	19	15.2	13.0	13.323
42.5	10.4	25	40.8	10.2	12.960
35.1	15.6	28	57.8	7.5	11.260
47.4	7.0	3	11.4	7.7	10.080
34.0	7.1	23	49.2	11.6	11.428
3.1	4.9	27	46.6	10.9	13.731

8

Comparing Fuller with Less Full Models

In Chapter 7, we provided initial examples of pairs of linear models linked by a fullness relation. One model, the fuller of the two, contained all of the explanatory variables in the less full model plus one or more additional ones. We also described a statistic whose sampling distribution can be used to conclude whether the fuller model is better than the less full one.

In this chapter, we expand the range of models that enjoy a fullness relation and, hence, can be compared using the Chapter 7 F-statistic. This expanded idea of relative fullness is important because it provides the key to translating our substantive hunches or hypotheses about our data into linear models that can be compared, thus contrasting or testing our hunches.

8.1
The Fuller/Less Full Relation

We have emphasized that the goal of modeling a response variable (y) is to find, from among a set of alternate models, the *best explanatory models* for that response. The set of alternatives may be very limited if we have fixed substantive questions to answer, or it may be broad if our questions are less focused or we are willing to let our data suggest additional models. Whatever the source or extent of our alternate models, the search for the best, once we have a sample of y observations, involves making comparisons among those models.

We emphasize here that the model comparisons that make the greatest contribution to modeling progress are those between models linked by a *fullness* relation. At each comparison, as we choose between fuller and less full alternatives, we learn something quite specific about what influences our response and how. Not all model pairs, as we saw in Chapter 7, enjoy a fuller/less full relation. Before we can take full advantage of our model comparison strategies, we need to know better just what kinds of models are linked by this fullness relation.

8.2
Models That Add or Delete *x*-variables

If the only difference between two linear models is that one or more explanatory variables have been deleted from one model to create the other, then, as we saw in Chapter 7, the models do have a fuller/less full relation. The model with the greater number of *x*s is the fuller of the two. Consider the two models illustrated at the top of Figure 8.1:

$$\mu(Income) = \beta_0 + \beta_1(Years\ Education) + \beta_2(Gender) \qquad \textbf{(Model A)}$$

and

$$\mu(Income) = \beta_0 + \beta_1(Years\ Education). \qquad \textbf{(Model B)}$$

Income, Years of Education, and Gender

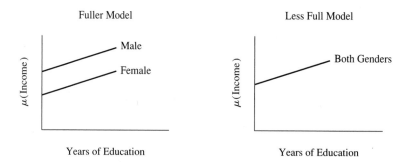

Response Time and Number of Trials

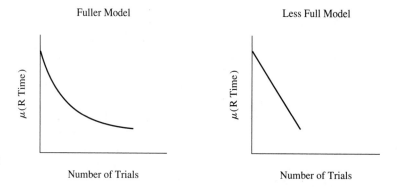

FIGURE 8.1
Fuller and Less Full Models

The comparison of the two models addresses the question,

■ Does Gender influence the annual income of those in the population sampled in addition to the influence of the Years of Education completed?

Similarly, the two models

$$\mu(\textit{Response Time}) = \beta_0 + \beta_1(\textit{No. Trials}) + \beta_2(\textit{No. Trials})^2 \quad \textbf{(Model A)}$$

and

$$\mu(\textit{Response Time}) = \beta_0 + \beta_1(\textit{No. Trials}) \qquad \textbf{(Model B)}$$

form a fuller/less full pair. The response here is the time required to report whether a visual display matches a verbal description. Response time is known to decrease with practice. The question addressed by the comparison of these two models is,

- Is there a constant rate of improvement in response speed with varying amounts of practice (the less full linear model) or does the amount of additional improvement change (decline) with larger amounts of practice (the fuller, quadratic model)?

The two response time models are sketched in the bottom part of Figure 8.1. Model B postulates a constant rate of improvement while Model A allows for a changing rate. The changing rate requires an additional parameter, establishing a fuller/less full relation between the two models.

Finally, here are two models of Attitude Towards Nuclear Power among United States Women as a function of the Region of Country in which they presently reside and the Region of Country in which they resided as primary school students:

$$\mu(\textit{Nuc Pwr}) = \beta_0 + \beta_1 nw2 + \beta_2 sw2 + \beta_3 ne2$$
$$+ \beta_4 ou1 + \beta_5 nw1 + \beta_6 sw1 + \beta_7 ne1 \qquad \textbf{(Model A)}$$

and

$$\mu(\textit{Nuc Pwr}) = \beta_0 + \beta_1 nw2 + \beta_2 sw2 + \beta_3 ne2. \qquad \textbf{(Model B)}$$

Region of Country is categorical, taking four levels for present residence (Northwest, Southwest, Northeast, and Southeast) and five levels for residence as student (Outside the U.S., Northwest, Southwest, Northeast, and Southeast). Our two linear models are the result of converting the region of residence to three dummy variables (*nw2*, *sw2*, and *ne2*) and the region of schooling to four (*ou1*, *nw1*, *sw1*, and *ne1*). Southeast is the comparison level for each of the dummy variable codings.

Model A is, again, fuller and Model B is less full. All of the *x*-variables in Model B are also in Model A, and Model A has some additional *x*s. A comparison of the two models addresses the substantive issue,

- Does region of childhood residence exert an influence on attitude towards nuclear power over and above the influence of region of present residence?

We can think of the less full model in each of these examples as the result of dropping one or more *x*-variables from the fuller model. As those *x*s are dropped from the model their accompanying slope parameters disappear as well. The resulting less full model has fewer parameters than the fuller one.

As an alternative to thinking of the less full model as the result of dropped *x*-variables and slope parameters, we can think of it as the result of *constraining* one or more fuller model slope parameters to be equal to 0. The result is the same, but we see in the following sections that the notion of imposing constraints on the parameters of the fuller model has broader implications for model development.

8.3
Models That Combine *x*-variables

We have just seen that *x*-variables can be dropped from an explanatory model to create a less full one. Another way in which a model can "give up" sources of influence is to combine two or more of them into a single new *x*-variable. Let's consider an example.

The following are two models for the length of Prison Term meted out as a function of the number of Prior Arrests of those convicted of armed robbery. In the first model, the Prior Arrests have been divided between Juvenile (younger than 18 years) and Adult Arrests:

$$\mu(\textit{Prison Term}) = \beta_0 + \beta_1(\textit{Juvenile Arrests}) + \beta_2(\textit{Adult Arrests}) \textbf{ (Model A)}$$

and

$$\mu(\textit{Prison Term}) = \beta_0 + \beta_1(\textit{Arrests}). \hspace{2cm} \textbf{(Model B)}$$

What would be the substantive motivation for these two models and for comparing them? The answers will be easier to see if we first rewrite Model B to make clear that the *x*-variable in that model is simply the sum of the two Model A *x*-variables, Juvenile and Adult Arrests:

$$\mu(\textit{Prison Term}) = \beta_0 + \beta_1(\textit{Arrests}) = \beta_0 + \beta_1(\textit{Juvenile Arrests} + \textit{Adult Arrests})$$
$$= \beta_0 + \beta_1(\textit{Juvenile Arrests}) + \beta_1(\textit{Adult Arrests}). \hspace{0.5cm} \textbf{(Model B)}$$

Now, let's recall our definition of the slope parameter in linear models as the mean increase in the response associated with a one-unit increase in that *x*-variable (the values of any other *x*s being held constant). Both Models A and B have slope parameters for two *x*-variables: the number of Juvenile Arrests and the number of Adult Arrests. The two models do differ in the following way: Model A permits the two slope parameters to take different values. In substantive terms, this means that Model A postulates that each additional Juvenile Arrest may have a different (smaller?) influence on the outcome of sentencing than each additional Adult Arrest. By contrast, Model B gives the same "weight" to Juvenile and Adult Arrests; each additional Juvenile Arrest is postulated to have the same impact as each additional Adult Arrest.

Model A is the fuller and Model B the less full model. The less full model has fewer parameters (two rather than three) than the fuller one. And, most importantly, this reduction in parameters is occasioned by replacing two *x*-variables in the fuller model with their sum. Equivalently, we can think of the less full model as the result of *constraining* the two fuller model parameters β_1 and β_2 to be equal, for $\beta_1 = \beta_2$ or for $\beta_1 - \beta_2 = 0$.

In any event, the substantive question,

- Do Adult Arrests have a different influence on Prison Term than Juvenile Arrests?

is answered by comparing Models A and B. The *F*-statistic of Chapter 7 provides a way of making the comparison on the basis of a sample of observations.

8.4
Models That Constrain Parameters

We stated alternative models for Prison Term and then developed the substantive question that gave rise to those two models. Let's look at a second example. This time, though, we'll consider the substantive issue first and develop models from that.

- The Admissions Committee of Farwest Medical College assigns a Priority Score to each applicant. This Priority Score is intended to take into account three pieces of information:
  1. score on the Medical College Admissions Test (*mcat*),
  2. undergraduate grade-point average in the liberal arts (*lagpa*), and
  3. undergraduate grade-point average in the sciences (*scigpa*),

Furthermore, they tell applicants that the Science GPA is "twice as important" to the Priority Score as the Liberal Arts GPA.

One way of finding out whether the relative importance of the two academic performance measures is as advertised would be to compare two models for the Priority Score. One model,

$$\mu(Priority) = \beta_0 + \beta_1(mcat) + \beta_2(lagpa) + \beta_3(scigpa) \qquad \textbf{(Model A)}$$

is indifferent to the relative influence of *scigpa* and *lagpa*. The two slope parameters, β_2 and β_3, may differ by any amount. The second model, though, postulates that the influence of *scigpa* is twice that of *lagpa* by requiring that $\beta_3 = 2\beta_2$:

$$\mu(Priority) = \beta_0 + \beta_1(mcat) + \beta_2(lagpa) + 2\beta_2(scigpa) \qquad \textbf{(Model B)}$$
$$= \beta_0 + \beta_1(mcat) + \beta_2(lagpa + 2\,scigpa)$$
$$= \beta_0 + \beta_1(mcat) + \beta_2(nugpa).$$

Once again, Model A is the fuller and Model B the less full model and the *F*-statistic provides the vehicle for comparing the models and concluding whether the weight given *scigpa* is, in practice, twice that given *lagpa*.

We can think of the less full model, in this example, as the result of combining the two undergraduate grade indices into one, replacing the two *x*-variables in the fuller model (*lagpa* and *scigpa*) with a single one ($nugpa = lagpa + 2\,scigpa$). The combined *x* is no longer a simple sum but a *weighted sum*. That is, each fuller model *x* is multiplied by some weight before summing: (1)*lagpa* + (2)*scigpa*.

Because of the way in which the substantive problem unfolded, however, it is easier to see the less full model as the result of imposing a constraint on the parameters of the fuller model. The *constraint* is that $\beta_3 = 2\beta_2$ or that $\beta_3 - 2\beta_2 = 0$.

The second form emphasizes that there is a *linear constraint* on the model parameters. A linear constraint on the fuller model parameters is one that can be written formally as

$$\Gamma = \sum_{j=1}^{p+k} C_j \beta_j, \qquad \textbf{(8.1)}$$

where $p + k$ is the number of parameters in the fuller linear model, C_j is the constraint coefficient (or weight) for the jth parameter, and Γ is the value *postulated* for the resulting weighted sum of the $p + k$ parameters. From the present example, we have, as an illustration of Equation [8.1],

$$\Gamma = (0)\beta_0 + (0)\beta_1 + (-2)\beta_2 + (1)\beta_3 = 0.$$

Both the C_js and Γ for Equation [8.1] are needed to specify fully the constraint on the fuller model βs.

8.5
Linear Constraints and Weighted Sums of Variables

We are ready now to state the general conditions under which a second model will be less full than a starting or fuller model. These conditions can be given in terms of either the x-variables in the fuller model or the β-parameters of the fuller model.

To set the stage, we'll assume the fuller model has $p + k$ parameters and the less full model has p parameters. (In each case, we include the intercept in our count.) Thus, the difference in the number of parameters is k. This difference may be as small as 1 or as large as $(p + k - 1)$. In the latter case, we have $p = 1$.

8.5.1   Less Full Model x-variables

One way of assuring that the new model is less full is to require that each of the new model xs be a *weighted sum* of the old model xs. We can express this restriction in the form of an equation:

$$z_j = \sum_{i=0}^{p+k-1} [w_{j,i} x_i], \text{ for } j = 1, (p-1), \qquad \textbf{(8.2)}$$

where x_1 to $x_{(p+k-1)}$ are the xs in the fuller (starting) model and z_1 to $z_{(p-1)}$ are the explanatory variables in the less full (new) model. The $w_{j,i}$ s are the weights.

The Equation [8.2] weights often are quite simple ones. If an x-variable is simply to be carried over from the fuller to the less full model, all but one of the weights would be 0 and the exceptional weight would take the value 1. For example, from the medical school admission Priority Score illustration the $(p - 1) = 2$ variables in the less full model are expressed as weighted sums of the $(p + k - 1) = 3$ xs in the fuller model in the following ways:

$$mcat = (1) \ mcat + (0) \ lagpa + (0) \ scigpa$$
$$nugpa = (0) \ mcat + (1) \ lagpa + (2) \ scigpa.$$

Equation [8.2] actually isn't needed to create most of the variables we want to include in less full models. We introduce it as a useful test. If we are uncertain about a fuller/less full relation between two models, we can ask if each of the x-variables in the model with fewer parameters *can be created* as a weighted sum of the *x*-variables in the larger model. As an obvious example, we know that

$$\mu(Income) = \beta_0 + \beta_1(Age) \qquad \text{(Model I)}$$

cannot be less full relative to

$$\mu(Income) = \beta_0 + \beta_1(Years\ Education) + \beta_2(Gender) \qquad \text{(Model II)}$$

even though it has fewer parameters. There is no way Age, the single *x*-variable of Model I, can be created as a weighted sum of Years Education and Gender, the *x*s of Model II.

Other instances are less obvious. For example,

$$\mu(Income) = \beta_0 + \beta_1(Age) \qquad \text{(Model I)}$$

would be less full relative to

$$\mu(Income) = \beta_0 + \beta_1(Years\ Employed) + \beta_2(Years\ Unemployed). \qquad \text{(Model II)}$$

if we knew Age was simply the sum of Years Employed and Years Unemployed, so that *Age*= (1) *(Years Employed)* + (1) *(Years Unemployed)*.

8.5.2   The Model Unit Variable

In thinking about the *x*-variables of one model as weighted sums of the *x*s of another, it can be helpful to have a *second way* of looking at the role of the intercept term in a linear model. We'll illustrate this with the example of the last paragraph.

We can rewrite Models I and II as

$$\mu(Income) = \beta_0(1) + \beta_1(Age) \qquad \text{(Model I)}$$

and

$$\mu(Income) = \beta_0(1) + \beta_1(Years\ Employed)$$
$$+ \beta_2(Years\ Unemployed). \qquad \text{(Model II)}$$

We've multiplied each of the intercept terms by "1." This, of course, does not change the value of the right-hand sides of these equations. What it does tell us, though, is that we can look at the intercept as the "slope" parameter for another *x*-variable in the model, an *x* that *always takes the value "1."* Because it is always equal to 1 or unity, we call this *x* the *unit variable*. It is really a constant rather than a "variable" and we don't give its "slope" (the intercept) the usual interpretation. But we can remember that there is this "extra" *x*, the unit variable, in the fuller model. It is another *x* that can enter into the weighted sum that produces less full model *x*-variables from fuller model ones.

Let's see how we can use this unit variable in the fuller/less full relation. In our previous example we said that Model I would be less full relative to Model II if Age were the sum of the Years Employed and the Years Unemployed. Having to count each of the years of infancy, childhood, and adolescence either as a Year Employed or a Year Unemployed, though, gives those variables rather unrealistic definitions. It makes better sense to "start counting" not at birth but sometime later on. For example, we might count as years employed or unemployed only those after

18 years of age. With this new definition of Years Employed and Years Unemployed, *can we say* whether

$$\mu(Income) = \beta_0(Unit) + \beta_1(Age) \qquad \textbf{(Model I)}$$

is less full relative to

$$\mu(Income) = \beta_0(Unit) + \beta_1(Years\ Employed)$$
$$+ \beta_2(Years\ Unemployed)? \qquad \textbf{(Model II)}$$

Yes, we can. We can regard each of the *x*-variables in Model I (a less full model) as a weighted sum of the *x*-variables in Model II (fuller with respect to Model I) as follows:

$$Unit^* = (1)(Unit) + (0)(Years\ Employed) + (0)(\text{Years Unemployed})$$

and

$$Age^* = (18)(Unit) + (1)(Years\ Employed) + (1)(Years\ Unemployed).$$

Model I has fewer *x*-variables than Model II but each of them can be expressed as a weighted sum of the *x*s in Model II. (We've marked each less full *x*-variable with an "*" to distinguish them from fuller model *x*-variables.)

The importance of this is that we can compare these two models with the *F*-statistic of Chapter 7.

Equation [8.2] anticipated the value of associating a unit variable with the intercept term. It provides for weighting a variable x_0, which is just this unit variable. If we associate a unit variable with the intercept, it will facilitate our notation to rewrite Equation [8.2], now letting β_1 denote the intercept and x_1 the unit variable:

$$z_j = \sum_{i=1}^{p+k}[w_{j,i}\ x_i], \ \text{for } j = 1, p. \qquad \textbf{(8.2)}$$

In this notation, z_1 most likely also will be a unit variable, associated now with the intercept in the less full model.

8.5.3   Linear Constraints on Fuller Model Parameters

The *second way* of establishing the fuller/less full model relation is to show that the less full model, with its *p* parameters, is the result of imposing *k* linear constraints on the $p + k$ parameters of the fuller model.

To allow for more than one linear constraint, we can adjust the notation of Equation [8.1] slightly to give

$$\Gamma_i = \sum_{j=1}^{p+k} C_{i,j}\ \beta_j, \ \text{for } i = 1, \dots, k. \qquad \textbf{(8.3)}$$

We can see illustrations of this in several of our examples.

As a first illustration, the less full model,

$$\mu(Nuc\ Pwr) = \beta_0 + \beta_1 nw2 + \beta_2 sw2 + \beta_3 ne2, \qquad \textbf{(Model B)}$$

with its $p = 4$ parameters, is the result of imposing on the $(p + k) = 8$ parameters of the fuller model,

$$\mu(Nuc\ Pwr) = \beta_0 + \beta_1 nw2 + \beta_2 sw2 + \beta_3 ne2 + \beta_4 ou1 + \beta_5 nw1 + \beta_6 sw1 + \beta_7 ne1,$$

(Model A)

these $k = 4$ linear constraints:

$$\Gamma_1 = (0)\beta_0 + (0)\beta_1 + (0)\beta_2 + (0)\beta_3 + (1)\beta_4 + (0)\beta_5 + (0)\beta_6 + (0)\beta_7 = 0,$$
$$\Gamma_2 = (0)\beta_0 + (0)\beta_1 + (0)\beta_2 + (0)\beta_3 + (0)\beta_4 + (1)\beta_5 + (0)\beta_6 + (0)\beta_7 = 0,$$
$$\Gamma_3 = (0)\beta_0 + (0)\beta_1 + (0)\beta_2 + (0)\beta_3 + (0)\beta_4 + (0)\beta_5 + (1)\beta_6 + (0)\beta_7 = 0,$$

and

$$\Gamma_4 = (0)\beta_0 + (0)\beta_1 + (0)\beta_2 + (0)\beta_3 + (0)\beta_4 + (0)\beta_5 + (0)\beta_6 + (1)\beta_7 = 0.$$

In a second illustration, the fuller model,

$$\mu(Prison\ Term) = \beta_0 + \beta_1(Juvenile\ Arrests) + \beta_2(Adult\ Arrests), \quad \textbf{(Model A)}$$

with its $(p + k) = 3$ parameters constrained by the following $k = 1$ linear equation,

$$\Gamma_1 = (0)\beta_0 + (1)\beta_1 + (-1)\beta_2 = 0,$$

provides a less full model with $p = 2$ parameters:

$$\mu(Prison\ Term) = \beta_0 + \beta_1(Juvenile\ Arrests) + \beta_1(Adult\ Arrests)$$
$$= \beta_0 + \beta_1(Juvenile\ Arrests + Adult\ Arrests)$$
$$= \beta_0 + \beta_1(Arrests).$$

Finally, as we saw earlier, the single ($k = 1$) linear constraint,

$$\Gamma_1 = (0)\beta_0 + (0)\beta_1 + (2)\beta_2 + (-1)\beta_3 = 0,$$

imposed on the $(p + k) = 4$ parameters of the fuller model,

$$\mu(Priority) = \beta_0 + \beta_1(mcat) + \beta_2(lagpa) + \beta_3(scigpa), \quad \textbf{(Model A)}$$

gives this less full model with $p = 3$ parameters:

$$\mu(Priority) = \beta_0 + \beta_1(mcat) + \beta_2(lagpa) + 2\beta_2(scigpa) \quad \textbf{(Model B)}$$
$$= \beta_0 + \beta_1(mcat) + \beta_2(lagpa + 2\ scigpa)$$
$$= \beta_0 + \beta_1(mcat) + \beta_2(nugpa).$$

Each linear constraint reduces by 1 the number of parameters in the less full model.

8.5.4 Reciprocity of Linear Constraints and Weighted Sums

Imposing linear constraints on the parameters of a fuller linear model and forming a smaller set of x-variables, each a weighted sum of the xs in the fuller model, are two sides of the same coin.

Imposing linear constraints on the fuller model's parameters *implies* the less full model will have *x*s that are weighted sums of fuller model *x*-variables. We see this in at least two of the previous examples. The linear constraint $\beta_2 = \beta_1$ led to a less full model with *Arrests = (Juvenile Arrests + Adult Arrests)*. And the linear constraint $\beta_3 = 2\,\beta_2$ gave rise to the variable *nugpa = lagpa + (2) scigpa*.

Similarly, replacing two or more fuller-model *x*s with their weighted sum implies linear constraints on the fuller model parameters. Thus, replacing Years Employed and Years Unemployed in the fuller model,

$$\mu(Income) = \beta_0 + \beta_1(Years\ Employed) + \beta_2(Years\ Unemployed), \qquad \textbf{(Model II)}$$

with a weighted sum in which the two have equal weight,

$$Age = 18 + (1)Years\ Employed\ + (1)Years\ Unemployed,$$

is the same as imposing the linear constraint $\beta_1 = \beta_2$ on the fuller model.

To show this, we start with the model including the weighted sum, the less full model,

$$\mu(Income) = \beta_0 + \beta_1(Age), \qquad \textbf{(Model I)}$$

and substitute for Age:

$$\mu(Income) = \beta_0 + \beta_1(18 + Years\ Employed + Years\ Unemployed)$$
$$= [\beta_0 + \beta_1(18)] + \beta_1(Years\ Employed) + \beta_1(Years\ Unemployed).$$

The constant, $\beta_1(18)$, is absorbed into the new intercept as it does not depend upon the value of any variable and we are left with a model that is identical to the fuller model except that the two slope parameters have been constrained to be equal:

$$\mu(Income) = \beta_0 + \beta_1(Years\ Employed) + \beta_1(Years\ Unemployed). \qquad \textbf{(Model I)}$$

If weighted sums imply linear constraints and vice versa, *do we need both* ways of looking at model relations? The answer is "Yes". Two of the basic stages to modeling are model formulation and model comparison. *Model formulation* requires translating our substantive ideas into linear models, and, at this stage, linear constraints often provide the easiest way of spelling out model relations. *Model comparison,* on the other hand, requires computing statistics over observations on the *x*- and *y*-variables, and, at this later stage, the definition of one variable as a weighted sum of other variables provides what is required. We must be prepared to go back and forth between the two representations of the relation if we are to formulate and test our explanatory ideas.

8.6
Motivation for a Less Full Model

Section 8.5 emphasized the mechanics of developing a less full model by imposing linear constraints on our linear model parameters or by replacing *x*-variables with a smaller number of weighted sums of those *x*s. Behind the mechanics must be some substantive hypothesis or, at least, a hunch that this will lead to a "better" model. What are the motivations for the mechanics?

First, we emphasize going from a fuller to a less full model. We value *parsimony*. The less complicated the model, the better—provided, of course, that the less-complicated model does as good a job—by our *F*-statistic criterion—of explaining the response as does the more complicated one. Our basic measure of model "complicatedness" is the number of parameters in the model which we seek to reduce where we can. This is clear certainly where we can drop *x*-variables and their slope parameters from a model. The resulting model provides a more economical explanation of the response; it depends upon fewer influences.

Simplification also occurs when, although we can't drop *x*s, we can reduce the number of model parameters by setting some equal to others or by otherwise "fixing" relations among them. Thus, a model that gives *equal weight* to Juvenile and Adult Arrests,

$$\mu(Prison\ Term) = \beta_0 + \beta_1(Juvenile\ Arrests) + \beta_1(Adult\ Arrests),$$

is *less complicated* than one that requires different weights for the two variables,

$$\mu(Prison\ Term) = \beta_0 + \beta_1(Juvenile\ Arrests) + \beta_2(Adult\ Arrests).$$

Once we see that the route to simple models is to reduce the number of parameters, we see better the role of linear constraints. What are the *substantive interpretations* of the βs in the model? How big, how small, how equal, how different should they be—given our ideas about how the *x*s influence the response? Using linear constraints to develop these ideas insures that we develop models that have a fuller/less full relation and can be compared.

8.7
Summary

Our emphasis in this chapter was on seeing the less full model as the result of constraining one or more parameters of a fuller model. This orientation encourages us to begin modeling a response variable with the "fullest" model and to seek ways in which that model can be simplified while still providing an explanation of the response. As we saw in Chapter 1, we are guided in that simplification by a mixture of substantive and data-based "hunches."

Exercises

1 The following data are for bloodstream cortisol levels (at 1600 hours) for a set of normals and four sets of differentially diagnosed psychotics. Begin with a full model, normal as the comparison level, and see how much simplification is possible. At the end, which psychotic groups differ in cortisol level from one another and from normals? Data from the five groups are arranged by column:

```
Column 1:   Normal
       2:   Major Depression
       3:   Bipolar Depression
       4:   Schizophrenia
       5:   Atypical
```

1.0	1.0	1.0	0.5	0.9
1.0	3.0	1.0	0.5	1.3
1.0	3.5	1.0	1.0	1.5
1.5	4.0	1.5	1.0	4.8
1.5	10.0	2.0	1.0	
1.5	12.5	2.5	1.0	
1.5	14.0	2.5	1.5	
1.5	15.0	5.5	1.5	
1.5	17.5		1.5	
1.5	18.0		2.0	
1.5	20.0		2.5	
1.5	21.0		2.5	
1.5	24.5		5.5	
2.0	25.0		11.2	
2.0				
2.0				
2.0				
2.0				
2.0				
2.0				
2.0				
2.5				
2.5				
3.0				
3.0				
3.0				
3.5				
3.5				
4.0				
4.5				
10.0				

2   The prices of 48 stocks listed on the London Stock Exchange are given for four dates in the fall of 1990. Does history help make stock market predictions? Use 26 October prices as the response. Will the 28 September prices taken together with the 12 October prices give better predictions than the 12 October prices by themselves? If the two sets of prices are useful, is it worthwhile adding a third x-variable, the 14 September prices?

	Sept. 14	Sept. 28	Oct. 12	Oct. 26
Abbey National	211	196	229	214
Argyll Group	235	238	239	244
Ass Brit Foods	405	404	399	390
Barclays Bank	323	310	349	349
BAT Inds	529	538	546	549
BICC	350	353	358	361
BOC Group	461	453	478	469
BPB Inds	174	177	185	164
British Airways	160	145	137	143
BP	367	345	349	340
British Telecom	287	264	276	262
Burmah Cast	512	464	496	468
Cadbury Schweppes	321	307	310	312
Cookson Group	101	78	67	74
Enterprise Oil	650	651	666	637
General Accident	450	423	482	446
GKN	328	300	308	301
Grand Metropolitan	564	532	560	564
GRE	178	172	188	176
Hammerson 'A'	572	523	550	555
Hawker Siddeley	473	406	379	396
ICI	829	808	824	815
Ladbroke	261	237	280	275
Lasmo	473	460	459	457
Lloyds Bank	258	240	281	256
Lucas Inds	129	115	116	115
Maxwell Comm	167	146	134	150
Midland Bank	235	195	192	190
NW Water	223	227	232	233
P&O dfd	509	465	533	489
Prudential Corp	203	194	204	199
Rank Org	558	544	615	593
Reckitt & Colman	1195	1187	1278	1214
Reed Intl	382	329	333	347
RMC Group	503	510	624	580
Rothmans	680	656	689	693
Royal Insurance	390	355	395	378
Sainsbury	302	289	307	306
Sears	86	83	83	84

	Sept. 14	Sept. 28	Oct. 12	Oct. 26
Smithkline Beecham	542	521	559	590
Standard Chartered	355	269	273	238
Sun Alliance	276	273	312	309
Tesco	226	219	233	229
Thorn EMI	616	587	613	622
Trusthouse Forte	229	232	262	257
Ultramar	362	340	339	324
United Biscuits	319	309	314	312
Whitbread 'A'	429	403	441	448

3 Here are data for which some quite interesting models may be developed. For each of several islands in the Galapagos, we are given the count of different Plant Species found and, among those found, the number native to that island. What might influence the number of nonnative plants found? We know something of the sizes of these islands, their nearest neighbors, and how separated they are from their neighbors. Develop and assess three or more models relating island characteristics to their plant specialization.

Island	No. Species	No. Native Species	Area (km^2)	Elevation (m)	Distance to Nearest Island (km)	Area of Nearest Island (km^2)
Baltra	58	23	25.09		0.6	1.84
Bartolome	31	21	1.24	109	0.6	572.33
Caldwell	3	3	0.21	114	2.8	0.78
Champion	25	9	0.10	46	1.9	0.18
Coamano	2	1	0.05		1.9	903.82
Daphne Major	18	11	0.34	119	8.0	1.84
Daphne Minor	24		0.80	93	6.0	0.84
Darwin	10	7	2.33	168	34.1	2.85
Eden	8	4	0.03		0.4	17.95
Enderby	2	2	0.18	112	2.6	0.10
Española	97	26	58.27	198	1.1	0.57
Fernandina	93	35	634.49	1494	4.3	4669.32
Gardner(1)	58	17	0.57	49	1.1	58.27
Gardner(2)	5	4	0.78	227	4.6	0.21
Genovesa	40	19	17.35	76	47.4	129.49
Isabela	347	89	4669.32	1707	0.7	634.49
Marchena	51	23	129.49	343	29.1	59.56
Onslow	2	2	0.01	25	3.3	0.10
Pinta	104	37	59.56	777	29.1	129.49
Pinzon	108	33	17.95	458	10.7	0.03
Las Plazas	12	9	0.23		0.5	25.09

Island	No. Species	No. Native Species	Area (km^2)	Elevation (m)	Distance to Nearest Island (km)	Area of Nearest Island (km)
Rabida	70	30	4.89	367	4.4	572.33
San Cristobal	280	65	551.62	716	45.2	0.57
San Salvador	237	81	572.33	906	0.2	4.89
Santa Cruz	444	95	903.82	864	0.6	0.52
Santa Fe	62	28	24.08	259	16.5	0.52
Santa Maria	285	73	170.92	640	2.6	0.10
Seymour	44	16	1.84		0.6	25.09
Tortuga	16	8	1.24	186	6.8	17.95
Wolf	21	12	2.85	253	34.1	2.33

9

Assessing a Model's Adequacy: Individual Observations

The goal of modeling is to find the best models for some response variable given a set of explanatory variables. Chapters 7 and 8 introduced the idea of comparing a fuller and a less full model to determine which is the better of the two. Actually, we have learned how to compare the *fits* of these two models to a sample of observations. We begin this chapter by describing this idea of model fit.

Our *F*-statistic comparison of models focuses on the overall fits of the fuller and less full models. The overall fit of a model may be our first concern, but we can often gain insights into how our model might be improved by looking at the fit in finer detail, examining how individual observations are fit by the model. That is the topic of this and the following chapter.

In this chapter, we stress three considerations. The first is whether one or more *design points*—patterns of *x*-variable scores—have the potential to exert an inordinate *influence* on the model. Such design points are said to possess *high leverage*.

A second consideration is whether some *y*-variable observations are so poorly fit by our explanatory model that they are *outliers* when compared with the rest of the data. The search for outliers focuses on the *residuals*, the differences between *y* scores and their estimated means, under the model. The identification of one or more outliers can be used to improve the model.

The third consideration is that particular *x* and *y* scores may combine, in our sample, to give to certain observations a great deal of *influence* on our estimates of the linear model parameters, the *β*s. This would be undesirable because we wish to interpret model parameters as descriptive of the populations from which we sampled, not just of a few highly influential data points.

In this chapter, we describe techniques for identifying high leverage design points, response outliers, and influential observations. In the final section, we discuss what should be done when such potentially troublesome data points are located.

9.1
Fitted Values and Residuals

Before beginning our study of individual observations, let us review a little. In Section 7.6, we described the *i*th *residual* as the difference between the *i*th *y* score and its estimated mean,

$$\hat{\epsilon}_i = y_i - \hat{\mu}(y_i),$$

where that estimated (conditional) mean is a linear function of the scores on the k x-variables at the ith sample point,

$$\hat{\mu}(y_i) = \widehat{\beta}_0 + \sum_{i=1}^{k} \widehat{\beta}_j x_{ij}.$$

The estimated response means, $\hat{\mu}(y_i)$, for $i = 1, \dots, N$, are called *fitted values*. Fitted values certainly is an easier term to use than estimated conditional means and we shall adopt it! These fitted values depend on the explanatory model and, loosely speaking, if they are close to the corresponding y_i observations we say the model provides a good fit. If the fitted values are close to the y observations, the residuals are small; therefore, a good fitting model produces small residuals. Large residuals accompany a poorer fitting model.

We already have seen how the size of residuals relates to the goodness of a model. The smaller the conditional response variance, the better the model. Our estimate of the conditional response variance for a model with k explanatory variables depends on the sum of the squares of the residuals:

$$\hat{\sigma}^2[y \mid Model] = \left[\frac{1}{(N-k-1)} \right] \sum_{i=1}^{N} \hat{\epsilon}_i^2 = \left[\frac{1}{(N-k-1)} \right] \text{SSR } (Model).$$

The smaller the sum of the squares of the residuals, the better the model fits the observations. We prefer models with small residuals.

9.2
Leverage of Design Points

Once we have a model that is overall better than one or more models with which it has been compared, we need to look at the fit of that model to the observations in some detail. The overall goodness of fit may hide some problems that, if identified, can help us improve our model. For example, the estimated response variance may overstate the goodness of fit if some y observations are well fit, but only *artifactually so*. Overly well fit y observations frequently are associated with *high leverage* design points, so the identification of these design points can help us with our model refinement.

What do we mean by leverage, why can it be dangerous, and how do we assess it?

We have seen in earlier chapters how to calculate the fitted value of an observation. We have a formula to follow in making the calculation, of course, but the important thing about that formula is that it tells us how to put together the x and y scores to get the fitted value. Without specifying just how they are put together, we can describe the fitted value as a *function* of x and y scores,

$$\hat{\mu}(y_i) = g(x, y).$$

Now, it turns out that we can be rather precise about how the fitted value is a function of the y- and x-variables. Though we don't use this formula actually to compute fitted values, the fitted value can be shown to be a linear function of the y scores,

$$\hat{\mu}(y_i) = h_{i1}y_1 + h_{i2}y_2 + \cdots + h_{ii}y_i + \cdots + h_{iN}y_N, \tag{9.1}$$

in which the weights, the h_{ij}s, depend *only on the x scores*.

According to Equation [9.1], we can think of each of the N fitted values as a weighted sum of the N y scores. The weight, h_{ij}, expresses the importance of the jth y observation in fitting the ith observation. In particular, h_{ii} is the weight given to y_i in fitting y_i.

The size of this *self-weight* is important. If a lot of weight is given to the actual value of y_i in fitting it, we can expect two things to be true:

- Dependence of $\hat{\mu}(y_i)$ on y_i means the fitted value and the observed value should be close. The fit should be good.

- Dependence of $\hat{\mu}(y_i)$ on y_i means the fitted value will not be influenced much by the other data points. As a result, the good fit doesn't reflect any systematic influence of xs on y.

A large h_{ii} suggests that the good fit of a model to that y observation is artifactual—it does not reflect the explanatory role of the x-variables. To the extent that the overall good fit of the model, the smallness of the estimated response variance, is due to artifactually well fit individual observations, we can be led to believe that we have a better model than we really do.

The h_{ii}s are called *hat diagonals*. In many statistical packages, the output from the regression commands includes or can include hat diagonals.

9.2.1   Size of the Hat Diagonal

High leverage design points, those yielding large h_{ii}, have the potential to disrupt our regression solution. How can we recognize such points and, more importantly, what can we do to avoid them when we design studies?

Limits to the Hat Diagonal

The value of the hat diagonal for any design point always lies in the interval,

$$\left(\frac{1}{N}\right) \le h_{ii} \le \left(\frac{1}{r}\right),$$

where N is the total number of observations in the sample and r is the number at the same design point as the ith observation. If a design point is represented by only a single observation h_{ii} may be as large as 1.0.

The inequality just described says two things about leverage. First, the leverage of points tends to be smaller as the overall sample size goes up—$1/N$ gets smaller as N gets larger. The more observations we have, the less important any one tends to be.

The second point is that we can reduce the leverage associated with any design point by including more observations at that design point—as r gets larger, $(1/r)$ gets smaller. We will return to this point shortly.

Leverage with a Single Explanatory Variable

If our model has a single measured x-variable, then the leverage associated with each design point—each distinct value of x—can be calculated by this formula:

$$h_{ii} = \frac{1}{N} + \frac{[x_i - M(x)]^2}{N \, \text{Var}(x)}. \tag{9.2}$$

The farther x_i is from the average, $M(x)$, the greater will be the leverage of that design point; h_{ii} is computed, from Equation [9.3], by adding to the minimum leverage value, $(1/N)$, an amount that is a function of the squared distance of x_i from $M(x)$. The squared contribution means that the leverage goes up more rapidly the farther the value of x is from $M(x)$.

Figure 9.1 provides an illustration of the impact on a regression solution of the leverage effect described by Equation [9.2]. The x-variable is Years of Education, the y-variable is Annual Income, and we imagine a sample of $N = 28$ observations. Of these, 9 are drawn from among those with 12 years of education, 9 from among those with 13 years, 9 from among those with 14 years, and 1 from among those with 22 years. The mean of the resulting x scores is $M(YrsEd) = 13.32$ yrs and the hat diagonal values for 27 of the 28 sample points are quite small—0.05, 0.04, and 0.04 for observations based on 12, 13, and 14 years of education, respectively. However, the h_{ii} for the 28th point, that for the 22 years of education, is quite large—0.82.

The effect of this large leverage is illustrated in Figure 9.1. The fitted value for the 28th point depends so heavily on the value of the 28th y score that the estimated regression slope will be determined almost exclusively by the 28th y value; it will take almost no account of the x/y relation in the remaining 27 sample points! The figure shows this by suggesting two possible, but quite different, values of y for this isolated design point.

If we want a wide spread of x scores in our design, we should make certain that the largest or smallest of these are not single, isolated points.

Leverage and the Categorical Explanatory Variable

Consider now a design in which the explanatory information is provided by a categorical variable taking k levels. Our design includes exactly k design points. In our linear model, these would be represented by the k distinct patterns of scores on $(k - 1)$ dummy variables. What is important from a leverage standpoint is how the total number of sample observations is *distributed over the k design points*, the k levels of our categorical variable.

If we represent the total number of sample observations as the sum of the number at each level,

$$N = N_1 + N_2 + \cdots + N_k,$$

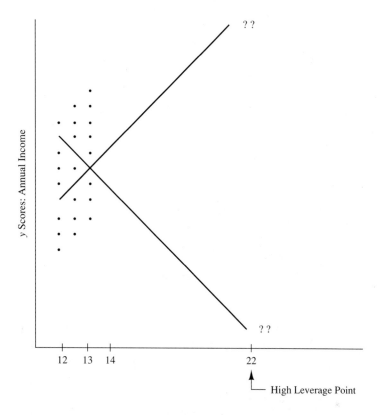

? ?

? ?

12   13   14   22

↑
High Leverage Point

x Scores: Years of Education

FIGURE 9.1
Potential Effect of
a High Leverage
Point

the leverage of the *i*th sample point is given by

$$h_{ii} = \frac{1}{N_j} \qquad (9.3)$$

where the *i*th sample point is one of the N_j at the *j*th explanatory level.
   Equation [9.3] teaches two lessons:

- If the number of observations in the sample is the same at each treatment or category level, $N_1 = N_2 = \cdots = N_k$, then every observation has exactly the same leverage, $h_{ii} = 1/N_k$.

- By contrast, if the levels are disproportionately represented in the design, Equation [9.3] tells us that observations at the category level with the smallest number of observations will have the greatest leverage.

   Figure 9.2 provides an extreme example. In the situation pictured, the attitude towards paid maternity leave of the single male in the sample will *determine completely* the estimated slope of the regression line or, equivalently, the estimated magnitude of the gender difference in attitude.

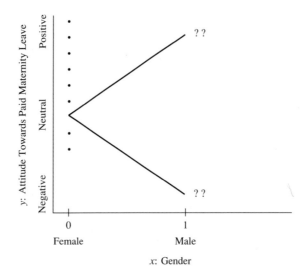

y: Attitude Towards Paid Maternity Leave

FIGURE 9.2
Potential Effect of
a High Leverage
Level

Unless there is a good substantive reason to give one level of a factor more influence in the fitting of an explanatory model, we should strive to provide equal numbers of sample observations at the several levels of any category.

Leverage and Multiple *x*-Variables

Although the h_{ii} is difficult to describe for multiple x designs, the point made by Equation [9.2], though not the equation itself, generalizes to design points based on two or more measured x-variables. The leverage of a point, h_{ii}, will be larger for points that are farther removed from the middle of their distribution.

Figure 9.3 is a scatterplot of two x-variables. The concentric ovals laid over the points connect points of equal leverage. The leverage increases as we move out from the center.

While there is not a simple formula to express leverage for points in multiple x-variable models, the computation of h_{ii} is automatic with many regression programs.

9.2.2   Leverage and the Growth-Study Data

Some of these points about leverage can be illustrated using the Growth-Study sample data of earlier chapters. We begin with the explanatory model (for age-18 heights) that includes only age-2 heights (*ht2*) as explanatory. Table 9.1 lists the age-2 heights (*ht2*), leverage (h_{ii}) values, and case numbers for the 28 observations. Case number refers to the order in which observations appeared in Table 7.1.

To make it easier to see the point made in Section 9.2.1, the tabled observations have been sorted on *ht2*. According to Equation [9.2], the leverage values increase as we consider observations farther away from the sample x-mean. Thus, in Table 9.1, we see the value of h_{ii} decreasing from the 0.2203 associated with the shortest

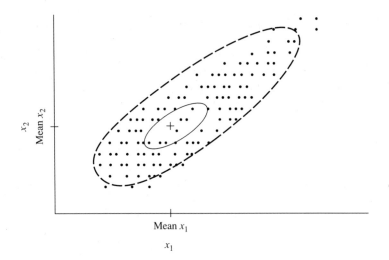

FIGURE 9.3
Increasing Lever-
age of Design
Points

boy in the sample (81.30 cm) to 0.0357—for an *ht2* score of 88.10 cm, very close to
the mean of $M(ht2) = 88.16$—and then increasing again to reach 0.0999 for the two
tallest boys (at 92.20 cm each).

The largest of the h_{ii} values in Table 9.1 are far smaller than the one we noted
for the artificial Years of Education example. In fact, none of the *ht2* leverage values
are large enough to cause concern. But, what would we do if they were?

The first thing to do with the h_{ii}s, certainly, is to use them to check if the *x* scores
are correct. A very large h_{ii} may signal an observation that was incorrectly recorded
or entered into the regression program.

The major importance of the leverage computation is that it allows us to check
our design. Do we have the design points that we intended? Are they represented
in the numbers we intended? Do we have unexpected design points (a possibility
when the design is the result of sampling *x* scores as well as *y* scores)? Are there
any design points inconsistent with the model we are interested in? Although h_{ii}
is typically computed together with the regression solution, when *y* scores are also
available, the leverage values depend only on the sample *x*-variable data. In some
situations, then, they can be computed before response data are collected.

Next, it should be remembered that a large value of h_{ii}, in itself, may not be
bad. Leverage indicates the *potential* of a design point to influence the regression
solution. That potential gets converted into an actual influence when the data point
is associated, in the solution, with a value of the response variable. We return to this
issue later in this chapter.

Table 9.2 shows h_{ii} values for the 28 Growth-Study sample observations when
the design for our model calls for observing both height and weight at age 2 as
explanatory of age-18 height. The data have been sorted by size of the hat diagonals.
The h_{ii} values now reflect how far a data point is away from the center of the age-2
"sizes," where size takes both weight and height into account. The minimum possible
value, $(1/28) = 0.0357$, would result if we had a data point that was at the average

of both *wt2*, M*(wt2)* = 13.5 kg, and *ht2*, M*(ht2)*= 88.16 cm. The closest of the 28 observations, *wt2* = 14.2 kg and *ht2* = 88.40 cm yields an h_{ii} of 0.0439.

The most atypical observation, the one farthest from the center of the size distribution, is case number 13 with age-2 weight of 17.20 kg, height of 87.70 cm, and hat diagonal of 0.3270. He is the heaviest, though not the tallest 2 year old in the sample. In fact, his height is very nearly in the middle of the distribution. He stands out as much because the two correlated measures *tend not to agree* as because one of them is extreme.

While we have no reason to doubt the accuracy of the measures in this instance—male infant no. 13 is just very chubby—h_{ii} provides a basis, in general, for challenging the *x* scores. Now, if on checking back we were to find an error in the *ht2* or *wt2* score for this sample point, we could correct it before continuing.

We have not yet said what might constitute a "big" hat diagonal. The sum of the hat diagonals over the *N* observations will be *k*, the number of parameters in our

T A B L E   9.1

Leverage (h_{ii}) as a Function of Age-2 Heights (*ht2*)

ht2	h_{ii}	Case No.
81.30	.2203	20.
82.20	.1750	7.
83.80	.1102	8.
83.80	.1102	27.
84.20	.0972	11.
86.20	.0507	28.
86.40	.0478	3.
86.40	.0478	17.
86.70	.0440	5.
87.10	.0401	23.
87.40	.0380	10.
87.60	.0369	4.
87.70	.0365	13.
88.10	.0357	6.
88.40	.0359	12.
89.60	.0439	14.
89.70	.0451	25.
90.00	.0490	16.
90.00	.0490	18.
90.20	.0521	1.
90.60	.0591	21.
91.00	.0674	9.
91.40	.0770	2.
91.40	.0770	15.
91.40	.0770	19.
91.40	.0770	24.
92.20	.0999	22.
92.20	.0999	26.

linear model. Thus, from Equation [9.2], we can deduce that the sum of hat diagonals for the linear model with one measured x-variable is 2. And, from Equation [9.3], we can deduce that the sum of hat diagonals in the one categorical variable model is k, the number of category levels. Thus, the absolute size of the hat diagonal depends on the number of model parameters. If the sum of hat diagonals is k, then the average hat diagonal value must be k/N. A rule of thumb is to think of hat diagonals greater than about twice the average as worth investigating. That is, a lower bound for interesting hat diagonals is $2(k/N)$.

The hat diagonal plays an important role in the analysis of individual observations in modeling. In addition to what it can tell us directly about individual design points, h_{ii} combines with other regression information to improve our understanding of the fit of a model. We see this in the following sections.

T A B L E 9.2

Leverage Values Based on Age-2 Weights and Heights

h_{ii}	wt2	ht2	Case No.
.0439	14.20	88.40	12.
.0446	13.70	89.60	14.
.0450	12.70	87.40	10.
.0474	12.70	86.70	5.
.0515	12.60	86.40	3.
.0561	13.60	90.20	1.
.0587	13.30	90.00	18.
.0595	14.30	90.60	21.
.0606	12.20	87.10	23.
.0696	12.00	86.20	28.
.0776	14.20	91.40	15.
.0787	14.80	87.60	4.
.0800	14.30	86.40	17.
.0835	13.80	91.40	19.
.0856	11.90	88.10	6.
.1029	14.20	92.20	26.
.1117	12.60	83.80	27.
.1185	11.40	84.20	11.
.1211	15.90	90.00	16.
.1233	15.90	91.40	24.
.1254	13.20	83.80	8.
.1279	13.40	92.20	22.
.1326	12.70	91.40	2.
.1610	11.50	89.70	25.
.1781	11.50	82.20	7.
.2054	16.90	91.00	9.
.2228	11.30	81.30	20.
.3270	17.20	87.70	13.

9.3
Residuals and Residual Plots

The basic tools of residual analysis are graphic. We use plots of the residuals against empirical or theoretical values to spot potential violations of our model assumptions. The single most useful of these graphical techniques for a simple linear regression model, one with a single *x*-variable, is the scatterplot of residuals,

$$\hat{\epsilon}_i = y_i - \hat{\mu}(y \,|\, x = x_i) = y_i - (\widehat{\beta}_0 + \widehat{\beta}_1 x_i),$$

against the values of the *x*-variable. We call this a *residual plot*. We can examine the residual plot for evidence of *nonlinearity* of the explanatory-response variable relation, *unequal response variance* at different levels of the explanatory variable, *lack of normality* in the conditional distribution of the residuals, or the presence of anomalous observations—*outliers*—very badly fit by the model.

9.3.1   Raw Residual Plots

Figure 9.4 is the residual plot for our example, with *ht2* the *x* and *ht18* the *y*. Traditionally, the *x*-variable describes the horizontal or *X*-axis and the residuals describe the vertical or *Y*-axis in residual plots. Residuals can be produced automatically by many regression programs. Scanning Figure 9.4, there is no evidence of nonlinearity (at all levels of *x*, the residuals are symmetric, about 0), nor of nonnormality (residuals are symmetric and there are proportionally more small in absolute value than large), nor are there any points markedly displaced from the mass of points (outliers). There is a suggestion of variability of residuals increasing as the value of *x* increases (variance heterogeneity).

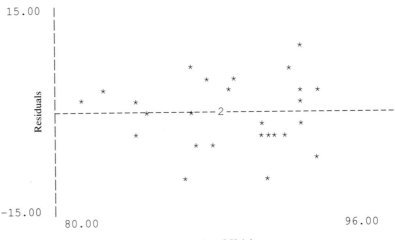

FIGURE 9.4

Raw Residual Plot:
ht18 Residuals on
ht2 Scores

For models with a single categorical explanatory variable, the linearity of the explanatory-response relation is not at issue, but the residuals from the model should still be plotted against the k levels of the category to check for outliers, heterogeneity of variance, and nonnormality. For plotting purposes, the k levels can be represented as separated points along the X-axis. This is conveniently accomplished by plotting the residuals against the k fitted values for the observations; the fitted values are the same for all observations at each level of the category. Figure 9.5 is the residual plot for the Spatial Problem-solving Training example in Chapter 6. The three columns of asterisks describe the three distributions of residuals for the Lecture, Control, and Video conditions, respectively. Figure 9.5 offers no evidence of nonnormality, outliers, or variance differences for the three groups.

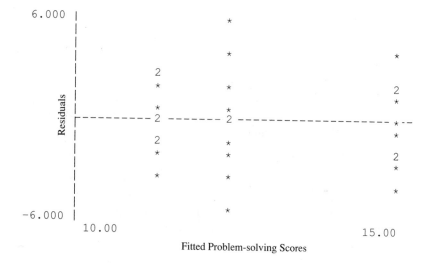

F I G U R E 9.5
Raw Residual Plot: Problem-solving Residuals Lecture, Control, & Video

Fitted Problem-solving Scores

The plotting symbols "2," "3," and so on appear when two, three, or more observations are so close to one another as to appear in the same place in the plot.

For models employing two or more x-variables, either measured or based on different categorical variables, it is a good idea to prepare both a *complete model* residual plot as well as separate residual plots for each explanatory variable. The complete model residual plot displays the residuals against the fitted values for the model and allows a check for outliers and model correctness. The separate plots, each based on the regression solution for a model with a single measured x or a single categorical variable, facilitate the search for an understanding of model failure and the location of a better model.

9.3.2 Improved Residuals

In developing and fitting linear models, we have made a number of assumptions. We've assumed a sample of independent observations from several conditional response populations all with population histograms having Normal characteristics and a common variance. We've also assumed that the means of these conditional response populations are linearly related to the *x*s in the model. We may be mistaken in the conclusions we draw about our models if these assumptions are unwarranted.

The residuals from a model can provide clues about any violation of these assumptions. We study them both graphically and numerically. While the *raw residuals*, displayed in Figures 9.4 and 9.5, are sometimes used for this purpose, it is better first to make two adjustments to them. These adjusted residuals may be requested in certain statistical packages or they may be computed from formulae presented below.

For one thing, we saw in the preceding section that high leverage design points, those with large hat diagonals, are likely to be better fit than others, however influential the *x*s may be. Another way of stating this is that the sampling variability of the residual—the sample-to-sample variability in the size of the residual we would observe if we were hypothetically to repeat the study over and over again—is smaller for a high leverage point than for a low leverage point. The relation between leverage and residual sampling variability is expressed in this equation:

$$\sigma^2(\hat{\epsilon}_i) = (1 - h_{ii})\sigma^2(y \,|\, Model). \tag{9.4}$$

As h_{ii} approaches its upper limit of 1.0, the sampling variability of the residual at that design point approaches 0. Before we can interpret our residuals, we need to correct for these differences in variability. A small raw residual, if it occurs in connection with a very high leverage design point, may signal a *y* observation that actually is quite badly fit by our model.

We use the relation of Equation [9.4] to correct the raw residuals. If each residual were divided by its sampling SD, the resulting corrected residuals would all have the same sampling variance, 1.0. While we don't know the true value of $\sigma^2(y \,|\, Model)$, the conditional response variance, we can substitute our estimate of it into Equation [9.4]. When we use the result to estimate the sampling SD for the raw residual, the corrected residual,

$$r_i = \frac{\hat{\epsilon}_i}{\sqrt{(1 - h_{ii})\hat{\sigma}^2(y \,|\, Model)}}, \tag{9.5}$$

is referred to (e.g., Weisberg, 1985) as a Studentized residual. The name reminds us that we have substituted an estimate for the unknown σ^2 and that, as a result, the sampling distribution for the corrected residual will be more nearly like one of Student's *t*-distributions than a Normal distribution.

The r_is of Equation [9.5] are no longer influenced directly by any differences in design-point leverage. They may be contaminated, though, in a secondary way. Our estimate of the conditional response variance,

$$\hat{\sigma}^2[y \,|\, Model] = \left(\frac{1}{N-k}\right) \sum_{i=1}^{N} \hat{\epsilon}_i^2,$$

for a k-parameter linear model is based on the raw residuals. Now, if a y observation is fit "too well" by a model, as it might if it were at a very high leverage point, it will contribute only a small residual. This small residual, in turn, makes the variance estimate smaller than it would be otherwise. On the other hand, if a y observation is fit "too poorly" by a model, as it would be if it were one of the outliers described in the next section, it will contribute a large residual and, hence, lead to a larger estimate of the conditional response variance.

In either event, we have a better idea of how well the individual y observation is fit by the model if the estimate of response variance used in correcting the corresponding residual, in Equation [9.5], ignores the (over- or under-) contribution of that particular observation. Thus, this doubly-corrected residual, t_i, replaces $\hat{\sigma}^2(y \,|\, Model)$, the usual estimate of the conditional response variance, with $\hat{\sigma}_{(i)}^2(y \,|\, Model)$, the estimate that would result if all of the linear model parameters were estimated from the sample of $(N-1)$ observations, excluding the ith one.

Fortunately, the t_is can be obtained without having to redo the regression solution N additional times, dropping one observation at a time. Weisberg (1985) has shown that the doubly-corrected residual can be computed from r_i by

$$t_i = r_i \sqrt{\frac{(N-k-1)}{(N-k-r_i^2)}}. \tag{9.6}$$

Weisberg refers to the residual of Equation [9.5] as an *internally Studentized* residual (the contribution of the ith observation is *included* in the correction) and the t_i of Equation [9.6] as an *externally Studentized* residual (the ith observation's contribution is *excluded* or deleted and an alternative name for t_i is the *Studentized deleted residual*).

Some regression programs produce internally or externally Studentized residuals (sometimes called standardized residuals) automatically.

These Studentized residuals have a variety of uses. In this chapter, we use them to aid in locating y outliers and highly influential data points. In Chapter 10, we employ them in residual plots to investigate how well a model complies with our model assumptions of linearity of explanatory relation, homogeneity of conditional response variance, and Normality of conditional y distribution.

9.4
Outliers

The notion of leverage was introduced to permit us to identify potentially suspect x scores or design points. We use the concept of *outlier* to identify potentially suspect y observations.

An outlier is a y observation that is very badly fit by a model, so badly fit that we think it may not have been sampled from the y population with which it is associated by its x scores. It may represent something quite different than the x/y relation we are trying to model.

Operationally, an outlier is a y observation that produces a very large Studentized residual. We use two tools, the residual plot and a boxplot of residuals, to aid us in identifying potential outliers.

We are a little fuzzy here, intentionally, in our provisional identification of outliers. In the more technical regression literature greater precision is given the concept. Here, though, our interest in outliers is primarily to insure that we look, one more time, for potential problems in our data. We will examine more observations than we need to in this way, but we are consequently less likely to miss seeing a problem.

9.4.1   Potential Outliers: Example 1

Figure 9.6 is the externally-Studentized residual plot corresponding to the raw residual plot of Figure 9.4.

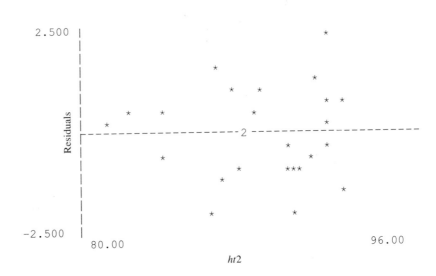

FIGURE 9.6
Studentized Residuals for *ht18* Against *ht2*

The largest residual in Figure 9.6 is associated with a point in the upper right corner of the plot. Visually, the point does not appear to be displaced from the main body of the plot very substantially. So far, we do not see any outliers in this data set.

We take another graphic look at the distribution of these residuals in the form of a boxplot, presented as Figure 9.7.

The boxplot suggests that the largest Studentized residual of 2.453 stands out enough to warrant attention; it is well above the end of the "whisker."

The suspect data point is provided by a boy with recorded age-2 and age-18 heights of 91.4 cm and 195.1 cm, respectively. We check these and find no reason to doubt their accuracy.

FIGURE 9.7

Boxplot of Stu-
dentized Residuals:
ht18 on *ht2*

```
                      -2.023
                      X -------------|-------------|
                                     |    *        |------- X
                      |-------------|
```
                                                                    2.453
                                                                      o

9.4.2   Significance of the Largest Residual

No obvious problem is found with the data for the sample point identified by the boxplot, but is the value of the residual so large that we should continue to worry about it? The Studentized residual, t_i, can be thought of as an observation sampled from a Student's t distribution, that with 26 d.f. (28 observations with 2 degrees of freedom lost for estimating the 2 parameters β_0 and β_1). What can we say about our value of 2.453? Is it so large that we should conclude that it does not belong to the same population of residuals as do the others?

Tabled values for the t-distribution with 26 d.f. tell us that values beyond ± 2.06 occur 5% of the time and values beyond ± 2.78 occur 1% of the time. Before we can relate these traditionally critical t values to our observed value of t_i, we need to distinguish between two ways in which we might have come to observe that particular t_i.

If we had reason to single out *this data point in advance* of examining the values of residuals, we would know that values such as ± 2.06 or ± 2.78 are large. In that case, we might well conclude that the t_i of 2.453 is an "improbably large" value.

However, if we have picked out a data point precisely *because it shows the largest residual*, then values of ± 2.06 or ± 2.78 are not as improbable. That's because we are no longer interested in the probability that *a particular residual* will be as big as ± 2.453. We're concerned with the probability that *the largest of 28 independent residuals* will be this big. Clearly, if we get 28 chances at finding a value as large as 2.453, it is more probable that we will succeed than if we only get one chance at it. In these circumstances, an observation has to be farther out in the tail of the t-distribution to be regarded as improbably large.

In fact, rather than asking that it be among the 5% or 1% of the values in the population, it is appropriate to ask that it be among the largest $(5/N)\%$ or $(1/N)\%$, where N is the sample size (the number of t_i values we have to search through before we can be certain we have found the largest of them).

Tables of the t-distributions for such small tail values are not widely available. To make outlier-detection values of t-distributions easily available, Table 9.3 was specially computed. Or, if you have access to a statistical package that computes t-distribution quantities, you can specify the small tail probabilities.

For our 28 observation sample and referring, conservatively, to the tabled values for a sample of size 30, the largest residual would have to exceed ± 3.48 to be among the most extreme 5% and be larger than ± 4.09 to be among the most extreme 1%. Our observed largest t_i of 2.453 is quite unspectacular. There is neither graphic, substantive, or statistical reason to treat it as an outlier.

Where the largest residual is so large as to pass this test, it might be of interest whether the second largest is also an outlier. The procedure for detection is the same, although the sample size should be interpreted as $(N - 1)$ rather than N in selecting a Table-9.3 entry. This idea generalizes to the third largest, and so on among the Studentized residuals.

9.4.3   Potential Outliers: Example 2

We look next at an example in which the presence of one or more outliers will be clearer.

Table 9.4 presents hypothetical data from a study of university faculty salaries, listing for 50 randomly chosen faculty members their Years of Service (number of years in teaching or other post-degree professional employment), the x-variable, and their Monthly Salaries, the response.

For this data set, the slope parameter is estimated at $\widehat{\beta}_1 = 99.92$ dollars/year and its SE at 13.63 dollars/yr. That is, in the population of faculty from which this sample was drawn, we would estimate on the basis of these data that for each additional Year of Service, the expected Monthly Salary would increase by about \$100. We could be a bit more precise by calculating a confidence interval (CI) for this rate of change,

$$CI[\beta_1, 90\%] = 99.92 \pm (13.63)(1.68)$$
$$= [77.02, 122.82].$$

We are 90% confident that Monthly Salary increases on the average between \$77 and \$123 for each additional Year of Service.

Figure 9.8 gives the (externally-Studentized) residual plot, a scatterplot of the residuals against the x values. Does the plot suggest any outliers?

T A B L E **9.3**

Critical Values of the Largest Studentized Residual

Parameters k:	Extreme 5%					Extreme 1%				
	2	3	4	5	6	2	3	4	5	6
Sample, N:										
10	3.83	4.03	4.32	4.77	5.60	5.04	5.41	5.96	6.87	8.61
15	3.58	3.65	3.73	3.83	3.95	4.44	4.55	4.69	4.86	5.08
20	3.51	3.54	3.58	3.62	3.67	4.23	4.29	4.35	4.42	4.50
25	3.49	3.51	3.53	3.55	3.58	4.14	4.17	4.20	4.24	4.28
30	3.48	3.49	3.51	3.52	3.54	4.09	4.11	4.13	4.15	4.18
35	3.48	3.49	3.50	3.51	3.52	4.06	4.07	4.09	4.11	4.12
40	3.49	3.49	3.50	3.51	3.52	4.04	4.05	4.06	4.08	4.09
50	3.51	3.51	3.52	3.52	3.53	4.03	4.03	4.04	4.05	4.06
75	3.56	3.56	3.56	3.56	3.56	4.03	4.04	4.04	4.04	4.05
100	3.60	3.60	3.60	3.60	3.61	4.48	4.49	4.49	4.49	4.49

Even the quickest glance at the residual plot draws attention to two data points—in the upper left hand corner—that are, relative to all others, very badly fit by this model. We verify the outlying nature of these two with a boxplot of the Studentized residuals.

This boxplot, Figure 9.9, clearly identifies two very large positive residuals. And, Table 9.5 displays the x and y scores for the five cases with the largest (absolute) Studentized residuals. Both of the two very largest residuals (for cases numbered 2 and 4) exceed the Table 9.3 5% and 1% critical values (3.51 and 4.03 for $k = 2$ and $N = 50$, respectively). They are statistical outliers.

Both outlying observations are characterized by low scores on the x-variable (Years of Service of 1 and 2) and large, underfit y scores (Monthly Salaries of $6,240 and $5,910 that the model fits as $2,750 and $2,850, respectively). They correspond, then, to two faculty members with (a) very few Years of Service and

T A B L E **9.4**

Faculty Salary Data: Years of Service and Monthly Salary

Years	Salary	Years	Salary	Years	Salary
1	2140	12	3210	20	4400
1	6240	14	3240	20	4590
2	1890	15	2660	20	5060
2	5910	15	4160	21	5120
3	2200	15	4500	22	5230
3	2490	15	4540	23	5150
4	2590	16	3230	24	5150
4	2720	16	4090	25	4730
5	2320	16	4440	25	5460
6	2890	16	4810	25	5630
6	2950	18	4320	27	5520
6	3430	18	4840	27	5580
7	2750	19	4110	28	5940
8	4000	19	4770	28	5950
9	3280	20	3210	29	5370
9	3740	20	4250	30	5880
11	3340			35	6410

T A B L E **9.5**

Characteristics of the Largest Residuals: Faculty Salary

Residual	Years	Salary	Case No.
1.207	16	3230	24
1.735	20	3210	32
1.796	15	2660	20
4.327	2	5910	4
5.293	1	6240	2

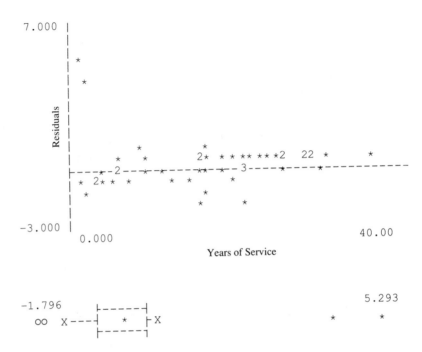

FIGURE 9.8
Faculty Salaries:
Studentized Residuals Against Years of Service

FIGURE 9.9
Boxplot of Studentized Residuals:
Faculty Salary

(b) Monthly Salaries much in excess of what would be expected on the basis of this service.

The two data points look very much as if they might not belong to the same population from which the other 48 faculty members were drawn. They are outliers.

9.5
Influential Observations

The residual focuses our attention on the y score and its possible failure to be fit adequately by our explanatory model, i.e., to be an outlier. Leverage, as indexed by the hat diagonal (h_{ii}), depended only on the x scores and asked us to consider the potential a design point had to influence our model or its interpretation. In this section, we introduce a statistic that takes both x and y into account and tells us, in effect, how great has been the *actual influence* on the regression solution of an individual data point.

9.5.1   Cook's D_i Statistic

The measure is Cook's distance, or D_i statistic (Cook 1977). It is based on the following ideas. We have estimates of the regression coefficients, our $\hat{\beta}_j$s, which we obtained using all N observations in our sample. The βs could also be estimated leaving out one of the observations (the ith one)and basing the calculations on the

x and y scores for the remaining $(N - 1)$ data points. Let's call these new estimates the $\widehat{\beta}_{(i)j}$s.

The two sets of estimates *may be different*. If leaving out the ith data point produces a big difference in the $\widehat{\beta}$s or a big distance between them, then that data point has a big *influence* on the regression solution. Alternatively, if the two sets of estimates are quite close, the ith data point exerts only minimal influence. Cook's D_i is related to the sum of squared distances separating the two sets of parameter estimates,

$$\sum_{j=1}^{k} [\widehat{\beta}_{(i)j} - \widehat{\beta}_j]^2,$$

and takes into account differences in all k of the parameters, including the intercept as well as the x slopes. The larger D_i, the greater the influence of the ith data point.

The computation of the D_i statistic is simpler than the ideas behind it suggest. We use a formula (Weisberg 1985) that links D_i to the leverage (h_{ii}) and the (internally) Studentized residual (r_i) of Equation [9.5]:

$$D_i = r_i^2 \left(\frac{1}{k}\right) \left[\frac{h_{ii}}{1 - h_{ii}}\right]. \tag{9.7}$$

Equation [9.7] tells us that large values of D_i are the result of a large r_i (positive or negative), a large h_{ii}, or both. While D_i neatly draws leverage and residual together, it is important to examine all three indices in evaluating most models.

9.5.2 Growth Study Influence Statistics

Figure 9.10 is a boxplot of the D_i statistics for the boys' heights example. The boxplot singles out one value, 0.2105, as possibly large. In fact, a D_i of this size is not very large. Observations with D_i values substantially smaller than 1.0 generally do not have a large impact on the regression solution.

Table 9.6 brings together all of the diagnostic statistics for the Growth-Study sample—leverages, residuals, and influence statistics. An examination of the entries shows that the largest influence statistic, $D_i = 0.2105$, is for case number 2. It is this same case that earlier produced the largest (Studentized) residual. Given the form of Equation [9.7], it is the large residual that is responsible for the large D_i.

The two observations with the largest leverages, cases 20 and 7, do not have large D_i statistics. Their h_{ii} values are not large enough to guarantee that they will have an appreciable influence on the regression solution, particularly as they were not accompanied by large residuals.

FIGURE 9.10   .6214E-06
Boxplot of D_i .2105
Statistics: Boys'
Heights Data

9.5.3   Faculty Salary Influence Statistics

Let's return to our second example, that of the influence of Years of Service on the Monthly Salary for a sample of university faculty. Earlier, two potential outliers had been noted in the data. When Cook's influence statistic is computed, we note, again, two aberrant values.

Figure 9.11 shows the results, first in boxplot form and then as a stem-and-leaf diagram. The latter provides a quite dramatic picture: 48 values smaller than 0.10, one of 0.49, and another of 0.72.

Below are listed the first five cases containing all of the diagnostic information for the 50 data points. It shows that large D_i statistics belong to the same two cases as stood out in the search for outliers, the second and fourth cases. The D_i statistics in this example are appreciably larger than the largest in the boys' heights example. It could be that cases 2, 4, or both have had a considerable influence on the regression

T A B L E   9.6
Individual Observation Diagnostics: Growth-Study Data

ht2	h_{ii}	ht18	fit	$\hat{\epsilon}_i$	t_i	D_i
90.20	.05	179.00	182.43	−3.43	−.70	.01
91.40	.08	195.10	184.34	10.76	2.45	.21
86.40	.05	183.70	176.41	7.29	1.54	.06
87.60	.04	178.70	178.31	.39	.08	.00
86.70	.04	171.50	176.89	−5.39	−1.11	.03
88.10	.04	181.80	179.11	2.69	.54	.01
82.20	.18	172.50	169.76	2.74	.60	.04
83.80	.11	174.60	172.29	2.31	.48	.01
91.00	.07	190.40	183.70	6.70	1.42	.07
87.40	.04	173.80	178.00	−4.20	−.85	.01
84.20	.10	172.60	172.93	−.33	−.07	.00
88.40	.04	185.20	179.58	5.62	1.15	.02
87.70	.04	178.50	178.47	.03	.01	.00
89.60	.04	177.60	181.48	−3.88	−.79	.01
91.40	.08	183.50	184.34	−.84	−.17	.00
90.00	.05	178.10	182.12	−4.02	−.82	.02
86.40	.05	177.00	176.41	.59	.12	.00
90.00	.05	172.90	182.12	−9.22	−2.00	.09
91.40	.08	188.40	184.34	4.06	.84	.03
81.30	.22	169.40	168.33	1.07	.24	.01
90.60	.06	180.20	183.07	−2.87	−.59	.01
92.20	.10	189.00	185.60	3.40	.71	.03
87.10	.04	182.40	177.52	4.88	1.00	.02
91.40	.08	185.80	184.34	1.46	.30	.00
89.70	.05	180.70	181.64	−.94	−.19	.00
92.20	.10	178.70	185.60	−6.90	−1.49	.12
83.80	.11	169.60	172.29	−2.69	−.56	.02
86.20	.05	166.80	176.09	−9.29	−2.02	.10

Boxplot

```
.1838E = 05

      ||                                                        .7156
      |:
      *|X**                                    *                   *
      || 2
```

Stem-and-Leaf

```
00 |  000000000000000000000000000000001111111111111233345
01 |
02 |
03 |
04 |  9
05 |
06 |
07 |  2
```

FIGURE 9.11

Distribution of D_i
for Faculty Salary
Data

solution. If so, what should be done about it? We examine this question in the next section.

x	y	$\hat{\mu}(y)$	$\hat{\epsilon}_i$	h_{ii}	t_i	D_i
1.	2140.00	2749.70	−609.70	.07	−.74	.02
1.	6240.00	2749.70	3490.30	.07	5.29	.72
2.	1890.00	2849.62	−959.62	.07	−1.16	.05
2.	5910.00	2849.62	3060.38	.07	4.33	.49
3.	2200.00	2949.55	−749.55	.06	−.90	.03

9.6
Resolving Troublesome Data Points

We have described three techniques for inspecting individual data points for evidence that one or more of those data points may play a "special" role in the fitting of an explanatory model. These lead to the identification of (a) high leverage design points, (b) response observations that are outliers, and (c) combinations of x and y scores that give some data points great influence on the fit of the model. In some sense, the finding of potentially suspect points is the easier part of our task. The harder part is to decide what we should do once we have found such evidence.

9.6.1 Change of Design

We noted that the leverage or potential influence statistic, h_{ii}, depends only on the x scores. If we compute these hat diagonals in advance of the collection of response data we will be alerted to the presence of potential problems in the design of our study. Even though the h_{ii}s are traditionally computed as part of a regression solution, we do not have to have "real" y scores to assess leverage. We can provide a regression program such as SPIDA with any data in place of the to-be-collected y scores and obtain the h_{ii} results.

The detection of high-leverage design points calls for a redesign of the study to better equalize the hat diagonals.

We may be able to change the design, even after the study is underway and some y observations have been collected. An examination of h_{ii} values may suggest the need to add data points before concluding a study. One should take care to make this judgment on the h_{ii} values alone, without looking at the associated y scores or residuals. It is one thing to decide more men should be added to the study because there are proportionately fewer of them than of women. It is quite another to decide to collect data for more men because the y scores for those already sampled are judged to be either too small or too large!

A second way in which troublesome data points may signal the need for a design change is if we detect some commonality among those points. If, for example, they turned out to be observations on younger animals and age was not already an explanatory variable, this would be a clear signal to assess the impact of including age—adding it to the design.

9.6.2 Correction of Data

Perhaps the happiest resolution of finding extraordinary h_{ii} or Studentized residuals is to discover that a clerical error has been made and a score has been incorrectly entered into the analysis. Suppose that case no. 27 is really 13 rather than 133 years old, or that the height of case no. 12 is 70 cm, not 7 cm. The data can be corrected and analyzed anew.

Errors of this kind are frustratingly common and offer the strongest argument for case analysis of the kind described in this chapter. The most thorough proofreading does not guarantee that an error will not reach the analysis stage. And, it is not unknown for a computer gremlin to corrupt correctly entered data.

9.6.3 Modification of Data

What can we do when we discover that an item of data is bad, but we can't establish, at least exactly, what the correct value should be? We may have to throw it out, but we may also have some clue about, at least, the direction in which the datum should be adjusted.

Survey respondents are asked to report their age and, subsequently, the number of years they have worked full time since reaching the age of 16. One respondent reports his age as 28 and the number of years worked (since age 16) as 20. Perhaps the latter could be recoded as 12? What would be the rationale?

Because there is some judgment needed in modifying data in this way, it is imperative that we describe those judgments whenever we communicate our analyses or interpret them to others. They, in turn, may suggest to us a better way of resolving our uncertainties!

9.6.4 Elimination of Cases

This represents the severest of decisions and, whatever the basis for making it, should always be reported together with any description of model development and evaluation.

Some data may be patently unusable. Our automatic pH meter fails in the middle of series of trials and registers a number of quite impossible values. No correction is possible and we have to ignore those trials.

Some observations may appear, after the fact, to be inappropriate to include. The faculty salary example of this chapter is wholly contrived, so we are free to argue that we might have found that the two faculty members whose salaries were so badly underestimated by our Years of Service model were, in fact, two distinguished, visiting professors. They were hired for only a short period of time. Their salaries were paid from a special alumni fund, rather than from the general university budget, and those salaries were not subject to the same constraints as were placed on other faculty salaries. In short, we may adduce ample evidence that these two faculty were quite different from the remainder of the sample.

Our conscience may be untroubled at dropping the two observations and redoing the analysis on the remaining 48 sample points. We should report what we have done and why we have done it. Equally importantly, however, we should think about what it means. We may need to acknowledge, to ourselves as well as to others, that we are now going on to model salaries for normal faculty members. This ought to include, of course, a good faith effort at describing what we mean by normal in this context.

9.6.5 Parallel Modeling

The least neat but often most justifiable (if not unavoidable) conclusion is that we can neither dismiss nor correct certain troubling observations. We must, as it were, live with them. Here our obligation is to report why they are troubling (h_{ii}, t_i, D_i, or other evidence) and how they may impact our modeling.

This latter point often takes the form of modeling both with and without the observations in question and then confronting the differences between the two results. We'll call this parallel modeling.

Let's examine the impact of the two most influential data points (and outliers) on the linear model for Faculty Salaries.

The estimated regression equation based on all 50 faculty members is

$$\hat{\mu}(Monthly\ Salary\mid Years\ of\ Service) = \$2,650 + \$100\ (Years\ of\ Service).$$

That based on all but the second case is

$$\hat{\mu}(Monthly\ Salary\mid Years\ of\ Service) = \$2,357 + \$114\ (Years\ of\ Service).$$

That based on all but the fourth is

$$\hat{\mu}(Monthly\ Salary\mid Years\ of\ Service) = \$2,408 + \$111\ (Years\ of\ Service).$$

That based on all but the second and fourth cases is

$$\hat{\mu}(Monthly\ Salary\mid Years\ of\ Service) = \$2,072 + \$127\ (Years\ of\ Service).$$

Removing case 2 and/or case 4 leads to steeper slope estimates and smaller estimates of the intercept.

Figure 9.12 depicts the two regression lines: one based on the Full sample—all 50 cases—with endpoints labeled "F," and a second one for the Reduced sample—the 48 cases remaining after cases 2 and 4 have been dropped from the analysis—with endpoints labeled "R."

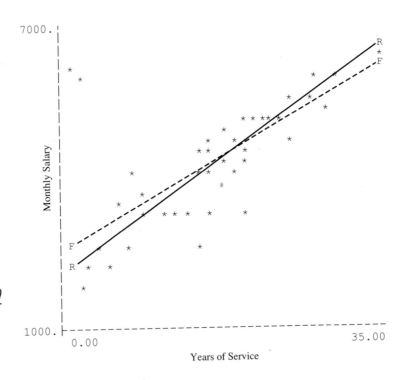

FIGURE 9.12

Faculty Salaries: Scatterplot & Estimated Regression Lines

The slope estimate when both cases are dropped ($127.20) is right at the upper end of the 95% CI for β_1 based on the 50-case sample: $99.92 ± (2.01)($13.63) = [$72.52, $127.32]. The full sample estimate of the slope ($99.92) is well outside the

95% CI based on the 48 cases: $\$127.20 \pm (2.01)(\$7.90) = [\$111.32, \$143.08]$. There can be no doubt that the impact of those two observations on the slope estimate is a real one.

Furthermore, the fit of the model to the data is considerably better for the 48 sample points than for the full sample. The estimated conditional response SD is $856.70 when all 50 cases are used, but only $469.90 when the sample is limited to the 48 cases.

Figure 9.13 gives the raw residual plots, above for the 50-case sample and below for the 48 cases. The two are plotted to the same scale so that the lessened variability in residuals for the reduced model is highlighted.

If we have reason to dismiss the two strangers we have a much more impressive model. In any event, having identified the two disparate points we are obliged to report the impact of their inclusion or exclusion on the model.

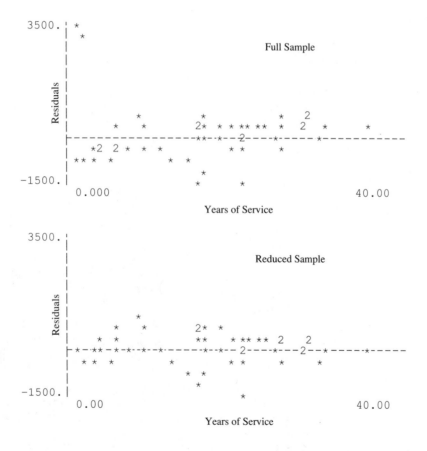

FIGURE 9.13
Raw Residual Plots:
Full and Reduced
Faculty Salary
Samples

9.7
Summary

The estimated conditional response variance gives us an idea of how well, overall, an explanatory model fits a set of response observations. We shouldn't stop there, however. It is important to go on to examine the fit in finer detail. This chapter is the first of two devoted to that. It focuses on the use of three indices—leverage or the hat diagonal, Studentized residuals, and Cook's influence statistic—to point to individual observations that may inordinately influence the fit of the model. In Chapter 10, we look further at residuals for evidence that the assumptions of linear modeling have been met. We also look at ways of improving a model that fails to meet those assumptions.

Exercises

1   This is an exercise in finding outliers. Here are data on typical Body Weight (column 3, in kg) and Brain Weight (column 4, in gm) for an assortment of animals. Does Body Weight strongly influence Brain Weight? Use residual plots to spot any potential outliers and interpret the results. (Because of the wide variability in scores, a preliminary logarithmic transformation of both variables may help bring the data into range.)

Species	Body Weight (kg)	Brain Weight (gm)
1 Mountain Beaver	1.350	8.100
2 Cow	465.000	423.000
3 Grey Wolf	36.330	119.500
4 Goat	27.660	115.000
5 Guinea Pig	1.040	5.500
6 Diplodocus	11700.000	50.000
7 Asian Elephant	2547.000	4603.000
8 Donkey	187.100	419.000
9 Horse	521.000	655.000
10 Potar Monkey	10.000	115.000
11 Cat	3.300	25.600
12 Giraffe	529.000	680.000
13 Gorilla	207.000	406.000
14 Human	62.000	1320.000
15 African Elephant	6654.000	5712.000
16 Triceratops	9400.000	70.000
17 Rhesus Monkey	6.800	179.000
18 Kangaroo	35.000	56.000
19 Hamster	0.120	1.000
20 Mouse	0.023	0.400
21 Rabbit	2.500	12.100

22 Sheep	55.500	175.000
23 Jaguar	100.000	157.000
24 Chimpanzee	52.160	440.000
25 Brachiosaurus	87000.000	154.500
26 Rat	0.280	1.900
27 Mole	0.122	3.000
28 Pig	192.000	180.000

2 Here we have, for a selection of popular U.S. magazines, data on the number of advertising pages sold during the first nine months of 1990 and the advertising income. Use your outlier detection techniques to identify any magazines whose incomes are very badly over- or underestimated by their page sales. Can you interpret the results?

Magazine	Pages Sold	Income
Business Week	2845.15	160326035
People	2494.61	235476537
Forbes	2485.10	108139559
Bride's	2354.94	41814684
Fortune	2320.36	111347345
TV Guide	2186.78	236131981
Vogue	2159.14	78218413
The Economist	1953.38	16995384
Modern Bride	1892.42	30851147
Sports Illustrated	1806.71	227289831
Time	1793.96	246748515
New York	1774.58	28759371
Elle	1590.63	47027305
Cosmopolitan	1578.02	94341991
Newsweek	1542.73	170638646
Entrepreneur	1504.95	14450795
The New Yorker	1472.83	37849662
GQ	1403.82	34220045
Glamour	1375.27	69992476
Rolling Stone	1351.60	50458141
U.S. News \& World Report	1324.73	105721620
Architectural Digest	1306.54	34839841
American Way	1273.38	17425033
Good Housekeeping	1224.98	116537952
Family Circle	1218.11	99365045

10

Assessing a Model's Adequacy: Checking Assumptions

In Chapter 9, we examined the fit of our model to see if it was unduly influenced by a few individual observations. Here, we continue to examine the fit, now looking for evidence that our model and data conform to the several assumptions of the linear model. Specifically, we look for evidence that (a) the relation of each of the explanatory variables (xs) to the (conditional) mean of the response variable (y) is *linear*, (b) the conditional response populations have *constant variance*, (c) the histograms for the conditional response populations have certain *Normal* random variable characteristics, and (d) the response variable observations are *independent*. Where we find evidence that an assumption has not been met, we consider how the failure might be corrected by a transformation of one of our variables.

We discussed potential problems with individual observations first. If not detected and resolved before we look for modeling violations they may mislead us about one or another of the assumptions. Similarly, the several assumptions are taken up in this chapter in the order in which they should be checked in a typical linear model.

The presence in our data of an undetected nonlinear explanatory relation can lead us to conclude that the conditional response variance is heterogeneous, not constant. Similarly, heterogeneous variances (or a nonlinear relationship) can suggest that we have sampled from non-Normal response populations.

In examining the fit of a model to our data, then, we look first for outliers, next for any evidence of nonlinearity, then for heterogeneity of response variance, and lastly for hints of non-Normality. Our acceptance of the assumption of the independence of response observations must rely, almost exclusively, on our knowledge of how those observations were sampled. We cannot detect violations of this assumption from the data alone. We will make some suggestions in this chapter, however, about certain limited checks on independence that can be made on the data.

At each stage, we are challenged to see if we can improve our model by bringing it more in line with our linear modeling assumptions. As we strive to improve our model, however, it is important that we keep two factors in mind. First, adjustments to the model must make substantive sense. Transforming the y-variable, say, by using the logarithm of the response may give a better fitting model, but one for which there may be no theoretical justification. Worse yet, such a transformation might starkly conflict with a physical or biological mechanism responsible for the explanatory-response relation. Second, model improvements suggested by examining a sample of data are necessarily dependent on those data. We should recognize that a correction—OK for this sample—may be incorrect for the population, and that it may reflect certain idiosyncracies in our particular set of observations.

10.1
Residuals and Modeling Assumptions

In Chapter 9, we computed and examined the residuals—the differences between the response observations and the values fitted to those observations by the model. They were important to us there in alerting us to potentially troublesome data points in our sample. These residuals are also a major source of information about whether the modeling assumptions have been met. In this chapter, we will learn both graphical and computational ways of using the residuals for this purpose.

None of the four assumptions is explicitly about residuals. Yet we depend heavily on their evidence in the checks we make. How can that be? The residual part of a response observation is the result of subtracting from it the fit of our model to that observation—the estimate of the mean for y in the conditional population from which that observation was drawn:

$$\widehat{\epsilon}_i = y_i - \widehat{\mu}(y \mid Model \ \& \ ith \ design \ point \ data). \qquad \textbf{(10.1)}$$

Now, subtracting the same number from each observation in a population changes neither the variance of those observations nor the shape of their histogram. As a result, residuals themselves are observations from populations that, if our modeling assumptions are correct, all have the same variance and all have Normal modality, symmetry, and kurtosis. In fact, by subtracting out what we think to be the only differences among the y observations—that they come from populations with different means—we make it easier to see whether the variances and shapes do remain constant.

Similarly, the fitted values for our model depend on our assumption of a linear relation between the y mean and the x-variables,

$$\widehat{\mu}(y \mid Model \ \& \ ith \ design \ point \ data) = \widehat{\beta}_0 + \sum_{j=1}^{k-1} \left(\widehat{\beta}_j x_{ij} \right). \qquad \textbf{(10.2)}$$

When we subtract these fits from the y observations, we are subtracting out the presumed linear relations. If the x/y relation is nonlinear, that nonlinearity would be highlighted in the residuals.

The residuals not only contain the information we need to assess our modeling assumptions, but in a form that makes it easier to make those assessments.

Our use of residuals in checking model assumptions is almost entirely graphical. That is, we plot the residuals in ways designed to shed light on the assumptions. Often these plots take the form of scatterplots and we preview this use here. Later, in the section on assessing the Normality assumption, we introduce a second residual plot, the quantile-quantile or QQ plot.

10.1.1   Residual Plots for Models with a Single Explanatory Variable

If our model has only one measured or categorical x-variable, we form a scatterplot by plotting the values of the residual (along the vertical or Y-axis) against the values of the single *x* (along the horizontal or *X*-axis). As in Chapter 9, it is better to use the Studentized residuals rather than the raw residuals for these plots.

10.1.2 Residual Plots for Models with Several Explanatory Variables

If our explanatory model has more than one measured *x*-variable, we examine two kinds of residual scatterplots. The first plots the residuals against the fitted values (estimated means) for the complete model and is useful in our homogeneity of variance assessment. The second, *partial residual plots*, are made up for each measured *x* and are used in checking the linearity assumption.

Plotting Residuals Against the Model's Fitted Values

Figure 10.1 is a scatterplot from the Boys'-growth study of earlier chapters. The externally Studentized residuals and fitted values—estimates for each data point of $\mu(ht18)$—were obtained for the model in which expected Adolescent Height, $\mu(ht18)$, was postulated to be a linear function of both Infant Height *(ht2)* and Infant Weight *(wt2)*. These two sets have been plotted against each other in Figure 10.1, the residuals along the *Y*-axis and the fitted values along the *X*-axis.

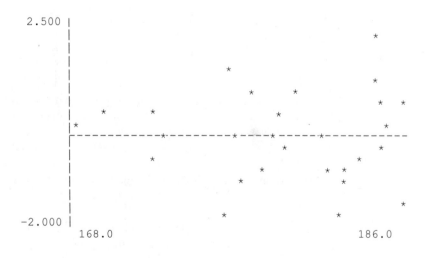

Boys'-growth Study

FIGURE 10.1
Scatterplot: Externally Studentized Residuals (*Y*-axis) v. Fitted Values (*X*-axis)

Partial Residual Plots for Each Explanatory Variable

In evaluating the relation to $\mu(y)$ of any one of the measured *x*s, it is important to adjust for any other explanatory variables in the model. We do this in the following way. For our linear model, each y observation can be written, based on Equations [10.1] and [10.2], as

$$y_i = \widehat{\beta}_0 + \sum_{j=1}^{k-1}(\widehat{\beta}_j x_{ij}) + \widehat{\epsilon}_i. \tag{10.3}$$

Now we are interested in whether the model provides the best representation of the relation of a particular x, say the ℓth one, to $\mu(y)$. To focus on that, we subtract from each y observation the modeled influence on it of all of the other x-variables (including the unit variable intercept) in the model. From Equation [10.3], this gives us

$$y_i - [\widehat{\beta}_0 + \sum_{j \neq \ell}(\widehat{\beta}_j x_{ij})] = \widehat{\beta}_{i\ell} x_{i\ell} + \widehat{\epsilon}_i. \tag{10.4}$$

On the right-hand side of Equation [10.4], we have that part of the y observation that does not depend on the other $(k - 1)$ sources of influence. In the partial residual plot, these values are plotted (on the Y-axis) against the values of the ℓth x-variable (along the X-axis). A residual plot would be prepared for each of the measured xs in our model.

These *partial residual plots* provide graphic summaries of the relations of the several measured xs within our model to the response. We use them to check on the linearity of the x/y relations.

Figure 10.2 displays the two partial residual plots for the boys' Growth-Study model:

$$\mu(ht18_i) = \beta_0 + \beta_1 ht2_i + \beta_2 wt2_i.$$

The top panel is the scatterplot of

$$\widehat{\beta}_1 ht2_i + \widehat{\epsilon}_i$$

against $ht2$. Superimposed on this scatterplot, connecting the points labeled "B," is the line with slope $\widehat{\beta}_1$, the linear relation assumed by the model. Notice that the Y-axis coordinates of this plot can be obtained from the right-hand side of Equation [10.4] once the residuals and regression slope estimates have been found. We inspect the scatter of points about this line for any evidence that the influence of $ht2$ on $ht18$ is nonlinear.

The bottom panel to Figure 10.2 is the scatterplot of

$$\widehat{\beta}_2 wt2_i + \widehat{\epsilon}_i$$

against $wt2$ with the partial regression line $\widehat{\beta}_2$ superimposed on it. Neither partial residual plot suggests a nonlinear patterning to the plotted points. Many statistical packages have facilities for preparing plots of this kind.

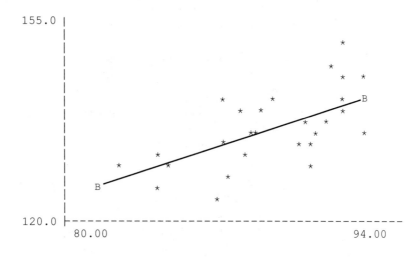

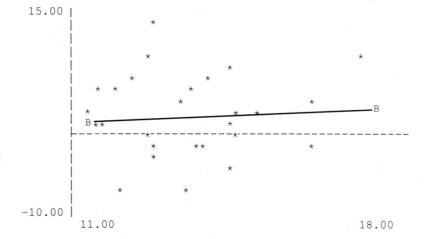

FIGURE 10.2
Partial Residual
Plots: Infant Height
(Top) & Infant
Weight (Below)

10.2
Assessing the Linearity of Regression

We begin the task of checking our model assumptions by asking if each of the measured *x*-variables in our model, conditional on the values of other *x*-variables in the model, is related *linearly* to the *y*-variable mean. Because any one of the dummy variables we may have introduced into our model takes only two values, 0 and 1, it will be linearly related to $\mu(y)$ automatically. We need not check on our dummy variables.

Before we *look* at any residual or scatterplot for evidence of linearity, we need to ask what we already know about the relation of a particular *x* to our *y*.

10.2.1   Is the Form of the Relation Known?

What do we know, on substantive grounds, about the form of the relation between our x and the mean of the response? Our answers to this question will fall into one of four categories:

- The relation is known to be linear. Example: The length of time taken to decide whether a word is a verb or adjective increases as a steady, linear function of the number of letters in the word.

- The relation is known to be nonlinear and the form of the relation is known as well. Example: The speed of a falling object increases as the square of the amount of time it has been falling.

- The relation is known to be nonlinear but the form of the relation is not specified. Example: Store managers' inventory adjustments become more accurate the longer they have been on the job. However, the amount of improvement is not steady, it changes as well with time.

- It is not known whether the relation is linear or not. Example: Doctors' incomes will vary as a function of the number of years they have practiced.

If the relation is in the first category, plot inspection should verify the linear relation. If it is in the second, we may be able to *transform* the x- or y-variable so that the relation is a linear one. For the example, the model

$$\mu(speed \mid time) = \beta_0 + \beta_1(time)$$

will not capture the nonlinear relation of time and speed, but the model

$$\mu(speed \mid time) = \beta_0 + \beta_1(time) + \beta_2(time)^2$$

will. This second model is still a *linear model*, one we know how to estimate and evaluate, because the model parameters are either additive (β_0) or multiplicative (β_1 and β_2) constants. Not all nonlinear relations can be converted to linear models.

Our interest in this section focuses on the third and fourth categories above. If we know the relation to be nonlinear, but we don't know its form, we see what we can learn about that form. If we are in doubt about linearity, we see what we can do when we "discover" that the x/y relation is apparently nonlinear.

10.2.2   Alternatives to a Linear Relation

When we use our sample data to describe the form of the x/y relation, we need to keep in mind that the description holds only for the range of x scores relevant to our study design. If we have data on annual sales volume (y) for a sample of life insurance agents with from 2 to 7 years experience (x), we can learn about the shape of the relation only over that range of experience; we know nothing about how sales volume might change between 10 and 15 years of experience.

To say that the x/y relation is linear is to say that the mean of y changes at a *constant rate* as the value of x changes. The alternative is that the rate of change in the y mean does not remain constant across the range of x. How might the rate of change depart from constancy? Figure 10.3 illustrates three alternatives of special interest. Each of the four panels describes a hypothetical relation between years of selling experience and average annual sales volume (again for life insurance agents, though now the range of x is broader, from 2 to 35 years experience).

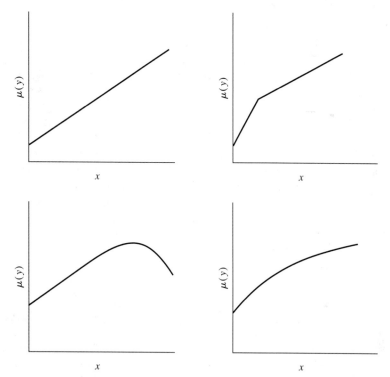

FIGURE 10.3

Examples of Linear and Nonlinear Regression Lines

The panel at the upper left of Figure 10.3 describes a linear relation. For each additional year of experience, the annual sales volume increases, on the average, by the same amount. In each of the other three panels, the average year-to-year increase in sales volume differs from one stage of the agent's career to another.

What distinguishes the panel in the upper right of Figure 10.3 from the two below it is the abruptness with which the rate of change in annual sales volume changes. Year-to-year increases are constant from two to five years, then they shift to a lower rate for the remainder of the agent's career. By contrast, there is a smooth shift in the amount by which the year-to-year sales volume changes in the two bottom panels. What distinguishes between the latter two is that there is a reversal in the rate of change in the average y—from positive to negative—in the lower left panel while the mean y in the lower right panel continues to increase throughout the x range.

We discriminate among these three departures from linearity in the way we treat them.

Should the Linear Regression Be Segmented?

The shift from one constant rate of change to another depicted in the upper right panel of Figure 10.3 describes a piecewise linear or *segmented regression*. The overall regression is made up of two separate linear segments. The possibility of segmented regression is suggested by an x/y scatterplot (in the case of models with a single x) or partial residual plot (in the case of a multiple-x model) with a pronounced "dog's leg" shape to the scatter of points. Chapter 13 provides details on formulating and fitting a segmented model.

A critical consideration in choosing to develop a segmented model is its substantive support. Segmented regression implies, in effect, that there is one influence "mechanism" operating over part of the x range and a second, different one operating over another part. Some substantive reason for the shift from one mechanism to another must be available if we are to prefer the abrupt to the smooth shift in strength of x influence.

In the life insurance agent example our segmented regression model would make sense if we knew, for example, that over the first five years agents were always "partnered" with more experienced agents and that after five years they worked "solo." The slope of the "early" regression line would describe partnership behavior, that for the "later" line solo performance.

The appearance of a "dog's leg" in the scatterplot should be a signal to ask whether there is a *reason* for an abrupt shift in influence. Failure to find a reason should direct our attention to one of the smooth alternative models described in the following sections.

Is There a Response Peak or Valley Within the Explanatory Variable Range?

If the shift in influence is a gradual, smooth one we ask whether the shift results in a reversal of the direction of influence. Does the x/y scatterplot or partial residual plot describe a peak or valley? Does the mean of y appear first to increase and then decrease (a peak) or to increase following a decrease (a valley)?

The regression described in the lower left panel to Figure 10.3 includes a peak. Expected annual sales volumes increase year by year (at a decreasing rate) over the first 30 years of the agent's career. After that, sales volumes tend downwards. Like segmented regression, modeling a peak or valley should make substantive sense. Why might the direction of influence of x on y change within this range of x? A possible explanation of the reversal in the life insurance agent example would be that, in the later part of their careers, agents devote progressively less energy or time to selling with the consequent slowing of growth of sales followed by growing decreases in volume.

If the explanation is prompted by the data rather than prior information, we need to be alert to supporting data. Is it true, for example, that older agents contact fewer potential clients?

Introducing a Squared Explanatory Variable

If the regression curve has a single peak or valley in the range of x, the x-y relation often is modeled effectively as *quadratic*, rather than linear. That is, the y mean is modeled as a function of x and of the square of x. The nonlinearity apparent in the plot will be accommodated if we replace the model,

$$\mu(y) = \beta_0 + \cdots + \beta_\ell x_{i\ell} + \cdots,$$

with one that has an additional x-variable, the square of the x producing the peak or valley:

$$\mu(y) = \beta_0 + \cdots + \beta_\ell x_{i\ell} + \cdots + \beta_q x_{i\ell}^2. \tag{10.5}$$

The quadratic relation of Equation [10.5] is discussed more thoroughly in Chapter 13. In particular, suggestions are given there on the interpretation of the parameters in a model that includes a squared x-variable.

Should there be both a y peak *and* a y valley within the range of x, we may be able to model the x-y relation as *cubic* by including the cube as well as the square of x in the explanatory model. Substantively, cubic relations with their double reversal of the direction of influence are very rare. Models in which a particular explanatory variable is present in a squared, cubed, or even higher powered form are called *polynomial regression* models. Quadratic and cubic models are the most common examples. Chapter 13 describes the special precautions to be taken when introducing a cubed or higher powered variable into a model.

Is the Nonlinear Relation Without Reversal?

The commonest nonlinear x-y relation is a smooth one but *without a reversal* in the direction of influence. The direction is positive (or negative) throughout the range of x with the strength of that influence gradually increasing (or decreasing).

Figure 10.4 displays, in stylized form, the four forms that such a nonlinear regression curve might take. The curves in the upper left and lower right show a positive x-y relation, while those in the lower left and upper right reflect a negative relation. The life insurance agent example at the bottom right of Figure 10.3 illustrates one of these: Expected annual sales volume increases year by year throughout the agent's career, but at a diminishing rate.

We detect nonlinear relations of this kind from similarly shaped swarms of points in the x-y scatterplot or the partial residual plots.

A Power Transformation of an Explanatory Variable

The smooth but nonreversing nonlinear x-y relation often is "straightened out" if we can replace the x-variable with a *power* of that x. That is, where the relation of the ℓth x-variable to y takes this nonlinear form, often we can "linearize" the relation if we replace the model

$$\mu(y) = \beta_0 + \cdots + \beta_\ell x_{i\ell} + \cdots$$

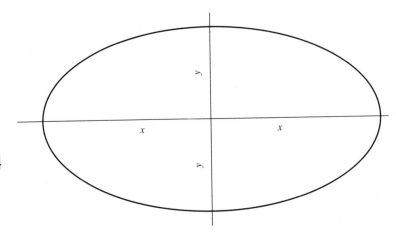

F I G U R E 10.4
Four Examples of
Nonlinear Nonre-
versing Regression
Curves

with this one:

$$\mu(y) = \beta_0 + \cdots + \beta_\ell x_{i\ell}^a + \cdots \tag{10.6}$$

where a is an appropriately chosen power to which to raise the ℓth x-variable, its *power coefficient.*

The power coefficient is another parameter of the model and, like the βs, it must be estimated from the sample. We suggest use of an estimate described more fully by Weisberg (1985). It is obtained as follows.

First, we find $\widehat{\beta}_\ell$, the estimate of the slope parameter for the to-be-powered, ℓth, variable in the usual linear model:

$$\mu(y) = \widehat{\beta}_0 + \sum_{j=1}^{k-1} (\widehat{\beta}_j x_{ij}). \tag{10.7}$$

Next, we find $\widehat{\eta}$, the estimate of the slope parameter for the *added variable,*

$$[x_{i\ell} \log(x_{i\ell})],$$

a product of scores on the ℓth x-variable and the *natural logarithms* of those scores, in a second model

$$\mu(y) = \widehat{\beta}_0 + \sum_{j=1}^{k-1} (\widehat{\beta}_j x_{ij}) + \widehat{\eta}[x_{i\ell} \log(x_{i\ell})]. \tag{10.8}$$

With these results in hand, our estimate of a is provided by

$$\widehat{a} = 1.0 + \left(\frac{\widehat{\eta}}{\widehat{\beta}_\ell} \right). \tag{10.9}$$

Because we need to take logarithms of the scores on the ℓth variable, it is essential that these scores all be greater than 0. If there are negative or 0 scores on the ℓth x-variable, it will be necessary to first add a constant to each score to make them all positive before computing the added variable and obtaining the η estimate from Equation [10.8].

In practice, the estimated a found by Equation [10.9] can be rounded to the nearest one-half before being used in Equation [10.6]. This gives reasonable interpretations to the power transformations, which are often squares or square roots or reciprocals of squares or square roots. If the rounded value of $\hat{a}$ is 1.0, no power transformation is indicated. If $\hat{a}$ rounds to 0, it is common to replace the ℓth x-variable with its natural logarithm:

$$\mu(y) = \beta_0 + \cdots + \beta_\ell \log(x_{i\ell}). \tag{10.10}$$

That is, we use a logarithmic rather than a power transformation of the ℓth x. Finally, estimates of a outside the range -2 to $+2$ should be treated as suspect. Try rounding them back to -2 or $+2$.

Estimation of the power coefficient can be carried out automatically with some statistical packages.

10.2.3   An Example of Nonlinearity: Faculty Salaries and Publication Counts

We illustrate the choice of an approach to "linearizing" the x-y relation using a hypothetical example. Table 10.1 lists the Monthly Salary (*sal*) and Number of Scholarly Publications (*pub*) for a sample of 50 university professors.

Of interest is the influence of publication record on salaries. How should it be modeled?

Let's assume that we started modeling knowing only that there ought to be an influence. It could be linear or nonlinear and our initial model is the linear one:

$$\mu(sal \mid pub_i) = \beta_0 + \beta_1 pub_i.$$

T A B L E 10.1

Sample Data: Monthly Salaries and Numbers of Scholarly Publications

pub	sal	pub	sal	pub	sal	pub	sal	pub	sal
2	2140	2	1890	5	2490	8	2200	10	2720
10	2590	10	2320	13	2890	15	3430	25	2950
20	2750	25	2660	30	3280	33	3340	35	3210
35	3240	37	3210	40	3230	45	4090	50	4250
45	4000	55	3740	55	4110	65	4540	65	4440
70	4400	70	4500	75	4160	75	4810	75	4320
75	4770	80	4590	80	5120	85	5060	90	5150
95	4840	100	4730	100	5580	100	5230	100	5150
110	5460	110	5630	120	5520	120	5940	130	5370
140	5950	150	5880	180	6410	190	5910	200	6240

The overall fit of this model to these data is very good. The slope parameter, β_1, is estimated at \$23.27/publication with a standard error of only \$1.21/publication. There clearly is a strong linear component to the relation of *pub* to expected *sal*.

A residual plot, however, suggests that, strong as this linear component might be, the explanatory role of *pub* may be more complex. Figure 10.5 plots the externally Studentized residuals from the linear model against *pub*. If the linear model were appropriate, we should expect to see the residuals randomly distributed across the plot with positive and negative residuals equally common at all levels of pub. Instead, we see some indication of a systematic relation of the residuals to the value of *pub*: The linear model appears to have overestimated *sal* for sample members with either very few or very many publications (giving rise to negative residuals) and underestimated salary for those with publication counts in the middle of the range.

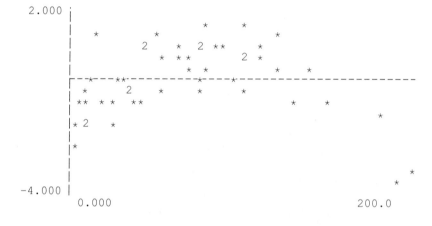

FIGURE 10.5

Scatterplot: Linear-model Residuals (*y*) v. Number of Publications (*x*)

The residual plot of Figure 10.5 suggests a nonlinear, fairly smoothly curved *x-y* relation, rather than a linear one. To see if there is a response peak (or valley) in the range of our *x*, we look at the scatterplot of *sal* against *pub*. This is reproduced as Figure 10.6. Monthly salaries appear to increase throughout the range of publication counts.

The indication of Figure 10.6 is that the *x-y* relation might be linearized by a power transformation of *x*. We will estimate a power coefficient.

The slope parameter for *pub* in the linear model has as its estimate in this sample

$$\widehat{\beta}_1 = 23.27.$$

We then add to our linear model the product variable [*pub* log(*pub*)], giving us the model

$$\mu(sal \,|\, pub_i) = \beta_0 + \beta_1 pub_i + \eta[pub_i \log(pub_i)].$$

Estimating the parameters of this extended model gives

$$\widehat{\eta} = -14.79.$$

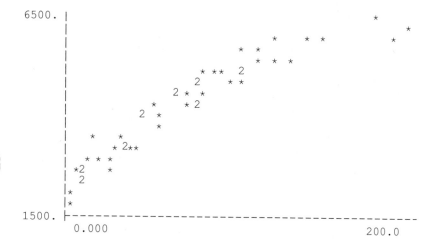

FIGURE 10.6
Scatterplot:
Monthly Salary
(*y*) v. Number of
Publications (*x*)

Substituting these results into Equation [10.9], the power coefficient is estimated at

$$\widehat{a} = 1.0 + \left(\frac{-14.79}{23.27} \right) = 1.0 - 0.64 = 0.36.$$

Rounded, we have an estimated power coefficient of (1/2).

Raising a variable to the (1/2) power is the same as taking the (positive) square root of that variable. So, the suggested new model is this one:

$$\mu(sal) = \beta_0 + \beta_1 [\sqrt{pub}],$$

replacing each *pub* score by its square root.

The overall fit of this nonlinear model is somewhat better than our linear one: The estimated conditional response standard deviation for the linear model was $421.90; for the square-root model it was $298.40. More importantly, we have dealt with the nonlinearity in the relation. Figure 10.7 plots the (externally Studentized) residuals from the square-root model against values of *pub*. There is no longer any hint of nonlinearity in this plot.

When we transform a variable, as we have here, we should go back to Chapter 9 and perform our checks on individual observations. Have we inadvertently made our new model more dependent on a few aberrant observations? Here, fortunately, the reverse is true. The square-root model would appear to be less influenced. Following are listed the values of the largest leverage points (h_{ii}), residuals (t_i), and influential points (D_i) for the two models:

	h_{ii}	t_i	D_i
Linear Model	0.16	−3.08	0.66
Square–root Model	0.10	2.26	0.20

For each index, the square-root model appears better able to accommodate even the most extreme data points in the sample.

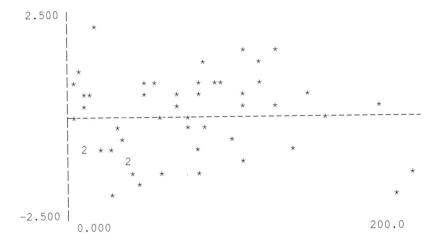

FIGURE 10.7

Scatterplot: Square-root-model Residuals (y) v. Number of Publications (x)

10.3
Assessing Homogeneity of Response Variance

The second of the model assumptions to be assessed is that of equal response variances across all of the conditional response populations sampled in our study. The expected value may change from population to population—that is, what we are modeling—but the variance should remain constant. If that assumption is violated, our use of the F- and t-statistics to compare the fits of models may be inaccurate.

We have two ways of assessing homogeneity of variance. The first is useful when the design of our study gives us many observations at each of a few design points. This is the case for models in which the explanatory variable is categorical and the sample size is fairly large; for example, 8 or more observations at each level of x. We need a second approach to homogeneity of variance assessment when the design gives us only a few (perhaps only one) observations at each of many design points. Models with one or more measured x-variables are of this kind.

10.3.1   When the Set of Design Points Is Small

For the first technique, we will have samples from relatively few (k) conditional response populations. If the y variances differ among these k conditional response populations, then we should expect to see bigger deviations from the (estimated) means of these conditional response populations for some levels than for other levels of k.

We can evaluate this possibility by using a version of these deviations as the y variable itself in a model comparison, what is sometimes called the *Levene test* (Madansky 1988). Let's assume a categorical variable with k levels and that we have fitted the model

$$\mu(y_i \,|\, Level) = \beta_0 + \beta_1 x_{i1} + \cdots + \beta_{k-1} x_{i(k-1)}$$

where $x_1, \ldots x_{(k-1)}$ is a set of dummy variables for $(k-1)$ of the k levels. The raw residuals from that model,

$$\widehat{\epsilon}_i = y_i - \widehat{\mu}(y_i \,|\, Level) = y_i - [\widehat{\beta}_0 + \widehat{\beta}_1 x_{i1} + \cdots + \widehat{\beta}_{k-1} x_{i(k-1)}],$$

are estimated deviations from means. For the Levene test, we use the *absolute values* of these residuals,

$$z_i = |\widehat{\epsilon}_i|, \tag{10.11}$$

as the y-variable scores in a comparison of the fits of two models. The fuller of the two models employs the original $(k-1)$ dummy variables,

$$\mu(z_i \,|\, Level) = \beta_0 + \beta_1 x_{i1} + \cdots + \beta_{k-1} x_{i(k-1)},$$

while the less full is the null model,

$$\mu(z_i \,|\, Level) = \beta_0.$$

We compare the fits of these two models in the usual way, by means of the F ratio. A large F, leading to rejection of the less full model, provides evidence of heterogeneity of variance. The logic of the Levene test is that the absolute values of the residuals will be larger where the underlying conditional response variance is larger. It is easy to apply in the model comparison context as it rests on a model comparison itself. All we need do is create a new y-variable, by Equation [10.11], from readily available residuals.

In Figure 10.8, we trace through how a statistical package like SPIDA could be used for this homogeneity of variance test on the Problem-solving example of Chapter 6. The y-variable is the number of spatial problems correctly solved following training. At the top of the figure, we repeat some of the results of fitting the model with two dummy variables, one coding the Video Training level, the other the Lecture level. The third treatment, Control, provides the comparison level. The fitted values (14.7 for Video subjects, 11.2 for Lecture subjects, and 12.2 for Control subjects) and residuals are displayed in the second panel. The residuals are both positive and negative, of course, as they have a mean of 0.

In the third panel of Figure 10.8, the *absolute values* of the original model residuals are displayed along with the x-variables for that model, the two dummy variables. The absolute values of the residuals become the y scores for the Levene test analyses; the original dummy variables are the Levene full model x-variables.

Fitting the full model to the absolute deviations gives *a residual sum of squares*, RSS: 60.768. It is simplest in a statistical package like SPIDA to obtain the sum of squares of residuals for the null model—the sum of squares about the overall sample mean—by squaring the estimated standard deviation, StDev: 1.485, (to give the estimated variance) and then multiplying by the appropriate degrees of freedom, $(N-1)$. Here, the null-model sum of squares of residuals is 63.952. The Levene test is completed by comparing the fits of these two models. The F-ratio is computed as

$$F = \frac{[63.952 - 60.768]/2}{60.768/27} = \frac{1.592}{2.251} = 0.707.$$

Full Model: Problem-solving Scores as the Response

```
regress($inp,y=1,x=(2,3),res=1)=:$outp
```

```
Response: ProbSolvScores
  Column Name         Coeff   StErr  p-value        SS

       0 Constant     12.2    0.842   0.000      4838.7
       2 Video         2.5    1.190   0.045        60.0
       3 Lecture      -1.0    1.190   0.408         5.0

  df:27              RSq:0.254 s:2.662          RSS:191.3
```

Full Model: *y* and *x* Data, Fit, and Residuals

```
$inp,$outp
 11 1 0 14.7 -3.7
 12 1 0 14.7 -2.7
 19 1 0 14.7  4.3
 13 1 0 14.7 -1.7
 17 1 0 14.7  2.3
 15 1 0 14.7  0.3
 17 1 0 14.7  2.3
 14 1 0 14.7 -0.7
 13 1 0 14.7 -1.7
 16 1 0 14.7  1.3
 11 0 1 11.2 -0.2
 14 0 1 11.2  2.8
 10 0 1 11.2 -1.2
  9 0 1 11.2 -2.2
 12 0 1 11.2  0.8
 13 0 1 11.2  1.8
 10 0 1 11.2 -1.2
  8 0 1 11.2 -3.2
 14 0 1 11.2  2.8
 11 0 1 11.2 -0.2
  7 0 0 12.2 -5.2
 18 0 0 12.2  5.8
 16 0 0 12.2  3.8
 11 0 0 12.2 -1.2
  9 0 0 12.2 -3.2
 10 0 0 12.2 -2.2
 13 0 0 12.2  0.8
 14 0 0 12.2  1.8
 12 0 0 12.2 -0.2
 12 0 0 12.2 -0.2
```

FIGURE 10.8
Heterogeneity of
Variance Test:
Problem-solving
Example

Levene Test: Absolute Values of Residuals

```
$dev:=abs($outp[;2])
$inp2:=$dev,$inp[;2,3]
$inp2
 3.7 1 0
 2.7 1 0
 4.3 1 0
 1.7 1 0
 2.3 1 0
 0.3 1 0
 2.3 1 0
 0.7 1 0
 1.7 1 0
 1.3 1 0
 0.2 0 1
 2.8 0 1
 1.2 0 1
 2.2 0 1
 0.8 0 1
 1.8 0 1
 1.2 0 1
 3.2 0 1
 2.8 0 1
 0.2 0 1
 5.2 0 0
 5.8 0 0
 3.8 0 0
 1.2 0 0
 3.2 0 0
 2.2 0 0
 0.8 0 0
 1.8 0 0
 0.2 0 0
 0.2 0 0
```

Levene Test: Full Model for Deviations

```
regress($inp2,y=1,x=(2,3),res=1)=:$outp2
```

```
Linear Regression Analysis
Response: AbsDev
 Column Name          Coeff StErr p-value        SS
```

Column	Name	Coeff	StErr	p-value	SS
0	Constant	2.44	0.474	0.000	127.308
2	Video	-0.34	0.671	0.616	0.024
3	Lecture	-0.80	0.671	0.243	3.200

```
df:27            RSq:0.05 s:1.5              RSS:60.768
```

FIGURE 10.8
(Continued)

Levene Test: Null Model for Deviations

```
desc($inp2[;1])$

 Col Name        Size Mean StDev Min Max

   1 Residuals    30 2.06 1.485 0.2 5.8

29*(1.485^2)
 63.952
```

Levene Test: *F*-ratio Computation and Evaluation

```
$fnum:=(63.952-60.768)/2
$fden:=60.768/27
$fnum,$fden,$fnum/$fden
 1.592 2.251 0.707
```

FIGURE 10.8
(Continued)

```
prob(0.707,type=3,df1=2,df2=27)
 0.502
```

As this is less than 1.0, we are assured it is rather nearer the middle of the *F*-distribution than in the upper tail. In fact, SPIDA reports that 50.2% of the *F*-distribution with 2 and 27 degrees of freedom is greater than 0.707. There is no evidence here, then, of differences in conditional response variance among the three populations sampled.

10.3.2   When the Set of Design Points Is Large

Now for the second technique. The Levene test "works" because we know from what limited number of conditional response populations our observations were drawn and, hence, where to look for possible differences in variance. But if we have one or only a few response observations from a large number of conditional response populations, our task is more difficult. To spot deviations from constant response variance in sample data from studies with a large number of design points depends on our having some idea as to what the nonconstancy might be related. In this section, we consider three such possibilities.

Case 1: Correlated Response Variances and Means

One heterogeneity of variance situation that we can recognize is that in which a model gives fitted values and conditional response variances that are *correlated*. In these situations, the variance of *y* either increases as its conditional mean gets larger (positive correlation) or it decreases as the mean increases (negative correlation).

We have two tools for spotting this kind of heterogeneity of variance. The first is the plot of residuals against fitted values. Correlated variances and fitted values will produce scatterplots like those in Figure 10.9. The overall shape of the scatterplot resembles a fan, opening to the right if the correlation is positive (first panel) or to the left if the correlation is negative.

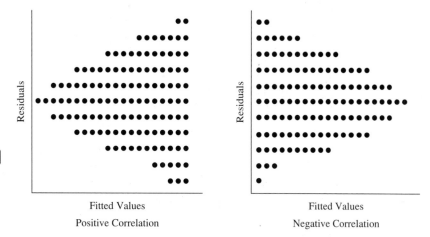

FIGURE 10.9
Scatterplots: Residuals (*y*-axis) v. Fitted Values (*x*-axis)

The second tool, analogous to the Levene test of the preceding section, is to use the fitted values and residuals in two new models, comparing the fits. These new models have the absolute values of the residuals as the new *y*-variable. The fuller of the two new models has the fitted values from the original model as a single *x*-variable. The less full model is the null model. If the model comparison rejects the less full model we have evidence that the conditional response variances are not constant but are systematically related to the conditional means.

When response variances and means are correlated, it is often possible to transform the response variable so that, for the new *y*, the conditional variances are homogeneous. Transformations that have this effect are called *variance stabilizing transformations*. Three of the best known of these transformations are described in Table 10.2. These and similar transformations are performed easily in most statistical packages.

We may start with a square root transformation and see if the resulting residual plot shows evidence of constant variance. If "fanning" is still present, a stronger transformation can be tried out.

Case 2: Apparently Nonindependent Design Points

Our only real assurance that response observations are independent lies in having sampled randomly. We cannot count on any evaluation of the data, once collected, to alert us to problems with this assumption. Having said that, however, there are occasions when a residual plot can point to nonindependence.

Detecting nonindependence from the residuals requires that we have some idea from where the nonindependence comes. For example, we might suspect that the order in which the observations were collected is important, that obserations adjacent to one another may not be independent of each other. This would be the case, for example, if a poll taker questioned both the husband and the wife in each household sampled, rather than choosing one of the two at random. This source of nonindependence could be recognized if we were to plot residuals from our model against the order of collection. A systematic pattern to the residuals, adjacent observations having residuals of the same size rather than "random" ones, would suggest nonindependence.

If our response observations are not independent, then our linear regression model is not appropriate to the data. We can sometimes compensate for this nonindependence by including the source of the nonindependence in the model. We do this in Chapter 14 for studies using repeated measures. Here we will continue to assume that we have sampled the y-scores randomly in composing our sample.

T A B L E 10.2

Some Variance Stabilizing Transformations

1 Square-root Transformation

   sqrt(y), if all values of y are positive

   sqrt($y + c$), where c is a constant added to each value of y to make them all positive

Useful when the extent of the correlation is only moderate

2 Logarithmic Transformation

   log(y), if all values of y are positive

   log($y + c$), c again chosen to make all values positive

Useful when the extent of the correlation is greater

3 Reciprocal Transformation

   $1/y$, if all values of y are positive

   $1/(y + c)$, c chosen so $(y + c)$ is always positive

An even stronger transformation than the logarithmic one

Case 3: Inconsistent Design Points

A final instance in which the residual plot can point to systematic nonhomogeneity of response variance is that in which a particular design point or points—usually at the "edge" of our design—are markedly inconsistent with the others.

Forty fifth-grade students are assigned, at random, ten apiece to four study conditions. The students are allowed five minutes, ten minutes, fifteen minutes, or one hour to study a four-paragraph text. They are then asked 12 factual questions about the text and each student's y score is the number of questions correctly answered. The response SD is about the same (2 points) for the 5-, 10-, and 15-minute groups but considerably smaller (only 0.10 point) in the 1-hour group.

The pattern of responses at one hour of study is *inconsistent* with the patterns at shorter intervals. Inconsistent design points are most likely to occur at the *edges of a design*, where the values of one or more x-variables cross over into a region where response variability is markedly affected. It is at these edges that we should look.

Having detected one or more inconsistent design points, what should we do? The short answer is that we should eliminate them. But, before we do that we must satisfy ourselves (and describe to the readers of our research) that there is a reason for the inconsistency.

An Example of Variance Heterogeneity: Faculty Salaries and Ages

Our data here are from a second, hypothetical population of university professors. This time, we are interested in modeling Monthly Salary as a function of Age. The Salary observations were, in fact, "constructed" to show greater variability with increasing age. This heterogeneity is reflected in the residual plot shown in Figure 10.10; though distributed about 0, the residuals are more tightly clustered for ages up to about 45 than above that.

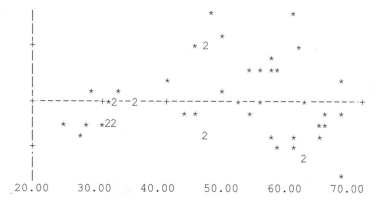

FIGURE 10.10
Scatterplot: Salary
Residuals (y-axis)
v. Age (x-axis)

We begin to correct the nonconstant variance problem by using the "weakest" of the transformations suggested in Table 10.2. We replace the Salary observations with their (positive) square roots. The residual plot for this square-root model is shown in Figure 10.11.

Moving from left to right in the residual plot, we still see some increasing variability and move up to a stronger transformation. In Figure 10.12, we see the result of replacing the Salaries with their logarithms.

Variance instability appears to be better controlled, judging by the residual plot of Figure 10.12. However, we now see a nonlinear pattern in the residuals. As a result of transforming the response variable to secure constant variance, we have introduced a nonlinearity in the x/y relation.

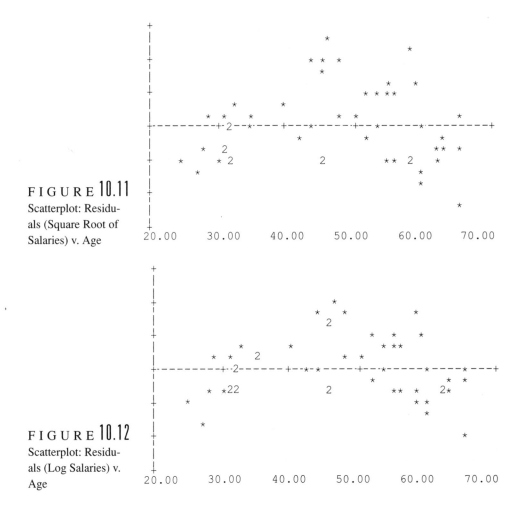

FIGURE 10.11

Scatterplot: Residuals (Square Root of Salaries) v. Age

FIGURE 10.12

Scatterplot: Residuals (Log Salaries) v. Age

Since the form of nonlinearity displayed in Figure 10.12 is very much the same as we observed in the earlier study of Salary as a function of Number of Scholarly Publications, we will transform the x-variable as we did there.

Our final model, then, is one in which the mean of the logarithm of Monthly Salaries is a linear function of the square root of Age.

$$\mu[\log (Monthly\ Salary)] = \beta_0 + \beta_1\sqrt{Age}.$$

The residual plot for this model is given in Figure 10.13. The plot shows constant variance and no discernible nonlinearity.

Because the scale we use for the response changed over the four models we just described, we cannot compare the conditional response variances to judge whether the final model also provides a better overall fit to the sample data. There is some evidence in this direction. The R^2 increased mildly, from 0.64 in the first linear model to 0.80 in the final model.

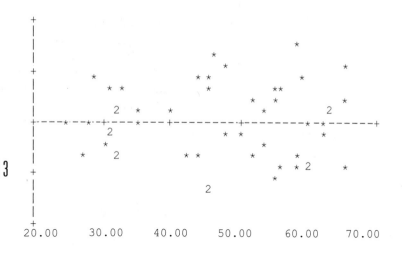

FIGURE 10.13
Scatterplot: Residuals (Log Salaries from Square-Root Age) v. Age

10.4
Assessing Normal Characteristics of Response

Our last check is on the Normal characteristics of the conditional response populations from which we've sampled.

10.4.1 An Overall Check on Normality

Our assumption is that each of the conditional response population histograms has characteristics in common with the density function of a *Normal random variable*. Our samples almost never include enough observations from each conditional population to let us assess this assumption directly. Rather, we do it indirectly and, as a result, less precisely.

We assume that *each residual* represents an observation from a population with a mean of 0 (the result of subtracting the estimated mean from each *y* observation) and some constant variance (now that we are satisfied as to that point). Our overall *Normality* check takes this form: "Can we think of the residuals as having been sampled, as well, from an idealized population that has Normal characteristics?"

A New Residual Plot: The Normal QQ Plot

To help us evaluate the residuals with respect to Normality, we introduce a special way of plotting the residuals. This plot is different from a scatterplot. It is an example of a *quantile-quantile* (or QQ) plot.

The idea behind a QQ plot is this. Let's assume we have two lists of scores, each the same length. We sort each list from smallest to largest in size. Then we plot the smallest value in each list against each other, then the next smallest against each other, and so on, the last point plotted being the largest in each list against each other. The result is a quantile-quantile plot; we've plotted the quantiles (the sorted values) in one list against the quantiles in another. The shape of the QQ plot tells us something about how similar the histograms are for the two lists.

We're interested in comparing the histogram of our residuals with the idealized one for a Normal random variable having the same mean and variance as our residuals. The QQ plot of interest is one that results when we plot our residuals (ordered from smallest to largest) against the values we would expect as the smallest, next smallest, and so on up to the biggest if we had really sampled from a Normal random variable.

Calculating those expected values is a task beyond the level of this text, but many statistical packages include either a quantile plotting command or a facility for generating the needed Normal random variable scores. In SPIDA, for example, the normal scores command gives the expected Normal scores against which the (standardized or Studentized) residuals can be plotted.

If our sample of residuals has a "Normal-like" histogram, the QQ plot will take the form of a fairly straight line. Departures from Normality will result in a pronounced curvature of the QQ plot, usually at one or both ends of the plot.

Skewness and Kurtosis

We can supplement our graphic check on the Normal character of our residual histogram with a pair of computational checks. The density function for the Normal random variable we've seen in earlier chapters is symmetric rather than skewed. Its peak is in the middle rather than being displaced towards one end of the range of scores. *Skewness*, like the mean or variance, is a statistical characteristic of a list or distribution of scores and can be computed as

$$g_1 = \sqrt{N} \frac{\sum_{i=1}^{N} \left(x_i - M(x)\right)^3}{\left\{\sum_{i=1}^{N} \left(x_i - M(x)\right)^2\right\}^{3/2}}. \tag{10.12}$$

In the numerator of Equation [10.12], we enter the sum of the *cubes* of the distances separating the scores from their sample mean. And, the term in the denominator is the sum of the squares of the distances from the mean raised to the 3/2 power. That is, the sum of squared deviations is first cubed and then the square root is obtained. Of course, most statistics packages will produce the skewness statistic automatically, saving the effort of computing from scratch in this fashion!

The skewness statistic of Equation [10.12] is 0 for distributions of numbers symmetric about their mean. It is negative for distributions with long tails stretching to the left, *negatively skewed*, and positive for distributions with long tails stretching to the right, *positively skewed*. For moderately large samples, N larger than about 100, a rough test of the size of g_1 can be made: a value outside the bounds

$$\pm 2\sqrt{\frac{6}{N}}$$

is evidence of asymmetry and, hence, of non-Normality.

Not all symmetric distributions, of course, are Normal. The Normal random variable can be roughly characterized as having a certain proportion of its scores concentrated in a middle peak and a remaining proportion equally spread between the two tails. Other symmetric distributions, in comparison with the Normal, will have either a greater peak and lesser tails or a lesser peak and greater tails. The first are said to be *platykurtic* while the second are *leptokurtic*. The degree of *kurtosis* of a symmetric distribution of scores is assessed by

$$g_2 = N \frac{\displaystyle\sum_{i=1}^{N} (x_i - M(x))^4}{\left\{ \displaystyle\sum_{i=1}^{N} (x_i - M(x))^2 \right\}^2}. \tag{10.13}$$

In the numerator of Equation [10.13], we have the sum of the fourth power of deviations about the mean and in the denominator the square of the sum of squares of these deviations. For a Normal random variable, g_2 will take the value 3.0; g_2 will be less than this for platykurtic distributions and greater for leptokurtic ones. As with the skewness statistic, g_2 can be evaluated for significance. Roughly, if N is large, a value of g_2 outside the range

$$3.0 \pm 2\sqrt{\frac{24}{N}}$$

is suggestive of non-Normality. More sensitive evaluations of skewness and kurtosis are possible (see, for example, Madansky 1988).

10.4.2 Transforming the Non-Normal Response Variable

If the residuals from our model appear to be "Normal" by these tests, this is evidence in support of our assumption of Normal characteristics for the conditional response populations. If our QQ plot or our skewness or kurtosis statistics, however, suggest the residuals are not like observations from a Normal random variable, we should see if we can transform our *y*-variable so that it meets this model assumption.

A Power Transformation of the Response

Replacing the *y*-variable in our model with that *y* raised to a power will often give the needed Normal characteristics. That is, the assumption may be justified if we replace *y* with, for example, its square root, square, or reciprocal. All of these are power transformations; we've raised *y* to a power of 2, 1/2, or −1 in these examples. The trick, of course, is to know to what power we should raise *y*.

Selecting a Coefficient for the Power Transformation

The Box and Cox transformation (Weisberg 1985) allows us to replace our *y* with the power that will best "Normalize" the conditional response populations. This best power usually is found by trying out several different values, then picking the one that gives the "closest to Normal" results. This can involve a fair amount of computing unless your statistical package includes a built-in command to do that work.

A Non-Normal Example: Faculty Salaries and Time Since Doctorate

Our third contrived data sample is one in which we wish to model faculty Monthly Salaries as a function of Years Since Doctorate. We have again a random sample of 50 hypothetical professors. The salary data were constructed here so that the residuals would display a non-Normal shape. Figure 10.14 gives the Normal QQ plot for the residuals from the linear model,

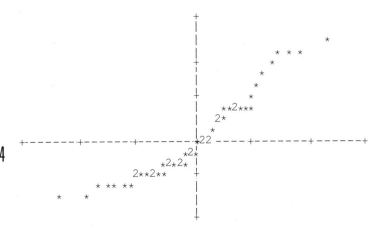

FIGURE 10.14

Normal QQ Plot: Salary Residuals from Year of Doctorate

$$\mu(Monthly\ Salary) = \beta_0 + \beta_1 (Years\ Since\ PhD).$$

The residuals are plotted along the Y-axis and the corresponding Normal quantities along the X-axis. This Normal QQ plot departs from a straight line. There is a pronounced "flattening," particularly at the lower end of the plot.

Flattening at both ends indicates a distribution of residuals more closely distributed about 0 than would a sample from a Normal random variable. On the other hand, "verticality" at both ends of the QQ plot—turning in of the ends towards the Y- rather than the X-axis—suggests residuals more spread out than would Normal observations. Flatness at just one end is symptomatic of a nonsymmetric residual distribution—longer than Normal in one direction and perhaps shorter in the other.

The flattening at both ends of our QQ plot in Figure 10.14 indicates that there are too few large negative and positive residuals compared with what we'd expect if they were a sample from a Normal random variable.

The Box-Cox facility in SPIDA suggests a power coefficient—after rounding—of $1/2$. We may find more Normal residuals, then, if we replace our y-variable,

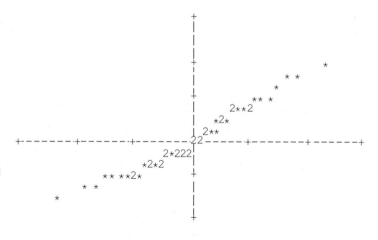

F I G U R E 10.15
Normal QQ Plot:
Residuals of Square
Root of Salary

Monthly Salaries, with its square root:

$$\mu[\sqrt{Monthly\ Salaries}] = \beta_0 + \beta_1\ (Years\ Since\ PhD).$$

Figure 10.15 is the Normal QQ plot for the residuals from this model. The plot is quite linear, particularly in comparison with that for the original residuals, Figure 10.14. While the change in response variable precludes comparing the two models in any detail, we note that R^2 is effectively unchanged. We have corrected for non-Normality without compromising the overall fit of the model.

Finally, Figure 10.16 is the residual plot for the square root transformed model. We see no evidence in this plot that the square root transformation of y has introduced any nonlinearity to the x/y relation nor that it has produced heterogeneity of response variance.

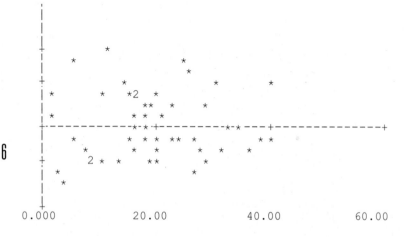

F I G U R E 10.16
Scatterplot: Resid-
uals (Square Root
of Salary) v. Years
Since PhD

10.5
Residuals and Modeling Strategies

When we improve the fit of our model on the basis of an examination of the residuals, that improvement is very much "data dependent." As a result, the model that results is a hypothesis rather than a confirmatory model. We must look to new data to verify the modifications we have made. The data that suggested the change cannot be used to validate the change.

10.6
Summary

The suitability of a model depends only in part on the overall fit of that model to a set of data. We must look as well at how that model fits particular regions of the design space or, even, individual data points. This more detailed examination of fit is necessary if we are to be assured that our assumptions about the model—linearity of relation, homogeneity of response variance, and Normality of residual histograms—are supported. A major tool for this examination is the residual plot and in this chapter we discuss how to use that plot to identify model problems. We also present suggestions for improving a model once these problems have been identified.

Exercises

1   For the data about snow geese flock size of Chapter 5 is there any evidence of heterogeneity of variance? Do the observers' estimates increase in variability with the true size of the flocks?

2   The data following are more than 250 years old. A gun is fired at a mark on a target from varying ranges. The bullet strikes the target at some distance from that mark. Are the sizes of the "misses" related to the ranges? And, with reference to this chapter, is the variability in the sizes of the misses a function of the range? We might expect to see greater scatter at greater firing distances.

Distance (in.)	Range (ft.)
1.500	9.00
1.750	9.00
0.350	6.00
1.300	9.00
0.675	2.00
1.075	4.00
1.250	6.00
1.450	8.00
0.600	2.00

Distance (in.)	Range (ft.)
0.925	4.00
1.200	6.00
1.550	8.00
1.900	9.00
0.100	9.00
0.300	0.25
0.350	0.25
1.700	9.00
0.225	0.25
0.650	2.00
1.000	4.00
1.175	6.00
0.300	0.25
2.000	9.00
2.100	9.00

3 For a sample of first births to recently married couples, we have the following data. Column 1 gives the husband's income at marriage and column 2 gives the number of months separating marriage and pregnancy. We are interested in how income influences pregnancy planning. The data may need both transformation to linearity and attention to any influential observations.

Income	Months to Pregnancy
5775	16.20
9800	35.00
13975	37.20
4120	9.00
25015	24.40
12200	36.75
7400	31.75
9340	30.00
20170	36.00
22400	30.80
4608	9.70
24120	20.00
19625	38.20
18000	41.25
13000	44.00
5400	9.20
6440	20.00
9000	40.20
18180	32.00
15385	39.20
18000	39.20
22400	27.90

Income	Months to Pregnancy
24120	22.30
5400	11.70
9340	32.50

11

Categorical Explanatory Variables: ANOVA Models

This and the following two chapters expand the range of multiple-x models that we can bring to bear on the study of complexly determined responses in biological and behavioral studies. Often we want to model the joint influence of two or more xs and in these chapters we focus on the forms this joint influence can take. This chapter concentrates on models with two or more categorical sources of influence on our response variable.

11.1
Two Categorical Influences: Additive Model

In Chapter 6, we learned how to develop models for a categorical explanatory variable. Now we extend those techniques to cover situations in which we have two or more categorical variables. How should we represent these sources of potential influence in our linear models, how do we compare the resulting models, and how do we interpret a selected model?

We begin with an example.

11.1.1 Example: Spatial Problem Solving

Our example is provided by an extension of a problem introduced in Chapter 6. There, we considered the results of assigning 30 students at random among three Spatial Problem-solving Training conditions—Lecture, Video, and Control. The groups were found to differ in their subsequent Problem-solving Performance.

We now redefine the study slightly. The 30 students are equally divided between females and males and the 15 *within each Gender* are distributed randomly among the three Training conditions.

Table 11.1 shows the Problem-solving scores for the 30 students, now classified by Gender as well as by Training condition.

Our interest is in the extent to which Problem-solving scores are influenced by either or both of two categorical variables, Gender and Training condition.

TABLE 11.1
Spatial Problem-solving Scores as a Function of Training Condition and Gender

Training Condition	Gender: Female					Male				
Videotape	11	12	13	14	15	13	16	17	17	19
Lecture	10	11	13	14	14	8	9	10	11	12
Control	7	11	12	14	16	9	10	12	13	18

11.1.2 Dummy Variable Scoring

We now have two categorical variables, Training condition at three levels and Gender at two levels. How can we include them in linear models? As a natural extension of Chapter 6's treatment of the single categorical variable, we can start by developing a set of *dummy variables* for Gender just as we did for Training condition. We'll then see how to include both sets in a model.

Gender has only two levels, Female and Male, so only a single dummy variable will be needed. We must decide, though, which level to make the comparison level. Let's take Male as the comparison level. Thus, our dummy variable will be one that takes the value "1" for each Female subject and "0" for each Male subject.

We'll again take the Control Training condition as the comparison level of the Training condition categorical variable. Let's define, then, x_1 as the dummy variable for the Video condition ("1" for Video-condition subjects, "0" for all others), x_2 as the the dummy variable for the Lecture condition ("1" for Lecture-condition subjects, "0" for others), and x_3 as our dummy variable for Female ("1" for Females, "0" for the comparison-level Males).

Now, we can write a model that includes all three of these variables:

$$\mu(\textit{Problem Solving} \mid \textit{Training, Gender}) = \beta_0 + \beta_1 x_1 + \beta_2 x_2 + \beta_3 x_3. \qquad \textbf{(11.1)}$$

What interpretation should we give the parameters of this model?

We can start with the intercept term, β_0. We know that it has to be the response mean when *all* the x-variables take the value 0. In this instance, all the model xs are 0/1 dummy variables. Because x values of 0 are in our design space, the intercept has meaning to us. When the dummy variables all take the value "0" we are at the comparison level of each of the categorical explanatory variables.

For the model of Equation 11.1, β_0 is the expected value of Problem Solving when Training is at the Control level *and* Gender is at the Male level:

$$\beta_0 = \mu(\textit{Problem Solving} \mid \text{Control, Male}).$$

The combination of the comparison levels of the two categorical variables defines a *comparison condition*. The slope parameters in models with a single set of dummy variables represent deviations of the response means from that at the comparison level. In the same vein, the slope parameters in models with two or more sets of dummy variables assess the deviation of the response means from that for the comparison condition.

We see this for the model of Equation 11.1 when we trace what happens when values of "1" are taken by one or two of the dummy variables as appropriate to the different treatment conditions in the study. The results are summarized in Table 11.2. The slope parameter β_1 is the difference in the response mean between Video and Control training, β_2 is the difference between Lecture and Control training, and β_3 is the difference between Females and Males.

Full Model

The model of Equation [11.1] provides for the explanatory influence of Gender to be *added to* that of Training condition. We think of it as a fuller model, one whose fit to the observations we will want to compare with that of at least one constrained or less full model.

T A B L E **11.2**

Conditional-response Means and the Parameters of the Model Using Dummy Variable Coding

Treatment Condition	Conditional Response Mean
Control, Male $x_1 = 0,$ $x_2 = 0,$ $x_3 = 0$	β_0
Video, Male $x_1 = 1,$ $x_2 = 0,$ $x_3 = 0$	$\beta_0 + \beta_1$
Lecture, Male $x_1 = 0,$ $x_2 = 1,$ $x_3 = 0$	$\beta_0 + \beta_2$
Control, Female $x_1 = 0,$ $x_2 = 0,$ $x_3 = 1$	$\beta_0 + \beta_3$
Video, Female $x_1 = 1,$ $x_2 = 0,$ $x_3 = 1$	$\beta_0 + \beta_1 + \beta_3$
Lecture, Female $x_1 = 0,$ $x_2 = 1,$ $x_3 = 1$	$\beta_0 + \beta_2 + \beta_3$

Constrained Models

The fit of the fuller model, with its two categorical variables might be compared with that of models that contain only one of the two. In Chapter 6, we developed a model that included, for these sample data, only Training condition as explanatory. Equation [11.2] describes this model, using the same dummy variables used above:

$$\mu(Problem\ Solving \mid Training) = \beta_0 + \beta_1 x_1 + \beta_2 x_2. \qquad \textbf{(11.2)}$$

The model of Equation [11.2] is a *constrained* version of that of Equation [11.1]. The slope for the Gender dummy variable (Female) is constrained to be 0.

We can give a substantive interpretation to this constraint by referring to Table 11.2. If $\beta_3 = 0$, then, in terms of the fuller model:

$$\mu(Problem\ Solving \mid Male,\ Control) = \mu(Problem\ Solving \mid Female,\ Control),$$

$$\mu(Problem\ Solving \mid Male,\ Video) = \mu(Problem\ Solving \mid Female,\ Video),$$

and

$$\mu(Problem\ Solving \mid Male,\ Lecture) = \mu(Problem\ Solving \mid Female,\ Lecture).$$

In other words, the constraint leading to the model of Equation [11.2] is that there is no male-female difference in Problem Solving *under any of the three Training conditions.*

Model Comparisons

How do the fits of the two models compare? Does the fuller model provide a better fit by including Gender?

Table 11.3 summarizes the parameter estimates for the two models obtained with a statistics package. It is easy to see from these results that the constrained model does not provide a poorer fit. The estimate for the Female slope parameter in the fuller model is not large relative to its standard error (SE); it is roughly one-half an SE away from (below) 0. As a result, we have no reason to believe that the population value, β_3, could not be 0.

In fact, the contribution of Gender to this model is so slight that the conditional-response variance is actually estimated to be larger for the fuller model, $2.701 \times 2.701 = 7.295$, than for the less full one, $2.662 \times 2.662 = 7.085$. Again, this is evidence that the fuller model does not provide a better fit.

The larger estimated conditional response SD, $\widehat{\sigma}(y \mid X)$, in the fuller model might be unexpected. The sum of squared residuals (SSR) can never be larger for the fuller than for the less full model; here we have SSR $= 189.7$ for the fuller model and SSR $= 191.3$ for the less full one. Usually, the smaller sum of squared residuals for the fuller model is sufficient to offset the decrease in degrees of freedom and produce an estimated conditional-response variance that is also smaller. We would then turn to the F-ratio test to evaluate whether that smaller estimate is sufficiently smaller that we should prefer the fuller model with more parameters. Here, we have no need for the F-ratio; the larger variance estimate for the fuller model tells us all we need to decide in favor of the constrained model.

T A B L E 11.3

Fitting the Training-plus-gender and Training-only Models

Fuller Model			Less Full Model		
Parameter	Estimate	SE	Parameter	Estimate	SE
β_0	12.43	0.99	β_0	12.20	0.84
β_1	2.50	1.21	β_1	2.50	1.19
β_2	−1.00	1.21	β_2	−1.00	1.19
β_3	−0.47	0.99			

$$\hat{\sigma}(y\,|\,X) \quad 2.70 \qquad\qquad \hat{\sigma}(y\,|\,X) \quad 2.66$$

Degrees of Freedom $\qquad$ Degrees of Freedom
$30 - 4 = 26$ $\qquad\qquad$ $30 - 3 = 27$

11.1.3 Alternative Scoring: Effect Coding

Dummy variable coding is just one way of introducing a categorical variable into a linear model. It is a good choice, certainly, where one of the levels is a natural control or comparison level. There are alternative codings of categorical levels, though, that may be better under other circumstances. The most common alternative to dummy variable coding is *effect coding*.

Purpose of Effect Coding

Effect coding takes its name from the idea that the several levels of a categorical variable have different size *effects on the response*. These differential effects are to be assessed relative to some overall size for the response, "averaged" over the category levels.

The idea of effect coding, and its interpretation, will be clear if we consider a specific example. Let's look again at the Problem Solving example, letting Training condition be the only categorical variable. The *overall size* of the categorical variable's effect is defined as the average of the conditional means:

$$\beta_0 = \frac{\mu(y\,|\,Video) + \mu(y\,|\,Lecture) + \mu(y\,|\,Control)}{3}.$$

Further, for *each level* there is an *effect size*, the difference between the conditional mean at that level and the overall size of the categorical variable's effect,

$$\beta_1 = \mu(y\,|\,Video) - \beta_0,$$
$$\beta_2 = \mu(y\,|\,Lecture) - \beta_0,$$

and

$$\beta_3 = \mu(y\,|\,Control) - \beta_0.$$

Thus each conditional response mean can be expressed as the sum of an overall size and an effect size:

$$\mu(y \mid Video) = \beta_0 + \beta_1,$$
$$\mu(y \mid Lecture) = \beta_0 + \beta_2,$$

and

$$\mu(y \mid Control) = \beta_0 + \beta_3.$$

Because the effect sizes are the *deviations* of the conditional means from their average, some will be positive and others negative. In fact, the effect sizes will sum to 0:

$$\beta_1 + \beta_2 + \beta_3 = 0.0.$$

To implement effect coding we must take into account the fact that the effect sizes sum to 0. The "sum to zero" condition imposes a *constraint* on the effect size parameters that we need to heed. Otherwise, we would have too many parameters in our models. Here, for example, we've defined four parameters—the overall size and three effect sizes—though we will have response observations from only three conditional populations. One way we use the sum to 0 property is to select one of the categorical levels as an *omitted level*, one whose effect size is simply the negative of the sum of the effect sizes of all the other levels:

$$\beta_1 + \beta_2 + \beta_3 = 0.0$$

allows us to describe the effect size for, say, the Control level as

$$\beta_3 = -(\beta_1 + \beta_2).$$

In this way, we reduce the total number of parameters to the number of distinct conditional response means to be estimated.

Implementing Effect Coding

How do we implement effect coding in practice? We create a set of effect coding variables in very much the same way we created dummy variables.

For each level of the categorical variable, except the omitted level, we create a new variable. This variable takes the value 1 for observations at that level, the value -1 for observations at the omitted level, and the value 0 for observations at all other levels.

Our Training-condition, categorical variable has three levels. If we designate the Control condition as the omitted level we'll need two effect coded variables: one for the Video condition, x_1, and one for the Lecture condition, x_2. The first, x_1, will contain 1s for the 10 observations under the Video condition, 0s for the 10 observations under the Lecture condition, and -1s for the 10 observations under the Control condition. And, x_2 will contain 1s for the Lecture-condition observations, 0s for the Video-condition observations, and -1s, again, for the Control-condition observations.

As a result, the model,

$$\mu(\text{Problem Solving} \mid \text{Training}) = \beta_0 + \beta_1 x_1 + \beta_2 x_2, \qquad \textbf{(11.2)}$$

hypothesizes these conditional means:

$$\mu(\text{Problem Solving} \mid \text{Video}) = \beta_0 + \beta_1,$$
$$\mu(\text{Problem Solving} \mid \text{Lecture}) = \beta_0 + \beta_2,$$

and

$$\mu(\text{Problem Solving} \mid \text{Control}) = \beta_0 - (\beta_1 + \beta_2).$$

The magnitudes of the Video, Lecture, and Control effects are given by β_1, β_2, and $-(\beta_1 + \beta_2)$. Together, they *sum to 0*: $\beta_1 + \beta_2 - (\beta_1 + \beta_2) = 0$. The intercept, β_0, is the *average* of the three expected values. We can see this from their sum:

$$\begin{bmatrix} \mu(\text{Problem Solving} \mid \text{Video}) \\ +\mu(\text{Problem Soving} \mid \text{Lecture}) \\ +\mu(\text{Problem Solving} \mid \text{Control}) \end{bmatrix} = \begin{bmatrix} [\beta_0 + \beta_1] \\ +[\beta_0 + \beta_2] \\ +[\beta_0 - \beta_1 - \beta_2] \end{bmatrix} = 3\beta_0.$$

The parameters of the model of Equation [11.2] have sample estimates consistent with their definitions:

$$\widehat{\beta}_0 = \frac{\text{M}(\text{Problem Solving} \mid \text{Video}) + \text{M}(\text{Problem Solving} \mid \text{Lecture}) + \text{M}(\text{Problem Solving} \mid \text{Control})}{3},$$

$$\widehat{\beta}_1 = \text{M}(\text{Problem Solving} \mid \text{Video}) - \widehat{\beta}_0,$$

and

$$\widehat{\beta}_2 = \text{M}(\text{Problem Solving} \mid \text{Lecture}) - \widehat{\beta}_0.$$

Additive-model Effect Coding

If we take Male *and* Control as the omitted levels for the two categorical variables, the linear model of Equation [11.1],

$$\mu(\text{Problem Solving} \mid \text{Training, Gender}) = \beta_0 + \beta_1 x_1 + \beta_2 x_2 + \beta_3 x_3,$$

can be written in terms of three effect-coded variables. Effect-coded variable x_1 and x_2 are as defined above, while x_3 is the effect-coded variable for Female, 1 for observations on females and -1 for observations on males. As the Gender categorical variable has two levels, only one effect-coded variable is needed. Also, because there are only two levels, no level is coded 0.

Table 11.4 shows the relation of the four model parameters of Equation [11.1] to the conditional means, based on our effect coding of the two categorical variables. The intercept term, β_0, is now the average of the six conditional means.

Comparing Effect and Dummy Coding

Effect and dummy coding give rise to slopes and intercepts with *different interpretations* even though they provide the same fit to the observations. Table 11.5 summarizes the parameter estimates and fits, under dummy variable and effect coding of the additive model (Training Condition and Gender) and the Training-Condition-only model.

The two codings give the same estimates of the response means for the six conditions. For the additive model, these can be worked out from Table 11.2 for dummy variable coding and from Table 11.4 for effect coding.

T A B L E **11.4**

Conditional-response Means and the Parameters of the Model

Using Effect Coding

Treatment Condition	Conditional Response Means	
Control, Male $x_1 = -1,$ $x_2 = -1,$ $x_3 = -1$	$\beta_0 - (\beta_1 + \beta_2)$	$-\beta_3$
Video, Male $x_1 = 1,$ $x_2 = 0,$ $x_3 = -1$	$\beta_0 + \beta_1$	$-\beta_3$
Lecture, Male $x_1 = 0,$ $x_2 = 1,$ $x_3 = -1$	$\beta_0 \qquad + \beta_2$	$-\beta_3$
Control, Female $x_1 = -1,$ $x_2 = -1,$ $x_3 = 1$	$\beta_0 - (\beta_1 + \beta_2)$	$+\beta_3$
Video, Female $x_1 = 1,$ $x_2 = 0,$ $x_3 = 1$	$\beta_0 + \beta_1$	$+\beta_3$
Lecture, Female $x_1 = 0,$ $x_2 = 1,$ $x_3 = 1$	$\beta_0 \qquad + \beta_2$	$+\beta_3$

The six estimated means are

Female, Video Training:	14.47	Female, Control:	1.97
Male, Video Training:	14.93	Male, Control:	12.43
Female, Lecture Training:	10.97		
Male, Lecture Training:	11.43		

Because the two codings involve the same number of model parameters and give the same fit for an observation, the overall fits—as represented in Table 11.5 by the estimated conditional SDs for *y*—are identical.

The estimated intercept for the additive model using dummy variable coding is the estimated response mean for the comparison condition, Male/Control (12.43). For effect coding, the intercept is estimated by the average of the response means over all six conditions: $[(1/6)(14.47 + 14.93 + 10.97 + 11.43 + 11.97 + 12.43) = 12.70]$.

TABLE 11.5
Fitting the Training-plus-gender and Training-only Models

Dummy Variable Coding

	Fuller Model			Less full Model		
Parameter	Estimate	SE	Parameter	Estimate	SE
β_0	12.43	0.99	β_0	12.20	0.84
β_1	2.50	1.21	β_1	2.50	1.19
β_2	−1.00	1.21	β_2	−1.00	1.19
β_3	−0.47	0.99			

$\hat{\sigma}(y\,|\,X)$ 2.70 $\hat{\sigma}(y\,|\,X)$ 2.66

Degrees of Freedom   Degrees of Freedom
$30 - 4 = 26$ $30 - 3 = 27$

Effect Variable Coding

	Fuller Model			Less Full Model		
Parameter	Estimate	SE	Parameter	Estimate	SE
β_0	12.70	0.49	β_0	12.70	0.49
β_1	2.00	0.70	β_1	2.00	0.69
β_2	−1.50	0.70	β_2	−1.50	0.69
β_3	−0.23	0.49			

$\hat{\sigma}(y\,|\,X)$ 2.70 $\hat{\sigma}(y\,|\,X)$ 2.66

Degrees of Freedom   Degrees of Freedom
$30 - 4 = 26$ $30 - 3 = 27$

Similar comparisons can be made between the estimated slope parameters for the two codings. For example, x_3 is coded 1 for females and 0 for males in the dummy coding. The two genders are separated by one unit on this variable and, as a result, the slope parameter of x_3, β_3, is estimated by the difference between the model's estimates of the response means for females and males: $[(14.47 - 14.93) = (10.97 - 11.43) = (11.97 - 12.43) = -0.46]$. With effect coding, x_3 is coded 1 for females and -1 for males. The genders are now separated by *two units* and, consequently, this x's slope parameter is estimated by one-half the difference between the model's estimates of the female and male average values $[\text{e.g.},(1/2)(14.47 - 14.93) = -0.23]$.

Similar comparisons can be made between the codings for the training-condition-only model. The overall fits are, again, identical. As a result, we could compare the additive model and Training-only models using either dummy variable or effect coding and the results would be the same.

11.1.4   Choice of Coding for Categorical Variable

Dummy variable and effect coding provide two ways of coding categorical variables, equivalent when judged from the point of view of the overall fits of the coded models. The parameters, though, have somewhat different interpretations and one coding may be preferred in certain circumstances.

Dummy variable coding identifies one level—or combination of levels if more than one categorical variable is to be included in a model—as a comparison condition. As such, it is an ideal coding when one level is a natural comparison level, for example, a *control condition* or a *standard treatment*.

Under effect coding, the intercept is defined as an average over all levels or conditions. This averaging is most meaningful when the levels embrace all the members of some *natural set*. Male/Female is a good example, as would be Freshman/Sophomore/Junior/Senior for undergraduates at a U.S. university, or NW/SW/NE/SE for a geographic quartering of observations.

Not all categorical variables either include a natural comparison level or exhaust a natural set of categories. When we code the levels of such a category in our models, the interpretation of the intercept, whether we choose dummy variable or effect coding, may seem a little artificial.

One final word on the choice of coding. Dummy variable and effect coding *should not be mixed* in the same model. As we have seen in the Problem Solving example, the combination of comparison levels when two categorical variables are given dummy variable representation gives rise to a comparison condition interpretation of the intercept. Similarly, the combination of omitted levels defines an omitted condition when both variables are effect coded. No simple interpretation of the intercept is possible, though, if one set of categories is dummy variable coded and the other is effect coded.

The importance of consistent coding of categorical variables within a model is highlighted in the next section.

11.2
Two Categorical Variables: Interactive Model

The additive model for two categorical variables is fuller, of course, than a model that includes but one of the two. There is, however, a two-categorical variable model that is even *fuller* than this additive one. And, it is a model that is often of considerable substantive interest to us.

11.2.1   Additive Model's Restricted Fit

Our additive model for the two categorical variables does not provide the fullest possible interesting model for the response means. Why this is true can be described quite simply. The additive model has *fewer parameters* than there are conditional populations from which we have sampled.

The design for our Spatial Problem-Solving study provided samples from six conditional-response populations:

(Problem-solving Scores | Female, Video Training)
(Problem-solving Scores | Male, Video Training)
(Problem-solving Scores | Female, Lecture Training)
(Problem-solving Scores | Male, Lecture Training)
(Problem-solving Scores | Female, Control Training)
(Problem-solving Scores | Male, Control Training).

The additive model of Section 11.1, whether developed for dummy variable coding or effect coding, estimated the means of these six populations as a function of just *four parameters*:

$$\mu(Problem\ Solving\,|\,Training, Gender) = \beta_0 + \beta_1 x_1 + \beta_2 x_2 + \beta_3 x_3. \tag{11.1}$$

Estimating Each Mean Independently

Where our design samples several times from each of a small number of conditional response populations it is important to have as the *fullest model* the one that estimates independently the means of each of those response populations.

The additive model does not provide *independent estimates* of the conditional means. This is clear in our Problem-solving example; the difference in the estimated means for Gender levels, female and male, was the same for each of the three Training conditions. That difference was $\widehat{\beta}_3$ for dummy variable coding and $2\widehat{\beta}_3$ for effect coding, regardless of the training condition.

For our model to provide independent estimates of six means, it must be a model with no fewer than six parameters. One way of constructing a six parameter model for the Problem-solving example is to treat the six conditional populations from which we sampled as the levels of a *single categorical variable*. We can then code the levels of this category, using either dummy variable or effect coding. This would give us five 0/1 (or −1/0/1) variables and a six parameter model:

$$\mu(Problem\ Solving \mid Training,\ Gender) = \beta_0 + \beta_1 x_1 + \beta_2 x_2 + \beta_3 x_3 + \beta_4 x_4 + \beta_5 x_5.$$
(11.2)

As an example of this, we could use dummy variable coding for the six Training/Gender combinations, letting Male, Control be the comparison level and assigning five dummy variables to the other levels as follows:

$$x_1 : (Female,\ Video) \quad x_2 : (Male,\ Video)$$
$$x_3 : (Female,\ Lecture) \quad x_4 : (Male,\ Lecture)$$
$$x_5 : (Female,\ Control).$$

When we estimate the six parameters for this model from the data of Table 11.1 we find that the intercept is estimated by the average of the five Problem-solving scores for Male, Control students,

$$\widehat{\beta_0} = \mathrm{M}(Problem\ Solving \mid Male,\ Control) = 12.40,$$

and each of the five slope parameters is estimated by the difference between the average Problem-solving score for students at that level and the average at the comparison level. For example,

$$\widehat{\beta_4} = \mathrm{M}(Problem\ Solving \mid Male,\ Lecture) - \mathrm{M}(Problem\ Solving \mid Male,\ Control)$$
$$= 10.00 - 12.40 = -2.40.$$

Improvement in Fit: A Fuller Model?

The estimated conditional-response variance for our six-parameter dummy-variable model is given from a regression program as $(2.480 \times 2.480) = 6.1504$. This estimate is *smaller* than the 7.295 obtained earlier for the additive, four-parameter one. To compare the fits of the two, though, the two have to enjoy a fuller/less full relation. If we are to do this we must satisfy ourselves that the additive model of Equation [11.1] is the result of constraining the six-parameter model of Equation [11.3].

What might those constraints be?

Table 11.6 shows the means of the six conditional-response populations sampled in terms of the six parameters of the Equation [11.3] dummy variable model.

T A B L E 11.6

Conditional-response Population Means: Six-parameter Dummy Variable Model

Response Population	Means
Female, Video	$\beta_0 + \beta_1$
Male, Video	$\beta_0 + \beta_2$
Female, Lecture	$\beta_0 + \beta_3$
Male, Lecture	$\beta_0 + \beta_4$
Female, Control	$\beta_0 + \beta_5$
Male, Control	β_0

First, we'll use the tabled means to look at the *differences* in the means for Females and Males for each of the three Training conditions. These are

$\mu(Problem\ Solving \mid Female, Video) - \mu(Problem\ Solving \mid Male, Video) = \beta_1 - \beta_2$

$\mu(Problem\ Solving \mid Female, Lecture) - \mu(Problem\ Solving \mid Male, Lecture)$

$$= \beta_3 - \beta_4, \text{ and}$$

$\mu(Problem\ Solving \mid Female, Control) - \mu(Problem\ Solving \mid Male, Control) = \beta_5.$

Next, we recall that for the additive model, the difference in the estimates of the means for Females and Males was the *same* for each of the three training conditions.

Imposing this equality on the differences in modeled means for the six-parameter dummy variable model results in the following set of relations among the parameters:

$$\beta_1 - \beta_2 = \beta_3 - \beta_4 = \beta_5.$$

The two equalities can be expressed as the two constraints

$$\beta_1 - \beta_2 = \beta_5 \text{ and}$$

$$\beta_3 - \beta_4 = \beta_5$$

or as

$$\beta_1 = \beta_5 + \beta_2 \text{ and}$$

$$\beta_3 = \beta_5 + \beta_4.$$

If we substitute the right-hand sides of these last two equalities for β_1 and β_3 in Equation [11.3], we have this constrained model:

$\mu(Problem\ Solving \mid Training, Gender)$

$$= \beta_0 + (\beta_5 + \beta_2)x_1 + \beta_2 x_2 + (\beta_5 + \beta_4)x_3 + \beta_4 x_4 + \beta_5 x_5.$$

When we gather together the separate terms for each of the parameters remaining in this model we have

$\mu(Problem\ Solving \mid Training, Gender)$

$$= \beta_0 + \beta_2(x_1 + x_2) + \beta_4(x_3 + x_4) + \beta_5(x_1 + x_3 + x_5).$$

But $(x_1 + x_2)$ is just a dummy variable coding Video treatment, $(x_3 + x_4)$ is a dummy variable coding Lecture treatment, and $(x_1 + x_3 + x_5)$ is a dummy variable coding Female. As a result, this last model is *identical to the additive model* of Equation [11.1], except for the change in name of the parameters and variables.

What we have just illustrated is that the additive four-parameter model can be found by imposing two constraints on the six-parameter, combined-categories, dummy variable model. These constraints have been identified using both of the techniques of Chapter 8: (a) replacing some of the parameters in the fuller linear model with linear functions of the remaining parameters, and (b) replacing the variables in the fuller model with a smaller number of linear combinations of those variables.

The six-parameter model is fuller with respect to the additive model. With the fuller/less full relation established, we are ready to compare the fits of the two models using the F-ratio statistic of Chapter 7,

$$F = 1 + \left(\frac{N-p}{k}\right)\left[\frac{\widehat{\sigma}^2(y \mid less\ full) - \widehat{\sigma}^2(y \mid fuller)}{\widehat{\sigma}^2(y \mid fuller)}\right]. \tag{7.23}$$

In this equation, N is the number of sample observations, p is the number of parameters in the less full model, and k is the number of constraints imposed on the parameters of the fuller model; the fuller model has $(p + k)$ parameters. For our comparison, $N = 30, p = 4, k = 2$, and the two conditional-response-variance estimates are

$\widehat{\sigma}^2(y \mid less\ full\ model) = 7.295$ (for the additive model) and
$\widehat{\sigma}^2(y \mid fuller\ model)\quad = 6.1504$ (for the 6-parameter, dummy variable model).

Substituting these values into the F statistic gives

$$F = 1 + \left(\frac{26}{2}\right)\left[\frac{7.295 - 6.1504}{6.1504}\right] = 3.419.$$

Is this a large value for the statistic if the constraints giving rise to the less full model are correct? To answer this, we refer our calculated value to the sampling distribution of F with $k = 2$ and $N - (p + k) = 24$ degrees of freedom. Referring to the table values, we see that only 5% of the sampling distribution is larger than 3.40. The call is a close one, but the result of the comparison is that we choose the fuller model as the better fitting of the two.

11.2.2   Explanatory Source Interaction

How are we to interpret the additive model's lack of fit, relative to the fuller, six-parameter model?

The additive model takes its name from the idea that the influences of the two categorical variables can simply be *added together*. That is, we sought a Gender effect on Problem Solving that could be added directly to the Training Condition effect we found earlier. That simple addition does not provide a good fit, though, to the six conditional populations sampled.

Where the influences of two categorical variables cannot be simply added together, we say that the two *interact* with each other in influencing the response. That is, the influence of one categorical variable is not constant across all levels of the second. Rather, it varies. We can interpret the Training Condition/Gender interaction we've just found in this way:

> *The influence of Gender on Problem Solving is not the same at all levels of Training Condition.*

11.2.3   Coding Interaction More Directly

The six-parameter dummy variable model, by providing independent estimates of the six conditional-response-population means allows the two categorical variables to interact. The additive model does not. We can safely refer to the six-parameter model now as an *interaction model*. The interactions, if they are present in the populations, have been brought into the model.

The question of whether two influence sources interact or not is of substantive importance in a lot of studies. As a result, we need a convenient way of developing models that either include or exclude specific interactions. The use of dummy variables to embrace interactions, in the way we did in the last section, does not provide the most convenient modeling of interactions. We develop an alternative here.

Dummy Variable Coding

If we use dummy variable coding for each of the two categorical variables separately, the additive model can be extended quite simply to include any potential interaction between them. We illustrate with the Problem-solving example.

The additive model for the two categorical variables, the one we have been working with, is one based on three variables,

$$\mu(Problem\ Solving \mid Training, Gender) = \beta_0 + \beta_1 x_1 + \beta_2 x_2 + \beta_3 x_3, \qquad \textbf{(11.1)}$$

where x_1 and x_2 are dummy variables coding two of the three levels of Training Condition (Video and Lecture) and x_3 is a dummy variable coding one of the two levels of Gender (Female).

We can form the six-parameter interaction model from this by adding two additional variables. We simply let x_4 be the *product* of x_1 and x_3, and x_5 be the product of x_2 and x_3.

When we fit the resulting model,

$$\mu(Problem\ Solving \mid Training, Gender) = \beta_0 + \beta_1 x_1 + \beta_2 x_2 + \beta_3 x_3 + \beta_4 x_4 + \beta_5 x_5,$$
$$\textbf{(11.3)}$$

we find that it provides *exactly the same fit* to the data as did that six-parameter dummy variable model of the preceding section. That is, the two give the same estimates for each of the six conditional response means and, hence, the same estimate for the conditional response variance: $\widehat{\sigma}^2(y \mid X) = 2.480 \times 2.480 = 6.1504$. The details of the fit of the interaction model to our sample observations are given in Table 11.7.

The Female-male difference in modeled response means is no longer constant across Training conditions. It ranges from -3.40 for the Video condition to 2.40 for Lecture training to -0.40 for the Control groups.

The two variables that were added to the model, x_4 and x_5, can be thought of as *interaction variables*. The fuller/less full relation between the additive and interaction models is clear now. The additive model is less full by virtue of our having "dropped" two variables (and their parameters) from the interaction model.

T A B L E 11.7

Fitting the Interaction Model: Dummy Variable Product Variables

Estimates of Model Parameters

Parameter	Estimate	Standard Error
β_0	12.40	1.109
β_1	4.00	1.568
β_2	-2.40	1.568
β_3	-0.40	1.568
β_4	-3.00	2.218
β_5	2.80	2.218

$$\hat{\sigma}(y \mid X)\, 2.480$$
Degrees of Freedom $30 - 6 = 24$

Estimates of Conditional Response Means

Population	x_1	x_2	x_3	x_4	x_5	Estimated Mean
Female, Video	1	0	1	1	0	$12.40 + 4.00 - 0.40 - 3.00 = 13.00$
Male, Video	1	0	0	0	0	$12.40 + 4.00 \qquad\qquad = 16.40$
Female, Lecture	0	1	1	0	1	$12.40 - 2.40 - 0.40 + 2.80 = 12.40$
Male, Lecture	0	1	0	0	0	$12.40 - 2.40 \qquad\qquad = 10.00$
Female, Control	0	0	1	0	0	$12.40 \qquad\qquad - 0.40 = 12.00$
Male, Control	0	0	0	0	0	$12.40 \qquad\qquad = 12.40$

The rule for creating interaction variables from the sets of dummy variables for the two categorical variables is simple. We form the product of each of the dummy variables in the set associated with the first categorical variable with each of the dummy variables in the set associated with the second categorical variable. If the first has I levels and the second has J levels, the result is $(I - 1)(J - 1)$ product variables. The dummy variable additive model has $1 + (I - 1) + (J - 1)$ parameters. Adding the product or interaction variables, the resulting interaction model will have $1 + (I - 1) + (J - 1) + (I - 1)(J - 1) = IJ$ parameters. This is exactly the number of parameters needed, one for each of the IJ populations from which we have sampled observations. This rule, and the corresponding one for effect coding given next, both assume that our design is *fully crossed*, that we have at least one observation at each pairing of a level from the first categorical variable with a level from the second. Later in this chapter, we look at designs in which this condition is not satisfied.

Effect Coding

We can extend the additive model based on effect coded variables for the two categorical variables in exactly the same way. That is, we can begin with an additive model that includes $(I - 1)$ effect coded variables for the I-level category and $(J - 1)$ effect coded variables for the J-level category. Adding the $(I - 1)(J - 1)$ product variables—each a product of one of the $(I - 1)$ effect coded variables for the first set of categories with one of the $(J - 1)$ effect coded variables for the second set—gives us the interaction model.

Table 11.8 gives the effect coded interaction-model results corresponding to the dummy variable results of Table 11.7. We see estimates of the six conditional means and of the conditional-response variance that are identical.

The choice of effect coding or dummy variable coding has been discussed earlier. Inasmuch as the parameters for the interaction variables are not themselves easily interpreted, a point we will return to, the choice of coding scheme should be based on what makes for an easier understood additive model. Again, however, dummy variable and effect coded variables should not be mixed in the same model.

T A B L E **11.8**
Fitting the Interaction Model: Effect Coded Product Variables

Estimates of Model Parameters

Parameter	Estimate	Standard Error
β_0	12.70	0.4528
β_1	2.00	0.6403
β_2	−1.50	0.6403
β_3	−0.233	0.4528
β_4	−1.467	0.6403
β_5	1.433	0.4528

$\hat{\sigma}(y\,|\,X)$ 2.480
Degrees of Freedom
$30 - 6 = 24$

Estimates of Conditional Response Means

Population	x_1	x_2	x_3	x_4	x_5	Estimated Mean
Female, Video	1	0	1	1	0	12.70 +2.00 −0.233 −1.467 = 13.00
Male, Video	1	0	−1	−1	0	12.70 +2.00 +0.233 +1.467 = 16.40
Female, Lecture	0	1	1	0	1	12.70 −1.50 −0.233 +1.433 = 12.40
Male, Lecture	0	1	−1	0	−1	12.70 −1.50 +0.233 −1.433 = 10.00
Female, Control	−1	−1	1	−1	−1	12.70 −2.00 +1.50 −0.233 +1.467 −1.433 = 12.00
Male, Control	−1	−1	−1	1	1	12.70 −2.00 +1.50 +0.233 −1.467 +1.433 = 12.40

11.2.4   Modeling with Interactions

We have seen two ways in which interactions may be explicitly "coded" in a model fuller than the additive one. The explicit coding not only makes it easier to see the fuller/less full relation but, with interactive computing facilities such as SPIDA, it is simple to develop and add product variables to models.

How should we organize our modeling when there is the possibility of an interaction between two categorical variables?

Model Comparisons

We usually begin by comparing the fits of the interactive and additive models. That is, our initial substantive concern about the two categorical influences is "Do they interact with one another or are their influences on the response simply additive?" If we reject the interaction model, we can then go on to ask whether—in the additive model—a better fitting model is provided by including both, rather than just one of the sets of categories.

In our example when we compared in Section 11.2.1 the interactive and additive models, we found the additive model inadequate. We chose not to reject the interactive model.

Role of the Fullest Model in Comparisons

Even where the interaction model is rejected, it frequently continues to play a role in our subsequent modeling. This will be true where sampling follows a *design*.

In the present example, our design called for us to sample, an equal number of times, from each of six response populations. We knew in advance exactly which response populations would be sampled and how many times. If our sampling does not follow a *design*, we often do not know, until sampling is completed, just how many or which conditional response populations have been sampled. The growth study is an example of an undesigned sample.

Where sampling *has followed a design* and where we have several response observations in the sample from each of a small number of response populations, we will follow a slightly different procedure in comparing fuller and less full models. Our goal in comparing models in this case is to understand the relations among the means of those response populations. Our model comparison strategy, though, requires that we estimate both the means and the variances of our conditional-response populations.

In Chapter 7, we obtained as Equation [7.24] a test statistic for comparing a fuller and a less full model. We'll rewrite it here in this form:

$$F = \frac{F_{num}}{F_{den}}$$

where

$$F_{num} = \frac{\text{SSR}(\textit{less full model}) - \text{SSR}(\textit{fuller model})}{k}$$

and

$$F_{den} = \frac{\text{SSR}(\textit{fuller model})}{N - (p + k)}.$$

It will be useful now to think of the numerator term, F_{num}, as estimating the difference in fits of the two models being compared and the denominator term, F_{den}, as our *best provisional estimate* of the variance common to our conditional-response populations.

With undesigned samples we *do not know which conditional response populations* we've sampled from. We are searching for a model to tell us just that. As a result, our estimate of the common conditional response variance always is dependent on our choice of model. Put another way, the denominator of Equation [7.24] will always be based on the fuller of the two models being compared.

By contrast, with designed samples, where the *conditional response populations are known*, our estimate of the common conditional-response variance will be based on the fullest model. F_{den} will be obtained from the fullest model for all model comparisons. This gives us an alternative F-statistic for model comparison:

$$F = \frac{\left(\frac{1}{k}\right)\{\text{SSR}(\textit{less full}) - \text{SSR}(\textit{fuller})\}}{\left(\frac{1}{N-p}\right)\text{SSR}(\textit{fullest})}. \tag{11.4}$$

In Equation [11.4], k is the difference in the number of parameters in the two models being compared; the fuller of the two has k more parameters than the less full one. The fullest model, however, has p parameters, the number of response populations sampled. The sampling distribution of the F-ratio of Equation [11.4], when the less full model is correct, is well approximated by the density function of the F-random variable with k numerator and $(N - p)$ denominator degrees of freedom.

Where the fuller of the two models being compared is the fullest model, as in the comparison of the additive and interactive models in Section 11.2.1, Equations [7.24] and [11.4] are identical. Although we prefer Equation [11.4] when a few response populations have been sampled according to design, other texts recommend Equation [7.24] in all model comparisons.

11.2.5   Interpreting the Interaction Model Parameters

We have emphasized throughout being able to give interpretation to the slope parameters in our linear models. How can we interpret the magnitudes of the "slope" parameters associated with the interaction terms in the models—the β_4 and β_5 of Table 11.7 or 11.8?

The short answer is that we can't. Or, at least, not very easily. The reason for this lies in our standard interpretation of the slope parameter in a multiple-x model. It is the increase in the mean value of the response associated with a one unit increase in a particular x, provided that all other xs are held constant. The trouble is that we can't visualize a one-unit change in the interaction variable without an *accompanying change* in at least one other x-variable. The interaction variables, for both dummy variable coding and effect coding, are products of other xs. Thus, the interaction x cannot change without a change in one of the xs entering into that product!

In fact, we take the position that *none* of the parameters of an interaction model should be interpreted. This does not mean that the interaction model is the wrong model. It does mean that the interaction model *should be rewritten* before any interpretation is attempted. We have already seen that the same model—in terms of its fit to our sample observations—can be written in different ways. The six-parameter dummy variable model of Section 11.2.1 and the dummy variable and effect coded interaction models of Sections 11.2.3 were equivalent. They gave the same estimates of means and of conditional-response variance; each model produced the same SSR. In the section following, we introduce an alternative to the interaction model called a *modular model*. The modular model provides the same fit as the interaction model. Its parameters, though, are much more easily interpreted.

11.2.6   A Modular Model for Interaction

Let's recall why the interaction model has that name. Our two categorical variables are said to interact with each other in influencing the response; their effects are not simply additive. Put another way, the influence of one of the categorical variables *changes from level to level* of the second.

In the context of our present example, we could say that the effect of *Training Condition* (whether Videotape, Lecture, or Control) on *Problem Solving* is different for men than for women. In linear model terms:

There is a different linear model linking mean Problem Solving to Training Condition for each of the two levels of Gender.

Let's see what those two models might look like. We'll use dummy variable coding for the *Training Condition*, taking the Control condition as the comparison one. Our two linear models could be expressed as

$$\mu(Problem\ Solving\ |\ Female, Training\ Condition) = \beta_1 + \beta_3 x_3 + \beta_5 x_5 \quad \textbf{(11.5)}$$

and

$$\mu(Problem\ Solving\ |\ Male, Training\ Condition) = \beta_2 + \beta_4 x_4 + \beta_6 x_6.$$

The Videotape Training condition is coded 1 and the other two are coded 0 by variables x_3 (for females) and x_4 (for males). Similarly, the Lecture condition is coded 1 and the other two are coded 0 by variables x_5 (female model) and x_6 (male model). If *Gender* and *Training Condition* interact, then either $\beta_3 \neq \beta_4$ or $\beta_5 \neq \beta_6$, or both. That is, the effect of Videotape or Lecture or both (compared with the Control treatment) is *different* for Males than for Females.

Notice that there are six parameters in the two models of Equation [11.5]. These two models are called *modules* because each is a model for only some of the conditional response populations of interest to us. If we can assemble these modules, with all of their distinct parameters, into a *single model appropriate to all* of our conditional response populations, the result is called a *modular model. Modular models* were pioneered in connection with linear models for categorical responses by Forthofer and Lehnen (1979), but they are equally useful in modeling a measured response.

Table 11.9 shows us how a modular model is constructed. In the upper part of the table, the two modules of Equation [11.5] are described. And in the lower part, they are *joined* in a modular model. It is a six-parameter model giving the same means for the six conditional-response populations as the separate by-gender models:

$$\mu(y \mid Gender, Training) = \beta_1 x_1 + \beta_2 x_2 + \beta_3 x_3 + \beta_4 x_4 + \beta_5 x_5 + \beta_6 x_6. \qquad \textbf{(11.6)}$$

T A B L E 11.9

A Modular Model for the Interaction of Gender and Training Conditions

Model for Females: $\beta_1 + \beta_3 x_3 + \beta_5 x_5$

Population	x_3	x_5	Response Mean
Videotape	1	0	$\beta_1 + \beta_3$
Lecture	0	1	$\beta_1 + \beta_5$
Control	0	0	β_1

Model for Males: $\beta_2 + \beta_4 x_4 + \beta_6 x_6$

Population	x_4	x_6	Response Mean
Videotape	1	0	$\beta_2 + \beta_4$
Lecture	0	1	$\beta_2 + \beta_6$
Control	0	0	β_2

Modular Model: $\beta_1 x_1 + \beta_2 x_2 + \beta_3 x_3 + \beta_4 x_4 + \beta_5 x_5 + \beta_6 x_6$

Population	x_1	x_2	x_3	x_4	x_5	x_6	Response Mean
Videotape, Female	1	0	1	0	0	0	$\beta_1 + \beta_3$
Lecture, Female	1	0	0	0	1	0	$\beta_1 + \beta_5$
Control, Female	1	0	0	0	0	0	β_1
Videotape, Male	0	1	0	1	0	0	$\beta_2 + \beta_4$
Lecture, Male	0	1	0	0	0	1	$\beta_2 + \beta_6$
Control, Male	0	1	0	0	0	0	β_2

How was the modular model of Equation [11.6] formed? The two "intercepts," β_1 and β_2—one for each gender—are accommodated in the modular model by including a 0/1 variable for *each* of the two levels of *Gender*; the new x_1 takes the value of 1 for all Females and 0 for all Males, while the new x_2 takes the value of 1 for all Males and 0 for all Females. This is *different from including dummy variables* for *Gender* in the model. Dummy variable coding produces a 0/1 variable for all category levels except the comparison level. In the modular model, we need a 0/1 variable for *each level* of one of the interacting categorical variables.

The new variables x_3 through x_6 can be formed as "product variables," in the same way that the interaction variables of Section 11.2.3 were formed. If we let z_1

and z_2 be dummy variables coding Videotape and Lecture training, respectively, for all respondents, Male and Female, (as might have been used for our earlier additive and interactive models) then (a) x_3 is the product of x_1 with z_1, (b) x_4 is the product of x_2 with z_1, (c) x_5 is the product of x_1 with z_2, and (d) x_6 is the product of x_2 with z_2.

The variables needed for the modular model are constructed easily with interactive statistical packages such as SPIDA.

We said that our modular model included two "intercepts," one for Females and one for Males. While β_1 and β_2 have intercept interpretations, when we ask most regresssion commands to fit this modular model, we must specify that it is a "no-constant" or "no-intercept" model. That is, because we have already provided for our intercepts by including x_1 and x_2, we don't want the regression machinery to add its own intercept. (Technical Note: Whenever a weighted sum of two or more x-variables produces a variable having the same value for every observation in the sample, an intercept is not needed. Here the sum of x_1 and x_2 give a variable that is everywhere equal to 1.)

Fit of the Modular Model

Table 11.10 summarizes the fit of the modular model of Equation [11.6]. It should be noted that the estimated conditional response variance and the modeled means for the six populations are identical to those reported for the interaction models in Tables 11.7 and 11.8. The modular model is equivalent to either interaction model. All have six unconstrained parameters and allow the six conditional response population means to be estimated independently.

Simplifying the Modular Model

We reached this modular model because in the comparison of the interaction and additive models we chose the interactive model. With which new models might we compare this modular model?

We recall that for the interaction model to be preferred, the effect of one or more of the *Training Condition* levels on problem solving is different for the Males than for the Females. Now we want to find out for which levels this is true. The estimates of Table 11.10 reveal a relatively small Male-female difference for the Control level (0.40 score points) compared with that for the other two levels (2.40 score points for Lecture Training and 3.40 score points for Videotape Training). A starting point, then, is to constrain the two Control means to be identical.

If we constrain β_2 to be equal to β_1, the modular model of Equation [11.6] changes to:

$$
\begin{aligned}
\mu(y \mid Gender, Training) &= \beta_1 x_1 + \beta_2 x_2 + \beta_3 x_3 + \beta_4 x_4 + \beta_5 x_5 + \beta_6 x_6 \\
&= \beta_1 x_1 + \beta_1 x_2 + \beta_3 x_3 + \beta_4 x_4 + \beta_5 x_5 + \beta_6 x_6 \quad \textbf{(11.7)} \\
&= \beta_1 (x_1 + x_2) + \beta_3 x_3 + \beta_4 x_4 + \beta_5 x_5 + \beta_6 x_6 \\
&= \beta_1 + \beta_3 x_3 + \beta_4 x_4 + \beta_5 x_5 + \beta_6 x_6.
\end{aligned}
$$

T A B L E **11.10**

Fitting Interactions with A Modular Model

Estimates of Model Parameters

Parameter	Estimate	Standard Error
β_1	12.00	1.109
β_2	12.40	1.109
β_3	1.00	1.568
β_4	4.00	1.568
β_5	0.40	1.568
β_6	−2.40	1.568
$\hat{\sigma}(y\,|\,X)$	2.480	

Degrees of Freedom
$30 - 6 = 24$

Estimates of Conditional Response Means

Population	x_1	x_2	x_3	x_4	x_5	x_6	Estimated Mean		
Female, Video	1	0	1	0	0	0	12.00	+ 1.00	= 13.00
Male, Video	0	1	0	1	0	0	12.40	+ 4.00	= 16.40
Female, Lecture	1	0	0	0	1	0	12.00	+ 0.40	= 12.40
Male, Lecture	0	1	0	0	0	1	12.40	− 2.40	= 10.00
Female, Control	1	0	0	0	0	0	12.00		= 12.00
Male, Control	0	1	0	0	0	0	12.40		= 12.40

In the second line, we replace β_2 with its equivalent β_1. Because they now have the same slope parameters, this allows us to add together x_1 and x_2 in the third line. Finally, as the sum of these two x-variables is a constant value of 1 for every sample observation, β_1 is simply the (single) intercept for our new model.

Fitting the model of Equation [11.7], a no-*Gender* difference for Control-level Training model, we obtain the results summarized in Table 11.11. The SSR for this five parameter model,

$$\text{SSR(Equation [11.7])} = 2.433^2 \times 25 = 147.99,$$

exceeds that for the modular model of Table 11.10,

$$\text{SSR(Modular)} = 2.480^2 \times 24 = 147.61,$$

by only a very small amount and the value of the F-ratio of Equation 11.4—were we to compute it—would also be quite small. There is no appreciable decrement in our model's ability to account for the data when we constrain the Control Training-level effect to be the same for Males and Females.

T A B L E 11.11

Fitting the Model of Equation [11.7]

Estimates of Model Parameters

Parameter	Estimate	Standard Error
β_1	12.20	0.769
β_3	0.80	1.333
β_4	4.20	1.333
β_5	0.20	1.333
β_6	−2.20	1.333
$\hat{\sigma}(y\,|\,X)$	2.433	

Degrees of Freedom

$30 - 5 = 25$

Estimates of Conditional Response Means

Population	x_3	x_4	x_5	x_6				Estimated Mean
Female, Video	1	0	0	0	12.20	+ 0.80		= 13.00
Male, Video	0	1	0	0	12.20	+ 4.20		= 16.40
Female, Lecture	0	0	1	0	12.20		+ 0.20	= 12.40
Male, Lecture	0	0	0	1	12.20		− 2.20	= 10.00
Female, Control	0	0	0	0	12.20			= 12.20
Male, Control	0	0	0	0	12.20			= 12.20

The results in Table 11.11 suggest the model might be further simplified. In particular, the estimates of β_3 and β_5 are each quite small compared with their standard errors. This suggests, in turn, that the fit of the present five parameter model be compared against that of one in which, additionally, β_3 and β_5 are each constrained to be 0. Substantively, this new model specifies that, in addition to there being no *Gender* difference for the Control level, there are no Video- or Lecture-level effects for Females. The fit to this three-parameter model is summarized in Table 11.12.

The SSR for this three-parameter model, SSR(Three Parameter Model)= $2.358^2 \times 27 = 150.1$, is quite close to that for the two fuller models and any formal comparison based on the F-statistic would lead to our preferring the more parsimonious three-parameter model.

The estimates of the three parameters and their standard errors, listed in Table 11.12, do not suggest any further model simplification; β_4 and β_6 are distinct from each other and both are distinct from 0. Substantively, we would conclude that Video Training enhances and Lecture Training degrades the *Problem-solving* performance of Males (relative to the Control condition) but neither affects the performance of Females.

TABLE 11.12
Fitting the Three Parameter Model

Estimates of Model Parameters

Parameter	Estimate	Standard Error
β_1	12.45	0.527
β_4	3.95	1.179
β_6	−2.45	1.179
$\widehat{\sigma}(y\,|\,X)$	2.358	

Degrees of Freedom
$30 - 3 = 27$

Estimates of Conditional Response Means

Population	x_4	x_6		Estimated Mean	
Female, Video	0	0	12.45		= 12.45
Male, Video	1	0	12.45	+ 3.95	= 16.40
Female, Lecture	0	0	12.45		= 12.45
Male, Lecture	0	1	12.45	− 2.45	= 10.00
Female, Control	0	0	12.45		= 12.45
Male, Control	0	0	12.45		= 12.45

11.3
Factorial Designs

The study design summarized in Table 11.1 is an example of a *factorial design*. The factorial design requires both two or more categorical explanatory variables and response observations at combinations of the levels of those variables. If all possible combinations are present, the design is *fully crossed* or a *complete factorial*. If some combinations are missing, it is an incomplete factorial. The *Training Condition-gender* study was an example of a 3 × 2 complete factorial design; each of the three *Training-condition* levels was paired with each of the two levels of *Gender*.

11.3.1 Modeling a 2 × 2 × 2 Factorial Design

Let's consider a second factorial design, one involving three rather than just two categorical variables. The addition of a third set of categories will extend our understanding of the role of interactions in models.

Student Ethnicity, School Type, and Year of Graduation

In the upper part of Table 11.13, we have (wholly fictitious) data for a three-factor study. Tabled are Scholastic Aptitude Test Mathematical (SATM) test scores for

T A B L E 11.13

Influence of *Ethnicity, School Type,* and *Year of Graduation* on Performance on the *SAT Mathematical Test*

		1983				1988		
Graduation Year:								
Student Ethnicity:	White		Asian-American		White		Asian-American	
School Type:	Private	Public	Private	Public	Private	Public	Private	Public
	65	28	62	70	71	56	83	85
	78	49	51	60	68	55	37	83
	73	53	56	53	72	35	65	55
	63	32	66	81	55	64	78	77
	58	57	48	61	58	69	68	81
	50	49	36	65	68	43	65	81
	68	54	76	65	78	48	72	58
	67	62	61	65	49	74	64	101
Avg	65.2	48.0	57.0	65.0	64.9	55.5	66.5	77.6

Full-Interaction Model: Dummy-Variable Coding

1. Private (P)	1	0	1	0	1	0	1	0
2. Asian-American (A)	0	0	1	1	0	0	1	1
3. 1988 (88)	0	0	0	0	1	1	1	1
4. P × A	0	0	1	0	0	0	1	0
5. P × 88	0	0	0	0	1	0	1	0
6. A × 88	0	0	0	0	0	0	1	1
7. P × A × 88	0	0	0	0	0	0	1	0

was chosen randomly from among all those seniors who were (a) White or Asian-American, (b) enrolled in a Public or Private school, and (c) graduated in 1983 or 1988. The three factors, each at two levels, give rise to our $2 \times 2 \times 2 = 8$ groups, a complete factorial design. Further, we have eight *replications* of each of the factor-level combinations; from each of the eight conditional-response populations, we've sampled eight students.

The sample averages vary, suggesting that the response-population means may differ as well. We hope to identify systematic differences in these conditional means by modeling.

To provide explanatory variables for our linear structural models, we will use dummy variables to code the levels of the three factors. The comparison levels are chosen to be Public schools, White students, and 1983 graduation year. Because each of the three factors has only two levels, one dummy variable (coded for the non-comparison level) is sufficient for each of the categorical variables. At the bottom of Table 11.13 is a summary of the dummy variable coding for Private schools (P), Asian-American students (A), and 1988 graduation (88). The rows numbered 1 through 3 give the values of these dummy variables for observations from the eight different groups.

Higher-order Interactions

Also at the bottom of Table 11.13 (rows 4 through 6) are the product variables needed to provide for the possible interactions of School Type with Ethnicity ($P \times A$), of School Type with Year of Graduation ($P \times 88$), and of Ethnicity with Year of Graduation ($A \times 88$). Again, because each categorical variable is at two levels, there is exactly one product variable for each interaction: $(2 - 1) \times (2 - 1) = 1$. These product variables, between the dummy variables coding each pair of categorical variables, are computed in the same way as we described in the preceding section. They are interaction variables.

The three interactions $P \times A, P \times 88$, and $A \times 88$ are termed *first order interactions*. We would interpret a particular one of them, say $P \times A$, as being sensitive to whether the influence of Ethnicity on SATM performance is the same for Private as for Public schools. Or, this same interaction could be thought of as reflecting whether the influence of School Type on SATM is the same for Asian-American students as it is for Whites. There are two ways of looking at each first-order interaction and we will have to be guided by substantive knowledge to decide "which makes better sense."

When more than two categorical variables are represented in a design, there is the possibility not only of first-order but of higher-order interactions. What do such interactions mean? In the present example, a second-order interaction between Ethnicity, School Type, and Year of Graduation might be understood as indicating that the first-order interaction between Ethnicity and School Type is itself different for the two levels of Year of Graduation.

Interaction variables for higher-order interactions are formed in the same way as those for the first-order interactions. If categorical variables A, B, and C are present at a, b, and c levels, respectively, and represented by $(a - 1), (b - 1)$, and $(c - 1)$ dummy variables, then the first-order interaction between A and B would be represented by $(a - 1) \times (b - 1)$ product variables, that between A and C by $(a - 1) \times (c - 1)$ product variables, that between B and C by $(b - 1) \times (c - 1)$ product variables, and that between A, B, and C by $(a - 1) \times (b - 1) \times (c - 1)$ product variables; these last are formed between dummy variables representing all three sources. Here, where $a = b = c = 2$, there is but $(2 - 1)(2 - 1)(2 - 1) = 1$ product variable for the second-order interaction.

The product variable for the second-order interaction is just the product of the three-dummy variables Private, Asian-American, and 1988. The scores on that second-order interaction variable are indicated on the last line of Table 11.13. For the three-categorical variable design, the number of dummy variables coding the categorical variable levels plus the number of first-order interaction variables plus the number of second-order interaction variables plus one (for the intercept) describe a model with as many parameters as there are combinations of levels of the factors, $a \times b \times c$. This full interaction model is a fullest model and allows us to unconstrainedly estimate the response means in all of the $a \times b \times c$ response populations sampled.

For our $2 \times 2 \times 2$ design, the full interaction model is

$$\mu(SATM \,|\, Ethnicity,\, School,\,\&\, Year)$$
$$= \beta_0 + \beta_1 x_1 + \beta_2 x_2 + \beta_3 x_3 + \beta_4 x_4 + \beta_5 x_5 + \beta_6 x_6 + \beta_7 x_7 \qquad \text{(11.8)}$$

with the x_is as defined in Table 11.13.

The principles for constructing and including higher-order interaction variables in models generalize to higher orders than second (i.e., if four categorical variables are present in a design, the fullest- or full-interaction model must include four sets of second-order interaction variables and one set of third-order interaction variables.) Higher-order interaction variables can be constructed from effect-coded variables for the categorical variables in the same way they are from dummy variables. As we noted earlier, we choose to code all of the categorical variables either with dummy variables or with effect coding. We do not mix them when we wish to compute product variables among them.

Modeling the $2 \times 2 \times 2$ Design

In the absence of strong theoretical information to the contrary, we model the factorial design with the goal of achieving the most parsimonious representation of the influence of the categorical variables on the response, consistent with the data. An interaction model is less parsimonious than an additive model and a model with higher-order interactions is less parsimonious than one with only first-order interactions.

A first priority, then, is to determine which, if any, interactions are needed to describe the influence of the categorical variables. Table 11.14 describes the fits of the first two models to be compared—the full-interaction Model 1 and Model 2 with all first-order interactions but without the second-order interaction.

The best estimate of the conditional response population variance common to the eight populations sampled is given by the fit to the fullest model, the full-interaction model (Model 1),

$$\hat{\sigma}^2(y \,|\, fullest\ model) = 11.80^2 = 139.24.$$

This will be our *denominator term* for any F-ratios we use to compare subsequent fuller and less full models in this study. The degrees of freedom associated with the fullest model, $64 - 8 = 56$, will be the denominator degrees of freedom used in evaluating these F-ratios.

Continuing with our examination of the fit of Model 1 to our sample, we observe that the estimate of the slope parameter for the second order interaction, β_7, is quite small relative to its standard error, yielding a t-ratio of $4.75/11.80 = 0.40$. This is small enough (considerably less than 2.0 or even 1.5) that we don't need a formal F-ratio comparison of the full-interaction model and the no-second-order-interaction model to conclude that there is no need to include a second-order interaction in our explanatory model. This gives us Model 2.

Are any of the potential first-order interactions for pairs of categorical Xs needed in our explanatory model? In the fit to Model 2, we see that the estimate for β_5, the slope parameter for School Type $\times$ Graduation Year, is smaller than its standard error. This interaction can be dropped from the model. A formal comparison of the

T A B L E 11.14

Evaluating the Second-order Interaction: Ethnicity × School Type × Year Example

Model 1: Full Interactions

	Estimates of Model Parameters	
Parameter	Estimate	Standard Error
β_0	48.00	4.173
β_1	17.25	5.902
β_2	17.00	5.902
β_3	7.500	5.902
β_4	−25.25	8.346
β_5	−7.875	8.346
β_6	5.125	8.346
β_7	4.750	11.80

$\widehat{\sigma}(y \mid X)$ 11.80

Degrees of Freedom: $64 - 8 = 56$

Model 2: All First-order Interactions

	Estimates of Model Parameters	
Parameter	Estimate	Standard Error
β_0	48.59	3.875
β_1	16.06	5.073
β_2	15.81	5.073
β_3	6.312	5.073
β_4	−22.88	5.858
β_5	−5.500	5.858
β_6	7.500	5.858

$\widehat{\sigma}(y \mid X)$ 11.72

Degrees of Freedom: $64 - 7 = 57$

fits of Models 2 and 3—the latter without this last interaction and summarized in Table 11.15—can be made with the *F*-ratio of Equation [11.7]:

$$F = \frac{7939.62 - 7829.43}{139.24} = 0.79.$$

The result, a ratio less than 1, offers no evidence that the interaction omitted from Model 2 is important. We prefer Model 3 to Model 2.

Table 11.15 summarizes the fit not only of Model 3 but of two further models. Model 4 differs from Model 3 by omitting the Ethnicity × Year of Graduation interaction. The slope estimate for the corresponding slope parameter in Model 3 had a small *t*-ratio, $7.500/5.852 = 1.28$, again less than 1.5.

T A B L E   **11.15**

Evaluating the First-order Interactions: Ethnicity, School Type, and Year

Model 3: Ethnic Interactions Only

Parameter	Estimate	Standard Error
	Estimates of Model Parameters	
β_0	49.97	3.584
β_1	13.31	4.138
β_2	15.81	5.068
β_3	3.563	4.138
β_4	−22.87	5.852
β_6	7.500	5.852

$\widehat{\sigma}(y \mid X)$ 11.70

Degrees of Freedom: $64 - 6 = 58$

Model 4: Single Interaction, School Type × Ethnicity

Parameter	Estimate	Standard Error
	Estimates of Model Parameters	
β_0	48.09	3.289
β_1	13.31	4.161
β_2	19.56	4.161
β_3	7.313	2.942
β_4	−22.87	5.884

$\widehat{\sigma}(y \mid X)$ 11.77

Degrees of Freedom: $64 - 5 = 59$

Model 5: No Interactions

Parameter	Estimate	Standard Error
	Estimates of Model Parameters	
β_0	53.81	3.270
β_1	1.875	3.270
β_2	8.125	3.270
β_3	7.312	3.270

$\widehat{\sigma}(y \mid X)$ 13.08

Degrees of Freedom: $64 - 4 = 60$

Correspondingly, the comparison of the fits of Models 3 and 4 gives us this F-ratio:

$$F = \frac{8173.44 - 7939.62}{139.24} = 1.68.$$

A value of F greater than about 4.0 is needed to conclude (for the F with 1 and 56 degrees of freedom at the 5% level) that the omitted term is important to our model. We prefer Model 4 to Model 3.

When we attempt to eliminate the last possibility of an interaction, between Ethnicity and Type of School, we are brought up short. The t-ratio is rather larger than 2.0 for the estimate of β_4 in Model 4: $-22.87/5.884 = -3.89$. When we compare the fits of Model 4 with Model 5 without this one interaction, the shift in fit is dramatic:

$$F = \frac{10265.18 - 8173.44}{139.24} = 15.02.$$

With 1 and 56 degrees of freedom, F ratios of 7.1 or greater occur less than 1% of the time when the less full model is correct. Clearly, the influence of Type of School on SATM scores must be different for Asian-American than for White students. We prefer Model 4 to Model 5.

A Modular Model

Finding that an interaction is important to an explanatory model does not explain the interaction and, in fact, requires that we continue our search for a best model. As for the earlier 3×2 factorial study, we now want to replace Model 4 with an equivalent *modular model*.

The significant interaction was between Type of School and Ethnicity of Student. This means we can choose to construct the model either out of separate "modules" for the levels of School Type or out of separate modules for the levels of Student Ethnicity. If we choose the first, our modular model will describe the *influence of Ethnicity* on the performance of students from the several School Types. If we choose the latter, our model will describe the *influence of School Type* on the performance of students of varying Ethnicity.

Neither model would be incorrect. The second modularization may be more natural, describing the impact of different School Types. We will replace Model 4 with such a modular equivalent.

The modules, one for each level of Ethnicity, are these:

$$\mu(SATM \mid Asian\text{-}American, School, Year) = \beta_1 + \beta_3 x_3 + \beta_4 x_1$$

and

$$\mu(SATM \mid White, School, Year) = \beta_2 + \beta_3 x_3 + \beta_5 x_1.$$

Here, our newest x_1 and x_3 remain dummy variables for Type of School and Year of Graduation, respectively. The modules specify that there are separate intercepts (β_1 and β_2) as well as separate School Type slopes (β_4 and β_5) for the Ethnicity levels but a *single* Year of Graduation slope, (β_3). There is no interaction between Ethnicity and Year postulated in these modules, as there was none in Model 4.

The modules require five parameters, just as there were five parameters in Model 4. The two modules are included in a single model of this form:

$$\mu(SATM \mid Ethnicity, School, Year) = \beta_1 x_2 + \beta_2 z_1 + \beta_3 x_3 + \beta_4 (x_2 \times x_1) + \beta_5 (z_1 \times x_1).$$

Here, x_2 is our old 0/1 variable taking the value 1 for Asian-American students and 0 for Whites; z_1 is a new 0/1 variable, taking the value 1 for Whites and 0 for Asian-Americans. The product variable ($x_2 \times x_1$) will be 0 for Whites and will take the value of the School Type dummy variable for Asian-Americans. This is reversed for the product variable $(z_1 \times x_1)$; it will be 0 for all Asian-American students and equal to the value of x_1, the dummy variable for School Type, for White students.

The fit of this modular model to our sample is summarized in Table 11.16. The estimate of $\sigma(y \mid X)$ for this model is identical to that for Model 4. If the parameter estimates of the two models were used to estimate the y means of the eight conditional-response populations, the two sets of estimates would also be the same. Our modular model is indeed the equivalent of Model 4.

We developed the modular alternative to provide a way either of interpreting the five-parameter model or of simplifying it. Our modular model seems a good stopping place. The two intercepts are distinct from each other (the two are separated by almost six times their common SE) and all of the t-ratios for slopes are small enough to suggest that no further model simplification is in order.

How do we interpret our final model? SATM is influenced by Ethnicity, Year of Graduation, and Type of School. These influences are described at the bottom of Table 11.16.

T A B L E   **11.16**

Evaluating the Modular Model: School Type Within Ethnicity

Model 6: Year, Ethnicity, School Within Ethnicity

Parameter	Estimates of Model Parameters Estimate	Standard Error
β_1	67.66	3.289
β_2	48.09	3.289
β_3	7.313	2.942
β_4	−9.562	4.161
β_5	13.31	4.161

$$\hat{\sigma}(y \mid X) \quad 11.77$$

Degrees of Freedom: $64 - 5 = 59$

Estimated Conditional Response Means

Group	Estimated Mean			
White, Public, 1983	48.09			= 48.09
Asian-American, Public 1983	67.66			= 67.06
White, Public, 1988	48.09	+ 7.31		= 55.40
Asian-American, Public, 1988	67.66	+ 7.31		= 74.97
White, Private, 1983	48.09		+ 13.31	= 61.40
Asian-American, Private, 1983	67.66		− 9.56	= 58.10
White, Private, 1988	48.09	+ 7.31	+ 13.31	= 68.71
Asian-American, Private, 1988	67.66	+ 7.31	− 9.56	= 65.41

- Asian-American students graduating from Public high schools in 1983 had SATM scores that averaged 19.57 points higher than their White colleagues: *67.66 − 48.09 = 19.57.*

- Students graduating in 1988 earned SATM scores that averaged 7.31 points higher than those for 1983 graduates.

- The effect of a Private education was different for Asian-Americans than for Whites. On the average, SATM scores for White high school graduates of Private schools were 13.31 points higher than for their Public school colleagues. Asian-American Private school graduates, on the other hand, earned SATM scores 9.56 points lower than their Public school counterparts.

11.3.2 Search Strategies for Complete Factorial Design Models

What strategies might we use to identify a parsimonious explanatory model for complete factorial designs? First, using either dummy variables, or effect coded variables for the levels of each categorical variable, we create a full interaction model. This model includes dummy (or effect) variables and products of dummy or effect variables. It has just as many parameters as the product of the numbers of levels of the several categorical variables. Or, as many parameters as there are response populations sampled.

In the search for a parsimonious model, we first ask which, if any, interactions among the categorical variables are necessary for adequate explanation. Models with interactions are less parsimonious than those without. Higher-order interactions, in turn, are more complex than first-order ones so we examine the higher-order ones initially. If no interactions are needed, an additive model results and the search for further simplification centers on the following twin questions:

- Do all of the levels of a particular categorical variable have the same impact on the response? If so, then that categorical variable plays no role in our explanatory model.

- Do some of the levels of a particular categorical variable have the same impact on the response? If so, the explanatory model should combine those levels, provided such combination is substantively sensible.

If one or more interactions are needed, we rewrite the model as a modular model. The modules chosen for this will reflect both the interactions identified as essential and the substantive interpretation of the model. These are the possibilities in the case of a three-factor (*A* at *a* levels, *B* at *b* levels, and *C* at *c* levels) design:

- A second-order interaction is needed. The modular model may best be expressed in modules of one of the first-order interactions; for example, a module for each of the $(a \times b)$ "levels" that result when all levels of *A* are crossed with all levels of *B*. Each module would include an intercept and a slope for each of $(c-1)$ levels of *C*. In our Ethnicity × School × Year example, a significant second-order interaction might have led to a module for each Ethnicity × Year level with slope parameter(s) for the non-comparison level(s) of School.

- All first-order interactions are needed. This is the most difficult to interpret of the models for this design. No modular model will be fully satisfactory. Choose one of the categorical variables, say A, and construct a module for each level. This module will have an intercept and slopes for each (noncomparison) level of B, for each (noncomparison) level of C and for each of the $(b-1) \times (c-1)$ product variables between the (noncomparison) levels of B and C. The intercepts and B and C slopes are allowed to differ from module to module (i.e., they vary from level to level of A, reflecting the $A \times B$ and $A \times C$ interactions) but the $B \times C$ slopes must be the same in each module (i.e., there is a $B \times C$ interaction but it does not vary from one level of A to another; there is no $A \times B \times C$ interaction).

- Two first-order interactions are needed. Modules are formed for each level of the categorical variable that enters into both interactions. Assuming the interactions are $A \times B$ and $B \times C$, modules are formed for each level of B. These modules each have intercepts and slopes for each of the $(a-1)$ and $(c-1)$ noncomparison levels of A and C.

- One first-order interaction is needed. Modules are formed for each level of either of the categorical variables contributing to the interaction. Ease of interpretation from a substantive point of view will determine which one is chosen. Assuming the interaction is $A \times B$ and we choose to construct modules for each level of A, each of these modules will include an intercept term, a slope for each noncomparison level of B, and a slope for each noncomparison level of C. The intercepts and B slopes can vary from module to module, but the C slopes will be constrained to be the same in every module.

In seeking simplification of any of these modular models, we ask if certain intercepts might be the same or if certain slopes might be the same. The choice of parameters to be "pooled" should make substantive sense, of course. In considering slopes that might be pooled, they should either be slopes for the same level of a categorical variable but from different modules, or slopes for different levels of the same categorical variable within a particular module. And, in the case of the modular model for second-order interaction where there are intercepts for each $A \times B$ combination, the sensible poolings would be of levels of A within a level of B or of levels of B within a level of A. In the complicated case of all first-order interactions, any pooling of the $B \times C$ slopes ought to follow similar rules.

11.3.3 Models for Incomplete Factorial Designs

A full interaction model, made up systematically of dummy variables and products of dummy variables, works for complete factorial designs. Where the design is *incomplete*, where some combinations of categorical-variable levels are not included, the fullest model must be constructed differently.

If, for example, the performance of Asian-American Stdents had been observed only in Public high schools, our SATM study would have involved samples from only six response populations:

> White Students, Public Schools, 1983 Graduates
> White Students, Public Schools, 1988 Graduates
> White Students, Private Schools, 1983 Graduates
> White Students, Private Schools, 1988 Graduates
> Asian-American Students, Public Schools, 1983 Graduates
> Asian-American Students, Public Schools, 1988 Graduates.

As we have samples from six populations, our fullest model will have six unconstrained parameters.

One way of constructing the fullest model is to think of one made up again of modules. We have specified that the School Type × Ethnicity pairings are incomplete. As a result, we could start with modules for the two levels of Ethnicity, for the two levels of School Type, or for the three levels of School Type × Ethnicity. For ease of interpreting the parameters, the last may have the edge. The three modules would look like this:

$$\mu(SATM \mid Private\ School\ Whites,\ Year) = \beta_1 + \beta_4 x_3$$
$$\mu(SATM \mid Public\ School\ Whites,\ Year) = \beta_2 + \beta_5 x_3$$
$$\mu(SATM \mid Public\ School\ Asian\text{-}Americans,\ Year) = \beta_3 + \beta_6 x_3$$

where x_3 is a dummy variable for one of the two levels of Year of Graduation (say, 0 for 1983 graduates, 1 for 1988 gradautes).

The complete modular model would look like this:

$\mu(SATM \mid Ethnicity,\ School,\ Year)$
$$= \beta_1 z_1 + \beta_2 z_2 + \beta_3 z_3 + \beta_4 (z_1 \times x_3) + \beta_5 (z_2 \times x_3) + \beta_6 (z_3 \times x_3)$$

where z_1 is 1 for Private School Whites and 0 for others, z_2 is 1 for Public School Whites and 0 for others, and z_3 is 1 for Public School Asian-Americans and 0 for others.

In considering simplifications to this fullest model, a substantively reasonable set of questions would include the following:

> Are β_1 and β_2 different?
> Are β_2 and β_3 different?
> Are β_4 and β_5 different?
> Are β_5 and β_6 different?

Comparing either β_1 and β_3 or β_4 and β_6 involves shifting levels of both Ethnicity and School Type. Such comparisons would appear to have little substantive support.

11.4
Nested Designs

The factorial design, complete or incomplete, is the most common one for studies with two or more categorical variables. Less common are studies in which the levels of a second set of categories are not crossed, fully or otherwise, with a first set but are nested within them.

Consider two categorical variables, Therapy (assuming, say, three levels corresponding to three distinct therapies) and Clinic (with levels corresponding to geographically separated clinics offering one or more of the therapies). If the levels of Clinic are fully crossed with those of Therapy, it would mean that we have observations for each therapy at each clinic. If the levels of Clinic are incompletely crossed with those of Therapy, then certain, usually only a few, of the possible crossings would not be present. Finally, if the levels of Clinic are said to be nested within those of Therapy, then *different* clinic levels are associated with *each* level of Therapy.

Figure 11.1 illustrates the three designs. In the top panel, the same set of clinics are associated with each therapy. The same is true in the middle panel except that Clinic 4 does not offer Therapy B and Clinic 1 does not offer Therapy C. In the bottom panel, however, completely different clinics (different levels of the Clinic variable) offer the three therapies; no clinic offers two or more of the therapies.

	Therapy Levels		
	Therapy A	Therapy B	Therapy C
Clinics Fully Crossed			
	Clinic 1	Clinic 1	Clinic 1
	Clinic 2	Clinic 2	Clinic 2
	Clinic 3	Clinic 3	Clinic 3
	Clinic 4	Clinic 4	Clinic 4
Clinics Incompletely Crossed			
	Clinic 1	Clinic 1	
	Clinic 2	Clinic 2	Clinic 2
	Clinic 3	Clinic 3	Clinic 3
	Clinic 4		Clinic 4
Clinics Nested			
	Clinic 1	Clinic 5	Clinic 9
	Clinic 2	Clinic 6	Clinic 10
	Clinic 3	Clinic 7	Clinic 11
	Clinic 4	Clinic 8	Clinic 12

FIGURE 11.1
Illustrating Fully and Incompletely Crossed and Nested Designs for Two Categorical Variables

11.4.1　Nested Designs: Motivation

In the factorial design, the two or more categorical variables are often of equal substantive importance to us. By contrast, we usually have only a limited interest in the nested categorical variable.

For our Clinics-within-Therapies example, the main focus is on the alternative therapies. Is one superior to the others? We include observations—the response variable is some measure of "success," assessed for individual patients—from different clinics for each therapy because of two interrelated concerns:

- We don't want to judge the effectiveness of a therapy by how it is provided in a particular clinic. This would risk confounding clinic effectiveness with therapy effectiveness.

- We are also interested in whether different clinics have about the same success with a given therapy. Or, does success vary quite a bit from clinic to clinic?

Because we are not interested in comparing clinics as such, we do not need to have them practice the same therapies. This may make it easier for us to organize the study; it could be prohibitive to require each clinic to offer all therapies of interest. Different clinics can be "assigned" to different therapies. Of course, to make the therapy comparisons most useful, we will not want the clinics assigned to, say, Therapy A to differ systematically from those assigned to either of the other therapies. Random allocation of clinics among the therapies is desirable.

11.4.2 Modeling the Nested Design

Our search for the best explanatory model will reflect, of course, our differential interest in the nested variable (clinics) and those within which it is nested (therapies). The modular model idea developed earlier in this chapter provides a very good way of initiating and organizing this search.

Nested Design: A Fullest Model

A fullest model needs to have exactly as many unconstrained parameters as response populations sampled in the study. Each combination of categorical variable levels corresponds to a response population. For the three panels of Figure 11.1, there are 12, 10, and 12 response populations sampled; those are the numbers of Therapy/Clinic combinations present in each design.

We write a fullest, 12-parameter model for the Clinics-nested-within-Therapies design as a modular model with a module for each therapy. Within each module, we use effect coding for the Clinic levels nested within that Therapy level. The modules will look like this:

$$\mu(Success \mid Therapy\ A, Clinic) = \beta_1 + \beta_2 x_2 + \beta_3 x_3 + \beta_4 x_4$$
$$\mu(Success \mid Therapy\ B, Clinic) = \beta_5 + \beta_6 x_6 + \beta_7 x_7 + \beta_8 x_8$$
$$\mu(Success \mid Therapy\ C, Clinic) = \beta_9 + \beta_{10} x_{10} + \beta_{11} x_{11} + \beta_{12} x_{12}$$

where, for example, x_2, x_3, and x_4 are effect coded variables for Clinics 2, 3, and 4 with Clinic 1 the omitted level for clinics practicing Therapy A. That is, x_2 takes the value 1 for observations from Clinic 2, -1 for observations from Clinic 1, and 0 for observations from Clinics 3 and 4. Effect coded variables x_6 through x_8 and x_{10} through x_{12} are similarly coded, with Clinics 5 and 9 the omitted levels in the last two sets of clinics.

The coding choices here equate the intercepts, β_1, β_5, and β_9, with the averages (across assigned Clinics) of the mean Success for the three Therapies, respectively. The slope coefficients correspond to the effects of the different Clinics relative to the appropriate one of these means; for example,

$$\mu(Success \mid Therapy\ B,\ Clinic\ 8) = \beta_5 + \beta_8.$$

The effect for an omitted Clinic level, of course, is the negative of the sum of the effects of the other Clinics (levels) at that same Therapy level:

$$\mu(Success \mid Therapy\ C,\ Clinic\ 9) = \beta_9 - (\beta_{10} + \beta_{11} + \beta_{12}).$$

To assemble the three modules into a single modular model,

$$\mu(Success \mid Therapy,\ Clinic) = \beta_1 x_1 + \beta_2 x_2 + \beta_3 x_3 + \beta_4 x_4$$
$$+ \beta_5 x_5 + \beta_6 x_6 + \beta_7 x_7 + \beta_8 x_8$$
$$+ \beta_9 x_9 + \beta_{10} x_{10} + \beta_{11} x_{11} + \beta_{12} x_{12},$$

we need to add the 0/1 variables x_1, x_5, and x_9 to code observations from the three Therapy levels, respectively, and to add scores of 0 to the nine effect coded variables for those observations from Clinic levels assigned to other therapies. For example, x_3 is 1 for observations from Clinic 3, -1 for observations from Clinic 1, and 0 for observations from Clinics 2 and 4 *and* for observations from Clinics 5 through 12 as well.

Nested Design Model Comparisons

Given the fullest model of Equation [11.9], our main interest is in determining whether β_1, β_5, and β_9 are all of about the same magnitude or whether one Therapy level is associated with greater Success. Before doing that, however, we attempt to simplify as much as possible the Clinic level effects (within therapies) present in the model:

- Which of β_2, β_3, and β_4 can be set equal to 0 or to one another?
- Which of β_6, β_7, and β_8 can be set equal to 0 or to one another?
- Which of β_{10}, β_{11}, and β_{12} can be set equal to 0 or to one another?

In short, how many parameters, of an initial nine, are needed to care for within-Therapy-level Clinic differences?

Once the between-Clinics (within-a-Therapy) questions have been resolved into a model with, perhaps, many fewer than 12 parameters, we can ask whether there are Therapy-level differences: are β_1, β_5, and β_9 the same or different?

11.5
Fixed and Random Factors

In this chapter, as well as in Chapter 6, we regard the levels of each categorical variable as *fixed*. Those levels either have been chosen by the researcher, or they are the only levels of interest, or we are not interested in generalizing our results beyond the levels present in our study. For example:

- In the Spatial Problem-Solving example, the researcher was specifically interested in the efficacy of Videotape and Lecture training, relative to a Control condition. These formed the three levels of interest for the categorical variable, Training.

- Also in the Spatial Problem-Solving example, and in the earlier example of SAT Verbal test scores, Male and Female are the only levels of Gender and are, hence, the levels of interest.

- In the most recent example, only three specific Therapies (A, B, and C) were offered and they provided the levels of the categorical variable, Therapy.

The same can be said for Public and Private as levels of Type of School and for White and Asian-American as levels of Ethnicity of Student. We assume those to be levels specifically of interest to the researcher.

For some categorical variables in some designs, however, the relevance of the specific selection or representation of levels either may be in doubt or may not be true. The Clinics variable of our last example raises this question. Twelve clinics were allocated (by preference, randomly) four apiece to three therapies. But, how were the 12 clinics selected in the first place? Here are two alternate scenarios, many others certainly are possible.

- There are exactly 12 clinics in Canada treating patients for whom therapies A, B, and C were developed. All 12 are used in the study.

- Twelve clinics are selected at random from among 150 that agreed to participate in the study.

By the first scenario, the Clinic levels would be of specific interest—they embrace all of the relevant possibilities. Under the second scenario, however, it is difficult to believe that our researcher would have specific interest in the 12 participating clinics. They are best regarded as only randomly representative of clinics that might have been selected.

Where the levels of a categorical variable are random selections from some larger set of potential levels, that categorical variable is called a *random* (rather than *fixed*) factor. Typically, the researcher is not interested in the size of the "effect" for any of the specific levels chosen, only in the variability of these effect sizes. The Success of patients in any particular clinic is not important. What is important is the variability in patient Success from clinic to clinic within any Therapy level. Roughly, in our linear model terms, the modeling focus shifts from estimating the slopes associated with individual levels to estimating the variance of those slopes. The techniques for doing that are taken up in the random effects analysis of variance.

We will not take up random effects here, for two reasons. First, truly randomly chosen levels are exceedingly rare. Even where the levels studied are not specifically of interest, they are often the only levels conveniently available for study. Twelve clinics, 10 classrooms, 14 streambeds, or (to anticipate Chapter 14) 25 patients are available as "sites" for our research. We have no interest in these specific sites, nor have they been randomly selected from some larger population. The levels of a categorical variable may be fixed, then, as much by availability as by interest.

Our second reason for steering away from the modeling techniques for truly random effects is that they are both more complex and more specific than the linear modeling we have developed for fixed effects. Because our (fixed-effects) linear models are so versatile, we prefer to stress this simpler approach. For the reader interested in learning more about random-effects models, there are many good introductions, among them Kirk (1982).

11.6
Summary

This chapter develops explanatory models for studies in which two or more categorical variables potentially influence the response. The response populations sampled correspond to combinations of levels of these variables and a fullest model will have as many unconstrained parameters as there are such populations in a study's design. Two classes of designs are described, factorial (or crossed) and nested. For factorial designs, an important explanatory question is whether two (or more) categorical variables interact with one another. For nested designs, a preliminary question of the importance of the nested variable is resolved before turning to the usually more important question of the explanatory role of the other categorical variable(s). A revised F-ratio for model comparison is introduced, one which takes into account the role of the fullest model in estimating the variance common to the response populations sampled.

Exercises

1 The data for this exercise are the following fertility figures. Births per 1,000 women of childbearing age are given for sampled areas within geographic regions of the U.S. They are given separately for 1975 and 1985. Treat the data as observations in a 2×5 factorial design. Is there an interaction? If there is, form and simplify a modular model—a module for each of the two years. Otherwise, simplify the additive model. What conclusions do you draw?

```
! Column 1: North East 1985
!        2: Mid West 1985
!        3: South Atlantic 1985
!        4: South Central 1985
!        5: West 1985
!        6: North East 1975
!        7: Mid West 1975
!        8: South Atlantic 1975
!        9: South Central 1975
!       10: West 1975
```

```
!  1    2    3    4    5    6    7    8    9   10
14.5 14.9 15.5 14.2 15.9 14.2 14.7 14.0 15.8 14.0
15.5 14.7 15.5 14.0 14.7 13.3 15.4 12.7 14.6 14.4
15.0 15.7 15.8 14.9 17.9 14.1 15.0 13.7 15.8 14.7
14.1 15.2 15.1 16.6 24.6 11.9 14.7 13.9 18.3 20.7
13.5 15.4 12.5 14.9 17.4 11.3 14.3 15.3 16.0 17.8
13.9 16.1 14.3 18.2 16.4 11.6 14.4 14.6 17.5 16.1
14.6 14.3 15.6 16.1 17.5 13.1 14.4 16.1 15.4 19.5
14.0 15.3 16.1 18.8 18.4 12.5 14.3 15.8 17.2 18.3
13.5 17.1 14.4      17.0 12.5 16.6 12.4      15.5
     17.1           19.1      16.5           18.1
     15.9           18.6      15.4           17.3
     16.2           22.8      14.9           25.7
                    16.4                     14.6
```

2 Here are data for another two-way factorial design. The response variable consists of scores on an Ethnic Sensitivity Inventory earned by police officers following completion of an in-service course. Data are classified by the amount of training given the officers and by the "beat origins" of the officers—whether their pre-course assignment was to a Middle-class, Working-class, or Central-city area. Evaluate the need for a modular model and simplify the model. What do you conclude from your simplest model?

```
Col 1: Officers from Middle-class Beats,  5 hours training
Col 2: Officers from Middle-class Beats, 10 hours training
Col 3:    ``              ''           , 15 hours training
Col 4: Officers from Working-class Beats, 5 hours training
Col 5:    ``              ''           , 10 hours training
Col 6:    ``              ''           , 15 hours training
Col 7: Officers from Central-city Beats, 5 hours training
Col 8:    ``              ''           , 10 hours training
Col 9:    ``              ''           , 15 hours training
 1  2  3  4  5  6  7  8  9
53 42 32 39 70 47 62 49 68
57 38 58 53 49 64 52 53 72
37 47 59 55 42 64 41 67 55
48 54 50 56 51 46 59 46 57
49 43 52 51 47 53 58 53 47
```

3 Below are the percentage of slaughter weight (excess over 70%) that became dressed weight for samples of swine of different breeds and genders. Treat this as a 2×5 factorial design. Look for and evaluate any gender $\times$ breed interaction. Then, simplify either the additive or modular model. What conclusions do you reach about breed? About gender?

Breed

1		2		3		4		5	
Male	Female	M	F	M	F	M	F	M	F
13.3	18.2	10.9	14.3	13.6	12.9	11.6	13.8	10.3	12.8
12.6	11.3	3.3	15.3	13.1	14.4	13.3	14.4	10.3	8.4
11.5	14.2	10.5	11.8	4.1		12.6	4.9	10.1	10.6
15.4	15.9	11.6	11.0	10.8		15.2		6.9	13.9
12.7	12.9	15.4	10.9			14.7		13.2	10.0
15.7	15.1	14.4	10.5			12.4		11.0	
13.2		11.6	12.9					12.2	
15.0		14.4	12.5					13.3	
14.3		7.5	13.0					12.9	
16.5		10.8	7.6					9.9	
15.0		10.5	12.9						
13.7		14.5	12.4						
		10.9	12.8						
		13.0	10.9						
		15.9	13.9						
		12.8							
		14.0							
		11.1							
		12.1							
		14.7							
		12.7							
		13.1							
		10.4							
		11.9							
		10.7							
		14.4							
		11.3							
		13.0							
		12.7							
		12.6							

12

Auxiliary Variable Models: Enhancing Model Sensitivity

In this and the following chapter, we look at studies in which one or more of the apparently explanatory variables (x-variables) is regarded as playing primarily an auxiliary role in our explanatory models. Although such *auxiliary variables* will appear in our linear models in the same way as do other x-variables, we treat them differently in developing model comparisons. Typically, we are not interested in estimating how great an influence the auxiliary variable has on the response. In this way, the auxiliary is unlike the usual x-variable.

The function of the auxiliary variable in a model is to help us *better understand* how one or more "truly explanatory" variables work. We have, in this sense, only an indirect interest in the auxiliary variable.

One important way in which auxiliary variables can help is by *increasing model sensitivity*. We sometimes include an auxiliary variable in our explanatory model to reduce the conditional response variance, $\sigma^2(y\,|\,X)$. This inclusion, we will see in this chapter, makes the model more sensitive to the role of those x-variables in which we are interested.

A second, common reason to include an auxiliary variable in a model is to *moderate the influence* of a particular explanatory variable. That is, the regression slope for an x-variable of interest may not be constant; it may change systematically, together with the value of a second, auxiliary variable. We call this auxiliary variable a *moderator variable*. In Chapter 13, we describe several ways to use moderator variables in explanatory models.

12.1
Increasing Model Sensitivity: Some General Ideas

We start by looking again at a pair of linear explanatory models, one with a single x-variable,

$$\mu[y\,|\,x_1 = x_{i1}] = \beta_0 + \beta_1 x_{i1}, \qquad \textbf{(Model 1)}$$

and one with a second x,

$$\mu[y\,|\,x_1 = x_{i1}, x_2 = x_{i2}] = \beta_0 + \beta_1 x_{i1} + \beta_2 x_{i2}. \qquad \textbf{(Model 2)}$$

Our principal concern is whether x_1 has an influence on the y-variable. Could β_1 be 0, in which case x_1 would have no explanatory role? We can explore this within the context of either model.

To answer this question based on Model 1, we must decide whether our estimate, $\widehat{\beta}_1$, is a likely sample from a sampling distribution with mean

$$\mu(\widehat{\beta}_1) = 0$$

and variance

$$\sigma^2(\widehat{\beta}_1) = \frac{\sigma^2[y \mid x_1]}{N \, \text{Var}[x_1]}, \tag{4.4}$$

where $\sigma^2[y \mid x_1]$ is the conditional-response variance, the variance in the population of y scores at each x_1 score, and $\text{Var}[x_1]$ is the sample design variance of the x_1 scores.

Similarly, to answer the question based on Model 2, we would decide whether the estimated slope (now estimated from Model 2), $\widehat{\beta}_1$, is a likely sample from a distribution with mean,

$$\mu(\widehat{\beta}_1) = 0$$

and variance

$$\sigma^2(\widehat{\beta}_1) = \frac{\sigma^2[y \mid x_1, x_2]}{N \, \text{Var}[x_{1.2}]}, \tag{7.16}$$

where, now, $\sigma^2[y \mid x_1, x_2]$ is the conditional response variance at each design point, each combination of x_1 and x_2 scores of interest to us, and $\text{Var}[x_{1.2}]$ is the variance for our sample design of the partial variable, $[x_{1.2}]$. This last is the variance "remaining in x_1" when that in common with x_2 has been partialed out.

If the left-hand side of Equation [7.16] is markedly smaller than the left-hand side of Equation [4.14], then Model 2 will be more sensitive to the departure of β_1 from 0 than will Model 1.

What will make the sampling variance of $\widehat{\beta}_1$ smaller for Model 2 than for Model 1? Let's examine the right-hand sides of Equations [4.14] and [7.16].

First, this goal will be aided if the numerator term for Equation [7.16] is smaller than the numerator term for Equation [4.14]. This will be true if the added x-variable, x_2, "helps" x_1 explain the response.

Second, it would help if the denominator in Equation [7.16] were larger than the denominator in Equation [4.14]. Unfortunately, this cannot happen. The variance of the partial variable $[x_{1.2}]$ can never be larger in any sample than the variance of x_1 in that same sample of observations. In fact, the denominator of Equation [7.16] can be considerably smaller; the inclusion of x_2 will partial out an appreciable part of the x_1 variance *if the two are highly correlated*. At best, the two denominator terms will be equal if x_1 and x_2 are uncorrelated in the sample.

Thus, the inclusion of a second x-variable in a model will increase the model's sensitivity to the influence of the first x if that second x reduces the conditional response variance and is (relatively) uncorrelated with the first x. Such a "second x" is a *sensitivity-increasing auxiliary variable* .

This basic idea of increasing sensitivity by including an appropriately chosen auxiliary variable has been presented for one explanatory and one auxiliary variable. The idea generalizes to models with multiple explanatory or multiple auxiliary variables.

Increasing Model Sensitivity: A Warning

Designs that increase model sensitivity commonly are advocated in the experimental-design literature. They either sharpen sensitivity for a fixed sample size or provide an acceptable degree of sensitivity for a reduced sample size. Increased sensitivity or decreased experimental cost are desirable goals. A technical discussion of the factors contributing to model sensitivity or *power of model comparisons* is provided in the Advanced Topics Appendix at the end of the book.

There is, however, "no free lunch"; there can be a down side to the use of auxiliary variables. There are two aspects to this down side. In Chapter 7, we made the point that the interpretation of the slope parameter for a given *x*-variable *changes* when we add a second *x*-variable to the explanatory model. Thus, the β_1 in Model 1 is the "increase, on average, in the value of the response variable for a one-unit increase in x_1," while the β_1 in Model 2 is the "increase, on average, in the value of the response variable for a one-unit increase in x_1, *provided that we hold constant the value of* x_2." There is, or may be, a not-so-subtle difference in the substantive importance of these interpretations. Let's rename y, x_1, and x_2, our response, explanatory and auxiliary variables, Annual Income, Years of Education and Parents' Socioeconomic Status. Now, in Model 1, β_1 is the "increase, on average, in Annual Income for an additional Year of Education," and, in Model 2, β_1 is the "increase, on average, in Annual Income for an additional Year of Education among those who share the same Parental Socioeconomic Status." Often we would like to interpret an estimate of the Model 2 β_1 as if it were an estimate of the Model 1 β_1. When can we do this?

If we were assured that the two β_1s had the same value, a value unknown to us, then it certainly would make good sense to use Model 2 to estimate this value rather than Model 1. Model 2 produces an estimate with a smaller SE. But, if the "true" values of the β_1s are different, then a $\widehat{\beta}_1$ obtained from Model 2 will be a *biased estimate* of the Model 1 β_1. Our estimate is systematically larger (or, smaller) than it ought to be if we use Model 2.

Are the substantive implications of the two β_1s the same? Do we have reason to believe the values of the two parameters are the same? Without such assurance, we certainly cannot interpret the estimate of β_1 from Model 2 as though it were an estimate of the Model 1 β_1. Obvious care is called for in interpreting sensitivity-increasing model results.

12.2
Increasing Model Sensitivity: An Example

Let's provide a substantive context, a research design, within which we can look at increasing model sensitivity.

We are interested in the influence of the length of time that photographs of infant faces are displayed to participants in a study on the accuracy of their judgments as to whether or not they have seen those photographs before.

Our research design calls for 32 participants to study a set of 20 infant photographs. Subsequently, they are shown, in random order, 10 of these previously studied photographs together with 10 new ones and they are asked whether each one is or is not one they studied previously. For this second recognition phase of the research, participants are distributed, eight apiece, among four Display-time levels; each photograph is exposed for either 1 sec, 2 secs, 4 secs, or 8 secs. Display-time is a *categorical* explanatory variable, taking four levels. The response variable, Recognition Accuracy, takes scores in the range 0 through 20, the number of photographs correctly reported as previously seen or unseen.

Recognition Accuracy, we have reason to believe, will be influenced by factors other than Display Time. In particular, we know that there is individual variability in the *rate at which visual information is taken up* and that this can influence the accuracy of judgments about whether displays are familiar or unfamiliar. Faster processors tend be more accurate. Perhaps a measure of visual information uptake can be used *auxiliarly* to increase the sensitivity of our research on the influence of Display Time. We say "auxiliarly" because we assume the explanatory importance of *Information-uptake* rate to be already established; our focus is on Display Time.

Let's assume that an appropriate measure of visual information uptake is provided by assessing Reading Speed. In particular, we'll assume we can obtain for our participants scores on a paper-and-pencil test of reading speed, scores that can be translated, roughly, as "words of standard-difficulty English prose read per minute under standard conditions."

We'll use the data from a hypothetical study involving these three variables—Display Time, Reading Speed, and Recognition Accuracy—throughout this chapter to describe three ways of using an auxiliary variable to increase sensitivity in a model.

12.3
Technique 1: Blocking

One approach to increasing model sensitivity involves *blocking* on the auxiliary variable. Briefly, this means identifying each response observation with a block (or level) of our auxiliary variable. The auxiliary is treated as *categorical* and is represented in our model in the same way a categorical explanatory variable would be. For blocking, the auxiliary might be essentially categorical (e.g., gender or country of origin) or we might choose to "categorize" the scores on a measured auxiliary. For our example, we'll need to do the latter.

12.3.1   Design of a Blocked Auxiliary Variable Study

We'll assume the Reading Speed scores are available prior to our assigning of participants to levels of Display Time. This is not necessary for blocking but it will make the blocking more effective as we explain later in this section. We begin by dividing the participants into blocks, based upon their Reading Speed scores. This is illustrated in the upper part of Table 12.1.

Assigned to Block 1 are those 8 participants with the highest Reading Speed scores from 125 to 141. In Block 2, are the next 8 fastest readers. The slower readers are in Block 3 and the slowest in Block 4. Where there are ties on the auxiliary, as there are here, it may be necessary to divide participants with the same score between blocks. For example, of the four with Reading Speed scores of 101, one has been (randomly) "promoted" to Block 2 to provide equal numbers in the blocks.

Next, the participants within each *block* are distributed over the several Display Time levels. Because there is some range of Reading Speed scores within a block, the assignment to Display Time level is best done *randomly*. At the top of Table 12.1,

T A B L E **12.1**

Blocking of Display Time Participants on Reading Speed

1. Reading Speed Scores

	Display Time			
Reading Speed	1 sec	2 secs	4 secs	8 secs
Block 1	125	141	133	131
	135	126	127	139
Block 2	115	119	125	121
	123	118	120	116
Block 3	107	107	107	114
	101	112	113	110
Block 4	101	78	97	89
	101	82	87	101

2. Recognition Accuracy Scores

	Display Time			
Reading Speed	1 sec	2 secs	4 secs	8 secs
Block 1	13	14	17	17
	16	15	18	18
Block 2	10	11	14	16
	8	9	12	17
Block 3	8	9	12	16
	8	10	11	15
Block 4	8	8	11	13
	7	8	11	16

let us assume then that, in the random assignment of Block 1 participants to Display Times, the two with Reading Speed scores of 125 and 135 words per minute got assigned to the 1-sec display.

Distributing the participants within each block over the levels of our "treatment" tells us something about how to form blocks. The number of observations in a block should be a multiple of the number of treatment levels. In this way, each block (natural or categorized level of the auxiliary variable) can be equally represented across the explanatory variable or treatment levels. And the number of blocks should be chosen with two competing goals in mind: The blocks should be "small" enough that, where categorization of scores is needed, the auxiliary-variable scores within the block are close together, and, at the same time, the number of blocks should be kept small to control the number of parameters in the model.

Blocking in this way insures that auxiliary blocks and explanatory levels are uncorrelated. In the preceding section, we noted the desirability of having the two *x*-variables uncorrelated.

One last point about the present design. The blocked design described here is actually a *randomized blocks design.* Within each block, respondents were randomly assigned to Display Time conditions. Such random assignment provides a measure of assurance that it is unlikely that any third influence will be confounded with Display Time.

In the bottom half of Table 12.1 are the response scores for our blocked auxiliary-variable study. For example, the two participants who were in Block 2 of the Reading Speed scores and were randomly assigned to a Display Time of 4 secs earned Recognition Accuracy scores of 12 and 14. We use these data in the balance of this section.

12.3.2 Model Comparisons in the Blocked Design

In the blocked auxiliary-variable design, we do not anticipate an interaction between the auxiliary and explanatory categorical variables. If we did, we would regard the auxiliary variable as explanatory; i.e., we would be interested in its explanatory role, and we would model along the lines outlined in Chapter 11. Here, without an interaction, the fullest model is additive, based on dummy (or effect-coded) variables for both categorical variables.

For our example, we define this starting model as

$$\mu(Accuracy \mid Time, Speed) = \beta_0 + \beta_1 x_1 + \beta_2 x_2 + \beta_3 x_3 + \beta_4 x_4 + \beta_5 x_5 + \beta_6 x_6,$$

(Model A)

where x_1, x_2, and x_3 are dummy variables for the 2-secs, 4-secs and 8-sec Display Times, and x_4, x_5, and x_6 are dummy variables for Blocks 2, 3, and 4 of the Reading Speed scores.

The fit of the data at the bottom of Table 12.1 to Model A is summarized in the upper part of Table 12.2. The general picture presented is that Recognition Accuracy decreases with decreases in Reading Speed (from Block 1 to Block 2, etc.) and increases with increases in Display Time (from 1 sec to 2 secs, etc.).

In evaluating any preset substantive hypotheses or in seeking a more parsimonious model, *we ignore* β_4, β_5 and β_6, the slope parameters for blocks. We do not

T A B L E 12.2

Regression Results for Display Time: Blocking on Reading Speed

Model A: Full

degrees of freedom: $32 - 7 = 25$
sigma   = **1.212**
R-square   = **.9047**
***F*-stat**   = **39.54**   **(6 over 25 d.f.)**
condition = **5.312**

var	coef	sdev	
1	.7500	.6062	(2-sec display dummy variable)
2	3.500	.6062	(4-sec display dummy variable)
3	6.250	.6062	(8-sec display dummy variable)
4	−3.875	.6062	(Block 2 dummy variable)
5	−4.875	.6062	(Block 3 dummy variable)
6	−5.750	.6062	(Block 4 dummy variable)
const	13.38	.5671	$\hat{\mu}[Accuracy \mid 1\text{-sec display, Block 1}]$

Model B: Constrained

degrees of freedom: $32 - 6 = 26$
sigma   = **1.255**
R-square   = **.8988**
***F*-stat**   = **46.20**   **(5 over 26 d.f.)**
condition = **4.490**

var	coef	sdev	
1	3.125	.5303	(4-sec display dummy variable)
2	5.875	.5303	(8-sec display dummy variable)
3	−3.875	.6124	(Block 2 dummy variable)
4	−4.875	.6124	(Block 3 dummy variable)
5	−5.750	.6124	(Block 4 dummy variable)
const	13.75	.4841	$\hat{\mu}[Accuracy \mid 1 \text{ or } 2 \text{ secs, Block 1}]$

constrain our estimates of these in any way. In the sensitivity-increasing design, our model simplification, whether substantive or data-based, should be directed at the influence of the explanatory, not the auxiliary, variable. (The magnitudes of the block slope estimates relative to their standard errors suggest, however, that our auxiliary variable is *doing its job*. The slopes are not 0; Recognition Accuracy is influenced by blocked Reading Speed.)

We treat Model A, then, as if it were the *fullest model* for a single categorical variable study. We concentrate on the slope parameters for levels of Display Time.

With no preset hypothesis in mind, we ask whether any of these slope parameters might be equal to 0 or to one another. Based on the fit to Model A, the most natural comparison would be to a model, Model B, in which the slope for the dummy variable coding the 2-sec Display Time is constrained to be 0. Substantively, this is the same as asking whether the influences of the 1-sec display (the comparison level) and the 2-sec display could be the same.

The fit of this *constrained model*, Model B, appears at the bottom of Table 12.2. The F-ratio comparison of the fits of Model A (the fuller) and Model B (the less full),

$$F = \frac{(26)1.225^2 - (25)1.212^2}{1.212^2} = 1.56,$$

is too small to be significant with 1 and 25 degrees of freedom. Model B is our preferred model. There is no obvious simplification of Model B and we can take it as our final blocked auxiliary-variable model for Display Time. Display times in excess of 2 secs increase recognition accuracy. Increase Display Time from 2 to 4 secs and Recognition Accuracy increases by about 3 points. Increase Display Time from 4 to 8 secs and there is an additional increase in Recognition Accuracy of a bit less than 3 more points ($5.875 - 3.125 = 2.75$).

12.3.3   Interpretation of Model Parameters

We need to remember the earlier warning, though, about the interpretation of auxiliary-variable model parameters. In the present context, we should say that we expect a gain of 3 points in Recognition Accuracy, for instance, when Display Time is increased from 2 to 4 secs within any particular Reading Speed block.

12.3.4   Modeling for Nonindependent Blocking

Because within each Reading Speed block study participants were evenly distributed among the Display Time levels, blocks and levels were independent in the design just analyzed. This independence permits the most straightforward interpretation of the results—the effects of the two categorizations are not confounded with one another.

Blocking could have had results that would make interpretation more difficult. If we had blocked on Reading Speed *after* assignments to Display Time level had been made, disproportionately large numbers of Block 1 (high Reading Speed) participants might have been assigned to one Display Time, and large numbers of Block 4 (low Reading Speed) participants to another. The two categorical variables would not be independent, and, if we were to follow the modeling strategy outlined before, the two sources of influence (Reading Speed and Display Time) would be inextricably correlated.

Under these circumstances, an alternate modeling strategy may serve us better. It is one that requires that we look more closely at the role of the auxiliary variable. As a consequence, it requires that we start with a model with quite a few more parameters. In this strategy, our fullest, beginning model is a *modular* one, based on a module for each explanatory variable level. In the context of our example, this model could be

$$\mu\,(Accuracy \mid Time,\, Block) = \beta_1 x_1 + \beta_2 x_2 + \beta_3 x_3 + \beta_4 x_4 \qquad \textbf{(Model C)}$$
$$+ \beta_5 x_5 + \beta_6 x_6 + \beta_7 x_7 + \beta_8 x_8$$
$$+ \beta_9 x_9 + \beta_{10} x_{10} + \beta_{11} x_{11} + \beta_{12} x_{12}$$
$$+ \beta_{13} x_{13} + \beta_{14} x_{14} + \beta_{15} x_{15} + \beta_{16} x_{16}.$$

Here, x_1, x_5, x_9, and x_{13} are 0/1 variables coding the four levels of Display Time, and x_2 to x_4, x_6 to x_8, x_{10} to x_{12} and x_{14} to x_{16} are dummy variables for three of the four blocks within each of the Display Time levels. That is, x_2, for example, is 0 for all observations outside a Display Time of 1 sec as well as for observations at Blocks 1, 3, and 4 within that Display Time (i.e., x_2 is a dummy variable coding Block 2 within the 1-sec display time). You may recognize **Model C** from Chapter 11 as the modular-model equivalent of a fully crossed factorial design model.

Our major interest, of course, is in the four intercept parameters, β_1, β_5, β_9, and β_{13}. Before tackling them, however, we try to simplify our 16-parameter model as much as possible towards the 8-parameter model we started with for the design in which auxiliary and explanatory levels were independent of one another. This simplification takes the form of asking to what extent the influence of a particular block is the same across Display Time levels. For example, how many of the parameters β_2, β_6, β_{10}, and β_{14} can be constrained to be equal? If each set of four can be reduced to a single parameter, we are back to **Model A** and we need not worry about any interaction between auxiliary and explanatory variables. Where we can't achieve that simplification, our models will be more complex and necessarily more complicated in their interpretation.

The lesson is clear. Whenever possible, block first on the auxiliary variable, then randomly assign from each block across explanatory variable levels.

12.4
Technique 2: Concomitant Variable Analysis

A second way of using the information about Reading Speed differences among participants is to include the Reading Speed measure directly as a single auxiliary or *concomitant variable* rather than using it to block or categorize observations.

Although we will use the data of Table 12.1 to illustrate concomitant variable modeling, it is important to note that we would not be likely to have assigned participants to treatments at random from within blocks unless we were to use the blocking in the subsequent modeling. For concomitant variable modeling, we would be much more likely to have assigned participants to treatment without regard to their Reading Speed scores. Indeed, we might not have measured Reading Speed until after assignments were made. Ideally, however, we would have made the assignments at random to offer protection against the assignments being correlated with Reading Speed or any third (but unobserved) influence.

In any event, our starting fullest model for concomitant variable analysis would take this form:

$$\mu(Accuracy \,|\, Time, Speed) = \beta_0 + \beta_1 x_1 + \beta_2 x_2 + \beta_3 x_3 + \beta_4 x_4. \qquad \textbf{(Model D)}$$

As in the blocked Model A, x_1, x_2 and x_3 are dummy variables for three of the Display Time levels (2 secs, 4 secs, and 8 secs, respectively). The fourth variable, x_4, carries our Reading Speed scores.

The fit of Model D to the data of Table 12.1 is summarized in the top half of Table 12.3. The slope parameter for the concomitant variable, Reading Speed, is clearly positive; its estimate is more than six times its estimated SE. And there is clear evidence that longer Display Times lead to better Recognition Accuracy; the estimates of the slope parameters for the three dummy variables are all positive and progressively larger for longer displays.

T A B L E 12.3

Regression Results, Reading Speed as Concomitant Variable

Model D: Fullest Concomitant Variable

degrees of freedom: $32 - 5 = 27$
sigma   = **1.651**
R-square   = **.8092**
F-stat   = **28.62**   (4 over 27 d.f.)
condition = **3.756**

var	coef	sdev	
1	1.131	.8273	(2-sec display dummy variable)
2	3.485	.8253	(4-sec display dummy variable)
3	6.052	.8258	(8-sec display dummy variable)
4	.1219	.0186	(Reading Speed)
const	−4.088	2.187	(Intercept)

Model E: Constraining 2 secs and 1 sec to Same Effect

degrees of freedom: $32 - 4 = 28$
sigma   = **1.676**
R-square   = **.7960**
F-stat   = **36.41**   (3 over 28 d.f.)
condition = **2.752**

var	coef	sdev	
1	2.922	.7264	(4-sec display dummy variable)
2	5.492	.7282	(8-sec display dummy variable)
3	.1201	.0188	(Reading Speed)
const	−3.323	2.147	(Intercept)

T A B L E 12.3
(Continued)

Model F: No Display Time Influence

degrees of freedom: $32 - 2 = 30$
sigma = 2.861
R-square = .3632
F-stat = 17.11 (1 over 30 d.f.)
condition = 2.028

var	coef	sdev	
1	.1323	.0320	(Reading Speed)
const	−2.599	3.655	(Intercept)

As with the modeling of the blocked design results, the only more parsimonious model to be suggested by the fit to Model D is one in which the influences of 1-sec and 2-sec displays are constrained to be the same. That is, the dummy variable for the 2-sec level is postulated to have a slope of 0. The fit for this constrained Model E is given in the middle part of Table 12.3.

The F-ratio comparison of the two fits,

$$F = \frac{(28)1.676^2 - (27)1.651^2}{1.651^2} = 1.85,$$

is small enough for 1 and 27 degrees of freedom so that we will again prefer the more parsimonious Model E.

If we were interested in evaluating the hypothesis of no difference among the Display Times rather than in seeking parsimony in an explanatory model, we would compare the fits of Model D and of a model that contains only Reading Speed (i.e., the three dummy-variable slopes are all constrained to be 0). The fit to this latter model, denoted Model F, is given at the bottom of Table 12.3. The F-ratio for the comparison of these two models is

$$F = \frac{(30)2.861^2 - (27)1.651^2}{(3)1.651^2} = 21.03,$$

and it is hugely significant with 3 and 27 degrees of freedom. Display Time is influential, at least when we control for Reading Speed.

12.5
Technique 3: Analysis of Covariance

Our independent blocking and concomitant variable models implicitly assumed that the influences of the explanatory variables and auxiliary variables are *additive*. Where our sole interest in the auxiliary variable is in its sensitivity-increasing potential, this assumption may be appropriate. However, we sometimes *seek assurance* that the auxiliary variable functions only in this way, that it does not impact the explanatory variables nor interact with them.

This assurance is unnecessary when blocking has *preceded* treatment assignment and assignments are made randomly from within each block. At the conclusion of Section 12.3, suggestions were given for exploring the possibility of an interaction between explanatory and auxiliary variables where blocking is handled more clumsily. In this section, we extend the analysis of the concomitant variable design to include the possibility of such an interaction.

12.5.1 Single Auxiliary Variable Slope Model

Concomitant variable analysis will be extended in two ways. We begin with an expansion of the concomitant variable model, developing an *even fuller* one in which the additive relation between the influences of the auxiliary and the categorical explanatory variables is expanded to be interactive.

In the context of the example, this is our original concomitant variable model:

$$\mu(Accuracy \,|\, Time, Speed) = \beta_0 + \beta_1 x_1 + \beta_2 x_2 + \beta_3 x_3 + \beta_4 x_4, \qquad \textbf{(Model D)}$$

where x_1, x_2, and x_3 are dummy variables for three of the Display Time levels (2 secs, 4 secs, and 8 secs, respectively) and x_4 is the concomitant (auxiliary) variable, Reading Speed.

It is an *additive* model; the y-mean is modeled as the sum of a Display Time component and a Reading Speed component:

Display Time	$\mu(Accuracy \,|\, Time, Speed) =$
1 sec	$\beta_0 \qquad\; + \beta_4 x_4$
2 secs	$\beta_0 + \beta_1 + \beta_4 x_4$
4 secs	$\beta_0 + \beta_2 + \beta_4 x_4$
8 secs	$\beta_0 + \beta_3 + \beta_4 x_4$

The Display Time component depends only on the Display Time level to which a participant has been assigned and the Reading Speed component depends only on the Reading Speed score. Display Time level cannot affect the contribution of the Reading Speed and vice versa.

An alternate additive five parameter model, providing exactly the same fit to the observations as Model D, is

$$\mu(Accuracy \,|\, Time, Speed) = \beta_1 x_1 + \beta_2 x_2 + \beta_3 x_3 + \beta_4 x_4 + \beta_5 x_5, \qquad \textbf{(Model G)}$$

where x_1 to x_4 are 0/1 variables coding the four levels of Display Time and x_5 is Reading Speed.

The fits of Models D and G to the example data are summarized in Table 12.4. Not only are the overall fits of the two models (i.e., the two SSRs, estimated conditional-response variances, or "sigmas") identical but the reader can verify that the models give exactly the same fit for any combination of Delay Time and Reading Speed scores.

Model G is the same additive model as Model D. We introduce Model G because it will be easier to extend.

> **TABLE 12.4**
> Alternative Concomitant Variable Models

Model D: Intercept and Three Dummy Variables

degrees of freedom: $32 - 5 = 27$
sigma   = 1.651
R-square   = .8092
F-stat   = 28.62   (4 over 27 d.f.)
condition = 3.756

var	coef	sdev	
1	1.131	.8273	(2-sec display dummy variable)
2	3.485	.8253	(4-sec display dummy variable)
3	6.052	.8258	(8-sec display dummy variable)
4	.1219	.0186	(Reading Speed Slope)
const	−4.088	2.187	(Intercept)

Model G: Four 0/1 Variables for Display Time

degrees of freedom: $32 - 5 = 27$
sigma   = 1.651
condition = 16.21

var	coef	sdev	
1	−4.088	2.187	(1-sec display intercept)
2	−2.957	2.131	(2-sec display intercept)
3	−.6032	2.189	(4-sec display intercept)
4	1.964	2.216	(8-sec display intercept)
5	.1219	.0186	(Reading Speed slope)

In both models, there is a single slope parameter for the auxiliary variable (or *covariate*). An equivalent name for the additive model in the *analysis of covariance* context is the *single-slope covariate* model.

12.5.2   Separate Covariate Slopes Model

A convenient way to introduce the idea of an *interaction* between the covariate (a measured auxiliary variable) and the "treatment" (a categorical explanatory variable) is to allow the slope parameter for the covariate to change from level to level of the treatment. Such a model would say that the effect of a one-unit change in the covariate is not necessarily the same for all levels of treatment. There is the possibility of an interaction.

It is a straightforward matter to develop a *separate-slopes* model from Model G. For our Recognition Accuracy example, the separate slopes model will look like

$$\mu(Accuracy \mid Time, Speed) = \beta_1 x_1 + \beta_5 z_1 \qquad \textbf{(Model H)}$$
$$+ \beta_2 x_2 + \beta_6 z_2$$
$$+ \beta_3 x_3 + \beta_7 z_3$$
$$+ \beta_4 x_4 + \beta_8 z_4,$$

where x_1 to x_4 are as defined for Model G, 0/1 variables for the four Display Time levels, and z_1 to z_4 are the following four product variables:

$$z_1 = x_1 \times x_5$$
$$z_2 = x_2 \times x_5$$
$$z_3 = x_3 \times x_5$$
$$z_4 = x_4 \times x_5,$$

with x_5 the Reading Speed variable. That is, z_j is a variable containing Reading Speed scores for observations at the jth Display Time level and 0s for observations from the other three levels.

With variables defined in this way, Model H is a combination of four separate models, one for each of the Display Time levels:

$$\mu(Accuracy \mid 1 \ sec, Speed) = \beta_1 + \beta_5 (Reading \ Speed \ score),$$
$$\mu(Accuracy \mid 2 \ sec, Speed) = \beta_2 + \beta_6 (Reading \ Speed \ score),$$
$$\mu(Accuracy \mid 4 \ sec, Speed) = \beta_3 + \beta_7 (Reading \ Speed \ score),$$

and

$$\mu(Accuracy \mid 8 \ sec, Speed) = \beta_4 + \beta_8 (Reading \ Speed \ score).$$

Model H provides for *separate intercepts and separate covariate slopes* for each level of the categorical explanatory variable or treatment.

12.5.3 Testing for Covariate/Explanatory Interaction: Single or Separate Slopes

An essential part of the *analysis of covariance* is to test the hypothesis that the slope for the covariate is the same at all treatment levels. It is a test of the additivity of the measured auxiliary and categorical explanatory variables. We will think of it as a comparison of the fits of the fuller Model H and the less full Model G. The two enjoy a fuller/less full relation as Model G can be seen to be the result of constraining the four slope parameters of Model H to be equal.

Table 12.5 describes the fits of the single and separate covariate slopes models to the example data. We are interested in whether the four slope estimates of Model H all could be estimates of the same, common slope parameter. The F-ratio for model comparison,

$$F = \frac{(27)1.651^2 - (24)1.596^2}{(3)1.596^2} = 1.63,$$

falls short of what would be required to reject the hypothesis of a single slope. We prefer Model G (or the equivalent Model D) with its fewer parameters.

There is *no evidence of an interaction* between the covariate (auxiliary variable) and the categorical explanatory variable. The influence of Reading Speed is not modified by the Display Time.

T A B L E 12.5

Analysis of Covariance: Separate or Single Covariate Slopes

Model H: Separate Covariate Slopes

degrees of freedom: $32 - 8 = 24$
sigma   =   **1.596**
condition =   **19.00**

var	coef	sdev	
1	−13.46	5.236	(1-sec display intercept)
2	−.8258	3.173	(2-sec display intercept)
3	−2.541	4.366	(4-sec display intercept)
4	6.357	4.407	(8-sec display intercept)
5	.2045	.0461	(1-sec Reading-speed slope)
6	.1026	.0283	(2-sec Reading-speed slope)
7	.1390	.0381	(4-sec Reading-speed slope)
8	.0838	.0380	(8-sec Reading-speed slope)

Model G: Single Covariate Slope

degrees of freedom: $32 - 5 = 27$
sigma   =   **1.651**
condition =   **16.21**

var	coef	sdev	
1	−4.088	2.187	(1-sec display intercept)
2	−2.957	2.131	(2-sec display intercept)
3	−.6032	2.189	(4-sec display intercept)
4	1.964	2.216	(8-sec display intercept)
5	.1219	.0186	(Single Reading-speed slope)

12.5.4   Testing for Covariate Bias

A second consideration in the analysis of covariance, the second extension of con-comitant variable analysis referred to at the beginning of this section, is that par-ticipants assigned to different treatment levels might *systematically differ* on their covariate (auxiliary variable) scores. If this is true, covariate and treatment influ-ences on the response variable are confounded. It will then be difficult to judge whether the *y*-mean was influenced by a treatment *or* by pretreatment differences on the covariate.

Assignment to treatment levels at random is designed to minimize the likelihood that those assigned to different treatments will differ in any other respect. Random-ization may not be possible in certain situations and then we should check for any covariate/treatment confounding.

The straightforward way to make the check is to regard the auxiliary variable as a response variable susceptible to the influence of the treatments, the levels of the categorical explanatory variable. For our example, then, Reading Speed becomes the *y*-variable with Display Time levels providing a set of dummy *x*-variables. We see the results of fitting such a model in Table 12.6. The *F*-statistic reported by our regression command is that for comparing the fit of this model with that of one in which the slope parameters for the dummy variables coding the Display Time levels are *all constrained* to be 0. The exceedingly small value, $F = .1129$, offers no evidence that Reading Speed scores differ over the Display Time levels.

T A B L E 12.6

Analysis of Covariance: Covariate (Reading Speed) as Response

degrees of freedom: $32 - 4 = 28$
sigma   = **16.80**
R-square = **.0119**
F-**stat**   = **.1129** **(3 over 28 d.f.)**
condition = **3.732**

var	coef	sdev	
1	−3.125	8.399	(2-sec display dummy variable)
2	.1250	8.399	(4-sec display dummy variable)
3	1.625	8.399	(8-sec display dummy variable)
const	113.5	5.939	(Intercept)

12.5.5   Completing the Analysis of Covariance

The two checks completed, we proceed with the analysis in this example exactly as discussed earlier for the *concomitant variable* approach. Had the single covariate slope model failed, we would have to examine the *seperate covariate slopes model* more closely to see which slopes, as well as which intercepts, might be combined.

The resulting model and its interpretation are likely to be *more complex* than they would be if a single slope were appropriate.

Where there is *covariate bias*, the analysis of the covariate must be reported together with that of the intended response variable. Again, the implications of any manipulation of the explanatory variable are more complicated than they otherwise would be.

12.6
Summary

We have developed in this chapter three approaches to including an auxiliary variable in a model so as to make that model more sensitive to the influence of a categorical explanatory variable. The auxiliary variable can be used as a basis for blocking observations, as an added or concomitant variable, or as a covariate in the analysis of covariance. In all instances, our inclusion of the auxiliary variable is predicated on the belief that it will increase certainty about the response but will be unrelated or nearly so to the x-variables of interest to us.

Exercises

1 The batting performance of a sample of Major League players follows. Players are identified as American League (al) or National League (nl) and as batting Left- (l) or Right- (r) handed. The number of season hits is given in the final column for each batter. We are interested in how hitting may have differed between leagues or batting stances. An important covariate, of course, is the number of times each player was at bat. This is given in Column 3 of the data table. Perform an analysis of covariance. Are the regression slopes, hits regressed on at bats, the same in the four groups, league crossed with handedness? What is your general conclusion?

League	Handedness	At bat	Hits
al	l	266	55
al	l	505	156
al	l	385	103
al	l	621	205
al	l	270	74
al	l	373	99
al	l	253	60
al	l	498	152
al	l	475	139
al	l	217	54
al	l	233	54
al	l	409	112
al	l	455	120

League	Handedness	At bat	Hits
al	l	361	94
al	l	320	96
al	l	375	102
al	l	245	75
al	l	239	65
al	l	353	85
al	l	631	191
al	r	223	51
al	r	300	71
al	r	360	86
al	r	241	62
al	r	514	127
al	r	399	121
al	r	535	135
al	r	391	104
al	r	564	156
al	r	484	115
al	r	375	110
al	r	461	136
al	r	545	158
al	r	396	104
al	r	541	148
al	r	519	141
al	r	441	133
al	r	239	53
al	r	414	98
al	r	378	111
nl	l	594	168
nl	l	588	196
nl	l	368	74
nl	l	511	121
nl	l	375	86
nl	l	253	54
nl	l	276	67
nl	l	604	203
nl	l	335	79
nl	l	215	50
nl	l	355	85
nl	l	374	107
nl	l	361	99
nl	l	428	118
nl	l	266	67
nl	l	287	64
nl	l	408	102
nl	l	343	111

League	Handedness	At bat	Hits
nl	l	476	113
nl	l	251	63
nl	r	542	145
nl	r	455	110
nl	r	462	130
nl	r	258	64
nl	r	458	106
nl	r	572	147
nl	r	510	160
nl	r	570	177
nl	r	304	78
nl	r	482	117
nl	r	325	111
nl	r	377	98
nl	r	259	74
nl	r	230	50
nl	r	537	132
nl	r	549	155
nl	r	606	176
nl	r	482	152
nl	r	573	159
nl	r	432	115

2 Using the Galapagos Island plant speciation data from the exercises in Chapter 8, conduct one or more analyses of covariance. For example, Total Number of Plants could be a covariate where Number of Native Species is the response variable. Similarly, you might choose to use Area or Distance as covariates in other models. Phrase and justify the covariance models before conducting any calculations.

13

Auxiliary Variable Models: Moderating Explanatory Variable Influence

In the discussion of the analysis of covariance in the last chapter, we ask if the covariate *interacted* with the categorical treatment variable to influence the response. We hoped that the answer would be "no." An interaction between the sensitivity-increasing auxiliary variable and the explanatory variable would signal a complication to the x-y relation; the explanatory variable's influence on the response would no longer be a simple direct one. Rather, the level of the explanatory variable would appear, as well, to affect the influence of the auxiliary on the response variable. Such a complication is unanticipated and usually unwanted in situations where we use the analysis of covariance.

In this chapter, we develop models for substantive questions in which the interaction of an auxiliary with an explanatory variable is *anticipated* and, perhaps, desirable from a substantive point of view. In this second role, we ask if an auxiliary variable *moderates* the explanatory influence of another variable, the explanatory variable of interest. For example, we may be interested in whether regular physical exercise moderates the influence of job-related stress on perceived psychological well-being. We might anticipate that the effect of stress on perceived well-being is less for those who regularly exercise than for those who do not. Exercise status is an auxiliary variable. We are not interested in its direct influence; we may already know about that. Rather, we are interested in how it may affect the *relation* between stress (the explanatory) and psychological well-being (the response).

13.1
Auxiliary Variables in Interaction

We have encountered the idea of interaction twice so far. In Chapter 11, we learned that two categorical variables might interact. That is, their joint influence on a response might be nonadditive. In substantive terms, this means that the influence of a certain treatment (i.e., the level of one of the categorical explanatory variables) might not be a constant; rather, it could differ among groups (i.e., the levels of a second categorical variable). In our Chapter 11 example, we asked whether the effect of Problem Solving Training strategies was the same for Female as for Male students.

Then, in Chapter 12, we asked, in connection with the analysis of covariance, whether there is an interaction between treatment (again, a categorical explanatory variable) and a measured covariate (or auxiliary variable). Such an interaction would take the form of different slopes for the measured covariate at different treatment levels. Again, the extent of influence of one variable, the covariate, on the response would vary from level to level of the other variable, the categorical explanatory variable.

In this chapter, we extend our study of interaction to other substantive questions. The basic modeling question, though, will remain the same: Does the influence on the *y*-variable of one *x*-variable depend upon the level of a second *x*-variable? Here, the second *x*-variable is called a moderating auxiliary variable, or *moderator variable*. The use of this term signals that the two variables are not substantively equal. Our interest in the moderator variable is in how it "helps" the explanatory variable to explain the response variable.

13.1.1   Moderation

We say that the influence on a response of an explanatory variable, Variable A, is moderated by an auxiliary variable, Variable B, if Variable A's influence differs from one level of Variable B to another. Put in modeling terms, Variable B is a *moderator variable* if the regression slope for Variable A changes systematically as the value of Variable B changes. The moderator variable may be, as may be the explanatory variable, either categorical or measured. Where the explanatory variable is categorical, its "slope" refers to the slope coefficients for the dummy or other variables used to code its levels.

13.1.2   Moderator Variable Designs

In this chapter we discuss four situations in which the influence of an explanatory on a response variable might be modeled as moderated by a third, auxiliary variable. What distinguishes among the four is

- whether the moderator is categorical or measured and
- whether the moderator is external or internal.

The *categorical/measured* distinction is one with which we are already familiar. The *external/internal* distinction is between a moderator that is not itself an explanatory variable (hence, it is *external* to the set of explanatory variables) and one that is an explanatory variable (i.e., an *internal* moderator.)

The first design to be discussed involves an *external, categorical* moderator.

13.2

Group Regression: External Categorical Moderation

Our first moderated regression example is called *group regression*. The basic idea is that the regression slope for an explanatory variable may be different for different *groups of observational units*. The grouping variable is categorical and we are not interested in the direct influence of groups on the response.

13.2.1 Example: Physics Course Performance

Let's examine the following situation:

Performance in a high-school physics class is known to be influenced, linearly, by the scores earned by students on a mathematics achievement test. The better a student's knowledge of school mathematics, the higher the grade to be expected in the physics course.

We have a model that looks like this:

$$\mu(Physics\ Grade \mid x_1 : Math\ Achievement\ Score) = \beta_0 + \beta_1 x_{i1}, \qquad \textbf{(13.1)}$$

where β_1 is positive. Now, the question of interest is whether this same model is appropriate when students are grouped by Gender, Males and Females.

13.2.2 Alternative Models

Equation [13.1] includes slope and intercept parameters. If it can be used equally well with Male and Female students, we will say we have a *single-slope, single-intercept* model relating Math Achievement to Physics Grades; the same slope and the same intercept can be used with each of the groupings, Males and Females. What are the alternatives to this model? Logically, we entertain the possibility that we may need different slopes and/or different intercepts for the two Gender levels. Figure 13.1 pictures these different group regressions.

At the upper left is the *single-slope, single-intercept model*,

$$\mu(Physics\ Grade \mid Math\ Achievement, Gender) = \beta_0 + \beta_1 x_{i1}, \qquad \textbf{(13.2)}$$

with x_{i1} the Math Achievement score for the ith student in the sample. Gender doesn't enter into this model at all.

At the upper right in Figure 13.1 is the *single-slope, separate-intercepts model*. It consists of two *modules*, one for each gender, which might be written this way:

$$\mu(Physics\ Grade \mid Math\ Achievement, Male) = \beta_{0M} + \beta_1 x_{i1}$$

and

$$\mu(Physics\ Grade \mid Math\ Achievement, Female) = \beta_{0F} + \beta_1 x_{i1}.$$

The slopes are the same, β_1, but the intercepts differ, giving rise to parallel regression lines. As the figure verifies, this model postulates a constant difference in

Single Slope
Single Intercept

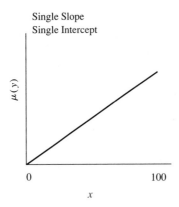

Single Slope
Separate Intercepts

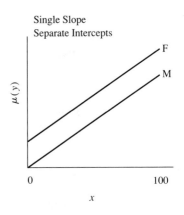

Separate Slopes
Single Intercept

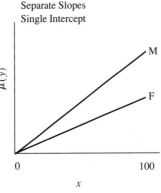

Separate Slopes
Separate Intercepts

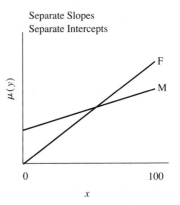

FIGURE 13.1
Two-Group Regressions: Influence of Math Achievement on Physics Grades for Male and for Female High-school Students

Physics Grades, $\beta_{0F} - \beta_{0M}$, between Male and Female students at all levels of Math Achievement.

The two modules can be expressed as a single *modular model*,

$$\mu(Physics\ Grade \mid Math\ Achievement,\ Gender) = \beta_0 + \beta_1 x_1 + \beta_2 z_1, \qquad \textbf{(13.3)}$$

with z_1 a dummy variable for, say, the Female level of Gender. That is, our third parameter, β_2, is the difference in the two Gender intercepts, the constant vertical distance between the two regression lines.

The *separate-slopes, single-intercept model* is pictured in the bottom left of Figure 13.1. It is based in two modules,

$$\mu(Physics\ Grade \mid Math\ Achievement,\ Male) = \beta_0 + \beta_{1M} x_1$$

and

$$\mu(Physics\ Grade \mid Math\ Achievement,\ Female) = \beta_0 + \beta_{1F} x_1,$$

that can be assembled into a single regression model,

$$\mu(Physics\ Grade \mid Math\ Achievement,\ Gender) = \beta_0 + \beta_1 (z_1 \times x_1) + \beta_2 (z_2 \times x_1),$$
$$\textbf{(13.4)}$$

with z_2 a second 0/1 variable coding the Male level of Gender. That is, the product variable $(z_1 \times x_1)$ contains a Math Achievement score if the observation is for a Female student and a 0 if for a Male. Similarly, $(z_2 \times x_1)$ is 0 for Females and a Math Achievement score for Males. We'll defer interpretation of this model. As pictured in Figure 13.1, it might describe a growing discrepancy between the two genders.

Finally, at the bottom right of Figure 13.1, is a sketch of the *separate-slopes, separate-intercepts model*. The two modules,

$$\mu(Physics\ Grade \mid Math\ Achievement, Male) = \beta_{0M} + \beta_{1M}x_1$$

and

$$\mu(Physics\ Grade \mid Math\ Achievement, Female) = \beta_{0F} + \beta_{1F}x_1,$$

give us this four-parameter regression model:

$$\mu(Physics\ Grade \mid Math\ Achievement, Gender) \tag{13.5}$$
$$= \beta_0 + \beta_1(z_1 \times x_1) + \beta_2(z_2 \times x_1) + \beta_3 z_1,$$

where β_0 is the Male intercept and $(\beta_0 + \beta_3)$ is the Female intercept.

Looking at Figure 13.1, the difference between the two *separate-slopes* models is whether the two regression lines meet when the x-variable is equal to 0 (single intercept) or when it takes some different value. In either event, the meeting point might be outside the range of explanatory values of interest to us.

13.2.3 Model Comparisons

The fuller/less-full relations among the four group regression models will be easier to understand if they are presented as a *fullest model* and *constraints* on that model. The fullest model, of course, is the one that postulates separate slopes and separate intercepts for the groups. For our example, it is the two-slopes, two-intercepts model of Equation [13.5]. We will rewrite it slightly, though, to make the separate slopes and intercepts somewhat more obvious:

Model A: separate slopes, separate intercepts.

$$\mu(Physics\ Grade \mid Math\ Achievement, Gender) \tag{13.6}$$
$$= \beta_1 z_1 + \beta_3(z_1 \times x_1) + \beta_2 z_2 + \beta_4(z_2 \times x_1).$$

Now β_1 is the Female intercept and β_2 the Male intercept, and β_3 is the Female slope and β_4 the Male slope. It is worth noting that this model is fullest only if we restrict our interest to models in which the mean Physics Grade is represented as a *linear function* of Math Achievement: $\mu(Physics\ Grade) = a + b(Math\ Achievement)$. If the shape of the relation of $\mu(y)$ to x is at question, then the fullest model, as we see later in this chapter, may well be more complicated.

The single-slope, separate-intercepts model is obtained from this fullest model by constraining the *slopes to all be equal*. Here that means requiring that $\beta_3 = \beta_4$. Remembering the definition of the product variables, this constraint leads to writing the constrained model from Equation [13.6] as

Model B: single slope, separate intercepts

$\mu(Physics\ Grade\ |\ Math\ Achievement,\ Gender)$ **(13.7)**

$$= \beta_1 z_1 + \beta_3(z_1 \times x_1) + \beta_2 z_2 + \beta_3(z_2 \times x_1)$$
$$= \beta_1 z_1 + \beta_2 z_2 + \beta_3(z_1 \times x_1 + z_2 \times x_1)$$
$$= \beta_1 z_1 + \beta_2 z_2 + \beta_3((z_1 + z_2) \times x_1)$$

or

$$\mu(Physics\ Grade\ |\ Math\ Achievement,\ Gender) = \beta_1 z_1 + \beta_2 z_2 + \beta_3 x_1.$$

Similarly, the separate-slopes, single-intercept model could be obtained from the fullest model by constraining the intercepts to be equal—$\beta_1 = \beta_2$ in our example. Entering this constraint into Equation [13.6] gives

Model C: separate slopes, single intercept

$\mu(Physics\ Grade\ |\ Math\ Achievement,\ Gender)$

$$= \beta_1 z_1 + \beta_3(z_1 \times x_1) + \beta_1 z_2 + \beta_4(z_2 \times x_1)$$
$$= \beta_1(z_1 + z_2) + \beta_3(z_1 \times x_1) + \beta_4(z_2 \times x_1)$$

or

$$\mu(Physics\ Grade\ |\ Math\ Achievement,\ Gender) = \beta_1 + \beta_3(z_1 \times x_1) + \beta_4(z_2 \times x_1).$$
(13.8)

The *least-full model*—the single-slope, single-intercept model—can be obtained either by constraining the intercept parameters in the single-slope, separate-intercepts model, or by constraining the slope parameters in the separate-slopes, single-intercept model. It is most natural, as we see in the next section, to further constrain the single-slope, separate-intercepts model. Here, we constrain the model of Equation [13.7], requiring that $\beta_1 = \beta_2$. This leads to

Model D: single slope, single intercept

$$\mu(Physics\ Grade\ |\ Math\ Achievement,\ Gender) = \beta_1 z_1 + \beta_1 z_2 + \beta_3 x_1$$

or

$$\mu(Physics\ Grade\ |\ Math\ Achievement,\ Gender) = \beta_1 + \beta_3 x_1.$$
(13.9)

Now we have the alternate models as constrained forms of fullest or fuller models. How should we make comparisons among them? Our recommendation is to begin with a comparison between the fullest, separate-slopes, separate-intercepts model and the less-full single-slope, separate-intercepts model:

Comparison I: separate slopes, separate intercepts (fuller) v. single slope, separate intercepts (less full).

This comparison goes directly to the question of *moderation*. Are separate slopes needed? Does the slope for the explanatory variable, Math Achievement, differ across the levels of Gender?

If this comparison favors the more parsimonious model, that with a single slope, we next ask if we can have a single intercept as well:

Comparison II: single slope, separate intercepts (fuller) v. single slope, single intercept (less full).

That is, once we have established that a single slope is sufficient, we ask if a single equation will fit the data.

In general, we attempt to *simplify the slope structure* of an explanatory model before addressing hypotheses about intercepts. The "in general" addresses the usual case where the explanatory variable value of 0 is outside our *design space*, outside the range of values in which we are interested. When that is true, testing for equality of intercepts serves only to reduce the number of parameters we need to estimate in a final model; the equality of some or all intercepts is of no substantive importance.

However, when 0 *is in the design space*, it may be an important value. We may have specific hypotheses about the regression lines when the explanatory variable is equal to 0. Consider this example:

Hours of Practice at some cognitive task explains subsequent Task Performance and may be moderated by grouping Ss by age into Teens, Twenties, and Thirties.

A natural question, one of substantive importance, would be whether the three groups have the same Performance *when given no Practice*. Equality of intercepts, here, would be an interesting possibility.

13.2.4 Interpretation of Group Regression Model

Our final model, after all model comparisons, will have one or more intercepts and one or more slopes. Interpretation is simplest, of course, for the one-intercept, one-slope model. One regression line works for all groups.

If there is a single slope but *different intercepts*, the group regression model is an additive model; the explanatory and auxiliary variables do not interact, although each may influence the response. In single-slope models a final question is whether that slope could be 0; does the explanatory variable influence the response?

If the final model is one that includes *separate slopes*, interpretation requires further exploration. When regression slopes differ, those lines will cross at some value of the explanatory variable. This is illustrated in the bottom two illustrations of Figure 13.1. Important to the interpretation of the final model is whether this crossing occurs within or outside the range of explanatory values that are of interest or, indeed, are possible.

If we assume that 0 is below the range of interesting Math Achievement scores, the bottom-left figure illustrates a situation in which the regression lines cross below that range. The implication from that figure, then, is that the discrepancy in Physics Grades steadily increases over the range of interest of Math Achievement scores. Similarly, if the crossing point is above that range, then the regression lines converge towards each other as the *x*-variable increases—the difference between groups diminishes.

However, if the crossing of regression lines is within the range of Math Achievement scores that is of interest to us, the implication is that the Physics Grade advantage in our model actually *shifts* from one group to another. Thus, in the lower-right diagram of Figure 13.1, a crossing within the design space of Math Achievement scores would imply that with lower Achievement scores Men earn higher Physics Grades than Women, but with higher Achievement scores Women do better than Men.

To determine if two regression lines cross above, below, or within the *x*-variable range of interest, compute the estimated *y*-variable mean at the two ends of the range and for the two groups. Thus, a finding in our present example that the regression slopes for Math Achievement were different for Female students than for Males and the knowledge that the Math Achievement score range of interest was from 10 to 80 would lead us to compare the Male-Female difference at the low end, between

$$\widehat{\mu}(Physics\ Grade\,|\,Math\ Achievement = 10, Male)$$

and

$$\widehat{\mu}(Physics\ Grade\,|\,Math\ Achievement = 10, Female),$$

with the Male-Female difference at the high end, between

$$\widehat{\mu}(Physics\ Grade\,|\,Math\ Achievement = 80, Male)$$

and

$$\widehat{\mu}(Physics\ Grade\,|\,Math\ Achievement = 80, Female),$$

to determine whether that difference was converging, diverging, or crossing over.

13.3
Segmented Regression: Internal Categorical Moderation

In group regression modeling, the grouping is on a different dimension than the one assessed by the explanatory variable whose regression intercepts and slopes are of interest. Thus, in the above section, we asked if the regression of high-school Physics Grades on Mathematics Achievement test scores was different for Male students than for Females.

The grouping, though, can be on the *same dimension* as the explanatory variable. If so, the regression is described as *segmented*.

Segmented regression can also be described as *piecewise linear regression*. That is, the regression is not smoothly curvilinear, as in the examples studied in Chapter 10. Rather, the slope of the regression line is thought to change, rather *abruptly*, at one point (or perhaps at two or more points) within the range of our explanatory variable. As a result, the slope of regression may differ from group to group. What sets this situation apart from group regression is that the groups correspond to ranges of the explanatory variable itself; they are not defined by an external categorical auxiliary variable. To reinforce the distinction, we'll refer to this new modeling scenario as *segmented regression*.

13.3.1   Example: Annual Income and Years of Education

We might, to take an example, have reason to suspect that among 40-year-old U.S. males, the slope of the regression of Annual Income on Years of Education is neither constant (a single regression line) nor constantly changing (a curvilinear regression). Rather, we might hypothesize *two regression lines*, a less-steep one covering the high-school years and a steeper one for the college years. That is, each additional Year of *high-school* Education makes a certain, positive contribution to expected Annual Income; each additional Year of *college* Education also makes a positive but larger contribution. This hypothetical situation is sketched in Figure 13.2.

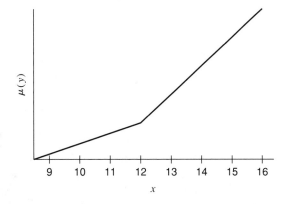

F I G U R E 13.2
Regression of Annual Income on Years of Education

Two separate regression lines *intersect* at Years of Education equal to 12. The less-steep line describes the regression for Years of Education less than 12; the more-steep line describes the regression for more Years of Education.

13.3.2   The Segmented Regression Model

How do we capture the *x-y* relation of Figure 13.2 in a linear model? We can take what we learned about group regression and begin with a *separate-intercepts, separate-slopes* model, one like that of Equation [13.6]:

$$\mu(Annual\ Income\,|\,Years\ of\ Education) = \beta_1 z_1 + \beta_3(z_1 \times x_1) + \beta_2 z_2 + \beta_4(z_2 \times x_1),$$

where for our example:

$z_1 = 1$ if Years of Education is 12 or fewer, and $z_1 = 0$ if otherwise;

$z_2 = 1$ if Years of Education is greater than 12, and $z_2 = 0$ if otherwise;

and

x_1 = Years of Education.

This model is, in effect, two separate linear models:

$$\mu(Annual\ Income\,|\,Years\ of\ Education <= 12) = \beta_1 + \beta_3(Years\ of\ Education)$$

and

$$\mu(Annual\ Income \mid Years\ of\ Education > 12) = \beta_2 + \beta_4(Years\ of\ Education).$$

Equation [13.6], though, is not quite what we want for segmented regression. It describes the situation in the lower-right corner of Figure 13.1, two regression lines each with their own intercepts and slopes. Those two lines, though, cross at an *indeterminate* point. We want our two regression lines to cross precisely when Years of Education is 12. How can we insure that?

The easiest way to model regression lines meeting at a prespecified value of an *x*-variable is to first *subtract that value* from each *x*-variable score. Why that helps will become clear. For our example, this means replacing x_1 with a new variable:

$$w_1 = (Years\ of\ Education - 12).$$

This new variable will be 0 when Years of Education is 12. And, a one-unit increase in w_1 still corresponds to an additional Year of Education. Using w_1, we can write a model for those whose Education terminated at high-school graduation or earlier:

$$\mu(Annual\ Income \mid Years\ of\ Education <= 12) = \beta_0 + \beta_1(Years\ of\ Education - 12).$$
$$\textbf{(13.10)}$$

The intercept of this model is

$$\beta_0 = \mu(Annual\ Income \mid Years\ of\ Education = 12)$$

as that corresponds to a *(Years of Education* − 12) = w_1 value of 0. The slope parameter, β_1, is the expected increase in Annual Income associated with an additional Year of high-school Education. A one-unit increase in w_1 corresponds to a one-*Year of Education* increase.

The corresponding model for those 40-year-old males with some college education is

$$\mu(Annual\ Income \mid Years\ of\ Education > 12) = \beta_0 + \beta_2(Years\ of\ Education - 12).$$
$$\textbf{(13.11)}$$

The slope parameter is postulated to be different from that in Equation [13.10]; a *steeper slope* is thought to characterize the regression line for those with college education. But the two equations have the *same intercept* because we have from Equation [13.11]

$$\beta_0 = \mu(Annual\ Income \mid Years\ of\ Education = 12).$$

The two regression lines cross for Years of Education = 12, for $w_1 = 0$.

Assembling Equations [13.10] and [13.11] into a single, segmented regression model gives

$$\mu(Annual\ Income \mid Years\ of\ Education) = \beta_0 + \beta_1(z_1 \times w_1) + \beta_2(z_2 \times w_1).$$
$$\textbf{(13.12)}$$

It is a single-intercept, separate-slopes model, given our redefinition of the explanatory variable so that it takes the value 0 at the postulated point of intersection of the regression lines.

13.3.3 Model Comparison in Segmented Regression

Do the two regression lines have the same or different slopes? That is the primary question associated with segmented regression. Put another way, does our segmented regression model, allowing two slopes, fit the data better than a single-slope model?

The model of Equation [13.12] is the fuller of two models to be compared. The less full is one constrained to have the slope parameters equal, $\beta_1 = \beta_2$:

$$\mu(Annual\ Income\,|\,Years\ of\ Education) = \beta_0 + \beta_1(z_1 \times w_1) + \beta_1(z_2 \times w_1)$$
$$= \beta_0 + \beta_1(z_1 \times w_1 + z_2 \times w_1)$$

or

$$\mu(Annual\ Income\,|\,Years\ of\ Education) = \beta_0 + \beta_1 w_1. \tag{13.13}$$

13.3.4 Use of Segmented Regression

Segmented regression is one way of approaching the analysis of an apparent but unsuspected nonlinear regression. Its best use, however, is when there is reason in advance to suspect a *natural segmentation* in the way in which the response variable is influenced by the explanatory measure. It is very difficult to "see" a segmented regression in a scatterplot, and the decision to pursue segmented modeling should always be supported by reasons external to the data.

13.4
Moderated Regression: External Measured Moderation

In group regression and its specialized form, segmented regression, the influence upon the *y*-variable mean of a change in the *x*-variable score is moderated by the *group* (internal or external) into which an observation falls. For a change of the same magnitude in *x*, the change in the *y* mean may be greater for some groups than for others.

In linear modeling, the notion of a *moderated influence* is more often associated with situations in which the regression slope for an explanatory variable is thought to change, not with respect to groups, but with respect to the value of a second, measured auxiliary variable. This auxiliary variable is called a *moderator variable*. The moderator variable moderates the influence of the explanatory variable.

13.4.1 Example: Income Moderating Counseling Success

Clients entering short-term counseling are administered an instrument measuring Readiness to Benefit from Counseling. There is a strong, positive linear relation between scores on this precounseling measure and self-ratings by clients of Counseling Success at the termination of counseling. Certainty about perceived counseling success is increased if readiness for counseling is known. At the same time, there is reason to believe that rated Counseling Success is also influenced by client economic self-sufficiency (our old friend, Annual Income).

We are interested in how Annual Income helps. Does it directly influence Counseling Success, or does it *moderate* the influence of Readiness for Counseling? Among those with low Annual Incomes, for example, small differences in Readiness could presage large differences in Success. Whereas, for high Income clients, those same Readiness differences might not be reflected at all in Success; Income might play a moderating role.

13.4.2   Modeling Moderation Through a Measured Variable

Where our moderator variable was categorical, as it was for group or segmented regression, we modeled the moderating role with, in effect, a different model (or explanatory module) for each level of the categorical auxiliary variable. The intercept and slope could then differ from level to level of the moderator. How can we carry this idea over to the measured auxiliary variable?

We can't model *measured moderation* in exactly the same way. That is, we can't introduce a separate slope and intercept parameter for *each value* of the measured auxiliary variable. We will not have enough observations in our sample to permit this. So, to control the number of "moderation" parameters in our model, we make some assumptions about how that moderation occurs—we have to model that as well.

Remember our basic notion of moderation is that the slope parameter for the x-variable of interest (and, perhaps, the intercept) changes as the value of the moderator variable changes. A common way of implementing this idea without introducing too many new parameters is to assume that the change in the slope (and intercept) is a *linear function* of the changing value of the moderator. In this way, we don't have to introduce moderation parameters for each value of the measured auxiliary variable. We need add only the parameters required for these linear functions. Let's see how this works.

We begin, for our example, with the usual model for the influence of Readiness on Success,

$$\mu(Counseling\ Success \mid Readiness) = \beta_0 + \beta_1(Readiness\ score), \qquad \textbf{(13.14)}$$

with its intercept and slope parameters. Now we introduce our linear moderation idea, that those parameters should not be *fixed constants*; rather, their values ought to each be some *linear function* of Annual Income. That is, we postulate that the intercept and slope in Equation [13.14] can be expressed as

$$\beta_0 = \alpha_1 + \alpha_2(Annual\ Income) \qquad \textbf{(13.15)}$$

and

$$\beta_1 = \alpha_3 + \alpha_4(Annual\ Income). \qquad \textbf{(13.16)}$$

When we introduce the right-hand sides of Equations [13.15] and [13.16] as replacements for the Equation [13.14] parameters, we get the following:

$\mu(Success \mid Readiness, Moderated)$

$$= (\alpha_1 + \alpha_2[Income]) + (\alpha_3 + \alpha_4[Income]) \times (Readiness)$$

or expanded,

$\mu(Success \mid Readiness, Moderated)$

$$= \alpha_1 + \alpha_2(Income) + \alpha_3(Readiness) + \alpha_4(Income \times Readiness)$$

or, in our more familiar β notation,

$\mu(Success \mid Readiness, Moderated)$ **(13.17)**

$$= \beta_0 + \beta_1(Income) + \beta_2(Readiness) + \beta_3(Income \times Readiness)$$

We've added only two parameters to include the *linear moderation* in our model. It should be noted that in Equation [13.17] this moderation results in the inclusion in our model of a *product variable*; that is, *(Income × Readiness)* has as its values the product of scores on the Annual Income and Readiness for Counseling variables. We've encountered product variables before. First, products of dummy (or effect-coded) variables were used to construct interaction models in Chapter 11. Then, in the analysis of covariance section of Chapter 12, product variables were formed between a measured covariate and treatment dummy variables. Here we have a third variety of product variable, between two measured variables. Product variables in a model always signify an interaction or moderation.

One more word about the simplified Equation [13.17]. We cannot tell from examining the right-hand side of this equation whether we intend Income to moderate Readiness, or Readiness to moderate Income. Substantively, we know the direction of moderation in which we are interested but, once we have fit the model of Equation [13.17], we shall not be able to interpret that fit, as we see below, until we reaggregate the estimated parameters in the forms of Equations [13.15] and [13.16]. This is a general comment about linear models. We often want to leave them in unsimplified form in order to improve ease or correctness of interpretation.

13.4.3   Model Comparisons in Moderated Regression

Equation [13.17] is the starting point in modeling moderated regression. The flow of model comparisons may be clearer if we rewrite that equation in a way that makes the moderation question obvious:

$\mu(Success \mid Readiness, Moderated)$ **(Model A)**

$$= (\beta_0 + \beta_1[Income]) + (\beta_2 + \beta_3[Income]) \times (Readiness).$$

Does Income moderate the influence of Readiness? The answer depends on the comparison of the fit of this fuller model with that of a model for which the influence of Readiness does not depend on the level of Income, one in which the parameter β_3

is constrained to be 0:

$$\mu(Success \,|\, Readiness, Moderated) = \beta_0 + \beta_1(Income) + \beta_2(Readiness).$$

(Model B)

If moderation of regression is the *sole question of interest*, this one comparison is all that is needed. If, however, we are uncertain about the explanatory role of Income—does it moderate the influence of Readiness or does it have a *direct influence*—or we seek the most parsimonious model, this comparison would be followed up by asking next if the parameter β_1 might be set to 0 without compromising the model's fit. That is, we would compare the fit of Model B with that of the further constrained model,

$$\mu(Success \,|\, Readiness, Moderated) = \beta_0 + \beta_2(Readiness),$$

(Model C)

in which Income plays no role at all.

13.4.4   Interpreting Moderated Regression Models

How do we interpret the slope parameters we estimate for moderated regression models? What is most challenging, perhaps, is the parameter β_3 associated with the product variable *Income × Readiness*.

Two problems arise. First, what is the *metric of this product variable*? What would a unit change in that variable look like? It is a very complicated variable, and it is present, not to satisfy our intrinsic interest in that product, but as a side effect of postulating a moderating effect. So we would be puzzled by any interpretation we could give to β_3, even if we arrived at it easily.

A second problem is that our usual slope interpretation has the proviso attached that "other *x*-variables remain fixed" while that variable changes value by one unit. But how can *Income × Readiness* change by one unit while both *Readiness* and *Income* remain constant? It can't.

The interpretation of *slope coefficients for product variables* is always difficult. We saw this first in Chapter 11 where we chose to reexpress any interaction model as an equivalent, modular one. The interaction model included products of dummy or effect coded variables. This raised, at least implicitly, the same problems we face here. Earlier in this chapter, we used the *modular-model* approach to make interpretable models that arise in connection with group and segmented regression applications. In those applications, a categorical auxiliary variable (the grouping or segmenting variable) can interact with a measured explanatory variable. Before "modularization," these interactions appeared in our models as products of dummy and measured variables.

Where there are products of measured *x*-variables, we don't have the same freedom to reexpress our model. There is no modular model alternative to Model A shown before. What we can do, though, is recognize that the moderation hypothesis *precludes* an independent interpretation of the parameters β_2 and β_3. Both are needed to understand the influence of Readiness on Success. The expression,

$$(\beta_3 + \beta_3[Income]) \times (Readiness),$$

abstracted from Equation [13.17] (or from Model A) accurately reflects the idea that the slope parameter for Readiness is not constant but is a function of Income.

What is most sensible to report and interpret, then, are *selected values* of

$$(\widehat{\beta}_2 + \widehat{\beta}_3[Income]),$$

the nonconstant slope-parameter "estimate" for Readiness. These selected values should span the range of Income that is of interest.

13.5
Polynomial Regression: Internal Measured Moderation

In Chapter 10, we described the inclusion in a model of the square of an x-variable or, on rare occasions, the cube when the influence relation is nonlinear. When we include such higher-order terms, we describe the models as polynomial.

Now, polynomial regression—certainly *quadratic regression*—can be thought of as moderated regression where the moderator variable is identical to the moderated explanatory variable.

In particular, the quadratic model

$$\mu(y \mid x = x_i) = \beta_0 + \beta_1 x_i + \beta_2 x_i^2 \qquad \textbf{(13.18)}$$

with its regression slope for a squared term can be written equally well in the form

$$\mu(y \mid x = x_i) = \beta_0 + [\beta_1 + \beta_2 x_i]x_i. \qquad \textbf{(13.19)}$$

The single regression "slope", $[\beta_1 + \beta_2 x_i]$, describes again the expected change in y associated with a unit change in x. However, this amount is not constant; the regression is nonlinear.

As with moderated regression, reporting selected values of $[\widehat{\beta}_1 + \widehat{\beta}_2 x_i]$ ought to contribute to a better understanding of how a change in the value of the x-variable influences the mean of the y-variable than any attempt to report and interpret $\widehat{\beta}_1$ and $\widehat{\beta}_2$ separately.

13.6
Summary

When the influence of a measured explanatory variable changes with the value of an auxiliary variable, we speak of the influence as moderated. In this chapter, we have examined four examples of such moderation, depending on whether the auxiliary variable is categorical or measured and on whether or not it is external to the moderated variable. The examples in this chapter complete our survey begun in Chapter 11 of designs in which two or more variables might be thought to interact in their influence on the response. Though developed in the context of modeling a measured response, the principles are equally appropriate to the modeling, in Chapters 15 through 19, of the categorical or counted response.

Exercises

1   Do military cadets have broader shoulders than male students in general? Shoulder width is related, of course, to general body size. Below are measures of Height and Shoulder Width for a sample of students classified as either Cadets (1 in column 3) or Students (0 in column 3). Use the separate slopes separate intercepts approach to the modeling of the influence of Height on Shoulder Width.

Height	Shoulder Width	Group
163	38.5	1
163	39.9	1
171	38.5	1
171	40.5	1
171	42.0	1
173	40.4	1
175	39.8	1
176	40.5	1
186	41.6	1
177	41.3	1
178	43.5	1
179	43.9	1
180	42.1	1
180	42.3	1
169	37.1	0
169	38.3	0
170	40.3	0
172	36.4	0
178	42.0	0
179	39.9	0
179	41.1	0
180	38.8	0
183	39.7	0
187	42.9	0

2   In surgery, it is sometimes inconvenient to obtain blood pressure readings from the arm. Can the leg be used as well? Use the following data to see how well Arm BP can be estimated from Leg BP. Participants in the study were divided into two groups. In one group, the BP recordings were made following administration of Curare (1 in column 3). Use the separate slopes separate intercepts approach to the understanding of the relationship.

Arm BP	Leg BP	Group
95	95	0
105	130	0
120	140	0
95	110	0
95	115	0
70	100	0
85	110	0
95	115	0
85	110	0
110	110	0
125	145	1
100	120	1
105	130	1
110	130	1
70	95	1
65	90	1
70	100	1
80	105	1
95	125	1
55	70	1
75	100	1
50	80	1
75	70	1

3 The strike-out performances of a sample of pitchers in the two Major Leagues are given below. Using number of strike-outs as the response and number of batters faced as the explanatory variable, test for separate slopes and separate intercepts relating to League and to time of season. We have data for each pitcher for April appearances and for September/October outings. What is your conclusion?

League	Batters Faced April	Strike-Outs April	Batters Faced Sep/Oct	Strike Outs Sep/Oct
al	143	12	135	14
al	142	16	65	3
al	54	11	68	18
al	143	25	102	23
al	31	5	93	19
al	107	8	126	14
al	96	13	129	19
al	69	9	147	28
al	118	10	98	6
al	82	28	120	17
al	183	21	90	19
al	25	7	62	9
al	99	12	62	12
al	71	5	34	5
al	52	9	67	18
al	156	28	138	29

League	Batters Faced April	Strike-Outs April	Batters Faced Sep/Oct	Strike Outs Sep/Oct
al	12	3	49	13
al	157	15	49	10
al	62	10	59	7
al	116	26	189	32
al	62	13	50	16
al	14	2	55	20
al	103	14	11	1
al	72	14	47	6
al	30	8	40	4
al	163	24	196	48
al	28	10	55	27
al	64	5	7	0
al	134	29	115	21
al	41	7	19	2
al	60	11	26	2
al	90	19	90	25
nl	52	6	35	13
nl	37	7	59	12
nl	59	10	54	10
nl	66	3	70	12
nl	127	21	152	40
nl	85	20	53	9
nl	142	30	133	27
nl	53	4	29	3
nl	141	12	74	8
nl	123	23	93	18
nl	96	8	127	26
nl	92	18	145	33
nl	140	31	159	35
nl	21	5	56	14
nl	61	13	53	9
nl	120	17	155	25
nl	46	7	43	6
nl	42	18	47	18
nl	120	23	103	20
nl	34	3	51	4
nl	137	23	150	29
nl	57	7	116	20
nl	158	38	126	22
nl	39	6	25	2
nl	100	13	63	14
nl	159	15	104	19
nl	131	20	111	17
nl	45	9	6	1

14

Introduction To Modeling Repeated Observations

An important consideration in fitting models is the assumed *independence* of the response observations making up our samples. Not all experimental or observational designs provide such independence. In fact, an important class of designs, *repeated-measures designs*, owes its importance to allowing us to collect and analyze observations that lack independence, multiple-response observations on individual observational units or subjects. In this chapter, we see how the model representation ideas of Chapter 12 can be used to make these significant repeated-measures designs accessible to our linear-models analysis.

14.1
Repeated Measures

Consider this hypothetical experiment. We are interested in the efficacy of a particular weight-reduction program. From among a large group of volunteers, all interested in losing weight and willing to commit to a three-month program, we randomly select 20 participants. Then, for the three-month duration of the study, our sampled volunteers' weights are obtained at monthly intervals. At the study's end, we have four weight observations, on each of the 20 participants, a total of 80 response observations.

What distinguishes this study from those we have studied thus far is that we have *several response observations* for each participant. Heretofore, each observational unit contributed a single *y*-variable score. Study designs in which each of our sampled observational units—whether individual, family, classroom, geographic unit, or enterprise—is assessed more than once on the same response variable are called *repeated-measures designs*.

Repeated-measures designs fall into two major classes. The first, exemplified by our hypothetical weight reduction study, calls for repeated-measures at different points in time. The intent of this design is to allow us to study the *change* or *time course* of the response. How much weight is lost? At what rate? Is the rate of weight loss constant or diminishing?

The second class of repeated-measures designs calls for the same response to be measured *under different treatment conditions*. Consider a second example. We are interested in how the size of the type in which a passage is printed influences the reading speed of fifth-grade students. We randomly sample 25 students from some large student population. These students are allowed 10 minutes to begin reading a narrative printed in 12-point type. At the end of this time, we record the number of words read. Then these *same students* are allowed 10 minutes to read a second narrative printed in smaller, 10-point type. Again, the number of words read in the 10 minutes is recorded. The study is a repeated-measures one because we have not one, but two responses for each student—one based on reading 12-point text and one on reading 10-point text. How much farther did the students read in the 12-point narrative than in the 10-point one?

14.1.1   Advantages of the Repeated-measures Design

Why would we want to have more than one *y*-variable score on an individual observational unit? Even to someone who knows very little about experimental design, it would seem quite natural to make several measurements if what we are interested in is *change*. What more reasonable way is there to answer the question "How much weight was lost?" than to measure weight before and after? For *time-course* questions, then, repeated measures would seem to be an obvious approach.

For questions relating to *different treatment conditions*, however, we have an alternative: separate groups. We could have randomly assigned some fifth graders to the 10-point condition and others to the 12-point one. In the resulting "two group" design, there would be no repeated measures; each fifth grader would contribute only one reading-speed score. What advantages would the *repeated-measures* design have over the *separate-groups* design?

There are two potential advantages: economy and power. Depending on the treatments involved, it may be far more economical (in terms of time if not expense) to "reuse" the same subjects for all treatments than to use "new" subjects for each treatment. This would certainly be true if there were any appreciable recruitment, orientation, or training costs associated with each participant. More importantly, the repeated-measures design often has greater power than the comparable separate-groups one. For example, using a repeated-measures design, we are more likely to detect that fifth graders read, on average, 25 more words per minute in 12-point type than in 10-point type. Later in this chapter, we'll see, in our linear modeling, why it is that there is a power advantage to the repeated-measures design.

14.1.2   Disadvantages of the Repeated-measures Design

A potential disadvantage to the reuse of subjects is that they may have been changed by their earlier use; they may enter a second treatment condition in a different state then when they entered the first treatment.

In our hypothetical type-size study, we hope to learn which size type, 10 or 12 point, leads to more rapid reading. We want to compare the effects of the two treatments. But, for the comparison to be valid in the repeated-measures context, we must be able to assume that an earlier treatment does not affect the response to a later treatment. Put another way, we want the reading speed for 10-point text not to be influenced by the subjects earlier having read 12-point text. In experimental design parlance, we do not want either *period* or *carryover effects*.

The risk of a carryover effect is very obvious in repeated-measures studies where the treatment conditions involve administering different drugs. The effects of earlier-administered drugs may be long-lasting enough to potentiate, suppress, or interact with the effects of later administered drugs. A common precaution is to provide between treatments a *washout period*, time for a previous drug's action to be damped out.

The influence of an earlier treatment on responses to later treatments can be more indirect. Simply because the subject is required to make the same response repeatedly, later responses may be contaminated. A subject's performance may improve because the study provided her with an opportunity to *practice* the response. Or performance may decline as a subject becomes *habituated*—fatigued or bored. Unless we are specifically interested in practice or fatigue effects, we should design repeated-measures studies around these possibilities. If the response task is a novel one, we must provide ample opportunity for the response to be practiced in advance of the study proper. If subjects are likely to become fatigued or bored, we must limit the number of treatment conditions in which they are used.

All of these precautions still may not rule out a *period effect*. It may be inevitable, for example, that a second administered drug will be less potent than it would have been were it administered first. To provide for this possibility, different treatment orders can be administered to different, randomly chosen subsamples of subjects. The result is a *counterbalanced* design. The reading speed example would benefit from counterbalancing; some students would read the 12-point text first and others would start with the 10-point materials. Later in this chapter, we discuss the modeling of a simple example of this counterbalanced design.

Apart from these experimental design issues, our major concern with the repeated-measures design is that the response observations are no longer fully *independent* of one another.

14.1.3 Nonindependent Response Observations

In developing a statistical rationale for comparing the fits of linear models, we have stressed three assumptions about our sampled response observations. Inferences based on our F-ratio model comparison statistics assume that the N response observations are drawn from conditional response populations that all have (a) the same variance and (b) histograms with Normal random variable characteristics. And we assume that the N observations have all been sampled independently of one another.

We have had little to say about the independent sampling assumption thus far. As long as each subject contributes a single y score, the random sampling of subjects from extant populations (for observational studies) or the random assignment to treatment levels of subjects randomly drawn from some single large population (for experimental studies) is sufficient to insure the independence of *y* scores. When each subject contributes two or more *y* scores, however, random sampling or assignment, while necessary, is no longer sufficient to provide the needed independence.

Independence is a key concept in probability and, hence, in statistical inference. Two observations are said to be independent of one another if knowledge of the value of one of the observations does not alter the probability that the second will take any particular value. Here is a simple example: The outcomes of two successive flips of a coin are independent of one another. Knowing that the first flip came up "Heads" does not make "Heads" any more or less likely on the second flip. What happens on the second flip is independent of what happened on the first flip.

Now, let's advance this idea to the random sampling from a population situation. We'll tie it to our reading speed example by considering the potential population of reading-speed scores for all fifth graders reading 12-point text. Let's assume that that population's histogram has Normal characteristics, a mean of 150 words per minute, and a standard deviation of 20 words per minute. We sample at random one observation from this population. This gives us someone named Anita who reads at 180 words per minute. We sample a second time, again at random. This time we come up with someone named George.

If our population is at all large (as it surely is if it contains the reading-speed scores of all fifth graders), then removing Anita does not alter the population. George is still a random draw from the same population from which we selected Anita, a population with mean of 150 w.p.m., an SD of 20 w.p.m., and Normal attributes. This is important. Because Anita's selection did not change the population, it makes no difference to what the randomly chosen George's score might be that Anita reads at 180 w.p.m., or at 120 w.p.m., or at any other level. Knowing Anita's score can't change our minds about what George's score might be. Anita's and George's scores are independent of one another. Because the scores are produced by different subjects we call them *between-subjects* scores. Given random selection from a larger population, accompanied by random assignment in the case of experiments, between-subjects scores are independent of one another.

While Anita's reading speed for 12-point text doesn't help us to know George's reading speed for that same material, it *is informative* about Anita's reading speed for 10–point text. If she is a rapid reader with one kind of material, she is likely to be a rapid reader with the second as well; the two observations are not independent in the sense that Anita's and George's scores are. Anita's 10-point and 12-point reading speed scores are *within-subjects scores*. Within-subjects scores do not have independence conferred upon them by the random selection of subjects.

Study designs in which all of the response observations are between subjects and, thus, independent by virtue of random selection (and random assignment for manipulated studies) fit naturally into the linear modeling approach we have been developing. Within-subjects or repeated-measures designs have this added complexity of nonindependent observations. Such designs are common enough and, more importantly, useful enough that we need to learn how to model their response variables as well.

The analysis of repeated-measures designs can be a fairly involved topic. There are special forms of the analysis of variance adapted to it, and a multivariate analog to analysis of variance—called *multivariate analysis of variance*—provides a popular alternative. Choice between these as well as their use depends upon the response observations satisfying certain distributional requirements. When these requirements are not met, a variety of "corrective" steps have been proposed in the statistical literature. All this places both approaches beyond the scope of this book. Learning about them, however, would be a logical next step for those wanting to learn more about modeling, particularly of designed studies. Good introductions to these advanced repeated measures analyses are provided by Kirk (1982) and by Bowerman and O'Connell (1990) and a very complete survey is presented by Crowder and Hand (1990).

Our approach to modeling within-subjects responses takes two forms. For some repeated-measures studies, our substantive interest is in a *single-response variable*, one that may be a combination of two or more of the repeated measures. In these cases, of course, we can use the between-subjects techniques with which we are already familiar. This situation commonly arises when we have only two response measures on each subject.

A more general approach to within-subjects designs is based on an idea developed in Chapter 12, that of *blocking on an auxiliary variable*. This approach directly confronts the source of nonindependence and allows us to model repeated measures quite serviceably within our familiar linear-regression model fitting and comparison tradition.

14.2
A Single Response Variable from Repeated Measures

A very common experimental design is the *pretreatment posttreatment* design. A response variable is measured, on each subject, both before and after some kind of intervention. The motivation for the design is that we think the magnitude of the posttreatment response will depend, in part, upon the magnitude of the pretreatment response.

Let's say we are interested in a "new" technique for teaching sixth-grade arithmetic. We can assign, at random, samples of students to both the old and new techniques and then measure their levels of achievement at the end of the sixth grade. But we know that how much was learned in the sixth grade, and hence the end-of-year achievement, depends not only on the teaching but on what amount of arithmetic achievement students bring with them. So we assess our students' arithmetic achievement at the beginning of the sixth grade as well.

The pretreatment posttreatment design is analyzed typically in one of three ways:

1 separate analyses of pretreatment and posttreatment scores,

2 analysis of gain scores, or

3 analysis of covariance.

14.2.1 Separate Analyses of Pretreatment and Posttreatment Scores

Our substantive interest may be in the posttreatment Achievement scores. We want to know by how much, on average, the achievement of students taught by the new technique exceeds that of those taught by the old technique. That is, if x_1 is a dummy variable coding the new technique, we might be interested in a confidence interval for β_1 in this End-of-year Achievement model:

$$\mu(\textit{End-of-year Achievement}) = \beta_0 + \beta_1 x_1.$$

We want to attribute the magnitude of β_1 in this model to the new technique and not to pretreatment differences in the achievement levels of students assigned to the two teaching techniques. We could check on this by comparing the fits of the following two models for a second response variable, Beginning-of-year Achievement:

$$\mu(\textit{Beginning-of-year Achievement}) = \beta_2 + \beta_3 x_1$$
$$\mu(\textit{Beginning-of-year Achievement}) = \beta_2.$$

If the data support constraining β_3 to be 0, we have evidence that the pre-sixth-grade achievements of the two student groups were not different.

14.2.2 Analysis of Gain Scores

Alternatively, our substantive focus may be on the amount by which achievement scores *increased* from the beginning to the end of the sixth grade. How much larger was this gain, on average, for students in new technique classes than it was for those taught by the old technique? Our y-variable for the Gain score analysis is the difference between posttreatment and pretreatment scores. If x_1 is again a dummy variable coding the new teaching technique, we are interested in establishing a confidence interval for β_1 in this model:

$$\mu(\textit{Gain in Arithmetic Achievement}) = \beta_0 + \beta_1 x_1.$$

14.2.3 Analysis of Covariance of Posttreatment Scores

Finally, we might adopt the analysis-of-covariance or moderated-regression approach introduced in Chapters 12 and 13. We would use the pretreatment scores as an auxiliary variable covariate and the posttreatment scores as the y-variable. This would allow us to study how the pretreatment score level might "moderate" or interact with the treatment.

We'd start with a separate-slopes, separate-intercepts model for End-of-year Achievement:

$$\mu(\textit{End-of-year Achievement}) = \beta_0 + \beta_1 x_1 + \beta_2(x_1 \times z) + \beta_3(x_2 \times z)$$

where x_1 and x_2 are 0/1 variables coding, respectively, the new and old teaching techniques and z is the set of Beginning-of-year Achievement scores. As a result, the product variable $(x_1 \times z)$ has Beginning-of-year scores for students in the new technique classes and 0s for those in the old. And $(x_2 \times z)$ has Beginning-of-year scores for old technique students and 0s for new technique students.

Our first model comparison is between the fits of this four-parameter model and of one in which the separate Beginning-of-year slopes are constrained to be equal:

$$\mu(\textit{End-of-year Achievement}) = \beta_0 + \beta_1 x_1 + \beta_2 z.$$

In the analysis of covariance context, we hope to be able to accept this less-full model, indicating the absence of an interaction between covariate (Beginning-of-year Achievement) and treatment (Teaching Technique).

Note that in this second model, β_1 is, as it was in the separate analysis of End-of-year Achievement scores, the expected End-of-year advantage for the new technique. However, it now has the conditional interpretation *for a student with a particular Beginning-of-year Achievement score.*

So, we have three approaches to the same set of data. No one of the three is the correct one. The choice depends upon the substantive question: Are we interested in gain, in posttreatment response level, or in posttreatment response level adjusted for pretreatment level?

14.2.4 Example: Gain in Plasma Concentration During a Fun Run

Columns 1 and 2 of Table 14.1 give for 11 randomly chosen finishers of the Tyneside Great North Run their prerace and postrace plasma concentrations, respectively (Dale et al., 1987). A numerically greater concentration (measured in pmol/liter) indicates greater body dehydration.

The 11 runners have been ordered from lowest to highest Prerace Plasma Concentration. The third column in the table gives, for each runner, the Gain in Plasma Concentration, the result of subtracting the Prerace Concentration from the Postrace Concentration.

T A B L E **14.1**

Plasma Concentrations for Sampled Great North Run Participants

Prerace	Postrace	Gain (Post – Pre)
4.3	29.6	25.3
4.6	25.1	20.5
5.2	15.5	10.3
5.2	29.6	24.4
6.6	24.1	17.5
7.2	37.8	30.6
8.4	20.2	11.8
9.0	21.9	12.9
10.4	14.2	3.8
14.0	34.6	20.6
17.8	46.2	28.4

All of the Gain scores in the sample are positive, but the sample is a small one. Can we infer that the average gain in the population of runners is positive? Our linear model is simply

$$\mu(Plasma\ Concentration\ Gain) = \beta_0 \qquad\qquad \textbf{(14.1)}$$

and we want to know whether we should conclude that β_0 is greater than 0. Our estimate of β_0, for this model, is simply the sample mean of the Gain in Plasma Concentration:

$$\widehat{\beta_0} = 18.736\ \text{pmol/l.}$$

And the standard error for this estimate is

$$SE(\widehat{\beta_0}) = 2.512\ \text{pmol/l.}$$

Our less-full model constrains β_0 to be 0. The easiest way to make the model comparison is to compute the t-statistic for β_0 in our fuller model and evaluate it for significance. This gives $t = 18.736/2.512 = 7.5$, a value that is highly significant for 10 degrees of freedom. (The t can be squared to give an F value from the F-distribution with 1 and 10 degrees of freedom: $F = 55.6$, a value that is similarly significant.)

What would separate prerun and postrun analyses of these data tell us? What would the results of an analysis of covariance look like?

14.3
Blocking on Individual Subjects

To provide a more general approach to repeated-measures designs, we will extend an idea developed in Chapters 12 and 13. There we introduced the use of *auxiliary variables* in models to reduce conditional response variance or to study the moderating influence on an explanatory variable. The auxiliary variable appears in our models much as an explanatory variable does but we are uninterested in interpreting the parameter for the auxiliary variable.

While it has these functions, the inclusion of an auxiliary variable in a model, as was just noted in connection with the analysis of covariance, alters the interpretation of the influence or effect of explanatory variables in the model. An example of the use of an auxiliary *blocking variable* will reinforce this point.

Let's say we are interested in how the positioning of a warning light on an aircraft's control panel influences the time it takes the pilot to take action effective to extinguish that warning light. Three positions of the warning light are to be tested: Central, High, and Low. Age is known to influence how quickly we respond to signals to shift our attention—enough so that we want to "control for" this age effect when we study other influences on attention-switching. We could do this in a variety of ways. One way, of course, is to conduct our study with pilots all of the same age. Another way is to block our pilot subjects on age before assigning them to treatments.

We'll assume 30 pilot subjects. We arrange them in age from youngest to oldest and then allocate them among five blocks. Block 1 consists of the six youngest pilots, Block 2 of the six next youngest, and so on with Block 5 holding the six oldest pilots. We now randomly assign pilots to Light Position treatments *within* blocks. The six pilots in Block 1 (the youngest six) are randomly assigned, two apiece to the three Light Positions. The same is done with each of the other four blocks. At the conclusion, 10 pilots have been assigned to each Light Position, two from each of the Age Blocks.

One way of writing a linear model for this design is

$$\mu(Response\ Speed | Position) = \beta_1 x_1 + \beta_2 x_2 + \beta_3 x_3 + \beta_4 x_4 + \beta_5 x_5 + \beta_6 x_6 + \beta_7 x_7$$

where x_1 through x_5 make up a set of 0/1 variables coding the five Age Blocks, x_6 is a dummy variable (0/1) for High Light Position, and x_7 is a dummy variable for Low Light Position. Given this coding, we are treating the Central Light Position as the reference treatment category. Our interest is in the parameters β_6 and β_7. They give the deviations of the mean Response Speeds to, respectively, High and Low Light Positions from the mean Response Speed to a Central Light Position, but *for pilots in the same Age Block*. Model comparison would focus on constraints on one or both of these two parameters. But note the conditional nature of the interpretations of these slopes; they tell us the differences in expected Response Speeds are for pilots of the "same age."

We will use this blocking *with its consequent conditional interpretation* of explanatory variable effects to counteract the nonindependence of within-subjects observations. In particular, we will form a block for *each subject*. Within each of these blocks are the repeated measures for an individual subject. We add to our models blocking variables for these *subject blocks*, just as we added variables for the *Age Blocks* in the *Response-speed* example. Let's develop our *Weight-loss* example to see how this works.

Our design called for 20 volunteers weighed at entrance to the weight loss program and again at the end of one, two, and three month's participation. We can represent this *within-subjects* design with this linear model:

$\mu(Weight \mid Length\ of\ Participation)$

$$= \beta_1 x_1 + \cdots + \beta_{20} x_{20} + \beta_{21} x_{21} + \beta_{22} x_{22} + \beta_{23} x_{23}$$

where x_1 through x_{20} are 0/1 variables coding the 20 subjects and x_{21}, x_{22}, and x_{23} are 0/1 variables coding, respectively, One-month, Two-months and Three-months participation. The reference or omitted category (among the four weight measurements) is the Zero Month so that weight comparisons are against subject's Initial Weight.

Given this coding, $\widehat{\beta}_1$ through $\widehat{\beta}_{20}$ are the Initial weights of the 20 study participants. The modeled difference between Initial and One-month weights *for an individual participant* is $\widehat{\beta}_{21}$. Similarly, $\widehat{\beta}_{22}$ is the modeled change in weight from Initial to Two Months *for an individual*, and $\widehat{\beta}_{23}$ is the modeled change for a participant over the full three months. Note the condition *for an individual* in these interpretations. Constraints on β_{21} through β_{23}, or model comparisons based on such constraints, will be *within-subjects* constraints or comparisons, appropriate to the within-subjects nature of the categorical explanatory variable: Initial, One-month, Two-month, and Three-month weights.

14.4
A Single Within-subjects Categorical Variable or Factor

This blocking principle is useful in modeling any within-subjects explanatory influence, whether it is studied alone, or in combination with other within-subjects, or between-subjects explanatory sources. We'll begin with the simplest situation—a single within-subjects categorical variable or factor.

Note that the term "factor" can be used as a synonym for "categorical explanatory variable." A factor takes two or more levels. It may be either a within-subjects factor (each subject is observed at all levels) or a between-subjects factor (different subjects are observed at each level). We prefer the term "categorical explanatory variable" here but use the term "factor" on occasion for the sake of brevity.

Let's revisit the data of Table 14.1. We have Prerace and Postrace Plasma Concentrations for each of 11 runners. These are our response variable scores and we can assemble them into a single column of 22 scores, the Pretest scores, say, at the top of the column and the Posttest scores in the bottom half. The two halves correspond, of course, to the two levels of a categorical explanatory variable, and we can begin our modeling by introducing a dummy variable to code one of the two "treatment" levels. Let's take x_1 as that dummy variable, 0 for the 11 Prerace observations, and 1 for the 11 Postrace observations.

If Prerace and Postrace observations were independent one of another, as they would be if the two sets of observations were made on different samples of runners, we would be ready to write the usual between-subjects linear model,

$$\mu(Plasma\ Concentration \mid Occasion) = \beta_0 + \beta_1 x_{i1},$$

and go on to "test" whether the slope parameter, β_1, might be 0. This we would do by comparing the fit of this fuller model with that of the less full (null) model:

$$\mu(Plasma\ Concentration \mid Occasion) = \beta_0.$$

However, the treatments are applied *within subjects*, since each runner is measured both before and after the fun run. As a result, we need to modify this model. We replace the single, overall intercept with a complete set of 0/1 variables coding each of the 11 different runners. This gives us the within-subjects linear model:

$$\mu(Plasma\ Concentration \mid Occasion, Runner) = \beta_1 x_{i1} + \sum_{j=2}^{12} \beta_{ij} x_j, \qquad \textbf{(14.2)}$$

where x_j, for $j = 2, 3, \ldots, 12$, are the 0/1 variables for the 11 runners. In this model, x_1 remains a 0/1 variable, 0 for Prerace observations and 1 for Postrace observations.

Our interest is still in β_1 but now we evaluate the fit of this fuller within-subjects model against that of this less full one:

$$\mu(Plasma\ Concentration \mid Runner) = \sum_{j=2}^{12} \beta_j x_{ij}. \qquad \textbf{(14.3)}$$

When we fit the model of Equation [14.2] using linear regression, the estimates of β_1 and of its SE are exactly the values found in our analysis of Change in Plasma Concentration for the single parameter of Equation [14.1], $\widehat{\beta}_0$ and its SE:

$$\widehat{\beta}_1 = 18.735 \text{ pmol/l and } SE(\widehat{\beta}_1) = 2.512 \text{ pmol/l}.$$

The SSR for the fit to the fuller model of Equation [14.2] is 346.923 $(\text{pmol/l})^2$ with $(22 - 12) = 10$ d.f., and the SSR for the less full model of Equation [14.3] is 2277.705 $(\text{pmol/l})^2$ with 11 d.f. The model comparison F-ratio is the same 55.6 observed in the change score analysis.

The point here is that model comparisons involving within-subjects influences can be made employing models that contain 0/1 x-variables (auxiliary variables) for individual subjects. This is a direct extension of the similar use of 0/1 auxiliary variables for *blocking* on other potential influences.

We have illustrated the analysis of a single within-subjects factor (categorical explanatory variable) for the simplest case, where that categorical variable has only two levels. Except for the inclusion of the subject blocking variables in place of a simple intercept, model comparison follows the same principles and strategies developed for between-subjects explanatory variables. We'll reinforce this continuity in the next section as we take up a slightly more complicated within-subjects design.

14.5
Two or More Within-subjects Categorical Explanatory Variables

Repeated measures may follow a more complicated design. Table 14.2 describes an example of a 2×2 repeated-measures factorial design. We are interested in whether a fuel additive improves car mileage (miles per gallon of fuel). For each of four different cars, we assess fuel use and mileage both with and without the fuel additive. Because we suspect the additive's effectiveness (if any) may be influenced by other driving conditions, we arrange to collect data for the four cars when driven both at sea level (Low Altitude) and at an elevation of 5,000 ft (High Altitude).

T A B L E **14.2**

Fuel Efficiency (mpg) of Cars Operated With and
Without Additive at Low and High Altitudes

	Low Altitude		High Altitude	
	Additive	No Additive	Additive	No Additive
Car 1	26.0	23.8	28.2	20.3
Car 2	10.4	8.2	12.6	7.9
Car 3	31.5	31.2	31.2	28.8
Car 4	15.6	12.4	18.6	13.5

We note that the four cars require very different amounts of fuel. Fuel consumptions under the four "treatments" will not be independent. We must model efficiency *conditional on choice of car*. We begin with a fullest model, one that allows for an interaction between Additive and Altitude and also blocks on the cars:

$$\mu(mpg \mid Additive, Altitude, Car) = \sum_{j=1}^{4} \beta_j x_j + \beta_5 x_5 + \beta_6 x_6 + \beta_7 x_7. \qquad \textbf{(14.4)}$$

Here x_1 through x_4 are 0/1 variables coding the four cars, x_5 is a 0/1 variable coding the Additive level of the Additive/No-Additive variable, x_6 is a 0/1 variable for the High-Altitude level of the High-/Low-Altitude variable, and x_7 is the product variable, $x_5 \times x_6$. The comparison treatment, given this coding, is No Additive at Low Altitude. The model is a simple one; it excludes the possibility of carryover effects or of car wear from trial to trial, for example.

The fuel efficiency data coded in this way for linear regression appear in Table 14.3. Because we have included a full set of 0/1 variables for all values of "Cars," we need to specify "no constant" to our regression program. Alternatively, we could have dummy coded all but one of the cars and included an intercept. As there is no reason to think of one of the subjects—here cars—as a comparison level, it is often easier to use the no constant convention.

The fit of this fullest, seven-parameter model is given at the top of Table 14.4. There are $(16 - 7) = 9$ degrees of freedom for the fit. We included an "interaction" variable, x_7, in our initial model to allow us to compare the fit of this interaction model with one that postulates no interaction—by constraining β_7 to be 0. The fit of this less-full model appears as the second panel to Table 14.4. We can make the model comparison for the simple constraint $\beta_7 = 0$ either by computing a t-statistic from the fuller model estimates,

$$t = 3.050/1.372 = 2.223,$$

or by using our more general F-ratio model comparison statistic from the residual sums of squares of the fuller and less-full model fits,

T A B L E **14.3**

Fuel Efficiency Data Coded For Linear Regression

y	x_1	x_2	x_3	x_4	x_5	x_6	x_7
26.0	1	0	0	0	1	0	0
10.4	0	1	0	0	1	0	0
31.5	0	0	1	0	1	0	0
15.6	0	0	0	1	1	0	0
23.8	1	0	0	0	0	0	0
8.2	0	1	0	0	0	0	0
31.2	0	0	1	0	0	0	0
12.4	0	0	0	1	0	0	0
28.2	1	0	0	0	1	1	1
12.6	0	1	0	0	1	1	1
31.2	0	0	1	0	1	1	1
18.6	0	0	0	1	1	1	1
20.3	1	0	0	0	0	1	0
7.9	0	1	0	0	0	1	0
28.8	0	0	1	0	0	1	0
13.5	0	0	0	1	0	1	0

$$F = \frac{26.240 - 16.938}{16.938/9} = 4.943.$$

In either event, the tail probability evaluates to 0.053, just slightly larger than 0.05.

Accepting the less full model on this evidence, we next go on to ask if the *Altitude* factor might be dropped. The fit of this No-altitude model appears in the third panel to Table 14.4. As the increase in RSS is so small, rising only to 26.49 from the 26.24 in the Altitude and Additive model, we can opt for the further reduced model. When we attempt to constrain the contribution of *Fuel Additive* to 0, however, the RSS increase is substantial and the resulting F-statistic,

$$F = \frac{75.49 - 26.49}{16.938/9} = 26.036,$$

is very significant on 1 and 9 degrees of freedom. Thus, this series of model comparisons leads to the inference that *Fuel Additive* but not *Altitude* contributes to fuel efficiency. Based on our final model (Model 3), the use of the *Fuel Additive* increases miles per gallon of fuel by about 3.5. (A rough 95% CI for this increase, extending two SEs either way, would run from 2.0 to 5.0.)

T A B L E **14.4**

Regression Models: Interaction Approach to Fuel Efficiency

Model 1: Interaction

Column Name		Coeff	SE	P Value	SS
2	Car1	23.462	0.907	0.000	2415.722
3	Car2	8.662	0.907	0.000	382.202
4	Car3	29.562	0.907	0.000	3763.823
5	Car4	13.913	0.907	0.000	903.003
6	Additive	1.975	0.970	0.072	49.000
7	HiAltit	−1.275	0.970	0.221	0.250
8	Add × Alt	3.050	1.372	0.053	9.303

d.f.:9   s:1.372   RSS:16.938

Model 2: Altitude Plus Fuel Additive

Column Name		Coeff	SE	P Value	SS
2	Car1	22.70	0.992	0.000	2415.722
3	Car2	7.90	0.992	0.000	382.202
4	Car3	28.80	0.992	0.000	3763.823
5	Car4	13.15	0.992	0.000	903.003
6	Additive	3.50	0.810	0.002	49.000
7	HiAltit	0.25	0.810	0.764	0.250

d.f.:10   s:1.62   RSS:26.24

Model 3: No Altitude

Column Name		Coeff	SE	P Value	SS
2	Car1	22.825	0.868	0	2415.722
3	Car2	8.025	0.868	0	382.202
4	Car3	28.925	0.868	0	3763.823
5	Car4	13.275	0.868	0	903.003
6	Additive	3.500	0.776	0	49.000

d.f.:11   s:1.552   RSS:26.49

Model 4: No Altitude or Fuel Additive

Column Name		Coeff	SE	P Value	SS
2	Car1	24.575	1.254	0	2415.722
3	Car2	9.775	1.254	0	382.202
4	Car3	30.675	1.254	0	3763.823
5	Car4	15.025	1.254	0	903.003

d.f.:12   s:2.508   RSS:75.49

Because our interaction term was so "close to significant," it is instructive to reanalyze the data beginning with a *modular model* rather than the interaction one described earlier. Our interest is in the Fuel Additive, and it would seem natural to develop a modular model having modules for the (two) levels of Altitude. This would allow us to examine the Fuel Additive influence *within Altitude levels*.

The modular model will have, as did the interaction model, seven parameters:

$$\mu(Mileage \mid Additive, Altitude, Car) = \sum_{j=1}^{4} \beta_j x_j + \beta_5 x_5 + \beta_6 x_6 + \beta_7 x_7, \quad \textbf{(14.4)}$$

where x_1 through x_4 again are 0/1 variables coding the four Cars, x_5 is a dummy variable for the High level of Altitude (continuing to make Low Altitude the comparison level), and x_6 and x_7 are 0/1 variables coding Fuel Additive (present) for, respectively, Low-altitude and High-altitude observations. x_7 is the product of the Fuel Additive and High-altitude 0/1 variables, and x_6 is the product of the Fuel Additive variable and a 0/1 variable coding Low altitude.

These modular model variables are displayed in Table 14.5. The fit of the modular model to these data are given at the top of Table 14.6.

T A B L E 14.5
Fuel Efficiency Data Coded for Modular Model

y	x_1	x_2	x_3	x_4	x_5	x_6	x_7
26.0	1	0	0	0	0	1	0
10.4	0	1	0	0	0	1	0
31.5	0	0	1	0	0	1	0
15.6	0	0	0	1	0	1	0
23.8	1	0	0	0	0	0	0
8.2	0	1	0	0	0	0	0
31.2	0	0	1	0	0	0	0
12.4	0	0	0	1	0	0	0
28.2	1	0	0	0	1	0	1
12.6	0	1	0	0	1	0	1
31.2	0	0	1	0	1	0	1
18.6	0	0	0	1	1	0	1
20.3	1	0	0	0	1	0	0
7.9	0	1	0	0	1	0	0
28.8	0	0	1	0	1	0	0
13.5	0	0	0	1	1	0	0

Our seven-parameter modular model fits as well as the seven-parameter interaction model did. The two are equivalent in fit. The estimated slope coefficients for the modular model suggest that β_6, the influence of the Fuel Additive at Low Altitude might be 0. When we introduce this constraint, our less full model (second half of Table 14.6) fits with an RSS of 24.739. Evaluating the increase in RSS with our

T A B L E **14.6**

Regression Models: Modular Model Approach to Fuel Efficiency

Model 1: Modular

	Column Name	Coeff	SE	P Value	SS
2	Car1	23.462	0.907	0.000	2415.722
3	Car2	8.662	0.907	0.000	382.202
4	Car3	29.562	0.907	0.000	3763.823
5	Car4	13.913	0.907	0.000	903.003
6	HiAltit	−1.275	0.970	0.221	0.250
7	Additive:Low	1.975	0.970	0.072	7.801
8	Additive:High	5.025	0.970	0.000	50.501
d.f.:9			s:1.372		RSS:16.938

Model 2: No Additive Influence at Low Altitude

	Column Name	Coeff	SE	P Value	SS
2	Car1	24.450	0.879	0.000	2415.722
3	Car2	9.650	0.879	0.000	382.202
4	Car3	30.550	0.879	0.000	3763.823
5	Car4	14.900	0.879	0.000	903.003
6	HiAltit	−2.263	0.963	0.041	0.250
8	Additive:High	5.025	1.112	0.001	50.501
d.f.:10			s:1.573		RSS:24.739

model comparison F-statistic,

$$F = \frac{24.739 - 16.938}{16.938/9} = 4.145,$$

we find a tail probability of 0.072 (a probability similarly noted for the t test of β_7 in the regression output for the modular model).

Examining the fit of this second model, no further simplification is obvious. We conclude that there is both an Altitude influence—mpg falls by about 2 at High Altitude—and a Fuel Additive influence, the latter only at High Altitude, where fuel efficiency increases by about 5 mpg.

The two sequences of model comparisons lead to somewhat different conclusions. The "final" model in Table 14.4, Model 3, describes two Fuel Efficiency levels: Fuel Additive and No Fuel Additive. But the "final" model, Model 2, in Table 14.6 describes *three* Fuel Efficiency levels: Low Altitude, High Altitude/No Additive, and High Altitude/Fuel Additive. Why is there a difference?

We obtained different answers because, in part, we asked different questions of the data. The "no interaction" model comparison we first made (Table 14.4) constrains the Fuel Additive influence to be *the same* at Low and High Altitudes. In terms of the modular model, we constrain β_6 and β_7 to be equal. The "no Fuel Additive influence at Low Altitude" comparison described in Table 14.6, however, only constrains β_6 to be 0. Equally importantly, we obtained different answers because at least one of our model comparisons provided only weak support for one model over the other. When we compared Models 1 and 2 in Table 14.4, we found the Fuel Additive × Altitude interaction to be nonsignificant but *just, p* = 0.053.

Our question was whether the Fuel Additive was effective. A conservative answer is that the Fuel Additive is effective at High Altitude. Less conservatively, it *may* be effective at Low Altitude.

We proceeded with the analysis of this 2×2 *within-subjects factorial design* very much as we would have if it had been a 2×2 between-subjects design. The sole difference is that our models included a 0/1 variable for each subject rather than a single intercept term. When a design includes explanatory sources some of which are *between subjects* and others that are *within subjects*, modeling becomes more complex. We examine designs of this mixed type in the next section.

14.6
Mixed Models: Within- and Between-subjects Variables in the Same Design

Let's change our Fuel Additive/Altitude study design. Instead of measuring Fuel Efficiency for the *same cars* at both Low and High Altitude, let's assume the 4 cars tested at High Altitude are *different* from those used at Low Altitude. Each car, though, is driven both with and without the Fuel Additive. Table 14.7 summarizes the data.

We refer to Altitude in this new design as a between-subjects categorical explanatory variable; different subsets of cars are used at the two levels of Altitude (High and Low). On the other hand, Fuel Additive is a within-subjects variable; each car is operated at both Fuel Additive levels (Present and Absent).

How shall we represent this mixed design as a linear model? We can begin by ignoring the between-subjects variable and writing a simple within-subjects model. We'll let this model include 0/1 variables for each of the 8 cars and a dummy variable for one of the Fuel Additive levels (Present):

$$\mu(mpg \mid Additive, Cars) = \sum_{j=1}^{8} \beta_j x_j + \beta_9 x_9.$$

But, we don't have a simple sample of 8 cars; we have *two sets* each of 4 cars. One set is operated at Low Altitude, and a second set at High Altitude. The car levels are *nested* within levels of the between-subjects factor, Altitude. As a result, our model needs to distinguish between the two sets as well as among individual cars within these sets. A way to do this is to replace the initial x_1 through x_8 with (1) an intercept, (2) dummy variables coding all but one level of Altitude, and (3) two sets of dummy variables, one set coding 3 of the 4 Low Altitude cars and one set coding 3 of the 4 High Altitude cars. For specificity, we'll let x_1 code High Altitude cars, x_2 through x_4 code cars 1 through 3 (3 of the 4 Low Altitude cars), and x_5 through x_7

T A B L E 14.7

Fuel Efficiency (mpg) of Cars Operated With and Without Additive

Low Altitude

	Additive	No Additive
Car 1	26.0	23.8
Car 2	10.4	8.2
Car 3	31.5	31.2
Car 4	15.6	12.4

High Altitude

	Additive	No Additive
Car 5	28.2	20.3
Car 6	12.6	7.9
Car 7	31.2	28.8
Car 8	18.6	13.5†

code cars 5 through 7 (3 of the 4 High Altitude cars). The resulting model looks like this:

$$\mu(mpg \mid Additive, Altitude, Cars) = \beta_0 + \beta_1 x_1 + \sum_{j=2}^{7} \beta_j x_j + \beta_8 x_8, \qquad \textbf{(14.5)}$$

with x_8 now the Fuel Additive (Present) dummy variable. Given our choice of dummy variables for Altitude, Fuel Additive, and Cars, the intercept has the following interpretation:

$$\beta_0 = \mu(mpg \mid No\ Additive,\ Low\ Altitude,\ Car\ 4).$$

Each of the other βs represents a change in this expectation associated with a different Car, presence of the Fuel Additive, or operation at High Altitude.

The model summarized by Equation [14.5] reflects only the *additive* contributions of Altitude and Fuel Additive to Fuel Efficiency. We'd like to investigate whether the two *interact*—whether the Fuel Additive has a differential effect depending upon Altitude. We provide for this in the usual way, adding interaction variables that are the products of dummy variables coding the two sources of influence. Here, Altitude and Fuel Additive each have but two levels and, hence, are represented by single dummy variables. We need to add just one product variable for the possible interaction: $x_9 = x_1 \times x_8$. Thus, the fullest model for our mixed (within- and between-subjects) design,

$$\mu(mpg \mid Additive, Altitude, Cars) = \beta_0 + \beta_1 x_1 + \sum_{j=2}^{7} \beta_j x_j + \beta_8 x_8 + \beta_9 x_9, \qquad \textbf{(14.6)}$$

has ten parameters. The x and y scores for this model are given in Table 14.8.

The construction of this fullest linear model deserves comment. It serves as a paradigm for models for similar, mixed designs. The linear model includes

- an intercept;
- dummy variables (0/1) for all but one of the between subjects "levels";
- dummy variables for all but one subject within each of the between-subjects levels;
- dummy variables for all but one of the within-subjects "levels"; and
- products of dummy variables for between-subjects levels and within-subjects levels.

T A B L E **14.8**

Fuel Efficiency Data Coded for Mixed Design

y	x_1	x_2	x_3	x_4	x_5	x_6	x_7	x_8	x_9
26.0	0	1	0	0	0	0	0	1	0
10.4	0	0	1	0	0	0	0	1	0
31.5	0	0	0	1	0	0	0	1	0
15.6	0	0	0	0	0	0	0	1	0
23.8	0	1	0	0	0	0	0	0	0
8.2	0	0	1	0	0	0	0	0	0
31.2	0	0	0	1	0	0	0	0	0
12.4	0	0	0	0	0	0	0	0	0
28.2	1	0	0	0	1	0	0	1	1
12.6	1	0	0	0	0	1	0	1	1
31.2	1	0	0	0	0	0	1	1	1
18.6	1	0	0	0	0	0	0	1	1
20.3	1	0	0	0	1	0	0	0	0
7.9	1	0	0	0	0	1	0	0	0
28.8	1	0	0	0	0	0	1	0	0
13.5	1	0	0	0	0	0	0	0	0

If the between-subjects levels are defined by a single categorical variable, the first set of dummy variables may be replaced by effect-coded variables. If the between-subjects levels result from the crossing of two or more categorical variables—as would be the case if cars were classified not only by Altitude but also by Size or Origin (Domestic/Foreign) or some other characteristic—then the first set of dummy variables would include products of dummy variables as well (or effect-coded variables and their products).

The same holds true for the dummy variables coding within subjects levels. To facilitate the simplification and interpretation of interactions, it is a good idea to use a common scheme—either dummy variable or effect coding—for coding the levels of all categorical variables that might interact.

It is convenient to organize the x-variables as we have done here. This facilitates model comparisons, as we ask first about the interaction of between- and within-subjects variables, then about within-subjects variables, and last about between-subjects influences.

We begin at the top of Table 14.9 with the fit of our fullest, 10-parameter model to the Fuel Efficiency data. The RSS is 9.838 on $(16 - 10) = 6$ degrees of freedom. This model includes the Altitude $\times$ Fuel Additive interaction variable, x_9, and we compare the fit of this model with that of the noninteractive model in which β_9 is constrained to be 0. The model comparison F-statistic,

$$F = \frac{19.14 - 9.838}{9.838/6} = 5.673,$$

has a tail probability of $p = 0.055$ for the F-distribution with 1 and 6 degrees of freedom. We opt for the less complicated additive model.

Next, we compare the fits of Models 2 and 3, asking if the Fuel Additive influence can be constrained to 0 as well. The model comparison F-statistic,

$$F = \frac{68.14 - 19.14}{9.838/6} = 29.884,$$

has a very small tail probability ($p = 0.002$) and we conclude the Fuel Additive effect is a real one.

T A B L E **14.9**

Regression Models: Mixed Model Approach to Fuel Efficiency

Model 1: Interaction

	Column Name	Coeff	SE	P Value	SS
0	Constant	13.013	1.012	0.000	6408.003
2	HiAlt	0.525	1.432	0.726	0.250
3	Car1	10.900	1.280	0.000	67.000
4	Car2	−4.700	1.280	0.010	238.521
5	Car3	17.350	1.280	0.000	301.023
6	Car5	8.200	1.280	0.000	45.100
7	Car6	−5.800	1.280	0.004	217.601
8	Car7	13.950	1.280	0.000	194.602
9	Additive	1.975	0.905	0.072	49.000
10	Alt × Add	3.050	1.280	0.055	9.303
d.f.:6		RSq:0.991	s:1.28		RSS:9.838

Model 2: Altitude Plus Fuel Additive

Column	Name	Coeff	SE	P Value	SS
0	Constant	12.25	1.240	0.000	6408.003
2	HiAlt	2.05	1.654	0.255	0.250
3	Car1	10.90	1.654	0.000	67.000
4	Car2	−4.70	1.654	0.025	238.521
5	Car3	17.35	1.654	0.000	301.023
6	Car5	8.20	1.654	0.002	45.100
7	Car6	−5.80	1.654	0.010	217.601
8	Car7	13.95	1.654	0.000	194.602
9	Additive	3.50	0.827	0.004	49.000
d.f.:7		RSq:0.983	s:1.654		RSS:19.14

Model 3: No Fuel Additive

Column	Name	Coeff	SE	P Value	SS
0	Constant	14.00	2.064	0.000	6408.003
2	HiAlt	2.05	2.918	0.502	0.250
3	Car1	10.90	2.918	0.006	67.000
4	Car2	−4.70	2.918	0.146	238.521
5	Car3	17.35	2.918	0.000	301.023
6	Car5	8.20	2.918	0.023	45.100
7	Car6	−5.80	2.918	0.082	217.601
8	Car7	13.95	2.918	0.001	194.602
d.f.:8		RSq:0.94	s:2.918		RSS:68.14

Model 4: No Within Subjects

Column	Name	Coeff	SE	P Value	SS
0	Constant	19.888	3.179	0.000	6408.003
2	HiAlt	0.250	4.496	0.956	0.250
d.f.:14		RSq:0	s:8.992		RSS:1131.988

Model 5: No Altitude

Column	Name	Coeff	SE	P Value	SS
2	Constant	20.013	2.172	0	6408.002
d.f.:15			s:8.688		RSS:1132.238

Finally, we want to evaluate the Altitude influence on mileage. As Altitude (in this Mixed Model design) is a between-subjects explanatory variable we evaluate *after removing from the model* both the individual subjects' *x*-variables (the blocking variables for individual cars within Altitude groups) as well as all of the within-subjects sources of influence. This fullest between-subjects model is

$$\mu(mpg|Altitude) = \beta_0 + \beta_1 x_1,$$

encompassing just the dummy variable for High Altitude and an intercept (for the comparison, Low Altitude, level).

Information about the fit of this model is given under the fit of Model 4 in Table 14.9. The RSS and d.f. for *the fullest between-subjects model*, the fullest one excluding subject and within-subject influences, are given by the corresponding *increases* over Model 3, the model that includes the subject blocking variables but none of the *x*-variables for within-subjects categorical variables or for interactions of within- and between-subjects variables. That is, the correct RSS and d.f. for Model 4 are

fullest between-subjects model RSS: $1131.988 - 68.14 = 1063.848$

fullest between-subjects model d.f.: $14 - 8 = 6$.

The big increase over that for Model 3 is testimony to the *between-cars* variability in mpg, a source we needed to control in evaluating within-subjects influences or interactions of within- and between-subjects influences.

These corrected fullest between-subjects model values play two roles in our assessment of between-subjects explanatory influences:

- the corrected RSS and d.f. for the fullest between-subjects model are used in the denominator of the *F*-ratio for all subsequent between-subjects model comparisons, and

- the reported SEs for slopes and intercepts must be corrected for the use of incorrect (as reported) RSS and d.f.

In our example, the denominator of the between-subjects *F*-ratios is given by

$$\widehat{\sigma}^2(y \mid \textit{Fullest Between-subjects Model}) = \frac{1063.848}{6} = 177.308.$$

The "denominator" degrees of freedom for the *F*-ratio comparisons will be the corrected d.f. for the fullest between-subjects model—6 in the example.

The reported SEs for slopes and intercepts in the between-subjects models are computed using the reported RSS and d.f. They can be corrected by multiplying each by the following adjustment factor:

$$\sqrt{\frac{\text{Corrected RSS} \times \text{Reported d.f.}}{\text{Corrected d.f.} \times \text{Reported RSS}}}.$$

In our example, the adjustment factor is computed to be

$$\sqrt{\frac{1063.848 \times 14}{6 \times 1131.988}} = 1.481.$$

Thus, the correct SE for the HiAlt slope in Model 4 is not the reported 4.496 but $(4.496) \times (1.481) = 6.659$.

We assess the importance of Altitude, finally, by constraining the High Altitude "slope," β_1, to be 0. The fit of this less full Model 5 is given at the bottom of Table 14.9. Comparing the fits of Models 4 and 5, the F-ratio,

$$F = \frac{1132.238 - 1131.988}{1063.848/6} = \frac{0.250}{177.308} = .0014,$$

is exceptionally small, providing no evidence to support the inclusion of Altitude in the model. Note that the numerator term is just the difference in reported sums of squares of residuals. There is no need to correct each before subtracting.

Our choice of model, before examining the between-subjects influences, was the nine-parameter Model 2 of Table 14.9. As it was parameterized, that model included a High Altitude x-variable. Now that we know that there is no need to distinguish between High and Low Altitude efficiencies, we can re-parameterize this model. We want the model to account for car-to-car variability but not to assign any of this variability to High-/Low-altitude differences. An easy way to do this is to replace x_1 through x_7 with a set of dummy variables for 7 of the 8 cars. (Or we could drop the intercept and include 0/1 variables for each of the 8 cars.) The fit to this final model, Model 6 is given in Table 14.10. It has the same overall fit as did Model 2 and it gives the same parameter estimate for the Fuel Additive influence, $\widehat{\beta}_8 = 3.50$ mpg. All we have done is declare that Altitude need not play a part in the between cars structure of the model.

Not surprisingly, as we used the same numbers, we conclude that the Fuel Additive increases mileage by about 3.50 mpg.

T A B L E 14.10

Final Fuel Efficiency Model

Model 6: No Altitude by Additive Interaction, No Altitude Influence

Column Name		Coeff	SE	P Value	SS
0	Constant	14.30	1.240	0.000	6408.003
2	Car1	8.85	1.654	0.001	54.600
3	Car2	−6.75	1.654	0.005	234.000
4	Car3	15.30	1.654	0.000	257.923
5	Car4	−2.05	1.654	0.255	60.270
6	Car5	8.20	1.654	0.002	45.100
7	Car6	−5.80	1.654	0.010	217.601
8	Car7	13.95	1.654	0.000	194.602
9	Additive	3.50	0.827	0.004	49.000
d.f.:7		RSq:0.983	s:1.654		RSS:19.14

Mixed Model: General Flow of Modeling

Let's review the linear modeling for the mixed model, with both within-subjects factors (the levels are repeated measures on the same subjects) and between-subjects factors (the levels are assessed on different subjects). We'll assume the within-subjects categorical variable, A, has I levels, and the between-subjects categorical variable, B, has J levels. Each subject contributes I response observations and the total number of subjects, N, is divided among J groups:

$$N = N_1 + N_2 + \cdots + N_J.$$

With this notation, we can see what enters into each successive model.

Model AB

The fullest model, one which allows for interaction between the influences of the within-subjects factor, A, and the between-subjects factor, B, will have the following terms:

- an intercept;
- $(J - 1)$ variables (dummy or effect coded) for all but the comparison level of the between-subjects variable, B;
- $(N - J)$ variables (dummy or effect coded) for individual subjects, omitting one subject at each of the J between-subjects levels;
- $(I - 1)$ variables (dummy or effect coded) for all but the comparison level of the within-subjects variable, A; and
- $(I - 1) \times (J - 1)$ interaction variables, each the product of an A-level variable and a B-level variable. Both sets should be dummy or effect coded.

The total number of parameters in Model AB is $N + (I - 1) + (I - 1) \times (J - 1)$. The total number of observations is $N \times I$. The degrees of freedom for the model is the difference between these:
d.f.$_{AB} = N \times (I - 1) - (I - 1) - (I - 1) \times (J - 1)$. In the Fuel Efficiency example, $N = 8$ cars, $I = 2$ Fuel Additive levels, and $J = 2$ Altitude levels. As a result, Model AB has $8 - 1 - 1 = 6$ degrees of freedom. We designate the sum of squares of residuals for this model SSR$_{AB}$.

The ratio of SSR$_{AB}$ to d.f.$_{AB}$ is the within-subjects fullest-model estimate of the conditional response variance and is the denominator term for all F-ratios comparing models with within-subjects terms.

Model A + B

This model provides for the influence of both the within- and between-subjects factors but not of their interaction. Thus, it has all of the terms of Model AB except the $(I - 1) \times (J - 1)$ interaction variables:

- an intercept;

- $(J - 1)$ variables (dummy or effect coded) for all but the comparison level of the between-subjects variable, B;
- $(N - J)$ variables (dummy or effect coded) for individual subjects, omitting one subject at each of the J between-subjects levels; and
- $(I - 1)$ variables (dummy or effect coded) for all but the comparison level of the within-subjects variable, A.

Model A + B, then, has $(I - 1) \times (J - 1)$ more degrees of freedom than Model AB: $\text{d.f.}_{A+B} = (N - 1) \times (I - 1)$. For the comparison of Models A + B (the less full) and AB (the fuller), the numerator of the F-statistic is the ratio

$$\frac{\text{SSR}_{A+B} - \text{SSR}_{AB}}{\text{d.f.}_{A+B} - \text{d.f.}_{AB}}.$$

The denominator of the F-statistic is the ratio of SSR_{AB} to d.f._{AB}. The degrees of freedom for the comparison statistic are $(I - 1) \times (J - 1)$ for the numerator and d.f._{AB} for the denominator.

Acceptance of the less-full Model A + B leads to its comparison with Model B_w following. Acceptance of the fuller Model AB suggests restructuring that model in *modular form* before seeking further simplification. For this mixed model, the modular model is best made up of modules for each level of the between-subjects factor. We describe it next.

Model B_A

The finding of a significant $A \times B$ interaction is a signal to model the influence of the within-subjects factor, A, *modularly* or separately at each level of the between-subjects factor, B. The modular model replacement for the fullest Model AB would have these terms:

- J variables (dummy), one for each level of the between-subjects factor, B (the slopes for these variables are the separate intercepts);
- $(N - J)$ variables (dummy or effect coded) for individual subjects, omitting one subject at each of the J between-subjects levels; and
- $J \times (I - 1)$ product variables, each the product of one of the J "intercept" variables and a dummy variable for one of the noncomparison levels of the within-subjects variable, A. The slope parameters for these variables assess the influence of a particular within-subjects level for a particular between-subjects level.

The number of terms is the same as for Model AB. The J between-subjects intercepts replace the single intercept and the $(J - 1)$ dummy or effect-coded variables for the between-subjects factor. And the $J \times (I - 1)$ product variables replace the $(I - 1)$ dummy variables for the within-subjects factor and the $(I - 1) \times (J - 1)$ interaction variables. The slope structure of this modular model is simplified first, always using the fullest model SSR and d.f. in the denominator of the F-ratio. Once the slope structure has been simplified, all of the product variables may be dropped from the model to give the equivalent of Model B_w following. That provides a starting place for any simplification of the intercept structure.

Model B$_w$

Assuming our tentative model to be the additive Model A + B, we next ask whether the within-subjects factor, B, needs to be included in the model. Our fuller model for the comparison is Model A + B and the less-full is the one that results from dropping from Model A + B the indicator variables for the levels of the within-subjects factor. Model B$_w$ includes these terms:

- an intercept;
- $(J - 1)$ variables (dummy or effect coded) for all but the comparison level of the between-subjects variable, B; and
- $(N - J)$ variables (dummy or effect coded) for individual subjects, omitting one subject at each of the J between-subjects levels.

The model comparison statistic has as its numerator the ratio

$$\frac{\text{SSR}_{Bw} - \text{SSR}_{A+B}}{\text{d.f.}_{Bw} - \text{d.f.}_{A+B}}.$$

The d.f. difference will be $(I - 1)$. The denominator in the F-ratio is again the conditional response variance estimate from Model AB with its degrees of freedom.

Accepting the less full Model B$_w$ leads to Model B$_b$ following. Accepting the fuller Model A + B, we would seek to simplify the model by combining related levels of B.

If, alternatively, we have been simplifying the slope structure of the modular model, we will want to fit Model B$_w$ when that simplification is completed. This Model B$_w$ will have an additional dummy variable for the Jth between-subjects level instead of the single intercept indicated above.

Model B$_b$

Once we are satisfied that we have the best model representation for the influence of the levels of the within-subjects variable, A, we turn our attention to the between-subjects variable, B. As the models to be compared are now all between-subjects models, we must first define a new fullest model. Model B$_b$ is Model B$_w$ stripped of its $(N - J)$ variables for individual subjects, leaving either:

- an intercept; and
- $(J - 1)$ variables (dummy or effect coded) for all but the comparison level of the between-subjects factor, B, or
- J variables (dummy), one for each level of the between-subjects variable, B.

The difference in the fits of Models B$_w$ and B$_b$ is due, of course, to *between-subjects variability*. And it is this assessment of between-subjects variability that we use to estimate the conditional response variance for between-subject model comparisons. The denominator of the F-ratio for between-subjects model comparisons is given by

$$\frac{\text{SSR}_{Bb} - \text{SSR}_{Bw}}{(N - J)}.$$

Null Model

Finally, we ask if the between-subjects variable, B, is needed to model the response variable. For our model comparison, Model B_b is the fuller, and the less full is the Null Model, consisting solely of

- an intercept.

The Null Model has a sum of squares of residuals, SSR_0, and a d.f. of 1. The numerator of the F-ratio for the model comparison is

$$\frac{SSR_0 - SSR_{Bb}}{(J-1)}.$$

The denominator is the between-subjects conditional response variance estimate described before, and the d.f.s for evaluating the F-ratio $(J-1)$ and $(N-J)$. If the comparison favors the fuller model we would search for simplifications of the pattern of influence of the levels of the between-subjects variable, B.

14.7
Coding Efficiencies for Repeated-measures Model Comparisons

The key to including within-subjects or repeated measures designs in the linear model framework has been to *block on individual subjects*. To accomplish this, we have included a separate x-variable in the model for each subject on which there are repeated measures. If there are many subjects, this means many blocking variables. It can be tiresome preparing large numbers of blocking variables and, in some instances, a regression program may be unable to accommodate all of them. Fortunately, a computational shortcut is available that will give nearly all of the modeling information provided by the blocking variable designs.

It is easy to describe how to implement the shortcut and only slightly harder to explain how to interpret the modeling fits that result from the shortcut's use. The shortcut is

instead of including in the linear model dummy *variables* for each subject, include a *single variable* with scores equal to the average of each subject's (repeated) responses.

When this shortcut is employed, the linear-regression results are substantially the same as would be obtained if a complete set of subject 0/1 x-variables was used:

- the RSS is the same for both models and
- the slope estimates for within subjects and interaction x-variables are the same for both models.

But, for this new "average response" model,

- the model degrees of freedom are reported incorrectly;
- the conditional response variance (or SD) is estimated incorrectly; and
- the SEs for the within-subject and interaction x-variable slopes are incorrect.

All of these errors have a common source. Our "average response" model includes *too few x-variables*. It includes a single "blocking" variable (that with average subject responses) rather than one for each subject. It is an easy matter, though, to adjust the reported model d.f. to reflect the appropriate number of blocking variables and then to use the corrected d.f. to adjust, in turn, the conditional response variance, and SEs. This adjustment procedure is illustrated here as we repeat one of the earlier analyses.

Table 14.11 repeats the Plasma Concentration example data from Table 14.1. The third column now reports each runner's average Plasma Concentration. Table 14.12 shows x and y scores for the "blocking on subjects" model,

$$\mu(Plasma\ Concentration|Occasion, Runner) = \beta_1 x_1 + \sum_{j=2}^{12} \beta_j x_j. \qquad \text{(14.2)}$$

x_1 is a dummy variable coding Postrace observations and x_2 through x_{12} are dummy variables for the 11 different runners. The table also shows the "average-response" model,

$$\mu(Plasma\ Concentration \mid Occasion, Runner) = \beta_0 + \beta_1 x_1 + \beta_2 x_2. \qquad \text{(14.7)}$$

x_1 again codes Postrace observations, but x_2 is the average-response x-variable. The blocking on subjects model has 12 parameters, the average response model only 3. The latter has nine too few x-variables.

T A B L E **14.11**

Plasma Concentrations for Sampled Great North Run Participants

Prerace	Postrace	Average: (Post + Pre)/2
4.3	29.6	16.95
4.6	25.1	14.85
5.2	15.5	10.35
5.2	29.6	17.40
6.6	24.1	15.35
7.2	37.8	22.50
8.4	20.2	14.30
9.0	21.9	15.45
10.4	14.2	12.30
14.0	34.6	24.30
17.8	46.2	32.00

The fits of these two models are reported as Table 14.13. The RSS for the two are identical, 346.923, as are the estimates of the Postrace increase in Plasma Concentration, $\widehat{\beta}_1 = 18.736$. The degrees of freedom for the average response model are reported as 19, reflecting the fact that our linear-regression program "sees" only three parameters to be estimated. This is because we included an intercept and a response average (giving two parameters) rather than a dummy variable for each runner (which would require 11 parameters.) As a result, the reported d.f. for the average-response model is $(11 - 2) = 9$ too large. The correct model d.f. is 10 as reported for the blocking-on-subjects fit.

T A B L E 14.12
Blocking-on-subjects and Average-response Variables:
Plasma Concentration of Runners Pre- and Postrace

Blocking on Subjects

y	x_1	x_2	x_3	x_4	x_5	x_6	x_7	x_8	x_9	x_{10}	x_{11}	x_{12}
4.3	0	1	0	0	0	0	0	0	0	0	0	0
4.6	0	0	1	0	0	0	0	0	0	0	0	0
5.2	0	0	0	1	0	0	0	0	0	0	0	0
5.2	0	0	0	0	1	0	0	0	0	0	0	0
6.6	0	0	0	0	0	1	0	0	0	0	0	0
7.2	0	0	0	0	0	0	1	0	0	0	0	0
8.4	0	0	0	0	0	0	0	1	0	0	0	0
9.0	0	0	0	0	0	0	0	0	1	0	0	0
10.4	0	0	0	0	0	0	0	0	0	1	0	0
14.0	0	0	0	0	0	0	0	0	0	0	1	0
17.8	0	0	0	0	0	0	0	0	0	0	0	1
29.6	1	1	0	0	0	0	0	0	0	0	0	0
25.1	1	0	1	0	0	0	0	0	0	0	0	0
15.5	1	0	0	1	0	0	0	0	0	0	0	0
29.6	1	0	0	0	1	0	0	0	0	0	0	0
24.1	1	0	0	0	0	1	0	0	0	0	0	0
37.8	1	0	0	0	0	0	1	0	0	0	0	0
20.2	1	0	0	0	0	0	0	1	0	0	0	0
21.9	1	0	0	0	0	0	0	0	1	0	0	0
14.2	1	0	0	0	0	0	0	0	0	1	0	0
34.6	1	0	0	0	0	0	0	0	0	0	1	0
46.2	1	0	0	0	0	0	0	0	0	0	0	1

T A B L E   14.12
(Continued)

Average Response

y	x_1	x_2
4.3	0	16.95
4.6	0	14.85
5.2	0	10.35
5.2	0	17.40
6.6	0	15.35
7.2	0	22.50
8.4	0	14.30
9.0	0	15.45
10.4	0	12.30
14.0	0	24.30
17.8	0	32.00
29.6	1	16.95
25.1	1	14.85
15.5	1	10.35
29.6	1	17.40
24.1	1	15.35
37.8	1	22.50
20.2	1	14.30
21.9	1	15.45
14.2	1	12.30
34.6	1	24.30
46.2	1	32.00

The use of an inflated model d.f. in the average response model gives rise to an incorrect computation of the conditional response SD (s in Table 14.13) and the SE for the Post Race slope. Let's see how these errors can be corrected. In general, the conditional response SD is estimated by

$$s = \sqrt{\frac{\text{RSS}}{\text{df}}}. \tag{14.8}$$

This formula gives, for the data reported from the average response model fit,

$$s = \sqrt{\frac{346.923}{19}} = \sqrt{18.259} = 4.273.$$

The estimate is too small. We should divide the RSS by the correct model d.f.:

$$s = \sqrt{\frac{346.923}{10}} = \sqrt{34.6923} = 5.890.$$

The resulting, correct s is the same as reported in the fit of the blocking-on-subjects model.

An alternative way of correcting s is to multiply the average-response model estimate by an adjustment factor, the square root of the ratio of the incorrect to the correct model d.f.s:

$$s(Adjusted) = s(Average\ Response\ Model)\sqrt{\frac{\text{d.f. } (Average\ Response\ Model)}{\text{d.f. } (Correct)}}$$

$$s(Adjusted) = (4.273)\sqrt{\frac{19}{10}} = (4.273)\sqrt{1.9} = (4.273)(1.378) = 5.89. \quad \textbf{(14.9)}$$

T A B L E **14.13**
Fits to Fullest Models, Plasma Concentration

Blocking-on-subjects Model

Column	Name	Coeff	SE	P Value	SS
1	Postrace	18.736	2.512	0.000	1930.782
2	S1	7.582	4.350	0.112	574.605
3	S2	5.482	4.350	0.236	441.045
4	S3	0.982	4.350	0.826	214.245
5	S4	8.032	4.350	0.095	605.520
6	S5	5.982	4.350	0.199	471.245
7	S6	13.132	4.350	0.013	1012.500
8	S7	4.932	4.350	0.283	408.980
9	S8	6.082	4.350	0.192	477.405
10	S9	2.932	4.350	0.516	302.580
11	S10	14.932	4.350	0.006	1180.980
12	S11	22.632	4.350	0.000	2048.000

d.f.:10   s:5.89   RSS:346.923

Average-response Model

Column	Name	Coeff	SE	P Value	SS
0	Constant	−9.368	3.028	0.006	6966.920
1	Postrace	18.736	1.822	0.000	1930.782
2	Subj.Avg.	1.000	0.154	0.000	770.185

d.f.:19   RSq:0.886   s:4.273   RSS:346.923

Because the too-small s is a multiplier in the SEs for the linear model parameters, the latter are underestimated as well. They are corrected, however, by a multiplication by the same adjustment factor:

$$SE(\widehat{\beta}\mid Adjusted) = SE(\widehat{\beta}\mid Average\ Response\ Model)\sqrt{\frac{\text{d.f. } (Average\ Response\ Model)}{\text{d.f. } (Correct)}}.$$

(14.10)

Thus, we can adjust the SE for the Postrace increase in Plasma Concentration reported for the average-response model:

$$SE(\widehat{\beta}_1 \mid Adjusted) = (1.822)\sqrt{\frac{19}{10}} = (1.822)(1.378) = 2.511.$$

This is the same result as reported for the blocking-on-subjects fit:

$$SE(\widehat{\beta}_1 \mid Blocking\text{-}on\text{-}subjects\ Model) = 2.512.$$

Three simple steps, then, are all that are needed to get correct blocking-on-subjects model standard deviation and SE estimates from the fit to the easier-to-describe average response model:

- correct the model d.f. reported for the average response model;
- use the correct and incorrect d.f.s to calculate an adjustment factor; and
- multiply the estimated conditional response SD and model-parameter SEs by the adjustment factor.

To find the correct model d.f., we *subtract* from the reported d.f. for the average response model the *difference* between the number of subjects with repeated measures and the number of between-subjects parameters in the average response model. In our Plasma Concentration example, the reported d.f. for the average response model was 19. The number of subjects with repeated measures, the number of runners, was 11. And the average response model included two between-subjects parameters, the intercept and the slope for the average response (Subj.Avg.). As a result, the correct d.f. is

$$19 - (11 - 2) = 19 - 9 = 10.$$

And the adjustment factor by which reported SDs and SEs should be multiplied is the square root of the ratio of the reported to the correct d.f.:

$$\sqrt{\frac{19}{10}} = 1.378.$$

For repeated-measures designs, such as the Plasma Concentration one, with *no* between-subjects x-variables, the average response model will have just the two between-subjects parameters: intercept and slope for subject average. For repeated measures designs that are *mixed* and have a between-subjects structure as well, we will include correspondingly more between-subjects parameters in the average response model. We'll illustrate this by constructing an average response model for the second of our two Fuel Efficiency studies.

The fit reported for Model 1 in Table 14.14 is taken from Table 14.9 (Model 1). It is the fit of the model whose variables are displayed in Table 14.8. Two groups of 4 cars were employed, one at Low Altitude and one at High Altitude. Each car was tested with and without the *Fuel Additive*. "HiAlt" is a between-subjects variable; it distinguishes between groups of subjects (cars).

T A B L E **14.14**

Fits to Fullest Model, Fuel Efficiency

Model 1: Blocking on Subjects

	Column Name	Coeff	SE	P Value	SS
0	Constant	13.013	1.012	0.000	6408.003
2	HiAlt	0.525	1.432	0.726	0.250
3	Car1	10.900	1.280	0.000	67.000
4	Car2	−4.700	1.280	0.010	238.521
5	Car3	17.350	1.280	0.000	301.023
6	Car5	8.200	1.280	0.000	45.100
7	Car6	−5.800	1.280	0.004	217.601
8	Car7	13.950	1.280	0.000	194.602
9	Additive	1.975	0.905	0.072	49.000
10	Alt × Add	3.050	1.280	0.055	9.303

d.f.:6   RSq:0.991   s:1.28   RSS:9.838

Model 2: Average Response

	Column Name	Coeff	SE	P Value	SS
0	Constant	−0.987	0.746	0.212	6408.003
2	HiAlt	−1.525	0.669	0.044	0.250
3	CarAvg	1.000	0.029	0.000	1063.848
4	Additive	1.975	0.669	0.013	49.000
5	Alt × Add	3.050	0.946	0.008	9.303

d.f.:11   RSq:0.991   s:0.946   RSS:9.838

When we construct an average response model to correspond to Model 1, we will want to retain HiAlt as one of the sources of influence. As a result, the average response model will have *three* between-subjects parameters: the intercept (constant), the slope parameter for the average response x-variable (CarAvg in the Table 14.14), and the slope parameter for HiAlt. In correcting the d.f., we subtract from 11 (the reported d.f. for the average-response model) the difference between 8 (the number of cars) and 3 (the number of between subjects parameters in the average response model). Thus, the correct number of d.f. is $11 - (8 - 3) = 6$, as reported for the blocking-on-subjects analysis.

Applying the adjustment factor of Equations [14.9] and [14.10], we obtain corrected estimates:

$$s(Adjusted) = (0.946)\sqrt{\frac{11}{6}} = (0.946)(1.3540) = 1.28$$

and

$$SE(Alt \times Add\ Slope) = (0.946)(1.354) = 1.28.$$

Both results agree with the estimates obtained from the larger blocking-by-subjects model.

Model comparison based on the F-statistic,

$$F = \frac{[\text{SSR}(Less\ Full) - \text{SSR}(Fuller)]/[\text{d.f.}\ (Less\ Full) - \text{d.f.}(Fuller)]}{[\text{SSR}(Fullest)/\ \text{d.f.}(Fullest)]},$$

works well with average-response models. The d.f.s for fuller and less full models need not be corrected; they will differ appropriately by the number of fuller model parameters constrained. However, the d.f. for the fullest model—d.f.(Fullest)—used in the denominator of F must be the corrected value. In the following section we illustrate the use of average-response models for model comparison in repeated-measures studies.

14.8
Covariates in Repeated-measures Designs

In the repeated measures designs considered so far, all of the explanatory variables, other than the "stand-in"subject average have been $0/1/-1$ variables, coding levels, or combinations of levels (product variables) of categorical variables. However, *measured sources of influence*, or covariates, can also be included, quite usefully, in models for repeated-measures studies. That is, the motivation for the Analysis of Covariance developed in Chapter 12 extends to certain repeated measures designs as well. In this section we look at the simplest of two classes of covariate designs for repeated-measures studies. In this first class, the same covariates are associated with each repeated-measures treatment. In the second class, different covariates accompany the responses on different occasions. We'll refer to these two classes, respectively, as *global* and *occasional* covariate designs. For information on occasional covariate designs, the reader may wish to continue reading in Judd and McClelland (1989).

14.8.1   Global Covariates in Mixed Repeated-measures Designs

The analysis of covariance was developed in Chapter 12 as a way of increasing the sensitivity of a study by controlling for an "extraneous" source of response variability. That is, the response variable is known to be influenced by some auxiliary variable as well as by the treatment or treatments of interest. By including the auxiliary variable (or covariate) in the model, we allow it to "soak up" some of the between-subjects response variability. In this way, the conditional response variance, against which treatment influences are assessed, is reduced. This increases the power of model comparisons involving the treatment.

The use of blocking-by-subjects x-variables (or their surrogate, the subject average variable) also controls for between-subjects response variability. Because it does so at the individual-subject level this is a more effective way of controlling for between-subjects variability than any covariate. For within-subjects models, there is no advantage to including a covariate in the model. However, for *mixed models*, those with interesting between subjects as well as within-subjects explanatory influences, a covariate can be useful. Although its presence will not affect model comparisons involving the repeated measures, the covariate can provide more powerful model comparisons involving between-subjects comparisons.

Let's reanalyze the Mixed Fuel Efficiency study data, introducing a covariate. The same cars are evaluated with and without a Fuel Additive, but different sets of cars are used at Low and at High Altitudes. Fuel Additive (present or absent) and its possible interaction with Altitude are repeated-measures influences. Between-cars variability is completely controlled for when these contributions to Fuel Efficiency are evaluated. However, the evaluation of the influence of the between-cars variable, Altitude, will be affected by the amount of between-car variability in the two sets of cars used. We can make the design potentially more sensitive to Altitude differences if we can reduce this between-car variability in Fuel Efficiency by including a covariate.

Larger engines consume more fuel and so we introduce engine size as a covariate. We take as the measure Engine Displacement, the volume in liters displaced by the pistons working in the engine's cylinders. Table 14.15 reproduces the Fuel Efficiency data of Table 14.7 adding the information on Engine Displacement for the 8 cars tested.

T A B L E **14.15**

Fuel Efficiency (mpg) of Cars Operated With and Without Additive

Low Altitude

	Engine	Fuel Efficiency (mpg)	
	Displacement	Additive	No Additive
Car 1	2.0	26.0	23.8
Car 2	3.8	10.4	8.2
Car 3	1.4	31.5	31.2
Car 4	2.5	15.6	12.4

High Altitude

	Engine	Fuel Efficiency (mpg)	
	Displacement	Additive	No Additive
Car 5	2.0	28.2	20.3
Car 6	3.8	12.6	7.9
Car 7	1.4	31.2	28.8
Car 8	2.5	18.6	13.5

Ignoring the covariate for the moment, we earlier developed the following linear model for these data:

$$\mu(mpg \mid Additive, Altitude, Cars) = \beta_0 + \beta_1 x_1 + \sum_{j=2}^{7} \beta_j x_j + \beta_8 x_8 + \beta_9 x_9, \quad \text{(14.6)}$$

where x_1 was 0/1 coding the High level of Altitude, x_2 through x_7 were 0/1 coding Cars 1 through 3 and Cars 5 through 7, x_8 was 0/1 coding the Fuel Additive Present level, and x_9 was a product of the two Altitude and Fuel Additive dummy variables, $x_9 = x_1 \times x_8$. The eight parameters associated with blocking on the individual cars were provided by β_0 through β_7. Within-subjects or repeated-measures parameters were β_8 and β_9.

We'll modify the model of Equation 14.6 first by substituting a single *average-response* variable for the collection of individual car xs,

$$\mu(mpg \mid Additive,\ Altitude,\ Cars) = \beta_0 + \beta_1 x_1 + \beta_4 x_4 + \beta_5 x_5 + \beta_6 x_6.$$

The Average Response is designated x_4 and the Fuel Additive (Present) and Altitude $\times$ Fuel Additive interaction variables are now x_5 and x_6, respectively. Now, we are ready to add our covariate, Engine Displacement, to the model. Anticipating an interest in evaluating whether the influence of increased Engine Displacement on Fuel Efficiency is the same at High as at Low Altitude, we'll introduce Engine Displacement as a pair of variables. We let x_2 carry the Engine Displacement scores for cars driven at Low Altitude and 0s for those driven at High Altitude. And x_3 is the "reverse": 0s for Low Altitude cars, Engine Displacement scores for High Altitude. The completed model, then, is a seven-parameter one,

$$\mu(mpg \mid Addit,\ Altit,\ Displ) = \beta_0 + \beta_1 x_1 + \beta_2 x_2 + \beta_3 x_3 + \beta_4 x_4 + \beta_5 x_5 + \beta_6 x_6.$$

(14.11)

Table 14.16 displays the variables associated with the model of Equation 14.11. Values of x_4 are averages over the two Fuel Additive levels at which each car was driven, e.g., $24.90 = (26.0 + 23.80)/2$. The fit of this fullest model is given at the top of Table 14.17. The RSS for this fullest model is exactly the same as reported for the Equation [14.6] model at the top of Table 14.9. Replacing the 6 individual car xs with covariate and average-response variables has not changed the overall fit of the model. As noted earlier, the d.f. for this fullest model is incorrectly calculated. Our covariance model has five between-subjects parameters (β_0 through β_4) rather than eight, the number of individual cars (subjects). Thus, the correct d.f. is $(8 - 5) = 3$ fewer than reported. The correct numbers of d.f.s for Models 1, 2, and 3 of Table 14.17 are $(9 - 3) = 6$, $(10 - 3) = 7$, and $(11 - 3) = 8$.

In fact, the fits of Models 1, 2, and 3 in Table 14.17 are identical to those of Models 1, 2, and 3 in Table 14.9. Since within-subjects "hypotheses" about the influence of the Fuel Additive or any interaction of the Fuel Additive's influence with that of Altitude involve comparisons among these models, the results would be the same whether or not the comparisons were carried out with the covariate in the models.

T A B L E **14.16**

Mixed-model Analysis of Covariance:
Fullest Model Variables

y	x_1	x_2	x_3	x_4	x_5	x_6
26.0	0	2.0	0.0	24.90	1	0
10.4	0	3.8	0.0	9.30	1	0
31.5	0	1.4	0.0	31.35	1	0
15.6	0	2.5	0.0	14.00	1	0
28.2	1	0.0	2.0	24.25	1	1
12.6	1	0.0	3.8	10.25	1	1
31.2	1	0.0	1.4	30.00	1	1
18.6	1	0.0	2.5	16.05	1	1
23.8	0	2.0	0.0	24.90	0	0
8.2	0	3.8	0.0	9.30	0	0
31.2	0	1.4	0.0	31.35	0	0
12.4	0	2.5	0.0	14.00	0	0
20.3	1	0.0	2.0	24.25	0	0
7.9	1	0.0	3.8	10.25	0	0
28.8	1	0.0	1.4	30.00	0	0
13.5	1	0.0	2.5	16.05	0	0

T A B L E **14.17**

Regression Models: Mixed-model Analysis of Covariance

Model 1: Fullest

	Column Name	Coeff	SE	P Value	SS
0	Constant	−0.987	4.438	0.829	6408.003
2	HiAlt	−1.525	1.628	0.373	0.250
3	Disp(LoAlt)	0.000	1.026	1.000	533.322
4	Disp(HiAlt)	0.000	0.934	1.000	424.309
5	Car_Avg	1.000	0.101	0.000	106.217
6	Addit	1.975	0.739	0.026	49.000
7	Alt × Add	3.050	1.045	0.017	9.303
d.f.:9		RSq:0.991	s:1.045		RSS:9.838

Model 2: No Altitude × Additive Interaction

	Column Name	Coeff	SE	P Value	SS
0	Constant	−1.75	5.863	0.771	6408.003
2	HiAlt	0.00	2.040	1.000	0.250
3	Disp(LoAlt)	0.00	1.357	1.000	533.322
4	Disp(HiAlt)	0.00	1.236	1.000	424.309
5	Car_Avg	1.00	0.134	0.000	106.217
6	Addit	3.50	0.692	0.000	49.000
d.f.:10		RSq:0.983	s:1.383		RSS:19.14

Model 3: No Fuel Additive Effect (Model B$_w$)

	Column Name	Coeff	SE	P Value	SS
0	Constant	0	10.528	1.000	6408.003
2	HiAlt	0	3.670	1.000	0.250
3	Disp(LoAlt)	0	2.442	1.000	533.322
4	Disp(HiAlt)	0	2.224	1.000	424.309
5	Car_Avg	1	0.241	0.002	106.217
d.f.:11		RSq:0.94	s:2.489		RSS:68.14

Model 4: No Within-subjects Influences (Model B$_b$)

	Column Name	Coeff	SE	P Value	SS
0	Constant	42.279	3.934	0.000	6408.003
2	HiAlt	−2.169	5.564	0.703	0.250
3	Disp(LoAlt)	−9.234	1.524	0.000	533.322
4	Disp(HiAlt)	−8.236	1.524	0.000	424.309
d.f.:12		RSq:0.846	s:3.812		RSS:174.357

Model 5: Homogeneity of Covariate Regression

	Column Name	Coeff	SE	P Value	SS
0	Constant	41.070	2.850	0.000	6408.003
2	HiAlt	0.250	1.847	0.894	0.250
3	Displac	−8.735	1.045	0.000	954.518
d.f.:13		RSq:0.843	s:3.695		RSS:177.469

Model 6: No Altitude Effect

	Column Name	Coeff	SE	P Value	SS
0	Constant	41.195	2.600	0	6408.003
3	Displac	−8.735	1.007	0	954.518
d.f.:14		RSq:0.843	s:3.563		RSS:177.719

This is a general principle. The global covariate has no effect on within-subjects modeling in mixed models. The global covariate may affect model comparisons that are between subjects, that relate to x-variables that differentiate among subjects. We can see the impact of the covariate when we compare the estimate of the conditional response variance for the fullest between-subjects model of Table 14.9,

$$\widehat{\sigma}^2(mpg \mid Altitude) = \frac{1131.988 - 68.14}{14 - 8} = \frac{1063.848}{6} = 177.308,$$

with our estimates for our covariance model of Table 14.17,

$$\widehat{\sigma}^2(mpg \mid Altitude, Displacement) = \frac{174.357 - 68.14}{12 - 8} = \frac{106.217}{4} = 26.554.$$

Clearly, Engine Displacement has absorbed a good deal of the between-cars variability in mileage.

We first ask in the analysis of covariance if the regression of the covariate on the response is the same at each of the treatment levels. In this example, we ask if we can constrain the two slopes β_2 and β_3 to be identical. To answer this, in Model 5 the two separate covariate x-variables have been combined into one (by adding them together.) The fits of Models 4 and 5 are not substantially different:

$$F = \frac{177.469 - 174.357}{(106.217/4)} = \frac{3.112}{26.554} = 0.117.$$

The rate of change of mpg with respect to engine displacement is the same for cars driven at Low as at High Altitude.

Is there an Altitude effect? Again the increase in RSS from Model 5 to Model 6 is so small,

$$F = \frac{177.719 - 177.469}{26.554} = \frac{0.250}{26.554} = 0.009,$$

that we accept the less full model. There is no Altitude effect.

The global covariate enters into the mixed-model analysis only where model comparison focuses on between-subjects variables.

14.9
Crossover Designs

Early in this chapter, we noted that one potential problem with the repeated-measures design was that the response on a particular trial might be influenced either by its position in the sequence of trials or by the effects of a treatment delivered on an earlier trial. The tracking down of such *period* and *carryover* effects can be a difficult analytic task. Repeated-measures designs in which each subject receives different treatments on different trials are called *crossover* designs. An excellent source on the design and analysis of crossover designs is Jones & Kenward (1989). In this section, we look at the analysis for a simple but common crossover design. Two treatments are to be compared. Both are to be administered to the same subjects inasmuch as between-subjects variability on the response variable may be quite large relative to the within-subject variability under different treatments. To provide a check on potentially invalidating carryover effects, the group of subjects is divided in two. One-half of the subjects receive the two treatments in one particular order (*AB*) and the other half receive them in the opposite order (*BA*).

Our example is adapted from Patel (1983). Two drugs, simply labeled *A* and *B*, were tested for effectiveness in relieving acute bronchial asthma. The response variable in the study is the volume of air forcibly expelled from the lungs in a one-second interval, Forced Expiratory Volume (*FEV*). Table 14.18 gives FEV values (in liters) for 17 patients. The 8 patients assigned to Group 1 were treated with Drug A during Trial 1 and Drug B during Trial 2. For the 9 patients in Group 2, the order of drug administration was reversed. We can note from the table that there is considerable between-patients variability in lung capacity. Because the repeated-measures design controls for this between subjects variability, it provides a more powerful way of comparing treatment effectiveness.

T A B L E **14.18**

Forced Expiratory Volumes Under Drugs A and B

Group 1 (Order: AB)				Group 2 (Order: BA)		
Patient	Period 1	Period 2		Patient	Period 1	Period 2
1	1.28	1.33		9	3.06	1.38
2	1.60	2.21		10	2.68	2.10
3	2.46	2.43		11	2.60	2.32
4	1.41	1.81		12	1.48	1.30
5	1.40	0.85		13	2.08	2.34
6	1.12	1.20		14	2.72	2.48
7	0.90	0.90		15	1.94	1.11
8	2.41	2.79		16	3.35	3.23
				17	1.16	1.25

14.9.1   The Fullest Crossover Model

To help us develop an initial explanatory model, the response-variable data from Table 14.18 have been organized into a single column of values, the first column of Table 14.19. Period 2 responses for the 17 patients are listed below the Period 1 responses in this column.

What influences are to be modeled? Primarily, we'll want to assess a Drug influence. Is there a difference in the effectiveness of Drugs A and B? Less important, but of interest, is whether there is a Period influence. Does drug treatment, whatever the specific drugs, become more or less effective with repetition? Because patients receive both drugs and because drugs are administered to each patient on two occasions, these two potential influences, Drug and Period, are *within-subjects* effects. In making these within-subjects comparisons, we will want to control for between-subject variability, either by blocking on subjects or by employing an *average-response* surrogate.

Finally, there is a *between-subjects* source of influence as well. Patients were divided into two Groups, corresponding to the two different orders in which the drugs were employed. Drug, Period, and Group are each at two levels and can be represented by appropriately coded dummy variables in our models. Our fullest model, an average response one, will include four explanatory variables:

- x_1, a dummy variable coding one level (Group 2: the AB drug order) of the Group factor;
- x_2, the patient's average response to the two drug treatments;
- x_3, a dummy variable coding one level (Period 2) of the Period factor; and
- x_4, a dummy variable coding one level (Drug B) of the Drug factor.

Scores on these four xs appear beside the corresponding y scores in Table 14.19. Together, they provide what is needed for a fullest model for this crossover design:

$$\mu(FEV \mid Drug, Period, Order) = \beta_0 + \beta_1 x_{i1} + \beta_2 x_{i2} + \beta_3 x_{i3} + \beta_4 x_{i4}. \quad \textbf{(14.12)}$$

T A B L E 14.19
Fullest Model Variables for the *FEV* Study

y	x_1	x_2	x_3	x_4
1.28	0	1.305	0	0
1.60	0	1.905	0	0
2.46	0	2.445	0	0
1.41	0	1.610	0	0
1.40	0	1.125	0	0
1.12	0	1.160	0	0
0.90	0	0.900	0	0
2.41	0	2.600	0	0
3.06	1	2.220	0	1
2.68	1	2.390	0	1
2.60	1	2.460	0	1
1.48	1	1.390	0	1
2.08	1	2.210	0	1
2.72	1	2.600	0	1
1.94	1	1.525	0	1
3.35	1	3.290	0	1
1.16	1	1.205	0	1
1.33	0	1.305	1	1
2.21	0	1.905	1	1
2.43	0	2.445	1	1
1.81	0	1.610	1	1
0.85	0	1.125	1	1
1.20	0	1.160	1	1
0.90	0	0.900	1	1
2.79	0	2.600	1	1
1.38	1	2.220	1	0
2.10	1	2.390	1	0
2.32	1	2.460	1	0
1.30	1	1.390	1	0
2.34	1	2.210	1	0
2.48	1	2.600	1	0
1.11	1	1.525	1	0
3.23	1	3.290	1	0
1.25	1	1.205	1	0

14.9.2 Testing for Carryover Effect

In the modeling of the typical mixed, between- and within-subjects effects design, we would follow the pattern of the earlier section, looking first at the within-subjects variability and then moving on to any between-subjects comparisons of interest. Because the between-subjects comparison in the crossover design is going to tell us how we should model what is of greatest interest to us, the Drug influence, we follow a different course here.

The Group factor enables us to compare the responses of two groups of patients. Patients in both groups are administered both drugs and are evaluated at both periods. The only difference between them is the order in which the two drugs are administered. The two groups ought not differ. If they do, it signals a complex interaction between the two drugs; Drug A, administered first, has a different influence on the response to the second administered drug, Drug B, than does Drug B, when administered first, on the response to Drug A. We have a much simpler model for the influence of our drugs if the order-of-administration groups do not differ. So we'd like to reject this complexity if possible at the outset of our analysis.

The influence of the levels of *Group* is evaluated first but in the same fashion as described earlier for the between-subjects factor in the mixed design. The difference in the fits of Models B_w and B_b gives us our estimate of the conditional response variance for any between-subjects comparisons. Here, the between Ss comparison of interest is that between Model B_b, a model allowing the different order of drug administration Groups to have an influence, and the Null Model, excluding that influence. In the context of this example, the three models are

$$\mu(FEV \mid Drug\ Order,\ Patient\ Diff) = \beta_0 + \beta_1 x_{i1} + \sum_{j=2}^{16} \beta_j x_{ij},$$

$$\mu(FEV \mid Drug\ Order) = \beta_0 + \beta_1 x_{i1}, \quad \text{and}$$

$$\mu(FEV) = \beta_0.$$

In these models, x_1 is a dummy variable for the *BA* order of drug administration group, and x_2 through x_{16} are dummy variables for 7 of the 8 *AB*-order patients and 8 of the 9 *BA*-order patients.

The regression output providing the fits of these models and the model comparison details are given in Table 14.20. Model B_w is fitted with an SSR of 2.548. Because we have used just three parameters for between-subjects influences (the intercept plus the slopes associated with the single Patient Average and the one Group dummy variable) rather than a blocking variable for each of the 17 patients, the reported d.f. of 31 is incorrect. The correct d.f. for Model B_w is $31 - (17 - 3) = 17$.

Model B_b yields an RSS of 15.189 and has (correctly reported) degrees of freedom of 32. The difference in the RSS for these two models is

$$SS(Patients\ Within\ Groups) = 15.189 - 2.548 = 12.641$$

while the degrees of freedom associated with this increase in RSS is the difference in correct d.f.s for the two models: $32 - 17 = 15$. It is the ratio of this sum of squares to its d.f. that forms our estimate of the conditional response variance for between-subjects comparisons. We'll use

$$\hat{\sigma}^2(FEV \mid Fullest\ Between\text{-}subjects\ Model) = 12.641/15 = 0.843$$

as the denominator term in the following model comparison.

The Null Model has only one parameter, the intercept, so its d.f. is $(34 - 1) = 33$. And the RSS for the Null Model is 17.41. The increase in RSS over Model B_b, the sum of square associated with the two order-of-drug administration Groups, is

$$SS(Groups) = 17.41 - 15.19 = 2.21.$$

T A B L E **14.20**

Regression Models: Testing for a Drug Order (Group) Effect

Model B$_w$

Column Name		Coeff	SE	P Value	SS
0	Constant	0	0.150	1	123.044
2	Group(BA)	0	0.107	1	2.221
3	Pt_Av	1	0.081	0	12.641
d.f.:31		RSq:0.854	s:0.287		RSS:2.548

Model B$_b$

Column Name		Coeff	SE	P Value	SS
0	Constant	1.631	0.172	0.000	123.044
2	Group(BA)	0.512	0.237	0.038	2.221
d.f.:32		RSq:0.128	s:0.689		RSS:15.189

Null Model

Column Name		Coeff	SE	P Value	SS
1	Constant	1.902	0.125	0	123.044
d.f.:33			s:0.726		RSS:17.41

This increase in RSS is based on just one d.f. difference in the two models, so SS(*Groups*) is the numerator in our *F*-ratio:

$$F = \frac{2.21}{0.843} = 2.635.$$

The degrees of freedom for evaluating this *F*-ratio are 1 (for the numerator) and 15 (for the denominator). As approximately 12.5 % of that *F*-distribution exceeds 2.635, we conclude there is no Group, carryover, or drug administration order influence on the response.

14.9.3 Assessing Drug and Period Influences

Assured of the lack of a complex interaction between the two levels of Drug, we can return to the Fullest model to assess the Drug and Period components of our model. The fit to the fullest model of Equation [14.12] appears at the top of Table 14.21. The sum of squares of residuals for this fullest model is reported (correctly) as 1.788. The d.f. for this model is reported as 29, incorrectly, we know because of the use of a surrogate (Patient Average) for a full set of subject-blocking variables. We obtain the corrected d.f. by subtracting from this reported d.f., 29, the difference between the number of patients, 17, and the number of between-patients parameters in our model. This latter is 3—the intercept plus the slopes for the Group dummy variable and for the Patient Average. The corrected d.f. for the fullest model, then, is $29 - (17 - 3) = 15$.

T A B L E   **14.21**

Regression Models: Assessing the Drug and Period Influences

Fullest Within-subjects Model

Column Name		Coeff	SE	P Value	SS
0	Constant	−0.059	0.144	0.686	123.044
2	Group(BA)	0.000	0.093	1.000	2.221
3	Pt_Av	1.000	0.070	0.000	12.641
4	Trial(2)	−0.139	0.085	0.114	0.202
5	Drug(B)	0.257	0.085	0.005	0.557
d.f.:29		RSq:0.897	s:0.248		RSS:1.788

No Drug Influence Model

Column Name		Coeff	SE	P Value	SS
0	Constant	0.077	0.154	0.620	123.044
2	Group(BA)	0.000	0.104	1.000	2.221
3	Pt_Av	1.000	0.079	0.000	12.641
4	Trial(2)	−0.154	0.096	0.119	0.202
d.f.:30		RSq:0.865	s:0.28		RSS:2.346

No Period (Trial) Influence Model

Column Name		Coeff	SE	P Value	SS
0	Constant	−0.132	0.140	0.353	123.044
2	Group(BA)	0.000	0.095	1.000	2.221
3	Pt_Av	1.000	0.072	0.000	12.641
5	Drug(B)	0.265	0.087	0.005	0.596
d.f.:30		RSq:0.888	s:0.255		RSS:1.952

The denominator term for all of our within-subjects model comparisons will be the conditional response variance estimated from the RSS and (corrected) d.f. for this fullest model:

$$\widehat{\sigma}^2(FEV \mid Fullest\ Within\text{-}subjects\ Model) = \frac{1.788}{15} = 0.119.$$

The comparison of the fits of this fullest model with one that omits the dummy variable for Drug will establish whether one of the two drugs is more effective. The RSS for the No Drug Influence model is given in Table 14.21 as 2.346. The increase in RSS, over that for the fullest model is $2.346 - 1.788 = 0.558$. The difference in the number of parameters between this No Drug and the fullest model is just 1 so we have as the F-ratio comparison statistic

$$F = \frac{0.558}{0.119} = 4.681.$$

When evaluated against the F-distribution with 1 and 15 d.f., this value is exceeded by only 4.7% of the distribution. We conclude that the two drugs are *not* equally effective.

Next, we ask if the influence of the drug administered first is different from that of the drug administered in the second period. Is there a Period or trial influence? The third model fitted in Table 14.21 is the No Period Influence Model. We ask whether its RSS, 1.952, is significantly greater than the RSS for the fullest model. (Note that as Drug was found to be important it was restored to the model.) The F-ratio statistic,

$$F = \frac{1.952 - 1.788}{0.119} = 1.376,$$

is exceeded in value by about 26% of the F-distribution with 1 and 15 d.f. The data provide no evidence, then, of a Period effect.

Had we found evidence of a group or carryover effect, any search for or interpretation of a period effect would not be possible. And, in the case of a carryover effect being found in this simple crossover design, the most appropriate follow-up would be to ignore the second trial or period data and test (between subjects) for a drug effect by comparing responses in the first trial. Jones and Kenward (1989) provide a thorough discussion of carryover and period effects.

The fit to a final model is given in Table 14.22. It is a within-patients model as the relevant influence, Drug, is a within-subjects factor. Both Group and Period, though, have been dropped. The RSS for this model is 1.952. The reported d.f. of 31 must be corrected. Seventeen "parameters," rather than two (an intercept and the Patient Average slope) are needed to control for between-subjects variability in this within-subjects model. Thus, the correct d.f. is $31 - (17 - 2) = 16$.

TABLE 14.22

Fit of Final Forced Expiratory Volume Model

Column Name		Coeff	SE	P Value	SS
0	Constant	−0.132	0.138	0.345	123.044
3	Pt_Av	1.000	0.065	0.000	14.863
5	Drug(B)	0.265	0.086	0.004	0.596
d.f.:31		RSq:0.888	s:0.251		RSS:1.952

Our interest in this final model is to describe the magnitude of the differential Drug influence. The slope estimate for Drug B is 0.265 liter. It is positive, meaning that Forced Expiratory Volume is about a quarter liter greater under Drug B than under Drug A. Let's see, though, about putting a confidence interval about this estimate. The reported SE of 0.086 liter is incorrect as it is based on the incorrect d.f. reported for the model. We know how to correct the SE, however:

$\mathrm{SE}(\widehat{\beta} \mid Adjusted)$

$$= \mathrm{SE}(\widehat{\beta} \mid Average\text{-}response\ Model) \sqrt{\frac{\text{d.f. } (Average\text{-}response\ Model)}{\text{d.f. } (Correct)}}.$$

(14.10)

Here, the corrected SE (*Drug B*) is

$$0.086\sqrt{\frac{31}{16}} = 0.12.$$

The sampling distribution for the slope estimate for Drug(level B) is the *t* distribution with 16 d.f. The middle 95% of this distribution is within 2.12 SE of the true slope. Thus, our 95% CI for the slope will extend from

$$(0.265 - [2.12] \times [0.120]) = 0.011 \text{ liter}$$

to

$$(0.265 + [2.12] \times [0.120]) = 0.519 \text{ liter}.$$

We are reminded that this slope estimate is for a *within-subjects* model. Hence, our interpretation is that the Forced Expiratory Volume will be greater *for an individual* under Drug B than for one under Drug A. The parameters of *between-subjects* models relate to the mean of the response variable in (different) populations of respondents. The parameters of *within-subjects* models relate to the mean of the response variable *for an individual respondent*.

14.10
Advanced Repeated-measures
Analysis: Beyond Blocking on Subjects

In this chapter we have presented the simplest approach to the analysis of repeated measures. The "blocking on subjects" notion has the advantage of being a direct extension of our "fixed-effects" linear model. All we've had to do is incorporate the "levels" of subject, another categorical explanatory variable, into our models when making comparisons among repeated measures *within* the same subjects. With that modification, we've had at our disposal all the technology developed in earlier chapters for linear models, their comparison, and the assessment of the strength of explanatory influences.

Unfortunately, this straightforward approach to repeated measures has some special requirements that are not always met. Where the number of repeated measures is greater than two, our approach strictly requires that there be a certain pattern to the correlations among the repeated measures. Often, this takes the form of requiring that the correlations between pairs of measurements be the same for all pairs. When this requirement is not met, our simple analysis may be suboptimal.

One situation in which the equal correlations assumption may not be warranted is where the repeated measurements are obtained at different points in time. Often, measures taken more closely in time will be more highly correlated with each other than will measures separated by greater lengths of time. For example, at the very beginning of this chapter, we described a study to evaluate the efficacy of a diet regime. Dieters selected at random were weighed at the start (y_0) and again at the end of one month (y_1), two months (y_2) and three months (y_3). We would expect the correlation to be stronger, say, between y_0 and y_1 (one month's separation in time) than between y_0 and y_3 (three months' separation.) These repeated measures may not be analyzed best by the techniques of this chapter. It may be that what is of interest can be better assessed after *transforming* the repeated measures into one or more "new" response variables that satisfy our modeling requirements. For example, in the diet program assessment, it may be sufficient for our purposes to study *separately* each of two derived variables:

$$Total\ Weight\ Loss:\ z_1 = y_0 - y_3$$

and

$$Weight\ Loss\ Gradient:\ z_2 = \left[y_0 - \left(\frac{y_1 + y_2}{2} \right) \right] - \left[\left(\frac{y_1 + y_2}{2} \right) - y_3 \right].$$

Modeling Total Weight Loss as the response variable allows us to assess overall weight loss. The second derived response variable will be negative if weight loss is greater during the second half of the program than in the first, positive if weight loss is greater during the initial month and a half, and 0 if the weight loss is constant over the two halves. Modeling this Weight Loss Gradient will inform us about the course of weight reduction. By transforming the original 4 y observations for each subject into two, the analysis method of this chapter can be applied.

Alternative analyses to the simple linear models approach described in this chapter have been developed but they are beyond the scope of this introduction to linear models. The reader interested in learning more about modeling repeated measures will find the monograph by Crowder and Hand (1990) particularly informative.

14.11
Summary

An important class of research designs calls for assessing a response variable on the same observational units either at different points in time or under different circumstances. The resulting response observations lack *independence,* an important assumption of linear modeling. In this chapter, an approach is outlined for bringing such designs under our linear model umbrella. That approach calls for *blocking on the individual subjects* or other observational units. Once developed, it is then shown that the same model results can be obtained with less coding difficulty by substituting a *subject average variable* for the individual subject dummy variables.

This chapter completes our coverage of models for the measured response variable. We have introduced a set of linear modeling tools, now extended to repeated measures, that permits the clear and efficient representation of almost any design in linear model form, whether for the measured response or for the categorical or counted responses to be introduced in the balance of this book. For the reader curious about the linear model representation of more complex measured-response designs, the work of Kirk (1982) contains much detail.

Exercises

1 Following are measurements of plasma citrate concentrations obtained from 10 subjects each measured at five times during the day: 8 a.m., 11 a.m., 2 p.m, 5 p.m., and 8 p.m. The study calls for a repeated-measures analysis. Begin with the fullest model and separate parameters for each of five time periods. Does there appear to be any time trend? If so, does it suggest how the model might be simplified?

Plasma Citrate Concentration

8am	11am	2pm	5pm	8pm
93	121	112	117	121
116	135	114	98	135
125	137	119	105	102
144	173	148	124	122
105	119	125	91	133
109	83	109	80	104
89	95	88	91	116
116	128	122	107	119
151	149	141	126	138
137	139	125	109	107

2 Following surgery on monkeys, the concentration of the substance phosphocreatine was measured on the regenerating left side of the spinal column (column 2 of the data) and on the unaffected, normal right side of the spinal column (column 3 of the data). Treat the data as an example of "change" or pre-posttreatment data: Normal to Regenerating.

Subject	Regenerating	Normal
1	5.6	7.4
2	4.3	8.0
3	12.5	10.9
4	8.9	20.6
5	4.6	16.8
6	6.1	31.8
7	5.0	15.9
8	18.0	22.6
9	9.8	17.6
10	10.6	15.2

3 Following are observations on the level of hemopexin in blood samples drawn from 12 women who are muscular dystrophy carriers and from 13 who are not. Here we present just the first three observations for each woman. Using these first three data points, carry out a mixed-model analysis. The within-subjects factor is occasions (1 through 3), and the between-subjects factor is the Carrier/Not Carrier distinction.

Carrier (C) / Noncarrier (N)	1	2	3
N	87.3	80.3	85.2
N	53.0	56.0	57.5
N	88.0	81.0	66.3
N	77.0	80.2	87.0
N	76.0	76.7	78.0
N	90.0	71.5	73.5
N	70.0	66.7	66.3
N	84.0	81.3	86.5
N	82.0	77.0	81.3
N	109.0	102.3	92.4
N	80.5	86.5	79.0
N	93.0	81.3	82.8
N	90.5	85.0	88.5
C	93.1	88.5	87.5
C	76.0	71.0	85.5
C	104.0	86.5	83.5
C	109.5	91.0	105.2
C	105.5	92.8	20.7
C	100.5	98.5	9.2
C	98.0	96.5	100.1
C	81.0	82.0	76.3
C	93.2	90.5	93.3
C	94.0	9.0	88.0
C	85.5	91.5	89.5
C	103.5	104.0	25.4

15

The Categorical Response Variable: Characteristics

Beginning with Chapter 2, we have been concerned with modeling responses that can be measured. Our response variables have had numeric scores—heights in cms, salaries in dollars per month, cognitive performances as the number of items correctly answered. For each, there was assumed to be a unit of measurement and we exploited that in the interpretation of our regression parameters.

Not all responses have a unit of measure. We may be interested in how level of education influences the choice among presidential candidates (a response variable that may have only two alternative "values," each a "name"). Or we may be interested in comparing the effectiveness of two drugs in relieving inflammation where relief is assessed by physicians on a scale consisting of the alternatives "None," "Limited," "Moderate," and "Total." This and the three following chapters are devoted to describing how to model response variables such as these, responses whose "scores" can only distribute observations among a limited number of categories rather than measure the strength of some attribute in those observations.

15.1
Categorical Responses: Population Characteristics

Before we can think about how an explanatory variable might influence a categorical response, we need to have some ways of describing categorical-response data. What about them is to be influenced? For purposes of modeling, we distinguish three types of categorical response variables. We describe the characteristics of each of these in this section.

15.1.1 Ordered Categories: No Unit of Measurement for the Response

The hallmark of the measured variable is that the scores on that variable possess a consistent *unit of measurement*. For example, three salmon swam through a water maze in 10 secs, 15 secs, and 25 secs respectively. We know from these results that the fish completing the maze in only 10 secs was faster than the one taking 15 secs who, in turn, was faster than the one requiring 25 secs. We also know, taking into account the properties of the second as a unit of measurement of time, that the difference in swimming times between the first and second fish (5 secs) is only one-half the size of the difference in times between the second and third fish (10 secs). The time-measurement unit "second" has a constant meaning to us and there were twice as many of them separating the performances of the second and third fish as there were separating the first and second.

Now consider this situation. Each judge at the Suquamish County Fair's Apple Pie Contest rates the entered pies on a seven-point scale, with a score of 1 indicating Not Acceptable and a score of 7 indicating Outstanding. That is, the judge assigns an integer number in the range [1, 7] to each pie. If judge A gives scores of 2, 3, and 5 to three pies, we can assume that she found the quality of the pie scored 5 higher than that of the one scored 3, and that, in turn, the pie scored 3 was of higher quality than the one scored 2. The judge's ratings *ordered* the pies by quality.

What we aren't likely to assume is that the difference in quality between the pies scored 3 and 5 is twice the difference in quality between the pies scored 2 and 3. For us to do so, we would need to be convinced that the differences between ratings of 2 and 3, between ratings of 3 and 4, and between ratings of 4 and 5 all correspond to the same difference in quality. We would have to know the judge was able to employ a constant unit of measurement in assessing pie quality. If we doubt there is such a unit of measurement, we cannot say the judge's ratings "measured" the quality of the pies. Instead, she assigned them to "categories" of quality.

While we can (and often do) use numbers for ordered categories, there is no special advantage to doing so. We would have the same information about the qualities of the pies if the judge's categories were named Not Acceptable, Barely Acceptable, Fair, Good, Very Good, Excellent, and Outstanding. These names serve equally well to label the seven ordered categories into which the pies' qualities are sorted by the judge. Numbers aren't mandatory as they are for measurement.

What would Judge A's ratings of all the apple pies entered at the Suquamish fair (a "population" of pie ratings) look like? It would consist of a certain number of 1s, some number of 2s, etc. We say, more formally, that there would be a certain *frequency* of 1s, of 2s, etc. Each level of the categorical variable has some frequency in the population. These frequencies are just counts. The sum of the frequencies over the levels of the ordered response categorical variable is just the total number of ratings in the population.

If we want to, we can divide the frequency at each level by the total number of ratings. The result is the *proportion* of ratings at each level. These proportions will sum, across the levels, to 1.0, accounting for all of the ratings.

Had our pie judge rated 50 entries, these might be the results:

	Category	Frequency (f)	Proportion (p)
Not Acceptable	1	5	0.10
	2	7	0.14
	3	8	0.16
	4	10	0.20
	5	10	0.20
	6	8	0.16
Outstanding	7	2	0.04
	Sum	50	1.00

The population of "scores" on a categorical variable can be described either by the set of frequencies for the several levels or by the set of proportions. We'll refer to these as *population frequencies* and *population proportions*. Frequencies are most useful when the population is small. Proportions have the advantage when the population is large or when we want to compare different-size populations.

When the categories are ordered, we can take this into account in reporting frequencies or proportions. Thus, from the table above we might say, "Twenty of the pies earned ratings of 5 or higher," or, "Forty percent (corresponding to a proportion of 0.40) of the pies were rated below 4." These are *cumulative frequencies* or *cumulative percentages*.

15.1.2   Nominal Categories: Nonorderable-response Alternatives

Not all sets of categories can be ordered. For example, these three outcomes characterize the responses possible in a taste test study: "Chose Coca-Cola," "Chose Pepsi-Cola," and "Chose Royal Crown Cola." The three levels of the categorical response correspond to distinguishable but nonorderable choices. That is, there is no obvious single dimension along which the three choices can be arranged, one between the other two.

The categorical response in this instance—choice of cola drink—is an example of a *nominal categorical variable*. The three "levels" are given distinctive "names." Those names, though, don't provide information about the arrangement of the categories.

We describe a population of nominal "scores" as we do a population of ordered "scores," with the frequencies or proportions of observations falling at each of the several levels. As there is no ordering of levels or categories, we do not usually accumulate proportions or frequencies across categories.

The proportions falling at the three levels of Choice of Cola in a population of university undergraduates might be something like

Category	Proportion (p)
Chose Coca-Cola	0.35
Chose Pepsi-Cola	0.45
Chose Royal Crown	0.20

The population is large, so we omit reference to the frequencies.

15.1.3   Dichotomies: Only Two Response Alternatives

We single out for special attention the categorical variable with only two levels. We refer to it as a *dichotomous variable*. What makes the dichotomous response special is that, having only two levels, an observation not falling into one level must fall into the other. As a result, we can "name" one level as the "opposite" of the other.

Some examples make the point. Three months into a course of treatment with an experimental drug, patients are rated as Improved or Not Improved. New Business Starts are assessed at the end of two years as Still in Business or No Longer in Business. After viewing a campaign video, potential voters describe themselves as More Favorable to the Candidate or No More Favorable to the Candidate.

In the categorical response population, the sum of the proportions over the category levels is a constant, 1.0. If there are only two levels, A and B, we have

$$p(\text{Level A}) + p(\text{Level B}) = 1.0$$

or

$$p(\text{Level B}) = 1.0 - p(\text{Level A})$$

or

$$p(\text{Level A}) = 1.0 - p(\text{Level B}).$$

If we know one of the proportions, we know the other one as well. If 75% of the patients Improved, we know that 25% were Not Improved. If the proportion of new enterprises Still in Business after two years is 0.40, then the proportion No Longer in Business must be 0.60.

The dichotomous response population can be characterized by a single number, *one of the two proportions*. As a shorthand, we can think of the two categories as Success and Failure and take p(success) as this key parameter of the population.

15.2
Certainty and the Categorical Response

Our goal in modeling is to express how, and to what extent the response variable is influenced by one or more explanatory variables. We early equated the idea of influence with an *increase in our certainty* about the "value" of the response. How can we use these same ideas of influence and certainty when the response is categorical rather than measured? Before answering that, let's review how we viewed certainty for the measured response.

15.2.1   Review: Certainty and the Measured Response

For the measured response, certainty and increase in certainty were tied up with the idea of *conditional response populations*. The conditional response population is the set of response scores for a population of potential respondents all of whom have the same pattern of scores on the explanatory variables in our model. It is a population of response scores, conditional upon that pattern of scores.

Each of these conditional, measured-response populations is characterized by a *mean* and a *variance*. The first tells us the size of score that is "typical" in that population while the second tells us how widely spread out around that typical value the scores in that population are. The smaller the variance, the more closely packed are the scores about the mean.

We said that an explanatory variable influenced or explained a measured response if the means of the conditional populations differed, that is, if we would make different predictions of the response for different patterns of x-variable scores. Or, to put it in the negative, if we were to predict the same value of y for each x score or each x-score pattern, those x scores would neither explain nor influence the y scores.

In comparing the fit of one model with that of another where the two are in a fuller/less full relation, we ask whether the fuller model, with its larger number of parameters, defines conditional response populations with smaller variances than do the conditional response populations defined by the less full model. We prefer the fuller model if it has a smaller conditional response variance. Prediction of the y-variable is more certain, then, than under the less full model.

15.2.2   Certainty and the Categorical Response: Proportions

The idea of conditional response populations will be just as useful with the categorical response as it has been with the measured one. We do need, however, a different way of characterizing these populations. They are not naturally characterized by means and variances.

Categorical response populations are characterized, rather, by *sets of proportions*. Thus, a conditional response population is described by the proportions at the different levels of the response when our model's x-variables take a particular set of values. As with the measured response, there will be a separate, albeit often hypothetical, conditional response population—a separate set of response proportions— for each explanatory score pattern of interest to us.

In modeling the measured response, we sought increased certainty about the response mean. An explanatory variable "explained" that response if there were differences among the response means, depending on the value of that explanatory variable. This idea generalizes to our categorical response variables. We will say that an explanatory variable "explains" a categorical response variable if the proportions at the several response levels are different, depending upon the explanatory variable score. If the explanatory variable does not influence the categorical response, the sets of proportions are the same in each conditional response population. We illustrate this idea in the following paragraphs.

Certainty and the Nominal Response

The response populations for a nominal response can be described by diagrams such as those making up Figure 15.1. In the upper-left panel is an aggregated-population description, reporting the proportions of voters in (mythical) Metropolitan Area Alpha who describe themselves as Democrats (D), Republicans (R), and Independents (I). It is a categorical analog to what we described earlier for observational studies as an unconditional population.

The three other panels show these political-party affiliation proportions broken down by or *conditional* upon educational background. In the upper-right corner is the display for voters with no more than a High-school education; in the lower left are the proportions at the three levels for those with at least some Undergraduate university or college education; and, in the lower right, we have the population of responses conditional upon an Advanced degree.

Because these are proportions displayed in the graphs, all four are conveniently made the same general size. Had we displayed frequencies, the graph in the lower right (for Advanced-degree holders) would be smaller than that in the lower left (for some college) which, in turn, would be smaller than that in the upper right (for voters with no more than a High-school education).

As a result of the disparate sizes of the three conditional populations, the unconditional- or aggregated-proportion graph (upper left) most closely resembles the conditional-proportion graph for the largest subpopulation, that in the upper right of Figure 15.1.

What Figure 15.1 illustrates is that political party preference is influenced by amount of education. The three conditional response graphs have different shapes.

Certainty and the Ordered Response

Everything we just said about Nominal response populations can be said as well for Ordered response populations. Because the several categories are ordered, though, we can characterize these populations in additional ways. Figure 15.2 gives proportion graphs for an aggregated or unconditional population of Supervisors Ratings of apprentice programmers as well as for the three contributing subpopulations, each conditional upon the year in which ratings were made. Supervisors rated the programmers' performances as Poor, Fair, Good, Very Good, or Excellent, and these five ordered levels of response are presented, left to right, in the four graphs.

The proportions conditional on the years 1985, 1986, and 1987 are presented in the upper-right, lower-left, and lower-right panels, respectively. The aggregated proportions, upper left in Figure 15.2, represents a pooling of the three conditional populations.

The proportions at the several levels changed over the years. Overall, the later-trained programmers received higher ratings.

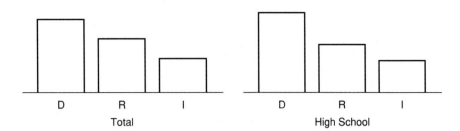

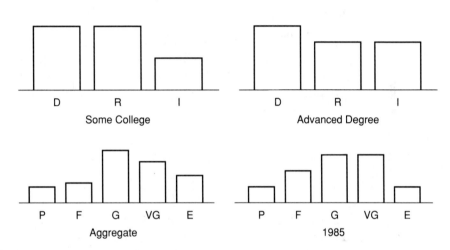

FIGURE 15.1
Aggregate and Conditional Proportions: Political Party Preference and Education
(D = Democrat, R = Republican, I = Independent)

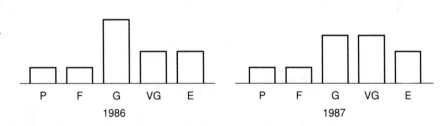

FIGURE 15.2
Conditional Proportions: Supervisors' Ratings and Year of Rating
(P = Poor, F = Fair, G = Good, VG = Very Good, E = Excellent)

Certainty and the Dichotomous Response

The dichotomous response variable has only two "levels." Each population is completely described by the proportions at each of those two levels. In fact, since the two proportions must sum to 1.00, each population is completely described by the proportion at one of the levels—the proportion at the other level being the difference between that and 1.0.

15.3
Modeling and the Categorical Response

We have just seen that the relevant property of categorical response populations is the proportions of observations falling into the different, alternative categories. *If these proportions shift* as we move from score to score or level to level of an explanatory variable, that variable is said to have an influence on our categorical response.

15.3.1   Proportions or Frequencies Expected for a Model

Our explanatory models for measured response variables gave us *estimates* of the conditional means (and variances) for the response. The explanatory models we develop for categorical variables will give us estimates of the proportions or frequencies (for fixed sample sizes) to be expected at the several response levels, again *conditional* on the values of our model's explanatory variables.

15.3.2   Assessing the Fit of a Model to the Observed Frequencies

To help us assess how good our explanatory model for a measured response is, we've learned to use a measure of agreement between the response values that actually occurred in our sample and the corresponding *fitted values*, conditional means estimated from our model. The *residual* is the difference between the two, and the *sum of squares of these residuals* provides our basic measure of how well the model "fits" the data. The larger the sum of squares, the poorer the fit.

In the same way, for our categorical response models, we will compare the observed frequencies in our sample with those *frequencies "expected" under the model*. The closer the agreement, the better the model.

15.3.3   Comparing the Fits of Two or More Models

The ideas of fuller and less full models developed earlier apply to models for categorical responses as well. As a result, we can *compare the fits* of two models to a set of observations and use this comparison as a basis for choosing one over the other.

The same ideas direct these comparisons. We seek to test hypotheses that can be expressed as a comparison between a pair of models or we seek to simplify an existing model, *searching for parsimony* in our explanation.

15.4
A Uniform Approach to Categorical Modeling

In the three chapters following, we develop a uniform approach to the explanatory modeling of the three types of categorical response: dichotomies, ordered categories, and nominal categories.

We begin with models for the response that takes only two values, the dichotomous response. Our approach to modeling the dichotomous response is called *logistic regression*. As we'll see in Chapters 16 and 17, this approach is very closely related to the linear-regression model we have been using for measured responses.

In Chapter 18, we extend logistic regression first to the *ordered* categorical response and then to the *nominal* response variable. An important advantage of the logistic regression approach is that it gives us the same range of model formulation and comparison tools that were developed for the measured response. Our models can include one or more measured, or categorical, influences or a combination of them. Our models may hypothesize interactions or moderating influences, and we can make use of the valuable tool of modular modeling.

In developing models for the categorical response, we will continue to stress the importance of interpretable model parameters and estimates. The most interpretable parameters for logistic regression and related models are those associated with *multiplicative models*. We will focus on the amount by which a "unit increase in an explanatory variable *multiplies the odds of success*."

15.5
Summary

This is a transitional chapter. We have completed our study of modeling strategies for the measured response. In Chapters 16 through 18, we see how essentially all of that strategy can be used when the potential responses are not along a scale of measurement but consist of a set of categories. In developing models for such categorical responses, we will be guided by whether those categories are ordered or simply distinctive and by the number of categories over which the response is distributed.

16

Logistic Regression: Modeling The Proportion of Successes

In this and the following chapter, we see how we can use what we have learned about modeling the multiple-valued, measured response to model the response that takes but two values. Such dichotomous responses are common. Therapy may be judged Successful or Not. Training may result in Improved or Unimproved performance. A particular anatomical feature may be Present in or Absent from sampled animal specimens.

However the two outcomes are labeled, it is important to learn what is associated with an *increased proportion* of the one and, consequently, a decreased proportion of the other. Does the proportion of therapeutic Successes increase with therapist's experience? Is training-group size important in determining the relative number of workers whose performance will be Improved by training? What is the impact of environmental aridity on the presence of enlarged bladders in a particular species?

This chapter and the next introduce a common procedure for modeling the dichotomous response variable. *Logistic regression* has very much in common with our linear regression modeling in that explanatory variables for logistic regression models can be measured, categorical, a mixture of the two, and can even include products and powers of other x-variables.

16.1
Simple Linear Regression: A Review

Because our approach to modeling the dichotomous response has so much in common with our modeling of the measured response, it will help us to review, briefly, some linear regression ideas. Though the ideas generalize, we'll assume for the review a linear model with just one x-variable.

16.1.1 Conditional Response Population Characteristics

Our simple (one x) linear regression model assumes that for each distinct x score there is a corresponding population of potentially observable scores on the measured response. We refer to these populations as *conditional response populations*. Each of these populations is assumed to have a common variance, $\sigma^2(y\,|\,x)$, the *conditional response variance*, and to have a histogram with Normal characteristics.

16.1.2   Sampling From Conditional Response Populations

For any particular study, observational or experimental, the collection of unique x scores or design points identifies a set of conditional response populations from which we sample. Our linear regression *estimation* and *inference* tactics assume that when we sample from these populations we do so *independently*. The response observations do not influence one another. Usually, we guarantee this by selecting respondents at random and, in the experimental case, assigning them at random among treatments.

16.1.3   The Linear Model

The several *design points* are linked to the conditional response populations by a *linear model*. Briefly stated, the linear model postulates that the means of these conditional populations are given by a linear function of the x scores. We may write this relation as

$$\mu(y\,|\,x = x_i) = \beta_0 + \beta_1 x_i \qquad \textbf{(16.1)}$$

and illustrate it as in Figure 16.1.

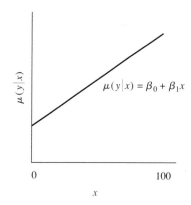

F I G U R E 16.1
The Linear Ex-
planatory Model

16.2
The Dichotomous Response: Censored Measurement

We are now ready to take all we know about the linear model for the measured response and use it to describe our approach to modeling the *dichotomous* response.

16.2.1   Censoring the Observed Measured Response

Let's assume that when we sample from any one of the conditional response populations (still for the Normal, constant variance, measured response) we don't actually see a measured score. Instead, the measured score is first *"censored."* This censoring involves a *critical value,* y_C, of the measured variable and produces a dichotomized response.

That is, if when we sample from one of the conditional measured response populations a value greater than y_C is selected, we observe only a *success,* one of two levels of the dichotomous response. All successes look alike to us. We do not observe the magnitude of the measured y. The occurrence of a success tells us only that the magnitude of the sampled response was greater than the critical value.

On the other hand, if the value of the measured score that is sampled falls at or below y_C, we observe a *failure.* Again, all failures look alike to us and tell us only that the magnitude of the underlying measured variable was not great enough to result in a success.

Success and failure are just *generic* names for the two levels of a dichotomous variable. Depending on the study, we may have, instead, Improved/Unimproved, Survived/Did Not Survive, Favors Candidate A/Does Not Favor Candidate A, Nests Above Timberline/Nests Below Timberline, or any *two-point classification.* When we think of these as censored observations, we have in mind some underlying attribute that is measurable, but perhaps only theoretically.

16.2.2   Characteristics of Censored Response Populations

We observe only successes and failures when our sampled observations from the measured y are censored in the way described. As a result, it is as if the conditional response populations consisted only of successes and failures. How can we describe such *conditional response populations?*

In Chapter 15, we noted that the dichotomous-response population could be described by a single parameter, the *proportion* of observations in the population that are at one of the two possible levels. Our *conditional response populations* made up of successes and failures are described by the *proportions of successes* in each. We express this as

$$p(\text{success} \mid x = x_i),$$

the proportion of successes when the explanatory variable takes the value x_i. This proportion can range from 0 (there are no successes in the conditional response population) to 1 (the response population consists entirely of successes).

16.2.3   Linear Regression and the Censored Response

Now, let's remember the *linear* part of our explanatory model and see what happens to it as the measured y is censored to a dichotomy. Let's assume that the explanatory relation is positive (the slope parameter, β_1, is positive). As Figure 16.1 depicts, the mean of y increases steadily as the value of x increases.

Conditional Proportions of Success

By assumption, the histograms for the conditional measured response populations all have the same size and shape. They all have the same "Normal" shape and their sizes are the same because they have the same variance. The histograms for the conditional response populations differ only in their *means*.

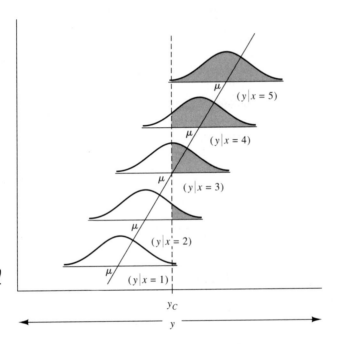

FIGURE 16.2

Censoring in the Conditional Response Populations

Figure 16.2 depicts the idealized histograms (Normal Curves) for a number of conditional response populations. Each summarizes a population of y scores for a particular value of x. In the figure, a histogram is shown for $x = 1, 2, 3, 4$, and 5. The five histograms are of the same size and shape, but each is centered over a different range of y scores. This is because the mean of the conditional response population increases with the value of the explanatory variable. The mean is indicated by a "μ" along the baseline of each histogram.

The area of each histogram corresponds to the totality of each conditional population. We think of each as having an area of one unit. At the bottom of Figure 16.2 is a y-variable scale. A vertical line drawn upwards from this scale will bisect each of the conditional histograms, dividing the area of each into two parts. The two parts have the following interpretation. The area to the left of the bisecting line is the proportion of observations in the conditional population having y scores at or below that value on the y scale at its intersection with the vertical line. The area to the right of the bisecting line is the proportion of observations in the conditional response population with y scores above the line's intersecting value on the y scale.

Now, we take the vertical line in Figure 16.2 as originating at the critical value, y_C, of the measured-response variable. The areas to the right in the five histograms correspond, then, to the *proportions of successes* in the five conditional response populations. The areas to the left of the line, similarly, reflect the proportions of failures. Figure 16.2 shows that as the mean of the measured response increases, as we move from $x = 1$ to $x = 5$, the proportion of successes also increases. An increasing proportion of observations is above the critical value.

Regression Curve: The Cumulative Normal Function

We are interested in how the proportion of successes increases as the value of x increases. The situation we are interested in is the one in which the *conditional mean* of the measured y is a *linear function* of the value of the measured x. When that is true, the proportion of successes in the conditional response population will be related to the value of x as shown in Figure 16.3.

The relation between $x = x_i$ and $p(\text{success} \mid x = x_i)$ is clearly *nonlinear*. The shape is *sigmoidal* ("S shaped"). The proportion of successes may change fairly rapidly in the middle of the x scale, but it approaches its lower and upper limits of 0 and 1 only very slowly.

16.3
Logistic Regression: An Introduction

Logistic regression provides a way of modeling the explanatory relation described by Figure 16.3. That relation is of interest to us, remember, because it represents the *usual linear regression model* except that the measured response has been *censored to provide only successes and failures.*

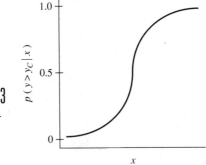

FIGURE 16.3
Relation of Proportion of Successes to Explanatory-variable Score

16.3.1   Straightening the Sigmoid

Logistic regression can be thought of as based on a *transformation of the proportion of successes*, a transformation that tends to *linearize* the relation between the transformed proportion and the *x*-variable.

Odds of Success   We have let the proportion of successes in a conditional response population be represented as $p(\text{success} \mid x = x_i)$. The proportion of failures in that same population can be expressed as

$$p(\text{failure} \mid x = x_i) = 1 - p(\text{success} \mid x = x_i). \tag{16.2}$$

Now, the *odds in favor of our observing a success* when we sample randomly from this response population are defined as the ratio of the proportions of successes and failures in that population:

$$\text{odds}(\text{success} \mid x = x_i) = \frac{p(\text{success} \mid x = x_i)}{1 - p(\text{success} \mid x = x_i)}. \tag{16.3}$$

For example, if the proportion of successes in a population is 0.75 and the proportion of failures is $(1 - 0.75) = 0.25$, then the odds in favor of observing a success when we sample once randomly from that population are

$$\text{odds}(\text{success}) = \frac{0.75}{0.25} = \frac{3}{1} = 3.$$

There are three times as many successes as failures in the population, so there are three chances that we will draw a success to every one that we will draw a failure. We say the odds in favor of success are "3 to 1" or 3/1.

If $p(\text{success})$ is greater than 0.50, then odds(success) will be greater than 1.0. If $p(\text{success})$ is smaller than 0.50 (failure is more common than success) odds(success) will be less than 1.0, but *never negative*.

Log-odds: Logarithm of Odds of Success

If we now take the *natural logarithm* of the odds, the result is called the "log-odds" of success:

$$\text{log-odds}(\text{success} \mid x = x_i) = \log_e[\text{odds}(\text{success} \mid x = x_i)]$$
$$= \log_e\left(\frac{p(\text{success} \mid x = x_i)}{1 - p(\text{success} \mid x = x_i)}\right). \tag{16.4}$$

The log-odds will be *positive* for odds greater than 1/1 (or for $p[\text{success}]$ greater than 0.50) and *negative* for odds less than 1/1 (or for $p[\text{success}]$ less than $p[\text{failure}]$). The log-odds will be 0.0 for odds of 1/1.

The log-odds of success also is known as the *logit transformation* of the proportion of successes.

The Logistic Function

The logit transformation of proportion of successes given by Equation [16.4] is such that the log-odds of success is very nearly a *linear function* of x whenever the proportion of successes is nonlinearly related to x in the way described by Figure 16.3.

That is, when a measured y is linearly influenced by x,

$$\mu(y \mid x = x_i) = \beta_0 + \beta_1 x_i, \tag{16.1}$$

but observation of y is censored so that only successes and failures are observed, the logit transformation of the proportion of successes will also be a *linear function* of that same x:

$$\text{log-odds}(\text{success} \mid x = x_i) = \alpha_0 + \alpha_1 x_i. \tag{16.5}$$

When the log-odds(success) is expressed in this way, as a linear function of one or more xs, it is described as a *linear logistic* (or simply *logistic*) function of the x-variables.

We have used αs as the intercept and slope parameters in the logistic function of Equation [16.5] to emphasize that they are numerically distinct from the βs in the related linear regression equation. If we were able to estimate the βs of the linear model (which would require that we observe an *uncensored* sample of the measured y), then $\widehat{\beta}_1$ would estimate the rate of increase (per unit of the x) in the mean of that measured y. By contrast, the estimated slope parameter of the logistic function estimates the *rate of increase* (again, per unit of x) *in the log-odds of success*.

Because we cannot observe the measured y, but only its censored form, we will have no further need to refer to the linear regression model. No confusion will arise, then, if we use ys and βs in the logistic function, rewriting Equation [16.5] as

$$\text{log-odds}(y_i = \text{success} \mid x = x_i) = \beta_0 + \beta_1 x_i. \tag{16.6}$$

Equation [16.6] is very important. It permits us, in this and the following chapters, to develop, assess, and compare *explanatory* models for the dichotomous response, now represented by the variable y, in the same way that we can for the measured response.

The results of this section hold as well for *multiple x-variable models*. That is, where the mean on the left of Equation [16.1] is a linear function of more than one explanatory variable and the response is observed only in a censored form, there is a corresponding logistic function of the form of Equation [16.6], linear in those same x-variables and expressing the influence of those on the log-odds of success.

16.4
Logistic Regression Models

In this section, we preview the range of models for the dichotomous y to which we can apply the logistic function. We'll refer to these as *logistic regression* models.

16.4.1   Simple Logistic Regression

The logistic function of Equation [16.6] describes a simple logistic regression model. The log-odds of success are postulated to be a linear function of a *single* explanatory variable.

For example, we might want to model the influence of age on criminal recidivism among males. We could take as our x-variable Age at First Felony Conviction and define success as No Second Felony Conviction (within 10 Years following this initial conviction). That leads to the logistic model:

log-odds(*No Second Conviction*) $= \beta_0 + \beta_1$(*Age at First Conviction*).

The slope parameter in our model should be *positive* if the rate of recidivism *decreases* with age.

16.4.2   Logistic Regression with Multiple Explanatory Variables

We developed the log-odds transformation of p(success) in the context of a single x-variable. But the ideas generalize to the dichotomous observation linearly influenced by more than one source of influence. If the mean of a measured, Normal, constant variance response is a linear function of more than one x-variable,

$$\mu(y \mid X) = \beta_0 + \sum_{j=1}^{k-1}(\beta_j x_{ij}),$$

and if observation of this y-variable is censored, yielding only successes and failures, then the log-odds of success will also be a linear function of those same x-variables:

$$\text{log-odds(success} \mid X) = \beta_0 + \sum_{j=1}^{k-1}(\beta_j x_{ij}). \qquad \textbf{(16.7)}$$

Because the log-odds may be modeled as a linear function of more than one explanatory variable, we have the same range of design possibilities for the dichotomous response that we had for the measured response.

Let's review some of those possibilities.

Single Categorical Explanatory Variable

As a first example of a multiple-x logistic regression model, let's assume that we are interested in the influence of Blood Type (A, B, AB, or O) on the success of an anticoagulant drug. Four hours after drug administration, a sample of blood is drawn from each participant. If the blood clots within three minutes, a drug "failure" is recorded. If No Clotting occurs within three minutes, a "success" is noted.

Our source of influence in this study is a categorical one, blood type. We can represent the levels of this categorical variable in a linear logistic model in the same way we did for a linear regression model. That is, we can code levels of the variable with dummy or effect coded variables.

If we use dummy variables to code all levels, we omit the intercept term in the model, giving us a logistic model that looks like this:

$$\text{log-odds}(No\ Clotting \mid Blood\ Type) = \beta_1 A_i + \beta_2 B_i + \beta_3 AB_i + \beta_4 O_i.$$

Here, if the *i*th study participant has type A blood, A_i takes the value 1; otherwise, A_i takes the value 0. Similar definitions hold for the other *x*-variables in this model, B, AB, and O. For each observation, one and only one of the four *x*s takes a value of 1; all others are 0. As a result, β_1, β_2, β_3, and β_4 are the log-odds of No Clotting for blood types A, B, AB, and O, respectively. We would be interested in whether the values of these four linear logistic parameters are the same or different.

Multiple Measured Explanatory Variables

As a second example, we might model Completion of Apprentice Training ("success" v. the noncompletion "failure") as a function of trainees' Ages and Years of Formal Education, two measured *x*-variables. An additive logistic model for the two follows:

$$\text{log-odds}(Completion \mid Age,\ Education) = \beta_0 + \beta_1\ Age + \beta_2\ Years\ Education.$$

Do either or both *x*-variables influence the proportion of apprentices who complete training?

Additional Designs

More complicated linear logistic models are possible if we include powers or products of *x*s in the model. All of the power and other transformations of *x*s—interactions, separate regressions, and moderations of influence—that we developed for the measured response are available for modeling the influence on a dichotomous response.

In this next example, we model, separately for male and female voters, the influence of Number of Siblings (brothers and sisters) on their intent to vote Yes (v. No) on a ballot issue increasing local school funding:

$$\text{log-odds}(Yes \mid Sex,\ Number\ Sibs) = \beta_1 x_{i1} + \beta_2 x_{i2} + \beta_3 x_{i3} + \beta_4 x_{i4},$$

where $x_1 = (0,\ \text{Males};\ 1,\ \text{Females})$, $x_2 = (0,\ \text{Females};\ 1,\ \text{Males})$, $x_3 = (0,\ \text{Males};\ \text{Number Sibs, Females})$, and $x_4 = (0,\ \text{Females};\ \text{Number Sibs, Males})$.

What would it mean for the female slope, β_3, to be greater than the male slope, β_4? What would a comparison of the two intercepts, β_1 and β_2, tell us?

16.4.3 Fuller and Less Full Models

We want, of course, not only to pose models but to make *comparisons* among them. We want to find the better among *alternative models*.

Because the range of models for logistic regression is as it was for linear regression, it may not be surprising that these models are interrelated in the same ways as well. In particular, the same "rules" that established a *fuller/less full* relation between two linear models work in the same way for logistic models.

Thus, the four-parameter logistic model just given above is fuller, relative to this three-parameter model:

$$\text{log-odds}(\textit{Yes} \mid \textit{Sex, Number Sibs}) = \beta_1 x_{i1} + \beta_2 x_{i2} + \beta_3 (x_{i3} + x_{i4}).$$

This less full model postulates different intercepts for male and female voters, but the *same slope*.

In the sections following, as we discuss estimating the logistic model parameters and determining how well a model fits a sample of observations, we'll compare fuller and less full models.

16.5
Fitting the Logistic Regression Model

Like the linear model for a measured response, the linear logistic model is expressed in terms of a set of *population parameters*, the βs of

$$\text{log-odds} \ (\textit{success} \mid X) = \beta_0 + \sum_{j=1}^{k-1} (\beta_j x_{ij}). \tag{16.8}$$

For linear logistic models to be useful, we must have some way of (1) *estimating* these k unknown parameters from a sample of observed successes and failures, (2) *assessing the fit* of the resulting estimated model to our data, (3) *comparing the fits* of two or more models, and (4) *inferring* the strength of explanatory influences in the populations sampled. These are the same tasks we faced for linear regression.

16.5.1   Modeled Frequencies of Successes and Failures

Our logistic models talk about the proportion of successes, the odds of success, and the log-odds of success in conditional populations. When we sample from such populations, the result is a finite number—often small—of successes and failures. We have to judge the "goodness" of a logistic model by its ability to "account for" the *observed successes and failures* that make up the sample.

Design Points

Our study—experimental or observational—causes us to sample, by design or otherwise, from each of several different conditional populations of successes and failures. Each distinct pattern of x scores included in our sample design, each design point, defines a *conditional response population*.

Expected Success Proportions

At each design point, our sample includes one or more observed successes and/or failures. For each design point, a logistic model will *estimate*—via the log-odds—the proportions of successes and failures in the corresponding conditional population. These estimated proportions, given a model, also are called *fitted* or *modeled* proportions.

It is the correspondence between the modeled success frequencies and the actual frequencies of successes (and failures) in the sample that determines how well the model fits the sampled data.

16.5.2 Logistic Regression in Statistical Packages

The logistic regression solution, unlike that for linear regression, cannot be described in terms of simple descriptive statistical computations. We must rely on a logistic regression command, now almost standard in statistical packages. In this section, we say a bit about the assumptions underlying the logistic regression estimates.

Three Assumptions: Independence, Dichotomy, and Linearity

Logistic regression parameter estimates and our interpretation of them are grounded in three assumptions about the sample of observations:

1 The N-sample observations are independent of one another. As with our linear models, we can assure this if we have randomly sampled from our populations of successes and failures.

2 Each sampled observation is from a population consisting only of a fairly large number of successes and a fairly large number of failures. This statement is really based on three assumptions:
   - Each population includes only successes and failures; there is no "third" or other possibility.
   - Each population includes some successes and some failures.
   - Each population is large enough that, when we sample one or more times from it, we do not change the proportions of successes and failures perceptibly in that population.

3 The log-odds of success is a linear function of the explanatory variables in the model.

The first and third assumptions are familiar from linear modeling. The second assumption plays the same role here as the linear model assumptions of conditional response variance constancy and Normality.

For the linear model, our conditional response populations differ only in their means—not in their variances nor in their histogram "shapes." For the logistic model, our conditional response populations differ only in their proportions of success.

An Iterative Fitting Approach

The numerical task of estimating the logistic model parameters is more difficult than that of estimating the linear model parameters. The linear parameters can be estimated directly, that is, we can write down formulae for their computation, even though we pass these formulae on to the computer for the actual computations. There are no comparable formulae for the logistic model parameters. They are *estimated iteratively.* This means we (actually, the computer again) start with some estimate of the βs, see how well the log-odds based on these estimates—via the logistic function—fit the observations, adjust the βs on this lack of fit, assess the fit of the new estimates, and continue in this way until we can't improve our estimates.

We clearly need a computer routine to keep track of the computing. Most statistical packages include a logistic regression command with a syntax resembling that of SPIDA's that will be used in our examples.

The 0/1 Response

To determine how well, at each stage, the logistic model parameter estimates fit our observations, it is convenient that the observed successes and failures be given numeric coding. The convention adopted by most logistic regression programs is to code each success as a 1 and each failure as a 0.

We'll use this convention throughout this and the next chapter in describing the fitting and comparing of logistic regression models. We'll see in Section 16.7 how the choice of a 0/1 scoring helps us assess the goodness of fit of a logistic model to our failure/success observations.

16.6
An Example: Law School Grades and Bar Examination Performance

Let's see now what a logistic regression problem and its computational solution look like. Our example is based on a study by Lee (1974), however, we have renamed the variables and taken the study out of Lee's medical setting.

16.6.1 Description of Data

The examination for admission to the Bar in State A included for the first time in 1986 a separately graded Ethics section. Overall, fewer than 30% of the candidates writing the Bar examination passed the Ethics section.

The law faculty at the University of A was interested in how the performance of students in that school's Professional Conduct course might explain passing or failing of the Ethics examination. Table 16.1 presents data for a random sample of 27 students who completed the course before writing the Bar examination.

T A B L E 16.1

Professional Conduct Course Grades and Ethics Examination Performance

Course Grade	Ethics Examination
70	Fail
70	Fail
72	Fail
72	Fail
74	Fail
74	Fail
74	Fail
76	Fail
76	Fail
76	Fail
78	Fail
78	Fail
78	Fail
80	Pass
82	Fail
82	Pass
82	Pass
84	Fail
84	Pass
86	Fail
88	Pass
90	Pass
94	Fail
96	Pass
100	Fail
100	Pass
100	Pass

Overall, 9 of the 27 candidates passed the Ethics examination. The tabled entries suggest that passing the examination may be associated with higher grades in the Professional Conduct course.

16.6.2 Modeling Goals

The study involves a single measured x-variable, Course Grade, and we are interested in whether and how that variable might influence the odds of Passing the Ethics examination. In particular, we are interested in three logistic models.

1 The Null Model.

$$\text{log-odds}(Passing) = \beta_0$$

The log-odds of Passing do not depend on Course Grade.

2   The Linear Model.

$$\text{log-odds}(Passing) = \beta_0 + \beta_1(Course\ Grade)$$

The log-odds of Passing is a linear function of Course Grade.

3   The Quadratic Model.

$$\text{log-odds}(Passing) = \beta_0 + \beta_1(Course\ Grade) + \beta_2(Course\ Grade^2)$$

The log-odds of Passing is influenced by Course Grade, but nonlinearly.

We could, of course, investigate nonlinear functions other than the quadratic one, if we have reason based on substantive theory or on sample diagnostic evidence to choose a particular nonlinear form. Here our interest is simply in determining whether a linear model is adequate and the comparison of the fits of linear and quadratic models will answer that question.

16.7
Assessing the Fit of a Logistic Regression Model

We have an overall index for determining the quality of our linear model for measured-response observations. It is based on the sum of squared differences between the response observations and the values "fit" to them by the linear model, the conditional means estimated from that model:

$$SSR = \sum_{i=1}^{N}[y_i - \widehat{\mu}(y \mid X)]^2 = \sum_{i=1}^{N}\widehat{\epsilon}_i^2.$$

We use this sum of squared residuals (SSR) to estimate the conditional response variance for the model. If the linear model has k parameters, the conditional response variance is estimated by

$$\widehat{\sigma}^2(y \mid X) = \frac{SSR}{N - k}.$$

This conditional response variance will be "small" if the linear model is good. It will be "large" if the model is a poor one.

A logistic regression model's fit to the observed failures (0s) and successes (1s) depends similarly on an index of the overall discrepancy between these observations and the model's "fit" to them.

16.7.1   Mean and Variance of a Population of 0s and 1s

Now that we have given numeric values to successes and failures, we can apply our earlier ideas about describing a population in terms of its mean and variance. What is the mean of a population of 0s and 1s? What will be its variance?

Below is a small set of 0s and 1s:

$$0, 1, 0, 1, 1, 1, 0, 1, 1, 0.$$

There are exactly six 1s and four 0s in this list. What is its mean? We add up the 10 numbers and divide that sum by 10. This gives us

Mean $= (0 + 1 + 0 + 1 + 1 + 1 + 0 + 1 + 1 + 0)/10 = 6/10 = 0.60.$

The mean of this set of 0/1 scores is the *proportion* of 1s in the list. Since it is the result of counting the number of 1s in the list, however long, and dividing that by the length of the list, this result will be true for any set of 0/1 scores.

In particular, this result is true for a *population* consisting of 0s and 1s. The mean of a 0/1 population is the proportion of 1s in the population, which we express this way:

$$\mu(0/1) = p(1). \qquad \textbf{(16.9)}$$

We interpret this equation as saying as well that if we have an estimate of the proportion of 1s (successes) we also have an estimate of the mean of the 0/1 population:

$$\hat{p}(1) = \hat{\mu}(0/1). \qquad \textbf{(16.10)}$$

The *variance* of a list of numbers is the mean of the squares of the differences between the numbers on the list and their mean. We subtract the mean of the list from each number, square the resulting differences, and then find the mean of those squared values. For the short list of 10 0/1 scores given above,

$$
\begin{aligned}
\text{Variance} &= (1/10)[(0 - 0.6)^2 + (1 - 0.6)^2 + (0 - 0.6)^2 + (1 - 0.6)^2 + (1 - 0.6)^2 \\
&\quad + (1 - 0.6)^2 + (0 - 0.6)^2 + (1 - 0.6)^2 + (1 - 0.6)^2 + (0 - 0.6)^2] \\
&= (1/10)[0.36 + 0.16 + 0.36 + 0.16 + 0.16 + 0.16 + 0.36 \\
&\quad + 0.16 + 0.16 + 0.36] \\
&= (1/10)[(4)(0.36) + (6)(0.16)] \\
&= [(0.4)(0.6)(0.6) + (0.6)(0.4)(0.4)] \\
&= [(0.6 + 0.4)(0.4)(0.6)] \\
&= [(1)(0.4)(0.6)] \\
&= [(1 - 0.6)(0.6)] = 0.24 \\
&= p(1)[1 - p(1)].
\end{aligned}
$$

The variance of a list of 0s and 1s is the product of the two proportions: Variance $= p(1)p(0)$. Again, this will be true even for "long" lists, populations of 0/1 scores:

$$\sigma^2(0/1) = p(1)[1 - p(1)].$$

16.7.2 Goodness of Fit Statistic: Deviance

We now have a way of talking about the estimated *mean* of a population of successes and failures.

Our overall *goodness of fit statistic* for the logistic model is called the *model Deviance*. It is based not on the squared differences between the response observations and their modeled means, but on their ratios.

First, we let $y_i = 1$, a success, and consider the ratio

$$\frac{y_i}{\hat{\mu}(y|x_i)} = \frac{1}{\hat{p}(1|x_i)}. \tag{16.11}$$

If the modeled proportion of successes, $\hat{p}(1|x_i)$, is close to 1, this ratio will also be close to 1. On the other hand, if the modeled proportion of successes is close to 0, this ratio will be considerably larger than 1. The ratio given by Equation [16.11] is close to 1 in value for a "well-fit" success and larger than 1 for a "poorly-fit" success.

Now, we let $y_i = 0$, a failure, and consider the ratio

$$\frac{1 - y_i}{1 - \hat{\mu}(y|x_i)} = \frac{1 - 0}{1 - \hat{p}(1|x_i)}. \tag{16.12}$$

If the modeled proportion of successes, $\hat{p}(1|x_i)$, is close to 0, this ratio will be close to 1. But, if the modeled proportion of successes is close to 1, this ratio will be considerably larger than 1. The ratio given by Equation [16.12] is close to 1 in value for a "well-fit" failure and larger than 1 for a "poorly-fit" failure.

Now, we can put together what we'd get for each success in our sample from Equation [16.11] with what we'd get for each failure from Equation [16.12] to obtain an overall assessment of the model's fit to the observed failures and successes. Let's start by simply adding all of the ratios together,

$$SR = \sum_{i=1}^{N_1} \frac{y_i}{\hat{\mu}(y \mid x_i)} + \sum_{i=1}^{N_0} \frac{1 - y_i}{1 - \hat{\mu}(y \mid x_i)}, \tag{16.13}$$

where the sample of N observations consists of N_1 successes and N_0 failures ($N = N_1 + N_0$).

This sum of ratios, SR, would be "close to N" if, overall, the N_1 successes and the N_0 failures were "well fit" by the logistic model. In contrast, SR would be "larger than N" if we had a poorly fitting logistic model.

Equation [16.14] can be converted into an equation with a single summation over all of the N sample observations by writing it in this form:

$$SR = \sum_{i=1}^{N} \left[y_i \left\{ \frac{y_i}{\hat{\mu}(y \mid x_i)} \right\} + (1 - y_i) \left\{ \frac{1 - y_i}{1 - \hat{\mu}(y \mid x_i)} \right\} \right]. \tag{16.14}$$

The first term in the summation enters in only if $y_i = 1$, and the second term only if $y_i = 0$. Equations [16.13] and [16.14] are identical, so long as y_i is either "0" or "1."

However, as with the F-ratio of earlier chapters, we'd like our goodness of fit statistic to have a sampling distribution that is simple, following the density function for a well understood, if hypothetical, random variable. If the ratios of the y_is to their estimated means are replaced in Equation [16.14] by the *natural logarithms* of those ratios, and if the resulting combined sums are multiplied by 2.0, the result,

$$Dev = 2 \left(\sum_{i=1}^{N_1} y_i \log \left[\frac{y_i}{\widehat{\mu}(y \mid x_i)} \right] + \sum_{i=1}^{N_0} (1 - y_i) \log \left[\frac{1 - y_i}{1 - \widehat{\mu}(y \mid x_i)} \right] \right), \qquad \textbf{(16.15)}$$

is termed the *Deviance*. For large samples the *Deviance* has a sampling distribution whose histogram is well matched by the probability density function of the Chi-squared random variable with degrees of freedom $(N - k)$, where N is the size of the sample and k is the number of β parameters in the logistic model.

When the logistic model is the correct model, repeated samples of N success/failure observations (always using the same set of design points) will produce a collection of *Dev* statistics whose histogram will "follow" this Chi-squared density function. The *Deviance* of Equation [16.15] is our goodness-of-fit statistic. It will take a small value when the model fits the observations well; it will be large when the model is a poor one. Replacing each ratio in Equation [16.13] with its logarithm does not destroy the logic; since the ratios are all 1.0 or larger, larger ratios give rise to larger logarithms.

Equation [16.15] can be simplified by replacing the y_is with explicit 1s and 0s, but we prefer to leave it in this form for consistency with later developments where the effective response observation is not 0 or 1, but a frequency of successes or of failures.

16.7.3   Deviance and Model Adequacy

For our linear regression models, each of the measured conditional response populations had two parameters, a mean, $\mu(y \mid x_i)$, and a variance, $\sigma^2(y \mid x)$. The size of this conditional response variance is usually not known to us. It can be large or small in absolute terms. This makes it difficult for us to tell from our model estimates of the conditional means alone whether we have a good model or not—the estimated conditional variance may be "large" either because the model is a poor one or because the y-variable we are trying to model has a large conditional variability, uninfluenced by any potential set of x-variables. We can judge our model only by comparing it with other models. Which one gives the smaller estimate of the conditional response variance?

By contrast, our 0/1 populations have only a single parameter; $p(1 \mid x_i)$ determines both the mean and the variance of the population. As a result, once we have estimates of these conditional $p(1 \mid x_i)$s for a logistic model, often we can tell, from the *Deviance* statistic, whether it is a "good" model or not. We need not compare it to other models. However, usually we want to because usually we will want to find, not just a good model, but the best among several alternatives.

The convention we will follow is that if the value of the *Deviance* statistic falls within the smallest 75% of the values making up the appropriate Chi-Squared probability distribution, it is a good model providing a good fit to the data. If the *Deviance* is larger, among the 25% that are the largest in the Chi-squared distribution, we say it does not provide a good fit. This good-fitting criterion is widely used for models with a categorical response; see, for example Forthofer & Lehnen (1979).

16.8
Comparing Logistic Regression Models

We have a way, then, of telling whether any particular model is a good one. What we want to do, as well, is to compare models and discover which is the better of two. Very much the same ideas that allowed comparisons among linear models are used with logistic models.

16.8.1   Deviance and the Fuller/Less Full Relation

First, the idea of a fuller/less full relation between models holds for logistic models exactly as it did for linear regression models. Assuming Model F is a $(k + q)$-parameter logistic model and Model L is a k-parameter model, following then the two stand in a fuller/less full relation to each other provided one of the statements is true.

- Model L is the result of constraining, linearly, the $k + q$ parameters of Model F. Examples: One Model-F parameter is constrained to be 0 (i.e., a Model-F x-variable is not present in Model L). Or, two Model-F parameters are constrained to be equal in value (i.e., two Model-F xs are hypothesized to have the same slopes).

- The k xs in Model L are all linear combinations of the $k + q$ x-variables in Model F. Examples: One or more Model-F x-variables are "dropped" (the remaining xs are each linear combinations of Model-F x-variables, being Model F xs themselves). Or, two Model-F xs are replaced by their sum in Model L (equivalent to constraining the two Model-F slope parameters to be equal).

Model F would be the fuller model, Model L the less full model. Each would have, for a particular sample of N success/failure observations, a *Deviance* as described in Section 16.7. The Model-F *Deviance* would be evaluated as an observation from a Chi-squared random variable with $(N - k - q)$ degrees of freedom, and the Model-L *Deviance* as one from a Chi-squared variable with $(N - k)$ degrees of freedom. It is possible that neither model would provide a "good" fit to the observations, in the sense of Section 16.7.

Where both are good (or adequate) we'd like to select the better of the two.

The *Deviance* for the less full model can be no smaller than the *Deviance* for the fuller model. A sensible result, the less full model with its fewer parameters cannot provide a better fit to the observations than the fuller one. The *Deviance difference*, the result of subtracting the fuller model *Deviance* from that for the less full model will always be a nonnegative quantity.

More importantly, the size of this *Deviance difference*,

$$Dev\ diff\,(Model\ F \mid Model\ L) = Dev(Model\ L) - Dev(Model\ F), \qquad \textbf{(16.16)}$$

can be used to compare the fits of the two models. The justification for it is this. If the less full model is the correct model, if it would be just as good as the fuller one when the true values of our logistic parameters are known, then "*Dev diff*" for a sample has a sampling distribution whose histogram is well described by the probability-density function for the Chi-squared random variable with q degrees of freedom, q being the difference in the number of parameters in the two models. Very large values of *Dev diff* are *unlikely* if the less full model really is the correct one. Very large values of *Dev diff* will lead us to prefer the fuller to the less full model. By very large we mean, typically, values that fall in the upper 5% or 1% of the Chi-squared distribution with q d.f.

16.8.2 Full, Intermediate, and Null Models

Again, as in linear modeling, we are likely to have for any substantive problem several models of interest. These can typically be arranged, though not always in a single hierarchy, from a fullest model (embracing all relevant x-variables), through several intermediate models, down to a null model, one that postulates that our success/failure ratios are not influenced by any of our explanatory variables.

Substantive questions and, to a lesser extent, our model estimates of parameters will suggest a number of comparisons to be made among these models. Typically, we begin with models of greater complexity—towards the fullest end—and seek less complexity, greater parsimony.

16.8.3 Results: Modeling the Bar Examination Example

For our Bar Examination study, we are interested in three models. Our fullest model is the three-parameter

Quadratic Model: $\text{log-odds}(Passing) = \beta_0 + \beta_1(Course\ Grade) + \beta_2(Course\ Grade^2)$.

The log-odds of Passing is influenced by Course Grade, but nonlinearly. There is one intermediate model called the

Linear Model: $\text{log-odds}(Passing\ Exam) = \beta_0 + \beta_1(Course\ Grade)$.

The log-odds of Passing is a linear function of Course Grade.
The final model is the

Null Model: $\text{log-odds}(Passing) = \beta_0$.

The odds of Passing do not depend upon Course Grade.

The fits to the quadratic, linear, and null models are given in Table 16.2 and the model *Deviance* and *Deviance differences* have been abstracted to Table 16.3.

Which model should we choose? The upper panel to Table 16.3 summarizes the fits. The quadratic and linear models each provide a good fit to the data; the p values listed for the *Deviances* are for the upper tail of the Chi-squared distributions and both are safely greater than 0.25 and, thus, in the lower 75% of the sampling distributions. The null model, on the other hand, fits poorly; the *Deviance* has a p value of only $0.13 < 0.25$.

T A B L E   **16.2**

Fits to Logistic Regression Models: Bar Examination Data

Quadratic Model

Response: Column	Column 2 Coeff	SE	P Value	Odds	0.95	CI	
0	−134.249	74.729	0.072				Constant
1	2.946	1.693	0.082	19.026	0.690	524.864	Linear
3	−0.016	0.010	0.093	0.984	0.966	1.003	Quadratic
d.f.: 24	Dev:22.224	%(0):66.667	#it:14				RSq: 0.353

Linear Model

Response: Column	Column 2 Coeff	SE	P Value	Odds	0.95	CI	
0	−12.758	4.992	0.011				Constant
1	0.145	0.059	0.015	1.156	1.029	1.298	Grades
d.f.:25	Dev:26.073	%(0):66.667	#it:9				RSq: 0.241

Null Model

Response: Column	Column 2 Coeff	SE	P Value	Odds	0.95	CI	
0	−0.693	0.408	0.09				Constant
d.f.:26	Dev:34.372	%(0):66.667	#it:8				RSq: 0

In the lower part of Table 16.3 are the *Deviance difference* model comparison statistics. The degrees of freedom associated with each model comparison are the difference in the numbers of parameters in the fuller and less full models. Large *Deviance differences* favor the fuller, more complex model. The *Deviance difference* of 3.85 between the Quadratic and Linear model fits is just large enough to fall within the upper 5% of the 1-d.f. Chi-Squared distribution. At the 5% level, we would prefer the (more complex) quadratic to the linear model; at the "more stringent" 1% level, we would prefer the (more parsimonious) linear model to the quadratic one.

T A B L E   **16.3**

Deviances and Deviance Differences: Models Fit to the Bar Examination Data

	Deviances		
Model	Deviance	Model d.f.	P Value
Quadratic	22.22	24	.5659
Linear	26.07	25	.4037
Null	34.37	26	.1259

	Model Comparisons		
Models Compared	Deviance Difference	d.f.	P Value
Quadratic-Linear	26.07 − 22.22 = 3.85	25−24 = 1	.0498
Linear-Null	34.37 − 26.07 = 8.30	26− 25 = 1	.0040
Quadratic-Null	34.37 − 22.22 = 12.15	26− 24 = 2	.0023

Had we occasion to compare either the quadratic or linear models with the null model, we should decide against the null model; both p values are well within the largest 1% of the relevant Chi-Squared distribution.

16.8.4   Interpreting the Selected Model

We should never choose our model solely on the basis of a statistical test—of the magnitude of the *Deviance difference* or the F-ratio. It is always a good idea to "have a look" at the model's fit and see if it makes sense or not. So, Figure 16.4 provides a look at the fit of the quadratic model. In the top half of the figure the fitted log-odds,

$$log \left\{ \frac{p(Passing)}{1 - p(Passing)} \right\},$$

are plotted against scores on the x-variable, Course Grade. In the bottom half, the fitted *p(Passing)* is plotted against Course Grades. Most logistic regression programs save the fits of models and they can be used in plots like this one.

We may be troubled at Figure 16.4 by the implications of our quadratic model. In the top part of the figure, the log-odds of Passing the exam increase over nearly the full range of Course Grades. At the upper end of the range of Course Grades, though, the log-odds of Passing the Bar exam *fall*. This reversal is more apparent in the lower part of the figure; the estimated probability of Passing the Bar exam decreases from a high of nearly 0.80 for a Course Grade of 94 to less than 0.60 for a Course Grade of 100.

We are likely to believe that, while the probability of Passing the Bar exam should never be 1.0, it should not drop with improving Course Grades. Our quadratic logistic regression model has been, perhaps, too sensitive in this small sample to a pair of Bar exam failures among students who earned relatively high Course Grades; as shown in Table 16.1, one student with a Course Grade of 94 and another with a grade of 100 failed the Ethics portion of the Bar exam.

Given (a) the substantive questionableness of the quadratic model's fit, (b) the closeness of the comparison between the linear and quadratic models (a p value only marginally less than .05), and (c) the adequacy of the linear model's fit to the observations (judged by the *Deviance* reported in Table 16.2), we might now prefer the more parsimonious Linear model. (We'll return to this example in the next chapter. To anticipate that, the quadratic model may not be the best nonlinear alternative. Indeed, in Chapter 10 it was described as the model of choice only when a response peak or valley is expected.)

The fit of the Linear model is depicted in Figure 16.5. In the top half of the figure is the plot of log-odds of Passing the Bar exam against Course Grades. This figure displays the linearity of the model,

$$\text{log-odds}(Passing) = \beta_0 + \beta_1(Course\ Grade). \tag{16.17}$$

In the lower part of Figure 16.5, the estimated probability of Passing the Bar exam is plotted against Course Grades. We see that the probability of Passing increases, across the range of Course Grades, reaching a high of 0.85 for a Course Grade of 100.

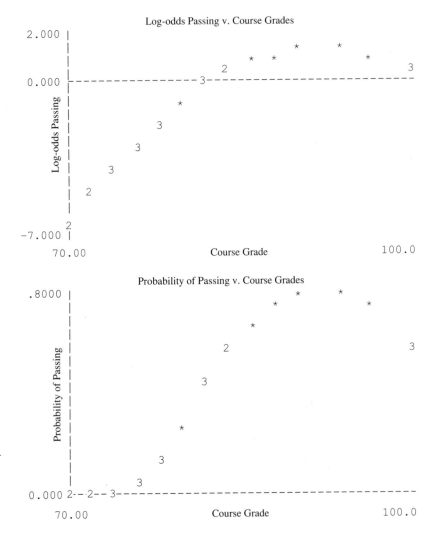

FIGURE 16.4

Fit of the Quadratic Model Relating Exam Success to Course Grades

The estimates of the two parameters for the linear model are given from Table 16.2 as

$$\widehat{\beta}_0 = -12.76 \quad \text{(with an SE of 4.99)} \tag{16.18}$$

and

$$\widehat{\beta}_1 = 0.145 \quad \text{(with an SE of 0.059).} \tag{16.19}$$

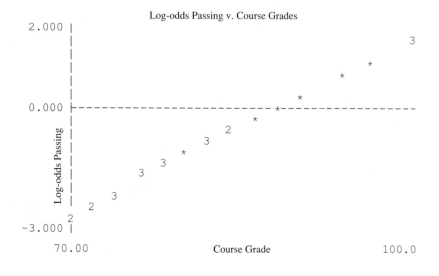

Log-odds Passing v. Course Grades

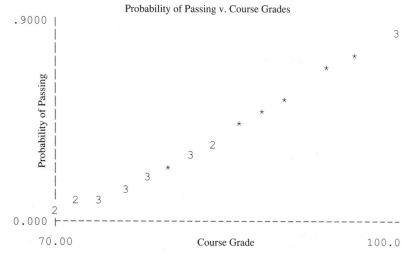

Probability of Passing v. Course Grades

FIGURE 16.5

Fit of the Linear Model Relating Exam Success to Course Grades

None of the Course Grades are in the vicinity of 0, so the estimated intercept has no natural interpretation. We can interpret the slope estimate in the usual form: An increase of one in the Course Grade is associated with an expected increase in the log-odds of Passing the Bar exam of about 0.14.

Unfortunately, the "*log-odds of Passing*" does not have the familiarity of the statements we were able to make about the influence on the measured y studied in earlier Chapters. It is hard for us to appreciate what a rate of increase of 0.14 per each x-variable unit actually means. Two things aid us, though, in understanding logistic regression models. First, we can "picture" the fit of a model as we have in Figures 16.4 to 16.5. Such plots, particularly those relating the probability of "success" to scores on an x, often provide the clearest statement of how the x-variable influences success. The second aid to interpretation is the topic of the next section.

16.9
Odds of Success: A Multiplicative Model

In Section 16.3, the log-odds of success relation,

$$\text{log-odds}(y_i \; success \mid x = x_i) = \beta_0 + \beta_1 x_i, \tag{16.6}$$

was introduced as a way of "capturing" for the censored y the linear relation that we would like to model between an explanatory variable and the mean of the completely measured version of that response.

Equation [16.6] led us to logistic regression, giving us a way to fit such models and to compare the fits of alternative models. Logistic regression is a powerful modeling tool; it allows us to propose, compare, test, modify, accept, or reject the same range of explanatory models for the dichotomous y that we have available to model the measured y. What logistic regression does not allow us to do is easily interpret models and their parameters.

The interpretation of a linear log-odds-of-success model is aided by knowing that there is an equivalent *multiplicative odds-of-success model*. Each logistic regression model, in which the influences of one or more xs are added together, can be reexpressed as a model in which these influences *multiply together*. And this multiplicative model is easier to understand.

16.9.1   Developing the Multiplicative Model

To describe the relation of the logistic to a multiplicative model, we'll start by rewriting Equation [16.6] slightly:

$$\log_e \left[\frac{p(success \mid x = x_i)}{1 - p(success \mid x = x_i)} \right] = \beta_0 + \beta_1 x_i. \tag{16.20}$$

There are several systems of logarithms in use, each distinguished by its choice of a *base number*. We are most familiar, probably, with base-10 logarithms. The base-10 logarithm of some number, a,

$$\log_{10}(a) = b,$$

is a second number, b. This second number is the *power* to which 10 (the base) must be raised to produce the first number, a. That is, for

$$\log_{10}(a) \text{ to be equal to b}$$

we must have

$$10^b = a.$$

For example, $\log_{10}(100) = 2$ inasmuch as $10^2 = 100$.

The left-hand side of Equation [16.20] defines the log-odds of success as a base e logarithm. It is unimportant to us why this base is used for log-odds; the value of e is about 2.72 and base-e logarithms are common in science. What is important is that the same power/logarithm relationship that holds for base 10 holds as well for base e. That is, for

$$\log_e \left[\frac{p(success \mid x = x_i)}{1 - p(success \mid x = x_i)} \right]$$

to be equal to $\beta_0 + \beta_1 x_i$, we must also have

$$\frac{p(success \mid x = x_i)}{1 - p(success \mid x = x_i)} = e^{[\beta_0 + \beta_1 x_i]}. \tag{16.21}$$

Equation [16.21] expresses the *odds of success,* on the left, as e raised to some power. This is the start of our multiplicative model. To get to that model, we will have to subject our equation to a little further algebraic manipulation.

First, a power term with a sum in the exponent, $e^{[a+b]}$, can be expressed as a product of power terms:

$$e^{[a+b]} = e^a e^b.$$

For example,

$$8 = 2^3 = 2^{[2+1]} = 2^2 2^1 = 4 \times 2 = 8.$$

We use this idea to rewrite Equation [16.21] as

$$\frac{p(success \mid x = x_i)}{1 - p(success \mid x = x_i)} = e^{\beta_0} e^{(\beta_1 x_i)}. \tag{16.22}$$

On the right, we have a product of two terms, each a power of e.

Next, we use the idea that a power term with a product in the exponent, $e^{(ab)}$, can be expressed as one power term raised to a second power:

$$e^{(ab)} = (e^a)^b.$$

As an example,

$$16 = 2^4 = 2^{(2)(2)} = \left(2^2\right)^2 = 4^2 = 16.$$

Applying this idea to the right of Equation [16.22] allows us to write

$$\frac{p(success \mid x = x_i)}{1 - p(success \mid x = x_i)} = e^{\beta_0} \left(e^{\beta_1}\right)^{x_i}. \tag{16.23}$$

Equation [16.23] is one version of our multiplicative model; the odds of success are expressed as a product of two terms, one an "intercept-type" or constant term, and the other taking different values for different values of x.

The βs are the intercept and slope of the log-odds model and it will make our multiplicative model easier to see and work with if we replace them with new parameters. We define

$$\gamma_0 = e^{\beta_0} \tag{16.24}$$

and

$$\gamma_1 = e^{\beta_1} \tag{16.25}$$

as *multiplicative parameters* and use them in a final version of the multiplicative model:

$$\frac{p(success \mid x = x_i)}{1 - p(success \mid x = x_i)} = \gamma_0 \gamma_1^{x_i}. \tag{16.26}$$

16.9.2 Interpreting Multiplicative Model Parameters

Equation [16.26] is simply a restatement of the log-odds or logistic regression model. It is of interest because its parameters are more easily understood than those of the log-odds model. In fact, they have interpretations that will seem quite familiar.

The lead multiplicative parameter, γ_0, has an "intercept-like" interpretation; γ_0 gives the odds of success when x takes 0 as its value. We can see this from Equation [16.26].

When $x_i = 0$ we have $\gamma_1^{x_i} = \gamma_1^0 = 1$ with the result that the right-hand side simplifies to γ_0.

What interpretation can be given γ_1? Will it be "slope-like"? In linear regression, the slope parameter said something about the impact of a 1-unit increase in x on the mean of y. How does a 1-unit change in x affect the value of Equation [16.26]?

Let's consider the effect of increasing by 1-unit the value of x, say from $x_i = 5$ to $x_i = 6$. We start with two forms of Equation [16.26]:

$$[Odds \ of \ Success \mid x_i = 5] = \gamma_0 \gamma_1^5$$

and

$$[Odds \ of \ Success \mid x_i = 6] = \gamma_0 \gamma_1^6.$$

The difference between the two is that γ_1 is raised to the sixth rather than the fifth power in the second equation. But, γ_1 raised to the sixth power is just γ_1 raised to the fifth power and then multiplied, one more time, by γ_1 :

$$\gamma_1^6 = \gamma_1^5 \gamma_1.$$

To get the Odds of Success when $x_i = 6$, we've just multiplied the Odds of Success when $x_i = 5$ by γ_1 one more time:

$$[Odds \ of \ Success \mid x_i = 6] = [Odds \ of \ Success \mid x_i = 5]\gamma_1.$$

The choice of $x_i = 5$ and $x_i = 6$ is unimportant; this relation would be the same for *any 1-unit increase* in x. The multiplicative parameter γ_1 is the amount by which the Odds of Success are to be *multiplied* when x increases by 1 unit. If $\gamma_1 = 2$, increasing x by one unit will double the Odds of Success. If $\gamma_1 = (1/2)$, increasing x by one unit will halve the Odds of Success. This *rate-of-change* parameter will always be *positive*; it will be larger than one when x is "positively" related to Success and less than 1 when x is "negatively" related to success. If $\gamma_1 = 1$, x does not influence the Odds of Success.

In our linear regression models, the slope parameter, β_1, can be described as an *additive rate-of-change-parameter*; it is the amount to be *added* to $\mu(y)$ when x

increases by 1 unit. Here, γ_1 is a *multiplicative rate-of-change-parameter*; it is the amount by which $[p/(1-p)]$ is to be multiplied when x increases by 1 unit.

For our example, the logistic regression parameters for the linear model were estimated in Table 16.2 to be

$$\widehat{\beta}_0 = -12.76 \text{(with an SE of 4.99)}$$

and

$$\widehat{\beta}_1 = 0.145 \text{(with an SE of 0.059)}.$$

The corresponding *multiplicative model parameter estimates* are

$$\widehat{\gamma}_0 = e^{-12.76} = 0.000003$$

and

$$\widehat{\gamma}_1 = e^{0.145} = 1.156.$$

The odds of Passing the Bar's Ethics exam are modeled, by our linear model, as increasing by about 15% for an increase of one point in the Course Grade in Professional Conduct. Based on Equation [16.26], the following odds of success are computed from that linear model:

$$[Odds\ of\ Passing \mid Course\ Grade = 88] = 1.002$$
$$[Odds\ of\ Passing \mid Course\ Grade = 90] = 1.339.$$

That is, the odds of Passing (Bar exam) are modeled to increase as we go from a Course Grade of 88 to 89,

$$(1.002)(1.156) = 1.158,$$

and, again, as we go from 89 to 90,

$$(1.158)(1.156) = 1.339.$$

16.9.3 The Two Models: Additive and Multiplicative

In effect, there are *two versions* of each logistic regression model, an additive one expressing the influence of one or more explanatory variables on the log-odds of success,

$$\log_e \left[\frac{p(success \mid x = x_i)}{1 - p(success \mid x = x_i)} \right] = \beta_0 + \beta_1 x_i, \qquad \textbf{(16.20)}$$

and a multiplicative one relating those same x-variables to the odds of success,

$$\frac{p(success \mid x = x_i)}{1 - p(success \mid x = x_i)} = \gamma_0 \gamma_1^{x_i}. \qquad \textbf{(16.26)}$$

We need both versions.

The additive (or linear) version is the one we use to assess the fit of the logistic model and to *compare the fits* of models. And it is by imposing constraints on the parameters of these linear versions that we implement hypotheses or explore more parsimonious models. The linear version provides the same richness of designs that we had for the measured *y*.

But, the parameters of the additive forms, because they speak to the *x*-variable's influence on a rather complicated response function—the log-odds of success—are typically uninterpretable. We must turn to the multiplicative version of a logistic regression model for *parameter interpretation* to gain an understanding of the influence of one or another explanatory variable—the influence now on the odds of success.

16.9.4   Logistic Regression Models with Multiple Explanatory Variables

In introducing logistic regression, this chapter has concentrated on models with but a single *x*-variable. However, all of the multiple-*x* models and modeling strategies of Chapters 7, 8, and 11 through 14 are available to us as we model the dichotomous response. Some of these multiple-*x* models are examined in the next chapter.

16.10
Summary

This chapter introduces logistic regression as a convenient way to model the influence of the values of one or more explanatory variables on the proportion of response observations falling into the "success" category of a *dichotomy*. Because the linear logistic regression model takes the same form as the more familiar linear regression model, the same range of *modeling strategies* is available for the dichotomous as for the measured *y*. Each logistic regression model has two versions, an *additive* one used for computing the fit of a model to the sample data and for comparing models, and a *multiplicative* one used for interpreting the influence of explanatory variables in selected models.

Exercises

1   Below are data for a sample of patients with coronary heart disease (CHD) and a sample of "normals" free of CHD. The participants are indicated by a 1 (no CHD) or a 2 (CHD) in column 1 of the data. Three risk factors are to be evaluated by way of logistic regression models, taking CHD as success and no CHD as failure. The risk factors are systolic blood pressure (column 2), blood-cholesterol level (column 3), and age (column 4). Fit at least one model in which you evaluate age as a moderator of the influence of systolic blood pressure, using the ideas of Chapter 13.

CHD Group	SBP	Chol	Age
1	135	227	45
1	122	228	41
1	130	219	49
1	148	245	52
1	146	223	54
1	129	215	47
1	162	245	60
1	160	262	48
1	144	230	44
1	166	255	64
1	138	222	59
1	152	250	51
1	138	264	54
1	140	271	56
1	134	220	50
2	145	238	60
2	142	232	64
2	135	225	54
2	149	230	48
2	180	255	43
2	150	240	43
2	161	253	63
2	170	280	63
2	152	271	62
2	164	260	65

2 The breadths and lengths were recorded of jellyfish collected at Dangar Island and Salamandar Bay, two sites on the Hawkesbury River in NSW Australia. Use the logistic regression model to determine whether length or breadth or both distinguish jellyfish from the two locales. The dichotomous response (*success v. failure*) is formed from the two locations. Interpret your logistic regression models.

Dangar Island		Salamander Bay	
Breadth	Length	Breadth	Length
6.5	8.0	12.0	14.0
6.0	9.0	15.0	16.0
6.5	9.0	14.0	16.5
7.0	9.0	13.0	17.0
8.0	9.5	15.0	17.0
7.0	10.0	15.0	18.0
8.0	10.0	15.0	18.0
8.0	10.0	16.0	18.0
7.0	11.0	14.0	19.0
8.0	11.0	15.0	19.0
9.0	11.0	16.0	19.0

Dangar Island		Salamander Bay	
Breadth	Length	Breadth	Length
10.0	13.0	16.5	19.0
11.0	13.0	18.0	19.0
12.0	13.0	18.0	19.0
11.0	14.0	16.0	20.0
11.0	14.0	16.0	20.0
13.0	14.0	17.0	20.0
14.0	16.0	18.0	20.0
15.0	16.0	19.0	20.0
15.0	16.0	15.0	21.0
15.0	19.0	16.0	21.0
16.0	16.0	21.0	21.0

17

Grouped Logistic Regression Models

In Chapter 16, we introduced the basic ideas of *logistic regression*, explanatory models for the dichotomous response. Two versions of the logistic model were examined: an *additive model* relating the log-odds transformation of success proportions to a linear function of our explanatory variables and a *multiplicative model* relating the odds of success to a product of influences. The additive model is used in assessing the fit of a logistic model and in comparing the fits of models. The multiplicative model parameters provide an interpretation of the role of explanatory variables in a selected model.

When the explanatory variables in a logistic regression are all *categorical*, we often group the observations before undertaking the analyses, hence *grouped logistic regression*. In grouped logistic regression, the use of dummy (or effect-coded) variables for the levels of the explanatory factors leads to particularly easily interpreted multiplicative versions of the models.

17.1
Design Points with Multiple Observations

We developed logistic regression in the context of linear regression models for censored measured response variable observations. This allowed us to take advantage of nearly all we have learned about linear models. Because the individual y observation is now either a 1 (success) or a 0 (failure) we frequently can simplify the computational side of our logistic models.

In particular, when we have more than one y observation at a *design point*, we do not require knowledge of the individual observations to fit and compare logistic models. All the needed information is contained in the *frequency* of successes and of failures at each design point. Or, since only successes and failures are possible, all we need to know is the *frequency of successes* at the ith design point (f_i) and *number of attempts* (resulting in successes or failures) at that design point (N_i). Note that i here indexes design points and not individual observations.

In other words, we can group our dichotomous responses, counting up the number of successes and the number of attempts at each design point. What is important to grouped logistic regression modeling is that we know how many successes there are out of how many attempts for each combination of *x-variable* scores.

17.1.1   Fitting the Design Points

The fit provided by the logistic model to our *individual* success/failure observations of Chapter 16 was of the form $\hat{\mu}(y_i \mid X_i) = \hat{p}(successes \mid X_{i.})$, the estimated *proportion of successes*, given a particular pattern of x-variable scores, designated $X_{i.}$ for the ith observation in our sample. As we have seen, that fit or estimated proportion could be "close" to a success (a 1) or to a failure, 0.

In grouped logistic regression, the fit of the model is not to individual 0s and 1s, but to the *observed frequencies* of successes at the different design points in the study. The fit to f_i, then, is no longer a proportion but an *estimated or modeled frequency*, $(\hat{f} \mid X_{i.})$, written more compactly as $\hat{f}_i$.

Estimated Frequency of Success

The conditional-response populations from which we sample are still populations of 0s and 1s, failures and successes. Each is characterized by the proportion of 1s in that population, conveniently represented as $p_i = p(y = 1 \mid X_{i.})$. Now, though, we sample more than one time from a conditional response population. If we sample, independently, N_i times from a large population in which the proportion of 1s is p_i, what should be our estimate of the frequency of 1s among the N_i responses?

If our sample responses are independent of one another, then (1) the proportion of 1s in the ith conditional response population remains at p_i throughout sample selection and (2) each time we sample from the ith population we sample at random from among the observations making up the population. That is, the *expected value* is p_i each of the N_i times we sample from the population. As a result, the expected frequency of 1s or successes is

$$\mu(f_i) = p_i N_i. \tag{17.1}$$

For example, if the proportion of 1s in a population is 0.50 and we sample 10 times from that population, we would expect to observe $(0.50)(10) = 5$ 1s (and 5 0s). Or, if the proportion of 1s is 0.25 and we sample 6 times, we would *estimate* the resulting frequency of 1s at $(0.25)(6) = 1.50$ (and of 0s at 4.5).

Estimating the frequency of successes for a logistic model follows the same reasoning except that we do not know the population parameter p_i but must estimate it from the data and model. Thus, the logistic model estimate of the frequency of successes to be observed when we sample N_i times from the ith conditional response population is

$$\hat{f}_i = \hat{p}_i N_i, \tag{17.2}$$

where $\hat{p}_i$ is the logistic model's estimate of the proportion of 1s in that population.

17.1.2   Deviance for Grouped Success

The overall goodness-of-fit statistic for modeling grouped success is again the *Deviance* statistic. For fitting individual observations, the *Deviance* statistic, in our present notation, took the form

$$Deviance = 2\left[\sum_{i=1}^{N_1} y_i \log\left(\frac{y_i}{\hat{p}_i}\right) + \sum_{i=1}^{N_0}(1-y_i)\log\left(\frac{1-y_i}{1-\hat{p}_i}\right)\right] \qquad \textbf{(16.15)}$$

where y_i is either a 1 or a 0.

We can think of Equation [16.15] as expressing the *Deviance* when we *sample once* from each of N conditional response populations; $N_i = 1$ for each population and, consequently $f_i(= y_i)$ can be only 0 or 1.

With that analogy in mind, the *Deviance* statistic for grouped success can be written in the combined sum form of Equation [16.14] as

$$Deviance = 2\sum_{i=1}^{m}\left[f_i \log\left(\frac{f_i}{\hat{f}_i}\right) + (N_i - f_i)\log\left(\frac{N_i - f_i}{N_i - \hat{f}_i}\right)\right] \qquad \textbf{(17.3)}$$

where the sum is now over the m distinct *design points*, rather than over the N individual observations. Strictly speaking, we ought to have allowed for separate summations in Equation [17.3] to care for any design points accompanied in the sample either by no successes ($f_i = 0$) or no failures ($N_i - f_i = 0$) inasmuch as log(0) formally is $-\infty$! In implementing Equation [17.3] computationally, we insure that we always set 0 log(0) equal to 0.

When the k-parameter logistic model used to estimate the conditional-response proportions,

$$\text{log-odds(success}\,|\,X_{i.}) = \beta_0 + \sum_{j=1}^{k-1}\beta_j x_{ij}, \qquad \textbf{(16.7)}$$

is the correct model, the *Deviance* statistic of Equation [17.3] has as its sampling distribution the Chi-squared distribution with $(m - k)$ degrees of freedom. Small values of *Dev* (in the lower 75% of the Chi-squared population) offer evidence that the logistic model used to estimate conditional response proportions and success frequencies is a "good" one.

17.1.3 Poorly Fit Success Frequencies

The *Deviance* is a measure of the overall fit of a logistic model. In evaluating a model, we are also interested in whether one or more design points may be poorly fit by the model or whether there is a pattern to the fit to the design points. That is, we'd like to perform some of the same checks on the fit of the logistic model as were developed in Chapters 9 and 10 for the linear model for the measured y.

Logistic regression provides an analog to the Studentized residuals of Chapter 9. The *standardized residual* for the ith design point is computed as

$$str_i = \frac{f_i - \hat{f}_i}{\sqrt{N_i \hat{p}_i(1 - \hat{p}_i)}}. \qquad \textbf{(17.4)}$$

The numerator gives the difference between the frequency of successes as observed and as fitted by the logistic model. The denominator is the model's *estimated standard deviation* for f_i. For an N_i which is reasonably large, str_i will be approximately Normal.

The sign of str_i indicates whether the model underestimated (positive residuals) the frequency of successes at the design point or overestimated them (negative residual). The pattern of standardized residuals can be inspected for signs of systematic over and underfitting by the model. Systematic lack of fit signals the need for a new model, the addition of new explanatory variables, or the transformation of current ones.

It is worth noting that, in the case of a measured explanatory variable, the presumed linearity of the logistic model,

$$\log\left[\frac{p_i}{1-p_i}\right] = \beta_0 + \beta_1 x_i, \tag{16.7}$$

can be checked in the grouped logistic regression setting. There, p_i (and $1 - p_i$) have *empirical estimates*, $\hat{p}_i = f_i/N_i$ and $(1 - \hat{p}_i) = (N_i - f_i)/N_i$ that do not depend on a model. If these are substituted on the left-hand side of Equation [16.7], the resulting values,

$$\log\left[\frac{f_i}{N_i - f_i}\right]$$

can be plotted against the corresponding values of x_i. Any systematic departure from linearity in this plot suggests that x should be transformed, as we did in Chapter 10 where we had a measured y.

17.1.4   Fuller and Less Full Model Comparisons

If two grouped logistic models are in a fuller/less full relation, then the *difference in Deviances*, each computed from Equation [17.3], is used to compare the fits of the two models. The fuller model with $k + q$ parameters has *Deviance, Dev(F)*, and the less full model with k parameters has *Deviance, Dev(LF)*.

$$Deviance\ difference = Dev(LF) - Dev(F)$$

provides the basis for model comparison. When the difference in *Deviances* is large (among the largest 5% or 1% of the Chi-squared distribution with q d.f.), we conclude the fuller model is better than the less full one. Otherwise, we prefer the more parsimonious less full model with its fewer parameters.

17.1.5   Reanalysis: Law School Grades and Bar Examination Results

Studies for which grouped logistic model analysis is appropriate can also be analyzed using the single success/failure observations as in Chapter 16. The grouped analysis is easier and provides us with diagnostic clues as noted in the last section.

However, the two types of analysis give the same model comparison results and, hence, will lead us to choose the same model.

Individual Observation Analysis Results

We illustrate this with a reanalysis of the Bar examination problem of Chapter 16. The results of the individual observations modeling are resummarized in Table 17.1.

The Chapter 16 comparison of the quadratic and linear models was based on a *Deviance difference* of 3.85. That difference was large enough to be just among the largest 5% when the less full (linear) model is the correct one. This provided evidence, until we looked at a picture of the fit, that the fuller model (quadratic) was the better of the two. In the upper half of Table 17.1 we see again that both models provide a good fit to the data; for example, Prob(*Deviance | quadratic model*) = 0.57 > 0.25 and Prob(*Deviance | linear model*) = 0.40 > 0.25.

T A B L E 17.1
Bar Examination Logistic Models: Individual Observation Analyses

Model	Deviance	d.f.	Prob(*Deviance* | *Model*)
Quadratic	22.22	24	0.57
Linear	26.07	25	0.40
Null	34.37	26	0.13

Model Comparisons

Models		Differences		
Fuller	Less Full	Deviance	d.f.	Prob(*Diff Dev* | *Less full Model*)
Quadratic	Linear	3.85	1	.0498
Linear	Null	8.30	1	.0040
Quadratic	Null	12.15	2	.0023

17.1.6 Grouped Analysis Results

There are two or more Ethics examination "scores" (pass or fail) for many of the Professional Problems Course Grades (design points). Thus, the individual observations of Table 16.1 have been grouped in Table 17.2.

Fourteen design points ($m = 14$) are represented in Table 17.2 with N_i ranging

T A B L E 17.2

Professional Conduct Course Grade and Ethics Examination Performance

Course Grade (x_i)	Number Writing Exam (N_i)	Number Passing Exam (f_i)
70	2	0
72	2	0
74	3	0
76	3	0
78	3	0
80	1	1
82	3	2
84	2	1
86	1	0
88	1	1
90	1	1
94	1	0
96	1	1
100	3	2

from 1 to 3. Let's look now at the results of evaluating the same three logistic models against these grouped observations. The three models are, from least full to fullest:

1 Null Model: log-odds(Passing Exam | *Course Grade*) = β_0;

2 Linear Model: log-odds(Passing Exam | *Course Grade*) = $\beta_0 + \beta_1 Grade$;

3 Quadratic Model: log-odds(Passing Exam | *Course Grade*) = $\beta_0 + \beta_1 Grade + \beta_2 Grade^2$.

The fits of the three logistic regression models are summarized in Table 17.3. The first thing to notice is that the model comparisons shown at the bottom of the table are identical to the model comparisons based on the individual observations that are summarized in Table 17.1.

The *Deviance differences*—what we rely on in making model comparisons—are the same whether we fit individual success/failure observations or success frequencies. However, the actual model *Deviances* and their degrees of freedom are not the same. Thus, in the top half of Table 17.3, the Linear model gives a *Deviance* of 15.7 with $(m - k) = (14 - 2) = 12$ d.f. The linear model fitted to the individual observations (Table 17.1) gives a *Deviance* of 26.1 with $(N - k) = 27 - 2 = 25$ d.f. And, while the fit to the individual observations is adequate ($P = 0.40 > 0.25$), the fit to the grouped observations is less satisfactory ($P = 0.21 < 0.25$).

An Additional Model Fit

In Chapter 16 our interest in comparing the quadratic and linear logistic models focused on whether the relation was *linear or nonlinear*. The two are in a fuller/less full relation and can be compared. Choosing the quadratic over the linear provides

T A B L E 17.3

Bar Examination Logistic Models: Grouped Observation Analyses

Model	Deviance	d.f.	Prob(*Deviance* | *Model*)
Quadratic	11.81	11	0.38
Linear	15.66	12	0.21
Null	23.96	13	0.03

Model Comparisons

Models		Differences		
Fuller	Less Full	Deviance	d.f.	Prob(*Dev Diff* | *Less full Model*)
Quadratic	Linear	3.85	1	.049
Linear	Null	8.30	1	.004
Quadratic	Null	12.15	2	.002

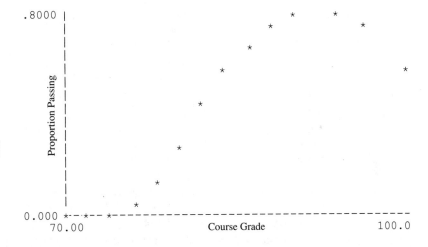

FIGURE 17.1

Proportion Passing Exam as a Function of Course Grade: Quadratic Logistic Model

evidence of a nonlinear relation, but it is not intended that it establish the quadratic as the most appropriate form for the nonlinear relation.

In fact, when we looked at the fit of the quadratic model to the observations, we saw substantive reasons for rejecting that model; for example, we rejected the idea that the probability of Passing the bar exam should decrease at the higher levels of Course Grade. The relation may be nonlinear, but the quadratic model is unacceptable.

Figure 17.1 displays again the fit of the quadratic model. The estimated proportion of successes (Passing the Ethics examination) increases, at first, with increasing Professional Conduct Course Grades, but it decreases over the highest range—above 96.

We would prefer a different nonlinear model—one in which the relation is *always increasing*, but with the rate of increase decreasing. That is, at the higher grade levels, the proportion Passing may level off, but it should not drop off.

From Chapter 10, we recall that while the quadratic transformation of the explanatory variable, is appropriate where the *direction of the relation changes* over the range of that variable a *power transformation* is preferred when the nonlinear relation does not produce a peak or valley in the design space. But, what should the power coefficient for course grades be? For logistic regression, there are not the built-in power estimation procedures that accompany many linear regression programs. Rather, we have to depend on substantive argument and trial and error.

Let's say that we do want a model in which the explanatory relation remains *positive but declines* in strength at the higher end of the Course Grade scale. In effect, we are saying that differences at the higher grades are not as important—as far as examination performance is concerned—as differences at the lower end of the scale.

To transform the Course Grade scale with this in mind means that we want a transformation in which the differences among the higher grades are "shrunk" and those among the lower grades "expanded." Power coefficients smaller than 1.0 will have this effect. For example, the three *variance stabilizing transformations* presented in Chapter 10 are all reasonable candidates: the square-root transformation corresponds to a power coefficient of 1/2, the logarithmic transformation corresponds to a power coefficient of 0, and the reciprocal transformation corresponds to a power coefficient of -1.

For our example, let's look at a *reciprocal transformation* of Course Grade.

Before applying any nonlinear power transformation to a variable, it is a good idea first to transform the variable linearly so that the range of the variable is one that allows the nonlinear transformation to have its effect. For example, nonlinear transformations will have little effect on a variable with a range from 1.0001 to 1.0005 or on one with a range from 20,011 to 20,015. In both instances, the ranges are quite small when compared with the typical magnitude of the scores—a range of 0.0004 for scores all about 1.000 in size and a range of 4 for scores all about 20,000 in size. The ratios of range to typical size in these examples are only $0.0004/1.0003 = .0004$ and $4/20,013 = .0002$.

A useful rule of thumb for the preliminary linear transformation is to produce scores that are all *positive* and extend from a low value of 1 or slightly higher to something in excess of 25, 50, or 100. The upper limit can be any conveniently chosen "large" number but the lower limit should not extend below 1.0. A good target range would be 1 to 100. With such a target, the transformed variable should have a *range to typical size ratio* exceeding 1.0 and often close to 2.0.

We linearly transform a variable by a combination of an addition (or subtraction) of one constant and a multiplication (or division) by a second constant. For example, if each of the scores in the range 1.0001 to 1.0005 were transformed by $[(x_i - 1.0000) \times 100,000]$ the transformed scores would run from 10 to 50. Or, the multiplication can precede the subtraction. Transforming this same range of scores by $[(x_i \times 100,000) - 100,009]$ produces scores that range from 1 to 41.

Similarly, the range 20,011 to 20,015 is converted by the linear transformation $[(x_i - 20,010.9) \times 20]$ to the range 2 to 82.

For our example, Course Grades range from 70 to 100. Before the reciprocal transformation is applied, we will linearly transform to scores that approach 1 at the low end. We choose simply to subtract 68 from each score, giving a resulting range from 2 to 32. This is an appropriate range for transformation.

Whenever we take reciprocals,

$$\frac{1}{x_i - 68},$$

we "turn around" the direction of the scale. The low score of 70 becomes

$$\frac{1}{70 - 68} = \frac{1}{2} = 0.50.$$

And the high score of 100 becomes

$$\frac{1}{100 - 68} = \frac{1}{32} = 0.03.$$

All the reciprocals are less than 1.0, so we can subtract each from 1.0 to get them back into the *right* order:

$$1 - \frac{1}{x_i - 68}$$

will take values from 0.50 (*Course Grade* of 70) to 0.97 (*Course Grade* of 100). Table 17.4 summarizes the overall fit of this reciprocal model:

$$\text{log-odds}(\text{Passing Exam} \mid Course\ Grade) = \beta_0 + \beta_1 \left(1 - \frac{1}{x_i - 68}\right).$$

The *Deviance* is of the same magnitude as reported for the quadratic model in Table 17.3 (11.81) but, with greater d.f. (12 rather than 11), is even closer to the middle of its Chi-squared sampling distribution: $\text{Prob}(Deviance \mid Reciprocal) = 0.47$ and $\text{Prob}(Deviance \mid Quadratic) = 0.38$.

Of course, the two models are not in a fuller/less full relation and cannot be compared statistically. Nonetheless, the reciprocal model would appear to give a good fit to the data.

T A B L E 17.4

Bar Examination Logistic Models: Reciprocal Transformation of Grades

Model	Deviance	d.f.	Prob(Deviance | Model)
Reciprocal	11.75	12	0.47
Null	23.96	13	0.03

Model Comparison

Model		Difference		
Fuller	Less Full	Deviance	d.f.	Prob(Diff Dev | Less Full Model)
Reciprocal	Null	12.21	1	.0005

Figure 17.2 sketches the relation of *p(Passing | Course Grade)* to Course Grade based on the reciprocal model. Note that it follows the postulated form. The proportion Passing continues to increase over the range of Course Grade, but the slope flattens out as higher Course Grades are considered.

Finally, lets look at the *standardized residuals* for the reciprocal model to see if there is any evidence of a systematic lack of fit. Figure 17.3 shows the plot of standardized residuals against our original explanatory variable scores (Course Grades).

The largest standardized residual is only -1.64 (lower right corner of Figure 17.3) and there is no discernible pattern to the residuals in the plot.

There is no reason to doubt the adequacy of the reciprocal model. We must remember, though, that it is a model suggested by the data; the linear model was first found to be inadequate, then we sought a reasonable form for a nonlinear explanatory relation. Before we proclaim the reciprocal model, we should evaluate it in a new sample of Course Grade/Bar examination performances.

FIGURE 17.2

Proportion Passing Exam as a Function of Course Grade: Reciprocal Logistic Model

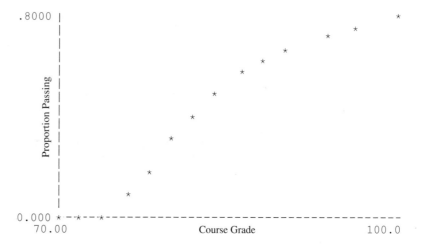

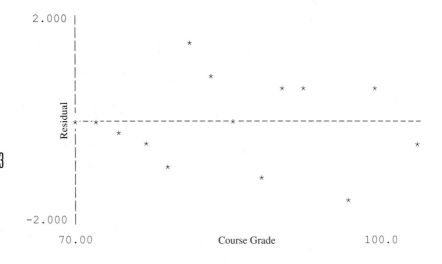

2.000

Residual

-2.000

70.00   Course Grade   100.0

FIGURE 17.3
Standardized
Residuals for Re-
ciprocal Logistic
Model: Bar Exami-
nation

17.2
Logistic Regression and Categorical Explanatory Variables

Our Chapter 16 example, just reanalyzed involved a measured *x*-variable—law school Course Grade. A more common use of grouped logistic regression is with studies with one or more *categorical explanatory variables* or factors. The design points in such studies correspond to a level or combination of *levels* on these factors.

We treat explanatory factors in logistic regression in essentially the same way we did in linear models for the measured *y*. Let's review, briefly, how we incorporate factors in models.

17.2.1 Dummy Variable Coding

The first technique we learned for bringing the multicategory variable into our linear models was to represent the *k*-level factor as a set of $(k - 1)$ dummy variables. One factor level is selected as the *comparison* level and 0/1 variables included in the explanatory model for each of the remaining levels. The dummy variable for the *i*th level is coded 1 whenever an observation is drawn from the conditional response population for that level, 0 otherwise.

We do the same for logistic models. Let's assume we have random samples of 50 bus drivers from each of the four North American West Coast Cities of Vancouver, Seattle, San Francisco, and Los Angeles and that we have classified each driver as Experienced (has driven for more than five years) or not experienced (has driven for five years or less). The design gives us 50 success/failure observations at each of four design points.

A *saturated* or fullest logistic model for these data is one with four unconstrained parameters. Thus, if we were to choose Seattle as the comparison (level of) City, the logistic model,

$$\text{log-odds}(Experienced \mid City) = \beta_0 + \beta_1 x_{i1} + \beta_2 x_{i2} + \beta_3 x_{i3}$$

where $x_1 = 1$ if driver is from Vancouver, 0 otherwise; $x_2 = 1$ if driver is from San Francisco, 0 otherwise; and $x_3 = 1$ if driver is from Los Angeles, 0 otherwise, is a saturated model. Estimating the four β parameters in this model provides *independent estimates* of the four success proportions:

$$p(Experienced \mid City = \text{Vancouver}),$$
$$p(Experienced \mid City = \text{Seattle}),$$
$$p(Experienced \mid City = \text{San Francisco}), \text{ and}$$
$$p(Experienced \mid City = \text{Los Angeles}).$$

Such a saturated model would estimate the four success frequencies *exactly*; the model *Deviance* would be 0. We would be interested in comparing the perfect fit of this model against the less perfect fit of a *constrained* model, a less full model in which we impose some constraints on the βs of the saturated model.

17.2.2   Effect Coding

An alternative coding of the k levels of a factor makes use of effect-coding variables. Again, one of the k levels is singled out; for effect coding, it is referred to as the *omitted level*. Then, $(k-1)\ 0/1/-1$ variables are introduced into the design. The coding follows the rules for dummy variables, except that observations from the omitted level are coded -1 on all $(k-1)$ effect-coding variables.

The same saturated model principle holds for effect coding. If we have success frequencies sampled from k response populations, then a logistic model with k freely estimated parameters will fit those data without any deviance.

The choice between dummy variable coding and effect coding rests, as it did for linear models, on the interpretation we wish to give the model intercept, β_0. Under dummy variable coding, the intercept is related to the explanatory "strength" of the comparison level. With effect coding, the intercept is the explanatory strength of the categorical variable, averaged over the k levels. The meaning of this distinction for logistic models will be made clearer in Section 17.6 when we discuss the multiplicative analog to the logistic model.

17.2.3   Interaction Terms as Products

If our design points are defined by the *intersection* of the levels of two or more factors, we frequently want to find out whether the factors *interact* with one another in their influence on the response. As in our linear models, these potential interactions can be represented in logistic models by the *products of dummy or effect variables* for the separate factors.

For example, we can extend our bus driver example by assuming that we know as well the gender of the sampled bus drivers. Our success response is still Experienced, but we now have two categorical influences, City and Gender. Assume that City is dummy coded as in the section above and that Gender is also dummy coded. The following logistic model accounts for the additive effects of the two categorical sources of influence:

$$\text{log-odds}(\textit{Experienced} \,|\, \textit{City, Gender}) = \beta_0 + \beta_1 x_{i1} + \beta_2 x_{i2} + \beta_3 x_{i3} + \beta_4 x_{i4}$$

where x_4 is the dummy variable for Gender. If male is the comparison level, the gender variable is scored 1 for women, 0 for men. The intercept in this model now refers to the comparison category defined by the two sets of dummy variables: Male, Seattle bus drivers.

The possibility of an interaction between the two factors (e.g., is the bus driver Experienced profile across Cities *different* for women than it is for men?) can be explored if we expand this additive model into an *interactive* one. We can do this by adding variables to the model that are products of the dummy variables for the two categories.

Because Gender provided only one dummy variable (x_4), we can create the interactive model by adding three variables, each the product of x_4 with one of the dummy variables for city (x_1, x_2, and x_3). If these product variables are identified as x_5, x_6, and x_7, then this is our interactive model:

$$\text{log-odds}(\textit{Experienced} \,|\, \textit{City, Gender}) = \beta_0 + \beta_1 x_{i1} + \beta_2 x_{i2} + \beta_3 x_{i3} + \beta_4 x_{i4}$$
$$+ \beta_5 x_{i5} + \beta_6 x_{i6} + \beta_7 x_{i7}.$$

This is another *saturated model*. We have Experienced frequencies from just eight response populations: male and female drivers in each of the four cities. The estimates of the eight parameters of the interactive model give us exactly fitting estimates of the eight observed Experienced proportions.

The *difference in Deviance* between the interactive and additive models, as we'll see in the example of Section 17.3, provides a test of the interaction hypothesis: Does the additive model fit significantly less well than the (perfectly fitting) interactive model?

17.2.4   All Levels Coding

If there is but a single factor in the model, an alternative to dummy or effect coding is 0/1 variables for all levels. We start with the dummy-variable coding and simply replace the intercept term in the model with a kth 0/1 variable for the (no longer) comparison level. Thus, if we redefine x_4 as 1 for Seattle and 0 for the other cities the dummy-variable model for cities can be replaced with this model:

$$\text{log-odds}(\textit{Experienced} \,|\, \textit{City}) = \beta_1 x_{i1} + \beta_2 x_{i2} + \beta_3 x_{i3} + \beta_4 x_{i4}.$$

Each of the four slope coefficients is associated with one of the four Cities. In fact, each gives the modeled *log-odds (Experienced)* for a particular level of City.

Like the four-parameter dummy-variable model, the all-levels coded model is saturated.

We employed all-levels coding, though perhaps not the name, in Chapter 11 when we first developed *modular models* to explore an interaction between explanatory factors. Modular models play their part in logistic regression as well.

17.3
Example: Death Penalty and Murder Convictions

We take as our example a set of data relating the imposition of the Sentence (Death or Non-death) on convicted murderers to (1) race of Victim and (2) race of Felon. We are interested in whether, and how, the proportion of successes (Non-death *Sentences*) varies over these four conditional response populations:

(*Sentence | Victim:* Black, *Felon:* Black),

(*Sentence | Victim:* Black, *Felon:* White),

(*Sentence | Victim:* White, *Felon:* Black), and

(*Sentence | Victim:* White, *Felon:* White).

Each response population consists of a certain proportion of Non-death Sentences (successes) and a remaining proportion of Death Sentences (failures).

17.3.1 Description of Data

Table 17.4 shows the samples from the four response populations. The data are for a southern U.S. state in the early 1970s and are reported in Radelet (1981).

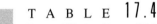

T A B L E 17.4

Race of Victim, Race of Felon, and the Death Sentence: Sample Data

Race		Frequency		
Victim	Felon	Non-death	Death	Total
Black	Black	97	6	103
Black	White	9	0	9
White	Black	52	11	63
White	White	132	19	151

17.3.2   Explanatory Models

To study the question of whether the proportion of Non-death Sentences is influenced by the races of Victim and Felon, we will consider five logistic models.

1 Interactive Model: Both race variables and the interaction between them are postulated to influence the proportion.

2 Additive Model: The two race variables are postulated to contribute additively but not interactively.

3 Race-of-victim Model: Race of Victim, but not race of Felon, is thought to influence proportions.

4 Race-of-felon Model: Race of Felon, but not race of Victim, is hypothesized to influence proportions.

5 Null Model: Proportion of Non-death Sentences is postulated to be uninfluenced by either race of Felon or Victim

Each of the two factors (race of *Victim* and race of *Felon*) takes only two levels, Black and White. For purposes of fitting and comparing models, we code each with a single effect-coded variable.

x_1: 1 if race of Victim is Black and -1 if White and
x_2: 1 if race of Felon is Black and -1 if White.

The choice of effect coding reflects that the levels—Black and White—exhaust the natural set of race categories. To allow for an interaction between the two race factors, we include in the interactive model a third *x*-variable:

$$x_3: \text{the product of } x_1 \text{ and } x_2.$$

The five explanatory models are expressed in terms of these three variables as follows:

1 Interactive Model: log-odds(Non-death *Sentence* | *Races*)
$$= \beta_0 + \beta_1 x_1 + \beta_2 x_2 + \beta_3 x_3$$
2 Additive Model: log-odds(Non-death *Sentence* | *Races*)
$$= \beta_0 + \beta_1 x_1 + \beta_2 x_2$$
3 Victim Race Model: log-odds(Non-death *Sentence* | *Races*)
$$= \beta_0 + \beta_1 x_1$$
4 Felon Race Model: log-odds(Non-death *Sentence* | *Races*)
$$= \beta_0 \qquad + \beta_2 x_2$$
5 Null Model: log-odds(Non-death *Sentence* | *Races*)
$$= \beta_0$$

For purposes of modeling, we equate a Non-death Sentence with a "success."

We see from these descriptions of the five models that the interactive model is fuller with respect to any one of the other four models, that the null model is less full with respect to any one of the other four models, and that the additive model is fuller with respect to either the Victim race or Felon race models. These relations form the basis of the model comparisons that will be of interest to us.

17.3.3   Model Fits and Comparisons

We have sampled from just four response populations, each characterized by the race of Victim (Black or White) and race of Felon (Black or White). As a result, the four-parameter interactive model is a *saturated model*, yielding estimates of the four p(Non-death *Sentences*) that are exactly equal to the observed sample proportions. The *Deviance*, correspondingly, is 0. Table 17.5 summarizes the fits of this and the four other models.

The top half of the table tells us that the interactive, additive, and race-of-Victim models provide adequate fits to the data. The *Deviances* for the latter two models are each small enough to fall within the lower 75% of their sampling populations, while the interactive model, by virtue of being a saturated model, fits perfectly. The race-of-Felon and null models, by contrast, do not provide acceptable fits to the observations.

We make our model comparisons here in the same way we did in Chapter 11 for similarly arranged linear models, seeking a parsimonious and simply interpretable model. We ask first whether the interaction between the two factors is a necessary part of the model. If it is not, we go on to ask whether either of the factors themselves might be "dropped" from the model. The flow for this example is summarized at the bottom of Table 17.5.

For the first model comparison, that between the interactive and additive models, the *difference in Deviances* is small enough that we should prefer the more parsimonious model, the one with fewer parameters. That is, we decide in favor of the additive model. Next, we ask whether we can drop either of the two factors (each represented here by a single *x*-variable) from the additive model. The comparison between the additive and race-of-*Victim* models evaluates the role of race of Felon in

T A B L E **17.5**

Death Sentence Logistic Models: Race of Victim and Race of Felon

Model	Deviance	d.f.	Prob(Deviance | Model)
Interactive	0.000	0	
Additive	0.701	1	0.40
Victim's Race	1.882	2	0.39
Felon's Race	7.910	2	0.02
Null	8.132	3	0.04

Model Comparisons

Models		Differences		
Fuller	Less Full	Deviance	d.f.	Prob(*Diff Dev* | *Less Full Model*)
Interactive	Additive	0.701	1	.402
Additive	Victim	1.181	1	.277
Additive	Felon	7.209	1	.007
Victim	Null	6.250	1	.012

the additive model. Again, the *difference in Deviances* is not so large that we should opt for the more complicated model.

On the other hand, when we compare the additive model with the race-of-Felon model, we see a large enough *difference in Deviances* to suggest that race of Victim should not be dropped from our explanatory model. The results of these two comparisons square with the fit data in the top of Table 17.5: the race-of-Victim model provides an adequate fit, the race-of-Felon model does not. Further evidence of the importance of race of Victim is provided by the last comparison at the bottom of Table 17.5. When the race-of-Victim model is compared with the null model, a *difference in Deviance* is produced that is large enough that we prefer the race-of-Victim model.

Our final model, then, is

Victim's Race Model: log-odds(Non-death *Sentence* | *Race*) $= \beta_0 + \beta_1 x_1$

where x_1 is $+1$ for a Black Victim and -1 for a White Victim

17.3.4 Modular Models in Logistic Regression

We noted in Chapter 11 that where an interaction between factors is found to be important to an explanatory model for a measured *y*, the interpretation of the model could often be improved by *rephrasing* the interactive model as a *modular* one. The same principle holds for interactions in logistic regression models. The Police Sensitivity Training problem in the exercises for this chapter provides an opportunity to develop and simplify such a modular model.

17.4
Multiplicative Models and Grouped Logistic Regression

In Chapter 16, we found that for any logistic regression model,

$$\text{log-odds}(success \,|\, X_i) = \beta_0 + \sum_{j=1}^{k-1} (\beta_j x_{ij}),$$

there is a corresponding *multiplicative model,* that expanding on Equation [16.26], takes the form

$$\text{odds}(success \,|\, X_i) = \gamma_0 \prod_{j=1}^{k-1} \gamma_j^{x_{ij}}, \qquad \textbf{(17.5)}$$

with the two sets of parameters related: $\gamma_j = e^{\beta_j}$. In Equation [17.5] the symbol

$$\prod_{j=1}^{k-1}$$

is read as "form the product among all the terms following, letting *j* range from 1 to $k - 1$." It is the *multiplicative* analog to the $\sum$ notation for summing.

The *parameters* of the *multiplicative model*, the γs, we learned, are usually easier to interpret than the additive parameters in the logistic model itself. In fact, the interpretation of these multiplicative parameters is particularly compelling for logistic models in which the xs are dummy variables, effect coded variables or products of these variables.

17.4.1   Interpreting Multiplicative Model Parameters

From Section 16.9, we have the following interpretations for the multiplicative model parameters.

γ_0—The modeled odds of success when all xs are equal to 0 and

γ_j—The modeled odds of success are multiplied by this amount when the jth x increases by 1 unit (and any other xs remain fixed).

Note that γ_0 is an intercept parameter and γ_j is a *multiplicative rate-of-change* parameter for the jth x.

These are general interpretations for multiplicative model parameters. For logistic models with factors, these parameters can be given specialized interpretations. How the factor levels have been coded in our model will dictate these interpretations.

Dummy Variable Parameters

Let's begin with a logistic model including only one categorical variable, the levels of which have been represented with dummy variables. For definiteness, we'll model the odds of Recidivism among samples of felons at first conviction in four geographic Regions of the U.S.A.: Northeast, Southeast, Northwest, and Southwest. We'll take the logistic regression model to be

$$\log\left[\frac{p(Recidivism)}{1 - p(Recidivism)}\right] = \beta_0 + \beta_1 x_1 + \beta_2 x_2 + \beta_3 x_3 \qquad \textbf{(17.6)}$$

where x_1 is a dummy variable coding Southeast, x_2 is a dummy variable coding Northwest, and x_3 is a dummy variable coding Southwest. Northeast is the *comparison level* for the Region factor.

The multiplicative model corresponding to Equation [17.6] is

$$\left[\frac{p(Recidivism)}{1 - p(Recidivism)}\right] = \gamma_0 \gamma_1^{x_1} \gamma_2^{x_2} \gamma_3^{x_3}. \qquad \textbf{(17.7)}$$

Our dummy variables, though, take only two values, 0 and 1. As a result, $\gamma_j^{x_j}$ must be either γ_j (when $x_j = 1$) or 1 (when $x_j = 0$). (Raising something to the 0 power always gives 1.) As a consequence, Equation [17.7] gives these four modeled odds of Recidivism:

$$\text{odds}[\text{Recidivism} \,|\, Northeast] = \gamma_0,$$
$$\text{odds}[\text{Recidivism} \,|\, Southeast] = \gamma_0 \gamma_1,$$
$$\text{odds}[\text{Recidivism} \,|\, Northwest] = \gamma_0 \gamma_2,$$

and

$$\text{odds}[Recidivism \,|\, Southwest] = \gamma_0\gamma_3.$$

The *multiplicative intercept* gives the modeled odds of success for the *comparison level* of the factor while the rate of change parameters are the *odds multipliers* for each of the other levels.

Effect Coded Variable Parameters

Now, we change the coding of the Region levels from dummy variables to effect coded variables. We still have Equation [17.6] as our logistic regression model:

$$\text{log-odds}[Recidivism \,|\, Region] = \beta_0 + \beta_1 x_1 + \beta_2 x_2 + \beta_3 x_3.$$

But the xs now are

$$x_1 : \text{an effect coded variable for Southeast;}$$
$$x_2 : \text{an effect coded variable for Northwest;}$$

and

$$x_3 : \text{an effect coded variable for Southwest.}$$

Northeast is now the *omitted level* of the Region factor. All three effect coded variables take the value -1 for Northeast observations.

Our multiplicative model for the odds of *Recidivism* is again given by Equation [17.7]:

$$\text{odds}[Recidivism \,|\, Region] = \gamma_0\gamma_1^{x_1}\gamma_2^{x_2}\gamma_3^{x_3}.$$

Now, the x_js can be -1 as well as 0 or 1. And, for $x_j = -1$,

$$\gamma_j^{x_j} \text{ can be expressed as } \gamma_j^{-1} \text{ or as } \left(\frac{1}{\gamma_j}\right).$$

That is, $\gamma_j^{x_j}$ is either γ_j, 1, or $\left(\frac{1}{\gamma_j}\right)$ depending on whether x_j is 1, 0, or -1.

For the four geographic Regions modeled using effect-coding variables, Equation [17.6] provides the following solutions:

$$\text{odds}[Recidivism \,|\, Northeast] = \frac{\gamma_0}{\gamma_1\gamma_2\gamma_3},$$
$$\text{odds}[Recidivism \,|\, Southeast] = \gamma_0\gamma_1,$$
$$\text{odds}[Recidivism \,|\, Northwest] = \gamma_0\gamma_2,$$

and

$$\text{odds}[Recidivism \,|\, Southwest] = \gamma_0\gamma_3.$$

The multiplicative intercept is now a *geometric average* of the four odds, the fourth root of the product of the four separate odds. It is also a "constant," scaled by different multipliers to get the separate odds. These effect coded multipliers are *constrained* so that their product is 1. The multipliers here are $\gamma_1, \gamma_2, \gamma_3$, and $1/(\gamma_1\gamma_2\gamma_3)$.

All Levels Coding of the Factor

A final way in which the four geographic Regions could be represented in our logistic regression model is through a set of four 0/1 variables, each coding one of the four levels. The logistic regression model would now be of this form:

$$\text{log-odds}[Recidivism \mid Region] = \beta_1x_1 + \beta_2x_2 + \beta_3x_3 + \beta_4x_4, \qquad \textbf{(17.8)}$$

with x_1, a 0/1 variable coding Southeast; x_2, a 0/1 variable coding Northwest; x_3, a 0/1 variable coding Southwest; and x_4, a 0/1 variable coding Northeast. All four regions are explicitly in the model, represented by 0/1 variables.

Our multiplicative model for the odds of recidivism, based on Equation 17.8, is now

$$\text{odds}[Recidivism \mid Region] = \gamma_1^{x_1}\gamma_2^{x_2}\gamma_3^{x_3}\gamma_4^{x_4}, \qquad \textbf{(17.9)}$$

which, for the allowable patterns of 0s and 1s, specializes to

$$\text{odds}[Recidivism \mid Northeast] = \gamma_4,$$
$$\text{odds}[Recidivism \mid Southeast] = \gamma_1,$$
$$\text{odds}[Recidivism \mid Northwest] = \gamma_2,$$

and

$$\text{odds}[Recidivism \mid Southwest] = \gamma_3.$$

There isn't a "single intercept" in the All Levels Coding model; rather, there is a separate intercept for each level of the factor.

Interaction Models

Where the x-variables can take only values of 0, 1, or -1, the odds of success can be modeled as the product of certain of the multiplicative parameters (or their reciprocals). We often construct interaction models by including xs that are products of two or more $0/1/-1$ variables. These products are also $0/1/-1$ variables and the modeled odds of success for interaction models are also *products of multiplicative parameters*.

This can be illustrated with our Death/Non-death Sentence example. The fullest model was the interaction model:

$$\text{log-odds (Non-death } Sentence \mid Race = \beta_0 + \beta_1x_1 + \beta_2x_2 + \beta_3(x_1 \times x_2).$$

The variables in this logistic regression interaction model are

$$x_1: 1 \text{ if Victim is Black}, -1 \text{ if Victim is White};$$
$$x_2: 1 \text{ if Felon is Black}, -1 \text{ if Felon is White};$$

and

$$(x_1 \times x_2): \text{Product variable, 1 or } -1.$$

The odds model (multiplicative) corresponding to this log-odds model and set of variables is

$$\text{odds(Non-death } Sentence \mid Race) = \gamma_0 \gamma_1^{x_1} \gamma_2^{x_2} \gamma_3^{(x_1 \times x_2)}. \tag{17.10}$$

Table 17.6 describes the patterns of x scores and odds computations for the interaction model.

The *interaction* model is a *saturated model* so the modeled odds reflect the observed data: For example, the odds of 16.2 to 1 in favor of Non-death Sentence for Black Victim/Black Felon reflects the relative frequencies of Non-death and Death Sentences for that category—$97/6 = 16.2$. As there were no Death Sentences in this sample for the Black Victim/White Felon category, our logistic regression program's modeled odds of 73,269 to 1 can only be taken as an estimate of some large but unspecifiable number (in [†]Table 17.6).

T A B L E 17.6
Interaction Model Odds for Death Sentence Example

Race					Odds of Non-death Sentence
Victim	Felon	x_1	x_2	$(x_1 \times x_2)$	
Black	Black	1	1	1	$\gamma_0\gamma_1\gamma_2\gamma_3 = (78.99)(13.78)(.1107)(.1342) = 16.2$
Black	White	1	-1	-1	$\gamma_0\gamma_1/\gamma_2\gamma_3 = (78.99)(13.78)/(.1107)(.1342) = $ [†]
White	Black	-1	1	-1	$\gamma_0\gamma_2/\gamma_1\gamma_3 = (78.99)(.1107)/(13.78)(.1342) = 4.7$
White	White	-1	-1	1	$\gamma_0\gamma_3/\gamma_1\gamma_2 = (78.99)(.1342)/(13.78)(.1107) = 7.0$

[†]The modeled odds are 73,269 to 1, but the data included no death sentences in this category.

17.4.2 Model Parameters for Selected Model

In describing the fits of the several logistic regression models to the death *Sentence* data, we concluded that the "best" model was the Victim race model:

$$\text{log-odds(Non-death } Sentence \mid Victim \text{ race}) = \beta_0 + \beta_1 x_1,$$

with $x_1 + 1$ for Black Victims and -1 for White Victims. The multiplicative model is

$$\text{odds(Non-death } Sentence \mid Victim \text{ race}) = \gamma_0 \gamma_1^{x_1}.$$

Here, x_1 is either $+1$ or -1, giving

$$\text{odds(Non-death } Sentence \mid Black \ Victim) = \gamma_0 \gamma_1$$

and

$$\text{odds(Non-death } Sentence \mid White \ Victim) = \gamma_0 / \gamma_1.$$

Our logistic regression program estimates these parameters at $\hat{\gamma}_0 = 10.41$ and $\hat{\gamma}_1 = 1.697$. These estimated parameters yield *modeled* odds of Non-death Sentences of

$$\text{odds(Non-death } Sentence \mid \text{Black } Victim) = (10.41)(1.697) = 17.7$$

and

$$\text{odds(Non-death } Sentence \mid \text{White } Victim) = (10.41)/(1.697) = 6.1.$$

That the Victim race variable is important to the fit to the data tells us that these two odds are different. One way of describing the relative magnitudes of two odds is to calculate an *odds ratio*. Here, the ratio of the (modeled) odds of Non-death Sentence for Black and White Victims is $17.7/6.1 = 1.697^2$ or 2.88.

The Victim race model estimates the odds that a convicted murderer of a Black person will receive a Non-death Sentence to be nearly three times the odds for one convicted of murdering a White person. Equivalently, the odds in favor of the Death Sentence are three times greater with a White than with a Black Victim.

17.5
Summary

This chapter extends the application of logistic regression models to designs where many successes and failures are recorded for each of a limited number of design points. These grouped logistic regression models have particularly simple interpretations when the design points correspond to levels of one or more categorical explanatory variables or factors. The idea of an odds ratio for comparing the influence of one factor level to another is introduced.

Exercises

1   Byssinosis is a lung affliction developed by workers exposed to dusts such as those found in cotton mills. The data set below relates the frequency of occurrence (f) among those exposed (N) to the factors of smoking, sex, race, length of employment, and type of workplace. Evaluate these potential influences.

f	N	Smoker (1=Yes)	Sex (1=Male)	Race (1=White)	Employment (1 = < 10 Yrs., 2 = 10–19 Yrs., 3 = ≥ 20 Yrs.)	Workplace Type (1 = most dusty, 2 = less dusty, 3 = least dusty)
3	37	1	1	1	1	1
25	139	1	1	0	1	1
0	5	1	0	1	1	1
2	22	1	0	0	1	1
0	16	0	1	1	1	1
6	75	0	1	0	1	1
0	4	0	0	1	1	1
1	24	0	0	0	1	1
8	21	1	1	1	2	1
8	30	1	1	0	2	1
0	0	1	0	1	2	1
0	0	1	0	0	2	1
2	8	0	1	1	2	1
1	9	0	1	0	2	1
0	0	0	0	1	2	1
0	0	0	0	0	2	1
31	77	1	1	1	3	1
10	31	1	1	0	3	1
0	1	1	0	1	3	1
0	1	1	0	0	3	1
5	47	0	1	1	3	1
3	15	0	1	0	3	1
0	2	0	0	1	3	1
0	0	0	0	0	3	1
0	74	1	1	1	1	2
0	88	1	1	0	1	2
1	93	1	0	1	1	2
2	145	1	0	0	1	2
0	35	0	1	1	1	2
1	47	0	1	0	1	2
1	54	0	0	1	1	2
3	142	0	0	0	1	2
1	50	1	1	1	2	2
0	5	1	1	0	2	2

f	N	Smoker (1=Yes)	Sex (1=Male)	Race (1=White)	Employment (1 = < 10 Yrs., 2 = 10–19 Yrs., 3 = ≥ 20 Yrs.)	Workplace Type (1 = most dusty, 2 = less dusty, 3 = least dusty)
1	33	1	0	1	2	2
0	4	1	0	0	2	2
1	16	0	1	1	2	2
0	0	0	1	0	2	2
0	30	0	0	1	2	2
0	4	0	0	0	2	2
1	141	1	1	1	3	2
0	1	1	1	0	3	2
3	91	1	0	1	3	2
0	0	1	0	0	3	2
0	39	0	1	1	3	2
0	1	0	1	0	3	2
3	187	0	0	1	3	2
0	2	0	0	0	3	2
2	258	1	1	1	1	3
3	242	1	1	0	1	3
3	180	1	0	1	1	3
3	260	1	0	0	1	3
0	134	0	1	1	1	3
1	122	0	1	0	1	3
2	169	0	0	1	1	3
4	301	0	0	0	1	3
1	187	1	1	1	2	3
0	33	1	1	0	2	3
2	94	1	0	1	2	3
0	3	1	0	0	2	3
0	58	0	1	1	2	3
0	7	0	1	0	2	3
1	90	0	0	1	2	3
0	4	0	0	0	2	3
12	495	1	1	1	3	3
0	45	1	1	0	3	3
3	176	1	0	1	3	3
0	2	1	0	0	3	3
3	182	0	1	1	3	3
0	23	0	1	0	3	3
2	340	0	0	1	3	3
0	3	0	0	0	3	3

2 Below is a table of frequencies based on interviews with male high school seniors. Treat College Expectation (Column 2) as the response and develop and evaluate one or more logistic regression models using other factors as explanatory. Interpret your results. The original study looked at the role of athletic participation in the college decision-making process.

Family Social Status 0: High, 1: Low	College Expectations 0: None, 1: Some	Parental Encouragement of Athletics 0: High, 1: Low	Academic Performance 0: High, 1: Low	Participation in Athletics 0: Some, 1: None	Frequency in Cell
0	0	0	0	0	2
0	0	0	0	1	2
0	0	0	1	0	10
0	0	0	1	1	23
0	0	1	0	0	2
0	0	1	0	1	4
0	0	1	1	0	2
0	0	1	1	1	16
0	1	0	0	0	38
0	1	0	0	1	55
0	1	0	1	0	21
0	1	0	1	1	22
0	1	1	0	0	6
0	1	1	0	1	12
0	1	1	1	0	4
0	1	1	1	1	2
1	0	0	0	0	8
1	0	0	0	1	12
1	0	0	1	0	45
1	0	0	1	1	91
1	0	1	0	0	4
1	0	1	0	1	23
1	0	1	1	0	28
1	0	1	1	1	76
1	1	0	0	0	44
1	1	0	0	1	61
1	1	0	1	0	37
1	1	0	1	1	30
1	1	1	0	0	9
1	1	1	0	1	23
1	1	1	1	0	10
1	1	1	1	1	6

3   Below are summary data for a binational sample of women who have undergone abortion. What factors influence their subsequent decision to accept fertility control? Age, number of living children, education, and country (India or Yugoslavia) are potential factors. Evaluate these.

Age of Women 1:< 25, 2: 25+	No. of Living Children 1: 0 or 1, 2: 2+	Education of Women 1: 0–6 yrs, 2: 7+ years	Country	No. of Women Accepting Fertility Control	No. of Women Not Accepting Fertility Control
1	1	1	India	4	8
2	1	1	India	2	1
1	1	2	India	14	7
2	1	2	India	7	3
1	2	1	India	17	1
2	2	1	India	175	9
1	2	2	India	12	2
2	2	2	India	90	5
1	1	1	Yugoslavia	12	21
2	1	1	Yugoslavia	13	9
1	1	2	Yugoslavia	112	155
2	1	2	Yugoslavia	40	39
1	2	1	Yugoslavia	8	3
2	2	1	Yugoslavia	63	36
1	2	2	Yugoslavia	13	9
2	2	2	Yugoslavia	96	66

18

Logistic Regression for Multiple Response Categories

The preceding two chapters showed how logistic regression permits us to extend our ideas of linear models to the response variable that is *dichotomous* rather than measured. In the present chapter, we see how logistic regression, in turn, can be extended, allowing us to model *categorical response variables* that take on more than two "values." We first develop regression models for the *ordered categorical response* and then for the response whose categories are distinguished only *nominally*. The techniques developed in this chapter are quite new and may not be available in all computational packages. These multi-category analyses, however, may be approximated with an ordinary logistic regression program.

18.1
The Ordered Categorical Response: Degrees of Success

The categories making up an *ordered categorical variable* are arranged in a distinct nonarbitrary order. Thus, the variable Rated Teaching Effectiveness with categories Poor, Fair, Good, Very Good, and Excellent is an ordered categorical variable, sometimes called an *ordinal variable*. The five categories form a distinct order. Fair must fall between Poor and Good, Good must fall between Fair and Very Good, and Very Good must fall between Good and Excellent. If we were to rearrange the categories into the sequence Fair, Very Good, Poor, Excellent, Good their orderedness would be lost.

In modeling the ordinal response, we should take the ordered nature of the categories into account. Until recently, the most common approach involved *scoring* the categories, that is, assigning numeric values to them. The resulting numeric scores were then used in models as though they were scores on a measured response. The approach had its drawbacks: (1) the resulting scores were far from satisfying the Normal characteristics requirement because they could take on only a small number of specific values, and (2) picking the score values could be quite arbitrary. If Poor is scored 1 and Fair 2, then should Good receive a score of 3 or 4 or what? Often successive integers were used as the scores, not because they were known to give the "correct" spacing to the categories but because some decision had to be made.

The scoring approach worked, in the sense that it allowed linear modeling of the ordered response but it was acknowledged to provide only an approximation to a more satisfactory solution.

18.2
Logistic Regression Models for the Ordered Response

As statisticians gained experience with logistic regression as a modeling tool, it was tempting to see how it might be applied to the modeling of the ordinal response as well. What made it tempting can be illustrated.

Assume that we want to model Rated Teaching Effectiveness as a function of instructor experience, measured by number of Years of Teaching. If we decide that Effective means a rating of Good or Better and that Ineffective means a rating of Poor or Fair, we could model Effectiveness, using the ideas of Chapters 16 and 17, as

$$\log\left[\frac{p(Good,\ Very\ Good,\ or\ Excellent)}{p(Poor\ or\ Fair)}\right] = \beta_1 + \beta_2\ (Years\ Teaching), \quad \textbf{(18.1)}$$

as a logistic regression or log-odds model with a corresponding *multiplicative* version,

$$\left[\frac{p(Good,\ Very\ Good,\ or\ Excellent)}{p(Poor\ or\ Fair)}\right] = \gamma_1\gamma_2^{(Years\ Teaching)}. \quad \textbf{(18.2)}$$

In Equation [18.2], γ_2 is the *odds multiplier* for Years of Teaching. Each additional year of teaching experience *multiplies* the odds of Effective teaching by γ_2.

Equations [18.1] and [18.2] describe one model of Rated Teaching Effectiveness. It is not a unique model because it depends on our decision to take the division point between Fair and Good as the division point between Ineffective and Effective as well. *If*, instead, we decide that to be Effective one has to be rated Very Good or Excellent, then our log-odds and odds models are

$$\log\left[\frac{p(Very\ Good\ or\ Excellent)}{p(Poor,\ Fair,\ or\ Good)}\right] = \beta_3 + \beta_4(Years\ Teaching) \quad \textbf{(18.3)}$$

and

$$\left[\frac{p(Very\ Good\ or\ Excellent)}{p(Poor,\ Fair,\ or\ Good)}\right] = \gamma_3\gamma_4^{(Years\ Teaching)}. \quad \textbf{(18.4)}$$

For Equation [18.4], γ_4 is a different odds multiplier for number of Years of Teaching. And, we have a third or a fourth odds multiplier if we take the "cut-point" for Ineffective/Effective teaching to be between Poor and Fair, or between Very Good and Excellent. The result is four different definitions of effective teaching and four (possibly) different odds multipliers for our explanatory variable, Years Teaching.

The straightforward logistic regression "solution" for the ordinal response, then, is an awkward one. First, it gives multiple estimates of an odds-multiplier for any *x*-variable. Should we believe one more than the others? Or, could they somehow be integrated into a single estimate? Second, we confront the fits of $(k - 1)$ different logistic regression models if our response has k ordered categories. How could these fits be aggregated into an overall fit? And, how could the fits, aggregated or not, be used in model comparison, say against the fits of a model that included Class Size as well as Years of Teaching as an explanatory variable?

It would be nice if, instead of having to wrestle with questions such as these, there were a logistic regression approach that (a) took into account all possible cut-points for the success/failure distinction but (b) yielded a unique odds multiplier for each x-variable, as well as an overall goodness of fit measure. We learn about just such an approach in the next section.

18.3
The Proportional Odds Model

Given wide currency by the British statistician Peter McCullagh (1980), the *proportional odds* model has become the most important technique for modeling the ordered categories response variable. For an ordinal response with J categories and a single x-variable, the proportional odds model can be written as follows:

$$\log\left[\frac{p(Categories\ 1\ through\ j|\ x_i)}{p(Categories\ j + 1\ through\ J|\ x_i)}\right] = \alpha_j + \beta x_i. \tag{18.5}$$

There is, as there was in the preceding section, a separate proportional odds equation for each possible cut point; j takes values from 1 through $(J - 1)$. But these equations differ only in their intercept terms, the α_js. The "slope" parameter for the x-variable is the *same* in all $(J - 1)$ equations. This means that there is a *single odds multiplier* in the multiplicative version of the model:

$$\left[\frac{p(Categories\ 1\ through\ j|\ x_i)}{p(Categories\ j + 1\ through\ J|\ x_i)}\right] = \kappa_j \lambda^{x_i}. \tag{18.6}$$

The odds of success are to be multiplied by λ for each unit increase in x. We no longer have to worry about a cut-point, about which of the J categories are associated with success and which with failure. We have a single parameter assessing the influence of an explanatory variable on our ordinal response. The multiplicity of *intersects*, the α_js or κ_js, in the proportional odds model usually is unimportant. As we have seen throughout this book, the intersect in many linear models has no substantively important interpretation.

Furthermore, the fit of the proportional odds model to a sample of observations gives the familiar *Deviance* statistic. Just as for the *Deviance* in ordinary logistic regression fits, it can be used to assess the goodness of fit of a proportional odds model to *grouped data* and to compare the fits of fuller and less full proportional odds models, whether for individual or grouped observations.

18.3.1 Example: Tonsil Enlargement and Streptococcus Pyogenes

Table 18.1 describes the tonsil sizes of a sample of 1,398 children aged 0–15 years with intact tonsils (Holmes & Williams 1954). Tonsils are classified as Not Enlarged, Enlarged, and Greatly Enlarged. The three categories define an ordinal variable, Tonsil Size. The researchers also ascertained whether or not each child was a carrier of *streptococcus pyogenes*. At issue is whether and to what extent Streptococcus contributes to tonsil enlargement.

At the bottom of Table 18.1, the data are repeated as coded for the proportional odds model fit. Our model has a single x, Streptococcus, which is a 0/1 variable taking the value 1 for Streptococcus Carriers and 0 for Noncarriers. The ordered response categories have been coded 1 (Not Enlarged), 2 (Enlarged), and 3 (Greatly Enlarged).

T A B L E **18.1**

Tonsil Size and *Streptococcus Pyogenes*

	Not Enlarged	Enlarged	Greatly Enlarged	Total
Streptococcus carriers	19	29	24	72
Noncarriers	497	560	269	1326
Total	516	589	293	1398

Data Coded for Proportional Odds Analyses

Tonsil Size (y)	Streptococcus (x)	Frequencies (f)
1	1	19
2	1	29
3	1	24
1	0	497
2	0	560
3	0	269

18.3.2 Conditional Multinomial Probabilities

Central to the proportional odds model and, indeed, to all of the models for the multicategory response, is the idea of *conditional multinomial probabilities*. Corresponding to each of the *design points* in our sample is a set of response category probabilities. They are described as *conditional probabilities* because they are conditional on the design point, on the values taken on by the x-variables in the model. For different design points, the response category probabilities are likely to differ. Calling the response set probabilities *multinomial* has a more technical significance but it directs our attention to the fact that there are multiple (more than two) response categories.

Let's link these ideas with our two examples. For the Rated Teaching Effectiveness illustration there is a set of five conditional probabilities associated with each value of Years of Teaching, the sole *x-variable*. That is, setting Years of Teaching equal to "5," points us to a particular *conditional population* of Teaching Effectiveness Ratings, that for instructors with 5 years of teaching experience. If we were to randomly sample an individual instructor from this population, there is a certain probability that we would obtain one whose teaching was rated Excellent,

$$p(Excellent \mid 5\ Years\ Teaching),$$

a certain probability that we would obtain one whose teaching was rated Very Good,

$$p(Very\ Good \mid 5\ Years\ Teaching),$$

and other probabilities for an instructor with a teaching effectiveness rating of Good, Fair, or Poor. Together, these five probabilities make up the set of conditional multinomial probabilities for the population of instructors with five years of teaching experience.

There would be a similarly defined set of five conditional multinomial probabilities for each of the conditional response populations of interest, for example, for each value of Years of Teaching covered in the study.

For our Tonsil Size example, there are only two conditional response populations: one for Carriers and one for Noncarriers. The first of these populations is marked by the three probabilities,

$$p(Not\ Enlarged \mid Carrier),$$
$$p(Enlarged \mid Carrier),$$

and

$$p(Greatly\ Enlarged \mid Carrier).$$

Again, these are the probabilities—having randomly selected from among children who are Streptococcus Carriers—of observing tonsils that are Not Enlarged, Enlarged, or Greatly Enlarged, respectively. Equally, they are the *proportions* of the population of children who are carriers with Not Enlarged, Enlarged, or Greatly Enlarged tonsils. A second set of probabilities or proportions describes the tonsils of the population of children who are Noncarriers.

A little notation assists in the further discussion of these multinomial conditional probabilities. We let the number of response categories be J and the number of design points be I. A particular response category will be denoted by j ($j = 1, 2, \ldots, J$) and a particular design point will be denoted by i ($i = 1, 2, \ldots, I$). With this notation, we can write

$$p(Response\ in\ Category\ j \mid Observation\ at\ Design\ Point\ i) = \pi_{j\mid i}. \qquad \textbf{(18.7)}$$

Whenever we sample from one of these *conditional multinomial populations* we observe one and only one of the response categories—a sampled child's tonsils are *either* Not Enlarged, Enlarged *or* Greatly Enlarged. The response categories are *mutually exclusive* (a response can fall into only one category) and *exhaustive* (a response must fall into one of the categories). As a result, for any multinomial population, the sum of the multinomial probabilities has to be 1:

$$\sum_{j=1}^{J} \pi_{j|i} = 1.0, \text{ for } i = 1, 2, \ldots, I. \tag{18.8}$$

The importance of Equation [18.8] is that *if* we knew the values of $(J - 1)$ of the multinomial probabilities for the ith design point, we would know the Jth probability as well. We could compute it simply by subtracting the sum of the $(J - 1)$ known probabilities from 1.0.

Put another way, if we know *none* of the J multinomial probabilities we really don't know just $(J - 1)$ of them! Equation [18.8] places *one constraint* on the J probabilities or parameters. As a result, there are only $(J - 1)$ unknown parameters for the ith conditional multinomial distribution. This, of course, is true of *each* of the I conditional distributions, one at each design point. In total, then, there are $I \times (J - 1)$ unknown multinomial parameters.

18.3.3 Estimation of Multinomial Probabilities

All of our linear explanatory models have as their purpose the estimation of the *parameters* of conditional response populations. When the response was *measured*, we needed estimates of $\mu(y \mid X_{i.})$, the means, and $\sigma^2(y \mid X)$, the variances, of the conditional response populations. When the response was *dichotomous* (or, *binomial*), we needed to estimate $p(Success \mid X_{i.})$, the proportion of successes in a conditional response population or, equivalently, the *probability* of obtaining a success from that conditional response population when we sample once at random. (With but two response categories, success and failure, the conditional probability of sampling a failure is automatically estimated whenever $p(success \mid X_{i.})$ is estimated: $p(failure \mid X_{i.}) = 1 - p(success \mid X_{i.})$. This is an application, for $J = 2$, of the principle of Equation [18.8].)

The conditional distribution of the multicategory or *multinomial* response has as its parameters the J conditional multinomial probabilities. All linear models for the multicategory or multinomial response have as their goal, then, the estimation of these probabilities. This estimation is, mathematically and computationally, even more complicated than it was for logistic regression. We will not dwell on any of the details of this estimation for any multinomial model, but will outline certain conditions that are placed on these estimates. These conditions are the same, essentially, as those placed on the estimates for measured and dichotomous response models:

1   The parameter estimates should be good ones. We'd like the estimates of the conditional multinomial probabilities to be "close" to the actual (but unknowable) values of those parameters. To this end, all of this chapter's linear models for the multicategory response have *maximum likelihood* (ML) parameter estimates. ML estimates were employed in earlier chapters for the measured and dichotomous models as well. They tend to be *unbiased* and to have small standard errors (SE). The use of maximum likelihood also helps secure our second parameter estimation condition.

2 The parameter estimates should facilitate the assessment of how well a model fits a sample of multinomial responses. Our ML estimated multinomial probabilities, the $\widehat{\pi}_{j|i}$s, can be used in the computation of a Model *Deviance* statistic. This *Deviance* for multinomial models is defined and computed as a natural extension to the *Deviance* of Chapters 16 and 17 for dichotomous response models.

Let $f_{j|i}$ be the *observed frequency* in our sample of responses at the ith design point that fall into the jth response category. And, let f_i be the total number of observations in the sample at the ith design point:

$$f_i = \sum_{j=1}^{J} f_{j|i}. \tag{18.9}$$

Then, the number of sample responses at the ith design point, *estimated* by some linear model to fall into the jth response category, is represented as

$$\widehat{f}_{j|i} = f_i \, \widehat{\pi}_{j|i} \tag{18.10}$$

where $\widehat{\pi}_{j|i}$ is the modeled probability of a response in category j given design point i. We refer to $\widehat{f}_{j|i}$ as the *modeled frequency* to contrast it with the observed frequency.

Finally, observed and modeled frequencies are used to compute the *Deviance* statistic:

$$Deviance = 2 \sum_{i=1}^{I} \sum_{j=1}^{J} \left[f_{j|i} \log \left(\frac{f_{j|i}}{\widehat{f}_{j|i}} \right) \right]. \tag{18.11}$$

Equation [18.11] is a direct extension of Equation [17.3], given in Chapter 17, for the dichotomous, $J = 2$ case.

Deviance, we recall, is a *goodness of fit* statistic. It takes smaller values for models that fit the sample data well and larger values for ill-fitting models. The *Deviance* statistic has a degrees-of-freedom parameter. For our multinomial linear models, the d.f. for the *Deviance* of Equation [18.11] is computed as

$$\text{d.f.}_{Dev} = I(J-1) - k \tag{18.12}$$

where k is the number of parameters in our linear model. Thus, the number of d.f. is the difference between the number of unknown conditional multinomial probabilities for the populations from which our sample was obtained, $I \times (J - 1)$, and the number of model parameters, k, used to estimate those probabilities.

3 The multinomial probability estimates must be consistent with a linear model. For the measured response, the estimated means for conditional response populations had to satisfy the linear model,

$$\widehat{\mu}(y \mid X_{i.}) = \widehat{\beta}_0 + \sum_{j=1}^{k-1} \widehat{\beta}_j x_{ij}.$$

And, for the dichotomous response, the estimates of the conditional probabilities of success had to satisfy a similar linear model,

$$\log\left[\frac{\widehat{p}(Success \mid X_{i.})}{(1 - \widehat{p}(Success \mid X_{i.}))}\right] = \widehat{\beta}_0 + \sum_{j=1}^{k-1} \widehat{\beta}_j x_{ij}.$$

For the *proportional odds model*, Equation [18.5],

$$\log\left[\frac{p(Categories\ 1\ through\ j \mid x_i)}{p(Categories\ j + 1\ through\ J \mid x_i)}\right] = \alpha_j + \beta x_i, \qquad \textbf{(18.5)}$$

shows the linear model that the estimated conditional multinomial probabilities must satisfy. The numerator and denominator on the left-hand side of Equation [18.5] are *cumulative probabilities*, sums of probabilities over categories. In our multinomial probability notation,

$$p(Categories\ 1\ through\ j \mid x_i) = \sum_{\ell = 1}^{j} \pi_{\ell \mid x_i}$$

and

$$p(Categories\ j + 1\ through\ J \mid x_i) = \sum_{\ell = j+1}^{J} \pi_{\ell \mid x_i}.$$

For consistency with the other linear models, we've substituted x_i for i indicating the design point as a score on a single x-variable. Assuming that x takes one of I distinct values, this gives us I design points. If we replace the multinomial probabilities with their estimates and then substitute the resulting estimated cumulative probabilities on the left-hand side of Equation [18.5], we have the linear model that the multinomial probability estimates must satisfy:

$$\log\left[\frac{\sum_{\ell=1}^{j} \widehat{\pi}_{\ell \mid x_i}}{\sum_{\ell=j+1}^{J} \widehat{\pi}_{\ell \mid x_i}}\right] = \widehat{\alpha}_j + \widehat{\beta} x_i. \qquad \textbf{(18.13)}$$

We'll make little use of this last, rather complicated equation. We have developed it simply to reinforce the idea that, for the proportional odds model, the estimated multinomial category probabilities *are linked* to a linear function of the x-variable(s). The proportional odds model is the first of this chapter's linear models for the multinomial response. Later models link a linear function of the xs to the multinomial probabilities in ways different from Equation [18.13].

18.3.4   Model Comparisons and Model Adequacy

If two multinomial linear models enjoy a fuller/less full relation, we have a basis for the comparison of their fits in the *difference* in the sizes of their *Deviances*. The

Deviance will be larger for the less full model and the *Deviance difference*,

$$\text{Dev diff(Model F | Model LF)} = \text{Dev(Model LF)} - \text{Dev(Model F)},$$

is positive. When the less full model is correct, that is, when the *constraints* imposed on the parameters of the fuller model to produce the less full one are correct, the *Dev diff* enjoys a Chi-squared probability distribution with d.f. equal to the difference in the number of parameters in the two models.

Large values of *Dev diff* lead to rejection of the less full model, small values lead to its acceptance.

The definition of the *Deviance Difference* and its use in model comparison are the same as they were for the dichotomous response in Chapters 16 and 17.

Deviance itself can be used to assess the adequacy of models for certain data. The data must be *grouped* and, ideally, the observations should be sufficiently numerous that each response category occurs several times for each design point. For large data sets, the *Deviance* can be interpreted as an observation of the Chi-squared random variable with the same degrees of freedom as calculated under Equation [18.12] for the *Deviance*. If the *Deviance* falls among the smaller 75% of the Chi-squared distribution, this is evidence that the model fits the data adequately. As in logistic regression, we seek, via model comparison, to find the adequate and most parsimonious model for our multinomial response data.

18.3.5 Proportional Odds Model Parameters: Tonsils Enlargement

We can now look further at a proportional odds model for the Tonsils Size data of Table 18.1. For this example, we have a single *x*-variable coded 1 for Carriers and 0 for Noncarriers. The categorical response has three ordered levels:

1 Not Enlarged,

2 Enlarged, and

3 Greatly Enlarged.

The three categories imply two cut-points with a linear (proportional-odds) model for each:

$$\log \left[\frac{p(\textit{Not Enlarged} \mid x_i)}{p(\textit{Enlarged} \text{ or } \textit{Greatly Enlarged} \mid x_i)} \right] = \alpha_1 + \beta x_i \qquad \textbf{(18.14)}$$

and

$$\log \left[\frac{p(\textit{Not Enlarged} \text{ or } \textit{Enlarged} \mid x_i)}{p(\textit{Greatly Enlarged} \mid x_i)} \right] = \alpha_2 + \beta x_i. \qquad \textbf{(18.15)}$$

Equation [18.14] is for the cut between categories 1 and 2 and Equation [18.15] is for the cut between 2 and 3. The two have different intercepts, but a common slope. Knowing that *x* is 0 for Noncarriers and 1 for Carriers allows us to write these more specialized equations:

$$\log\left[\frac{p(\textit{Not Enlarged} \mid \textit{Noncarrier})}{p(\textit{Enlarged} \text{ or } \textit{Greatly Enlarged} \mid \textit{Noncarrier})}\right] = \alpha_1,$$

$$\log\left[\frac{p(\textit{Not Enlarged} \mid \textit{Carrier})}{p(\textit{Enlarged} \text{ or } \textit{Greatly Enlarged} \mid \textit{Carrier})}\right] = \alpha_1 + \beta, \qquad \textbf{(18.16)}$$

$$\log\left[\frac{p(\textit{Not Enlarged} \text{ or } \textit{Enlarged} \mid \textit{Noncarrier})}{p(\textit{Greatly Enlarged} \mid \textit{Noncarrier})}\right] = \alpha_2,$$

and

$$\log\left[\frac{p(\textit{Not Enlarged} \text{ or } \textit{Enlarged} \mid \textit{Carrier})}{p(\textit{Greatly Enlarged} \mid \textit{Carrier})}\right] = \alpha_2 + \beta. \qquad \textbf{(18.17)}$$

The intercepts α_1 and α_2, give the log-odds of falling below each of the cut-points of our ordinal response for the comparison level, Noncarriers. The slope parameter, β, is the additive contribution to each of these log-odds for Carriers.

As with the logistic regression models of the preceding two chapters, these additive log-odds models have multiplicative odds model equivalents. Exponentiating on both sides of Equations [18.16] and [18.17] gives us

$$\left[\frac{p(\textit{Not Enlarged} \mid \textit{Noncarrier})}{p(\textit{Enlarged} \text{ or } \textit{Greatly Enlarged} \mid \textit{Noncarrier})}\right] = e^{\alpha_1} \quad = \kappa_1,$$

$$\left[\frac{p(\textit{Not Enlarged} \mid \textit{Carrier})}{p(\textit{Enlarged} \text{ or } \textit{Greatly Enlarged} \mid \textit{Carrier})}\right] = e^{\alpha_1}e^{\beta} = \kappa_1\lambda, \qquad \textbf{(18.18)}$$

$$\left[\frac{p(\textit{Not Enlarged} \text{ or } \textit{Enlarged} \mid \textit{Noncarrier})}{p(\textit{Greatly Enlarged} \mid \textit{Noncarrier})}\right] = e^{\alpha_2} \quad = \kappa_2,$$

and

$$\left[\frac{p(\textit{Not Enlarged} \text{ or } \textit{Enlarged} \mid \textit{Carrier})}{p(\textit{Greatly Enlarged} \mid \textit{Carrier})}\right] = e^{\alpha_2}e^{\beta} = \kappa_2\lambda. \qquad \textbf{(18.19)}$$

In the multiplicative form of the model, the intercepts ($\kappa_1 = e^{\alpha_1}$ and $\kappa_2 = e^{\alpha_2}$) give the odds of smaller tonsils for the comparison group, while the slope ($\lambda = e^{\beta}$) is the odds-multiplier for the Carriers. If Carriers of streptococcus are more likely than Noncarriers to have enlarged tonsils, λ should be less than 1. Equivalently, β should be negative.

18.3.6 Fitting the Proportional Odds Model: Tonsils Enlargement

Table 18.2 displays some details of the fit of our proportional odds model to the *Tonsils Size* data of Table 18.1 (The fit was computed in SPIDA with the ODREG

■ T A B L E 18.2
Proportional Odds Model: Tonsils Enlargement and Streptococcus

**Ordinal Regression
Response: Tonsil Size**

Column	Name	Coeff	SE	P Value	Odds	0.95	CI
0	Const 1	−0.509	0.056	0.000	0.601	0.538	0.672
0	Const 2	1.363	0.067	0.000	3.907	3.424	4.458
2	Carriers	−0.603	0.225	0.007	0.547	0.352	0.851

d.f.:1395 $\qquad$ −2LogL: 2955.495 $\qquad$ #iter:10

command.) In our notation, we have these estimates of the proportional-odds parameters for both the log-odds (additive) and odds (multiplicative) models:

$$\hat{\alpha}_1 = -0.509, \ \hat{\kappa}_1 = 0.601,$$
$$\hat{\alpha}_2 = 1.363, \ \hat{\kappa}_2 = 3.907,$$

and

$$\hat{\beta} = -0.603, \ \hat{\lambda} = 0.547.$$

The odds of Carriers having less enlarged tonsils are *modeled* as about one-half the odds for Noncarriers (i.e., $\hat{\lambda} = 0.547$). We can check this and other model results against the *empirical* or observed odds to get an idea as to whether the model is faithful to the data or not. From Table 18.1, we have these empirical odds:

$$\left[\frac{Not\ Enlarged\ |\ Carrier}{Enlarged\ or\ Greatly\ Enlarged\ |\ Carrier}\right] = \left[\frac{19}{29+24}\right] = 0.358,$$

$$\left[\frac{Not\ Enlarged\ |\ Noncarrier}{Enlarged\ or\ Greatly\ Enlarged\ |\ Noncarrier}\right] = \left[\frac{497}{560+269}\right] = 0.600,$$

$$\left[\frac{Not\ Enlarged\ or\ Enlarged\ |\ Carrier}{Greatly\ Enlarged\ |\ Carrier}\right] = \left[\frac{19+29}{24}\right] = 2.000,$$

and

$$\left[\frac{Not\ Enlarged\ or\ Enlarged\ |\ Noncarrier}{Greatly\ Enlarged\ |\ Noncarrier}\right] = \left[\frac{497+460}{269}\right] = 3.558.$$

The second and fourth of these odds are modeled as $\hat{\kappa}_1 = 0.601$ and $\hat{\kappa}_2 = 3.907$ while the first and third are modeled as $(0.601)(0.547) = 0.329$ and $(3.907)(0.547) = 2.137$.

We can compute the *Deviance* for this model. The SPIDA calculated estimates of the conditional multinomial probabilities are

$$\hat{\pi}_{NE|C} = 0.248, \hat{\pi}_{E|C} = 0.434, \hat{\pi}_{GE|C} = 0.319$$

and

$$\hat{\pi}_{NE|NC} = 0.376, \hat{\pi}_{E|NC} = 0.421, \hat{\pi}_{GE|NC} = 0.204.$$

The subscripts are coded: NE, E, and GE for Not Enlarged, Enlarged, and Greatly Enlarged, and C and NC for Carriers and Noncarriers. The above estimated multinomial probabilities were used by SPIDA via Equation [18.10] to give the following model-estimated frequencies:

$$
\begin{aligned}
\hat{f}_{NE|C} &= (0.248)(19 + 29 + 24) & &= (0.248)(72) = 17.831, [f_{NE|C} = 19], \\
\hat{f}_{E|C} &= (0.434)(72) & &= 31.227, [f_{E|C} = 29], \\
\hat{f}_{GE|C} &= (0.319)(72) & &= 22.941, [f_{GE|C} = 24], \\
\hat{f}_{NE|NC} &= (0.376)(497 + 560 + 269) & &= (0.376)(1326) = 497.970, [f_{NE|NC} = 497], \\
\hat{f}_{E|NC} &= (0.421)(1326) & &= 557.793, [f_{E|NC} = 560], \text{ and} \\
\hat{f}_{GE|NC} &= (0.204)(1326) & &= 270.237, [f_{GE|NC} = 269].
\end{aligned}
$$

The corresponding observed frequency is given in brackets following each of the estimates. The *Deviance* computed by Equation [18.11] is quite small, $Dev = 0.302$. The d.f. for this statistic, from Equation [18.12], is d.f. $= I \times (J - 1) - k = 2(3 - 1) - 3 = 4 - 3 = 1$. We have $I = 2$ design points, $J = 3$ response categories, and our proportional odds model has $k = 3$ parameters.

Our model *Deviance* of 0.302 evaluated against the Chi-squared distribution with one d.f. returns an upper tail probability of 0.68. This is substantially greater than 0.25 and we judge that the proportional odds model provides an adequate fit to the data.

18.3.7 Model Comparison: Tonsils Enlargement

Our three-parameter model fits the data adequately, but is it as parsimonious as it could be? In particular, we are interested in whether the odds of tonsils enlargement could be the same for Carriers as for Noncarriers. In terms of our proportional odds model, could the β of our model be constrained to be 0 (and, hence, the odds multiplier λ constrained to be 1)?

The constrained two parameter model specifies that the odds, hence the underlying multinomial probabilities, for the two groups of children are the same. We can work out estimates of these common multinomial probabilities from the data of Table 18.1:

$$\hat{\pi}_{NE|C} = \hat{\pi}_{NE|NC} = \left[\frac{19 + 497}{1398} \right] = 0.369,$$

$$\hat{\pi}_{E|C} = \hat{\pi}_{E|NC} = \left[\frac{29 + 560}{1398} \right] = 0.421,$$

and

$$\widehat{\pi}_{GE|C} = \widehat{\pi}_{GE|NC} = \left[\frac{24 + 269}{1398}\right] = 0.210.$$

These Null model probabilities lead to these estimated frequencies:

$$
\begin{aligned}
\widehat{f}_{NE|C} &= (0.369)(72) &&= 26.575, & [f_{NE|C} &= 19], \\
\widehat{f}_{E|C} &= (0.421)(72) &&= 30.335, & [f_{E|C} &= 29], \\
\widehat{f}_{GE|C} &= (0.210)(72) &&= 15.090, & [f_{GE|C} &= 24], \\
\widehat{f}_{NE|NC} &= (0.369)(1326) &&= 489.425, & [f_{NE|NC} &= 497], \\
\widehat{f}_{E|NC} &= (0.421)(1326) &&= 558.665, & [f_{E|NC} &= 560], \text{ and} \\
\widehat{f}_{GE|NC} &= (0.210)(1326) &&= 277.910, & [f_{GE|NC} &= 269].
\end{aligned}
$$

The *Deviance* of the Null model from Equation [18.11] is $Dev = 7.32$. The *Deviance difference* between the Carrier/Noncarrier and Null models is

$$Dev\ diff = 7.320 - 0.302 = 7.018.$$

Were the Null model the correct one, this would be an observation from the Chi-squared distribution with d.f. equal to the difference in the numbers of parameters in the two models. Our fuller model has three parameters. The less full has only two. The difference is one. The upper tail probability for 7.018 in the Chi-squared distribution with one d.f. is 0.008. It is well within the upper 1% so we reject the less full (Null) model. We need to estimate odds of Tonsils Enlargement separately for Carriers and for Noncarriers.

We accept as our final model, then, the three parameter proportional odds model: It provides an adequate fit to the data and it fits significantly better than does the Null model.

18.4
Proportional Odds with Multiple *x*-Variables

The proportional odds model has been introduced with a single explanatory variable. Like logistic regression models, of which they are extensions, the multinomial models of this chapter can have several *x*-variables. These may be measured, categorical (using dummy variables), or a mixture of the two. In short, we have the full range of explanatory models for the multinomial response as we had for the measured or dichotomous response. There is one exception. Because the model postulates different intercepts for different cut-points, many proportional odds programs cannot handle "no-constant" models.

Let's look at a second proportional odds example, this time one with more than a single *x*-variable. The data in Table 18.3 describe the Breast Development of a sample of 318 12 and 13-year-old Turkish girls (Neyzi, Alp. & Orhon 1975). Breast Development in this study was an ordinal variable, taking values from 1 (Undeveloped) through 5 (Fully Developed). The girls were further classified by the Socioeconomic Status of their parents. Four socioeconomic categories were used, with 1 the Highest and 4 the Lowest.

T A B L E **18.3**

Breast Development and Parental Socioeconomic Status

	Breast Development				
	(Least)				(Fullest)
Parental Socioeconomic Status	1	2	3	4	5
1 (Highest)	2	14	28	40	18
2	1	21	25	25	9
3	1	12	12	12	2
4 (Lowest)	6	17	34	33	6

We are interested in whether the stage of Breast Development is a function of the Socioeconomic Status (SES) of the family. Our influence source is a categorical one with four levels. We'll take SES level 1 to be the comparison level and introduce dummy variables for each of the other three levels in our proportional odds model.

Our initial, fullest proportional odds model will have four intercepts, one fewer than the number of response categories, and three slopes, one fewer than the number of levels for the explanatory factor:

$$\log\left[\frac{p(\text{Cat 1 of } Development \mid SES)}{p(\text{Cat 2–5 of } Development \mid SES)}\right] = \alpha_1 + \beta_1(SES\ 2) + \beta_2(SES\ 3) + \beta_3(SES\ 4),$$

$$\log\left[\frac{p(\text{Cat 1–2 of } Development \mid SES)}{p(\text{Cat 3–5 of } Development \mid SES)}\right] = \alpha_2 + \beta_1(SES\ 2) + \beta_2(SES\ 3) + \beta_3(SES\ 4),$$

$$\log\left[\frac{p(\text{Cat 1–3 of } Development \mid SES)}{p(\text{Cat 4–5 of } Development \mid SES)}\right] = \alpha_3 + \beta_1(SES\ 2) + \beta_2(SES\ 3) + \beta_3(SES\ 4),$$

and

$$\log\left[\frac{p(\text{Cat 1–4 of } Development \mid SES)}{p(\text{Cat 5 of } Development \mid SES)}\right] = \alpha_4 + \beta_1(SES\ 2) + \beta_2(SES\ 3) + \beta_3(SES\ 4).$$

The intercepts are the log-odds of lesser Breast Development for girls from SES level 1, while the slopes are increments to these log-odds for girls from other SES levels.

The data of Table 18.3 are coded in Table 18.4 for the proportional odds model.

The estimated proportional odds model parameters are given in Table 18.5. The increasing magnitude of the $\widehat{\alpha}$s is a characteristic of designs of this type, where the intercept is a log-odds for a comparison group. The log-odds of falling below the cutoff increase as the cutoff moves to the right and more and more categories fall below the cutoff.

All three estimated slopes appear to be non-0. Equivalently, the odds multipliers for SES 2, SES 3, and SES 4 all appear to be greater than 1.0: $\widehat{\lambda}_1 = 1.87$, $\widehat{\lambda}_2 = 2.60$, and $\widehat{\lambda}_3 = 2.02$. (The P values and CIs that appear as part of the ODREG output in SPIDA are based on the assumption that, for large enough sample sizes, the $\widehat{\alpha}$s and $\widehat{\beta}$s will have sampling distributions with normal histograms.) Delayed (lesser) Breast Development appears more characteristic of girls from SES levels 2, 3, and 4 than for those from SES 1.

T A B L E 18.4

Breast Development and SES Level: Coded Variables

Frequency	Development Category	SES Level	SES 2	SES 3	SES 4
2	1	1	0	0	0
1	1	2	1	0	0
1	1	3	0	1	0
6	1	4	0	0	1
14	2	1	0	0	0
21	2	2	1	0	0
12	2	3	0	1	0
17	2	4	0	0	1
28	3	1	0	0	0
25	3	2	1	0	0
12	3	3	0	1	0
34	3	4	0	0	1
40	4	1	0	0	0
25	4	2	1	0	0
12	4	3	0	1	0
33	4	4	0	0	1
18	5	1	0	0	0
9	5	2	1	0	0
2	5	3	0	1	0
6	5	4	0	0	1

T A B L E 18.5

Breast Development and SES Level: Proportional Odds Model Fits

Model 1: Separate Log-odds for Each SES Level

Column	Name	Coeff	SE	P Value	Odds	0.95	CI
0	Const 1	−3.971	0.364	0.000	0.019	0.009	0.038
0	Const 2	−1.717	0.211	0.000	0.180	0.119	0.272
0	Const 3	−0.314	0.188	0.095	0.730	0.505	1.056
0	Const 4	1.644	0.222	0.000	5.177	3.351	7.998
4	SES 2	0.626	0.272	0.021	1.870	1.097	3.188
5	SES 3	0.956	0.344	0.006	2.600	1.324	5.105
6	SES 4	0.705	0.261	0.007	2.024	1.214	3.372

df:311   −2LogL: 881.899   #iter:11

Estimated Multinomial Probabilities
Breast Development

	1	2	3	4	5
SES 1	0.018	0.134	0.270	0.416	0.162
SES 2	0.034	0.217	0.326	0.329	0.094
SES 3	0.047	0.272	0.337	0.276	0.069
SES 4	0.037	0.230	0.330	0.316	0.087

The estimated conditional multinomial probabilities for this proportional odds model appear at the bottom of Table 18.5. They can be used to obtain modeled frequencies and the latter compared with the observed frequencies in the *Deviance* statistic. The computed *Deviance* for this fullest model is

$$Dev(fullest) = 7.712.$$

The degrees of freedom for this *Dev* are $I \times (J - 1) - k = 4(5 - 1) - (4 + 3) = 9$. When we refer the *Dev* of 7.712 to the Chi-squared distribution with 9 d.f., we find an upper-tail probability of $0.563 > 0.25$. The proportional odds model provides an adequate fit to the data.

Can the seven-parameter model be simplified? Our interest is in the λs (or, the βs). An examination of their estimates in Table 18.5 suggests the following:

- all three odds multipliers are greater than 1.0;
- the three odds multipliers do not have a natural order—the $\hat{\lambda}$ for SES 3 is *not* between those for SES 2 and SES 4; and
- the CIs for the three $\hat{\lambda}$s are such that all three λs *could* fall within the same interval.

The second observation argues against substituting a measure/SES variable for the level dummy variables. The third observation, however, suggests that we might try setting all three βs (and, as a result, all three λs) equal to the same quantity.

Let's fit this latter model. We form a new x-variable for this constrained model by adding the three dummy variables of the fullest model together, producing a variable that is 0 for SES 1 and 1 for SES 2, 3, or 4. In Table 18.6, we have the ODREG fit to this constrained proportional odds model. The single odds multiplier, for SES levels 2 through 4, is estimated to be about 2: $(\hat{\lambda} = 2.055)$.

The *Deviance* for this less full model, obtained via the estimated multinomial probabilities and modeled frequencies, is

$$Dev(less\ full) = 8.605$$

with d.f. of $4(5 - 1) - (4 + 1) = 11$. (There are two fewer parameters in the less full model. Hence, its *Deviance* has two more d.f.) We first check this *Deviance* to see

T A B L E 18.6

Breast Development and SES Level: Proportional Odds Model Fits

Model 2: SES Level 1 vs. Levels 2 through 4

Column	Name	Coeff	SE	P Value	Odds	0.95	CI
0	Const 1	−3.966	0.364	0.000	0.019	0.009	0.039
0	Const 2	−1.714	0.211	0.000	0.180	0.119	0.272
0	Const 3	−0.314	0.188	0.095	0.730	0.505	1.056
0	Const 4	1.642	0.222	0.000	5.166	3.345	7.980
7	SES 2+	0.720	0.222	0.001	2.055	1.331	3.173

d.f.:313   −2LogL: 882.792   #iter:11

if the less full model provides an adequate fit to the data. The upper-tail probability of 8.605 in the Chi-squared distribution with 11 d.f. is 0.658 > 0.25. The less full model provides an adequate fit to the data.

Both the fullest and less full models are adequate. We can compute and evaluate the *Deviance difference* to determine which model has the stronger support. The *Deviance difference* is $(8.605 - 7.712) = 0.893$. If the less full model is correct, this will be an observation from the Chi-squared distribution with 2 d.f., the difference in the number of parameters in the two models. The upper-tail probability for 0.893 on 2 d.f. is 0.64 > 0.05, offering evidence that the constraint to the less full model is appropriate. Breast Development would appear to be advanced among Turkish girls from SES 1. The odds of lesser development are about twice as great for girls from SES levels 2, 3, or 4 than for those from SES 1. There appears, however, to be no difference in the rates of development among girls from SES levels 2, 3, and 4.

In this example, the odds of lesser Breast Development were modeled because the response categories had been ordered from Least Developed (1) to Fullest Developed (5). Had we wanted to model the odds of fuller Breast Development we simply could have reversed the order of the categories, arranging them from Fullest (1) to Least (5). The results of fitting a proportional odds model to the reversed category order are that the signs of the αs and βs would be *reversed* from what they were, and, as a result, the odds and odds multipliers, the κs and λs, would be the *reciprocals* of what they had been.

Thus, for our second Breast Development model, a reversal of response category ordering would have given $\widehat{\beta} = -0.720$ and $\widehat{\lambda} = (1/2.055) = 0.487$. The odds of *fuller* development are about one-half as great for girls from SES levels 2, 3, or 4 than for those from level 1. We reach the same conclusion but phrase it differently. You will want to think about whether there is a more natural way of expressing your results before electing a direction to the response category ordering.

18.5
An Alternative Cumulative Odds Model

The proportional odds model provides a very attractive approach to modeling the ordinal response. It provides, for each *x*-variable in our model, a uniquely defined and estimated odds multiplier, a single measure of the influence of an *x* on the ordered response. Unfortunately, the proportional odds assumptions are not met by all ordinal response data sets. There are instances in which the *Deviance* for the fullest proportional odds model of interest will be so large that we must reject this approach.

What can we do when this happens?

At the beginning of this chapter, we noted that "ordinary logistic regression" could be used in modeling the ordinal response. We could carry out a separate logistic regression for each success/failure cut-point. But, we noted, having a separate solution for each cut-point posed two problems for model comparison and interpretation:

1 each cut-point logistic regression provides its own estimate of a variable's influence on success and

2 each cut-point logistic regression provides its own goodness of fit statistic, the *Deviance*.

Failure of the proportional odds model to provide an adequate fit means that, in some sense, we must accept the first of these limitations. Our data *are inconsistent* with the proportional odds model assumption of a constancy of the slopes, the βs, across cut-points. Rather, the values of at least some of the βs change from cut-point to cut-point.

However, by judicious choice of our cut-point logistic regression model, we can ameliorate the impact of the second problem. In this section, we introduce a second linear model for cumulative odds, one that permits us to interpret the *sum* of the *Deviances* for the $(J - 1)$ individual logistic regressions as an overall goodness of fit for our linear model.

18.5.1   Logistic Regression for Continuation Ratios

Before describing this new model, let's review our conditional multinomial probability notation for the ordinal response. Our response variable consists of J mutually exclusive and exhaustive categories obeying a "natural order," $j = 1, 2, \ldots, J$. Our study design calls for sampling the response from I different populations, each associated with a different design point or x-score pattern. We express the (conditional) probability of observing response category j when we randomly sample from population $i(i = 1, 2, \ldots, I)$ as

$$p(Response\ in\ Category\ j \mid Observation\ at\ Design\ Point\ i) = \pi_{j|i}. \qquad \textbf{(18.7)}$$

For any design point i, the sum of these multinomial probabilities has to be 1:

$$\sum_{j=1}^{J} \pi_{j|i} = 1.0,\ \text{for}\ i = 1, 2, \ldots, I. \qquad \textbf{(18.8)}$$

If, again for a particular design point i, we sum these multinomial probabilities over *adjacent* categories, but not necessarily over all J categories, we compute a *cumulative* probability. In the proportional odds model, we dealt with two cumulative probabilities, the probability of being "below" the cut-point,

$$\sum_{\ell=1}^{j} \pi_{\ell|i},$$

and the probability of being "above" the cut-point,

$$\sum_{\ell=j+1}^{J} \pi_{\ell|i}.$$

It was the log of the *ratio* of these two cumulative probabilities for which the proportional odds approach offered a model linear in one or more *x*-variables:

$$\log \left[\frac{\sum_{\ell=1}^{j} \pi_{\ell|x_i}}{\sum_{\ell=j+1}^{J} \pi_{\ell|x_i}} \right] = \alpha_j + \sum_{m=1}^{q} \beta_m x_{im}, \ j = 1, 2, \ldots, J-1. \qquad \textbf{(18.20)}$$

As noted earlier, we could reverse the order of the response categories. This amounts to writing the proportional odds model in this form:

$$\log \left[\frac{\sum_{\ell=j+1}^{J} \pi_{\ell|x_i}}{\sum_{\ell=1}^{j} \pi_{\ell|x_i}} \right] = \alpha_j + \sum_{m=1}^{q} \beta_m x_{im}, \ j = 1, 2, \ldots, J-1. \qquad \textbf{(18.21)}$$

The model has $k = (J-1) + q$ parameters, a separate intercept for each of the $(J-1)$ cut-points but a single slope for each of the q *x*-variables.

This second form for the proportional odds is more easily compared with the *continuation ratio* model.

Equation [18.21] models the log odds of being *beyond the jth category* as opposed to being in *one of the first j categories*. The continuation ratio models the log odds of being *beyond the jth category* as opposed to being in *the jth category*:

$$\log \left[\frac{\sum_{\ell=j+1}^{J} \pi_{\ell|x_i}}{\pi_{j|x_i}} \right] = \alpha_j + \sum_{m=1}^{q} \beta_{jm} x_{im}, \ j = 1, 2, \ldots, J-1. \qquad \textbf{(18.22)}$$

Notice that it is not just the denominator of the ratio on the left-hand side that has changed from Equation [18.21] to Equation [18.22]. The continuation ratio model provides for *possibly different* slopes for the q *x*-variables at each cut-point. The notation β_{jm} implies that the slope for the mth *x*-variable may differ from one cut-point to the next. The continuation ratio model of Equation [18.22] has a total of $k = (J-1) + (J-1) \times q$ parameters.

The log-odds terms of Equation [18.22] are independent over the values of j, which makes it possible to obtain a useful overall *Deviance* statistic based on all $(J-1)$ of the log-odds.

An example will clarify the distinction between proportional odds and continuation ratio models.

18.5.2 Pneumoconiosis Among Coal Miners

Table 18.7 is taken from McCullagh and Nelder (1989) and relates the absence, presence, and severity of the lung disease pneumoconiosis to the number of years miners have worked at the coal face. Their analysis of these data establishes a nonlinear relation between Years Employed and the log-odds of Pneumoconiosis. The relation

T A B L E **18.7**

Years of Employment and Frequency of Pneumoconiosis Examination Outcomes Among Coal Miners

		Pneumoconiosis		
Years Employed	Log Years	Absent	Moderate	Severe
5.8	1.758	98	0	0
15.0	2.708	51	2	1
21.5	3.068	34	6	3
27.5	3.314	35	5	8
33.5	3.512	32	10	9
39.5	3.672	23	7	8
46.0	3.829	12	6	10
51.5	3.942	4	2	5

is straightened out if the explanatory variable is transformed logarithmically. We'll take Log Years (Employed) as our explanatory variable and ask how it influences the development of Pneumoconiosis. A 1-unit increase in this base-*e* logarithmic scale corresponds, roughly, to tripling the Years Employed.

The proportional odds model is expressed in two equations,

$$\log\left[\frac{Moderate \ or \ Severe \mid Years}{Absent \mid Years}\right] = \alpha_1 + \beta \ (Log \ Years)$$

and

$$\log\left[\frac{Severe \mid Years}{Absent \ or \ Moderate \mid Years}\right] = \alpha_2 + \beta \ (Log \ Years), \qquad \text{(18.23)}$$

with a total of three parameters.

The continuation ratio model is also expressed in two equations,

$$\log\left[\frac{Moderate \ or \ Severe \mid Years}{Absent \mid Years}\right] = \alpha_1 + \beta_1 \ (Log \ Years)$$

and

$$\log\left[\frac{Severe \mid Years}{Moderate \mid Years}\right] = \alpha_2 + \beta_2 \ (Log \ Years), \qquad \text{(18.24)}$$

with a total of four parameters, including a different slope parameter for Log Years employed in each equation.

Notice the choice of ordering of the three response categories. It reflects the assumption that workers, given continued exposure to the coal face, will tend to move from less-ill to more-ill states rather than the reverse. So, we choose to model the odds of becoming more ill (as opposed to not becoming more ill.)

Parameters for the two models differ not only in their number but in the interpretation we give to them as well. Since we tend to ground our parameter interpretations in the multiplicative versions of our logistic regression models, let's look at those here. For the proportional odds model, we have

$$\left[\frac{Moderate \text{ or } Severe \mid Years}{Absent \mid Years} \right] = \kappa_1 \lambda^{(Log\ Years)}$$

and

$$\left[\frac{Severe \mid Years}{Absent \text{ or } Moderate \mid Years} \right] = \kappa_2 \lambda^{(Log\ Years)},$$

while for the continuation ratio model we have

$$\left[\frac{Moderate \text{ or } Severe \mid Years}{Absent \mid Years} \right] = \kappa_1 \lambda_1^{(Log\ Years)}$$

and

$$\left[\frac{Severe \mid Years}{Moderate \mid Years} \right] = \kappa_2 \lambda_2^{(Log\ Years)}.$$

The multiplicative intercepts, the κs, are of no interest in either model. They model the odds of becoming more ill for Log Years employed $= 0$, a value outside our range of interest for the x-variable. How do we interpret the odds multipliers, the λs, though? For the proportional odds model, λ is the amount by which we multiply the odds of "becoming more afflicted with Pneumoconiosis" for each additional Log Year of coal face employment, that is, for a tripling of the period of employment. For the continuation ratio model, λ_1 is the amount by which we multiply the odds of becoming at least moderately afflicted with the disease (as opposed to staying free of it) for each additional Log Year. And λ_2 is the amount by which we multiply the odds of developing Severe Pneumoconiosis (as opposed to being only moderately afflicted).

18.5.3 Interpreting the Nonlinear Log-odds Model

The results of the proportional odds fit to the Pneumoconiosis data are given in Table 18.8. Because of the nonlinear transformation of Years Employed, the proportional odds parameter estimates are not easily interpreted. We can get a sense of the impact of Years Employed by computing a few odds. The odds of Moderate or Severe Pneumoconiosis are estimated from the model fit as

$$\left[\frac{Moderate \text{ or } Severe}{Absent} \right] = \exp[\widehat{\alpha}_1 + \widehat{\beta}\log(Years)] = \exp[-9.68 + 2.60\log(Years)].$$

This equation, and the companion following, are obtained by "exponentiating" the left- and right-hand sides of Equations [18.23]. For coal miners employed five years, the model estimates the odds of Pneumoconiosis at $1/250$. These odds increase

T A B L E **18.8**

Pneumoconiosis in Coal Miners: Proportional Odds Model Estimates

Ordinal Regression (Response: Severity)

Column	Name	Coeff	SE	P Value	Odds	0.95	CI
0	Const 1	−9.676	1.324	0	0.000	0.000	0.000
0	Const 2	−10.582	1.345	0	0.000	0.000	0.000
2	Ln Years	2.597	0.381	0	13.421	6.359	28.325

d.f.:368	−2LogL:408.548	#iter:14

to 1/40 at ten years, to 1/14 at 15 years, and to 1/7 at 20 years. One of every eight miners working twenty years will be afflicted.

The second odds estimate, the odds of Severe Pneumoconiosis are estimated by the model as

$$\left[\frac{Severe}{Absent \text{ or } Moderate}\right] = \exp[\widehat{\alpha}_2 + \widehat{\beta}\log(Years)] = \exp[-10.58 + 2.60\log(Years)].$$

After 5 years of employment, the odds of Severe Pneumoconiosis are 1/500. These odds increase to 1/100 at 10 years, to 1/34 at 15 years, and to 1/16 at 20 years. One in 17 coal face workers employed for 20 years will develop Serious Pneumoconiosis.

The *Deviance* for this proportional odds model is 5.027 with degrees of freedom of $8(3−1) − 3 = 13$. Three model parameters (two intercepts and one slope) are used to estimate the 16 unknown multinomial probabilities, two for each of the eight multinomial populations sampled. The upper tail probability of 5.027 in the Chi-squared distribution with 13 d.f. is 0.975. The model fits the data very well.

18.5.4   Fitting the Continuation-ratio Model

We can use a single logistic regression solution to fit the continuation ratio model. To accomplish this, we must arrange our data so that we have the ordered responses, successes, and failures (or attempts), for *all* $(J − 1)$ log-odds models coded as a single logistic regression problem.

Table 18.9 displays the Pneumoconiosis data of Table 18.7 arranged to satisfy the log-odds models of Equations [18.24]. The first column lists the number of successes, the numerator frequencies for Equations [18.24]. And the second column contains the number of attempts, the sums of the numerator and denominator frequencies. Thus, 0 of 98 coal miners employed 5.8 years had either Moderate or Severe Pneumoconiosis. And, in the second row, 3 of 54 workers employed at the coal face for 15.0 years had either Moderate or Severe Pneumoconiosis.

The top half, or top 8 rows, of Table 18.9 provides data for the first log-odds model,

$$\log\left[\frac{Moderate \text{ or } Severe \mid Years}{Absent \mid Years}\right] = \alpha_1 + \beta_1 \, (Log \, Years),$$

and the lower 8 lines provide data for the second model,

T A B L E 18.9

Logistic Regression Input for Continuation Ratio Model for Pneumoconiosis Data Set

1	2	3	4	5	6
0	98	1	0	1.758	0.000
3	54	1	0	2.708	0.000
9	43	1	0	3.068	0.000
13	48	1	0	3.314	0.000
19	51	1	0	3.512	0.000
15	38	1	0	3.676	0.000
16	28	1	0	3.829	0.000
7	11	1	0	3.942	0.000
0	0	0	1	0.000	1.758
1	3	0	1	0.000	2.708
3	9	0	1	0.000	3.068
8	13	0	1	0.000	3.314
9	19	0	1	0.000	3.512
8	15	0	1	0.000	3.676
10	16	0	1	0.000	3.829
5	7	0	1	0.000	3.942

$$\log\left[\frac{Severe \mid Years}{Moderate \mid Years}\right] = \alpha_2 + \beta_2 \,(Log\ Years).$$

Thus, the bottom line reports that 7 workers with 51.5 Years Employment had either Moderate or Severe Pneumoconiosis and, of that number, 5 were diagnosed Severe. The ninth line of the table contains a 0 in the second column. Most logistic regression programs will not accept data sets with entries indicating 0 attempts (sum of successes and failures) at any data point, and before completing the analysis this line was omitted from the data set.

Equations [18.24] correspond to what in an earlier chapter we described as a separate-intercepts, separate-slopes model. Taken together, there are two intercepts, α_1 and α_2, and two slopes, β_1 and β_2. Columns 3 through 6 of Table 18.9 display the x-variables associated with this model. The two intercepts are provided for by the 0/1 variables in columns 3 and 4. Separate slopes for Log Years are provided for by splitting the Log Years observations into two x-variables, columns 5 and 6.

The upper half of Table 18.10 gives the parameter estimates for the continuation ratio model of Equations [18.24]: $\widehat{\alpha}_1 = -9.609$, $\widehat{\alpha}_2 = -3.864$, $\widehat{\beta}_1 = 2.576$ and $\widehat{\beta}_2 = 1.136$. The estimates for α_1 and β_1 are in close agreement with those found for the corresponding intercept and the common slope for the proportional odds model. The first "halves" of the proportional odds and continuation ratio models are close in interpretation. The second "halves," however, are different and the estimate of β_2 is unlike the other slope estimates. It has to do with the transition from Moderate to Severe Pneumoconiosis and this would appear to be much less

T A B L E **18.10**

Logistic Regression Solution for the Continuation Ratio Model for Pneumoconiosis
Data Set

Model 1: Separate Log Years Slopes

Column	Name	Coeff	SE	P Value	Odds	0.95	CI
3	Const1	−9.609	1.339	0.000	0.000	0.000	0.000
4	Const2	−3.864	2.688	0.151	0.021	0.000	4.073
5	LnYears_1	2.576	0.386	0.000	13.144	6.165	28.027
6	LnYears_2	1.136	0.759	0.134	3.115	0.704	13.786

d.f.:11   −2LogL:4.878   %(0):72.185   #iter:13

Model 2: Single Log Years Slope

Column	Name	Coeff	SE	P Value	Odds	0.95	CI
3	Const1	−8.734	1.128	0	0.000	0.00	0.001
4	Const2	−8.051	1.180	0	0.000	0.00	0.003
5	LnYears	2.321	0.327	0	10.189	5.37	19.335

d.f.:12   −2LogL:7.627   %(0):72.185   #iter:13

influenced by Years of Employment.

$$\left[\frac{Severe}{Moderate}\right] = \exp[-3.864 + 1.136\log(Years)],$$

can be used to compute estimates of odds of Severe Pneumoconiosis for different
periods of employment as was done for the proportional odds model.

The *Deviance* for this fullest continuation ratio model was 4.878 with d.f. equal
to $15 - 4 = 11$. It is certainly a good fitting model.

A less full model, in which β_1 and β_2 are constrained to be equal, is fit in
the second half of Table 18.10. The combined slope estimate is $\widehat{\beta} = 2.321$. *Deviance* for the constrained model was 7.627 with 12 d.f. The *Deviance difference*,
$7.627 - 4.878 = 2.749$, evaluated as a Chi-squared observation with $12 - 11 = 1$
d.f., produces an upper-tail probability of $0.097 > 0.05$. This suggests that a single
slope may be acceptable.

Given, however, that β_1 and β_2 relate to two different kinds of transition—from
the absence to presence of the disease on the one hand, and from Moderate to Severe
conditions on the other—the constraint of equality may not have a good substantive
basis. The results of fitting the fuller model, though, suggest a second possible model
simplification of interest. The CI for β_2 is wide enough to include 0 (equivalently,
the CI for the odds multiplier, λ_2, overlaps 1.0). Constraining β_2 to be 0, by dropping
the corresponding *x*-variable, gives a less full model whose fit could be compared
against that of the fuller model.

The continuation ratio model provides an alternative to the single-slope assumption of the proportional odds model, but at the cost of a change in the interpretation
of the fitted slopes.

18.5.5   An Approximation to the Proportional Odds Model Fit

Fitting the proportional odds model requires a command or program unavailable in many statistical packages. The approach used to fit the continuation ratio model, putting $(J - 1)$ log-odds into a single logistic regression, offers a useful *approximation* to the proportional odds model. We illustrate the approximation by refitting the Tonsils Enlargement data.

Table 18.11 shows the tonsils data reorganized for logistic regression. Column 1 contains the success frequencies, column 2 the total attempts. Rows 1 and 2 are for the streptococcus Carriers. The row 1 successes are the Not Enlarged tonsils. The row 2 successes are the Not Enlarged or Enlarged (but not Greatly Enlarged) tonsils. This pattern is repeated in rows 3 and 4 for the Noncarriers.

Notice that, unlike the logistic regression setup for the continuation ratio models, the total attempts include all cases for each "cut." This makes for *nonindependence* here and, hence, only an *approximation* to the proportional odds-model results.

Column 3 contains a 0/1 variable coding Steptococcus and columns 4 and 5 0/1 variables for the two cuts between the ordered categories. In the logistic regression analyses, columns 3 through 5 will provide the *x*-variables. Because the two cut variables sum to a constant, the analyses will be done specifying "no constant."

The parameter estimates, both for the model with the Streptococcus *x*-variable and for the Null model are given in Table 18.12. The Streptococcus slope and the two intercepts for the fuller model are very close to those obtained with the proportional odds command and reported in Table 18.2. There, the Streptococcus β was -0.603.

Because the logistic regression command assumes independent observations and does not "know" the correct structure for these data, the *Deviance* is incorrectly reported. However, most logistic regression programs report enough information about modeled frequencies or probabilities under the model program to permit reconstruction of the correct modeled frequencies.

In this application, the correction takes advantage of the cumulative nature of the two sets of data. The logistic regression modeled frequencies for rows 1 and 3 give correct modeled frequencies for the Not Enlarged categories. The correct modeled frequencies for the Enlarged categories, though, are obtained by subtracting the logistic regression row 1 and row 3 modeled frequencies from the row 2 and row 4 modeled frequencies, respectively. And the correct modeled frequencies for the

T A B L E 18.11

Tonsils and Streptococcus Data Organized for Logistic Regression Approximation to Proportional Odds Model

1	2	3	4	5
19	72	1	1	0
48	72	1	0	1
497	1326	0	1	0
1057	1326	0	0	1

T A B L E 18.12

Logistic Regression Approximation to Proportional Odds Tonsils Data Set

Logistic Regression Analysis
Response: Smaller

Column	Name	Coeff	SE	P Value	Odds	0.95	CI
3	Carrier	−0.599	0.191	0.002	0.549	0.378	0.798
4	Cut1	−0.508	0.056	0.000	0.602	0.539	0.672
5	Cut2	1.363	0.067	0.000	3.909	3.427	4.458
d.f.:1	−2LogL:0.181		%(0):42.024		#iter:9		RSq:

Logistic Regression Analysis
Response: Smaller

Column	Name	Coeff	SE	P Value	Odds	0.95	CI
4	Cut1	−0.536	0.055	0	0.585	0.525	0.652
5	Cut2	1.327	0.066	0	3.771	3.316	4.290
d.f.:2	−2LogL:10.075		%(0):42.024		#iter:9		RSq:

Greatly Enlarged categories are the total frequencies for each of the two samples minus the logistic regression row 2 and row 4 modeled frequencies.

With these corrected modeled frequencies for the Streptococcus and Null models, the *Deviances* are computed:

$$Dev(Streptococcus\ Model):\quad 0.32,\quad d.f. = 4 - 3 = 1$$
$$Dev(Null\ Model):\quad\quad\quad 7.32,\quad d.f. = 4 - 2 = 2$$
$$Deviance\ difference:\quad\quad 7.00,\quad d.f. = 1$$

For the proportional odds model, the *Deviances* were 0.302, 7.320, and 7.018.

For this example, the logistic regression approach provided a very good approximation to the proportional odds calculations.

18.6
Nominal Response Categories: Polychotomous Logistic Regression

In this last section, we look at how logistic regression can be used to model the *nominal-response variable*. The technique to be illustrated is called *polychotomous logistic regression*.

Logistic regression models, as a linear function of one or more x-variables, the log-odds of falling into one response category rather than another. In ordinary logistic regression, there are but two response categories. In the case of an ordinal response, we've seen how to use the ordered nature of the response categories to compose two "super-categories" for logistic regression. But how can we pick a pair of categories to model when the categories possess no ordinal structure?

18.6.1 Polychotomous Logistic Regression

The approach of polychotomous logistic regression (PLR) is to select one of the J nominal-response categories as a *modal category* and to model the log-odds of each of the other categories against that one. This gives rise to $(J - 1)$ logistic regressions. They are fit *simultaneously*, however, and in a way to compensate for the lack of independence among the several regressions. An overall goodness of fit statistic, the *Deviance* again, is available. The *Deviance difference*, too, provides a mechanism for comparing the fits of fuller and less full models. The PLR technique is fully explained in Hosmer and Lemeshow (1989).

The idea of assessing the odds of a particular response *relative* to a modal one makes sense for a lot of nominal-response variables. Often the response categories include a "Normal" or "Standard" or, if not so-labeled, one that is the "Most Popular." A natural question to ask, then, is whether and to what extent an x-variable can explain *departure* from the Standard or Popular. As with other logistic regression models, there is a companion *multiplicative* model to facilitate interpretation.

18.6.2 Recoverability of Other Comparisons

The choice of a modal category may seem arbitrary. There may be comparisons of interest among the response categories other than those *relative* to the modal category. Does the PLR approach run the risk of missing something potentially important in forcing a choice of modal category and does it preclude making other comparisons?

Two points should be made. First, we noted earlier in the chapter that for J response categories and I design points there are underlying $I \times (J - 1)$ *conditional multinomial probabilities*. These are the underlying unknown population parameters that must be estimated in any multicategory logistic regression. They underlie any modeled log-odds or odds. The *Deviance* is based on those estimated conditional probabilities and, thus, indicates the overall goodness of fit of the explanatory structure, whatever set of category comparisons or odds are chosen for study.

Second, the linear model for other category odds can be recovered from any choice of modal category. This point can be illustrated. For simplicity, we'll assume a single x-variable and just three response categories: A, B, and C. Say we had chosen B as the modal category. PLR would estimate the parameters for these two linear models:

$$\log\left[\frac{p(A \mid x_i)}{p(B \mid x_i)}\right] = \beta_{0A} + \beta_{1A}x_i$$

and

$$\log \left[\frac{p(C \mid x_i)}{p(B \mid x_i)} \right] = \beta_{0C} + \beta_{1C} x_i.$$

Now, say we are interested in a further comparison, A and C. Can we model $\log \left[\frac{p(A \mid x_i)}{p(C \mid x_i)} \right]$?
It turns out we already have all we need to do that. Since the logarithm of a ratio is the difference between the logarithms of the numerator and denominator terms, we can write

$$\log \left[\frac{p(A \mid x_i)}{p(B \mid x_i)} \right] - \log \left[\frac{p(C \mid x_i)}{p(B \mid x_i)} \right] = \log \left[\frac{p(A \mid x_i)}{p(C \mid x_i)} \right].$$

Then, incorporating the two right-hand sides of the original log-odds give:

$$\log \left[\frac{p(A \mid x_i)}{p(C \mid x_i)} \right] = (\beta_{0A} - \beta_{0C}) + (\beta_{1A} - \beta_{1C}) x_i.$$

This result generalizes to a larger number of categories and to models with more than one *x*-variable.

18.6.3   Mammography Experience: An Example

Table 18.13 reports data (Hosmer & Lemeshow 1989) on the mammography experience of a sample of women. Mammography Experience is the response and the women are classified as "Never having had a mammogram," "Having had one within the past year," and "Having had one but more than a year ago." We treat the categories as nonordered.

To what extent can the varying mammography Experience of these women be explained by their beliefs in the efficacy of the procedure? The explanatory source here is the response to the questionnaire item "How likely is it that a mammogram could find a new case of breast cancer?" The women's responses were categorized as Not Likely, Somewhat Likely, and Very Likely.

In Table 18.14, the mammography data have been rearranged as input for an initial PLR model fit.

T A B L E   **18.13**
Mammography Belief and Experience

	Likelihood of Detection		
Experience	Not	Somewhat	Very
Never	13	77	144
Within the Past Year	1	12	91
Over One Year Ago	4	16	54

T A B L E 18.14

Mammography Experience: PLR Input Data

Frequency	Response	Not Likely	Somewhat	Very
13	1	1	0	0
1	2	1	0	0
4	3	1	0	0
77	1	0	1	0
12	2	0	1	0
16	3	0	1	0
144	1	0	0	1
91	2	0	0	1
54	3	0	0	1

We have three 0/1 variables coding the three levels of our categorical explanatory variable and the three response categories have been given numeric codes: 1 = Never, 2 = Within the Year, and 3 = Over a Year. The Never response category is both the most numerous and a natural comparison category. We are interested in whether and by how much differing beliefs about mammography affect the odds of having had one (as opposed to never having had one). Never will be the modal category in the PLR analyses.

The models to be fit, then, are these two:

$$\log\left[\frac{p(\textit{Within Year} \mid \textit{Belief})}{p(\textit{Never} \mid \textit{Belief})}\right] = \beta_{21}x_1 + \beta_{22}x_2 + \beta_{23}x_3$$

and

$$\log\left[\frac{p(\textit{Over a Year} \mid \textit{Belief})}{p(\textit{Never} \mid \textit{Belief})}\right] = \beta_{31}x_1 + \beta_{32}x_2 + \beta_{33}x_3.$$

Given the choice of coding for the xs the first of these log-odds will take the values of β_{21}, β_{22}, or β_{23} for Not, Somewhat, and Very Likely beliefs, respectively. A similar result holds for the second log-odds equation.

The PLR fit to this model (as given by the SPIDA command PLREG) is given at the top of Table 18.15. The first set of coefficients refers to the Within Year/Never odds and the second refers to the Over a Year/Never comparison.

The values listed in the "Odds" column are the multiplicative model parameters, $\gamma_{jk} = e^{\beta_{jk}}$.

We notice a steady progression in the

$$\left[\frac{p(\textit{Within Year})}{p(\textit{Never})}\right]$$

for the ordered Likely levels:

Not (0.077), Somewhat (0.156), and Very (0.632).

T A B L E **18.15**

PLR Model Fits to the Mammography Experience Data

Column	Coeff	SE	P Value	Odds	0.95	CI	Within v. Never
3	−2.565	1.038	0.013	0.077	0.010	0.588	Not Likely
4	−1.859	0.310	0.000	0.156	0.085	0.286	Somewhat Likely
5	−0.459	0.134	0.000	0.632	0.486	0.822	Very Likely
							Over v. Never
3	−1.179	0.572	0.039	0.308	0.100	0.944	Not Likely
4	−1.571	0.275	0.000	0.208	0.121	0.356	Somewhat Likely
5	−0.981	0.160	0.000	0.375	0.274	0.513	Very Likely

d.f.:406   −2LogL: 778.401   %Omit: 56.796   #iter: 7

Column	Coeff	SE	P Value	Odds	0.95	CI	Within v. Never
0	−4.345	0.848	0.000				Constant
6	1.290	0.297	0.000	3.634	2.029	6.508	How Likely
							Over v. Never
0	−2.070	0.655	0.002				Constant
6	0.351	0.242	0.147	1.420	0.884	2.280	How Likely

d.f.:408   −2LogL: 779.993   %Omit: 56.796   #iter: 12

Odds of having had a mammogram in the past year are almost tenfold greater for those who believe mammogram detection of cancer is Very Likely than for those who think it Not Likely. There is not a clear pattern, though, for the second odds, Over a Year v. Never.

Is this model a good one? In fact, it is a *saturated model*. There are $I \times (J - 1) = 3(3 - 1) = 6$ unknown multinomial probabilities underlying these data and PLR estimated 6 βs. One way of seeing that the model fits the data perfectly is to note that the estimated odds are exactly the same as the observed odds. For example, the observed odds of Within v. Never for those saying Very Likely, from Table 18.13 are 91 to 144, or 0.632.

Let's constrain the model now by assigning scores to the three How Likely categories: 1 = Not, 2 = Somewhat, and 3 = Very. This will reduce our model parameters from 6 to 4. The PLR fit to this less full model is given at the bottom of Table 18.15.

For the "scored" How Likely scale we obtain an estimated odds multiplier of 3.634 for the Within Year v. Never odds. A one-unit increase in this scale multiplies the odds of having had a mammogram within the past year threefold. Or, if we consider the influence of a change in score from Not Likely to Very Likely (two units), the odds are increased by a multiple of $(3.634)(3.634) = 13.2$. Again, this is close to a tenfold increase in odds of having a recent mammogram.

The How Likely odds multiplier is considerably smaller for the Over a Year/Never odds. In fact, the reported 95% CI for the odds multiplier overlaps 1.0, indicating uncertainty as to whether an increase in the How Likely score increases or decreases the odds of a less-recent mammogram. Belief in efficacy seems to influence recent but not distant behavior. The *Deviance* for the four-parameter model is 1.592, which, with $6 - 4 = 2$ d.f., signals a good-fitting model.

18.7
Summary

Logistic regression provides the same range of modeling possibilities for the dichotomous response as linear regression does for the measured response. In this chapter, techniques are introduced for extending the logistic regression approach to the multicategory response. The proportional odds model is perhaps the most promising of these extensions to the ordered categorical response, while polychotomous logistic regression opens the nonordered response to linear explanatory modeling.

Exercises

1 In the data set for U.S. colleges and universities used in the Chapter 7 exercises, one of the variables, Competitiveness, is an ordered categorical variable. Take this as an ordinal response in one or two simple proportional odds models. In one, Tuition Cost is the explanatory variable; in the other, student-to-faculty ratios is the explanatory variable. What influences Competitiveness?

2 The following data are from a study of rearing influences on deaths among newborn mice in different size litters. These data relate to the type of cage, a or b. For litters of different initial sizes (7, 8, 9, 10, or 11) the researcher recorded losses of (0, 1, or 2 or more) pups. The latter gives a three-level ordered categorical response. How is it influenced by litter size and cage type? Do those factors interact?

Litter Size	Cage type a, b	Number of litters showing 0 depletions	Number of litters showing 1 depletion	Number of litters showing 2+ depletions
7	a	58	11	5
7	b	75	19	7
8	a	49	14	10
8	b	58	17	8
9	a	33	18	15
9	b	45	22	10
10	a	15	13	15
10	b	39	22	18
11	a	4	12	17
11	b	5	15	8

3 The Swiss educational psychologist Piaget postulates stages of cognitive development. Part of this development is marked by whether the child has a sense that matter is conserved as it is moved about. According to Piagetian criteria, children can be classified as Nonconservers, Conservers, or Transitionals. The following data relate these classifications to the ages of children in one sample. Use a polychotomous logistic regression approach to explore the influence of age on this tripartite classification. This particular data set is troubling to some educational psychologists. Why might that be?

Piagetian stage. 0: Nonconserver, 1: Transitional, 2: Conserver	Age in months	Frequency
0	60	10
0	72	7
0	84	4
0	96	1
0	108	2
0	121	15
0	133	3
0	144	0
1	60	0
1	72	3
1	84	4
1	96	3
1	108	0
1	121	3
1	133	2
1	144	2
2	60	0
2	72	0
2	84	0
2	96	6
2	108	8
2	121	10
2	133	5
2	144	8

19

Poisson Regression for Counts in Time or Space

In this final chapter, we look briefly at linear models or regression extended to responses that are counts. Arguably, counts may be thought to possess a unit of measurement—a difference in the count of one is the same thing however large the count—and, hence, to fall within the treatment already given to the measured response. However, we learn here that the counting of independently-occurring events leads to response distributions in which the means and variances are strongly correlated. This, of course, violates one of the assumptions, homogeneity of variance, we are asked to make for modeling the measured response. Fortunately, there is a modeling approach, Poisson regression, that explicitly fits such response data.

19.1
Counting Independently Occurring Events

Consider events that occur separated either in time or in space: the number of clover blossoms in a quarter-acre of grass or the number of pieces of mail received at your residence on a Monday. Each clover blossom has its own position over the space of the land. The mail, while it may arrive at your home all at once, can be thought to enter your local delivery system one piece at a time over the period it is collected awaiting delivery. The contents of the Monday mail, then, are distributed in arrival time. Such counts, over a space or time period, can be of interest as response variables in biological or behavioral studies. Is the incidence of clover blossoms affected by the acidity of the soil in the grass plot? Is the size of the Monday mail influenced by season?

Where the events of interest can be thought to occur independently one of another—where the occurrence of an event at one point in time or space has no influence on whether that same event will or will not occur at another particular point in time or space—the count of those events is modeled effectively as an observation from a Poisson random variable. The Poisson random variable is discrete-valued, it can only take on the nonnegative integer values 0, 1, 2, ... In principle, the Poisson variable can take any positive integral value but "large" values have a very small probability of occurring. The probability function for the Poisson random variable has this form:

$$p(y) = \frac{e^{-\lambda}\lambda^y}{y!}, \quad \text{for } y = 0, 1, 2, \ldots, +\infty \tag{19.1}$$

where e is the numeric constant ($e = 2.718\ldots$), $y!$, read "y factorial," is the product of the integers from one to y inclusive (with the proviso that $0! = 1! = 1$) and λ is the Poisson variable parameter. The mean and the variance of the Poisson random variable are both equal to λ.

The parameter λ gives the number of events we would expect to see in a "unit" of time or space. More generally, we think of λ as a *rate parameter;* in any one unit of time or space, we may not see exactly λ events but we would expect, over a very large space or a very long period of time, to observe an event occurring at the rate of λ per unit of time or space.

From Equation [19.1], we have

$$p(y = 0) = \frac{e^{-\lambda}\lambda^0}{0!} = e^{-\lambda},$$

$$p(y = 1) = \frac{e^{-\lambda}\lambda^1}{1!} = p(y = 0)\left(\frac{\lambda}{1}\right),$$

$$p(y = 2) = \frac{e^{-\lambda}\lambda^2}{2!} = p(y = 1)\left(\frac{\lambda}{2}\right),$$

$$\ldots$$

$$p(y = m + 1) = \frac{e^{-\lambda}\lambda^{m+1}}{(m+1)!} = p(y = m)\left(\frac{\lambda}{m+1}\right). \tag{19.2}$$

The multiplier $\left(\dfrac{\lambda}{m+1}\right)$ is greater than one when $(m+1)$ is less than λ and less than one when $(m+1)$ exceeds λ. As a result, the probability of y increases over the range of y from $y = 0$ to $y = \lambda$ and decreases as $y > \lambda$.

Because $p(y)$ gets smaller as y gets larger, the Poisson random variable often is thought of as describing the occurrence of "rare" events. Large counts are not expected. In particular, as one of the Exercises in this chapter illustrates, the Poisson is useful in modeling the occurrence of rare events in finite populations. In fact, if the probability of the occurrence of an event to an individual in a finite population is either less than 0.05 or greater than 0.95, the Poisson provides a better model than the binomial random variable that underpins logistic regression.

19.2
Poisson Regression

Our interest here is in modeling observed counts, that is, in determining whether the value of λ, the rate of occurrence of some interesting event, is influenced by the value of one or more explanatory variables. Our vehicle for doing this is Poisson regression.

In Poisson regression, as in linear or logistic regression, we assume a link between a parameter of a conditional response population and the value of a "design point" in our study. In simple linear regression, this took the form

$$\mu(y \mid x = x_i) = \beta_0 + \beta_1 x_i,$$

where $\mu(y \mid x = x_i)$ is the mean of a population of measured-response observations, a population conditional on the explanatory variable x taking the value x_i. For (simple) logistic regression, the explanatory-variable conditional response population link was provided by

$$\log\left(\frac{p(success \mid x = x_i)}{1 - p(success \mid x = x_i)}\right) = \beta_0 + \beta_1 x_i,$$

where $p(success \mid x = x_i)$ is the proportion of successes in the population of successes and failures conditional on the explanatory variable taking the value x_i. The Poisson link we use takes the form

$$(\lambda \mid x = x_i) = e^{\beta_0 + \beta_1 x_i}, \tag{19.3}$$

or, taking logarithms on both sides of this equation,

$$\log(\lambda \mid x = x_i) = \beta_0 + \beta_1 x_i, \tag{19.4}$$

where $(\lambda \mid x = x_i)$ is the mean/variance parameter for the population of counted y responses conditional on the explanatory variable taking the value x_i. The use of the "logarithmic link" of Equation [19.4], rather than a straightforward linear one, $\lambda_i = \beta_0 + \beta_1 x_i$, insures that λ_i (and our estimate of it) is always positive, as it needs to be.

To take into account that we may be counting an event over a longer or shorter time period for different values of the explanatory variable, we extend the notation of Equations [19.3], and [19.4] slightly, to

$$(\lambda \mid x = x_i) = t_i e^{\beta_0 + \beta_1 x_i}, \tag{19.5}$$

and

$$\log(\lambda \mid x = x_i) = \log(t_i) + \beta_0 + \beta_1 x_i = [\log(t_i) + \beta_0] + \beta_1 x_i, \tag{19.6}$$

where t_i is, for the design point x_i, either

- the amount of time our count extends over,
- the size of the space our count extends over, or
- the size of the population.

This variable, t_i, is called *exposure time*. In Equations [19.5] and [19.6] $\lambda_i = (\lambda \mid x = x_i)$ is the *modeled mean number of events in time*, t_i. As the far right-hand side of Equation [19.6] suggests, we can think of the varying exposure times as influencing only the intercepts of our models. Typically, as in linear and logistic regression, our interest is in the slope parameter, β_1, or its multiplicative model analog. If we rewrite Equation [19.5], we have

$$(\lambda \mid x = x_i) = t_i e^{\beta_0 + \beta_1 x_i} = t_i \gamma_0 \gamma_1^{x_i} = (t_i \gamma_0) \gamma_1^{x_i}, \tag{19.7}$$

where $\gamma_0 = e^{\beta_0}$ and $\gamma_1 = e^{\beta_1}$.

The latter is the multiplicative analog of the slope parameter. It is the amount by which λ is to be multiplied when the value of x increases by one unit:

$$(\lambda \mid x = x_i)\gamma_1 = (\lambda \mid x = x_i + 1). \tag{19.8}$$

Here we will refer to γ_1 as a rate multiplier.

Equations [19.3] to [19.8] generalize to models in which the design points are a function of two or more x-variables. The x-variables may be measured or dummy variables, perhaps accompanied by product or power variables just as we've seen for linear models.

19.3
Model Fitting and Comparisons

Given samples of counts, y_i, and exposure times, t_i, from $i = 1, 2, , \ldots, I$ locations, time periods, or finite populations, each a design point associated with a pattern of x-variable scores, it is possible to obtain maximum likelihood estimates of the βs. Like the logistic regression estimates, those for Poisson slopes and intercepts are arrived at only through iterative computation; we cannot write down their equations. More and more statistical packages, however, include Poisson regression commands. We use the SPIDA package with its PREG command for the illustrations of this chapter.

Once the βs have been estimated, these estimates can be used in Equation [19.5] to obtain *modeled counts*,

$$\hat{y}_i = t_i e^{\hat{\beta}_0 + \hat{\beta}_1 x_i}. \tag{19.9}$$

The modeled and observed counts (the y_is) are used, as they were in Chapters 17 and 18, to calculate a model fit statistic, the *Deviance*. It is defined in the same way,

$$Dev = 2 \sum_{i=1}^{I} \left[y_i \log \left(\frac{y_i}{\hat{y}_i} \right) \right], \tag{19.10}$$

as in logistic regression. If the counts are of independent events and our k parameter model for the λ_is is the correct model, the sampling distribution for the *Deviance* of Equation [19.10] has a histogram well-approximated by the probability density function of the Chi-squared random variable with $(I - k)$ degrees of freedom. A *Deviance* in the lower 75% of that probability distribution provides evidence of a good-fitting model. A larger *Deviance* signals a poor fit. A poor fit may come about because the assumption of independence is unwarranted. When this is true, we say the counts reflect *overdispersion* relative to a Poisson random variable.

The fits of nested models, those enjoying a fuller/less full relation as developed in Chapter 8, are compared using the *Deviance difference* statistic. If the fuller model has $(k + p)$ parameters and the less full one k, then the difference in *Deviances* is

$$Dev\ diff = Deviance(\text{less full model}) - Dev(\text{fuller model}).$$

It has a sampling distribution, when the constraints leading to the less full model are correct, with the same shape as the density function for the Chi-squared random variable with p degrees of freedom. A large *Dev diff* is evidence in favor of the fuller model.

In short, the model fit and comparison rules are the same as for logistic regression.

19.4
Poisson Regression Model Interpretation

As with logistic regression, we have both a *logarithmic model,* Equation [19.6], and a *multiplicative model,* Equation [19.7]. Because the logarithmic model is linear in our explanatory variables, it is that model that we constrain to form less full from fuller models. But, because that model expresses the influence of one or more explanatory variables on the logarithm of a modeled count, the logarithmic model parameters are less easy to interpret than those of the multiplicative model. It is the γ_is we turn to, once we have chosen one or more models, to understand and communicate the role of our explanatory influences.

19.5
An Example of Poisson Regression Model Comparison

The data in Table 19.1 are Poppy Counts reported in Curnow, Mead, and Hasted (1992). Blocks refer to separate plots of land, each the same size. Each of the four blocks, in turn, is divided into six equally sized subplots with each subplot receiving one of six different Treatments. The counts of Table 19.1 are the counts of Poppies in each of the subplots, classified into two categories: Block in which located and Treatment administered.

Are the poppy counts influenced by Treatment when we control for (any) between-Block differences? In the spirit of Chapter 11, we begin with a fuller model that includes dummy variables for both Blocks and Treatments:

$$\log(\lambda_i) = t_i + \beta_0 + \sum_{j=1}^{8} \beta_j x_{ij} \quad \textbf{(Block and Treatment Model)}$$

T A B L E **19.1**
Poppy Counts: Treatment Subplots Within Blocks

Treatment	Block 1	Block 2	Block 3	Block 4
A	538	422	377	315
B	438	442	319	380
C	77	61	157	52
D	115	57	100	45
E	17	31	87	16
F	18	26	77	20

where x_1 to x_5 are dummy variables for Treatment levels A through E and x_6 through x_8 are dummy variables coding Blocks 1, 2, and 3. The comparison condition, then, is Treatment F applied to Block 4. The fit to this model is summarized in the top panel of Table 19.2. The model *Deviance* is computed at 256.3. This fuller model uses $k + p = 9$ parameters, the βs, to estimate $6 \times 4 = 24$ Poisson λs. As a result, we say the model fit has $24 - 9 = 15$ degrees of freedom.

T A B L E **19.2**

Poisson Regression Fits: Poppy Counts

Block-and-Treatment Model

Column Name	Coeff	SE	P Value	IDR	95	%CI
0 Constant	−5.924	0.091	0.000			
3 TrA	2.504	0.089	0.000	12.237	10.269	14.582
4 TrB	2.459	0.090	0.000	11.696	9.812	13.942
5 TrC	0.944	0.101	0.000	2.570	2.107	3.135
6 TrD	0.854	0.103	0.000	2.348	1.920	2.872
7 TrE	0.112	0.118	0.344	1.119	0.887	1.411
8 Bl1	0.374	0.045	0.000	1.453	1.330	1.587
9 Bl2	0.227	0.047	0.000	1.255	1.145	1.375
10 Bl3	0.294	0.046	0.000	1.342	1.226	1.468

d.f.: 15   Dev: 256.3   #iter:14   RSq:0.934

Block-only Model

Column Name	Coeff	SE	P Value	IDR	95	%CI
0 Constant	−4.283	0.035	0			
8 Bl1	0.374	0.045	0	1.453	1.330	1.587
9 Bl2	0.227	0.047	0	1.255	1.145	1.375
10 Bl3	0.294	0.046	0	1.342	1.226	1.468

d.f.: 20   Dev: 3803.325   #iter:7   RSq:0.019

Combined-treatments Model

Column Name	Coeff	SE	P Value	IDR	95	%CI
0 Constant	−5.867	0.067	0			
3 TrAB	2.425	0.062	0	11.297	10.011	12.749
4 TrCD	0.842	0.071	0	2.322	2.021	2.667
5 Bl1	0.374	0.045	0	1.453	1.330	1.587
6 Bl2	0.227	0.047	0	1.255	1.145	1.375
7 Bl3	0.294	0.046	0	1.342	1.226	1.468

d.f.: 18   Dev: 260.201   #iter:14   RSq:0.933

Our less full model, for evaluating Treatment influence, is obtained from the fuller model by constraining the βs for the Treatment dummy variables to all be 0. The resulting, Block-only model,

$$\log(\lambda_i) = t_i + \beta_0 + \sum_{j=1}^{3} \beta_j x_{ij} \qquad \textbf{(Block-only Model)}$$

has only three x-variables, dummy variables coding Blocks 1, 2, and 3. The fit to this model is summarized in the middle panel of Table 19.2. This four-parameter model has $24 - 4 = 20$ degrees of freedom and a huge *Deviance* of 3,803.325. There is little reason to evaluate the *Deviance difference* of $3,803.325 - 256.3 = 3,547$ against the probability distribution of the Chi-squared variable with $(9 - 4) = 5$ d.f. It is hugely significant. The less full model (Block-Only) fits the data much more poorly than the fuller model. There is a Treatment effect, even controlling for Block differences.

You will have noted that while Table 19.1 provides the y_i scores and the information needed to construct the Treatment and Block dummy variables, it is silent on the matter of the t_is, the exposure times. Because the subplots in which the poppy counts are made are all of the same size, all counts have the same "exposure time." The particular value we choose to represent this constant exposure time will not affect the slope estimates. We wanted a realistic t_i, however, and chose a value that might be a maximum y_i, the poppy count in a subplot completely filled with poppies. In particular, the analyses reported in Table 19.2 have $t_i = 10,000$.

Having set aside the block-only model, we return to the block and treatment model. Can it be made more parsimonious?

In large samples, the $\hat{\beta}$s have sampling distributions whose SEs can be approximated and whose histograms tend to have Normal random-variable characteristics. These *asymptotic standard errors* (SE) are reported together with the $\hat{\beta}$s (Coeff) in the Poisson regression output. We note in the top panel of Table 19.2 that the slope estimates for (the dummy variables for) Treatments A and B were quite close, within one SE of each other. So too were the slope estimates for Treatments C and D (0.944 and 0.854 with SEs of 0.101 and 0.103). And the slope estimate for Treatment E (0.112) was within one SE of 0; that is, Treatment E may have the same influence as the comparison level, Treatment F. All three of these suggestions were incorporated in a Combined-treatments model. The block-and-treatment Model contained five dummy variables for Treatments A through E. In the Combined-treatments model, x_1 and x_2 were added together to produce a dummy variable coding Treatment AB, x_3 and x_4 were added together to produce a dummy variable coding Treatment CD, and x_5 was dropped from the model so that the level it was coding, Treatment E, is joined with Treatment F in a new, combined-comparison level: Treatment EF.

The fit to the combined treatments model is given at the bottom of Table 19.2. This model is less full than the block-and-treatment model, the result of imposing three constraints on the fuller model βs ($\beta_1 = \beta_2$, $\beta_3 = \beta_4$, and $\beta_5 = 0$). The *Deviance difference* $(260.201 - 256.3) = 3.901$ can be regarded as an observation from the Chi-squared random variable with 3 d.f. (the difference in parameter counts for the two models) if the less full model is correct. Since 27.2% of the Chi-squared probability distribution consists of values greater than 3.901, a computation provided by SPIDA, we accept that the less full model (Combined Treatments) fits as well as the fuller one. We opt for the more parsimonious model.

Examining the slope estimates for our new treatment categories, Treatment AB and Treatment CD, does not suggest any further model simplification. How should we interpret the two slope estimates in the final model? We have for the Treatment AB dummy variable $\hat{\beta}_{AB} = 2.425$ (SE = 0.062) and $\gamma_{AB} = 11.297$ (the rate multiplier). The latter is our multiplicative-model parameter estimate and, given the dummy variable coding of the associated variable (0 or 1), it has a clear interpretation. Under this model Poppy Count under Treatment AB is expected to be 11.3 times the Poppy Count under Treatment EF. (An increase of one unit in x_1, from 0 to 1, moves us from the comparison level, Treatment EF, to Treatment AB.) The SE and assumed Normal character of the sampling distribution of $\hat{\beta}_{AB}$ are used to estimate a confidence interval (95% CI) for γ_{AB}. We are 95% confident that γ_{AB} is between 10.011 and 12.749.

Similarly, for the Treatment CD dummy variable, we have $\hat{\beta}_{CD} = 0.842$ and $\hat{\gamma}_{CD} = 2.322$. We should expect twice the number of poppies, per unit area, under Treatment CD as under Treatment EF.

The two model comparisons clearly establish, first, the importance of Treatment level to Poppy Count and, second, the equivalent influence of certain Treatment levels. A troubling part of the analysis, however, is that the fullest of our models, the block-and-treatment model, does not provide a good fit to the observed counts. The *Deviance* of 256.3 is very large relative to the probability distribution of the Chi-squared random variable with 15 degrees of freedom. It may be that poppies are not distributed independently in plots of ground. But see Exercise 1 below for another approach to these data.

19.6
Summary

This chapter provides a brief introduction to a regression model approach to the response variable that is a count. This technique, Poisson regression, is appropriate where the counts are made over time or space or within fairly large finite populations of subjects and where the events counted can be thought to occur independently of one another.

Exercises

1   Your first exercise centers on the Poppy data. One way of interpreting the poor fit of the block-and-treatment model is that it fails to provide for an interaction between Block and Treatment. The model is an additive one. The full-interaction model, with products of dummy variables added to the block-and-treatment model, is a saturated model. It will have 24 parameters, exactly the number of Poisson counts, and will give a perfect fit to the data, a *Deviance* of 0. Begin not with the full interaction model but with a modular model equivalent—an intercept for each Block level and slope parameters for five of six Treatments *within* each Block level—4 intercepts and

$4 \times 5 = 20$ slopes. Simplify this model by pooling slope variables until you reach a model that you think is a good final one. Interpret the multiplicative parameter estimates. Presumably, this will differ from either the block-and-treatment model or the combined treatments model in that at least some Treatment levels will have different influences in different Blocks.

2 The following data relate to the incidence of nonmelanoma skin cancer among women in Minneapolis/St. Paul, and Dallas/Ft. Worth. At issue is whether or by what amount the incidence of nonmelanoma skin cancer is greater in an area of greater sunlight (Dallas/Ft. Worth) than in an area of lesser sunlight (Minneapolis/St. Paul). As age also may be important, the data are blocked on Age levels as well. Column y_i gives the counts of skin cancer cases and column t_i the corresponding population sizes or exposures. Thus, 16 of the 123,065 Minneapolis/St. Paul women aged 25–34 contracted nonmelanoma skin cancer.

City	Age	y_i	t_i
St. Paul	15-24	1	172,675
St. Paul	25-34	16	123,065
St. Paul	35-44	30	96,216
St. Paul	45-54	71	92,051
St. Paul	55-64	102	72,159
St. Paul	65-74	130	54,722
St. Paul	75-84	133	32,185
St. Paul	85 +	40	8,328
Ft. Worth	15-24	4	181,343
Ft. Worth	25-34	38	146,207
Ft. Worth	35-44	119	121,374
Ft. Worth	45-54	221	111,353
Ft. Worth	55-64	259	83,004
Ft. Worth	65-74	310	55,932
Ft. Worth	75-84	226	29,007
Ft. Worth	85 +	65	7,583

Develop, compare, and evaluate models. Do they fit the Poisson independence assumptions? Obtain model estimates of nonmelanoma incidences, the $\hat{y}_i$s, and residuals, $y_i - \hat{y}_i$. As the mean of a Poisson random variable is also its variance, the quantities

$$str_i = \frac{y_i - \hat{y}_i}{\sqrt{\hat{y}_i}}$$

should have a variance close to 1.0 and can be useful in spotting any poorly-fitting observations. Are they suggestive in this problem?

1

Tables of Statistical Distributions

Table A.1.1   Central Proportions of t-Distributions

Table A.1.2   Critical Values of $F_{n,d}$ for Upper Tail Proportion: $\alpha = 0.05$

Table A.1.3   Critical Values of $F_{n,d}$ for Upper Tail Proportion: $\alpha = 0.01$

Table A.1.4   Upper Tail Proportions of Chi-Squared Distributions

T A B L E **A.1.1**
Central Proportions of *t*-Distributions

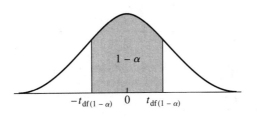

(1 − α) df	.80	.90	.95	.99
1	3.078	6.314	12.706	63.657
2	1.886	2.920	4.303	9.925
3	1.638	2.353	3.182	5.841
4	1.533	2.132	2.776	4.604
5	1.476	2.015	2.571	4.032
6	1.440	1.943	2.447	3.707
7	1.415	1.895	2.365	3.499
8	1.397	1.860	2.306	3.355
9	1.383	1.833	2.262	3.250
10	1.372	1.812	2.228	3.169
11	1.363	1.796	2.201	3.106
12	1.356	1.782	2.179	3.055
13	1.350	1.771	2.160	3.012
14	1.345	1.761	2.145	2.977
15	1.341	1.753	2.131	2.947
16	1.337	1.746	2.120	2.921
17	1.333	1.740	2.110	2.898
18	1.330	1.734	2.101	2.878
19	1.328	1.729	2.093	2.861
20	1.325	1.725	2.086	2.845
21	1.323	1.721	2.080	2.831
22	1.321	1.717	2.074	2.819
23	1.319	1.714	2.069	2.807
24	1.318	1.711	2.064	2.797
25	1.316	1.708	2.060	2.787

T A B L E A.1.1
(Continued)

df \ (1 − α)	.80	.90	.95	.99
26	1.315	1.706	2.056	2.779
27	1.314	1.703	2.052	2.771
28	1.313	1.701	2.048	2.763
29	1.311	1.699	2.045	2.756
30	1.310	1.697	2.042	2.750
35	1.306	1.690	2.030	2.724
40	1.303	1.684	2.021	2.704
45	1.301	1.679	2.014	2.690
50	1.299	1.676	2.009	2.678
60	1.296	1.671	2.000	2.660
70	1.294	1.667	1.994	2.648
80	1.292	1.664	1.990	2.639
90	1.291	1.662	1.987	2.632
100	1.290	1.660	1.984	2.626
120	1.289	1.658	1.980	2.617
140	1.288	1.656	1.977	2.611
160	1.287	1.654	1.975	2.607
180	1.286	1.653	1.973	2.603
200	1.286	1.653	1.972	2.601
∞	1.282	1.645	1.960	2.576

T A B L E A.1.2
Critical Values of $F_{n,d}$ for Upper Tail Proportion : $\alpha = 0.05$

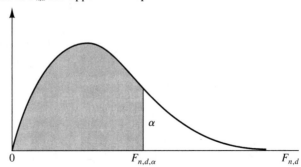

	n									
d		1	2	3	4	5	6	7	8	9
		Numerator Degrees of Freedom								
	1	161.4	199.5	215.7	224.6	230.2	234.0	236.8	238.9	240.5
	2	18.51	19.00	19.16	19.25	19.30	19.33	19.35	19.37	19.38
	3	10.13	9.55	9.28	9.12	9.01	8.94	8.89	8.85	8.81
	4	7.71	6.94	6.59	6.39	6.26	6.16	6.09	6.04	6.00
	5	6.61	5.79	5.41	5.19	5.05	4.95	4.88	4.82	4.77
	6	5.99	5.14	4.76	4.53	4.39	4.28	4.21	4.15	4.10
	7	5.59	4.74	4.35	4.12	3.97	3.87	3.79	3.73	3.68
	8	5.32	4.46	4.07	3.84	3.69	3.58	3.50	3.44	3.39
	9	5.12	4.26	3.86	3.63	3.48	3.37	3.29	3.23	3.18
	10	4.96	4.10	3.71	3.48	3.33	3.22	3.14	3.07	3.02
	11	4.84	3.98	3.59	3.36	3.20	3.09	3.01	2.95	2.90
	12	4.75	3.89	3.49	3.26	3.11	3.00	2.91	2.85	2.80
	13	4.67	3.81	3.41	3.18	3.03	2.92	2.83	2.77	2.71
	14	4.60	3.74	3.34	3.11	2.96	2.85	2.76	2.70	2.65
	15	4.54	3.68	3.29	3.06	2.90	2.79	2.71	2.64	2.59
	16	4.49	3.63	3.24	3.01	2.85	2.74	2.66	2.59	2.54
	17	4.45	3.59	3.20	2.96	2.81	2.70	2.61	2.55	2.49
	18	4.41	3.55	3.16	2.93	2.77	2.66	2.58	2.51	2.46
	19	4.38	3.52	3.13	2.90	2.74	2.63	2.54	2.48	2.42
	20	4.35	3.49	3.10	2.87	2.71	2.60	2.51	2.45	2.39
	21	4.32	3.47	3.07	2.84	2.68	2.57	2.49	2.42	2.37
	22	4.30	3.44	3.05	2.82	2.66	2.55	2.46	2.40	2.34
	23	4.28	3.42	3.03	2.80	2.64	2.53	2.44	2.37	2.32
	24	4.26	3.40	3.01	2.78	2.62	2.51	2.42	2.36	2.30
	25	4.24	3.39	2.99	2.76	2.60	2.49	2.40	2.34	2.28
	26	4.23	3.37	2.98	2.74	2.59	2.47	2.39	2.32	2.27
	27	4.21	3.35	2.96	2.73	2.57	2.46	2.37	2.31	2.25
	28	4.20	3.34	2.95	2.71	2.56	2.45	2.36	2.29	2.24
	29	4.18	3.33	2.93	2.70	2.55	2.43	2.35	2.28	2.22
	30	4.17	3.32	2.92	2.69	2.53	2.42	2.33	2.27	2.21
	40	4.08	3.23	2.84	2.61	2.45	2.34	2.25	2.18	2.12
	60	4.00	3.15	2.76	2.53	2.37	2.25	2.17	2.10	2.04
	120	3.92	3.07	2.68	2.45	2.29	2.17	2.09	2.02	1.96
	∞	3.84	3.00	2.60	2.37	2.21	2.10	2.01	1.94	1.88

Denominator Degrees of Freedom

T A B L E A.1.2
(Continued)

d \ n	10	12	15	20	24	30	40	60	120	∞
1	241.9	243.9	245.9	248.0	249.1	250.1	251.1	252.2	253.3	254.3
2	19.40	19.41	19.43	19.45	19.45	19.46	19.47	19.48	19.49	19.50
3	8.79	8.74	8.70	8.66	8.64	8.62	8.59	8.57	8.55	8.53
4	5.96	5.91	5.86	5.80	5.77	5.75	5.72	5.69	5.66	5.63
5	4.74	4.68	4.62	4.56	4.53	4.50	4.46	4.43	4.40	4.36
6	4.06	4.00	3.94	3.87	3.84	3.81	3.77	3.74	3.70	3.67
7	3.64	3.57	3.51	3.44	3.41	3.38	3.34	3.30	3.27	3.23
8	3.35	3.28	3.22	3.15	3.12	3.08	3.04	3.01	2.97	2.93
9	3.14	3.07	3.01	2.94	2.90	2.86	2.83	2.79	2.75	2.71
10	2.98	2.91	2.85	2.77	2.74	2.70	2.66	2.62	2.58	2.54
11	2.85	2.79	2.72	2.65	2.61	2.57	2.53	2.49	2.45	2.40
12	2.75	2.69	2.62	2.54	2.51	2.47	2.43	2.38	2.34	2.30
13	2.67	2.60	2.53	2.46	2.42	2.38	2.34	2.30	2.25	2.21
14	2.60	2.53	2.46	2.39	2.35	2.31	2.27	2.22	2.18	2.13
15	2.54	2.48	2.40	2.33	2.29	2.25	2.20	2.16	2.11	2.07
16	2.49	2.42	2.35	2.28	2.24	2.19	2.15	2.11	2.06	2.01
17	2.45	2.38	2.31	2.23	2.19	2.15	2.10	2.06	2.01	1.96
18	2.41	2.34	2.27	2.19	2.15	2.11	2.06	2.02	1.97	1.92
19	2.38	2.31	2.23	2.16	2.11	2.07	2.03	1.98	1.93	1.88
20	2.35	2.28	2.20	2.12	2.08	2.04	1.99	1.95	1.90	1.84
21	2.32	2.25	2.18	2.10	2.05	2.01	1.96	1.92	1.87	1.81
22	2.30	2.23	2.15	2.07	2.03	1.98	1.94	1.89	1.84	1.78
23	2.27	2.20	2.13	2.05	2.01	1.96	1.91	1.86	1.81	1.76
24	2.25	2.18	2.11	2.03	1.98	1.94	1.89	1.84	1.79	1.73
25	2.24	2.16	2.09	2.01	1.96	1.92	1.87	1.82	1.77	1.71
26	2.22	2.15	2.07	1.99	1.95	1.90	1.85	1.80	1.75	1.69
27	2.20	2.13	2.06	1.97	1.93	1.88	1.84	1.79	1.73	1.67
28	2.19	2.12	2.04	1.96	1.91	1.87	1.82	1.77	1.71	1.65
29	2.18	2.10	2.03	1.94	1.90	1.85	1.81	1.75	1.70	1.64
30	2.16	2.09	2.01	1.93	1.89	1.84	1.79	1.74	1.68	1.62
40	2.08	2.00	1.92	1.84	1.79	1.74	1.69	1.64	1.58	1.51
60	1.99	1.92	1.84	1.75	1.70	1.65	1.59	1.53	1.47	1.39
120	1.91	1.83	1.75	1.66	1.61	1.55	1.50	1.43	1.35	1.25
∞	1.83	1.75	1.67	1.57	1.52	1.46	1.39	1.32	1.22	1.00

Numerator Degrees of Freedom (column header); Denominator Degrees of Freedom (row label)

Source: From M. Merrington and C. M. Thompson, "Tables of Percentage Points of the Inverted Beta (*F*)-Distribution," *Biometrika,* 33, 1943, pp. 73–88. Reproduced by permission of the *Biometrika* Trustees.

T A B L E A.1.3

Critical Values of $F_{n,d}$ for Upper Tail Proportion : $\alpha = 0.01$

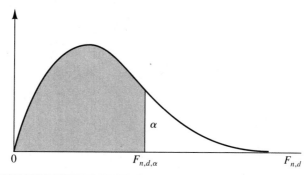

d	n				Numerator Degrees of Freedom				
	1	2	3	4	5	6	7	8	9
1	4,052	4,999.5	5,403	5,625	5,764	5,859	5,928	5,982	6,022
2	98.50	99.00	99.17	99.25	99.30	99.33	99.36	99.37	99.39
3	34.12	30.82	29.46	28.71	28.24	27.91	27.67	27.49	27.35
4	21.20	18.00	16.69	15.98	15.52	15.21	14.98	14.80	14.66
5	16.26	13.27	12.06	11.39	10.97	10.67	10.46	10.29	10.16
6	13.75	10.92	9.78	9.15	8.75	8.47	8.26	8.10	7.98
7	12.25	9.55	8.45	7.85	7.46	7.19	6.99	6.84	6.72
8	11.26	8.65	7.59	7.01	6.63	6.37	6.18	6.03	5.91
9	10.56	8.02	6.99	6.42	6.06	5.80	5.61	5.47	5.35
10	10.04	7.56	6.55	5.99	5.64	5.39	5.20	5.06	4.94
11	9.65	7.21	6.22	5.67	5.32	5.07	4.89	4.74	4.63
12	9.33	6.93	5.95	5.41	5.06	4.82	4.64	4.50	4.39
13	9.07	6.70	5.74	5.21	4.86	4.62	4.44	4.30	4.19
14	8.86	6.51	5.56	5.04	4.69	4.46	4.28	4.14	4.03
15	8.68	6.36	5.42	4.89	4.56	4.32	4.14	4.00	3.89
16	8.53	6.23	5.29	4.77	4.44	4.20	4.03	3.89	3.78
17	8.40	6.11	5.18	4.67	4.34	4.10	3.93	3.79	3.68
18	8.29	6.01	5.09	4.58	4.25	4.01	3.84	3.71	3.60
19	8.18	5.93	5.01	4.50	4.17	3.94	3.77	3.63	3.52
20	8.10	5.85	4.94	4.43	4.10	3.87	3.70	3.56	3.46
21	8.02	5.78	4.87	4.37	4.04	3.81	3.64	3.51	3.40
22	7.95	5.72	4.82	4.31	3.99	3.76	3.59	3.45	3.35
23	7.88	5.66	4.76	4.26	3.94	3.71	3.54	3.41	3.30
24	7.82	5.61	4.72	4.22	3.90	3.67	3.50	3.36	3.26
25	7.77	5.57	4.68	4.18	3.85	3.63	3.46	3.32	3.22
26	7.72	5.53	4.64	4.14	3.82	3.59	3.42	3.29	3.18
27	7.68	5.49	4.60	4.11	3.78	3.56	3.39	3.26	3.15
28	7.64	5.45	4.57	4.07	3.75	3.53	3.36	3.23	3.12
29	7.60	5.42	4.54	4.04	3.73	3.50	3.33	3.20	3.09
30	7.56	5.39	4.51	4.02	3.70	3.47	3.30	3.17	3.07
40	7.31	5.18	4.31	3.83	3.51	3.29	3.12	2.99	2.89
60	7.08	4.98	4.13	3.65	3.34	3.12	2.95	2.82	2.72
120	6.85	4.79	3.95	3.48	3.17	2.96	2.79	2.66	2.56
∞	6.63	4.61	3.78	3.32	3.02	2.80	2.64	2.51	2.41

Denominator Degrees of Freedom

T A B L E   A.1.3
(Continued)

d \ n	10	12	15	20	24	30	40	60	120	∞
				Numerator Degrees of Freedom						
1	6,056	6,106	6,157	6,209	6,235	6,261	6,287	6,313	6,339	6,366
2	99.40	99.42	99.43	99.45	99.46	99.47	99.47	99.48	99.49	99.50
3	27.23	27.05	26.87	26.69	26.60	26.50	26.41	26.32	26.22	26.13
4	14.55	14.37	14.20	14.02	13.93	13.84	13.75	13.65	13.56	13.46
5	10.05	9.89	9.72	9.55	9.47	9.38	9.29	9.20	9.11	9.02
6	7.87	7.72	7.56	7.40	7.31	7.23	7.14	7.06	6.97	6.88
7	6.62	6.47	6.31	6.16	6.07	5.99	5.91	5.82	5.74	5.65
8	5.81	5.67	5.52	5.36	5.28	5.20	5.12	5.03	4.95	4.86
9	5.26	5.11	4.96	4.81	4.73	4.65	4.57	4.48	4.40	4.31
10	4.85	4.71	4.56	4.41	4.33	4.25	4.17	4.08	4.00	3.91
11	4.54	4.40	4.25	4.10	4.02	3.94	3.86	3.78	3.69	3.60
12	4.30	4.16	4.01	3.86	3.78	3.70	3.62	3.54	3.45	3.36
13	4.10	3.96	3.82	3.66	3.59	3.51	3.43	3.34	3.25	3.17
14	3.94	3.80	3.66	3.51	3.43	3.35	3.27	3.18	3.09	3.00
15	3.80	3.67	3.52	3.37	3.29	3.21	3.13	3.05	2.96	2.87
16	3.69	3.55	3.41	3.26	3.18	3.10	3.02	2.93	2.84	2.75
17	3.59	3.46	3.31	3.16	3.08	3.00	2.92	2.83	2.75	2.65
18	3.51	3.37	3.23	3.08	3.00	2.92	2.84	2.75	2.66	2.57
19	3.43	3.30	3.15	3.00	2.92	2.84	2.76	2.67	2.58	2.49
20	3.37	3.23	3.09	2.94	2.86	2.78	2.69	2.61	2.52	2.42
21	3.31	3.17	3.03	2.88	2.80	2.72	2.64	2.55	2.46	2.36
22	3.26	3.12	2.98	2.83	2.75	2.67	2.58	2.50	2.40	2.31
23	3.21	3.07	2.93	2.78	2.70	2.62	2.54	2.45	2.35	2.26
24	3.17	3.03	2.89	2.74	2.66	2.58	2.49	2.40	2.31	2.21
25	3.13	2.99	2.85	2.70	2.62	2.54	2.45	2.36	2.27	2.17
26	3.09	2.96	2.81	2.66	2.58	2.50	2.42	2.33	2.23	2.13
27	3.06	2.93	2.78	2.63	2.55	2.47	2.38	2.29	2.20	2.10
28	3.03	2.90	2.75	2.60	2.52	2.44	2.35	2.26	2.17	2.06
29	3.00	2.87	2.73	2.57	2.49	2.41	2.33	2.23	2.14	2.03
30	2.98	2.84	2.70	2.55	2.47	2.39	2.30	2.21	2.11	2.01
40	2.80	2.66	2.52	2.37	2.29	2.20	2.11	2.02	1.92	1.80
60	2.63	2.50	2.35	2.20	2.12	2.03	1.94	1.84	1.73	1.60
120	2.47	2.34	2.19	2.03	1.95	1.86	1.76	1.66	1.53	1.38
∞	2.32	2.18	2.04	1.88	1.79	1.70	1.59	1.47	1.32	1.00

Denominator Degrees of Freedom

Source: From M. Merrington and C. M. Thompson, "Tables of Percentage Points of the Inverted Beta (F)-Distribution," *Biometrika,* 33, 1943, pp. 73–88. Reproduced by permission of the *Biometrika* Trustees.

T A B L E   **A.1.4**

Upper Tail Proportions of Chi-Squared Distributions

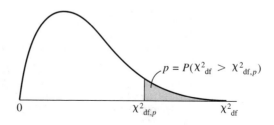

$$p = P(\chi^2_{df} > \chi^2_{df,p})$$

df \ p	.25	.20	.10	.05	.01
1	1.323	1.642	2.706	3.841	6.635
2	2.773	3.219	4.605	5.991	9.210
3	4.108	4.642	6.251	7.815	11.345
4	5.385	5.989	7.779	9.488	13.277
5	6.626	7.289	9.236	11.070	15.066
6	7.841	8.558	10.645	12.592	16.812
7	9.037	9.803	12.017	14.067	18.475
8	10.219	11.030	13.362	15.507	20.090
9	11.389	12.242	14.684	16.919	21.666
10	12.549	13.442	15.987	18.307	23.209
11	13.701	14.631	17.275	19.675	24.725
12	14.845	15.812	18.549	21.026	26.217
13	15.984	16.985	19.812	22.362	27.688
14	17.117	18.151	21.064	23.685	29.141
15	18.245	19.311	22.307	24.996	30.578
16	19.369	20.465	23.542	26.296	32.000
17	20.489	21.615	24.769	27.587	33.409
18	21.605	22.760	25.989	28.869	34.805
19	22.718	23.900	27.204	30.144	36.191
20	23.828	25.038	28.412	31.410	37.566
21	24.935	26.171	29.615	32.671	38.932
22	26.039	27.301	30.813	33.924	40.289
23	27.141	28.429	32.007	35.172	41.638
24	28.241	29.553	33.196	36.415	42.980
25	29.339	30.675	34.382	37.652	44.314

T A B L E **A.1.4**
(Continued)

df \ p	.25	.20	.10	.05	.01
26	30.435	31.795	35.563	38.885	45.642
27	31.528	32.912	36.741	40.113	46.963
28	32.620	34.027	37.916	41.337	48.278
29	33.711	35.139	39.087	42.557	49.588
30	34.800	36.250	40.256	43.773	50.892
35	40.223	41.778	46.059	49.802	57.342
40	45.616	47.269	51.805	55.758	63.691
45	50.985	52.729	57.505	61.656	69.957
50	56.334	58.164	63.167	67.505	76.154
60	66.982	68.972	74.397	79.082	88.379
70	77.579	79.715	85.527	90.531	100.425
80	88.129	90.405	96.578	101.879	112.329
90	98.646	101.054	107.565	113.145	124.116
100	109.143	111.667	118.498	124.342	135.807
120	130.050	132.806	140.233	146.567	158.950
140	150.895	153.854	161.827	168.613	181.840
160	171.672	174.828	183.311	190.516	204.530
180	192.400	195.743	204.704	212.304	227.056
200	213.096	216.609	226.021	233.994	249.445

T A B L E A.1.4
(Continued)

p df	.25	.20	.10	.05	.01
26	30.435	31.795	35.563	38.885	45.642
27	31.528	32.912	36.741	40.113	46.963
28	32.620	34.027	37.916	41.337	48.278
29	33.711	35.139	39.087	42.557	49.588
30	34.800	36.250	40.256	43.773	50.892
35	40.223	41.778	46.059	49.802	57.342
40	45.616	47.269	51.805	55.758	63.691
45	50.985	52.729	57.505	61.656	69.957
50	56.334	58.164	63.167	67.505	76.154
60	66.982	68.972	74.397	79.082	88.379
70	77.579	79.715	85.527	90.531	100.425
80	88.129	90.405	96.578	101.879	112.329
90	98.646	101.054	107.565	113.145	124.116
100	109.143	111.667	118.498	124.342	135.807
120	130.050	132.806	140.233	146.567	158.950
140	150.895	153.854	161.827	168.613	181.840
160	171.672	174.828	183.311	190.516	204.530
180	192.400	195.743	204.704	212.304	227.056
200	213.096	216.609	226.021	233.994	249.445

2

Advanced Topics

Matrix Formulation of Linear Models

Using the notation of vectors and matrices, the conventions of matrix algebra, make it possible to express our linear modeling results, whatever the number of explanatory variables. We begin by organizing our N sampled response observations into an N-element (column) vector, y. Similarly, the explanatory variable scores are organized into a matrix X with N rows, one row for each of our sample observations. This matrix is organized so that the ith row of X refers to the same observation as the ith element of y. Each column of X contains the scores on a particular x-variable. To simplify the notation and algebra, the first column of X is a column of ones. The second column contains scores on x_1. The third column has scores on x_2. As a result, X will have $(k + 1)$ columns; X is an N by $(k + 1)$ matrix. The entry at the intersection of the ith row and jth column of X, X_{ij}, is the score for the ith sample observation on explanatory variable x_{j-1}. Frequently, X is referred to as the *design matrix* for a linear model, and y as the *response vector*.

Next we define a $(k + 1)$-element vector, β, with unknown parameters as its elements. We use it to write, in matrix form, our linear model equation:

$$X\beta = \mu(y). \tag{1}$$

As X is $N \times (k + 1)$ and β is $(k + 1) \times 1$, the matrix product $\mu(y)$ is $N \times 1$; it is an N-element column vector. Each element of $\mu(y)$ is a sum of products between the elements of a row of X and the vector β:

$$\mu(y)_i = \sum_{j=1}^{k+1} X_{ij}\beta_j = \beta_1 1 + \beta_2 x_{i1} + \ldots + \beta_{(k+1)}x_{ik}.$$

The first element of β is the regression intercept and the remaining k elements are regression slopes. The vector $\mu(y)$ contains conditional response means, means for the conditional response populations from which the corresponding elements of y were sampled:

$$\mu(y)_i = \mu(y_i). \tag{2}$$

The elements of β are unknown population parameters to be estimated from the sample data making up the vector y and matrix X. The algebra of this estimation can be summarized as follows:

1   Form the matrix by vector product $X^{\mathrm{T}}y$, where X^{T} is the transposed form of X. The product will be a $(k + 1)$ element vector, each element of which is a sum of products between a column of X and the y vector. For $k = 1$, the linear regression model with a single x-variable, this product would have two elements:

$$(X^{\mathrm{T}}y)_1 = \sum_{i=1}^{N} X_{i1}\, y_i = \sum_{i=1}^{N} 1 y_i = \sum_{i=1}^{N} y_i$$

and

$$(X^{\mathrm{T}}y)_2 = \sum_{i=1}^{N} X_{i2}\, y_i = \sum_{i=1}^{N} x_i\, y_i.$$

For multivariable models the pattern will be the same, the first element will be the sum of response observations and each additional element a sum of products of those with scores on one of the x-variables.

2   Form the minor product moment of the *design matrix*, $X^{\mathrm{T}}X$. The resulting, symmetric, matrix will be $(k + 1)$ by $(k + 1)$. The diagonal elements of the matrix are sums of squares of columns of X, and the off-diagonal elements are sums of products between a pair of columns of X. For $k = 2$, where we have two explanatory variables, selected elements of $X^{\mathrm{T}}X$ would be

$$(X^{\mathrm{T}}X)_{11} = N,$$
$$(X^{\mathrm{T}}X)_{22} = \sum_{i=1}^{N} x_{i1}{}^2,$$
$$(X^{\mathrm{T}}X)_{23} = (X^{\mathrm{T}}X)_{32} = \sum_{i=1}^{N} x_{i1}x_{i2}.$$

3   Find the regular inverse of the product moment matrix, $(X^{\mathrm{T}}X)^{-1}$. Every square matrix of full rank has a regular inverse, a second matrix the same size as the first that, when used either as a premultiplier or postmultiplier of the original matrix, returns the identity matrix:

$$(X^{\mathrm{T}}X)^{-1}(X^{\mathrm{T}}X) = (X^{\mathrm{T}}X)(X^{\mathrm{T}}X)^{-1} = I.$$

The identity matrix, the matrix equivalent of the scalar 1, is 0 everywhere except along the main diagonal where all elements are 1s. Our $X^{\mathrm{T}}X$ will have a regular inverse so long as no one of our explanatory variables can be expressed as a linear combination of the remaining x-variables. In terms of partial variables, this requires that the SD for each partial variable be greater than 0.

The elements of the regular inverse of $X^{\mathrm{T}}X$ for $k > 1$ are not easily described. For $k = 1$, though, they would be

$$[(X^\mathsf{T}X)^{-1}]_{11} = \frac{\Sigma\, x_i^2}{N\, \Sigma\, x_i^2 - (\Sigma\, x_i)^2},$$

$$[(X^\mathsf{T}X)^{-1}]_{22} = \frac{N}{N\, \Sigma\, x_i^2 - (\Sigma\, x_i)^2}, \text{ and}$$

$$[(X^\mathsf{T}X)^{-1}]_{12} = [(X^\mathsf{T}X)^{-1}]_{21} = \frac{-\Sigma\, x_i}{N\, \Sigma\, x_i^2 - (\Sigma\, x_i)^2}.$$

4 Finally, the vector of estimated regression slopes and intercept is given by the matrix product

$$\hat{\beta} = (X^\mathsf{T}X)^{-1}(X^\mathsf{T}y). \tag{3}$$

Although some algebraic simplification is required, you may be interested to verify that the premultiplication of the $X^\mathsf{T}y$ vector given in step 1 by the $(X^\mathsf{T}X)^{-1}$ matrix given in step 3 does yield the intercept and slope estimates for the simple linear regression model presented in Chapter 4:

$$\hat{\beta}_2 = r(y, x)\frac{\mathrm{SD}(y)}{\mathrm{SD}(x)}$$

$$= \left(\frac{\mathrm{Cov}(y, x)}{\mathrm{SD}(y)\,\mathrm{SD}(x)}\right)\left(\frac{\mathrm{SD}(y)}{\mathrm{SD}(x)}\right) = \frac{\mathrm{Cov}(x, y)}{\mathrm{Var}(x)} = \frac{N\, \Sigma\, x_i y_i - \Sigma\, x_i\, \Sigma\, y_i}{N\, \Sigma\, x_i^2 - (\Sigma\, x_i)^2} \tag{4.1}$$

and

$$\hat{\beta}_1 = M(y) - \hat{\beta}_2 M(x) = (1/N)\, \Sigma\, y_i - \hat{\beta}_2(1/N)\, \Sigma\, x_i. \tag{4.2}$$

The vector of N estimated conditional response means is given by substituting the estimated vector $\hat{\beta}$ for β in Equation [1]:

$$X\hat{\beta} = \hat{\mu}(y). \tag{4}$$

An N-element vector of residuals is obtained by subtracting $\hat{\mu}(y)$ from y:

$$\hat{\epsilon} = y - \hat{\mu}(y) = y - X\hat{\beta}. \tag{5}$$

The minor product moment of the residual vector gives the sum of squares of residuals,

$$\mathrm{SSR} = \hat{\epsilon}^\mathsf{T}\hat{\epsilon} = (y - X\hat{\beta})^\mathsf{T}(y - X\hat{\beta}), \tag{6}$$

which, divided by $(N - k - 1)$, provides our estimate of the conditional response variance:

$$\frac{\mathrm{SSR}}{N - k - 1} = \frac{\hat{\epsilon}^\mathsf{T}\hat{\epsilon}}{N - k - 1} = \hat{\sigma}^2(y \mid X). \tag{7}$$

Finally, the estimated sampling variance-covariance matrix for the $(k + 1)$ regression parameter estimates results from multiplying each element of $(X^\mathsf{T}X)^{-1}$ by this conditional response variance:

$$C(\hat{\beta}) = \hat{\sigma}^2(y \mid X)(X^\mathsf{T}X)^{-1}. \tag{8}$$

The diagonal elements of $C(\hat{\beta})$ give the estimated sampling variances for our regression slope and intercept estimates. The square roots of these diagonal elements are our standard errors,

$$\sqrt{[C(\hat{\beta})]_{jj}} = \text{SE}(\hat{\beta}_j), \qquad [9]$$

used in developing CIs. The SE reported in Chapter 5 for the slope in the simple linear regression model,

$$\text{SE}(\hat{\beta}_2) = \sqrt{\frac{\hat{\sigma}^2(y\,|\,x)}{\text{Var}(x)N}}, \qquad [5.2]$$

can be re-created by application of Equations [8] and [9], noting again that

$$[(X^TX)^{-1}]_{22} = \frac{N}{N\,\Sigma\,x_i^2 - (\Sigma\,x_i)^2} = \frac{N}{N[N\,\text{Var}(x)]}.$$

The off-diagonal elements of $C(\hat{\beta})$ give the sampling covariances for pairs of $\hat{\beta}$ elements,

$$C(\hat{\beta})_{j\ell} = \hat{\text{Cov}}(\hat{\beta}_j, \hat{\beta}_\ell). \qquad [10]$$

The covariance here is over hypothetical resamples. Large positive or negative values, relative to the size of the corresponding SEs, indicate that our estimates of a pair of β elements are correlated one with another. This correlation can be estimated as

$$\hat{\rho}(\hat{\beta}_j, \hat{\beta}_\ell) = \frac{\hat{\text{Cov}}(\hat{\beta}_j, \hat{\beta}_\ell)}{\text{SE}(\hat{\beta}_j)\,\text{SE}(\hat{\beta}_\ell)}. \qquad [11]$$

It was noted before that, for simple regression models, those with a single x-variable, the off-diagonal element of the inverse of the product moment of the 2×2 design matrix took the form

$$[(X^TX)^{-1}]_{12} = [(X^TX)^{-1}]_{21} = \frac{-\Sigma\,x_i}{N\,\Sigma\,x_i^2 - (\Sigma\,x_i)^2}.$$

Interpreting this in the light of Equations [8], [10], and [11], we see that our estimates of the regression slope and intercept will be uncorrelated with each other only, if in the sampling design, $M(x) = 0$. More generally, we look to the magnitudes of the elements of $C(\hat{\beta})$ to tell us whether or by how much our estimates of pairs of slope parameters are correlated.

The fuller/less full model relations developed in Chapter 8 can also be expressed in matrix algebra form. If X is an N by $(p + k)$ design matrix and Z a second N by p design matrix, then the two are in a fuller/less full relation if we can link the two by a matrix equation of the form

$$Z = XW, \qquad [12]$$

where W is a $(p + k)$ by p matrix of weights. Each column of W contains the weights needed to convert the $(p + k)$ fuller-model variables into one of the less full model variables.

And if β is a $(p + k)$ vector of fuller-model regression parameters we can represent a collection of k linear constraints on those parameters as the matrix equation

$$C^{\mathrm{T}} \beta = \Gamma,$$

[13]

where C is a $(p + k)$ by k matrix (C^{T} is k by $p+k$) and Γ is a k-element vector. Each column of C contains the $(p + k)$ coefficients needed for a single constraint on β. For Equation [13] to impose k constraints on the full-model parameters, that is, for the constrained or less full model to have k fewer regression parameters, the matrix C must be of rank k. That is, no column of C can be a weighted combination of other columns of C.

We will return to the constraint matrix C later in the section in this Appendix on power.

Power of Model Comparisons

Equation 7.24,

$$F = \frac{\left(\frac{1}{k}\right)[\text{SSR}(\textit{less full model}) - \text{SSR}(\textit{fuller model})}{\left(\frac{1}{N - (p + k)}\right)\text{SSR}(\textit{fuller model})},$$

[7.24]

gives us a mechanism for comparing two models. We ask whether we can *infer* from our sample of y observations that the conditional response variance under the less full model really is larger than under the fuller model. If F is large enough, we'll conclude that at least some of the k extra parameters are needed and choose the fuller over the less full model. If our computed F is not so large, we'll infer that the less full model is just as good as the fuller one and opt for the model with fewer parameters.

Our F-ratio *inferences,* however, are just that. We are trying to infer something about the real world from a limited amount of information, from a sample. That sample *may* lead us to reject the less full model when it is the correct one, or to accept that model when we should hold out for some of the added complexity of the fuller model. We *may be wrong* in our inference. How likely is it that we will make an incorrect inference?

Incorrect Rejection of Less Full Model

In classical statistical hypothesis testing, two kinds of decision errors are identified. We make a similar distinction in modeling. One kind of error occurs when the less full model is correct, but we decide that we need at least some of the extra parameters associated with the fuller one for an adequate explanatory model. Let's see how that happens.

Our model comparison statistic, the F of Equation [7.24], has as its sampling distribution one of the F random variables *when the less full model is the true model*. We use this principle in our comparison strategy. It is our guide in deciding when the difference in size of the estimated conditional response variances (or of the SSRs) is too large for the less full model to be a reasonable choice. We say that if the value of F is so large that it or a larger value of F would occur only one time in twenty (5% of the time) or only one time in a hundred (1% of the time) when the less full model is correct, then such a result is so unlikely as to lead us to conclude that the less full model is not correct.

Thus, our model comparison strategy requires that we be wrong in this way, on the average, 5% of the time or 1% of the time when the less full model is correct depending upon our standard for interpreting the F ratio result. Because the sampling distribution of our F statistic includes a few very, very, large values—even when the less full model is correct—*we must accept some chance of making this kind of error* if we are to make comparisons and choices between a less full and fuller model. The most common choices for the chances are 5% and 1%. In modeling, we agree to reject the less full model even though, if it were correct, this would lead to a wrong conclusion 5% or 1% of the time.

Alternatives to the Less Full Model

It is convenient to think of the less full and fuller models as just two models. It helps to focus our attention in modeling. In fact, however, a fuller and less full model together describe a very large collection of possible models, not just two. Put another way, there are *many alternatives to the less full model* contained within our idea of the fuller one. And when we come to evaluate the seriousness of a second erroneous conclusion, incorrectly choosing the less full model, we'll want to do this in the context of which of those alternatives actually describes the world from which we have sampled.

We can appreciate the multiplicity of alternative models if we look again at the less full model as the result of imposing one or more *constraints* on the parameters of a fuller model. Let's consider a simple example. In Chapter 6, we examined, via a sample data set, the question of whether men and women high school seniors have the same or different expected values for the Scholastic Aptitude Test verbal score.

Our fuller model for this study looked like this:

$$\mu(SATV \mid Gender) = \beta_1 + \beta_2 x_i,$$

with x_i the value of a *Gender* dummy variable—$x_i = 0$ for Men, $x_i = 1$ for Women. In this model, β_1 is the mean for men, $\mu(SATV \mid Men)$, and β_2 is the amount by which the mean for women exceeds that for men, $\mu(SATV \mid Women) - \mu(SATV \mid Men)$. The less full model, stipulating that men and women have the same SATV means, is the result of constraining β_2 to be 0:

$$\mu(SATV \mid Gender) = \beta_1.$$

This constraint may be written using Equation [8.3],

$$\Gamma_i = \sum_{j=1}^{p+k} C_{i,j}\beta_j, \text{ for } i = 1, \ldots, k, \qquad \text{[8.3]}$$

as

$$\Gamma_1 = 0\beta_1 + 1\beta_2 = 0.$$

Here $k = 1$ and $(p + k) = 2$; only one constraint on the two parameters of the fuller model is needed to describe the less full model.

The less full model constrains β_2 to be equal to 0. The fuller model, however, allows β_2 to *be any value*, positive or negative, large or small. If we specify any particular value for β_2 *other than 0* we specify an *alternative model*, an alternative to the less full one.

Failure to Reject Less Full Model for Specified True Alternatives

A *second kind of model comparison error* occurs when we choose the less full model, but an alternative one is correct. That is, in the present example, we might conclude that $\beta_2 = 0$ when, in fact, $\beta_2 = 50$.

What is the chance that we will make this error? There is a specific answer for incorrectly rejecting the less full model. It depends solely upon the standard we establish for the F-ratio comparison, 5% or 1%. The chance that we will fail to reject the less full model when we should is *more complexly determined*. There is no single, simple answer.

The chance of not rejecting the less full model when we should depends upon five factors:

1 The choice of probability level for rejection of the less full model. If we increase this, say from 1% to 5%, we decrease the chance of not rejecting the less full model when we should. There is a tradeoff between the two.

2 The size of the conditional response variance. The greater the fuller model conditional response variance, the greater the chance we will fail to reject the less full model when we should.

3 The design of the study. In particular, how many observations are included in the sample and how those observations are distributed among the design points are important. The larger the sample, the smaller the chance of failing to reject an incorrect less full model. And for many model comparisons, a balanced design—equal numbers of observations at each design point—gives better protection against comparison error.

4 The constraints that we impose on the parameters of the fuller model. The number of constraints, for example, affects the chance of error.

5 How "close" the alternative model is to the less full model. The closer the two are, the greater the chance we will "miss" the alternative and opt, mistakenly, for the less full model.

In the Gender/SATV example, the less full model specifies a gender difference of 0. We shortly will see, as an instance of one of these principles, that it will be harder for us to reject this model when we sample from a real world in which the true gender difference in means is 25 points than when that difference is 50 points.

Model Comparison Power to Detect Alternatives

It is common now to refer to the *power of a model comparison* for a particular alternative rather than to the chance of failing to reject the less full model when that particular alternative is the correct model. Power is just the converse. It is the chance that the less full model *will be rejected* when a specified alternative is correct. If the chance of failing to reject the less full model when an alternative is correct is 10% for a particular alternative model, then the power to detect that alternative is 90%. Because it is just the flip side, power depends upon the same five factors just mentioned.

When we know the values of these five factors, we can compute the power of a model comparison. This is particularly important at the design stage of a study. It allows us to choose a design and sample size that will give us a good chance to identify those alternative models *that are important to us*. Even where we can't control the design, the power calculation will tell us that we had a good chance of spotting the alternative had it been correct or that our study lacked the power to do so.

The Noncentral *F*-sampling Distributions

It is customary to say that the *F*-ratio of Equation [7.24] has as its sampling distribution that of the *F*-random variable with k and $(N-p-k)$ degrees of freedom when the less full model is correct. But this description is not quite precise enough for a distinction we now draw. When the less full model is correct, the *F*-statistic of Equation [7.24] has as its sampling distribution that of the central *F*-random variable with k and $(N - p - k)$ degrees of freedom. It is the sampling distribution of these central *F*s that is also tabulated in an Appendix.

It is important to specify that it is a special class of *F*-distributions that describes the sampling distribution of the *F*-ratio when the less full model is the correct one. That is because when the less full model is *incorrect*, the *F* of Equation [7.24] has a different sampling distribution, that of a noncentral *F* with k and $(N - p - k)$ degrees of freedom *and noncentrality parameter* γ. The size of this noncentrality parameter depends upon the last four of the five factors outlined before. In short, the *F*-ratio has a *different sampling distribution* when a model alternative to the less full model is actually true.

We use the central *F*-distribution to tell us the *critical value* of the *F*-ratio; an *F*-ratio below the critical value leads us to select the less full model while one above the critical value leads us to reject it in favor of the fuller one. We choose a critical value such that the chance of an F-ratio larger than the critical value is 5% (or 1%) *if the less full model is correct.*

Because we can, in principle, specify the sampling distribution of F when a particular alternative model is true, we can use this distribution in a similar fashion. In particular, we'll use the noncentral F to find the chances of our F-ratio exceeding the selected critical value—and, hence, our rejecting the less full model—when a particular alternative to the less full model is correct. And that is precisely the power of our comparison to detect that alternative model.

Statistical Packages and the Noncentral F-distributions

To implement this approach to determine the power of a model comparison, we must be able to do two things. First, we must calculate or deduce this additional F-distribution parameter for noncentrality. Then, we need to determine the proportion of our particular noncentral F-distribution that is greater than our critical value. These, alas, are seemingly complex tasks. The noncentrality parameter depends on several factors and the number of noncentral F-distributions is potentially quite large. In the past, power computations have been made possible through the publication of collections of tables, specialized to particular study designs and to particular model comparisons. Notable among these are the books of Cohen (1987) and Kraemer and Thieman (1987). These can be consulted profitably for a variety of specific model comparisons.

However, in keeping with our goal of presenting linear models as a unifying structure for data analysis, we will describe the power computations in the most generalizable fashion. We have focused on the use of statistical computing packages (such as SPIDA which we use to illustrate regression and related computations) that allow for computing the noncentrality parameter and for obtaining noncentral F-probabilities.

The computation of a noncentrality parameter in the general case is best described in matrix calculational form as, for example, in Chapter 12 of Woodward, Bonett and Brecht, 1990. That formulation will be outlined here as it allows us to draw important conclusions about the impact of design factors on power. Although the multiplicity of noncentral F-distributions is so great as to preclude tabling (as for the central F-distribution 95% and 99% points), the needed noncentral F-tail probabilities may be available in your statistical package or, as in SPIDA, they may be generated by recursive calls to a central F-probability generator. The algorithm used by SPIDA for the examples described in this section is that given by Norton (1983).

Noncentrality Parameter Computation

The size of the noncentrality parameter is based on four of the power-influencing factors listed before:

1 the fuller model conditional response variance,

2 our study design (i.e., the design matrix for the fuller model),

3 the less full model constraints, and

4 the specific alternative to the less full model.

These four factors are conveniently linked to a value of the noncentrality parameter by a matrix calculation. That calculation seems complex but, once we have used it as a basis for showing the impact of different factors on power, it should become more understandable. Before presenting the noncentrality computation, we must define some constituents.

1 First, we need at least an estimate of the common conditional response variance under the fuller model, which we'll write as $\hat{\sigma}^2(y \mid X)$.

2 Next, we recall the notion of a *design matrix, X,* and some of the matrix calculations given earlier in this Appendix. The particular design matrix is that for the fuller model. This matrix will have a column for each x-variable in the fuller model, including usually a first column of "1"s for the intercept. It will have a row for each observational unit. The matrix X has N rows and $(p + k)$ columns. The linear algebraic formulation of the computation of $\hat{\beta}$ and $\text{SE}(\hat{\beta}_j)$ makes use of the minor product moment of the design matrix, $X^T X$, and its inverse, $(X^T X)^{-1}$. This last matrix plays a role in the computation of the noncentrality parameter.

3 The less full model is the result of constraining the parameters of the fuller model. That is, we require in the less full model that the $(p + k)$ regression parameters of the fuller model, written as the vector β, satisfy k linear constraints. These, we've seen earlier in this Appendix, are conveniently written as the matrix equation

$$C^T \beta = \Gamma_0, \tag{13}$$

where C is a $(p + k)$ by k matrix (C^T is k by $p + k$). Each column of C contains the $(p + k)$ coefficients needed for a single constraint on β. In many model comparisons, $k = 1$ and C is a column vector. We'll refer to C as the *constraint matrix.* On the right-hand side of Equation [13], Γ_0 is a k-element vector. Each column of C provides a set of weights for the elements of β. The corresponding element Γ_0 gives the value of this weighted sum of the β elements, *when the less full model is correct.* Typically, the elements of Γ_0 are 0s.

4 Our alternative model has associated with it a second k-element vector, Γ_A. Its elements correspond to what the left-hand side entries for Equation [13] would be if the alternative model, rather than the less full one, were correct. When the less full model is true, Γ_0 gives the values of the k weighted sums of the fuller model βs, and, when the alternative is true, Γ_A gives the values.

We now have defined all the terms that enter into the noncentrality parameter computation. The matrix calculation giving the noncentrality parameter looks like this:

$$\gamma = \left(\frac{1}{\hat{\sigma}^2(y \mid X)} \right) (\Gamma_A - \Gamma_0)^T (C^T (X^T X)^{-1} C)^{-1} (\Gamma_A - \Gamma_0). \tag{14}$$

While matrix equations such as this one accomplish a great deal, they disguise what they are doing! It is worth spending a few minutes with Equation [14] to see what is happening. To facilitate this, we consider the case of a single constraint, $k = 1$. In this case, Γ_0 and Γ_A are both scalars, C is a vector, and, consequently, $(C^T(X^TX)^{-1}C)$ is a scalar allowing Equation [14] to be rewritten as

$$\gamma_{(k=1)} = \frac{(\Gamma_A - \Gamma_0)^2}{\hat{\sigma}^2(y|X)(C^T(X^TX)^{-1})C)}. \qquad [15]$$

We have noted that the sampling variance-covariance matrix for the $\hat{\beta}$ elements can be expressed as

$$\text{Cov}(\hat{\beta}) = \hat{\sigma}^2(y|X)(X^TX)^{-1}. \qquad [8]$$

The diagonal elements of $\text{Cov}(\hat{\beta})$ are the sampling variances (squares of the SEs) for the $\hat{\beta}$ elements; the off-diagonals are covariances between pairs of $\hat{\beta}_j$s. Now, let's consider a single constraint on a set of, say, $k = 3$ regression parameters. In particular, let's say that we want to constrain the fuller model parameters such that $\beta_2 = \beta_3 = 0$. We write this in the form of a linear constraint as $\beta_2 - \beta_3 = 0$ or in the form of $C^T\beta = \Gamma_0$ as

$$0\ \beta_1 + 1\ \beta_2 - 1\ \beta_3 = 0,$$

where $C^T = (0\ 1\ -1)$ and $\Gamma_0 = 0$. We'll refer to $C^T\beta$ as the *left-hand side* of the constraint and to Γ_0 as the *right-hand side* of the constraint.

Just as the estimates $\hat{\beta}_2$ and $\hat{\beta}_3$ are subject to sampling variability, so is our estimate of the left-hand side of our constraint,

$$C^T\hat{\beta} = \hat{\beta}_2 - \hat{\beta}_3.$$

Because our constraint is linear, we can estimate its sampling variance by pre- and postmultiplying $\text{Cov}(\hat{\beta})$ by C^T and C, respectively:

$$\begin{aligned} \hat{\sigma}^2(C^T\hat{\beta}) &= C^T(\text{Cov}(\hat{\beta}))C \\ &= C^T[\hat{\sigma}^2(y|X)(X^TX)^{-1}]C = \hat{\sigma}^2(y|X)[C^T(X^TX)^{-1}C]. \end{aligned} \qquad [16]$$

But the far right-hand-side term of Equation [16] is the denominator of Equation [15], allowing us to rewrite the latter as

$$\gamma_{(k=1)} = \frac{(\Gamma_A - \Gamma_0)^2}{\hat{\sigma}^2(C^T\hat{\beta})} = \left(\frac{\Gamma_A - \Gamma_0}{\text{SE}(C^T\hat{\beta})}\right)^2. \qquad [17]$$

We can read this form. The noncentrality parameter is the square of the deviation of Γ_A (the value of the constraint under the alternative model) from Γ_0 (the value of the constraint under the less full model) scaled by the SE of the constraint. Scaling by the SE standardizes the metric of the constraint. The larger the difference between Γ_A and Γ_0 in the standard metric, the larger the value of the noncentrality parameter. Equation [14] generalizes this result for $k > 2$.

The difference $(\Gamma_A - \Gamma_0)$ is set by our choice of the less full and alternative models. The other influences on γ are captured in the "denominator" term,

$$\hat{\sigma}^2(C^T\hat{\beta}) = \hat{\sigma}^2(y|X)[C^T(X^TX)^{-1}C]. \qquad [16]$$

What affects its magnitude? We'll examine this question in the context of an example.

Power Computations: The Gender SATV Example

Let's see what the noncentrality and the power computations tell us about the Gender/SATV example. The noncentrality computations, carried out stepwise in SPIDA, are shown in Figure A.2.1. (In practice, SPIDA is able to compute the noncentrality parameter with a single command.)

A first thing we need is an estimate of the conditional response variance, $\sigma^2(y\,|\,X)$, for our fuller model. We'll use the estimate from the Chapter 6 analy-

FIGURE A.2.1

SPIDA Steps in the Calculation of Noncentrality Parameter

```
$sig2:=9765.10                        Full model conditional response variance (estimated).
$x1:=1+(0*(1;;50))                    x₁, a column of 50 ones.
$x2:=1+(0*(1;;22));0*(1;;28)          x₂, 22 ones followed by 28 0s in a second column.
$xmat:=$x1,$x2                        Joining the two columns into a matrix.
$xmat
  1 1                                 Rows 1-3 of the design matrix.
  1 1
  1 1
  . .
  1 0                                 Rows 48-50 of the design matrix.
  1 0
  1 0
$xtrx:=tran($xmat)#$xmat              Computing XᵀX.
$xtrx
  50 22                               The 2 by 2 XᵀX.
  22 22
$xtrxi:=inv($xtrx)                    Computing the inverse of XᵀX.
$xtrxi
   0.036 -0.036                       The inverse, (XᵀX)⁻¹
  -0.036  0.081
$cmat:=0;1                            Forming the constraint matrix.
$cmat
  0                                   One constraint, so C is a column vector.
  1
$cxxic:=tran($cmat)#($xtrxi#$cmat)    Forming Cᵀ(XᵀX)⁻¹C.
$cxxic
  0.081                               The result is a scalar.
$cci:=1/$cxxic                        The inverse of a scalar is its reciprocal.
$cci
 12.32
$gam0:=0                             Γ, under the less-full model.
$gama:=50                            Γ, under the alternative model.
$g:=($gama-$gam0)^2*$cci             Completing the numerator of the noncentrality.
$g
 30800
$nonc:=$g/$sig2                      The last step in computation.
$nonc
  3.154
```

ses: $\sigma^2(y|X) = 9765.10$. This is termed $\verb|$sig2|$ in the figure. In the fuller model,

$$\mu(SATV \,|\, Gender) = \beta_1 x_{1i} + \beta_2 x_{2i},$$

we have $(p + k) = 2$ parameters and associated x-variables—x_1 which is 1 for all observations (the unit variable associated with the intercept term) and x_2 which is 0 for men and 1 for women. In our Chapter 6 example, our sample consisted of 22 women and 28 men. The design matrix, X, would have 50 rows and 2 columns. The first column would contain only 1s. The second column would be a mixture of 28 0s and 22 1s, the 1s in rows corresponding to observations for women. The constructed design matrix is termed $\verb|$xmat|$ in the figure. Figure A.2.1 next describes the computation of X^TX and its regular inverse and displays each: $\verb|$xtrx|$ and $\verb|$xtrxi|$.

The single constraint $(k = 1)$ on the parameters of the fuller model that produces the less full model is obtained from

$$\Gamma_i = \sum_{j=1}^{p+k} C_{i,j}\, \beta_j, \text{ for } i = 1, \ldots, k \qquad \text{[8.3]}$$

as

$$\Gamma = 0\,\beta_1 + 1\,\beta_2 = 0.$$

We can collect the $C_{i,j}$s in a matrix,

$$C = \begin{pmatrix} 0 \\ 1 \end{pmatrix},$$

with a single column for the single constraint. This is $\verb|$cmat|$ in Figure A.2.1. From these results, $C^T(X^TX)^{-1}C$ and its inverse are then computed and displayed as $\verb|$cxxic|$ and $\verb|$cci|$, respectively. As $k = 1$, these are both scalar quantities.

The left-hand side of Equation [8.3] is 0 under the less full model. To link Γ more obviously with the less full model, we write

$$\Gamma_0 = 0.$$

The "0" subscript signifies that this is the value of the constraint *under the less full model.*

Lastly, but most importantly, we need to describe an alternative model, one we would like our F-ratio statistic to distinguish from the less full one. Alternative models, given our orientation to describing the less full model in terms of constraints on the parameters of the fuller model, correspond to alternative specifications of Γ (or of the several Γ_is if the less full model is defined by more than one constraint on the fuller one).

What alternative value of Γ is of interest to us? Here, Γ is the amount by which the expected value of the SATV distribution for Women exceeds that for Men.

What are the chances that we would reject the less full model when, say, the mean for women is actually 50 points higher than for men ($\Gamma_A = 50$) or when the mean for men exceeds that for women by 25 points ($\Gamma_A = -25$)? These are possible alternative models. Substantive considerations could tell us *how large* a difference between the genders is of interest. To give us something to work with, though, let's take the alternative model to be that the Γ of Equation [8.3] takes the value

$$\Gamma_A = 50$$

rather than $\Gamma_0 = 0$. The two are identified in Figure A.2.1 as $gam0 and $gama.

The computation is then completed in accordance with Equations [16] and [17] yielding a noncentrality parameter of $\gamma = 3.154$. In order to complete the calculation, we had to describe our fuller model, with X and $\hat{\sigma}^2(y|X)$; our less full model, with C and Γ_0; and our alternative model, with Γ_A. All three models are needed.

The F-ratio of Equation [7.24], the statistic we use to compare the fuller and less full models is compared to values of the central F-random variable with $k = 1$ and $(N - p - k) = 50 - 1 - 1 = 48$ degrees of freedom. We will prefer the less full model when F is small and the fuller when it is large. Large and small are relative to a *critical value of F.* We choose this critical value by first deciding on the acceptable chance of rejecting the less full model when it is correct. If we decide to set the chance of this error at 5%, then reference to the (central) F-tables gives us a critical value of $F = 4.043$.

We agree to use the F-ratio of Equation [7.24] to decide between the less full and fuller models. If F is less than or equal to 4.043, we choose the less full model. If F is greater than this critical value, we reject the less full model and accept the fuller one. There is a 5% chance that, if the less full model is correct, we will obtain a value of F greater than 4.043 and, consequently, reject the less full model for the added complexity of the fuller one.

How often will the F of Equation 7.24 take values greater than 4.043 *when the less full model is not the correct model?* The F-ratio then will have a noncentral F-distribution as its sampling distribution, with a noncentrality parameter dependent on how far the correct model is from the less full one.

For our SATV/Gender example, the less full model prescribes that $\Gamma_0 = \beta_2 = 0$; there is no gender difference in SATV means. If the true value of β_2 is 50 and not 0, then the F-ratio has as its sampling distribution that of the noncentral F with 1 and 48 degrees of freedom and, as just computed, a noncentrality parameter of $\gamma = 3.154$.

For the noncentral F with 1 and 48 degrees of freedom and the noncentrality parameter of 3.154, the proportion of the sampling distribution greater than 4.043 (the critical value) as computed within SPIDA is 0.412. There is, in other words, a 41% chance that we will reject the less full model (that $\beta_2 = 0$) when, in fact, $\beta_2 = 50$, the alternative.

We say that the *power* of our model comparison for this particular alternative ($\Gamma_A = 50$, rather than $\Gamma_0 = 0$) is 41%. We have only a 41% chance of rejecting the less full model's specification when this alternative provides the correct specification of the model.

The power of the model comparison, as stressed earlier, depends on several factors. We see the influence of four of these illustrated in Table A.2.1. Our initial example is on Line 2 of the table; for samples consisting of 22 Females and

T A B L E A.2.1

Model Comparison Power, SATV/Gender Example

				Critical Region	
		Alternative	Noncentrality	5%	1%
Line	Design	Model	Parameter	Power	Power
1	22F/28M	25	0.789	13.4%	2.8%
2		50	3.154	41.2%	19.3%
3		100	12.616	93.6%	80.2%
4	25F/25M	25	0.800	13.5%	
5		50	3.200	41.7%	
6		100	12.801	93.9%	
7	50F/50M	25	1.600	23.9%	
8		50	6.400	70.7%	
9		100	25.602	99.9%	
10	10F/10M	25	0.320	7.8%	
11		50	1.280	18.5%	
12		100	5.120	57.1%	

28 Males, an alternative model of $\beta_2 = 50$, and a critical value of F that sets the chance of a Type 1 Error at 5%, the power is 41.2%.

Choice of Critical Value

If we set the chance of falsely rejecting the less full model lower (or higher) than 5%, we correspondingly decrease (or increase) the power of our model comparison. This is illustrated on Line 2 of the table. Setting the chance at 1% rather than 5% requires that we increase the critical value of the F-ratio from 4.043 to 7.209. The chance that the F-ratio will be greater than 7.209 when our alternative model is correct is now only 19.3%. We've made it less likely that we will reject the less full model not only when it is the correct model (1% as opposed to 5%) but also when an alternative model is correct (19.3% as opposed to 41.2% for $\Gamma_A = 50$).

Choice of Alternative Model

The less full model specified that $\beta_2 = 0$. Our first alternative model specifies that $\beta_2 = 50$ SATV points. Lines 1 and 3 of Table A.2.1 illustrate the consequence of choosing an alternative model which is either *closer to* or *farther away from* the less full model than this initial choice. Line 1 specifies a model in which the Female/Male difference is chosen to be 25 SATV points, closer to the less full model. We see that this leads to a smaller noncentrality parameter—0.789 rather than 3.154—and to reduced power—13.4% rather than 41.2%. We are less likely to reject the less full model when the true difference is 25 points than when it is 50 points.

Line 3 shows the reverse of this. By selecting an alternative model farther from the less full one, we increase power. Chances of rejecting the less full model when the true difference is 100 points are a very high 93.6%.

Balance of Design

In the Chapter 6 example, the random selection of 50 high school students provided a sample consisting of 22 women and 28 men. Because the numbers of observations at the two design points are not the same, we say the study design is *unbalanced*. Balanced designs generally provide greater power. This point is illustrated, albeit marginally, by Lines 4, 5, and 6 of the table.

If the numbers of men and women are both 25, keeping the total number of observations at 50, the noncentralities of our alternative models are slightly increased and, in consequence, so are the powers of our model comparison. Our original design was only mildly unbalanced so the improvements are rather small, just a fraction of a percentage point in power for each of the alternative models.

Sample Size

A major reason for examining the power of model comparisons is to be able to answer the question, "Are there [going to be] enough observations in my sample that I can expect to detect interesting models?" Lines 7, 8, and 9 show the effect of increasing sample size. We assume a balanced design but now, instead of 25 women and 25 men, we assume twice that number of each, 100 in total. *Doubling the sample size in this way doubles the value of the noncentrality parameter.*

The sampling distributions for our *F*-ratio are now those with degrees of freedom parameters 1 and 98 rather than 1 and 48, and the 95% critical value is 3.939 rather than 4.043. And, importantly, the power of our fuller/less full model comparison has gone up for all three of our alternative models—for example, from 41.7% to 70.7% for $\beta_2 = 50$.

Lines 10, 11, and 12 show the result of choosing a smaller sample size. With just 10 women and 10 men, the power of our model comparison when $\beta_2 = 50$ is only 18.5%.

We noted that doubling the sample size, while keeping all other design conditions the same, doubled the size of the noncentrality parameter. Let's examine this effect in the context of the "denominator" term for the noncentrality parameter as given by Equation [16].

$$\sigma^2(C^T\hat{\beta}) = \sigma^2(y\,|\,X)[C^T(X^TX)^{-1}C]. \qquad [16]$$

What is the influence of a changed sample size? C will be unchanged. So, too, we assume will be the conditional response variance, $\sigma^2(y\,|\,X)$, as we have not changed the full model design. But assume we increase sample size by doubling the number of rows of X simply by adding the "old" X below itself. All of the elements of X^TX will be doubled and all of the elements of $(X^TX)^{-1}$ will be halved. The denominator of γ is halved; γ itself is doubled.

Other Influences

Table A.2.1 does not touch on one important influence on the power of model comparisons: the size of the conditional response variance. The relation of γ to

$\sigma^2(y\,|\,X)$ is straightforward. In the computation of the noncentrality parameter,

$$\gamma = \left(\frac{1}{\hat{\sigma}^2(y\,|\,X)}\right)(\Gamma_A - \Gamma_0)^{\mathrm{T}}(\mathrm{C}^{\mathrm{T}}(X^{\mathrm{T}}X)^{-1}\mathrm{C})^{-1}(\Gamma_A - \Gamma_0), \qquad [\textbf{8.6}]$$

we divide by our estimate of the fuller model conditional response variance, $\hat{\sigma}^2(y\,|\,X)$. If this estimate is too small, our noncentrality parameter, γ, is too large and we *overestimate* the power of our model comparison.

Using Power Calculations in Study Design

We want our study designs to be strong enough that we have a good chance of detecting important alternatives to the less full model. While we seek parsimony in our models, we also want them to reflect reality. A bias towards accepting the less full model leads to the adoption of overly simplistic explanatory views. Power calculations, carried out in advance of data collection, can help insure against that.

Three threats to adequate power should be addressed in the design of a study:

1 sample size,

2 estimation of response variance, and

3 control of response variance.

Before we address each of these, we need to pay attention to the idea of *important alternatives* to a less full model.

The Closest Important Alternative

Not every alternative to the less full model is of interest to us. For example, in the Gender/SATV example, we may be indifferent to whether the Female-Male difference in expected value of SAT verbal scores is 0, -2, or $+5$ points. The latter two are "close enough" to 0 that we would not distinguish them from "no difference between Males and Females." A difference of 100 points, on the other hand, we'd regard as a huge difference. When we ask whether the scores of Men and Women are the same or different on average, we need to have in mind what *same* and *different* mean. What differences are trivial and which consequential? How big does the real-world difference have to be before we think it important and, hence, that is should have a good chance of being noticed in our sample?

We'll refer to this difference as the *closest important difference* or, more generally, as the closest important alternative—to the less full model's "zero difference." We'll not be disappointed if differences smaller than this pass unnoticed; differences of this size or larger, though, we'd like to be reasonably certain of detecting. For our SATV example, we might decide that a 25-point difference is large enough of a difference to merit serious attention.

The closest important alternative tells us how to specify the alternative Γ_A in our power calculations. We need not make power computations for a range of alternatives; power and closeness to the less full model are linked. We can be confident that the power will be smaller for alternatives closer to the less full model and greater for alternatives farther from the less full model than our closest important alternative. (When there is but one constraint, we've seen via Equation [17] that the noncentrality parameter increases as the square of the difference between Γ_A and Γ_0.)

Now, how certain do we want to be that we will detect this closest important alternative? Only your judgement as to what is substantively consequential can be correct here. Rules of thumb, though, have been suggested. The power for the closest important alternative probably should be in the neighborhood of 75% to 90%. If it is important to detect an alternative, we ought to have something such as three chances in four or better of doing so.

The first steps, then, in power analysis are to specify the closest important alternative for a model comparison and the power we want the comparison to have for that alternative. Now, in planning most studies, we intend to make more than a single model comparison when the data are in. So we need to be prepared to think about closest important alternatives for several comparisons and the power of a design for each of these.

Multiple Constraint Alternatives

Our SATV example is of a fuller/less full model comparison involving a single constraint. That is, the less full model is specified by a single constraint on the fuller model. For such model comparisons, it is straightforward to specify a closest important alternative. When the less full model constrains the fuller one in several ways, deciding on a closest important alternative requires more thought.

As an example of a multiply constrained less full model, let's briefly revisit the Spatial Problem-Solving Instruction study of Chapter 6. Thirty students were randomly assigned, ten apiece, to three different instruction conditions—Videotape, Lecture, or Control. Taking the Control level of training as the comparison level and introducing dummy variables x_1 and x_2 to code the other two levels, a full model can be written as

$$\mu(Problem\ Solving\ Performance \mid Training) = \beta_0 + \beta_1 x_1 + \beta_2 x_2,$$

allowing the unconstrained estimation of expected performance under each of the three training conditions. Consider now a less full model specifying that all three training levels result in the same expected performance:

$$\mu(Problem\ Solving\ Performance \mid Training) = \beta_0.$$

Two constraints are needed to reduce the number of parameters from the fuller model's three to the less full's one:

$$\Gamma_{01} = 0\ \beta_0 + 1\ \beta_1 + 0\ \beta_2 = 0$$

and

$$\Gamma_{02} = 0\ \beta_0 + 0\ \beta_1 + 1\ \beta_2 = 0.$$

In matrix formulation, we'd write

$$C = \begin{bmatrix} 0 & 0 \\ 1 & 0 \\ 0 & 1 \end{bmatrix},$$

and

$$\Gamma_0 = \begin{bmatrix} 0 \\ 0 \end{bmatrix}.$$

To describe a model alternative to this less full one, we must supply another pair of values, Γ_{A1} and Γ_{A2}. Here are two ways in which we might describe a closest important alternative:

$$\Gamma_{A1} = 5 \text{ and } \Gamma_{A2} = 5 \qquad \textbf{Alternative 1}$$

$$\Gamma_{A1} = 10 \text{ and } \Gamma_{A2} = 0. \qquad \textbf{Alternative 2}$$

Alternative 1 specifies that we consider it important to detect when Videotape and Lecture training each lead to at least 5 points of improvement over Control training.

Alternative 2 states that it is important *only* to detect when Videotape instruction leads to at least 10 points of improvement. No interest is expressed in Lecture training's impact. However, if, as was true in this example, the number of students assigned to each training condition is the same, the power of our fuller/less full model comparison for alternative 2 is identical to its power for

$$\Gamma_{A1} = 0 \text{ and } \Gamma_{A2} = 10. \qquad \textbf{Alternative 2b}$$

That is, the power for the alternative "Videotape is 10 points better than Control" is the same as for the alternative "Lecture is 10 points better than Control." Thus, it is safe to interpret alternative 2 as describing the closest important alternative, as *either* Videotape or Lecture training leads to a 10-point improvement over Control training.

The purpose of the study, of course, dictates which of these forms makes more sense. Do we want to make sure that we detect when *both* experimental treatments "work" or when *at least one* of them does? The latter, symbolized as

$$\Gamma_A = \begin{bmatrix} 0 \\ 10 \end{bmatrix}, \qquad [18]$$

is a more common concern in treatment/control studies.

Determining Sample Size for Fixed Power

We've seen that sample size affects power. Indeed, the major contribution of power analysis to study design is that it allows us to determine a sample size that will be large enough to give us the desired chance of detecting the closest important and, hence, all more "distant" alternatives to the less full model.

The relation between the size of the sample and that of the noncentrality parameter is a direct one. If we keep the design "constant" we can automatically scale up (or down) the noncentrality parameter as we consider larger (or smaller) samples. We illustrate from the Spatial Problem Solving example.

We'll assume the fuller and less full models described before and that Equation [18] provides our closest important alternative. We'll also assume that the conditional response variance is $\sigma^2(Performance \mid Treatment) = 225$. Finally, we'll start with the design described above, 10 students apportioned to each of the training levels. For these selections, the noncentrality parameter is $\gamma = 2.963$.

For this initial design, the fuller/less full model comparison requires that we compute the F-ratio of Equation [7.24] and reject the less full if this ratio is larger than a chosen critical value. When the less full model is the correct one, this F-ratio has as its sampling distribution the central F with $k = 2$ and $(N - p - k) = 30 - 1 - 2 = 27$ degrees of freedom. If we choose a 95% level for this comparison, accepting that we will reject the less full model incorrectly on the average 5% of the time, the critical value is 3.356.

What are the chances that our F-ratio will exceed 3.356 when our closest important alternative model, not the less full one, is correct? The chances of an F-ratio larger than 3.356, when the sampling distribution is the noncentral F with degrees of freedom 2 and 27 and noncentrality parameter 2.963, is 28.7%. We have less than one chance in three of rejecting the model of equal expected values for the three treatments when, in fact, one of the experimental treatments produces an improvement of 10 points in problem-solving performance.

Let's say that we wanted to be 80% sure of detecting a real-world score difference, in treatment vs. control, of 10 points. We can't achieve that with 30 students, 10 assigned to each treatment. How many students will we need? If we assume that we are going to assign equal numbers to the three treatments, keeping our same balanced design, we can find an answer fairly easily. Thirty students aren't enough. What would our model comparison power for the closest important alternative be if we were to *double* the sample size, assigning 20 students to each of the three treatments? For this new design, the model comparison F-ratio will have as its sampling distribution the central F with 2 and 57 degrees of freedom when the less full model is correct and the noncentral F with 2 and 57 degrees of freedom and a noncentrality parameter of $(2)(2.963) = 5.926$ when the closest important alternative model is correct. (Note: k and p are unchanged while N has increased from 30 to 60. And doubling the total sample size while keeping the same design, we've learned, simply doubles the noncentrality parameter.)

For this 60-student design, the critical value of our F-ratio is the value in the central F with 2 and 57 d.f., above which only 5% of that sampling distribution lies. The central F tables give this critical value as 3.157. And the chances of an F-ratio larger than 3.157 when the closest important alternative model is the correct one is now 55.4%. We certainly have more power with our 60-student design than with the 30-student one; we've nearly doubled the chances of picking up a 10-point score difference. But, we're still short of the 80% certainty we sought. We need a sample larger than 60.

What about 90 students in total, triple the number in our original design? The F-ratio would now have the central F-distribution with 2 and 87 degrees of freedom when the less full model is correct and the 95% level critical value for that distribution is 3.1. When our closest important alternative model is correct, the F-ratio has a noncentral F sampling distribution, again with 2 and 87 d.f.s but with a noncentrality parameter of $(3)(2.963) = 8.889$. The chances of an F-ratio greater than 3.1 and, hence, of rejecting the less full model when the closest important alternative is correct, again calculated in SPIDA, is 75%.

We're very close to our goal now. If we increase the sample size just a bit more, from 30 to 35 in each treatment, calling for a total of 105 students, the 95% critical value (from the central F with 2 and 102 d.f.s) is 3.087. And the chances of exceeding 3.087 when the F-ratio's sampling distribution is the noncentral F with 2 and 102 d.f.s and noncentrality of $(35/10)(2.963) = 10.371$ is 81.8%. That's the chance of rejecting the less full when the closest important alternative model is correct and we use these larger samples.

Estimating the Conditional Response Variance

In the two examples we've considered this far, the SATV/Gender and Spatial Problem-solving Training studies, we've stated the conditional response variance fairly confidently. In many studies, we will have a good idea, in advance of collecting data for that particular study, of how large the conditional response variance will be. In other instances, that will not be true. We will be particularly uncertain, of course, when our response variable is one with which we don't have much experience.

Not having a good estimate of what the conditional response variance will be makes our power calculations problematic. But we can be forewarned. For a fixed design—not thinking now about changing sample size or model comparison or closest important alternative—the conditional response variance and noncentrality parameter have a simple relationship. Halving the conditional response variance doubles the noncentrality parameter; doubling the conditional response variance halves the noncentrality parameter.

We can use this relation in some "what if" calculations: "What would the power of our model comparison be if the response variance were, say, 100 rather than 75?" The idea can be illustrated by extending our sample size-setting example. In our final design, with 35 students in each of the training levels, we found that we achieved 81.8% power for the closest important alternative model, assuming the conditional response variance was 225—i.e., $\sigma(Performance \mid Training) = 15$ score points. What if that estimate were too low? What would the power be if $\sigma(Performance \mid Training) = 20$ and the conditional response variance were 400?

We calculated the noncentrality parameter for the 35 students per training condition design at $\gamma = 10.371$. But that was based on the $\sigma^2(y \mid X) = 225$ assumption. If $\sigma^2(y \mid X) = 400$, the correct noncentrality parameter is given by $(225/400)(10.371) = 5.834$. And with this smaller noncentrality parameter, the chances of rejecting the less full model when the closest important alternative is correct fall from 81.8% to 55.7%. Our model comparison would have considerably less power for this greater conditional response variance. If we felt conditional response variance were likely to be as large as 400 and we still wanted an 80% or better chance of detecting a 10-point training v. control difference, we would need to look for much larger samples than 35 in each treatment.

Controlling Conditional Response Variance

We have just seen how a smaller conditional response variance is associated with a larger noncentrality parameter and, hence, with greater power for any particular alternative to the less full model. This suggests that, where we can, we should try to reduce the conditional response variance before we make model comparisons. We can then have the power we desire without, perhaps, unacceptably or impossibly large sample sizes. In Chapters 11 through 13, but notably in Chapter 12, we introduced a number of multivariable designs that do help us control conditional response variance and, hence, achieve higher power.

References

Andrews, D. F. and A. M. Herzberg (1985). *Data: A Collection of Problems from Many Fields.* New York: Springer-Verlag.

Bowerman, B. L. and R. T. O'Connell (1990). *Linear Statistical Models: An Applied Approach.* Boston: PWS-Kent.

Cohen, J. (1987). *Statistical Power Analysis for the Behavioral Sciences.* Hillsdale, N.J.: Lawrence Erlbaum Associates.

Cook, R. D. (1977). Detection of influential observations in linear regression. *Technometrics, 19,* 15–18.

Cook, T. D. and D. H. Campbell (1979). *Quasi-experimentation.* Chicago: Rand McNally.

Cox, D.R. (1992). Causality: some statistical aspects. *Journal of Royal Statistical Society, Series A, 155,* 291–301.

Crowder, M. J. and D. J. Hand (1990). *Analysis of Repeated Measures.* London: Chapman & Hall.

Dale, G., J. A. Fleetwood, A. Weddell, R. D. Ellis and J. R. C. Sainsbury (1987). β endorphin: A factor in 'fun run' collapse? *British Medical Journal, 294,* 1004.

Forthofer, R. N. and R. G. Lehnen (1981). *Public Program Analysis: A New Categorical Data Approach.* Belmont, CA: Lifetime Learning.

Holmes, M. C. and R. E. O. Williams (1954). The distribution of carriers of *Streptococcus pyogenes* among 2413 healthy children. *J. Hygiene Camb.* 52, 165–179.

Hosmer, D. W. and S. Lemeshow (1989). *Applied Logistic Regression.* New York: Wiley.

Jones, B. and M. G. Kenward (1989). *Design and Analysis of Crossover Trials.* London: Chapman & Hall.

Judd, C. M. and A. McClelland (1989). *Data Analysis: A Model-comparison Approach.* San Diego: Harcourt Brace Jovanovich.

Kirk, R. E. (1982). *Experimental Design: Procedures for the Behavioral Sciences.* Monterey, CA: Brooks-Cole.

Kraemer, H. C. and S. Thieman (1987). *Statistical Power Analysis in Research.* Beverly Hills, CA: Sage.

Leamer, E. E. (1978). *Specification Searches.* New York: Wiley.

Lee, E. T. (1974). A computer program for linear logistic regression analysis. *Computer Prog. Biomed.* 4, 80–92.

Madansky, A. (1988). *Prescriptions for Working Statisticians.* New York: Springer-Verlag.

McCullagh, P. (1980). Regression models for ordinal data (with discussion). *Journal of the Royal Statistical Society, Series B.* 42, 109–142.

McCullagh, P. and J. A. Nelder (1989). *Generalized Linear Models (2d. Ed.).* London: Chapman & Hall.

Neyzi, O., H. Alp and A. Orhon (1975). Breast development of 318 12–13 year old

Turkish girls by socio-economic class of parents. *Ann. Hum. Biol.* 2, 49–59.

Norton, V. (1983). A simple algorithm for computing the non-central F distribution. *Applied Statistics,* 32, 84–85.

Patel, H. I. (1983). Use of baseline measurements in two-period crossover designs in clinical trials. *Communications in Statistics, Theory and Methods,* 12, 2693–2712.

Radelet, M. (1981). Racial characteristics and the imposition of the death penalty. *Amer. Sociol. Rev.* 46, 918–927.

Rubin, D. R. (1991). Practical implications of modes of statistical inference for causal effects and the critical role of the assignment mechanism. *Biometrics,* 47, 1213–1234.

Tuddenham. R. D. and M. M. Snyder (1954). Physical growth of California boys and girls from birth to age 18. *California Publications in Child Development,* 1, 183–364.

Weisberg, S. (1985). *Applied Linear Regression (2d. Ed.).* New York: Wiley.

Woodward, J. A., D. G. Bonett and M-L Brecht (1990). *Introduction to Linear Models and Experimental Design.* San Diego: Harcourt Brace Jovanovich.

Sources of Data Used in End-of-Chapter Exercises

Chapter 5

Exercise 1: Weisberg, S. (1985). *Applied Linear Regression. (2d. Ed.)* New York: Wiley.

Exercise 2: Andrews, D. F. & A. M. Herzberg (1985). *Data: A Collection of Problems from Many Fields.* New York: Springer-Verlag.

Chapter 6

Exercise 2: Dobson, A. J. (1983). *An Introduction to Statistical Modelling.* London: Chapman & Hall.

Exercise 3: Dolkart *et al.* (1971). *Diabetes, 20,* 162–167.

Chapter 7

Exercise 1: *The World Almanac and Book of Facts, 1990.* New York: Pharos Books.

Exercise 2: *Barron's Profiles of American Colleges, 17th. Ed.*

Exercise 3: Andrews & Herzberg (1985).

Chapter 8

Exercise 1: Rothschild *et al.* (1982). *British J. of Psychiatry, 141,* 471–474.

Exercise 2: *Times* of London, 14 Sept, 28 Sept, 12 Oct & 26 Oct 1990.

Exercise 3: Andrews & Herzberg (1985).

Chapter 9

Exercise 1: Rousseeuw & Leroy (1987). *Robust Regression and Outlier Detection.* New York: Wiley.

Exercise 2: *Parade Magazine,* December 1990.

Chapter 10

Exercise 1: Weisberg (1985).

Exercise 2: Andrews & Herzberg (1985).

Chapter 11

Exercise 1: *World Almanac, 1990.*

Exercise 3: Snedecor, G. & W. Cochran *Statistical Methods.* Ames, Iowa: Iowa State University Press.

Chapter 12

Exercise 1: *The Elias 1990 Baseball Analyst.*
Exercise 2: Andrews & Herzberg (1985).

Chapter 13

Exercise 3: *The Elias 1990 Baseball Analyst.*

Chapter 14

Exercise 1: Andersen, A. H., E. B. Jensen & G. Schou (1981). *International Statistical Review,* 49, 153–167.
Exercise 2: Osborn, J. F. (1979). *Statistical Exercises in Medical Research.*

Chapter 16

Exercise 1: Kleinbaum, D. G., L. L. Kupper & K. E. Muller (1988). *Applied Regression Analysis and Other Multivariable Methods.* Boston: PWS-Kent.
Exercise 2: Lunn, A. D. & D. R. McNeil (1991). *Computer-interactive Data Analysis.* New York: Wiley.

Chapter 17

Exercise 1: Lunn & McNeil (1991).
Exercise 2: Aickin, M. (1983). *Linear Statistical Analysis of Discrete Data.* New York: Wiley.
Exercise 3: Kleinbaum, Kupper & Muller (1988).

Chapter 18

Exercise 1: *Barron's Profiles of American Colleges, 17th. Ed.*
Exercise 2: Kleinbaum, Kupper & Muller (1988).

Chapter 19

Exercise 1: Curnow, R. N., R. Mead & A. M. Hasted (1992). *Statistical Methods in Agriculture and Experimental Biology (2d. Ed.).* London: Chapman and Hall.
Exercise 2: Gebski, V., O. Leung, D. McNeil & D. Lunn (1992). *SPIDA User's Manual, Version 6.* Eastwood NSW (Australia): Statistical Computing Laboratory.

Index

A

Addition of explanatory variables, 196–97
Additive model, 269–82
All levels coding, 451
Alp, H., 477, A33
Alternative (to less-full) model, A16–18, A20–22, A25
  closest important, A27
Analysis of covariance, 321–23, 353–54, 382–87
  assessing covariate bias, 326
  assessing interaction, 324–25
  separate slopes model, 323
  single slope model, 322–23
Analysis of variance, 25
  one-way, 148
Andrews, D. F., A33
Assessment selection, 12
Assumptions
  checking, 239–42
  linear regression, 57, 73, 94, 126, 160–61, 183, 239
  logistic regression, 419
Attribute manipulation, 13
Auxiliary variable, 311
  moderating an influence, 332
  sensitivity-increasing, 312
Average response model, 375–88
  adjustment factor, 378–80

B

Balanced design, A26
Blocking, 316, 501
  model search strategy, 316–18
  nonindependent, 318–19
  on an auxiliary variable, 314–18, 353
  on individual subjects, 356–59
Bonett, D. G., A19, A34
Bowerman, B. L., 353, A33
Box and whisker plot, 41
Brecht, M-L., A19, A34

C

Campbell, D. H., 19, 20, 22, A33
Carryover effect, 351, 389–91
Case elimination, 233
Categorical variable, 9
  explanatory variable, 119–21, 269–85
  levels of, 120
  response variable, 24, 399–407
Causality, 19–20
Censored measurement, 409–10
  linear model, 410–13
Certainty, 50, 71, 124, 402–03
  conditional, 44
  dichotomous response, 405
  nonordered response, 404
  ordered response, 404
  unconditional, 43

Chi-squared random variable, 92, 425, 504, A08–09
Cohen, J., A19, A33
Combining explanatory variables, 198, 200–204
Comparison condition, 270
Concomitant variable design, 319–21
Conditional response mean, 50, 56, 72–73, 183
  estimate, 75, 127
  estimation, A13
Conditional response population, 29–31, 59, 71–72, 90, 121–22, 154–56, 182, 409
Conditional response variance, 64, 72–73, 80–81, 183, A27, A30
  estimate, 84, 128
  estimation, A13, A31–32
Confidence interval, 104–105
  difference in means, 136–37, 144–46
  regression intercept, 110
  regression slope, 106–109, 113, 171–75, 187
  response mean, 132–33, 139–41
Confounding, 20
Constrained model, 125, 146–47, 175, 272, 280–81, A16–17
Constraining linear model parameters, 199–204
Constraint matrix, A20–22, A24
Constraints, within-subjects, 357
Construct selection, 12
Continuation ratio model, 482–83
  fitting, 486
Cook's Influence (Di) statistic, 228–31
Cook, R. D., 228, A33
Cook, T. D., 19, 20, 22, A33
Correlation
  product moment, 61, 66–69
  of means and variance, 256–58
  of regression parameter estimates, A14
Counted variable, 9
  response variable, 24, 34
Counterbalanced design, 351
Covariance, 61, 64–65
Cox, D. R., 20, A33
Critical value, A25
Crossover design, 387–94
Crowder, M. J., 353, 395, A33
Cumulative odds model, 481–82
Curnow, R. N., 501
Curve of regression, 50–51

D

Dale, G., 355, A33
Data correction, 232
Data modification, 232–33
Degrees of freedom, 83–84, 100

Deletion of explanatory variables, 196–97
Design change, 232
Design matrix, A11–12, A20
Design point, 439–40, 468–69
Deviance difference, 426–27, 442, 473, 500
Deviance statistic, 423–25, 440–41, 471–72, 491, 500
Dichotomous variable, 10
  response variable, 402, 409–10
Dummy variable, 270–73, 276–78
  coding, 360–61, 449, 501
  model, 134–36, 141–44

E

Effect coding, 273–78, 450
Errors of extrapolation, 56
Estimates of model parameters, 58, 71
  conditional response variance, 185
  regression intercept, 163, 185
  regression slope, 163, 185
  response mean, 163
  response variance, 164–65
Experimental studies, 18, 28, 45, 73, 88
Explanation, 28
Explanatory relation, 6, 14, 52–53
Explanatory variable, 6
Exploratory data analysis, 1
Exposure time, 499

F

F-distribution, *see* F-random variable
F-random variable, 178–80, A04–07, A16
  noncentral distribution, A18–19
F-statistic, 177–80, 188, A15, A30
Factorial design, 293–303
  incomplete, 302–303
  model search strategy, 301–302, 453–54
Fitted values, 211–12, 406
Fixed effects, 25–26, 306–308
Forthofer, R. N., 289, 425, A33
Full model, 124–25, 130, 146–47, 175, 271
Fuller model, 176–77, 195, 417, A20–22
Fuller/less full model relation, 195–205, 426–27, 473, 500, A14–15
Fullest model, 286

G

Gain scores, 353–54
Goodness of fit, 422
Group regression, 333–34
  model interpretation, 337–38
  model search strategy, 335–37

H

Hand, D. J., 353, 395, A33
Hasted, A. M., 501
Hat diagonal, 213
Herzberg, A. M., A33
Histogram
frequency, 38–39, 59, 122–23
probability density, 92–93
sampling distribution, 96
Holmes, M. C., 468, A33
Homogeneity of variance, 58
checking, 252–60
inconsistent design point,
258–60
Levene test, 252–56
non-independence, 258
Hosmer, D. W., 491, 492, A33

I

Independence of observations, 58, 497
Inference, 58
magnitude, 103–104
parameter value, 99, 103
relation, 103, 110
Influential observations, 228–31
Interaction, 279–82
higher order, 295
of explanatory and auxiliary variables, 331
of explanatory variables, 282–88,
360–61, 366, 450–51
Interaction variables
dummy variable coding,
283–84
effect coding, 285
regression slopes, 287–88
Interactive model, 279–82
Intercept, *see* Regression intercept
Interquartile range, 40

J

Jones, B., 387, 393, A33
Judd, C. M., A33

K

Kenward, M. G., 387, 393, A33
Kirk, R. E., 353, 395, A33
Kraemer, H. C., A19, A33
Kurtosis, 59, 263

L

Leamer, E. E., 15, A33
Least squares, 88
Lee, E. T., 420, A33
Lehnen, R. G., 289, 425, A33
Lemeshow, S., 491, 492, A33
Less full model, 176–77, 195, 200,
204–205, 417, A20–22
Level of aggregation, 11
Leverage, 212–13
explanatory categories, 214–16
magnitude, 213

multiple explanatory variables, 216
single explanatory variable, 214
Linear model
checking, 243–52
linear algebraic representation, 188
matrix formulation, A11–15
multiple explanatory categories,
138–49
multiple explanatory variables,
156–60, 181–88
two explanatory variables, 153–56,
161–65, 169–77
two-category explanatory
variable, 133–37
Linear regression, 52
Log-odds of success, 414
Logistic function of explanatory variables, 415
Logistic regression, 407, 413
iterative fitting, 420
ordered response, 466
models, 415–17
Logit transformation of success proportion, 414
all levels coding, 458
dummy variable coding, 456
effect coding, 457
interaction, 458–59

M

Madansky, A., 252, 263, A33
Maximum likelihood estimation, 470
McClelland, A., A33
McCullagh, P., 467, 483, A33
Mead, R., 501
Mean
population, 42
sample, 36
Mean line, 78, 80
Mean squared error (MSE), 82–84,
86–87
Measured variable, 8
response variable, 24, 32, 35
Median
sample, 37
Mixed models, 365–66
search strategy, 367–75
Modal category, 491
Model
confirmatory, 3, 266
explanatory, 1, 52
hypothesis, 3, 266
statistical, 1
structural, 53
summary, 2
Model comparison, 110–13, 137,
172–181, 188, 195–205, 272–
73, 282, 286–87, 290–93, 296–
300, 406, 426–27, 472–73
error, A16–17
Model development, 12
Model elements, 5

Model modification
major, 17
minor, 16
Model rejection, 15
Model revision, 17
Model selection, 16
Moderated regression, 341–42
model interpretation, 344
model search strategy, 343–44
Moderator variable, 332
designs, 332
Modular model, 288–93, 299–300,
363, 452
logistic regression, 455
Modules, 288–89
Monotonic explanatory relation, 247–
52
Multinomial probabilities
conditional, 468–69, 472, 491
estimation, 470–72
Multiple constraints, A28–29
Multiple correlation, 186–87
Multiple regression, *see* Linear model
Multiplicative model, 407, 432–35,
455, 474, 491, 501

N

Nelder, J. A., 483, A33
Nested design, 303–304
model search strategy, 305–306
Nested factors, 366
Neyzi, O., 477, A33
Nominal, *see* Nonordered
categories
Noncentrality parameter, A19–22,
A24, A30–31
Nonlinear model interpretation, 485–
86
Nonordered categories, 10, 120, 401
response categories, 490
Nonrandom assignment, 20
Nonrandom selection, 22
Nonreversing relation, *see* Monotonic
explanatory
relation
Normal characteristics of
response, 59
checking, 261–65
Normal random variable, 59, 92
Norton, V., A19, A34
Null model, 111–12, 125, 130, 137,
146–47, 175

O

O'Connell, R. T., 353, A33
Observational studies, 21, 28, 72, 80–
81, 85, 88
Odds multiplier, 407, 434–35
Odds of success, 407, 414, 432
Odds ratio, 460
Ordered categorical variable,
10, 32
categories, 120, 148–49, 399–401

response variable, 33
  response variable categories, 465
Orhon, A., 477, A33
Outlier, 16, 223–24
  test for significance, 225–28

P

Parallel modeling, 23–35
Parameters, 42
Parsimony, 204–205, 406
Partial explanatory variable, 161–64, 170, 184–85, 312
Partial residual plot, 241–43
Patel, H. I., 387, A34
Period effect, 351, 388, 391–92
Point of means, 78–79
Poisson random variable, 497–98
Poisson regression, 497–99
Polychotomous logistic regression, 490–91
Polynomial regression, 246, 345
Populations
  complete and subdivided, 47
Power of model comparison, 313, A15–18, A22–30, A32
Prediction, 23, 28, 86, 88
Pretreatment-posttreatment design, 353–54
Probability density function, 92–93
Product variables, 283–85, 450–51
Proportion of successes, 412–13
  modeled, 418–19
Proportional odds model, 467, 477
  an approximate fit, 489–90

Q

Quadratic regression, 246–47
Quantile-quantile (QQ) plot, 261–62, 264–65
Quartiles, 40

R

Radelet, M., 452, A34
Random assignment, 19
Random factors, 306–308
Random selection, 22
Rate of change, 53–54
  relation, 7
  parameter, 498–500
Reciprocal transformation, 446–47
Regression, 49–50, 57
  and correlation, 26
Regression intercept, 52, 55–56, 157–60, 183
  dummy variable, 134–36
  estimate, 75, 87
  estimation, A13

Regression line, 80
  estimate, 76–79, 86–87
Regression slope, 52–55, 74, 157–60, 184
  dummy variable, 134–37
  estimate, 75–77, 87
  estimation, A13
Repeated measures designs, 349
  advanced analyses, 394–95
  advantages and disadvantages, 350–51
  multiple within-subjects factors design, 359–61
  model search for, 362–65
  single within-subjects factor design, 358–59
Residual, 186, 211–12, 220–23, 240–42, 266, 406, A13
Residual plot, 220–21, 226–28, 240–42
Residual sum of squares, *see* Sum of squares of residuals
Response variable, 5
  between-subjects observations, 352
  nonindependent observations, 351
  within-subjects observations, 352
Response vector, A11–12
Rubin, D. R., 20, A34

S

Sample size, 103, 109, A26, A29–30
Sampling distribution, 88–93
  intercept estimate, 94–96, 169–70
  response mean estimate, 128–29
  response variance estimate, 97, 129–30
  slope estimate, 94–96, 169–170, 186
Scatterplot, 62–64, 67–68
SD Line, 78, 80
Segmented regression, 246, 338–40
  model search strategy, 341
Separate intercepts, 334
Separate slopes, 334
Single intercept, 334
Single slope, 334
Skewness, 39, 262
Slope, *see* Regression slope
Snyder, M. M., 35, 60, A34
SPIDA, 253–56, 264, 420, A19, A22–23
Standard deviation (SD), 37
Standard error, 95–96
  intercept estimate, 100
  Poisson rate parameter, 503
  regression slope, A14
  slope estimate, 100–103, 186
Standard scores, 66–68

Standardized residual, 441–42, 448
Statistics
  descriptive, 74
  inferential, 74
  parameter estimates, 74
Stem and leaf plot, 40
Student's *t*-random variable, 92, 100–101, 109, A02–A03
Studentized residual, 222–28
  external, 223
  internal, 222–23
Study design, A27
Sum of squares of residuals (SSR or RSS), 115, 186, 212, A13
Symmetry, 39, 59

T

t-distribution, *see* Student's *t*-random variable
Thieman, S., A19, A33
Transformation of variable, 16
  Box and Cox for normality, 263–65
  power of explanatory variable, 247–52, 446
  power of response, 263
  variance stabilizing response, 257–58
Tuddenham, R. D., 35, 60, A34

U

Unbiasedness of estimate, 94
Unconditional response population, 29–31, 72
Unconditional response variance, 72, 80–81
  estimate, 83
Unimodality, 59
Unit of measurement, 10, 33–34, 36, 120, 399
Unit variable, 201–203

V

Variable type, 8, 23
Variance
  population, 42
  sample, 37

W

Washout period, 351
Weisberg, S., 222–23, 229, 248, 263, A34
Williams, R. E. O., 468, A33
Woodward, J. A., A19, A34